M: Management

M: Management

7th Edition

Thomas S. Bateman
McIntire School of Commerce,
University of Virginia

Robert Konopaske
McCoy College of Business,
Texas State University

Mc
Graw
Hill

m: management

DIRECTOR: **MICHAEL ABLASSMEIR**

LEAD PRODUCT DEVELOPER: **KELLY I. PEKELDER**

EXECUTIVE MARKETING MANAGER: **DEBBIE CLARE**

LEAD CONTENT PROJECT MANAGER: **CHRISTINE VAUGHAN**

SENIOR CONTENT PROJECT MANAGER: **KERI JOHNSON**

SENIOR BUYER: **SUSAN K. CULBERTSON**

SENIOR DESIGNER: **MATT DIAMOND**

LEAD CONTENT LICENSING SPECIALIST: **JACOB SULLIVAN**

COVER IMAGE: **SHUTTERSTOCK**

COMPOSITOR: **SPi GLOBAL**

M: MANAGEMENT, SEVENTH EDITION

Published by McGraw Hill LLC, 1325 Avenue of the Americas, New York, NY 10121. Copyright ©2022 by McGraw Hill LLC. All rights reserved. Printed in the United States of America. Previous editions ©2020, 2018, and 2016. No part of this publication may be reproduced or distributed in any form or by any means, or stored in a database or retrieval system, without the prior written consent of McGraw Hill LLC, including, but not limited to, in any network or other electronic storage or transmission, or broadcast for distance learning.

Some ancillaries, including electronic and print components, may not be available to customers outside the United States.

This book is printed on acid-free paper.

1 2 3 4 5 6 7 8 9 LMN 26 25 24 23 22 21

ISBN 978-1-260-73518-5 (bound edition)
MHID 1-260-73518-4 (bound edition)
ISBN 978-1-264-20951-4 (loose-leaf edition)
MHID 1-264-20951-7 (loose-leaf edition)

All credits appearing on page or at the end of the book are considered to be an extension of the copyright page.

Library of Congress Cataloging-in-Publication Data

Names: Bateman, Thomas S., author. | Snell, Scott, 1958- author. |
    Konopaske, Robert, author.
Title: M : management / Thomas S. Bateman, McIntire School of Commerce,
    University of Virginia, Scott A. Snell, Darden Graduate School of
    Business, University of Virginia, Rob Konopaske, McCoy College of
    Business, Texas State University.
Description: 7th edition. | New York, NY : McGraw Hill LLC, [2022] |
    Includes index.
Identifiers: LCCN 2020039545 | ISBN 9781260735185 (bound edition) | ISBN
    9781264209507 (Instructor's edition) | ISBN 9781264209514 (loose-leaf
    edition) | ISBN 9781264209552 (ebook)
Subjects: LCSH: Management.
Classification: LCC HD31 .B369485 2022 | DDC 658—dc23
LC record available at https://lccn.loc.gov/2020039545

The Internet addresses listed in the text were accurate at the time of publication. The inclusion of a website does not indicate an endorsement by the authors or McGraw Hill LLC, and McGraw Hill LLC does not guarantee the accuracy of the information presented at these sites.

mheducation.com/highered

BRIEF Contents

Contents

RGR Collection/Alamy Stock Photo

Media for Medical SARL/Alamy Stock Photo

Stanislau Palaukou/Shutterstock

NYCStock/Shutterstock

Yoshikazu Tsuno/AFP/Getty Images

Jae C. Hong/AP Photo

John Lund/Blend Images LLC

Rawpixel.com/Shutterstock

Cody Duty/AP Photo

Chris Ryan/OJO Images/Getty Images

PAUL J. RICHARDS/Getty Images

Source: National Archives and Records Administration (NWDNS-306-SSM-4A-35-6)

Ariel Skelley/Blend Images

Kwame Zikomo/Purestock/SuperStock

Jennifer DeMonte/Getty Images

Christiane Oelrich/dpa/Alamy Stock Photo

Yuri Arcurs/E+/Getty Images

CHAPTER Changes

Overall, the seventh edition of *M: Management* is more streamlined and reader-friendly, with current content and a layout that is visually appealing to today's college learner. The endnotes of course are updated and expanded.

CHAPTER 1

- New chapter opener about Lynsi Snyder, CEO of In-N-Out Burger, practicing effective leadership and management.
- New example: Tricia Griffith, CEO of Progressive Insurance, fostering an environment of teamwork that motivates employees.
- New example: Capital One experiencing a massive data breach due to ineffective cyber controls.
- New example regarding Pacific Gas & Electric's outdated equipment causing several catastrophic wildfires in California.
- Updated Sustaining the Future feature showcasing REI's stewardship strategy.
- New example: Mary Barra, CEO of GM, using conceptual and decision skills to adapt to environmental changes to ensure the auto company's long-term success.
- New example of Nike and Starbucks operating their enterprises on a global scale.
- New example: Netflix, the largest global streaming service in the world, entertaining over 150 million subscribers with its locally produced content.
- Updated Take Charge of Your Career feature about the benefits of studying abroad.
- Updated statistics about global Internet usage.
- New example: Stitch Fix, IPSY, TikTok, and Snapchat are online success stories.
- Updated section about employee diversity and labor force trends.
- New example about Starbucks, Gatorade, and Nike allowing customers to customize products.
- New example: Walmart increasing the efficiency of employee scheduling by launching a new self-service app called My Walmart Schedule.

- New example: List of companies with strong sustainability performance like Corporate Knights, Banco do Brasil, and McCormick.
- New example about Patagonia's Worn Wear program repairing customers' outdoor gear and clothing to reduce waste.
- New example: Managers at Discount Tire delivering all six sources of competitive advantage.

CHAPTER 2

- Updated chapter opener about the importance of knowing how management practices have evolved over time.
- Edited exhibit that illustrates the evolution of management thought.
- Updated Sustaining the Future feature about companies embracing green power.
- Trimmed nonessential text, enhancing the student experience.

CHAPTER 3

- New chapter opener about Gordon Logan (founder of Sports Clips) creating a hair salon designed specifically for male customers.
- New example: Microsoft and Walmart paying millions to settle charges that the companies violated the U.S. Foreign Corrupt Practices Act.
- Updated list of federal regulatory agencies.
- New example: Escalating trade war against China and exit of the United Kingdom (Brexit) from the European Union affecting managers and organizations.
- Updated section about the stock market being an important economic influence.
- New example of mobile apps like Gusto for HR payroll services and Slack for instant messaging and team collaboration changing how business gets done.
- New Did You Know? feature suggesting that students texting during lectures leads to lower exam scores.

- Updated section on employee demographics and immigration trends.
- Updated Sustaining the Future feature: "Water for People."
- New example: IBM allowing both parents of a newborn or adopted child to take up to 20 weeks of parental leave.
- New example: Johnson & Johnson providing reservable lactation rooms for working mothers.
- New example of immersive virtual reality games like *Beat Saber* and *The Thrill of the Fight* getting players moving.
- New section about the United States-Mexico-Canada Agreement (USMCA).
- New example: Gillette learned that social media is hard to control after it posted a video about the #MeToo movement that backfired.
- Updated example of Whole Foods positioning itself as an alternative to traditional grocery stores.
- New example: PepsiCo, Dell, and Berkshire Hathaway monitoring events in the environment that may affect their businesses.
- New example about GMC Cadillac developing an electric car for the fast-growing Chinese auto market.
- New example: Ford adapts to changing regulations and customer tastes by using aluminum alloy in the body of its popular F-150 truck.
- New example: Fitppl, a health foods brand, taking voluntary actions by sponsoring organized volunteer cleanups of natural areas.
- New example: Ariana Grande sues Forever 21, claiming it used her unauthorized likeness in a social media campaign.
- New Take Charge of Your Career feature discussing how job seekers can assess whether they fit with an employer's organizational culture.

CHAPTER 4

- New example: Coca-Cola, Intel, and Best Buy enacting ethics policies related to employee use of social media.
- New example about Facebook selling without permission user data to Cambridge Analytica, a political consulting firm.
- New example: The Justice Department charges several people, including celebrities and university coaches, for participating in a college admissions scandal.
- New example of WhatsApp being used to circulate unconfirmed news about the Brazilian presidential election.
- New example: Kim Kardashian, a popular social media–based influencer, accumulating more than 140 million followers.
- Updated Did You Know? feature ranking 180 countries from most honest (New Zealand) to least honest (Somalia).
- New example: Rate of retaliation against employees reporting unethical behavior tripled over a 10-year period.
- Business leaders at Apple, Google, Intel, Facebook, and Ingersoll Rand remaining committed to the Paris Climate Accord's goal of limiting climate change.

- New example: Chick-fil-A fostering an ethical organizational climate by hiring individuals who are honest, respectful, and kind.
- Cognizant Technology Solutions Corp. paid $25 million to the U.S. government to settle a case involving attempted bribery of Indian government officials.
- New Take Charge of Your Career feature: "Want to find an ethical employer?"
- Updated example of Ethisphere Institute honoring companies like Hilton, L'Oréal, and Grupo Bimbo for making a positive impact on society.
- Updated example of 10,000 students and graduates from 300 colleges and institutions signing the MBA Oath to act with integrity.
- Updated example of New Belgium Brewery's sustainability practices.
- New example: LEGO identifying sustainable alternatives for its building bricks and product packaging.
- New example: Nintendo, Southwest Airlines, and Honda taking steps to reduce carbon emissions caused by their operations.
- Updated Sustaining the Future feature: "A College Built by and for the Poor."
- New example: Bloomberg Philanthropies bringing business leaders and scientists together to identify ways to replace coal with clean energy.
- Updated section on water scarcity and how companies are responding to the shortage.
- New example: Ben & Jerry's stops using ingredients dried with harmful herbicides.
- New example about IKEA working toward using 100 percent renewable energy and sourcing wood from only sustainable sources.
- New section on the circular economy, an economic system that is an alternative to the current "take-make-waste" industrial model.

CHAPTER 5

- New chapter opener about the unexpected effects of the COVID-19 pandemic reminding organizations to plan strategically for contingencies.
- New quote by Simon Sinek.
- New example: Mission statements from Life is Good, Patagonia, and Honest Tea.
- New example: Vision statements from Creative Commons, Alzheimer's Association, and Hilton.
- Updated example of McDonald's acting in alignment with its mission.
- New example of Florida Power & Light investing in nuclear, wind, and solar energy.
- New example about Denmark's Orsted and GE partnering to build offshore wind farms.

- New example: Anheuser-Busch InBev developing strategic plans to leverage its tangible and intangible assets.
- New example: IBM's nearly 10,000 patents are rare and valuable resources.
- New example about Jimmy John's core capability of fast sandwich production and delivery.
- New example: Apple creating appealing product designs to achieve competitive advantage.
- New example of In-N-Out Burger and Walmart using benchmarking to eliminate inefficiencies.
- New example about Five Guys following a concentration business strategy.
- New example: Procter & Gamble diversifying into unrelated product areas from hand soaps to laundry detergents to paper towels.
- New example of UK retailer Boots making changes to grow and maintain its competitive market position.
- New example about Tieks using a differentiation strategy by producing handwritten thank-you cards and colorful high-quality packaging.
- New example: Oatly's oat milk being popular among baristas who like the unique product's quality.
- Updated Sustaining the Future feature: "The Green Cities Movement."
- Updated section about the Wells Fargo fake customer account scandal.
- New example: Companies like Amazon, Alphabet, and Volkswagen spending heavily on research and development.
- New example: Amazon takes a risk and sells over 100 million Echo speakers with Alexa voice activation.

CHAPTER 6

- New chapter opener discussing Anne Wojcicki, the successful entrepreneur who founded 23andMe.
- New example of one-third of adults in Texas, Utah, California, and Colorado starting businesses.
- New example: Cindy Mi, CEO of VIPKID, connecting North Americans to teach over half a million Chinese students.
- New quote by Peter Drucker.
- Updated example about Shama Hyder and her company, Zen Media.
- Updated example: Bill Gross starting more than 150 companies.
- New example: Tiff's Treats, which started off as a hot-cookie delivery service, expanded to over 50 stores with over 1,000 employees.
- New example about Apoorva Mehta cofounding Instacart, a grocery home delivery service.
- New example: Guzman Energy providing affordable renewable energy to communities in the western United States.

- Updated example of Team Rubicon helping victims of Hurricane Dorian in the Bahamas.
- Updated Take Charge of Your Career: "You don't have to wait! You can be an entrepreneur while still in school."
- New example about Krispy Kreme being a successful franchise with over 1,000 stores.
- Updated Traditional Thinking—The Best Managers Today feature about crowdfunding websites like Kickstarter and Indiegogo.
- Updated example about the advertising support model used by Google and Facebook.
- New example about Society6 using an affiliate model to market its premium consumer goods to affiliates who decorate and sell them.
- New example: List of entrepreneurial frontiers including virtual reality, cryptocurrency, and robots powered by artificial intelligence.
- New quote by Richard Branson.
- Updated Did You Know? feature about the best U.S. cities for starting new businesses.
- New example: Uber expanding its service offerings to include Uber Eats food delivery service and Uber Mobility, rentable battery-powered bikes.
- New feature discussing the top three factors that predict start-up company success.

CHAPTER 7

- Updated chapter opener about the organizational restructuring of Activision Blizzard (owner of the *Call of Duty* and *Candy Crush* franchises).
- New quote by Stephen R. Covey.
- New example: Top management teams from Target, Airbnb, Amazon, and Nepris meeting regularly to make important decisions for their organizations.
- New example about Elon Musk, CEO of Tesla, flattening the company's management structure to improve communication and increase market responsiveness.
- New example: Fog Creek Software growing to a point where it needed middle managers positioned between programmers and top management.
- New example: Burgerville recycling oil into biofuel and using 100 percent renewable energy to power its operations.
- New example: Unilever organizing into four product divisions with more than 100 independent company divisions.
- Updated Take Charge of Your Career feature: "Land an internship."
- New example: China and India are the leading producers of motorcycles in the world.
- Updated Sustaining the Future case: "'Community Solutions' Goal to End Homelessness."
- New example: Hyundai Motor aligning with Uber to develop the S-A1, an autonomous personal air vehicle.

- Updated example about Bombardier Aerospace using a virtual network of suppliers to make its products.
- New example: Basecamp maintaining its agile, balanced, and anti-workaholic culture.
- New example of how Pizza Hut, Microsoft, *USA Today,* and Honeywell are learning organizations.
- New example: Mead Metals crediting ISO 9001 certification with helping it safely create high-quality products.
- New example about Apple using large batch technologies to make AirPods and Beats.
- New example: Panera using standardized production runs to deliver consistent food products to its customers.
- New quote by Albert Einstein.
- Trimmed nonessential text, enhancing the student experience.

CHAPTER 8

- Updated chapter opener about Enterprise hiring and training ambitious people, promoting from within, and putting customers and employees first.
- New example: Alcon, Southwest Airlines, and Toyota seeing their employees as adding unique value to customers.
- New example about employees contributing to hard-to-imitate cultures at Pipedrive, Google, and Airbnb.
- New example: Companies like Nielsen, Virgin Media, and Clarks leveraging data analytics to make more informed talent management decisions.
- New quote by Jim Collins.
- New example: Microsoft, Alphabet, Deloitte, and EY relying on H-1B employees to fill key positions.
- New example of managers at Mayo Clinic encouraging employees to be lifelong learners and to continually develop capabilities by taking on new roles.
- Updated example of Accenture's progress toward its goal of having a 50 percent female workforce by 2025.
- Updated example about JPMorgan Chase's "Veteran Jobs Mission" expanding to 230 companies with a goal of hiring one million veterans.
- Updated Did You Know? feature identifying the top reasons why employees leave their organizations.
- New example: Job candidates answering interview questions with the STAR method: describing the specific situation, required tasks, action taken, and results achieved.
- New example: Former CEOs of Bausch & Lomb, Yahoo!, and RadioShack adding false information to their résumés.
- Updated example: Nearly 85 percent of recruiters check candidates' information posted on social networking sites.
- Updated section discussing how 76,000 charges of illegal discrimination were filed in 2019, costing employers millions in settlements.
- New example: Uber agreeing to pay over $4 million to settle a sexual harassment and retaliation charge.

- New example: Dollar General settling a race discrimination charge for $6 million.
- New example of an Alaskan mining company settling charges for not providing advancement opportunities for women.
- Updated exhibit listing important training and development topics.
- New example: Companies like The Gap, Adobe, and Deloitte replacing their formal, annual performance appraisals with informal, frequent check-ins.
- New quote by Ken Blanchard.
- New Take Charge of Your Career: "Tips for receiving constructive feedback."
- New example: CEO pay is more than 278 times the average worker's pay.
- New exhibit titled: "HR executives cannot neglect safety and health."

CHAPTER 9

- New chapter opener about managing diversity being one of the biggest challenges and opportunities.
- New example of there being only 33 percent female representation at Google.
- New example: Federal contractor, SOS International, applying affirmative action policies to advance the inclusion of minorities, women, veterans, and the disabled.
- New quote by Ola Joseph.
- Updated section about changing diversity of the U.S. workforce.
- Updated section about women's earnings, pay gaps, and glass ceiling effects.
- New examples of female CEOs of *Fortune* 500 companies, including Safra Catz of Oracle and Tricia Griffith of Progressive.
- New Did You Know? feature highlighting some of Diversity Inc's Top 50 Companies for Diversity.
- Updated statistics regarding the participation of minorities and immigrants in the workplace.
- New example of successful immigrant entrepreneurs like Beto Perez of Zumba, Jan Koum of WhatsApp, and Mariama Levy of Verdi Consulting.
- New example: Hilton, Farmers Insurance, and Old Navy being awarded for their myriad diversity initiatives.
- New example: Companies like 3M, Yum! Brands, Lowe's, and Target employing corporate diversity officers.
- New example: Merck and Microsoft, among other companies, supporting minority internships.
- Updated section about people with mental and physical disabilities.
- New quote by Isabel Allende.
- New example: L'Oréal, Sodexo, and Lenovo listed on *Bloomberg*'s 2019 Gender-Equality Index.

- New example about Starbucks closing 8,000 stores to provide four hours of racial bias training to 175,000 employees.
- Updated Take Charge of Your Career: "Finding a mentor."
- New example: KFC in China adapting its menu by adding egg tarts, rice congee, and matcha ice cream among other items to match location-specific tastes.
- Updated Sustaining the Future case: "The Greenest Countries and Companies on Earth."

CHAPTER 10

- New chapter opener about effective leaders influencing the attainment of critical organizational goals.
- New example: Kenneth Frazier, CEO of Merck, creating value for stockholders while also delivering value in the form of vaccines and medicines to serve humanity.
- New Did You Know? feature about a Gallup survey reporting that manager coaching improves employees' work.
- New example of Richard Branson's vision about the world being powered entirely by renewable energy by 2050.
- New quote by Alan Mulally.
- New example: Employees of H-E-B grocery store chain giving their CEO, Charles C. Butt, a 99 percent approval rating on Glassdoor.
- New Traditional Thinking–The Best Managers Today feature about leaders needing influential managers to effect lasting change.
- New quote by John C. Maxwell.
- Updated Sustaining the Future feature about the The B Team encouraging business leaders to be a force for social, environmental, and economic good.
- New quote by Harvey Firestone.
- New example: Frances Hesselbein, former CEO of the Girl Scouts of America, continuing to be a transformational leader.
- New example about Dr. Anthony Fauci, leading expert on the coronavirus pandemic, exemplifying a Level 5 leader.
- New Take Charge of Your Career feature: "Hone your leadership skills."
- Trimmed nonessential text, enhancing the student experience.

CHAPTER 11

- New chapter opener about how motivating employees is an important managerial responsibility.
- New quote by Arthur Ashe.
- New example of goal setting at companies like Uber Eats, Grubhub, and DoorDash.
- New example: New Belgium Brewery dedicating itself to continuously improving its sustainability initiatives.
- New example of organic and natural beverage maker, Honest Tea, establishing a goal to improve people's health and well-being.

- New example: Google using the Objectives and Key Results (OKR) framework to motivate employee performance.
- New example: Aramark settling a $21 million lawsuit for unexpectedly canceling bonuses earned by frontline managers.
- Updated Sustaining the Future feature: "Stonyfield Organic Motivates Through Its Mission."
- New exhibit illustrating the potential consequences of making a mistake at work.
- New example: New Belgium Brewery celebrates employee tenure with anniversary milestones, including a one-week paid trip to Belgium after five years.
- New example about companies offering financial incentives to employees who live healthier lives, including weight loss, cholesterol management, and smoking cessation.
- New example: Enterprise develops its employees by assigning them to a management training program where they learn several functions.
- New Take Charge of Your Career feature: "Are you motivated to find a job you love?"
- New example: Anheuser-Busch, GEICO, and Blue Cross and Blue Shield rotating future leaders through multiple positions and locations to help them learn the businesses.
- New example: 3M encouraging employees to spend up to 15 percent of their time pursuing innovative ideas.
- New Did You Know? feature highlighting some of the best jobs in the United States.
- New example identifying the top three contributors to employee dissatisfaction.

CHAPTER 12

- New chapter opener discussing Stephanie Farsht leading innovative teams at Target to create positive culture change and enhanced customer service.
- New example: Teams at Papa & Barkley helping the company achieve sizable growth in revenue.
- New example: Tarang Amin crediting teamwork for helping build successful brands like Bounty, Pantene, and e.l.f. Cosmetics.
- New example of Amazon, 3M, and Boeing using teams to create new products faster.
- New example: Nestlé's In Genius program encouraging employees to pitch new innovative business ideas to senior management.
- New example: Software engineering teams at Google producing new products like Google Pixel, Google Translate, and Chromecast.
- Updated Sustaining the Future feature about teams making a social impact with design thinking.
- New example: Teams at Spotify deciding what projects to develop and how, resulting in innovative services like Rise and Secret Genius.

- New Did You Know? feature about virtual teams and enhanced communications technology potentially making face-to-face meetings obsolete.
- New quote by Dale Carnegie.
- Revised Traditional Thinking—The Best Managers Today feature about the evolving role of team leaders.
- New Did You Know? feature highlighting the differences between high- and low-performing teams at Google.
- New Take Charge of Your Career: "Build your teamwork skills now."
- Updated Did You Know? feature about the EEOC's mediation program to resolve complaints resulting in more than $165 million in monetary benefits to complainants.
- Trimmed nonessential text, enhancing the student experience.

CHAPTER 13

- New chapter opener about CEOs at organizations like Slack, Marriott, and the Dallas Mavericks needing to communicate empathy, support, and understanding to employees during the coronavirus pandemic in 2020.
- New exhibit illustrating how the Zoom videoconferencing app is being utilized as a two-way communication tool.
- New example indicating that one-third of companies are moving away from formal performance appraisals to frequent, informal check-ins with employees.
- New exhibit providing several tips for improving communication with someone who speaks a different native language.
- New example of some technology companies that have allowed ageism to negatively bias their decisions about hiring older employees.
- Updated example about average full-time employees spending about one-third of their day reading and answering emails.
- New example of team collaboration platforms growing in popularity like Asana, Ryver, Google's G Suite, Microsoft Teams, and Office 365 OneDrive.
- New Sustaining the Future feature: "Getting the Green Message Out with Social Media."
- New example: Tens of thousands of employees shifting to telework to adhere to social distancing rules during the coronavirus pandemic in 2020.
- New example: Deloitte giving its employees the choice to work outside the office and, when coming in, to reserve a workspace for the day (known as "hotdesking").
- New Study Tip feature: "Visiting your professor."
- New quote by John Kotter.
- New example: Google Cafés providing a space to encourage horizontal communication among employees and between teams.
- Trimmed nonessential text, enhancing the student experience.

CHAPTER 14

- New chapter opener about Julie Sweet, CEO of Accenture, taking several measurable steps to create a culture of equality.
- Updated section on General Motors' vehicle recall replacing faulty ignition switches.
- Updated Taking Charge of Your Career: "How to control without being too controlling."
- New example: Procter & Gamble's Worldwide Business Conduct Manual providing clear ethical and legal guidelines to employees around the world.
- New quote by Mark Twain.
- New example: Hertz using feedback from customer ratings of service and car quality to make corrections and improvements.
- New example: Bechtel, Caterpillar, Wipro, and Starwood Hotels & Resorts utilizing six sigma to address issues causing customer dissatisfaction.
- New Sustaining the Future feature: "The Gates Foundation: Do Even Good Intentions Need to be Controlled?"
- New example: 3M funding disruptive innovation, including Flex & Seal shipping material that requires no tape or filler, and residential roofing shingles containing smog-reducing granules to improve air quality.
- New example: Callie Field and her team at T-Mobile creating new and better ways to serve customers, decreasing the percentage of calls escalated to supervisors.
- New example about Starbucks relying on clan control to shape employee behavior by emphasizing satisfying customers more than pleasing managers.
- Trimmed nonessential text, enhancing the student experience.

CHAPTER 15

- New chapter opener discusses how coping effectively with major challenges requires bold and ethical leadership, dynamic strategic planning, new forms of intelligent organization, and sound control systems.
- New example: Global pharmaceutical companies like Roche, Eli Lilly, and Johnson & Johnson taking the unprecedented step to share information and resources to fight the coronavirus pandemic.
- Updated statistics about the Internet of Things (IoT).
- New examples of IoT devices like the Garmin smartwatch, Ring video doorbells, and Philips Hue personal lighting.
- New example: 3M, Nike, Google, and Merck achieving dominant competitive positions through early development and application of new technologies.
- New example of Amazon Web Services gaining a first-mover advantage in the cloud infrastructure market.
- New example: Netflix, LinkedIn, ESPN, and Airbnb relying on cloud service to store voluminous amounts of data generated from their applications.

- New example of Google Glass inspiring next-generation brands of smartglasses like North Focals, Vuzix Blade, and Solos.
- New example: Uber investing heavily in driverless car technology to make rides more efficient and prices lower for customers.
- New example: Samsung and Capital One acting as prospector firms, which are outward-looking and opportunistic.
- New Traditional Thinking—The Best Managers Today feature discussing the source of innovation in many organizations.
- Updated section about Intuit's Innovation Days.

- New Did You Know? feature about senior leaders communicating compelling stories to effect transformational change.
- New example of managers enlisting the support of employees regarding the need to work from home during the coronavirus pandemic.
- Updated Sustaining the Future feature about TerraCycle's new home recycling delivery service called Loop.
- New quote by C.S. Lewis.
- Updated Take Charge of Your Career: "Is a side hustle in your future?"
- Trimmed nonessential text, enhancing the student experience.

M: Management

chapter 1 Managing in a Global World

Learning Objectives

After studying Chapter 1, you should be able to

LO1 Describe the four functions of management.

LO2 Understand what managers at different organizational levels do.

LO3 Define the skills needed to be an effective manager.

LO4 Summarize the major challenges facing managers today.

LO5 Recognize how successful managers achieve competitive advantage.

fizkes/Shutterstock

Almost everyone has worked for a good supervisor, played for a good coach, or taken a class with a good professor. What made these managers effective? Did they have a plan and goals to guide people to accomplish what needed to get done? Were they organized and always prepared? Or maybe they were effective because of the way they motivated, inspired, and led employees, players, or students. Of course, they were probably good at keeping things under control and making changes when needed.

Effective managers in companies all over the world lead, plan, organize, and control to help employees reach their potential so organizations can thrive in the highly competitive global marketplace. Lynsi Snyder, CEO of fast-food chain In-N-Out Burger, has proven to be an effective *leader*. With a 99 percent approval rating by employees, Snyder was ranked in 2019 as one of the top 5 CEOs in the United States.[1] Over the past decade, she's expanded In-N-Out Burger's cultlike following to over 300 stores in six states. She's been able to do so, in part, by creating a constructive and positive work environment. In-N-Out Burger pays its employees an average of $13 an hour, 25 percent more than most competitors, and it offers strong job-training programs and benefit plans for part- and full-time staff. Says Snyder, "[M]y hope is that anyone who spends time as an In-N-Out Associate finds the experience valuable."[2]

Another secret to In-N-Out Burger's success has been not to chase the latest food craze or try to outmarket other fast-food restaurants with an unending number of menu options. Its success has been in doing the opposite: staying true to its core principles of making quality food with quality products. Many fast-food chains have recently introduced "never-frozen" ground beef in their stores; In-N-Out Burger has never used frozen meat in its 70-plus-year history. The chain still bakes its own buns each day and banned microwaves and heat lamps from its stores. These are *controlling* principles that help it deliver the consistent quality its loyal customers want. Says Snyder, "It's not [about] adding new products. Or thinking of the next bacon-wrapped this or that. We're making the same burger, the same fry. We're really picky and strategic. We're not going to compromise."[3]

But preserving those core values while also trying to expand the company's reach doesn't happen on its own. It requires careful *planning*. Since taking over the company in 2010, Snyder has taken a slow-but-steady approach to expansion. While Snyder opened more than 80 new stores and branched out from California into states such as Texas and Oregon, she wanted to make sure that adding locations didn't result in less quality. "I felt a deep call to make sure that I preserve those things that [my family] would want. That we didn't ever look to the left and the right to see what everyone else is doing, cut corners or change things drastically or compromise," says Snyder. "I really wanted to make sure that we stayed true to what we started with. That required me to become a protector. A guardian."[4]

In-N-Out Burger hasn't grown as quickly as some of its competitors, but it has grown smartly. The average In-N-Out location generates twice as much revenue as the average McDonald's, and it does so while sustaining a 20 percent profit margin, significantly higher than its competitors.[5] To maintain such efficiency requires effective *organizing*. Fast-food outlets sometimes boast as many as 80 different menu items at a time; In-N-Out serves fewer than 15. That has led to streamlined production and stronger quality control standards across its stores. Snyder hasn't rushed to flood the market with In-N-Outs nationwide, but her restraint and dedication to organizational efficiency promises a strong profit-generating store with each new opening.

● In-N-Out Burger's CEO Lynsi Snyder puts the four functions of management into action. Ethan Pines/The Forbes Collection/Contour RA/Getty Images

In business, there is no replacement for effective management. A company may fly high for a while, but it cannot maintain that success for long without good management. Our goal in this book is to help you learn what it takes to become an effective and successful manager. You will learn a wide variety of strategies and tactics, organized under the major themes described above. Along the way, we emphasize how the best managers differentiate themselves and achieve excellence in today's marketplace, including globalization, sustainability, entrepreneurship, diversity management, and more.

Elon Musk, CEO of the Boring Company, announces his plan to combine the start-up's hyperloop technology with SpaceX's plan to use its latest rocket program to create a transportation system to get anywhere on Earth in less than an hour. SpaceX/Getty Images

LO1 Describe the four functions of management.

1 | THE FOUR FUNCTIONS OF MANAGEMENT

Management is the process of working with people and resources to accomplish organizational goals. Good managers do those things both effectively and efficiently:

- To be *effective* is to achieve organizational goals.

- To be *efficient* is to achieve goals with minimal waste of resources—that is, to make the best possible use of money, time, materials, and people.

Unfortunately, far too many managers fail on both criteria or focus on one at the expense of another. The best managers maintain a clear focus on both effectiveness *and* efficiency.

Although business is changing rapidly, there are still plenty of timeless principles that make managers great and companies thrive. While fresh thinking and new approaches are required now more than ever, much of what we already know about successful management practices (Chapter 2 discusses historical

but still-pertinent contributions) remains relevant, useful, and adaptable to the current highly competitive global marketplace.

Great managers and executives like Lynsi Snyder of In-N-Out Burger not only adapt to changing conditions but also apply—passionately, rigorously, consistently, and with discipline—the fundamental management principles of planning, organizing, leading, and controlling. These four core functions remain as relevant as ever, and they still provide the fundamentals that are needed to manage effectively in all types of organizations, including private, public, nonprofit, and entrepreneurial (from microbusinesses to global firms).

As any exceptional manager, coach, or professor would say, excellence always starts with the fundamentals.

1.1 | Planning Helps You Deliver Value

Planning is specifying the goals to be achieved and deciding in advance the appropriate actions needed to achieve those goals. As Exhibit 1.1 illustrates, planning activities include analyzing current situations, anticipating the future, determining objectives, deciding what types of activities the company will engage in, choosing corporate and business strategies, and determining the resources needed to achieve the organization's goals. Plans set the stage for action.

Exhibit 1.1 Examples of planning activities

| Analyze current situation. | → | Anticipate the future. | → | Determine objectives. |
| Decide what actions to engage in. | → | Choose a business strategy. | → | Determine resources to achieve goals. |

For example, Elon Musk, CEO of Tesla and SpaceX, has ambitious plans to make life interplanetary.[6] The entrepreneur wants to be the first to colonize Mars, as early as 2024.[7] Before humans can survive on the Red Planet, several objectives need to be met. The first hurdle is transportation. SpaceX is planning to build a 31-engine, 387-foot-tall rocket (nicknamed "Starship") to carry about 100 human passengers on the six- to nine-month journey to Mars.[8] The second challenge is preparing the infrastructure on the planet to sustain human life. SpaceX plans to send multiple unpiloted cargo missions to ferry equipment, search for water, and build a fuel plant.[9] These cargo missions will be followed by astronaut-carrying missions. The third objective is to shuttle human passengers to the Red Planet.[10] Following the achievement of this goal, Elon Musk will likely make plans for other ambitious interstellar adventures.

In today's highly competitive business environment, the planning function can also be described as *delivering strategic value.* Value is a complex concept.[11] Fundamentally, it describes the monetary amount associated with how well a job, task, good, or service meets users' needs. Those users might be business owners, customers, employees, governments, and even nations. When Steve Jobs, founder and CEO of Apple, died on October 5, 2011, many people around the world experienced a sense of loss both for him as a person and for the value that his transformational Apple products

Effectively creating value requires fully considering a new and changing set of factors, including the government, the natural environment, global forces, and the dynamic economy in which ideas are king and entrepreneurs are both formidable competitors and potential collaborators. You will learn about these and related topics in Chapter 4 (ethics and corporate responsibility), Chapter 5 (strategic planning and decision making), and Chapter 6 (entrepreneurship).

management the process of working with people and resources to accomplish organizational goals

planning the management function of systematically making decisions about the goals and activities that an individual, a group, a work unit, or the overall organization will pursue

organizing the management function of assembling and coordinating human, financial, physical, informational, and other resources needed to achieve goals

1.2 | Organizing Resources Achieves Goals

Organizing is the process of assembling and coordinating the human, financial, physical, informational, and other resources needed to achieve goals. Organizing activities include attracting people to the organization, specifying job responsibilities,

> ## Out of clutter find simplicity. From discord find harmony. In the middle of difficulty lies opportunity.
>
> —Albert Einstein

provided. The better you meet users' needs (in terms of quality, speed, efficiency, and so on), the more value you deliver. That value is "strategic" when it contributes to meeting the organization's goals. On a personal level, you should periodically ask yourself and your boss, "How can I add value?" Answering that question will enhance your contributions, job performance, and career.

Traditionally, planning was a top-down approach in which top executives established business plans and told others to implement them. For the best companies, delivering strategic value is a continual process in which people throughout the organization use their knowledge and that of their external customers, suppliers, and other stakeholders to identify opportunities to create, seize, strengthen, and sustain competitive advantage. (Chapter 3 discusses the external competitive environment of business and how managers can influence it.) This dynamic process swirls around the objective of creating more and more value for the customer. For example, In-N-Out Burger provides value to customers by using only high-quality ingredients and maintaining consistency across its franchises.[12]

grouping jobs into work units, marshaling and allocating resources, and creating conditions so that people and things work together to achieve maximum success.

The organizing function's goal is to *build a dynamic organization.* Traditionally, organizing involved creating an organization chart by identifying business functions; establishing reporting relationships; and having a personnel department that administered plans, programs, and paperwork. Now and in the future, effective managers will be using new forms of organizing and viewing their people as their most valuable resources. They will build organizations that are flexible and adaptive, particularly in response to competitive threats and customer needs.

Tony Hsieh, CEO of Zappos, has built a dynamic and successful online shoe and retail business by changing the rules of how to organize and treat the company's diverse employees and customers. After he founded the business in 2000, Hsieh's entrepreneurial approach was rewarded when Amazon purchased Zappos in 2009 for $1.2 billion.[13]

Fast-forward to today. Hsieh has adopted a "holacracy" organizational model that takes decision making away from managers and places it in the hands of self-organizing circles of employees.[14] Instead of job descriptions, employees have one or more roles that support Zappos' goal to be more innovative and adaptable. Employees' roles and accountabilities are posted online to increase understanding of everyone's responsibilities.[15]

Employees aren't the only stakeholders who benefit from Hsieh's flexible and adaptive approach to organizing. Customers who call the online retailer often feel spoiled by the treatment they receive. Surprisingly, customer service employees at Zappos aren't told how long they can spend on the phone with customers. In a time when many call-in customer service operations are tightly controlled or outsourced, Hsieh encourages his employees to give customers a "wow" experience, such as staying on the phone with them for as long as it takes to connect and make them happy (the longest recorded phone call lasted 10 hours and 51 minutes), giving customers free shipping both ways, sending greeting cards to celebrate customers' marriages and birthdays, writing thank-you notes, or even sending a military care package to a customer in Afghanistan.[16]

Progressive employee- and customer-oriented practices such as those at Zappos help organizations organize and effectively deploy the highly dedicated, diverse, and talented human resources needed to achieve success. You will learn more about these topics in Chapter 7 (organizing for success), Chapter 8 (human resources management), and Chapter 9 (managing diversity and inclusion).

1.3 | Leading Mobilizes Your People

Leading is stimulating people to be high performers. It includes motivating and communicating with employees, individually and in groups. Leaders maintain contact with people, guiding and inspiring them toward achieving team and organizational goals. Leading takes place in teams, departments, and divisions, as well as at the tops of large organizations.

In earlier textbooks, the leading function described how managers motivate workers to come to work and execute top management's plans by doing their jobs. Today and in the future, managers must be good at *mobilizing and inspiring people* to engage fully in their work and contribute their ideas—to use their knowledge and experience in ways never needed or dreamed of in the past.

Tricia Griffith, CEO of Progressive Insurance since 2016, has created an environment that fosters teamwork and motivates her employees by "making them feel connected to the brand."[17] On Fridays, Griffith eats lunch in the cafeteria in order to meet employees, and employees can participate in the innovation garage, which allows employees to experiment with new ideas and get feedback from their peers. Under Griffith's leadership, Progressive has risen to become the third largest auto insurer in the United States, behind only State Farm and Geico.[18] In *Fortune*'s list of top companies to work for, Progressive ranked 76 out of 100.[19]

Like Tricia Griffith, today's managers must rely on a very different kind of leadership (Chapter 10) that empowers and

● Online retail giant Zappos' culture and work environment make it a fun place to work. Tribune Content Agency LLC/Alamy Stock Photo

motivates people (Chapter 11). Far more than in the past, great work must be done via great teamwork (Chapter 12), both within work groups and across group boundaries. Underlying these processes will be effective interpersonal and organizational communication (Chapter 13).

1.4 | Controlling Means Learning and Changing

Planning, organizing, and leading do not guarantee success. The fourth function, controlling, is about monitoring performance and making necessary changes in a timely manner. By controlling, managers make sure the organization's resources are being used properly and the organization is meeting its goals for quality and safety.

Control must include monitoring. If you have any doubts that this function is important, consider a monitoring lapse that caused over 100 million people's private data to be hacked.[20] Capital One's customer application information (with Social Security numbers) was hacked by Paige Thompson, a software engineer who formerly worked for Amazon Web Services, who exploited a "'misconfiguration' of a firewall on a web application."[21] The hack went undetected until Capital One was alerted by a tip received from its security hotline. The hack exposed 140,000 Social Security numbers, one million Canadian Social Insurance numbers, and 80,000 bank account numbers, as well as people's names, addresses, credit scores, balances, and other information.[22] Corporations must monitor customer data and continuously assess the processes in place to secure these data.

● Ursula Burns, chair and CEO of Xerox, attends a State Dinner at the White House in honor of Canadian Prime Minister Justin Trudeau. REX/Shutterstock

When managers implement their plans, they often find that things are not working out as planned. After two years of devastating wildfires, Pacific Gas & Electric, a California utility company, filed bankruptcy and faced lawsuits from stakeholders across the state for its role in the wildfires. Under California law, utilities companies are liable for wildfires caused by equipment, even when the company is not negligent in maintaining the equipment; in the past two years, PG&E equipment was blamed for starting more than 12 fires,[23] destroying thousands of homes and killing dozens of people.[24] To reduce the company's risk in the future, PG&E created a wildfire safety plan and pledged to spend up to $2.3 billion in 2019 to reduce wildfires.[25]

The plan called for PG&E to do more tree trimmings, conduct more equipment inspections, and have preventative blackouts on dry and windy days. PG&E has since hired a new board member and appointed a special independent safety advisor.[26]

Successful organizations, large and small, pay close attention to the controlling function. But today and for the future, the key managerial challenges are far more dynamic than in the past; they involve *continually learning and changing*. Controls must still be in place, as described in Chapter 14. But new technologies and other innovations (Chapter 15) make it possible to achieve controls in more effective ways, to help all people throughout a company and across company boundaries change in ways that forge a successful future.

Exhibit 1.2 provides brief definitions of the four functions of management and the respective chapters in which these functions are covered in greater detail.

1.5 | Managing Requires All Four Functions

As a manager in the ever-changing global economy, your typical day will not be neatly divided into the four functions. You will be doing many things more or less simultaneously.[27] Your days will be busy and fragmented, with interruptions, meetings, and firefighting. If you work with heavy digital users who constantly send texts and e-mails, then your workdays will require even more stop-and-go moments.[28] There will be plenty of activities that you wish you

Exhibit 1.2	The four functions of management	
Function	**Brief Definition**	**See Chapters**
Planning	Systematically making decisions about which goals and activities to pursue.	4, 5, and 6
Organizing	Assembling and coordinating resources needed to achieve goals.	7, 8, and 9
Leading	Stimulating high performance by employees.	10, 11, 12, and 13
Controlling	Monitoring performance and making needed changes.	14 and 15

top-level managers senior executives responsible for the overall management and effectiveness of the organization

middle-level managers managers located in the middle layers of the organizational hierarchy, reporting to top-level executives

frontline managers lower-level managers who supervise the operational activities of the organization

team leaders employees who are responsible for facilitating successful team performance

could be doing but can't seem to get to. These activities will include all four management functions.

Some managers are particularly interested in, devoted to, or skilled in one or two of the four functions. Try to devote enough time and energy to developing your abilities with *all four* functions. You can be a skilled planner and controller, but if you organize your people improperly or fail to inspire them to perform at high levels, you will not be realizing your potential as a manager. Likewise, it does no good to be the kind of manager who loves to organize and lead but doesn't really understand where to go or how to determine whether you are on the right track.

Good managers don't neglect any of the four management functions. You should periodically ask yourself whether you are devoting adequate attention to *all* of them.

The four management functions apply to your career and other areas of your life as well. You must find ways to create value; organize for your own personal effectiveness; mobilize your own talents and skills as well as those of others; monitor your performance; and constantly learn, develop, and change for the future. As you proceed through this book and this course, we encourage you to engage in the material and apply the ideas to your other courses (e.g., improve your leadership skills), your part-time and full-time jobs (e.g., learn how to motivate coworkers and delight your customers), and use the ideas for your own personal development by becoming an effective manager.

● Facebook overhauled its News Feed to focus on what friends and family share. JGI/Tom Grill/Getty Images

LO2 Understand what managers at different organizational levels do.

2 | FOUR DIFFERENT LEVELS OF MANAGERS

Organizations—particularly large organizations—have many levels. In this section, you will learn about the types of managers found at four different organizational levels:

- Top-level manager.
- Middle-level manager.
- Frontline manager.
- Team leader.

2.1 | Top Managers Strategize and Lead

Top-level managers are the organization's senior executives and are responsible for its overall management. Top-level managers, often referred to as *strategic managers,* focus on the survival, growth, and overall effectiveness of the organization.

Top managers are concerned not only with the organization as a whole but also with the interaction between the organization and its external environment. This interaction often requires managers to work extensively with outside individuals and organizations.

The chief executive officer (CEO) is one type of top-level manager found in large corporations. This individual is the primary strategic manager of the firm and has authority over everyone else. Others include the chief operating officer (COO), company presidents, vice presidents, and members of the top management team. As companies have increasingly leveraged technology and knowledge management to help them achieve and maintain a competitive advantage, they have created the position of chief information officer (CIO). A relatively new top manager position, chief ethics officer, has emerged in recent years. Emmanuel Lulin holds that position for L'Oréal. Lulin has been recognized as a champion for "ethics as a way of life within the company."[29]

Traditionally, the role of top-level managers has been to set overall direction by formulating strategy and controlling resources. But now, more top managers are called on to be not only strategic architects but also true organizational leaders. Like Eric Artz of REI, leaders must create and articulate a broader corporate purpose with which people can identify—and one to which people will enthusiastically commit.

2.2 | Middle Managers Bring Strategies to Life

As the name implies, middle-level managers are located in the organization's hierarchy below top-level management and above the frontline managers and team leaders. Sometimes called *tactical managers,* they are responsible for translating the general goals and plans developed by strategic managers into more specific objectives and activities.

Traditionally, the role of the middle manager is to be an administrative controller who bridges the gap between higher and lower levels. Today, middle-level managers break down corporate objectives into business unit targets; put together separate business unit plans from the units below them for higher-level corporate review; and serve as nerve centers of internal communication, interpreting and broadcasting top management's priorities downward and channeling and translating information from the front lines upward.

As a stereotype, not long ago, the term *middle manager* connoted mediocre, unimaginative people defending the status quo. Companies have been known to cut them by the thousands, and television often portrays them as incompetent (such as Michael Scott of NBC's *The Office*).[31] But middle managers are closer than top managers to day-to-day operations, customers, frontline managers, team leaders, and employees, so they know the problems. They also have many creative ideas—often better than their bosses'. Good middle managers provide the operating skills and practical problem solving that keep the company working.[32]

2.3 | Frontline Managers Are the Vital Link to Employees

Frontline managers, or *operational managers,* are lower-level managers who execute the operations of the organization. These managers often have titles such as *supervisor* or *sales manager.* They are directly involved with nonmanagement employees, implementing the specific plans developed with middle managers. This role is critical because operational managers are the link between management and nonmanagement personnel. Your first management position probably will fit into this category.

Traditionally, frontline managers were directed and controlled from above to make sure that they successfully implemented operations to support the company strategy. But in leading companies, their role has expanded. Operational execution remains vital, but in leading companies, frontline managers

are increasingly called on to be innovative and entrepreneurial, managing for growth and new business development.

Managers on the front line—usually newer, younger managers—are crucial to creating and sustaining quality, innovation, and other drivers of financial performance.[33] In outstanding organizations, talented frontline managers are not only *allowed* to initiate new activities but are *expected* to do so by their top- and middle-level managers. And they receive the freedom, incentives, and support to do so.[34]

2.4 | Team Leaders Facilitate Team Effectiveness

A relatively new type of manager, known as a team leader, engages in a variety of behaviors to achieve team effectiveness.[35] The use of teams (discussed in Chapter 12) has increased as organizations shift from hierarchical to flatter structures that require lower-level employees to make more decisions.[36] While both team leaders and frontline managers tend to be younger managers with entrepreneurial skills, frontline managers have direct managerial control over their nonmanagerial employees. This means that frontline managers may be responsible for hiring, training, scheduling, compensating, appraising, and if necessary, firing employees in order to achieve their goals and create new growth objectives for the business.

● Actor Steve Carell played Michael Scott, the sometimes-likeable but often incompetent middle manager on NBC's *The Office. RGR Collection/Alamy Stock Photo*

REI's Stewardship Strategy

It would be hard to come up with a better example of a company that fully embraces the idea of environmental stewardship than Recreational Equipment, Inc., or REI. Based in Kent, Washington, REI is the maker of an award-winning line of outdoor gear and clothing backed by a 100 percent satisfaction guarantee. Structured as a retail cooperative, the company offers its 18 million members a discount on all purchases and one vote in the election of board members for a one-time fee of $20. By hiring outdoor enthusiasts, it continues to operate with a passion for and commitment to outdoor adventure. It has appeared on *Fortune*'s *100 Best Companies to Work For* list every year since the list began.

REI's commitment to the environment is equally strong. From gathering community input before building its flagship store in Seattle to retrofitting existing facilities for the same energy efficiency it builds into its new ones, the company strives to design and operate each of its buildings to reduce operating costs and environmental impact. It operates seven facilities holding the coveted LEED certification for environmental sustainability and has long been at the forefront of the green building movement. REI generates its own energy via solar panels on more than two dozen of its buildings, and it partners with business groups dedicated to promoting action on climate change while protecting the economic health of their communities. In 2014 the company was named a Green Power Leader by the U.S. Environmental Protection Agency. It monitors energy used in the course of executive travel and employee commutes, supports responsible forestry in paper goods it needs for its operations, composts waste at its headquarters, and works with suppliers to eliminate packaging waste. Through all these efforts, REI now operates on 100 percent renewable power.

REI is a company that has fully embraced the idea of environmental stewardship.
Jonathan Weiss/Shutterstock

Each year the company produces a stewardship report; its 2018 report announced that more than 70 percent of its profits went back to the outdoor community, mostly in contributions to nonprofits and environmental groups. By making such investments, REI is living up to its core principle of putting "purpose before profits."

Discussion Questions

- REI earned record revenues of nearly $3 billion in 2018. To what extent do you think REI's environmentally responsible strategies help support its financial success?

- In a recent message to the company, CEO Eric Artz declared the company's "fight for life outside" initiative as one of its core values. All 13,000 REI employees pledged to do so. What kind of effect do you think this kind of collective call to action can have on a workforce? Could other companies learn from REI's example? Are there any risks?

Sources: Company website, https://www.rei.com/ stewardship, accessed March 4, 2020; "Fortune's 100 Best Companies to Work For 2020," *Fortune*, https://fortune.com/best-companies/2020/ search/; and company website, https://www .rei.com/stewardship/climate-change, accessed March 4, 2020.

In comparison, team leaders are more like project facilitators or coaches. Their responsibilities include organizing the team and establishing its purpose, finding resources to help the team get its job done, removing organizational impediments that block the team's progress, and developing team members' skills and abilities.[37] In addition, a good team leader creates and supports a positive social climate for the team, challenges the team, provides feedback to team members, and encourages the team to be self-sufficient.[38] Beyond their internally focused responsibilities, team leaders also need to represent the team's interests with other teams, departments, and groups within and outside the organization. In this sense, the team leader serves as the spokesperson and champion for the team when dealing with external stakeholders.

Team leaders are expected to help their teams achieve important projects and assignments. In some ways, a team leader's job can be more challenging than frontline and other types of managers' jobs because team leaders often lack direct control (e.g., hiring and firing) over team members. Without this direct control, team leaders need to be creative in how they inspire, motivate, and guide their teams to achieve success.

Exhibit 1.3 elaborates on the changing roles and activities of managers at different levels within the organization. You will learn about each of these aspects of management throughout the course.

2.5 | Three Roles That All Managers Perform

The trend today is toward less hierarchy and more teamwork. In small firms—and in large companies that have adapted to these highly competitive times—managers have strategic, tactical, and operational responsibilities and team responsibilities.

Shutterstock

Exhibit 1.3	Transformation of management roles and activities			
	Team Leaders	**Frontline Managers**	**Middle-Level Managers**	**Top-Level Managers**
Changing Roles	From operational implementers to facilitators of team effectiveness.	From operational implementers to aggressive entrepreneurs.	From administrative controllers to supportive controllers.	From resource allocators to institutional leaders.
Key Activities	Structuring teams and defining their purpose.	Attracting and developing resources.	Linking dispersed knowledge and skills across units.	Establishing high performance standards.
	Finding resources and removing obstacles so teams can accomplish their goals.	Creating and pursuing new growth opportunities for the business.	Managing the tension between short-term purpose and long-term ambition.	Institutionalizing a set of norms to support cooperation and trust.
	Developing team members' skills so teams can be self-managing.	Managing continuous improvement within the unit.	Developing individuals and supporting their activities.	Creating an overarching corporate purpose and ambition.

ASDF_MEDIA/Shutterstock

Sources: F. P. Morgeson, D. S. DeRue, and E. P. Karam, "Leadership in Teams: A Functional Approach to Understanding Leadership Structures and Processes," *Journal of Management* 36, no. 1 (January 2010), pp. 5–39; J. R. Hackman and R. Wageman, "A Theory of Team Coaching," *Academy of Management Review* 30, no. 2 (April 2005), pp. 269–87; and C. Bartlett and S. Goshal, "The Myth of the Generic Manager: New Personal Competencies for New Management Roles," *California Management Review* 40, no. 1 (Fall 1997), pp. 92–116.

They are *complete* businesspeople; they have knowledge of all business functions, are accountable for results, and focus on serving customers both inside and outside their firms. All of this requires the ability to think strategically, translate strategies into specific objectives, coordinate resources, and do real work with lower-level people.

Today's best managers can do it all; they are adaptive and agile and are "working leaders."[39] They focus on relationships with other people and on achieving results. They don't just make decisions, give orders, wait for others to produce, and then evaluate results. They get their hands dirty, do hard work themselves, solve problems, and create value.

What does all of this mean in practice? How do managers spend their time—what do they actually do? A classic study of top executives found that they spend their time engaging in 10 key activities, falling into three broad categories or roles:[40]

1. **Interpersonal roles:**

   - *Leader*—Developing effective strategies to achieve organizational goals.
     Example: The manager of a tech start-up motivates and leads seven employees.

   - *Liaison*—Maintaining a network of outside stakeholders and alliances that provide information and favors.
     Example: A human resources director attends monthly HR association meetings.

   - *Figurehead*—Performing symbolic duties on behalf of the organization, like greeting important visitors and speaking at important events.
     Example: The president of a university presides over a graduation ceremony.

2. **Informational roles:**

   - *Monitor*—Seeking information to develop a thorough understanding of the organization and its environment.
     Example: A financial analyst researches the financial health of a publicly traded company.

   - *Disseminator*—Sharing information between different people, like employees and managers; sometimes interpreting and integrating diverse perspectives.
     Example: A team leader in a management consulting firm shares her team's concerns with the managing partner.

   - *Spokesperson*—Communicating on behalf of the organization about plans, policies, actions, and results.
     Example: A public relations officer of a global company issues a news release detailing plans to expand into Pacific Rim countries.

3. **Decisional roles:**

   - *Entrepreneur*—Searching for new business opportunities and initiating new projects to create change.

   Example: A software engineer at a social networking website company identifies a new and more intuitive way to connect its users.

   - *Disturbance handler*—Taking corrective action during crises or other conflicts.
     Example: The owner of an amusement park implements new safety protocols after a malfunctioning ride injures a customer.

   - *Resource allocator*—Providing funding and other resources to units or people; includes making major organizational decisions.
     Example: The chief financial officer at a company determines the size of each division's budget for the upcoming fiscal year.

   - *Negotiator*—Engaging in negotiations with stakeholders inside and outside the organization.
     Example: An account executive from an advertising company negotiates the purchase price and terms of an advertising campaign with a team from a large client.

This classic study of managerial roles remains highly descriptive of what all types of managers do today. As you review the list, you might ask yourself, "Which of these activities do I enjoy most (and least)? Where do I excel (and not excel)? Which would I like to improve?" Whatever your answers, you will be learning more about these activities throughout this course.

LO3 Define the skills needed to be an effective manager.

3 | MANAGERS NEED THREE BROAD SKILLS

Performing management functions and roles, pursuing effectiveness and efficiency, and competitive advantage (discussed later in this chapter) are the cornerstones of a manager's job. However, understanding this fact does not ensure success. Managers need a variety of skills to *do* these things *well*. Skills are specific abilities that result from knowledge, information, aptitude, and practice. Although managers need many individual skills, which you will learn about throughout this text, three general categories are crucial:[41]

- Technical skills.

- Conceptual and decision skills.

- Interpersonal and communication skills.

First-time managers tend to underestimate the challenges of the many technical, human, and conceptual skills required.[42]

However, with training, experience, and practice, managers can learn to apply each of these skills to improve their effectiveness and performance.

3.1 | Technical Skills

A **technical skill** is the ability to perform a specialized task that involves a certain method or process. The technical skills you learn in college will give you the opportunity to get an entry-level position or change careers; they will also help you as a manager. For example, your accounting and finance courses will develop the technical skills you need to understand and manage an organization's financial resources.

Lower-level managers who possess technical skills earn more credibility from their subordinates than comparable managers without technical know-how.[43] Thus, newer employees may want to become proficient in their technical area (e.g., human resources management or marketing) before accepting a position as team leader or frontline manager.

3.2 | Conceptual and Decision Skills

Conceptual and decision skills involve the ability to identify and resolve problems for the benefit of the organization and everyone concerned. Managers use these skills when they consider the overall strategy of the firm, the interactions among different parts of the organization, and the role of the business in its external environment. Managers (like Mary Barra of GM) are increasingly required to think out of their comfort zones to make periodic and major changes in the way they do business to ensure the long-term success of their missions and organizations.

As you acquire greater responsibility, you will be asked often to exercise your conceptual and decision skills. You will confront issues that involve all aspects of the organization and must consider a larger and more interrelated set of decision factors. Much of this text is devoted to enhancing your conceptual and decision skills, but experience also plays an important part in their development.

3.3 | Interpersonal and Communication Skills

Interpersonal and communication skills influence the manager's ability to work well with people. These skills are often called *people skills* or *soft skills.* Managers spend the great majority of their time interacting with people,[44] and they must develop their abilities to build trust, relate to, and communicate effectively with those around them. Your people skills often make a difference in the levels of success you achieve. LinkedIn founder Jeff Weiner said, "The biggest skills gap in the United States is soft skills. . . . Everyone's so keenly focused on technology and AI. It's related though. . . . If you don't have that foundation in place, it becomes almost prohibitively complex to learn multiple skills at the same time."[45] Supporting this view, a study by the National Association of Colleges and Employers found that the ability to work in a team and written and verbal communication skills were the most desired skills sought in recent college graduates.[46]

Management professor Michael Morris emphasizes that it is vital for future managers to realize the importance of these skills in getting a job, keeping it, and performing well, especially in this era when so many managers supervise independent-minded knowledge workers. He explains, "You have to get high performance out of people in your organization who you don't have any authority over. You need to read other people, know their motivators, know how you affect them."[47]

As Exhibit 1.4 illustrates, the importance of these skills varies by managerial level. Technical skills are most important early in your career when you are a team leader and frontline manager. Conceptual and decision skills become more important than technical skills as you rise higher in the company and occupy positions in the middle and top manager ranks. But interpersonal and communication skills are important throughout your career, at every level of management. One way to increase the effectiveness of your interpersonal and communication skills is by being emotionally intelligent at work.

Good, successful managers often demonstrate a set of interpersonal skills known collectively as **emotional intelligence**[48] (or EQ). EQ combines three skill sets:

- *Understanding yourself*—including your strengths and limitations as a manager.

- *Managing yourself*—dealing with emotions, making good decisions, seeking feedback, and exercising self-control.

- *Working effectively with others*— listening, showing empathy, motivating, and leading.

technical skills the ability to perform a specialized task involving a particular method or process

conceptual and decision skills skills pertaining to the ability to identify and resolve problems for the benefit of the organization and its members

interpersonal and communication skills people skills; the ability to lead, motivate, and communicate effectively with others

emotional intelligence the skills of understanding yourself, managing yourself, and dealing effectively with others

Exhibit 1.4	Skill importance at different managerial levels		
	Technical Skills	Conceptual/ Decision Skills	Interpersonal/ Communication Skills
Top manager	Low	High	High
Middle manager	Medium	High	High
Frontline manager	High	Medium	High
Team leader	High	Medium	High

Source: Adapted from R. Katz, "Skills of an Effective Administrator," *Harvard Business Review* 52, no. 5 (September–October 1974), pp. 90–102.

The basic idea is that before you can be an effective manager of other people, you need to be able to manage your own emotions and reactions to others. Maybe you already have a high EQ, but if you feel that you could use some improvement in this area, observe how others connect with the people around them, handle stressful situations, and exercise self-control. This can help you build your own EQ so that you can be a more effective manager.

LO4 Summarize the major challenges facing managers today.

4 | MAJOR CHALLENGES FACING MANAGERS

When the economy is soaring, business seems easy. Starting up an Internet company looked easy in the 1990s, and ventures related to the real estate boom looked like a sure thing during the early 2000s. Eventually investors grew wary of dot-com start-ups, and the demand for new homes cooled as the United States experienced a major economic recession. At such times, it becomes evident that management is a challenge that requires constant adaptation to new circumstances.

What defines the competitive landscape of today's businesses? You will be reading about many relevant issues in the coming chapters, but we begin here by highlighting five key elements that make the current business landscape different from those of the past:

1. Globalization.

2. Technological change.

3. The importance of knowledge and ideas.

4. Collaboration across organizational boundaries.

5. Increasingly diverse labor force.

4.1 | Business Operates on a Global Scale

Far more than in the past, today's enterprises are global, with offices and production facilities all over the world. Corporations such as Starbucks and Adidas transcend national borders. A key reason for this change is the strong demand coming from consumers and businesses overseas. Companies that want to grow often need to tap international markets where incomes are rising and demand is increasing.

Nike got its start selling athletic shoes and apparel from a small town in Oregon.[49] Nike now sells products in 170 countries, with more than half its revenues coming from outside the United States.[50]

Globalization also occurs via cross-border partnership. Netflix created partnership agreements with cable and cell phone operators across the globe and expanded its reach to every country except China, Crimea, North Korea, and Syria.[51] Not only does Netflix offer local subscribers access to its massive database of movies, documentaries, and TV shows, but it also provided funding to local producers to create new content for global consumption. For example, *Elite* is a Spanish series produced by Zeta Audiovisual that stars Spanish actors.[52] Other global content funded by Netflix includes *Schitt's Creek,* a Canadian production by Daniel Levy, *Aggretsuko,* a Japanese animated series, and *Bodyguard,* a U.K.-based drama.[53] The global partner strategy is working. In 2018, for the first time, "international streaming revenues exceeded domestic streaming revenues."[54] Netflix is the largest global streaming service with over 151 million subscribers, only 60 million of whom live in the United States.[55]

Another factor that is making globalization both more possible and more prevalent is the Internet. It is estimated that by the end of 2019, there will be over 26 billion devices around the world connected to the Internet.[56] From 2000 to 2019, the largest increases in users of the Internet were from developing countries in Africa, the Middle East, Asia, Latin America, and the Caribbean.[57] As people in developing nations turn to the power of the web, they develop content in their own languages and create their own means of access, like Baidu, the search engine market leader in China that has over 70 percent of the search engine market share.[58]

The Internet is a powerful force for connecting people without regard to time and space. The Internet enables people to connect and work from anywhere in the world on a 24/7 basis. Laura Asiala, a manager for Dow Corning, based in Midland, Michigan, supervises employees in Tokyo, Seoul, Hong Kong, Shanghai, and Brussels. To keep in touch with them, she starts working at 5:00 a.m. some days and ends as late as midnight. She takes a break from 3:30 to 9:30 each day, and technology lets her communicate from home.[59]

China, with its 829 million Internet users,[60] is an attractive market for tech companies that want to expand internationally. Internet companies have struggled to operate and succeed in the Chinese market due to intense local competition, logistical challenges, and human rights concerns.

Involvement in company operations by the Chinese government has reached a new level. The state-run Xinhua News Agency announced that cybersecurity police would be embedded in large Internet companies to help guard against fraud and the "spreading of rumors." This policing effort is believed to be an effort on the part of the Chinese government to exert better control over the Internet in a country of over 1.4 billion people.[61]

Despite these challenges, LinkedIn entered the Chinese market in 2014 to try to attract some of the 140 million knowledge workers to its professional networking site. In exchange for being granted access to Chinese Internet users, LinkedIn agreed to censor content when asked to do so by government officials. In 2019, the company had 50 million registered users in China.[62] Time will tell whether LinkedIn can navigate successfully the myriad challenges in the world's largest Internet market.[63]

Take Charge of Your Career

Study abroad while you can

Do you have the cultural sensitivity, international perspective, and foreign-language skills to succeed in the global economy? If you truly want to become a global citizen, how can you get the skills and experience you need?

One obvious—and fun—way to develop this skill set is to study abroad. Colleges all over the country award students credit for these programs, and many options are available, from a one-week stay, to a summer- or a semester-long program, to full-year immersion programs. Through study abroad you can gain valuable exposure to a new culture, perfect a language you've studied or begin learning a new one, acquire marketable job skills, and make professional connections.

Cultural awareness and empathy are two skills that increasingly appear as top criteria for hiring managers. The modern workplace emphasizes inclusion and collaboration, so being aware of cultural differences, as well as being able to empathize—see things from the perspectives of other people—are critical skills to achieve these goals. Study abroad programs present you with opportunities to interact with people whose culture is different from your own, experience others' values and norms, and observe the way people of different backgrounds approach and solve problems. In navigating an unfamiliar environment, you'll increase your independence and self-reliance, enhance your problem-solving skills, overcome explicit or implicit stereotypes you may have formed, and develop patience, flexibility, and adaptability that will serve as assets in whatever career you pursue.

Currently only about 10 percent of U.S. students study abroad, a number some experts say is too low given our increasingly globalized economy and job market. Many of the critical health, energy, environmental, and political problems humans now face will best be solved by people who know how to communicate across cultures and understand that we work best when we work together. Why not be one of them?

Sources: A. Doyle, "Top Skills and Attributes Employers Look For." *The Balance,* January 22, 2020, https://www.thebalancecareers.com/top-skills-employers-want-2062481; and NAFSA, "Trends in U.S. Study Abroad," accessed March 4, 2020.

● Reed Hastings, the Netflix chief, had a global vision that disrupted the television industry. Ethan Miller/Getty Images

Smaller firms are also engaged in globalization. Many small companies export their goods. Many domestic firms assemble their products in other countries, using facilities such as Mexico's maquiladora plants. And companies are under pressure to improve their products in the face of intense competition from foreign manufacturers. Firms today must ask themselves, "How can we be the best in the world?"

For students, it's not too early to think about the personal ramifications. In the words of chief executive officer Jim Goodnight of SAS, the largest privately held software company in the world, "The best thing business schools can do to prepare their students is to encourage them to look beyond their own backyards. Globalization has opened the world for many opportunities, and schools should encourage their students to take advantage of them."[64]

4.2 | Technology Is Advancing Continuously

The Internet's impact on globalization is only one of the ways that technology is vitally important in the ever-changing business world. Technology both complicates things and creates new opportunities. The challenges come from the rapid rate at which communication, transportation, information, and other technologies change.[65]

Until recently, for example, desktop computers were a reliable source of income, not only for computer makers but also for the companies that make keyboards and a whole host of accessories like wrist rests and computer desks. But after just a couple of decades of widespread PC use, customers switched to laptops, tablets, and even smartphones for their computing needs, requiring different accessories and using them in different ways.[66] Any company that still makes desktops has to rethink its customers' wants and needs, not to mention the possibility that these customers may be doing their work at the airport or a local coffee shop rather than in an office.

Later chapters will discuss technology further, but here we highlight the rise of the Internet and its effects. Why is the Internet so important to business?[67]

- It enables managers to be mobile and connected 24/7.

- It fulfills many business functions. It is a virtual marketplace, a means to sell goods and services, a distribution channel, an information service, and more.

- It speeds up globalization. Managers can see what competitors, suppliers, and customers are doing on the other side of the world.

- It provides access to information, allows better-informed decisions, and improves efficiency of decision making.

- It facilitates design of new products and services, from smartphones to online banking services.

While these advantages create business opportunities, they also create threats as competitors capitalize on new developments.

At the beginning, Internet companies dazzled people with financial returns that seemed limitless. Today, investors and entrepreneurs have learned that not every business idea will fly, but many profitable online businesses have become a part of our day-to-day lives. Just a few years ago, it was novel to go online to order plane tickets, read the news, or share photos.

Some online success stories, such as Stitch Fix, IPSY, and Zappos, are purely Internet businesses. Other online companies added brick-and-mortar channels to their business strategies.

The Internet's impact is felt not only at the level of businesses as a whole but also by individual employees and their managers. Just as globalization has stretched out the workdays of some people, high-tech gadgets have made it possible to stay connected to work anytime and anywhere. Wi-Fi hotspots make connections available in shared working spaces, coffee shops, restaurants, hotels, airports, and libraries. Software lets users download and read files and e-mail on their phones and tablets.

Social media and networking are also challenging the way businesses operate and managers connect. Facebook, the largest online social network, has reported 2.376 billion monthly active users as of April 2019; nearly 90 percent of these users are located outside the United States and Canada.[68] Other popular social networking sites—like Instagram, Twitter, Snapchat, and TikTok—also connect people with one another.

Finding the time to build and maintain meaningful connections to a large and diverse network of contacts, clients, and other key stakeholders is a major challenge for managers today. While it can be time-consuming, connecting with people has never been easier because of online social networking sites that allow you to develop your social capital. The goodwill stemming from your social relationships is more important than ever and aids your career success, compensation, employment, team effectiveness, successful entrepreneurship, and relationships with suppliers and other outsiders.[69] Students should take time to build a large and diverse network while in school. This network may prove valuable in the future.

The stress comes when employees or their supervisors don't set limits on being connected. As out-of-office flex work becomes increasingly common, research suggests that individuals are using their smartphones to work longer hours during workday evenings and on weekends.[70] Users can and should decide when to turn off the devices. Jean Chatzky, an editor for *Money* magazine, realized that her device had become more of a distraction than a help and began reminding herself that the messages were not emergencies.[71] Thus, using technology effectively is more than a matter of learning new skills; it also involves making judgments about when and where to apply the technology for maximum benefit.[72]

4.3 | Knowledge Needs Managing

Companies and managers need new, innovative ideas. Because companies in advanced economies have become so efficient at producing physical goods, most workers have been freed up to provide services like training, entertainment, research, and advertising. Efficient factories with fewer workers produce the cereals and cell phones the market demands; meanwhile, more and more workers create software and invent new products. These workers, whose primary contributions are ideas and problem-solving expertise, are often referred to as *knowledge workers.*

Managing these workers poses some particular challenges, which we will examine throughout this book. For example, determining whether they are doing a good job can be difficult because the manager cannot simply count or measure a knowledge worker's output. Also, these workers often are most motivated to do their best when the work is interesting, not because of a carrot or stick dangled by the manager.[73]

Because the success of modern businesses so often depends on the knowledge used for innovation and the delivery of services, organizations need to manage that knowledge. **Knowledge management** is the set of practices aimed at discovering and harnessing an organization's intellectual resources—fully utilizing the intellects of the organization's people. Knowledge management is about finding, unlocking, sharing, and capitalizing on the most precious resources of an organization: people's expertise, skills, wisdom, and relationships.

Gorodenkoff/Shutterstock

Typically, knowledge management relies on software that lets employees contribute what they know and share that knowledge readily with one another. As a result, knowledge management may be the responsibility of an organization's information technology (IT) department, perhaps under the leadership of a chief information officer or chief knowledge officer.

4.4 | Collaboration Boosts Performance

One of the most important processes of knowledge management is to ensure that people in different parts of the organization collaborate effectively. This requires communication among departments, divisions, or other subunits of the organization. For example, BP tries to encourage managers to break out of the traditional corporate hierarchy to share knowledge freely across the organization while remaining fiercely committed to the performance of their individual business units. This emphasis on dual responsibilities for performance and knowledge sharing also occurs at pharmaceutical giant Glaxo-SmithKline, the large German industrial company Siemens, and the London-based steelmaker Ispat International.[74]

Toyota keeps its product development process efficient by bringing together design engineers and manufacturing employees from the beginning. Often, manufacturing employees can see ways to simplify a design so that it is easier to make without defects or unnecessary costs. Toyota expects its employees to listen to input from all areas of the organization, making this type of collaboration a natural part of the organization's culture. The collaboration is supported with product development software, including an online database that provides a central, easily accessible source of information about designs and processes. Along with this information, employees use the software to share their knowledge—best practices they have developed for design and manufacturing.[75] At Toyota, knowledge management supports collaboration and vice versa.

Customers, too, can be collaborators. Creating outstanding products and services can start with involving customers in company decisions. For example, Starbucks customers have a huge variety of drink options, and Zazzle customers can personalize products such as tote bags, pillows, and iPhone cases prior to purchasing them.[76]

4.5 | Diversity Needs to Be Leveraged

The labor force is becoming more and more diverse. This means that it is likely that your coworkers, customers, suppliers, and other stakeholders will differ from you in race, ethnicity, age, gender, physical characteristics, or sexual orientation. To be an effective manager, you'll need to understand, relate to, and work productively with these individuals. How diverse are we becoming at work? The following trends in the U.S. labor force are expected from 2016 through 2026:[77]

- The labor force will continue to grow more diverse.

- The share of women in the labor force will increase to just over 47 percent.

- Fast growth of "older workers" will occur to the point that approximately one out of four workers will be 55 and older.

- Hispanics will grow to about 20 percent, African Americans to nearly 13 percent, and Asians to approximately 7 percent of the labor force.

- A higher percentage of women than men will join the labor force.

- White (non-Hispanic) workers' participation in the labor force will decrease from 63 to 58 percent.

The increase in gender, racial, age, and ethnic diversity in the workplace will accentuate the many differences in employees' values, attitudes toward work, and norms of behavior. In addition to leveraging the strengths of diverse employees, effective managers need to find ways to connect with diverse customers, suppliers, and government officials, both in the United States and internationally. As will be discussed in greater detail in later chapters, managers need to be acutely aware of these differences and be prepared to prevent (or deal with) miscommunication, insensitivity, and hostility on the part of an employee, customer, or other stakeholder who doesn't embrace the benefits of diversity management.

Fortunately, effective managers and organizations are taking steps to address these concerns and leverage the diversity of their resources and talent in new ways. Members of Target's board of directors are 36 percent female and 45 percent racially diverse, while the store management workforce is 52 percent female and 33 percent racially diverse.[78] Target has also taken steps to make its products more diverse, including carrying clothing lines specifically designed for kids with sensory-processing difficulties and other physical disabilities, carrying more than 1,000 beauty products that address different skin tones and hair types, and sourcing products from diverse suppliers.[79]

Accounting, taxation, and consulting firm Deloitte LLP has undertaken several steps to break the "glass ceiling" and retain more of its talented female employees. The firm decreased the amount of travel for employees to allow them to have better work–life balance, created a Parents Transition Programme to help women and men with parental leave, and made diversity management a key priority for the entire organization. Deloitte created the Female Academy initiative, which features academic workshops, speakers, and events given to 25 promising female university students over the course of six weeks, to challenge and support them in their pursuit of creativity and growth.[80] By making a concerted effort to retain and value female employees, Deloitte is managing its talent in a more effective and efficient manner. Twenty-five percent of board members and 31 percent of the leadership team are women.[81]

Globalization, technological change, the monumental importance of new ideas, collaboration across disappearing boundaries, diversity—what are the effects of this tidal wave of new forces? The remainder of this chapter and the following chapters will answer this question with business and management principles, real-world examples, and insights from successful managers and leaders.

5 | SOURCES OF COMPETITIVE ADVANTAGE

Why do some companies lose their dominant positions while others manage to stay on top?[82] Blockbuster was a successful video rental chain until Netflix, cable companies, and online enterprises changed the delivery and pricing of videos and entertainment content. Then there's Eastman Kodak. For more than 100 years, it dominated the camera and film markets until being upended by the invention of digital photography, file sharing, and the like. On the other hand, how does a company like Apple continually excite customers with its "iGadget" offerings?[83] How does the Chinese electric car manufacturer BYD compete effectively in this emerging segment of the automobile industry? How does the Indian technology company Infosys compete effectively against its American rivals, Accenture and McKinsey?[84]

These successful companies have strong managers who know they are in a competitive struggle to survive and win. To do this, you have to gain advantage over your competitors and earn a profit. You gain competitive advantage by being better than your competitors at doing valuable things for your customers. But what does this mean, specifically? To succeed, managers must deliver the fundamental success drivers: innovation, quality, service, speed, cost competitiveness, and sustainability.

5.1 | Innovation Keeps You Ahead of Competitors

Founded in 2000, Baidu is the number one Chinese-language Internet search engine. With more than 40,000 employees[85] and nearly 20,000 of those working on research and development initiatives,[86] Baidu is hoping that its recent innovations—from driverless car technology to AI customer service—will help it maintain an innovative edge in China.[87]

Innovation is the introduction of new goods and services. Your firm must adapt to changes in consumer demand and to new competitors. Products don't sell forever; in fact, they don't sell for nearly as long as they used to because so many competitors are introducing so many new products all the time. Likewise, you have to be ready with new ways to communicate with customers and deliver products to them, as when the Internet forced traditional merchants to learn new ways of reaching customers directly. Globalization and technological advances have accelerated the pace of change and thus the need for innovation.

Sometimes, the most important innovation isn't the product itself but the way it is delivered. Borrowing an idea that has proved popular in Europe, Opaque's Dining in the Dark creates dining experiences in complete darkness.[88] Guests select gourmet meals from a menu in a lighted lounge and then are led into a dark banquet room by blind or visually impaired servers. The attraction is that diners experience the meal in a completely new way because they are forced to concentrate on their senses of taste, smell, and touch. The company is located in Santa Monica, California.[89]

Innovation is today's holy grail.[90] And like the other sources of competitive advantage, innovation comes from people, it must be a strategic goal, and it must be managed properly. Later chapters will show you how great companies innovate.

5.2 | Quality Must Improve Continually

Historically, quality pertained primarily to the physical goods that customers bought. It referred to attractiveness, lack of defects, reliability, and long-term dependability. The traditional approach to quality was to check work after it was completed and then eliminate defects. But then W. Edwards Deming, J. M. Juran, and other quality gurus convinced managers to take a more complete approach to achieving *total* quality. This includes several objectives:

- *Preventing* defects before they occur.

- *Achieving zero defects* in manufacturing.

- *Designing* products for quality.

The goal is to plan carefully; prevent, from the beginning, all quality-related problems; and live a philosophy of *continuous improvement* in the way the company operates. Deming and his ideas were actually rebuffed by U.S. managers; only when he found an audience in Japan, and Japan started grabbing big chunks of market share from the United States in vehicles, computer chips, and TVs, did U.S. managers start internalizing and practicing his quality philosophy.[91]

Providing world-class quality requires a thorough understanding of what quality really is.[92] Quality can be measured in terms

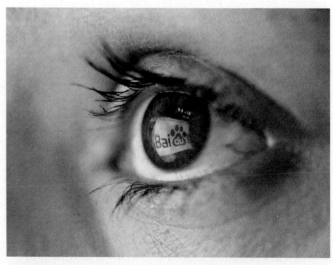

Iain Masterton/Alamy Stock Photo

of product performance, customer service, reliability (avoidance of failure or breakdowns), conformance to standards, durability, and aesthetics.

Quality is further provided when companies customize goods and services to the wishes of the individual consumer. Choices at Starbucks give consumers thousands of variations on the drinks they can order. Gatorade GX allows customers to create customized bottles. Nike's 90/10 pack sneakers give customers the opportunity to participate in designing their own shoes, and Icon Meals permits customers to create custom meal plans online.[93]

5.3 | Services Must Meet Customers' Changing Needs

As we noted in the discussion of quality, important quality measures often pertain to the level of service customers receive. This dimension of quality is particularly important because the service sector now dominates the U.S. economy. Services include intangible products like insurance, hotel accommodations, medical care, and entertainment. In recent years, Americans spent a higher percentage of their personal income on services than tangible goods.[94] The total number of jobs in service companies—not including retailing, wholesaling, and government workers—is nearly five times the number in manufacturing companies. And that pattern is expected to intensify. Between now and 2024, the fastest-growing job categories will be almost entirely services and retailing jobs, and the jobs expected to see the greatest declines are almost all in manufacturing.[95]

In a competitive context, **service** means giving customers what they want or need, when and where they want it. So service is focused on continually meeting the changing needs of

An important dimension of service quality is making it easy and enjoyable for customers to experience a service or to buy and use products. For example, Apple made it easy and enjoyable for online customers to sample their favorite music and then download it from the iTunes store. Amazon allows customers to look at a free sample of a book to help them decide whether they want to read and purchase the entire book. These innovations in service are changing the way companies do business.

5.4 | Do It Better *and* Faster

Google's culture, based on rapid innovation, is constantly trying to make improvements in its product. When Sheryl Sandberg (now chief operating officer of Facebook) was a vice president at Google, she once made a mistake by moving too fast to plan carefully. Although the mistake cost the company a few million dollars, Google cofounder Larry Page responded to her explanation and apology by saying he was actually glad she had made the mistake. It showed that Sandberg appreciated the company's values. Page told her, "I want to run a company where we are moving too quickly and doing too much, not being too cautious and doing too little. If we don't have any of these mistakes, we're just not taking enough risks."[97]

While it's unlikely that Google actually favors mistakes over money-making ideas, Page's statement expressed an appreciation that in the modern business environment, **speed**—rapid

> "Be everywhere, do everything, and never fail to astonish the customer."
>
> —Macy's Motto

customers to establish mutually beneficial long-term relationships. Service is also an important offering for many companies that sell tangible goods. Software companies, in addition to providing the actual programs, may help their customers identify requirements, set up computer systems, and perform maintenance.

Stores offer a shopping environment and customer service along with the goods on their shelves. To improve service for a wider customer base, Best Buy adjusted its store environment so it would be more inviting to female shoppers. The chain's loud music and emphasis on high-tech features had been aimed at young men, but the store found that women influence 9 out of 10 consumer electronics purchases. Best Buy lowered the volume, dimmed the lighting, and trained staff to discuss what customers want the technology to do for them, rather than merely pointing out bells and whistles.[96]

Chesnot/Getty Images

execution, response, and delivery of results—often separates the winners from the losers.

How fast can you develop and get a new product to market? How quickly can you respond to customer requests? You are far better off if you are faster than the competition—and if you can respond quickly to your competitors' actions.

Speed is no longer just a goal of some companies; it is a strategic imperative. Speed combined with quality is a measure that a company is operating efficiently. The Starbucks mobile app made ordering so much easier and faster that one-third of all U.S. Starbucks transactions are now done through the app. Through the app, customers can order and customize coffee, pay, and redeem rewards all before they arrive at the store. To increase delivery speed, Starbucks has "juggled employees' tasks to limit bottlenecks caused by in-store pickups of online orders."[98]

Speed isn't everything—you can't get sloppy in your quest to be first. But other things being equal, faster companies are more likely to be the winners, slow ones the losers.

5.5 | Low Costs Help Increase Your Sales

Walmart keeps driving hard to find new ways to cut billions of dollars from its already very low distribution costs. The retail giant is experimenting with using shelf-scanning robots to monitor inventory to reduce employee costs. The robots move through store aisles scanning the shelves for missing or mispriced inventory; a human worker responds only when an issue is found.[99] Walmart introduced an app called My Walmart Schedule that allows employees to pick up shifts and gives all employees the same weekly shift for 13 weeks. The core-hour schedule gives employees stability and predictability in their schedule and reduces the amount of time managers spend putting the schedules together.[100]

Walmart's efforts are aimed at cost competitiveness, which means keeping costs low enough so the company can realize profits and price its products (goods or services) at levels that are attractive to consumers. Toyota's efforts to trim product development processes are also partly aimed at cost competitiveness. Making the processes more efficient through collaboration between design and manufacturing employees eliminates wasteful steps and procedures. Needless to say, if you can offer a desirable product at a lower price, it is more likely to sell.

Managing your costs and keeping them down requires efficiency: accomplishing your goals by using your resources wisely and minimizing waste. Every company must worry about cost because consumers can easily compare prices on the Internet from thousands of competitors. Expedia, NexTag, PriceGrabber, Google Flights, and Google Shopping are only a few of the search tools that can generate lists of prices at which a product is available from various suppliers. Consumers looking to buy popular items—such as cameras, printers, and plane fares—can go online to research the best models and the best deals. If you can't cut costs and offer attractive prices, you can't compete.

● Walmart controls costs by continuously improving the efficiency and speed of its inventory management system. One of its distribution centers is pictured above. Susana Gonzalez/Bloomberg/Getty Images

5.6 | Sustainability

Reducing resource use and waste, especially resources that are polluting and nonrenewable, helps to achieve an important form of competitive advantage: sustainability. Although sustainability means different things to different people,[101] in this text we emphasize a long-term perspective on helping the natural environment and building tomorrow's business opportunities while effectively managing today's business.[102]

In the United States, corporate sustainability efforts have fluctuated as environmental laws are strengthened or loosened; overall, the worldwide trend has been in the direction of greater concern for sustainability. Many companies have discovered that addressing sustainability issues often produces bottom-line benefits. Companies with strong sustainability performance that have also become financial winners include Danish bioscience company Corporate Knights, financial services provider Banco do Brasil, French luxury-goods maker Kering, and U.S. food spice firm McCormick.[103] Patagonia does not want customers to discard their outdoor gear that has a broken zipper, tear in the sleeve, or chewed-up Velcro closure. Known as the Worn Wear program, the company hopes to keep its products out of landfills by offering free repairs with no questions asked. The program is working. In 2017, 14 employees from its Reno, Nevada, service center made more than 50,000 clothing repairs.[104] One vital thing sustainability accomplishes is to protect and create options for moving forward.[105] Done properly, sustainability allows people to live and work in ways that can be maintained over the long term (generations) without destroying our environmental, social, and economic resources.

5.7 | The Best Managers Deliver All Six Advantages

Don't assume that you can settle for delivering just one of the six competitive advantages: low cost alone or quality alone, for example. The best managers and companies deliver them all.

When Discount Tire was started by Bruce Halle he had no long-term business plan and was "just trying to make a living."[106]

Halle made several key decisions that gave Discount Tire its competitive edge through the years, including specializing exclusively on tires. He piloted new services like wheel alignments, battery replacements, and oil changes but quickly realized that those services slowed down the tire change process. Halle focused on "getting customers in and out quickly, winning their trust and gaining customers for life." Discount Tire creates loyal customers by offering key services free of charge, like tire air pressure checks and tire rotation and balancing.[107] Halle fosters a positive working environment by giving employees realistic and attainable goals, promoting from within the company, and placing no cap on earning power for managers. Employees are incentivized and rewarded for "treating customers right."[108]

Trade-offs may occur among the various competitive advantages, but this doesn't need to be a zero-sum game where one has to suffer at the expense of another. Many portrait businesses in the United States are run by one or two photographers who do it all—shoot photos, edit, sell and market, run a website and social media, optimize SEO, and more. Photo editing is one the most time-consuming tasks, so photographers are increasingly hiring professional editing companies like FixThePhoto and WeEdit. Photos to edit their images.[109] As long as the photographer communicates with the editor and chooses an editor with compatible style, the photographer's style and creative vision aren't sacrificed. Turning over those responsibilities to a vendor that specializes in performing them efficiently frees up the photographer to engage in other aspects of the business where the photographer's creativity and personal touch are more necessary.

Making decisions about outsourcing and cost savings are just some important ways to help your organization achieve competitive advantage. As you read this chapter, you learned about several of the challenges facing managers today and what functions and activities managers engage in at different levels of the organization. The next chapter (Chapter 2) looks back to help provide a lens for understanding how we got to where we are today. It provides a brief look at the evolution of management thought and practice.

Notes

1. Glassdoor, "Top CEOs 2019: Employees' Choice," https://www.glassdoor.com/Award/Top-CEOs-LST_KQ0,8.htm.

2. P. Bhardwaj, "In-N-Out Burger's Lynsi Snyder Is the Best Female CEO in America, According to an Analysis of More Than a Million Glassdoor Reviews," *Money,* June 19, 2019, https://money.com/highest-rated-ceo-lynsi-snyder-in-n-out/.

3. C. Sorvino, "Exclusive: In-N-Out Billionaire Lynsi Snyder Opens Up about Her Troubled Past and the Burger Chain's Future," *Forbes,* October 10, 2018, www.forbes.com/sites/chloesorvino/2018/10/10/exclusive-in-n-out-billionaire-lynsi-snyder-opens-up-about-her-troubled-past-and-the-burger-chains-future/#461f00fa4b9c.

4. C. Sorvino, "Exclusive: In-N-Out Billionaire Lynsi Snyder Opens Up about Her Troubled Past and the Burger Chain's Future," *Forbes,* October 10, 2018, www.forbes.com/sites/chloesorvino/2018/10/10/exclusive-in-n-out-billionaire-lynsi-snyder-opens-up-about-her-troubled-past-and-the-burger-chains-future/#461f00fa4b9c.

5. C. Sorvino, "Exclusive: In-N-Out Billionaire Lynsi Snyder Opens Up about Her Troubled Past and the Burger Chain's Future," *Forbes,* October 10, 2018, www.forbes.com/sites/chloesorvino/2018/10/10/exclusive-in-n-out-billionaire-lynsi-snyder-opens-up-about-her-troubled-past-and-the-burger-chains-future/#461f00fa4b9c.

6. C. Clifford, "Here's What It Will Be Like to Travel to Mars in Elon Musk's Spaceship," *CNBC,* November 29, 2017, www.cnbc.com.

7. N. Drake, "Elon Musk: In Seven Years, SpaceX Could Land Humans on Mars," *National Geographic,* September 29, 2017, www.nationalgeographic.com/news/2017/09/elon-musk-spacex-mars-moon-bfr-rockets-space-science/.

8. L. Grush, "Elon Musk Reveals Updated Design for Future SpaceX Mars Rocket," The Verge, September 17, 2018, www.theverge.com; and J. Porter, "Elon Musk Renames Big Falcon Rocket to Starship," *The Verge,* November 20, 2018, www.theverge.com.

9. K. Samuelson, "Elon Musk Just Revealed More about His Plan to Colonize Mars," *Time,* September 29, 2017, www.time.com.

10. S. Pham and J. Wattles, "Elon Musk Is Aiming to Land Spaceships on Mars in 2022," *CNNMoney,* September 29, 2017, www.money.cnn.com.

11. D. Lepak, K. Smith, and M. S. Taylor, "Value Creation and Value Capture: A Multilevel Perspective," *Academy of Management Review* 23 (2007), pp. 180–94.

12. C. Sorvino, "Exclusive: In-N-Out Billionaire Lynsi Snyder Opens Up about Her Troubled Past and the Burger Chain's Future," *Forbes,* October 10, 2018, www.forbes.com/sites/chloesorvino/2018/10/10/exclusive-in-n-out-billionaire-lynsi-snyder-opens-up-about-her-troubled-past-and-the-burger-chains-future/#461f00fa4b9c.

13. K. Palmer, "The Secrets to Zappos' Success," *U.S. News & World Report,* August 10, 2010, www.usnews.com.

14. B. Tomasian, "Q&A with John Bunch: Holacracy Helps Zappos Swing from Job Ladder to Job Jungle Gym," *Workforce,* March 29, 2019, www.workforce.com.

15. See www.zappos.com.

16. R. Warren, "10 Things to Know about Zappos Customer Service," Zappos, August 30, 2018, www.zappos.com; and K. Frantik, "Befriending a Soldier Named Gummy Bear," *Zappos,* November 8, 2017, www.zappos.com.

17. A. Jenkins, "Meet the CEO of the Insurance Company Growing Faster Than Apple," *Fortune,* November 15, 2018, www.fortune.com.

18. A. Jenkins, "Meet the CEO of the Insurance Company Growing Faster Than Apple," *Fortune,* November 15, 2018, www.fortune.com.

19. "100 Best Companies to Work For," *Fortune,* www.fortune.com, accessed August 9, 2019.

20. E. Flitter and K. Weise, "Capital One Data Breach Compromises Data of over 100 Million," *The New York Times,* July 29, 2019, www.nytimes.com.

21. E. Flitter and K. Weise, "Capital One Data Breach Compromises Data of over 100 Million," *The New York Times,* July 29, 2019, www.nytimes.com.

22. R. McLean, "A Hacker Gained Access to 100 Million Capital One Credit Card Applications and Accounts," *CNN Business,* July 30, 2019, www.cnn.com.

23. P. Eavis and I. Penn, "The Struggle to Control PG&E," *The New York Times,* February 13, 2019, www.nytimes.com.

24. I. Penn, "PG&E's Wildfire Plan Includes More Blackouts, More Tree Trimming and Higher Rates," *The New York Times,* February 7, 2019, www.nytimes.com.

25. P. Eavis and I. Penn, "The Struggle to Control PG&E," *The New York Times,* February 13, 2019, www.nytimes.com.

26. "PG&E Announces New Board Member and Appointment of Special Independent Safety Advisor," PG&E press release, April 22, 2019, www.pge.com.

27. T. Cappellen and M. Janssens, "Characteristics of International Work: Narratives of the Global Manager," *Thunderbird International Business Review* 52, no. 4 (July–August 2010), pp. 337–48.

28. E. Ofek and L. Wathieu, "Are You Ignoring Trends That Could Shake Up Your Business?" *Harvard Business Review* 88, no. 7 (July–August 2010), pp. 124–31; and M. Branscombe, "Tools That Will Discreetly Tap a Shoulder to Offer Help," *Financial Times,* October 8, 2008, p. 4.

29. See www.loreal.com; and "L'Oréal's Chief Ethics Officer Recognized for Leadership in Corporate Ethics—L'Oréal Group," January 22, 2016, www.loreal.com.

30. M. Schneider, "Google Got Rid of Its Bosses—and Then Brought Them Back for These 10 Reasons," *Inc.,* February 6, 2019, www.inc.com; J. Bariso, "Google Spent 10 Years Researching What Makes the 'Perfect' Manager—Here Are the Top 10 Traits They Found," *Business Insider,* June 23, 2019, www.businessinsider.com; and M. Harrell and L. Barbato, "Great Managers Still Matter: The Evolution of Google's Project Oxygen," Re:Work, February 27, 2018, https://rework.withgoogle.com.

31. "Business: In Praise of David Brent, Middle Managers," *The Economist* 400, no. 8748 (August 27, 2011), p. 56.

32. Q. N. Huy, "In Praise of Middle Managers," *Harvard Business Review,* September 2001, pp. 72–79.

33. L. A. Hill, "New Manager Development for the 21st Century," *Academy of Management Executive,* August 2004, pp. 121–26.

34. F. Hassan, "The Frontline Advantage," *Harvard Business Review* 89, no. 5 (May 2011), pp. 106–14.

35. J. R. Hackman and R. Wageman, "A Theory of Team Coaching," *Academy of Management Review* 30, no. 2 (April 2005), pp. 269–87.

36. S. E. Humphrey, J. R. Hollenbeck, C. J. Meyer, and D. R. Ilgen, "Trait Configurations in Self-Managed Teams: A Conceptual Examination of the Use of Seeding for Maximizing and Minimizing Trait Variance in Teams," *Journal of Applied Psychology* 92, no. 3 (2007), pp. 885–92.

37. J. R. Hackman and R. Wageman, "A Theory of Team Coaching," *Academy of Management Review* 30, no. 2 (April 2005), pp. 269–87.

38. F. P. Morgeson, D. S. DeRue, and E. P. Karam, "Leadership in Teams: A Functional Approach to Understanding Leadership Structures and Processes," *Journal of Management* 36, no. 1 (January 2010), pp. 5–34.

39. B. Joiner and S. Josephs, "Leadership Agility," *Leadership Excellence* 24, no. 6 (June 2007), p. 16; and L. R. Sayles, "Doing Things Right: A New Imperative for Middle Managers," *Organizational Dynamics,* Spring 1993, pp. 5–14.

40. H. Mintzberg, *The Nature of Managerial Work* (New York: Harper & Row, 1973).

41. R. L. Katz, "Skills of an Effective Administrator," *Harvard Business Review* 52 (September–October, 1974), pp. 90–102.

42. L. A. Hill, "New Manager Development for the 21st Century," *Academy of Management Executive,* August 2004, pp. 121–26.

43. S. J. Hysong, "The Role of Technical Skill in Perceptions of Managerial Performance," *Journal of Management Development* 27, no. 3 (2008), pp. 275–90.

44. H. Mintzberg, "The Manager's Job: Folklore and Fact," *Harvard Business Review* 53 (July–August 1975), pp. 49–61.

45. N. Thompson, "Jeff Weiner Explains the Most Important Challenge for Tech in the Next 25 Years," LinkedIn, October 12, 2018, www.linkedin.com.

46. D. J. Deming, "The Value of Soft Skills in the Labor Market," The National Bureau of Economic Research, *NBER Reporter* no. 4 (2017), www.nber.org/reporter.

47. F. Di Meglio, "Columbia Gets Personal," *Bloomberg Businessweek,* October 18, 2006, www.businessweek.com.

48. D. Coleman, R. Boyatzis, and A. McKee, *Primal Leadership: Realizing the Power of Emotional Intelligence* (Boston: Harvard Business School Press, 2002).

49. "Nike, Inc.: A Growth Company," Nike press release, http://media.corporate-ir.net/media_files/IROL/10/100529/nike-gs09/global.html, accessed August 17, 2019.

50. See www.nike.com.

51. "Where Is Netflix Available?" Netflix Help Center, www.netflix.com, accessed August 9, 2019.

52. "Elite Starts Production in Madrid for Season 2," Netflix Media Center, January 15, 2019, www.media.netflix.com.

53. J. Toomer, "The Best Foreign TV Shows on Netflix Right Now," UPROXX, June 18, 2019, www.uproxx.com.

54. L. Brennan, "How Netflix Expanded to 190 Countries in 7 Years," *Harvard Business Review,* October 12, 2018, www.hbr.org.

55. E. Lee, "Netflix Stock Tumbles as U.S. Subscribers Decrease after Price Increases," *The New York Times,* July 17, 2019, www.nytimes.com.

56. B. Marr, "5 Internet of Things Trends Everyone Should Know About," *Forbes,* February 4, 2019, www.forbes.com.

57. "Top 20 Countries with the Highest Number of Internet Users," Internet World Stats, June 30, 2019, www.internetworldstats.com.

58. J. Wong, "Bing, Baidu and a Big Mess for Chinese Search Engines," *The Wall Street Journal,* January 24, 2019, www.wsj.com.

59. S. Shellenbarger, "Time-Zoned: Working around the Round-the-Clock Workday," *The Wall Street Journal,* February 15, 2007, www.wsj.com.

60. CircleID Reporter, "Number of Chinese Internet Users Reaches 829 Million, More Than Double the Population of the US," Circle ID, February 28, 2019, www.circleid.com.

61. E. C. Economy, "The Great Firewall of China: Xi Jinping's Internet Shutdown," *The Guardian,* June 29, 2018, www.theguardian.com.

62. "Leading Countries Based on Number of LinkedIn Users as of July 2019," www.statista.com, accessed August 15, 2019.

63. Company website, "About Us," www.linkedin.com, accessed March 27, 2016; D. Dou, "China to Embed Internet Police in Tech Firms," *The Wall Street Journal,* August 5, 2015, www.wsj.com; and V. Luckerson, "Why China Is a Nightmare for American Internet Companies," *Time,* February 27, 2014, www.time.com.

64. T. Bisoux, "Corporate Counter Culture," *BizEd,* November–December 2004, pp. 16–20, quoted on p. 19.

65. G. Huber, *The Necessary Nature of Future Firms* (Thousand Oaks, CA: Sage, 2004).

66. J. Greene and C. Edwards, "Desktops Are So Twentieth Century," *BusinessWeek,* December 8, 2006, www.businessweek.com.

67. F. Cairncross, *The Company of the Future* (Cambridge, MA: Harvard Business School Press, 2002).

68. M. S. Reyes, "Scandals and Teen Dropoff Weren't Enough to Stop Facebook's Growth," *Business Insider,* April 26, 2019, www.businessinsider.com.

69. P. Adler and S. Kwon, "Social Capital: Prospects for a New Concept," *Academy of Management Review* 27 (2002), pp. 17–40.

70. J. Deal, "Always On, Never Done? Don't Blame the Smartphone," Center for Creative Leadership (White Paper), August 2013, www.ccl.org.

71. J. Chatzky, "Confessions of an E-mail Addict," *CNNMoney,* March 2007, www.money.cnn.com.

72. J. Chatzky, "Confessions of an E-mail Addict," *CNNMoney,* March 2007, www.money.cnn.com.

73. J. Cohen and J. Birkinshaw, "Make Your Knowledge Workers More Productive," *Harvard Business Review,* September 5, 2013, www.hbr.org; and R. Austin, "Managing Knowledge Workers," *Science,* July 21, 2006, www.sciencecareers.sciencemag.org.

74. M. Hansen and B. von Oetinger, "Introducing T-Shaped Managers: Knowledge Management's Next Generation," *Harvard Business Review,* March 2001, pp. 106–16.

75. "Toyota Headquarters Designed to Drive Innovation, Collaboration, CEO Says," *Biz Journals* (Video), June 24, 2015, www.bizjournals.com; and J. Teresko, "Toyota's Real Secret," *Industry-Week,* February 2007, www.industryweek.com.

76. See www.zazzle.com.

77. "Employment Projections, Chart of Civilian Labor Force, by Age, Sex, Race, and Ethnicity," Bureau of Labor Statistics, October 2017, www.bls.gov/emp/tables/civilian-labor-force-summary.htm.

78. See Target's 2018 Corporate Responsibility report at www.corporate.target.com.

79. See Target's 2018 Corporate Responsibility report at www.corporate.target.com.

80. See Deloitte's 2017/18 Annual Report at www.deloitte.com.

81. See Deloitte's 2017/18 Annual Report at www.deloitte.com.

82. R. Newman, "10 Great Companies That Lost Their Edge," *U.S. News & World Report,* August 19, 2010, https://money.usnews.com.

83. R. Newman, "10 Innovative Companies You Should Copy," *U.S. News & World Report,* August 19, 2010, https://money.usnews.com/.

84. R. Newman, "10 Innovative Companies You Should Copy," *U.S. News & World Report,* August 19, 2010, https://money.usnews.com/.

85. "#297 Baidu," *Forbes,* May 15, 2019, www.forbes.com/companies/baidu.

86. "A Closer Look at Baidu's Operating Cost Management," *Forbes,* December 4, 2017, www.forbes.com.

87. Globe Newswire, "Baidu Lays Out Vision to Empower a New Era of Intelligent Industry at Create 2019," NASDAQ, July 4, 2019, www.nasdaq.com.

88. Opaque Dark Dining company website, darkdining.com, accessed August 17, 2019.

89. Opaque Dark Dining company website, darkdining.com, accessed August 17, 2019.

90. R. I. Sutton, "The Weird Rules of Creativity," *Harvard Business Review,* September 2001, pp. 94–103.

91. O. Port, "The Kings of Quality," *BusinessWeek,* August 30, 2004, p. 20.

92. D. A. Garvin, "Manufacturing Strategic Planning," *California Management Review,* Summer 1993, pp. 85–106.

93. J. Scipioni, "Gatorade Chief Says New 'Customized' Sports Drink Is a Game-Changer," *Fox Business,* July 19, 2018, https://www.foxbusiness.com; D. Green and J. Avella, "Nike Lets Customers Add Glitter, Paint, and Wacky Laces to Their Sneakers," *Business Insider,* March 23, 2018, https://www.businessinsider.com; and B. Ladd, "The Next Big Trends in Food Are Being Driven by Amazon, Icon Meals, and Mercatus," *Forbes,* December 3, 2018, https://www.forbes.com.

94. U.S. Bureau of Labor Statistics, *Occupational Outlook Quarterly* 53, no. 4 (Winter 2009–10).

95. See www.bls.gov/emp/ep_table_203.htm.

96. M. Fetterman, "Best Buy Gets in Touch with Its Feminine Side," *USA Today,* December 20, 2006, www.usatoday.com.

97. A. Lashinsky, "Chaos by Design," *Fortune,* October 2, 2006, https://money.cnn.com.

98. J. F. Peltz, "How Starbucks Has Picked Up Steam Again," *Los Angeles Times,* July 28, 2019, www.latimes.com.

99. J. Vanian, "Why Walmart Is Testing Robots in Stores—and Here's What It Learned," *Fortune,* March 26, 2018, www.fortune.com.

100. M. Smith, "New Scheduling System Gives Associates More Consistency and Flexibility," Walmart, November 13, 2018, www.corporate.walmart.com.

101. J. Pfeffer, "Building Sustainable Organizations: The Human Factor," *Academy of Management Perspectives* 24 (2010), pp. 34–45.

102. S. L. Hart, *Capitalism at the Crossroads,* 3rd ed. (Upper Saddle River, NJ: Wharton School Publishing, 2010).

103. M. T. Hansen, H. Ibarra, and U. Peyer, "The Best-Performing CEOs in the World," *Harvard Business Review,* November 2014, http://hbr.org, p. 90.

104. A. Engel, "The Most Sustainable Companies in 2019," *The Washington Post,* August 31, 2018, www.washingtonpost.com.

105. B. Doppelt, *Leading Change Toward Sustainability* (Sheffield, UK: Greenleaf, 2010).

106. J. R. Hagerty, "Bruce Halle Overcame Early Stumbles to Create Discount Tire Chain," *The Wall Street Journal,* January 19, 2018, www.wsj.com.

107. D. L. Jacobs, "How to Get Rich without Being a Tech Titan," *Forbes,* March 19, 2012, www.forbes.com.

108. D. L. Jacobs, "How to Get Rich without Being a Tech Titan," *Forbes,* March 19, 2012, www.forbes.com.

109. Q. Decaillet, "Wedding Photographers: Get Your Life Back by Outsourcing Your Editing," Fstoppers, August 15, 2016, www.fstoppers.com.

The Evolution of Management

Learning Objectives

After studying Chapter 2, you should be able to

LO1 Describe the origins of management practice and its early concepts and influences.

LO2 Summarize the five classical approaches to management.

LO3 Discuss the four contemporary approaches to management.

LO4 Identify modern contributors who have shaped management thought and practice.

What is a chapter about history doing in a management textbook? It provides context for understanding how managerial practices have evolved over time. Today's taken-for-granted management practices—efficiency, division of labor, pay for performance efforts, cooperative work environments, equitable treatment of employees, decentralized decision making, empowerment, autonomy, and teamwork—originated and emerged from earlier management.

Many of the legendary contributors discussed in this chapter were colorful, interesting people. Frederick Taylor did not like seeing that processes at his company were disorganized and workers were slacking off. His ideas inspired the likes of Henry Ford, who perfected the assembly line and changed history. Lillian Gilbreth maintained quite a balancing act between her successful career, husband, and 12 children while still finding time to design kitchens and appliances as a consultant for General Electric. Henri Fayol saved a large mining and steel company that was on the brink of bankruptcy and turned it into a profitable, well-managed organization. He saved more than 10,000 employees' jobs.

Understanding the origins of management thought will help you understand the origins of the ideas and concepts presented in the chapters ahead. Although this chapter is titled "The Evolution of Management," it might be more appropriately called "Revolutions in Management" because it documents the wide swings in management approaches over the last 100 years. Parts of each of these approaches have survived and found their way into modern management perspectives. Thus, the legacy of past efforts, breakthroughs, and failures has become our guide to current and future management practice.

This chapter discusses the classical and contemporary approaches to management, as well as modern contributions from current and well-known management thought leaders.

1 | ORIGINS OF MANAGEMENT

For several thousand years, managers have wrestled with some of the same issues and problems that confront executives today. As far back as 5000 BC, the Sumerians practiced the management function of controlling (discussed in Chapter 1) by keeping records of tax receipts, real estate holdings, and lists of farm animals.[1] Here are some other examples of the early application and use of management functions:[2]

- Around 4000 BC, the Egyptians used planning, organizing, leading, and controlling to build their great pyramids; one pyramid took more than 100,000 laborers 20 years to complete.

- As early as 1100 BC, the Chinese applied the managerial concepts of delegation, cooperation, efficiency, organization, and control.

● The Egyptians needed all four management functions to build the pyramids. Alfredo Dagli Orti/Shutterstock

- In 500 BC, Sun Tzu discussed the importance of planning and leading in his book *The Art of War.*

- Around 400–350 BC, the Greeks recognized management as a separate art and advocated a scientific approach to work.

- Around 1436, the Venetians standardized production through the use of an assembly line and an inventory system to monitor the contents.

- In 1776, Adam Smith discussed control and the principle of specialization for manufacturing workers.

However, throughout history, most managers operated on a trial-and-error basis. The Industrial Revolution in the 18th and 19th centuries changed that. Fueled by major advances in manufacturing and transportation technologies like the steam engine, cotton gin, and railway networks and the availability of large numbers of low-skilled laborers,[3] businesses and factories grew in size and became more complex to operate. Managers who made minor improvements in management tactics produced impressive increases in production quantity and quality.[4]

The emergence of economies of scale—reductions in the average cost of a unit of production as the total volume produced increases—drove managers to strive for further growth. The opportunities for mass production created by the Industrial Revolution spawned intense and systematic thought about management challenges—particularly efficiency, production processes, and cost savings.[5] In the 1890s, the newly formed General Electric Company was able to mass-produce several new products (many invented or refined by Thomas A. Edison), including incandescent lightbulbs, electric fans, and phonographs.[6]

Toward the end of the Industrial Revolution, management emerged as a formal discipline. The first university programs to offer management and business education, the Wharton School at the University of Pennsylvania and the Amos Tuck School at Dartmouth, were founded in the late 19th century. By 1914, 25 business schools existed.[7]

1.1 | The Evolution of Management

Exhibit 2.1 provides a timeline depicting the evolution of management thought through the decades. This historical perspective is divided into two major sections: classical approaches and contemporary approaches. Many of these approaches overlapped as they developed, and they often had a significant impact on one another. Some approaches were direct reactions to the deficiencies of previous approaches. Others developed as the needs and issues confronting managers changed over the years. These efforts addressed the real issues facing managers and provided them with tools to solve future problems. Exhibit 2.1 will reinforce your understanding of the key relationships among the approaches and place each perspective in its historical context.

pieceofmind/Shutterstock

LO2 Summarize the five classical approaches to management.

2 | CLASSICAL APPROACHES

The classical period extended from the mid-19th century through the early 1950s. The major approaches that emerged during this period were systematic management, scientific management, bureaucracy, administrative management, and human relations.

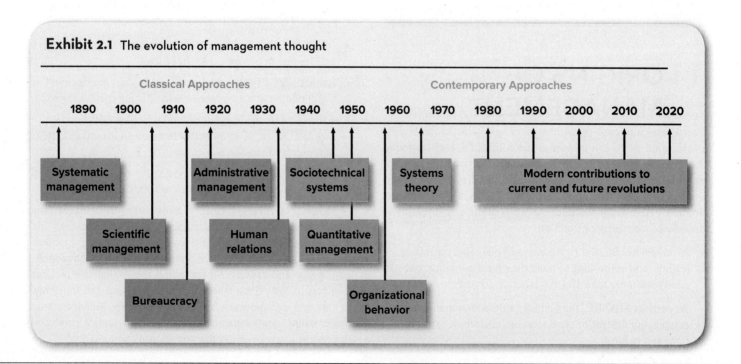

Exhibit 2.1 The evolution of management thought

2.1 | Systematic Management

During the 19th century, growth in U.S. business centered on manufacturing.[8] Early writers such as Adam Smith believed the management of these firms was chaotic, and their ideas helped to systematize it. Most work tasks were subdivided and performed by specialized labor. However, poor coordination caused frequent problems and breakdowns of the manufacturing process.

An Early Labor Contract

The following rules, taken from the records of Cocheco Company, were typical of labor contract provisions in the 1850s.

1. The hours of work shall be from sunrise to sunset, from the 21st of March to the 20th of September inclusively; and from sunrise until eight o'clock, P.M., during the remainder of the year. One hour shall be allowed for dinner, and half an hour for breakfast during the first mentioned six months; and one hour for dinner during the other half of the year; on Saturdays, the mill shall be stopped one hour before sunset, for the purpose of cleaning the machinery.

2. Every hand coming to work a quarter of an hour after the mill has been started shall be docked a quarter of a day; and every hand absenting him or herself, without absolute necessity, shall be docked in a sum double the amount of the wages such hand shall have earned during the time of such absence. No more than one hand is allowed to leave any one of the rooms at the same time—a quarter of a day shall be deducted for every breach of this rule.

3. No smoking or spiritous liquors shall be allowed in the factory under any pretense whatsoever. It is also forbidden to carry into the factory, nuts, fruits, etc., books, or papers during the hours of work.

Source: W. Sullivan, "The Industrial Revolution and the Factory Operative in Pennsylvania," The Pennsylvania Magazine of History and Biography 78 (1954), pp. 478–79.

The systematic management approach built specific procedures and processes into operations to ensure coordination of effort. Systematic management emphasized economical operations, adequate staffing, maintenance of inventories to meet consumer demand, and organizational control. These goals were achieved through

- Careful definition of duties and responsibilities.

- Standardized techniques for performing these duties.

- Specific means of gathering, handling, transmitting, and analyzing information.

- Cost accounting, wage, and production control systems to facilitate internal coordination and communications.

Systematic management emphasized internal operations because managers needed to meet the explosive growth in demand brought about by the Industrial Revolution. They focused on internal issues of efficiency, in part because the government did not regulate business practices significantly. Labor was poorly organized, and many managers were oriented more toward things than toward people.

Systematic management did not address all the issues 19th-century managers faced, but it tried to raise managers' awareness about the most pressing concerns of their job.

2.2 | Scientific Management

Systematic management failed to lead to widespread production efficiency. This shortcoming was apparent to a young engineer named Frederick Taylor, who was hired by Midvale Steel Company in 1878. Taylor discovered that production and pay were poor, inefficiency and waste were widespread, and most companies had tremendous unused potential. He concluded that management decisions were unsystematic and that no research to determine the best means of production existed.

In response, Taylor introduced a second approach to management, known as scientific management.[9] This approach advocated the application of scientific methods to analyze work and to determine how to complete production tasks efficiently. For example, U.S. Steel's contract with the United Steel Workers of America specified that sand shovelers should move 12.5 shovelfuls per minute; shovelfuls should average 15 pounds of river sand composed of 5.5 percent moisture.[10]

economies of scale
reductions in the average cost of a unit of production as the total volume produced increases

systematic management
a classical management approach that attempted to build into operations the specific procedures and processes that would ensure coordination of effort to achieve established goals and plans

scientific management
a classical management approach that applied scientific methods to analyze and determine the "one best way" to complete production tasks

● The fifteen millionth Ford Model T rolls off the assembly line in 1927. Henry Ford revolutionized automobile manufacturing by applying the principles of scientific management. Keystone/Getty Images

Taylor identified four principles of scientific management:

1. Management should develop a precise, scientific approach for each element of each job to replace general guidelines.

2. Management should scientifically select and place each worker so that the right person has the right job.

3. Management should cooperate with workers to ensure that jobs match plans and principles.

4. Management should ensure an appropriate division of work and responsibility between managers and workers.

To implement this approach, Taylor used techniques such as time-and-motion studies. With this technique, a task was divided into its basic movements, and different motions were timed to determine the most efficient way to complete the task.

After the "one best way" to perform the job was identified, Taylor stressed the importance of hiring and training the proper worker to do that job. Taylor advocated the standardization of tools, the use of instruction cards to help workers, and breaks to eliminate fatigue.

Another key element of Taylor's approach was the use of the differential piecerate system. Taylor assumed workers were motivated by receiving money. Therefore, he implemented a pay system in which workers were paid additional wages when they exceeded a standard level of output for each job. Taylor concluded that both workers and management would benefit from such an approach.

Henry L. Gantt worked with and became a protégé of Frederick Taylor's.[11] Like Taylor, he believed in scientific management and the need for management and labor to cooperate. He expanded on the piecerate system by suggesting that frontline supervisors should receive a bonus for each of their workers who completed their assigned daily tasks.[12] Gantt believed that this would motivate supervisors to provide extra attention and training to those workers who were struggling with meeting their output goals.

● Frederick Taylor was an early expert in management efficiency. Bettmann/Getty Images

Henry Gantt is also known for creating the Gantt chart, which helps employees and managers plan projects by task and time to complete those tasks. An interesting aspect of the chart is that it illustrates how some tasks need to be done during the same time period. Today, Gantt charts (available through Microsoft Project and other project software) are used in several fields for a wide variety of projects.[13] Exhibit 2.2 illustrates how students can use a Gantt chart to complete a semester-long team research project.

Frank B. and Lillian M. Gilbreth were a productive husband and wife team. Frank was a strong believer in Taylor's philosophies. While working as a supervisor of bricklayers, Frank Gilbreth developed a system to reduce costs and increase worker productivity by showing how employees could work smarter, not harder.[14] His analysis showed how the number of motions for the average bricklayer could be reduced from 18 to 4, allowing worker productivity to increase from 1,000 to 2,700 bricks laid each day.[15] This success inspired Gilbreth to use a motion picture camera (with a clock in the foreground) to capture the precise movements of workers as they accomplished tasks. These "motion studies" were used to identify and remove wasteful movements so workers could be more efficient and productive.

Lillian Gilbreth was an influential contributor in her own right to management thought and practice. Known as the "mother of modern management," she earned a PhD in psychology and later taught at Purdue University as a professor of

Exhibit 2.2 — Using a Gantt chart for a team research project at school

Step	Task	Assigned to	Aug	Sept	Oct	Nov	Dec
1	Review assignment.	All team members	-----8/28				
2	Meet as group to discuss and identify areas for clarification.	All team members	-----9/5				
3	Identify team leader.	All team members		-------9/8			
4	Meet with professor to clarify objectives of assignment.	Team leader		----9/12			
5	Meet as group to divide responsibilities.	Team leader and members		-------9/18			
6	Write sections 1–3.	Member B			--------------10/31		
7	Write sections 4–6.	Member C			--------------10/31		
8	Write introduction and conclusion and type bibliography.	Member D			--------------10/31		
9	Edit entire paper.	Team leader				-------11/15	
10	Prepare PowerPoint slides for presentation.	Member E				------11/20	
11	Practice/rehearse presentation.	Team leader and members				--------11/22	
12	Submit completed paper and deliver presentation.	Team leader and members					--12/1

management and was the first female professor in the engineering school.[16] While supportive of her husband's work, Lillian Gilbreth eventually focused less on the technical and more on the human side of management. She was interested in how job satisfaction motivated employees, how motion studies could be used to help disabled individuals perform jobs, and how fatigue and stress affected workers' well-being and productivity.[17]

Scientific Management and the Model T

At the turn of the century, automobiles were a luxury that only the wealthy could afford. They were assembled by craftspeople who put an entire car together at one spot on the factory floor. These workers were not specialized, and Henry Ford believed they wasted time and energy bringing the needed parts to the car. Ford took a revolutionary approach to automobile manufacturing by using scientific management principles.

After much study, machines and workers in Ford's new factory were placed in sequence so that an automobile could be assembled without interruption along a moving production line. Mechanical energy and a conveyor belt were used to take the work to the workers.

The manufacture of parts likewise was revolutionized. For example, formerly it had taken one worker 20 minutes to assemble a flywheel magneto. By splitting the job into 29 different operations, putting the product on a mechanical conveyor, and changing the height of the conveyor, Ford cut production time to 5 minutes.

By 1914, chassis assembly time had been trimmed from almost 13 hours to 1½ hours. The new methods of production required complete standardization, new machines, and an adaptable labor force. Costs dropped significantly, the Model T became the first car accessible to the majority of Americans, and Ford dominated the industry for many years.

Source: H. Kroos and C. Gilbert, *The Principles of Scientific Management* (New York: Harper & Row, 1911).

Famously, Lillian Gilbreth did all this while raising 12 children and running a consulting business. Some consider her to be the "first superwoman" to balance a remarkably successful career and family life.[18]

Scientific management principles were widely embraced. One of the most famous examples of the application of scientific management is the factory Henry Ford built to produce the Model T.[19]

The legacy of Taylor's scientific management approach is broad and pervasive. Most important, productivity and efficiency in manufacturing improved dramatically. He introduced scientific methods and research to manufacturing. The piecerate system gained wide acceptance because it more closely aligned effort and reward. Taylor also emphasized the need for cooperation between management and workers. And the concept of a management specialist gained prominence.

Despite these gains, not everyone was convinced that scientific management was the best solution to all business problems. First, critics claimed that Taylor ignored many job-related social and psychological factors by emphasizing only money as a worker incentive. Second, production tasks were reduced to a set of routine, machinelike procedures that led to boredom, apathy, and quality control problems. Third, unions strongly opposed scientific management techniques because they believed management might abuse their power to set the standards and the piecerates, thus exploiting workers and diminishing their importance. Finally, although scientific management resulted in intense scrutiny of the internal efficiency of organizations, it did not help managers deal with broader external issues such as competitors and government regulations, especially at the senior management level.

Weber believed bureaucratic structures can eliminate the variability that results when managers in the same organization have different skills, experiences, and goals. As illustrated in Exhibit 2.3, Weber emphasized a structured, formal network of relationships among specialized positions in an organization. Rules and regulations standardize behavior, and authority resides in positions rather than in individuals. As a result, the organization need not rely on a particular individual, but will realize efficiency and success by following the rules in a routine and unbiased manner.

According to Weber, bureaucracies are especially important because they allow large organizations to perform the many routine activities necessary for their survival. Bureaucratic positions foster specialized skills, eliminating many subjective judgments by managers. If the rules and controls are established properly, bureaucracies should be unbiased in their treatment of people, both customers and employees. Many organizations today are bureaucratic.

● Lillian Gilbreth focused her research and analysis on the human side of management. This "effort-versus-efficiency" research championed the human over the technical. Also one of the first to "have it all," she balanced her career with raising a family. Bygone Collection/Alamy Stock Photo

2.3 | Bureaucracy

Max Weber, a German sociologist, lawyer, and social historian, showed how management itself could be more efficient and consistent in his book *The Theory of Social and Economic Organizations.*[20] The ideal model for management, according to Weber, is the bureaucracy approach.

● German sociologist Max Weber believed that a bureaucracy approach would make management more efficient and consistent. Cci/Shutterstock

Exhibit 2.3 Characteristics of an effective bureaucracy

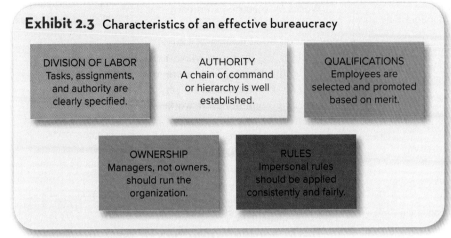

DIVISION OF LABOR
Tasks, assignments, and authority are clearly specified.

AUTHORITY
A chain of command or hierarchy is well established.

QUALIFICATIONS
Employees are selected and promoted based on merit.

OWNERSHIP
Managers, not owners, should run the organization.

RULES
Impersonal rules should be applied consistently and fairly.

Source: Adapted from M. Weber, *The Theory of Social and Economic Organization,* trans. T. Parsons and A. Henderson (New York: Free Press, 1947), pp. 324–41.

Bureaucracy can be efficient and productive. However, bureaucracy is not the appropriate model for every organization. Organizations or departments that need rapid decision making and flexibility may suffer under a bureaucratic approach. Some people may not perform their best with excessive bureaucratic rules and procedures.

Other shortcomings stem from faulty execution of bureaucratic principles rather than from the approach itself. Too much authority may be vested in too few people; the procedures may become the ends rather than the means; or managers may ignore appropriate rules and regulations. Finally, one advantage of a bureaucracy—its stability—can also be a problem. Once a bureaucracy is established, dismantling it is very difficult.

2.4 | Administrative Management

The administrative management approach emphasized the perspective of senior managers within the organization and argued that management was a profession and could be taught.

A broad framework for administrative management emerged in 1916, when Henri Fayol, a French mining engineer and executive, published a book about his management experiences. Fayol identified five functions and 14 principles of management. The five functions, which are very similar to the four functions discussed in Chapter 1, are planning, organizing, commanding, coordinating, and controlling. Exhibit 2.4 lists and defines the 14 principles. Although some critics claim Fayol treated the principles as universal truths for management, he actually wanted them applied flexibly.[21]

A host of other executives contributed to the administrative management literature. These writers discussed a broad spectrum of management topics, including the social responsibilities of management, the philosophy of management, clarification of business terms and concepts, and organizational principles. Chester Barnard's and Mary Parker Follett's contributions have become classic works in this area.[22]

Barnard, former president of New Jersey Bell Telephone Company, published his landmark book *The Functions of the Executive* in 1938. He outlined the role of the senior executive: formulating the purpose of the organization, hiring key individuals, and maintaining organizational communications.[23] Mary Parker Follett's 1942 book *Dynamic Administration* extended Barnard's work by emphasizing the continually changing situations that managers face.[24] Two of her key contributions—the notion that managers desire flexibility and the differences between motivating groups and individuals—laid

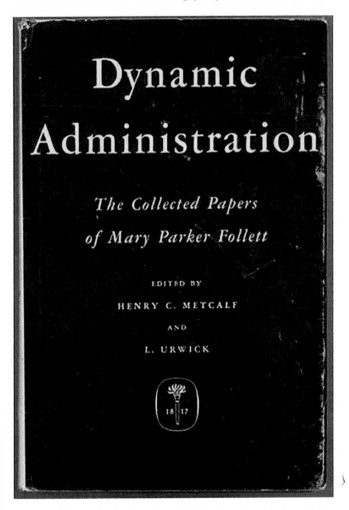

● Author of *Dynamic Administration* and other works, Mary Parker Follett was an influential writer, speaker, and management consultant.
Call Number: 658.01 F667d (Education Library and Storage Auxiliary)
Harper, New York. 320p. Publication Date: 1940
Dynamic Administration: The Collected Papers of Mary Parker Follett, Harper, 1942.

Exhibit 2.4 Fayol's 14 principles of management

1. *Division of work*—divide work into specialized tasks and assign responsibilities to specific individuals.
2. *Authority*—delegate authority along with responsibility.
3. *Discipline*—make expectations clear and punish violations.
4. *Unity of command*—each employee should be assigned to only one supervisor.
5. *Unity of direction*—employees' efforts should be focused on achieving organizational objectives.
6. *Subordination of individual interest to the general interest*—the general interest must predominate.
7. *Remuneration*—systematically reward efforts that support the organization's direction.
8. *Centralization*—determine the relative importance of superior and subordinate roles.
9. *Scalar chain*—keep communications within the chain of command.
10. *Order*—order jobs and material so they support the organization's direction.
11. *Equity*—fair discipline and order enhance employee commitment.
12. *Stability and tenure of personnel*—promote employee loyalty and longevity.
13. *Initiative*—encourage employees to act on their own in support of the organization's direction.
14. *Esprit de corps*—promote a unity of interests between employees and management.

the groundwork for the modern contingency approach discussed later in the chapter.

All the writings in the administrative management area emphasize management as a profession along with fields such as law and medicine. These authors offered many recommendations based on their personal experiences, which often included managing large corporations. Although these perspectives and recommendations were considered sound, critics noted that they might not work in all settings. Different types of personnel, industry conditions, and technologies may affect the appropriateness of these principles.

2.5 | Human Relations

A fifth approach to management, human relations, developed during the 1930s. This approach aimed at understanding how psychological and social processes interact with the work situation to influence performance. Human relations was the first major approach to emphasize informal work relationships and worker satisfaction.

This approach owes much to other major schools of thought. For example, many of the ideas of the Gilbreths (scientific management) and Barnard and Follett (administrative management) influenced the development of human relations from 1930 to 1955. In fact, human relations emerged from a research project that began as a scientific management study.

Western Electric Company, a manufacturer of communications equipment, hired a team of Harvard researchers led by Elton Mayo and Fritz Roethlisberger. They were to investigate the influence of physical working conditions on workers' productivity and efficiency in one of the company's factories outside Chicago. This research project, known as the *Hawthorne Studies,* provided some of the most interesting and controversial results in the history of management.[25]

The Hawthorne Studies were a series of experiments conducted from 1924 to 1932. During the first stage of the project (the Illumination Experiments), various working conditions, particularly the lighting in the factory, were altered to determine the effects of those changes on productivity. The researchers found no systematic relationship between the factory lighting and production levels. In some cases, productivity continued to increase even when the illumination was reduced to the level of moonlight. The researchers concluded that the workers performed and reacted differently because the researchers were observing them. This reaction is known as the Hawthorne effect.

This conclusion led the researchers to believe productivity may be affected more by psychological and social factors than by physical or objective influences. With this thought in mind, they initiated the other four stages of the project. During these stages, the researchers performed various work group experiments and had extensive interviews with employees. Mayo and his team eventually concluded that productivity and employee behavior were influenced by the informal work group.

Human relations proponents argued that managers should stress primarily employee welfare, motivation, and communication. They believed social needs mattered more than economic needs. Therefore, management must gain the cooperation of the group and promote job satisfaction and group norms consistent with the goals of the organization.

Abraham Maslow was a famous contributor to the field of human relations.[26] In 1943, Maslow suggested that humans have five levels of needs. The most basic needs are the physical needs for food, water, and shelter; the most advanced need is for self-actualization, or personal fulfillment. Maslow argued that people try to satisfy their lower-level needs and then progress upward to the higher-level needs. Managers can facilitate this process and achieve organizational goals by removing obstacles and encouraging behaviors that satisfy people's needs and organizational goals simultaneously.

Although the human relations approach generated research into leadership, job attitudes, and group dynamics, it drew heavy criticism.[27] Critics believed that one result of human relations—a belief that a happy worker was a productive worker—was too simplistic. While scientific management overemphasized the

human relations
a classical management approach that attempted to understand and explain how human psychological and social processes interact with the formal aspects of the work situation to influence performance

Hawthorne effect
people's reactions to being observed or studied, resulting in superficial rather than meaningful changes in behavior

Take Charge of Your Career

Use history to your advantage

Many senior executives and entrepreneurs have not only read many of the modern books by writers like Peter Drucker, Michael Porter, W. Chan Kim, and Renée Mauborgne (discussed later in this chapter), but they also know the classic works of Frederick Taylor, Elton Mayo, Abraham Maslow, Mary Parker Follett, and Douglas McGregor. By familiarizing yourself with these influential works, you can discuss them with senior managers, who will probably be impressed to discover that you have taken the time to learn "where we have come from."

You might take this approach a step further by learning everything you can about the *history of the industry* in which your organization competes. This may give you insights into your firm's growth and position relative to its competitors. Next you could dig into the *history of the company* and learn about the key people and founders who shaped its culture and direction. This will help you learn about the firm's values and how things really work inside its walls.

Last, try to learn about the *history of your supervisor and coworkers* since they joined the organization. This information will give you insight and could prove helpful in many ways. For example, maybe you find out that your supervisor was instrumental in stopping some unethical practices in the department a few years ago. This should tell you that she or he takes these issues very seriously, and thus you and your coworkers should do the same.

History is a source of information, and information is powerful when it is turned into actionable knowledge that can help you develop an excellent reputation and successful career.

GET AHEAD:
Learn the *history* of the industry, company, managers, and employees.

● Employees working at a Western Electric plant circa 1930. Courtesy of Western Electric from the Historical Archive.
FPG/Hulton Archive/Getty Images

sociotechnical systems theory an approach to job design that attempts to redesign tasks to optimize operation of a new technology while preserving employees' interpersonal relationships and other human aspects of the work

quantitative management a contemporary management approach that emphasizes the application of quantitative analysis to managerial decisions and problems

economic and formal aspects of the workplace, human relations ignored the more rational side of the worker and the important characteristics of the formal organization. However, human relations was a significant step in the development of management thought because it prompted managers and researchers to consider the psychological and social factors that influence performance.

> **LO3** Discuss the four contemporary approaches to management.

3 | CONTEMPORARY APPROACHES

The contemporary approaches to management include sociotechnical systems theory, quantitative management, organizational behavior, and systems theory. The contemporary approaches have developed at various times since World War II, and they continue to represent the cornerstones of modern management thought.

3.1 | Sociotechnical Systems Theory

Drawing on several classical approaches, sociotechnical systems theory suggests that organizations are effective when their employees (the social system) have the right tools, training, and knowledge (the technical system) to make products and services that are valued by customers.[28] Developed in the early 1950s by researchers from the London-based Tavistock Institute of Human Relations, sociotechnical systems theory explained how important it was to understand how coal miners' social behaviors interacted with the technical production system. The researchers found that when there was a good fit between these two important internal dimensions and the demands of customers external to the organization, the organizations could reach higher levels of effectiveness.[29]

While research on sociotechnical systems theory was a precursor to the total quality management (TQM) movement (discussed in other chapters), it also promoted the use of teamwork and semiautonomous work groups as important factors for creating efficient production systems. The researchers believed that workers should be given the freedom to correct problems at early stages of the production process rather than after products were made, when errors would create waste.[30]

Sociotechnical systems theory is being used by Oracle Utilities Opower, a company that collects, analyzes, and presents data in an easy-to-understand format for utilities companies and their customers. By combining knowledge of "Big Data" analytics with customer behavior, Oracle Utilities Opower provides visually appealing feedback (in the form of pie charts and easy-to-understand billing information) to customers regarding energy conservation and usage. In 2016, the company reported working with 95 utilities companies, earning 3 percent energy savings for their customers and reducing by 19 percent the number of billing-related calls from customers.[31]

3.2 | Quantitative Management

Although Taylor introduced the use of science as a management tool early in the 20th century, most organizations did not adopt the use of quantitative techniques for management problems until the 1940s and 1950s.[32] During World War II, military planners began to apply mathematical techniques to defense and logistic problems. After the war, private corporations began assembling teams of quantitative experts to tackle the complex issues confronting large organizations. This approach, quantitative management, emphasizes the application of quantitative analysis to management decisions and problems.

Quantitative management helps a manager make decisions by developing formal mathematical models of the problem. Computers facilitated the development of specific quantitative methods. These include such techniques as statistical decision theory, linear programming, queuing theory, simulation, forecasting, inventory modeling, network modeling, and breakeven analysis. Organizations apply these techniques in many areas, including production, quality control, marketing, human resources, finance, distribution, planning, and research and development.

One particular area of quantitative management known as "Big Data" (discussed in Chapter 15) is used to analyze patterns in structured and unstructured data.[33] The idea is that more accurate analyses and decision making can result in "greater operational efficiencies, cost reductions, and reduced risk."[34]

Despite the promise of quantitative management, managers do not use these methods as their primary way to make decisions. Typically, they use these techniques as a supplement or tool in the decision-making process. Many managers will use results that are consistent with their experience, intuition, and judgment, but they often reject results that contradict their beliefs. Also, managers may use these techniques to compare alternatives and eliminate weaker options.

Several explanations account for the limited use of quantitative management. Many managers have not been trained in using these techniques. Also, many aspects of a management decision cannot be expressed through mathematical symbols and formulas. Finally, many of the decisions managers face are nonroutine and unpredictable.

3.3 | Organizational Behavior

During the 1950s, a transition took place in the human relations approach. Scholars began to recognize that worker productivity and organizational success are based on more than the satisfaction of economic or social needs. The revised perspective, known as organizational behavior, studies and identifies management activities that promote employee effectiveness through an understanding of the complex nature of individual, group, and organizational processes. Organizational behavior draws from a variety of disciplines, including psychology and sociology, to explain people's behavior as they do their jobs.

During the 1960s, organizational behaviorists heavily influenced the field of management. Douglas McGregor's Theory X and Theory Y marked the transition from human relations.[35] According to McGregor, Theory X managers assume workers are lazy and irresponsible and require constant supervision and external motivation to achieve organizational goals. Theory Y managers assume employees *want* to work and can direct and control themselves.

An important implication for managers who subscribe to Theory X is known as *self-fulfilling prophecy*. This occurs when a manager treats employees as lazy, unmotivated, and in need of tight supervision; then the employees eventually fulfill the manager's expectations by acting that way. This cycle can have several negative implications for managers, employees, and organizations.

McGregor advocated a Theory Y perspective, suggesting that managers who encourage participation and allow opportunities for individual challenge and initiative would achieve superior performance. Other major organizational behaviorists include Chris Argyris, who recommended greater autonomy and better jobs for workers,[36] and Rensis Likert, who stressed the value of participative management.[37] Through the years, organizational behavior has consistently emphasized development of the organization's human resources to achieve individual and organizational goals.

Like other approaches, organizational behavior has been criticized for its limited perspective, although more recent contributions have a broader and more situational viewpoint. In the past few years, many of the primary issues addressed by organizational behavior have experienced a rebirth with a greater interest in leadership, employee engagement, and self-management.

3.4 | Systems Theory

The classical approaches as a whole were criticized because they (1) ignored the relationship between the organization and its external environment, and (2) usually stressed one aspect of the organization or its employees at the expense of other considerations. In response to these criticisms, management scholars during the 1950s stepped back from the details of the organization to attempt to understand it as a whole system.

These efforts were based on a general scientific approach called systems theory.[38] Organizations are open systems, dependent on inputs from the outside world, such as raw materials, human resources, and capital. They transform these inputs into outputs that (ideally) meet the market's needs for goods and services. The environment reacts to the outputs through a feedback loop; this feedback provides input for the next cycle of the system. The process repeats itself for the life of the system, and is illustrated in Exhibit 2.5.

Systems theory also emphasizes that an organization is one system in a series of subsystems. For instance, Southwest Airlines is a subsystem of the airline industry, and the flight crews are a subsystem of Southwest. Systems theory points out that each subsystem is a component of the whole and is interdependent with other subsystems.

Building on systems theory ideas, the contingency perspective refutes universal principles of management by stating that a variety of factors, both internal and external to the firm, may affect the organization's performance.[39] There is no "one best way" to manage and organize because circumstances vary.

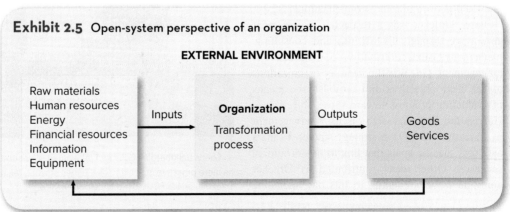

Exhibit 2.5 Open-system perspective of an organization

EXTERNAL ENVIRONMENT

Raw materials
Human resources
Energy
Financial resources
Information
Equipment

Inputs → **Organization** Transformation process → Outputs → Goods Services

contingencies factors that determine the appropriateness of managerial actions

Situational characteristics are called **contingencies**. Understanding contingencies helps a manager know which sets of circumstances dictate which management actions. You will learn recommendations for the major contingencies throughout this text. These important contingencies include

1. Circumstances in the organization's external environment.

2. The internal strengths and weaknesses of the organization.

3. The values, goals, skills, and attitudes of managers and workers in the organization.

4. The types of tasks, resources, and technologies the organization uses.

With an eye to these contingencies, a manager may categorize the situation and then choose the proper competitive strategy, organization structure, or management process for the circumstances.

Researchers continue to identify key contingency variables and their impact on management challenges. As you read the topics covered in each chapter, you will notice similarities and differences among management situations and the appropriate responses. This perspective should represent a cornerstone of your own approach to management. Many of the management strategies and tactics you will learn about throughout this course apply a contingency perspective.

> **LO4 Identify modern contributors who have shaped management thought and practice.**

decentralization, employees as assets (not liabilities), corporation as a human community, and the importance of knowledge workers in the new information economy.

Several CEOs have also left an impact on modern management thought. Former CEO Jack Welch transformed General Electric from a $13 billion company into a $500 billion company over a 20-year period.[42] Though sometimes criticized for his controversial practices such as massive layoffs and using forced rankings of employee performance,[43] he is widely viewed as having mastered "all of the critical aspects of leadership: people, process, strategy and structure."[44] You will learn about many exceptional leaders influencing current management thought and practice throughout this book and course.

Michael Porter, professor at Harvard University, is a well-known and influential expert on competitive strategy. He has published more than 125 research articles and 18 books on the subject and related areas, including *Competitive Strategy: Creating and Sustaining Superior Performance.* Two of his influential research articles are titled "What Is Strategy?" and "The Five Competitive Forces That Shape Strategy" (discussed in Chapter 3).[45]

Peter Senge of MIT Sloan School of Management has made major contributions to our understanding of organizational learning and change. In addition to founding the Society for Organizational Learning, Senge wrote *The Fifth Discipline: The Art and Practice of the Learning Organization,* which has sold more than 1 million copies worldwide (2006).[46]

Gary Hamel, professor, consultant, and management educator, was ranked as the "world's most influential business thinker" by *The Wall Street Journal.* Hamel has published numerous influential articles, including: "The Core Competence

4 | MODERN CONTRIBUTORS

In addition to the historical figures discussed above, several individuals from more recent times have influenced (through their leadership, interviews, speeches, and writing) the way management is practiced in today's organizations.

Peter Drucker was a respected management guru who, through his writings and consulting, made many lasting contributions to the practice of management. One was the need for organizations to set clear objectives and establish the means of evaluating progress toward those objectives.[40] He was the first person to discuss "management by objective" (MBO), a strategy whereby a manager sets specific goals that link to organizational success.[41] Other ideas contributed by Drucker continue to be influential to this day, including

● Sheryl Sandberg's book *Lean In: Women, Work and the Will to Lead* encourages women to be more proactive in seeking challenges at work, taking risks, and pursuing difficult goals. THIBAULT CAMUS/POOL/EPA-EFE/REX/Shutterstock

Traditional Thinking

Leaders adapt to change by relying on one or two favorite managerial approaches.

The Best Managers Today

Adapt to change by drawing on classic, contemporary, and modern managerial approaches to inform their decisions and actions.

of the Corporation" (with C. K. Prahalad) and "The Why, What, and How of Management Innovation." His book, *The Future of Management,* was named best business book of 2007 by Amazon.[47]

Sheryl Sandberg's book, *Lean In: Women, Work and the Will to Lead,* discusses the challenges women (including mothers) face in a workplace in which sexism and pay inequities remain. She encourages women to be more proactive in seeking challenges at work, taking risks, and pursuing difficult goals. Sandberg provides practical advice to women and tips regarding negotiation techniques and satisfying careers.[48]

W. Chan Kim and Renée Mauborgne are professors of strategy at INSEAD, one of the world's top business schools, and co-directors of the INSEAD Blue Ocean Strategy Institute in Fontainebleau, France. They wrote the international best-selling book *Blue Ocean Strategy,* in which they describe how to succeed by tapping entirely new markets with room to grow—"blue oceans" rather than "red oceans" full of cut-throat competitors.[49]

Professor Martin Davidson of the University of Virginia's Darden School of Business has changed how many executives approach inclusion and diversity in their organizations with his thought leadership. Davidson teaches, conducts research, and consults with global leaders to help them use diversity strategically to drive high performance. His book, *The End of Diversity as We Know It: Why Diversity Efforts Fail and How Leveraging Difference Can Succeed,* introduces a research-driven road map to help leaders more effectively create and capitalize on diversity in organizations.[50]

4.1 | An Eye on the Future

These historical perspectives have left legacies that affect contemporary management thought and practice. Their undercurrents continue to flow, even as the context and the specifics change.

Times do pass, and things do change. This may sound obvious, but it isn't to those managers who sit by idly while their firms fail to adapt to changing times. New technologies and flexible work arrangements like virtual teamwork, mobile communications, and social networking change how we work, produce goods, and deliver services. Change continually creates both new opportunities and new demands for reducing costs and for achieving greater innovation, quality, and speed.

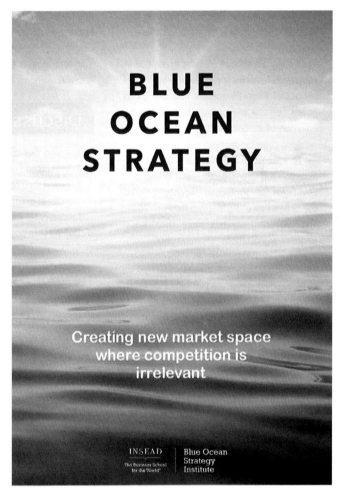

Kim and Mauborgne's *Blue Ocean Strategy* offers a systematic approach to reduce competition. The authors advise about how to create uncontested market spaces. https://www.blueoceanstrategy.com

Employee skills are also changing. Increasing global competition requires employees to develop key 21st-century skills such as problem solving, critical thinking, communication, collaboration, and self-management, along with a global perspective, foreign language proficiency, and cross-cultural knowledge.[51] Management knowledge and practices evolve accordingly.

The Organizational Environment and Culture

Learning Objectives

After studying Chapter 3, you should be able to

LO1 Describe the five elements of an organization's macroenvironment.

LO2 Explain the five components of an organization's competitive environment.

LO3 Understand how managers stay on top of changes in the external environment.

LO4 Summarize how managers respond to changes in the external environment.

LO5 Discuss how to use organizational cultures to overcome challenges in the external environment.

Andrés Romero Castro Photography/Alamy Stock Photo

W hen Gordon Logan founded Sport Clips, he wanted to change the haircut experience for men. He often felt out of place in salons designed for women, so he created a salon with men in mind. Through market research, Logan made some important discoveries: He found that many men were uncomfortable with salon smells and chemicals and reminisced about the camaraderie they felt when going to barbershops with their fathers. Logan also found little competition in the men's haircut market.[1]

Logan took advantage of this untapped market space to create a successful national franchise. Since the first Sport Clips opened in 1993, the franchise has grown to over 1,800 stores throughout the United States and Canada and is one of the fastest-growing franchise systems. Meanwhile, Sport Clips has earned a spot on *Entrepreneur*'s Franchise 500 list multiple times, most recently in 2019.[2]

True to his vision, Logan created a culture and environment where customers feel comfortable and workers can excel. Sport Clips provides men's haircuts, hair washes, hot face towels, shoulder massages—and that's all; no perms, no hair dying, no chemicals. This limited list of offerings with a straightforward pricing structure allows newly hired stylists to be trained faster, which is crucial for franchisees trying to scale a business.[3] To make the environment more fun and inviting to men, salons look like sports bars, complete with sporting events playing on TVs—minus the alcohol.

The core of Sport Clips culture is inspired by the words of former Notre Dame coach Lou Holtz: "Do Your Best. Do What's Right. Treat Others the Way They Want to Be Treated." That's exactly what the franchise does. In fact, Sport Clips has donated nearly $8 million through its "Help A Hero" program for veterans. And in 2019, it earned awards for Best Company for Women and Best Company Culture from Comparably.com.[4] It's little surprise that the International Franchise Association honored Logan by making him the 2020 inductee to its Hall of Fame for a lifetime of achievement in franchising.[5]

open systems
organizations that are affected by, and that affect, their environments (and other systems)

external environment
all relevant forces outside a firm's boundaries, such as competitors, customers, the government, and the economy

Executives like Logan must keep watch over their external environment, constantly monitoring developments outside their organizations. As we suggested in the first two chapters, organizations are open systems—that is, they are affected by and in turn affect their external environments. They use *inputs* like goods and services from their environment to create goods and services that are *outputs* to their environment. When we use the term external environment here, we mean more than an organization's customers, partnerships, or supplier relationships: The external environment includes all relevant forces outside the organization's boundaries.

Many external factors are uncontrollable. Managers and their organizations are battered by recession, government regulations, and competitors' actions. But their lack of control does not mean that managers can ignore such forces, use them as excuses for poor performance, or try to just get by. Managers must stay abreast of external developments and react effectively. In addition, as we discuss later, sometimes managers can influence components of the external environment.

This chapter discusses the major components of an organization's macroenvironment and competitive environment. It covers several methods that managers use to gather information to better understand environmental uncertainties. Next, the chapter discusses how leaders respond to and attempt to manage these uncertainties. It also examines the organization's internal environment, or culture, and how a culture can help the organization respond to its environment. Later chapters elaborate on many of the environmental forces introduced here.

● Gordon Logan, founder of Sport Clips, created the successful business after conducting market research that showed there was little competition in the men's haircut market. Wendy Yang/KRT/Newscom

macroenvironment the general environment; includes governments, economic conditions, and other fundamental factors that generally affect all organizations

1 | THE MACRO-ENVIRONMENT

All organizations operate in a macroenvironment, which includes the general elements in the external environment that potentially can influence strategic decisions. As Exhibit 3.1 illustrates, the five components of an organization's macroenvironment include laws and regulations, the economy, technology, demographics, and social values.

1.1 | Laws and Regulations Protect and Restrain Organizations

U.S. government policies impose strategic constraints on organizations but may also provide opportunities. The Tax Cuts and Jobs Act of 2017 reduced the corporate tax rate from 35 to 21 percent.[6] Many corporations benefited from this tax cut, which reduced their federal taxes to a negligible amount.[7]

study tip 3

Make brief outlines of chapters

At first it may sound like a waste of time, but making an outline of a chapter as you read it will help you later when it's time to study for an exam. A brief outline (for example, write the headings and key points from LO1, 1.1, 1.2, and so on) in your notebook or laptop gives you a "road map" for the whole chapter. The road map allows you to quickly see (and remember) how the different sections of the chapter interrelate and where the key concepts fit. Even though you can probably find an outline already done for you online, doing it yourself will help you better understand the material and thus increase your chances of getting higher grades on exams.

In your outlines, be sure to include the key terms (but don't write out the definitions—this will make the outline too long). On index cards or a study app like Quizlet, write the key term on one side and the full definition on the other. Keep them with you and practice them while eating lunch, exercising, and so forth. Being organized and disciplined will pay off!

The government can affect business opportunities through tax laws, economic policies, labor laws, and international trade rulings. In some countries, for example, bribes and kickbacks are common and expected ways of doing business. However, the *Foreign Corrupt Practices Act* (FCPA) prohibits Americans from bribing foreign officials.[8]

Microsoft paid more than $24 million to settle charges related to improper gift giving and payments and discounts given to governments in Hungary, Turkey, Saudi Arabia, and Thailand.[9] Walmart paid more than $144 million to the SEC and $138 million to the Department of Justice for failing to operate a sufficient anticorruption compliance program for more than a decade.[10]

But laws can also assist organizations. Because U.S. federal and state governments protect property rights, including copyrights, trademarks, and patents, it is economically more attractive to start businesses in the United States than in countries where laws and law enforcement offer less protection.

Regulators are specific government organizations in a firm's more immediate task environment. Some examples of regulatory agencies include:

- National Labor Relations Board (www.nlrb.gov).

- Federal Communications Commission (www.fcc.gov).

- Nuclear Regulatory Commission (www.nrc.gov).

- Occupational Safety and Health Administration (www.osha.gov).

- Environmental Protection Agency (www.epa.gov).

- Federal Reserve System (www.federalreserve.gov).

- Food and Drug Administration (www.fda.gov).

These agencies have the power to investigate company practices and take legal action to ensure compliance with laws. For example, the U.S. Department of Labor proposed changes in the way white-collar (executive, administrative, and professional) employees are classified. In the past, a manager of a restaurant would not be entitled to overtime pay for doing "nonmanagerial" duties like filling in for an absent cook, seating customers, and delivering plates to tables, because these activities were not considered part of her "primary duties." The proposed changes state that white-collar employees who make less than $47,476 per year are entitled to overtime pay.[11]

Often, the corporate community sees government as an adversary. However, many organizations realize that government can be a source of competitive advantage for a company or an entire industry. Public policy may prevent or limit new foreign or domestic competitors from entering an industry. Government may subsidize failing companies or provide tax breaks to some. Federal patents protect innovative products or production technologies. Legislation may be passed to support industry prices, thereby guaranteeing profits or survival.

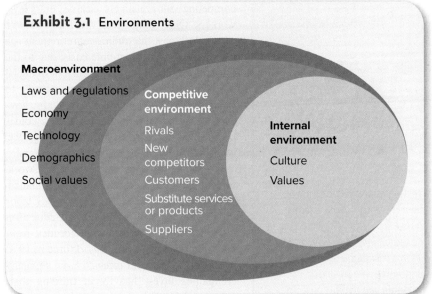

Exhibit 3.1 Environments

Macroenvironment

Laws and regulations

Economy

Technology

Demographics

Social values

Competitive environment

Rivals

New competitors

Customers

Substitute services or products

Suppliers

Internal environment

Culture

Values

The government may even intervene to ensure the survival of certain key industries or companies, as it did to help auto companies, airlines, and agricultural businesses.

1.2 | The Economy Affects Managers and Organizations

Although most Americans think in terms of the U.S. economy, the economic environment for organizations is much larger—created by complex interconnections among the economies of different countries. Several recent events have had far-reaching influence: For example, the escalating tariffs and trade war

● Venezuelan president Nicolás Maduro won reelection in 2018 despite leading his oil-rich nation into a shattering economic depression that prompted one of the worst migration crises in recent Latin American history. Molina86/Shutterstock

against China, the impending exit of the United Kingdom (Brexit) from the European Union, the pro-democracy protests in Hong Kong, and the humanitarian crisis at the Mexican border.

The economic environment dramatically affects managers' ability to function effectively, and influences their strategic choices. Interest and inflation rates affect the availability and cost of capital, growth opportunities, prices, costs, and consumer demand for products. Unemployment rates affect labor availability and the wages the firm must pay, as well as product demand. Steeply rising health care costs limit companies' ability to hire and raise the cost of doing business. Changes in the value of the dollar on world exchanges may make American products cheaper or more expensive than their foreign competitors.

The stock market is another important economic influence. When investors bid up stock prices, they are paying more to own shares in companies, so the companies have more capital to support their strategies. Observers of the stock market watch trends in major indexes such as the Dow Jones Industrial Average, Standard & Poor's 500, and NASDAQ Composite, which combine many companies' performance into a single measurement. In recent years, the indexes have reached record levels.[12] While some believe this bull market will continue for the foreseeable future, volatility remains a concern. In a single week in February 2020, the Dow plunged over 3,500 points (including the largest one-day drop in history).[13]

The stock market may also affect the behavior of individual managers. In publicly held companies, managers throughout the organization may feel required to meet Wall Street's earnings expectations. It is likely that you, too, will be asked to improve budget or sales numbers because your company does not want to disappoint "the Street." Such external pressures usually have a positive effect—they can help make firms more efficient and profitable. But failure to meet those expectations can cause a company's stock price to drop, making it more difficult for the firm to raise additional capital for investment. Managers' compensation also can be affected, particularly if they have been issued stock options. These pressures sometimes lead managers to focus on short-term results at the expense of the long-term success of their organizations, or even worse, to engage in unethical or unlawful behavior that misleads investors.[14]

1.3 | Technology Is Changing Every Business Function

A company cannot succeed without incorporating into its strategy the astonishing technologies that exist and are under development. As technology evolves, new industries, markets, and competitive niches develop. For example, the popularity of smartphones has spawned a fast-growing global app industry that topped 204 billion downloads in 2019, generating over $120 billion in revenue.[15] Many apps are changing the way people do business. Gusto streamlines payroll, benefits, time tracking, and paid time off for small businesses and also provides HR support.[16] Another example is Slack, the instant messaging and communications app used by millions of people and companies including Intuit, Lyft, and Airbnb.[17] Slack allows teams to organize and back up conversations, exchange files, and increase collaboration.[18]

In addition, new technologies provide more efficient ways to manage and communicate. Advanced information technology and telecommunication systems make information available when and where it's needed around the clock. Productivity software monitors employee performance and detects deficiencies. Telecommunications allow conferences to take place without requiring people to travel to the same location. As you will learn in Chapter 5, strategies developed around cutting-edge technological advances can create a competitive advantage.

1.4 | Demographics Describe Your Employees and Customers

Demographics are statistical characteristics of a group or population. An organization's customers, a university's faculty and staff, or a nation's current labor force can all be described statistically in terms of their members' ages, genders, education levels, incomes, occupations, and so forth.

Managers must consider workforce demographics in formulating their human resources strategies. The labor force participation rate measures the percentage of the population working or looking for work. From early 2007 (before the recession hit) to July 2019, this rate decreased from 66.4 to 63 percent.[20] The rate has hovered around 63 percent for the past decade due in part to an aging workforce plus fewer 25- to 54-year-olds seeking employment.[21]

Population growth influences the size and composition of the labor force. In the decade from 2014 to 2024, the U.S. civilian labor force is expected to grow at a relatively slow rate of half a percent annually, reaching nearly 163.8 million in 2024.[22]

The fastest-growing age group will be workers who are 75 years old and older, growing at a rate of 3.4 percent per year.[23] What does this mean for employers? They will need to find ways to retain and fully use the talents of their experienced workers while

Did You KNOW?

Texting during lectures may be hazardous to your grades. A research study published in *Research in Higher Education Journal* divided a group of undergraduate business students into two groups: One-half of participants were allowed to text during a lecture and the other half were not. Exam scores of the "texting" students were significantly lower than those of the other students.[19]

competing for relatively scarce entry-level workers. Older employees will likely be willing to work past the traditional retirement age of 65, at least on a part-time basis; due to the importance of work and existence of financial needs, one-third of Baby Boomers ages 67 to 72 have put off retirement.[24] Eventually, however, declining participation in work by older people will force managers to find replacements for these highly experienced workers.

The education and skill levels of the workforce are another demographic factor managers must consider. The share of the U.S. labor force with at least some college education increased steadily over several decades, from less than one-fourth of the workforce in 1970 to close to 70 percent today.[25] Even so, many companies invest heavily in training their entry-level workers and send them through their own corporate universities, common at hundreds of large organizations like Unilever, General Mills, Credit Suisse, Air Liquide, Novartis, and Apple.[26] Also, as college has become a more popular option, employers are having difficulty recruiting employees for jobs that require knowledge of a skilled trade, such as machinists and toolmakers.[27]

In June 2019, there were 7.3 million job openings in the United States, which is a positive sign;[28] however, there was evidence that many openings for some high-demand skills like IT stayed unfilled for longer periods of time.[29] This trend suggests that either employers are being choosy or applicants are underqualified, or both. However, as education levels improve around the globe, more organizations may send technical tasks to lower-priced but highly trained workers overseas.

Another factor influencing the U.S. population and labor force is immigration. In 2018, there were 28.2 million foreign-born individuals in the U.S. labor force, which represented about 17.4 percent of the total labor force.[30] Between now and 2065, future immigrants and their descendants will account for approximately 88 percent of U.S. population growth.[31]

The demographic importance of immigration intersects with legal issues governing who is permitted to work in the United States. For example, the federal government recently cracked down not only on undocumented workers but also on the managers who hired them. It established a new program by which businesses are required to check prospective hires' legal status by submitting their names to a database called "E-Verify."[32] Some companies have asked the U.S. government to admit more foreign workers with technical expertise that may be hard to find in the United States.

Immigration is one reason the labor force in the future will be more ethnically diverse than it is today. The biggest percentage of employment increases will be by Asian Americans and Hispanic populations, followed by African Americans.

Water for People

Approximately 2.2 billion (nearly 1 in 3) people in the world lack access to safe water. Twice that number live in areas without adequate sanitation. Many people—often women—walk hours every day to bring safe water home. The World Health Organization estimates that 2 million people die each year from waterborne diseases related to unsafe water and sanitation; the majority of these deaths are children under age 5.

Water for People, based in Denver, is an international nonprofit working across nine countries to bring safe water and sanitation to millions of people. CEO Eleanor Allen leads her team to achieve the organization's mission: "To promote the development of high-quality drinking water and sanitation services, accessible to all, and sustained by strong communities, business, and governments." Ultimately, Water for People wants to reach "everyone forever."

Water for People's values reflect its focus on "demonstrating integrity in all we do." Those values are accountability, courage, empowerment, partnership, and transparency. The organization transmits them to all stakeholders, including staff, volunteers, governing board members, field partners, donors and funding organizations, and other partners.

The United Nations adopted a plan called "The 2030 Agenda for Sustainable Development," which is comprised of 17 sustainable development goals (SDGs). Water for People focuses exclusively on SDG 6: Ensure availability and sustainable management of water and sanitation for all. To date, Water for People has brought reliable water services to over 3.6 million people. Its goal through 2021 is to increase its already significant impact 20 times over.

To achieve these results, Water for People deploys team members familiar with the culture and language of communities in Honduras, Guatemala, Nicaragua, Bolivia, Peru, Malawi, Rwanda, Uganda, and India. To choose a community with which to work, Water for People considers the strength of the region's commitment to work with it, the cost of the project, the availability of a reliable NGO (nongovernmental organization) partner, and the degree of support from the area's local government. The idea is for outside financing to diminish over time as costs decrease and local sources of funding take over.

In recognition of her innovative efforts to effect "lasting social change," Schwab Foundation named Allen a Social Entrepreneur of the Year. Says Allen, "Water changes everything. It lays the foundation for health, education and economic prosperity. That is social progress."

Discussion Questions

- Why must Water for People assess local commitment to supporting infrastructure improvements in water access and sanitation before beginning a project? Is it reasonable to expect communities to eventually take over the costs of improvements it makes? Why or why not?

- Water for People's CEO Eleanor Allen says enabling access to clean water "is social progress." What are some areas in which you have thought about making a difference? Do you envision ever starting a venture that matters to you?

Sources: "1 in 3 People Globally Do Not Have Access to Safe Drinking Water," World Health Organization, June 18, 2019, https://www.who.int/news-room/detail/18-06-2019-1-in-3-people-globally-do-not-have-access-to-safe-drinking-water-unicef-who; "Waterborne Disease Related to Unsafe Water and Sanitation," World Health Organization, https://www.who.int/sustainable-development/housing/health-risks/waterborne-disease/en/, accessed March 5, 2020; Organization website, https://www.waterforpeople.org/mission-and-history/, accessed March 5, 2020; Organization website, https://www.waterforpeople.org/strategic-plan/, accessed March 5, 2020; Organization website, https://www.waterforpeople.org/where-we-work/, accessed March 5, 2020; and H. Schwab, "Meet the Social Entrepreneurs of the Year 2017," World Economic Forum, March 29, 2017, www.weforum.org/agenda/2017/03/2017-social-entrepreneurs/.

In the last quarter of the 20th century, women joined the U.S. labor force in record numbers. Throughout the 1970s and 1980s, they became much more likely to take paying jobs. In the 1970s, only about one-third of women were in the labor force, but 60 percent had jobs in 1999. Since then, the women's labor force participation rate has declined slightly to about 59 percent.[33]

A more diverse workforce has many advantages, but managers have to ensure fairness for women and minorities with respect to employment, advancement opportunities, and compensation. They must recruit, retain, train, motivate, and effectively use people of diverse demographic backgrounds who have the skills to achieve the company's mission.

1.5 | Social Values Shape Attitudes Toward Your Company and Its Products

Societal trends regarding how people think and behave have major implications for management of the labor force, corporate social actions, and strategic decisions about products and markets. During the 1980s and 1990s, women in the workforce often chose to delay having children as they focused on their careers, but today more women are having children and then returning to the workforce. As a result, companies have created programs to support working parents. At IBM, both parents can take 20 weeks of parental leave anytime during the first year after the child is born or adopted.[34] Johnson & Johnson created reservable lactation rooms that allow mothers to work quietly, listen to music, and charge devices.[35]

A prominent issue today pertains to natural resources: drilling for oil in formerly protected areas in the United States. Firms in the oil industry like ExxonMobil, Royal Dutch Shell, BP, ConocoPhillips, and Chevron face considerable public opinion both in favor of preserving the natural environment and against U.S. dependence on other countries for fuel. Currently, the U.S. government is planning to allow oil drilling in nearly all waters off the U.S. coast.[36] Protection of the natural environment will factor into social concerns and many types of management decisions.

How companies respond to social issues may affect their reputation in the marketplace, in turn helping or hindering their competitiveness. The public health issue of childhood obesity

gave video games a bad name among those who want children to get off the couch and move. *Dance Dance Revolution* and Nintendo's *Wii Sports* led the way for video games that made the participant move to play. Now, virtual reality (VR) headsets have created immersive games that get players moving, including *Beat Saber* and *The Thrill of the Fight*.[37] Black Box specializes in in-person gyms with private fitness featuring private workout booths, lockers, showers, and a mobile app to track progress.[38]

LO2 Explain the five components of an organization's competitive environment.

2 | THE COMPETITIVE ENVIRONMENT

All managers are affected by the components of the macroenvironment just discussed. As Exhibit 3.2 illustrates, each organization also functions in a closer, more immediate competitive environment, consisting of rivalry among existing competitors and the threat of new entrants, the threat of substitute and complementary products, and the bargaining power of suppliers and buyers. This model was developed by Michael Porter, a Harvard professor and a noted authority on strategic management.[39]

According to Porter, successful managers do more than simply react to the environment; they act in ways that actually shape or change the organization's environment. Porter's model is an excellent method for analyzing the competitive environment and adapting to or influencing the nature of the competition.

2.1 | Rivals Can Be Domestic or Global

Among the various components of the competitive environment, competitors within the industry must first deal with one another. When organizations compete for the same customers and try to win market share at the others' expense, all must react to and anticipate their competitors' actions.

jennygiraffe/Shutterstock

Exhibit 3.2 Porter's five forces: The organization's competitive environment

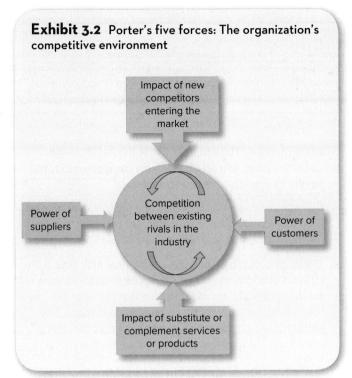

Source: Adapted from M. E. Porter, "The Five Competitive Forces That Shape Strategy," *Harvard Business Review*, www.hbr.org (January 2008), pp. 78–93.

Identify the Competition

The first question to consider is this: Who is the competition? Sometimes the answer is obvious. The major competitors in the market for mobile phones are Apple, Samsung, LG, Google, and Motorola.[40] But if organizations focus exclusively on traditional rivalries, they miss the emerging ones. Back in the 1990s, many of the large music companies were so busy competing against one another for sales and market share that they underestimated the long-term impact of new technologies like MP3 files and music swapping services like Napster. Then the launch of iTunes by Apple allowed customers to purchase (for about $.99) single songs, dealing yet another competitive blow to the traditional music industry. In-store sales of CDs have never recovered.

Apple's game-changing strategy didn't stop there. In 2007, Apple released its first iPhone, which played MP3 files along with performing countless other functions. The music player industry didn't expect a computer manufacturer (Apple) to create a smartphone with multifunctionality that could compete with stand-alone MP3 players.[41]

Competitors may include many types of companies:

- Small domestic firms, especially upon their entry into tiny, premium markets.

- Strong regional competitors.

- Big new domestic companies exploring new markets.

- Global firms, especially those that try to solidify their position in small niches (a traditional Japanese tactic) or can draw on an inexpensive labor force on a large scale (as in India and China).

- Newer ventures launched by all types of entrepreneurs.

Competition from other countries grew with worldwide reduction in international trade barriers. For example, the United States-Mexico-Canada Agreement (USMCA) was recently signed into law, effectively updating the 25-year-old North American Free Trade Agreement (NAFTA).[42] While still focused on promoting trade among the three countries, new provisions of the USMCA include requiring more automobile production in the United States and stronger labor rules in Mexico.[43]

Analyze How They Compete Once competitors are identified, the next step is to analyze how they compete. Competitors use tactics such as price reductions, new-product introductions, and advertising campaigns to gain advantage over their rivals.

Consider the market for athletic shoes. Nowadays, the Nike brand frequently comes to consumers' minds when it's time to purchase a new pair of shoes for the gym or sports. That wasn't always the case. For 30 years, Nike and Reebok competed fiercely with one another over the lucrative footwear market. Founded in 1964 by Phil Bowerman and Phil Knight, Nike quickly gained a foothold in the market by importing quality athletic footwear and "aggressively courting male customers."[44] Paul Fireman, who bought Reebok in 1984, instead focused on the growing market for female sneakers—a strategy that led to Reebok surpassing Nike in sales in 1987.

Nike took a different approach by signing the world-famous athlete, Michael Jordan, as a spokesperson for the company. The Air Jordan brand was a hit and earned the company annual sales of $1 billion. Nike later signed Naomi Osaka, Neymar Jr., LeBron James, Serena Williams, Kevin Durant, Cristiano Ronaldo, and others. Eventually, with the help of celebrity endorsements and strong branding, Nike beat out Reebok to become the $39 billion powerhouse that it is today.[45]

Competition is most intense when there are many direct competitors (including global contenders), industry growth is slow, and the product or service cannot be differentiated. New, high-growth industries offer enormous opportunities for profits. When an industry matures and growth slows, profits drop. Then intense competition causes an industry shakeout: Weaker companies are eliminated, and the strong companies survive.[46] We will discuss competitors and strategy further in Chapter 5.

2.2 | New Entrants Appear When Barriers to Entry Are Low

New entrants into an industry compete with established companies. A relatively new global industry, downloadable apps have become big business. In 2017, the most popular Google Android apps were FaceApp, What the Forecast?!!, Boomerang, TopBuzz Video, and Yarn. Top Apple iOS apps included Bitmoji, Snapchat, YouTube, Facebook Messenger, and Instagram.[47]

competitive environment the immediate environment surrounding a firm; includes suppliers, customers, rivals, and the like

If many factors prevent new companies from entering an industry, the threat to established firms is less serious. If there are few such barriers to entry, the threat of new entrants is greater. Major barriers to entry include:

- *Government policy*—When a firm's patent for a drug expires, other companies can enter the market. The patent recently expired on Merck's asthma and allergy medicine, Singulair. At the same time, several research projects to introduce new, patented medicines were delayed or failed, so Merck had to lay off thousands of employees to cut costs.[48]

- *Capital requirements*—Getting started in some industries, such as building aircraft or operating a railroad, may cost so much that companies won't even try to raise such large amounts of money. This helps explain why Boeing and Airbus have no direct competitors in manufacturing large, long-haul aircraft.[49]

- *Brand identification*—When customers are loyal to a familiar brand, new entrants have to spend heavily. Imagine the costs involved in trying to launch a new chain of fast-food restaurants to compete against Taco Bell or Panda Express. Similarly, Google's name change to Alphabet surprised many people because of its brand dominance in the search

● Nike spokesperson Serena Williams, whose celebrity endorsement enhances Nike's strong branding. Neale Cousland/Shutterstock

engine domain. The company hopes the name change and subsequent restructuring will encourage faster growth among its younger, less-known ventures.[50]

- *Cost disadvantages*—Established companies may be able to keep their costs lower because they are larger, have more favorable locations, and already have needed assets.

- *Distribution channels*—Existing competitors may have such efficient distribution channels that new entrants struggle to get their goods or services to customers. For example, established food products have supermarket shelf space. New entrants must displace existing products with promotions, price breaks, intensive selling, and other tactics.

2.3 | Customers Determine Your Success

Customers purchase the goods or services an organization offers. Without them, a company won't survive. Organizations that sell directly to customers are known as business-to-consumer (B2C) companies. You are a final consumer when you buy a book from Amazon or new home speakers from Bose.

Intermediate consumers buy raw materials or wholesale products and then sell to final consumers, as when Sony buys components from Seagate (hard drives) and Bosch (motion sensor chips) and uses them to make consoles. These organizations are referred to as business-to-business (B2B) companies. Types of intermediate customers include retailers, who buy from wholesalers and manufacturers' representatives and then sell to consumers, and industrial buyers, who buy raw materials (such as chemicals) to be converted into final products. Intermediate customers make more purchases than individual final consumers do.

Customers do much more than simply purchase goods and services. They can demand lower prices, higher quality, unique product specifications, or better service. They also can play competitors against one another, as occurs when a car buyer (or a purchasing agent) collects different offers and negotiates for the best price. Often, today's customers want to be actively involved with their products, whether personalizing a Coke bottle,[51] choosing the strap designs of custom Chaco sandals,[52] or receiving clothes chosen personally by a stylist at Stitch Fix.[53]

Social networking and media sites have further empowered customers. They provide an easy source of information—about both product features and pricing. In addition, today's social media users informally create and share messages about products, providing flattering free "advertising" at best or embarrassing and even erroneous bad publicity at worst.

Oreo Cookie ✓
@Oreo

Power out? No problem.
pic.twitter.com/dnQ7pOgC

← Reply ♻ Retweet ★ Favorite 🗨 Pocket ••• More

YOU CAN STILL DUNK IN THE DARK

16,075 RETWEETS   6,186 FAVORITES

Twitter

One college-age writer put it this way: "Social media has become the younger generation's primary means of interacting with the world." Some believe that "callouts" via social media provide important feedback to companies to improve their product or customer service.[54] However, social media can be hard to control and may even cause damage to a company's brand. Gillette posted a two-minute short film promoting the "ideals of the #MeToo movement."[55] The video received more than 14 million views, it got twice as many dislikes as likes, and viewers vowed to trash their Gillette products.[56] Today's companies may find it difficult to identify, much less respond to such unofficial messages.

As we discussed in Chapter 1, customer service means giving customers what they want or need in the way they want it. This usually depends on the speed and dependability with which an organization can deliver its products. Actions and attitudes that provide excellent customer service include the following:

• Speed of filling and delivering normal orders.

• Willingness to meet emergency needs.

• Merchandise delivered in good condition.

• Readiness to take back defective goods and resupply quickly.

• Availability of installation and repair services and parts.

• Service charges (i.e., whether services are free or priced separately).[57]

An organization is at a disadvantage if it depends too heavily on powerful customers—those who make large purchases or can easily find alternative places to buy. If you are a firm's largest customer and can buy from others, you have power over that firm and probably can negotiate with it successfully. Your firm's biggest customers, especially if they can buy from other sources, will have the greatest negotiating power over you.

2.4 | Competitors' Products Can Complement or Substitute for Yours

Besides products that directly compete, other products can affect a company's performance by being substitutes for or complements of the company's offerings. A *substitute* is a potential threat; customers use it as an alternative, buying less of one kind of product but more of another. For example, substitutes for coffee could be tea, energy drinks, cola, or water.

A *complement* is a potential opportunity because customers buy more of a given product if they also demand more of the complementary product. Examples include ink cartridges as a complement for printers; when people buy more printers, they buy more ink cartridges.

Substitutes Technological advances and economic efficiencies are among the ways that firms can develop substitutes for existing products. Internet offerings such as YouTube and Minecraft have attracted video game players away from their TV sets to interact with one another online. This example shows that substitute products or services can limit another industry's revenue potential.

Founded in Austin, Texas, in 1980, Whole Foods (purchased by Amazon in 2017) positions itself as a substitute to more traditional grocery chains like Kroger, HEB, and Albertsons. Providing natural and organic foods that cater to health-conscious consumers and vegetarians, Whole Foods grew dramatically to over 500 stores in the United States, Canada, and United Kingdom, earning more than $233 billion in 2018.[58]

Rumors of soon-to-be available substitutes can garner attention. Apple is rumored to be working on a secret iCar project that will focus on the driving technology behind autonomous driving cars.[59]

In addition to current substitutes, companies need to think about potential substitutes that may be viable in the future. For example, possible alternatives to fossil fuels include nuclear fusion, solar power, and wind energy. The advantages promised by each of these technologies are many: inexhaustible fuel supplies, inexpensive electricity, zero emissions, universal public acceptance, and so on. Yet each of these faces economic and technical hurdles.

● Solar power and wind energy are viable substitutes for fossil fuel.
narvikk/Getty Images

Complements Besides identifying and planning for substitutes, companies must consider complements for their products. Classic examples of complementary products include razors and razor blades and printers and cartridges. Revenues from the initial, one-time purchase (razor or printer) are surpassed by the ongoing need to purchase the complementary products (razor blades or cartridges). In another example, automobile manufacturers offer several products and services that are used in conjunction with their automobiles, including windshield wipers and maintenance requirements.

2.5 | Suppliers Provide Your Resources

Recall that organizations must acquire resources (inputs) from their environment and convert those resources into products or services (outputs) to sell. Suppliers provide the resources needed for production, and those resources may come in several forms:

- *People*—supplied by trade schools and universities.

- *Raw materials*—from producers, wholesalers, and distributors.

- *Information*—supplied by researchers and consulting firms.

- *Financial capital*—from banks and other sources.

But suppliers are important to an organization for reasons beyond the resources they provide. Suppliers can raise their prices or provide poor-quality goods and services. Labor unions can go on strike or demand higher wages. Workers may produce defective work. Powerful suppliers, then, can reduce an organization's profits, particularly if the organization cannot pass on price increases to its customers.

Organizations are at a disadvantage if they become overly dependent on any powerful supplier. A supplier is powerful if the buyer has few other sources of supply or if the supplier has many other buyers. Intel has a dominant hold on a key part of the microprocessor chip market. To maintain its market dominance, Intel announced the release of the Xeon Skylake processor for use in data centers. Navin Shenoy, manager of the company's data center group, called the release the company's "biggest data center platform announcement in a decade."[60] Intel's hold on the processor market is being challenged by other tech titans like Google, IBM, Microsoft, and Baidu.[61]

Switching costs are fixed costs buyers face if they change suppliers. For example, once a buyer learns how to operate a supplier's equipment, such as computer software, the buyer faces both economic and psychological costs in changing to a new supplier.

In recent years many companies have improved their competitiveness and profitability through supply chain management, the management of the entire network of facilities and people that obtain raw materials from outside the organization, transform them into products, and distribute them to customers.[62] Increased global competition requires managers to pay close attention to their costs; they can no longer afford to hold large inventories, waiting for orders to come in. Also, once orders do come in, some products sitting in inventory might be out of date.

Customers look for products built to their specific needs and preferences—and they want them delivered quickly at the lowest available price. This requires the supply chain to be not only efficient but also flexible, so that the organization's output can respond quickly to changes in demand.

Today, the goal of effective supply chain management is to have the right product in the right quantity available at the right place at the right cost. Uber Freight connects freight truck

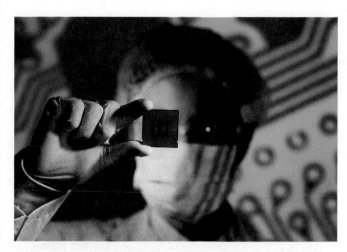

● According to Intel, the Xeon Skylake redesign brings greater CPU and GPU performance and reduced power consumption.
Dragon Images/Shutterstock

drivers with warehouse suppliers to decrease the amount of unpaid time drivers waste waiting for deliveries to load.[63] The truckers can rate suppliers based on the loading and unloading times plus the options for parking, bathrooms, and food.[64]

In sum, choosing the right supplier is an important strategic decision. Suppliers can affect manufacturing time, product quality, costs, and inventory levels.

The relationship between suppliers and the organization is changing in many companies. The close supplier relationship has become a new model for many organizations that use a just-in-time manufacturing approach. And in some companies, innovative managers are forming strategic partnerships with their key suppliers to develop new products and new production techniques.

> **LO3** Understand how managers stay on top of changes in the external environment.

3 | KEEPING UP WITH CHANGES IN THE ENVIRONMENT

If managers do not understand how the environment affects their organization, or cannot identify opportunities and threats that are likely to be important, their ability to make decisions and execute plans will be severely limited. For example, if little is known about customer likes and dislikes, organizations will have difficulty designing new products, scheduling production, or developing marketing plans. Timely and accurate environmental information is critical for running a business.

But information about the environment is not always readily available. Even economists have difficulty predicting whether an upturn or a downturn in the economy is likely. Managers find it difficult to forecast how well their own products will sell, let alone how a competitor might respond. In other words, managers often operate under conditions of uncertainty.

Environmental uncertainty means that managers do not have enough information about the environment to understand or predict the future. Uncertainty arises from two related factors:

- *Complexity*—the number of issues to which a manager must attend, and the degree to which they are interconnected. Industries (e.g., the automotive industry) with many different firms that compete in vastly different ways tend to be more complex—and uncertain—than industries with only a few key competitors (e.g., airplane manufacturers).

- *Dynamism*—the degree of discontinuous change that occurs within the industry. High-growth industries (e.g., smartphones) with products and technologies that change rapidly are more uncertain than stable industries where change is less dramatic and more predictable (e.g., utilities).[65]

switching costs fixed costs buyers face when they change suppliers

supply chain management the managing of the network of facilities and people that obtain materials from outside the organization, transform them into products, and distribute them to customers

environmental uncertainty lack of information needed to understand or predict the future

environmental scanning searching for and sorting through information about the environment

competitive intelligence information that helps managers determine how to compete better

To deal with environmental uncertainty, managers need methods for collecting, sorting through, and interpreting information about the environment. By analyzing forces in both the macroenvironment and the competitive environment, managers can identify environmental opportunities and threats.

3.1 | Environmental Scanning Keeps You Aware

The first step in coping with uncertainty in the environment is to identify what might be important. Organizations and individuals often act out of ignorance, only to later regret their actions. IBM had the opportunity to purchase the technology behind xerography but turned it down. Xerox saw the potential and took the lead in photocopying. Later, Xerox researchers developed the technology for the original computer mouse but failed to see its potential and missed an important opportunity.

To understand and predict changes, opportunities, and threats, organizations such as PepsiCo, Dell, and Berkshire Hathaway spend a good deal of time and money monitoring events in the environment. Environmental scanning includes searching for information that is not immediately evident and sorting through that information to interpret what is important. Managers ask questions such as these:

- Who are our current competitors?

- Are there few or many entry barriers to our industry?

- What substitutes exist for our product or service?

- Is the company too dependent on powerful suppliers?

- Is the company too dependent on powerful customers?[66]

Answers to these questions—based, as you might have noticed, on Porter's model—help managers develop competitive intelligence, the information necessary to decide how best to manage in the competitive environment.

Exhibit 3.3 describes two extreme environments: an attractive environment, which gives a firm a competitive advantage, and an unattractive environment, which puts a firm at a competitive disadvantage.[67] An example of an attractive environment is health technology, which is one of the most profitable industries in the United States.[68] On the other side of the spectrum is the newspaper publishing industry, which is being replaced by online media.[69]

scenario a narrative that describes a particular set of future conditions

benchmarking the process of comparing an organization's practices and technologies with those of other companies

forecasting method for predicting how variables will change the future

3.2 | Developing Scenarios Helps You Think About the Future

As managers try to determine the effects of environmental forces on their organizations, they often develop different portrayals of how the future might look—using different combinations of the many factors that form a total picture of the environment and the firm.[70] For example, tablet computers like the iPad were once heralded as a potential replacement for PCs and laptops in the workplace. Despite making some inroads (schools purchasing tablets for student use), tablets did not fully replace PCs, and global sales of tablets declined in recent years.[71]

Organizations sometimes develop a best-case scenario (the occurrence of events that are favorable to the firm), a worst-case scenario (the occurrence of unfavorable events), and one or more middle-ground alternatives. The value of scenarios is that they help managers develop contingency plans for what they might do given different outcomes.[72] For example, as a manager, you will be involved in budgeting for your area. You will almost certainly be asked to list initiatives you would eliminate in case of an economic downturn and new investments you would make if your firm does better than expected.

Effective managers regard the scenarios they develop as living documents, not merely prepared once and put aside. They constantly update the scenarios to take into account relevant new factors that emerge, such as significant changes in the economy or actions by competitors. Also, managers try to identify strategies that are the most robust across all of the different scenarios.

3.3 | Forecasting Predicts Your Future Environment

Whereas environmental scanning identifies important factors, and scenario development develops alternative pictures of the future, forecasting attempts to predict more precisely the changes in and the future values of important variables. For example, in making capital investments, firms forecast interest rates. In deciding to expand or downsize a business, firms may forecast the demand for goods and services and the supply and demand of labor. A few years ago, China overtook the United States as the largest market for GMC's Cadillac.[73] Sales of the luxury vehicle slowed in the United States but grew in China thanks to young Chinese consumers who like the wealthy status that Cadillac projects. Cadillac is now launching its first electric vehicle in China.[74]

Ultimately, forecasts may or may not be accurate, or they may not be accurate enough to help managers make good decisions. Because they extrapolate from the past to project the future, forecasts tend to be most accurate when the future ends up looking a lot like the past. We don't need sophisticated forecasting techniques in those instances. Forecasts are most useful when the future will look radically different from the past.

Unfortunately, that is when forecasts tend to be less accurate. The more things change, the less confidence we have in our forecasts. Here is some practical advice for using forecasts:

- Use multiple forecasts, and consider averaging their predictions.

- Remember that accuracy decreases as you go further into the future.

- Collect data carefully. Forecasts are no better than the data used to construct them.

- Use simple forecasts (rather than complicated ones) where possible.

- Keep in mind that important events often are surprises that sabotage the predictions.[75]

3.4 | Benchmarking Helps You Become Best in Class

Besides trying to predict changes in the environment, firms can study the best practices of other firms to understand their sources of competitive advantage. Benchmarking means identifying the best-in-class performance by a company in a given area—say, product development or customer service—and then comparing your processes with theirs. A benchmarking team collects information about its own company's operations and those of the other firm in order to determine gaps. These gaps serve as a point of entry to learn the underlying causes of

Exhibit 3.3	Attractive and unattractive environments	
Environmental Factor	**Attractive**	**Unattractive**
Competitors	Few; high industry growth; unequal size differentiated.	Many; low industry growth; equal size; commodity.
Threat of entry	Low threat; many barriers.	High threat; few entry barriers.
Substitutes	Few.	Many.
Suppliers	Many; low bargaining power.	Few; high bargaining power.
Customers	Many; low bargaining power.	Few; high bargaining power.

Sources: Adapted from S. Ghoshal, "Building Effective Intelligence Systems for Competitive Advantage," *Sloan Management Review* 28, no. 1 (Fall 1986), pp. 49–58; and K. D. Cory, "Can Competitive Intelligence Lead to a Sustainable Competitive Advantage?" *Competitive Intelligence Review* 7, no. 3 (Fall 1996), pp. 45–55.

performance differences. Ultimately, the team maps out a set of best practices that lead to world-class performance. We will discuss benchmarking further in Chapter 5.

> **LO4** Summarize how managers respond to changes in the external environment.

4 | RESPONDING TO THE ENVIRONMENT

For managers and organizations, responding effectively to their environments is almost always essential. Clothing retailers who pay no attention to changes in the public's style preferences, and manufacturers who fail to ensure they have steady sources of supply, are soon out of business. To respond to their environment, managers and companies have a number of options, which can be grouped into three categories:

1. Adapting to the environment.

2. Influencing the environment.

3. Selecting a new environment.

4.1 | Adapt to the External Environment

To cope with environmental uncertainty, organizations frequently adjust their structures and work processes. Exhibit 3.4 shows four different approaches that organizations can take in adapting to environmental uncertainty, depending on whether it arises from complexity, dynamism, or both.

When uncertainty arises from environmental complexity, organizations tend to adapt by decentralizing decision making. For example, if a company faces a growing number of competitors in various markets, if different customers want different things, if product features keep increasing, and if production

Exhibit 3.4 Four structural approaches for managing uncertainty

	Stable	Dynamic
Complex	Decentralized Bureaucratic (standardized skills)	Decentralized Organic (mutual adjustment)
Simple	Centralized Bureaucratic (standardized work processes)	Centralized Organic (direct supervision)

> **empowerment** the process of sharing power with employees to enhance their confidence in their ability to perform their jobs and contribute to the organization

facilities are being built in different regions of the world, executives probably cannot keep abreast of all activities and understand all the operational details of a business. In these cases, the top management team is likely to give lower-level managers authority to make decisions that benefit the firm. The term empowerment is used frequently today to talk about this type of decentralized authority.

To compete in volatile environments, organizations rely on knowledgeable and skilled workers. One way to develop such workers is to sponsor training programs. Alliances among employers, community colleges, universities, foundations, and nonprofit training programs are producing workers with much-needed skills in many industries. One program in New York, Per Scholas, trains individuals from economically distressed areas like the Bronx to obtain careers in information technology. Funded by grants from private foundations and the New York City Council, the program gained momentum through its collaboration with companies looking for skilled IT employees. Since its creation more than 20 years ago, Per Scholas has trained more than 7,000 low-income adults to obtain jobs in the technology field.[76]

Expanding from NYC to five other major metro areas in the United States, Per Scholas boasts a job placement rate of 85 percent of its graduates, who earn significantly higher average starting wages than what they would have earned without the training. One graduate, Cristina Rodriguez, works at Spectrum as a broadband specialist. Her new skills have empowered her to become a high-performing employee. "What feels great is when I resolve someone's issue," she says. Rodriguez, fluent in both English and Spanish, is able to solve customers' problems in both languages.[77]

Per Scholas' training programs have grown more successful in recent years because of their close association with companies that hire their graduates. For example, Per Scholas and Cognizant teamed up to open technology skills training facilities in the South Bronx and Dallas. The facilities offer customized technology courses that provide students hands-on training and career preparation skills, putting them in a direct hiring pipeline to Cognizant and other large IT firms.[78]

In response to uncertainty arising from a dynamic environment, organizations tend to establish more flexible structures. Today, the term *bureaucracy* generally has a bad connotation. While bureaucratic organizations may be efficient and controlled if the environment is stable, they tend to react slowly to changes in products, technologies, customers, or competitors. Because bureaucratic organizations tend to be formal and stable, they often cannot adjust to change or exceptional circumstances that "don't fit the rules." In these cases, more organic structures give organizations the flexibility to adapt. Organic structures are less formal than bureaucratic organizations; decisions are made through interaction and mutual adjustment among individuals rather than from a set of predefined rules.

● Per Scholas hosted hands-on workshops to help 1,500 older adults in New York City learn how technology can improve the quality of their lives.
Media for Medical SARL/Alamy Stock Photo

clothing season, retailers discount their merchandise to clear it out and make room for incoming inventories. These are examples of smoothing environmental cycles to level off fluctuations in demand.

Adapting at the Core While buffering and smoothing manage uncertainties at the boundaries of the organization, firms also can establish flexible processes that allow for adaptation in their technical core. For example, firms increasingly try to customize their goods and services to meet customers' varied and changing demands. Health care companies like UnitedHealthcare and Cigna offer a variety of coverage options to customers. Even in manufacturing, where it is difficult to change basic core processes, firms are creating flexible factories. Instead of mass-producing large quantities of a "one-size-fits-all" product, organizations can use mass customization to produce customized products at an equally low cost. For example, customers who purchase a Ford F-150 truck can choose from a wide variety of trims, engine sizes, safety features, and interior design features to customize the military-grade aluminum alloy body.[81] The process of mass customization involves the use of a network of independent operating units in which each performs a specific process or task such as making a dashboard assembly on an automobile. When an order comes in, different units join forces to deliver the product or service as specified by the customer.[82] Despite these examples of companies adapting their technical core to changing environments, organizational agility or the combination of flexibility, speed, nimbleness, and responsiveness is an elusive goal for many company leaders.[83]

4.2 | Influence Your Environment

In addition to adapting or reacting to the environment, managers and organizations can be more proactive and actually change the external environment. Two general types of proactive responses are independent action and cooperative action.

Independent Action A company uses independent strategies when it acts on its own to influence stakeholders or change some aspect of its current environment. As illustrated in Exhibit 3.5, several independent strategies are possible:[84]

- *Competitive aggression*—exploiting a distinctive competence or improving internal efficiency for competitive advantage (e.g., aggressive pursuit of green goals). Kohl's was the first U.S. retailer to achieve carbon neutrality or zero CO_2 emissions.[85]

- *Competitive pacification*—independent action to improve relations with competitors (e.g., helping competitors find raw materials). Austin Beerworks, a craft brewery, promotes the

buffering creating supplies of excess resources in case of unpredictable needs

smoothing leveling normal fluctuations at the boundaries of the environment

flexible processes methods for adapting the technical core to changes in the environment

Adapting at the Boundaries Because they are open systems, organizations are exposed to uncertainties from both their inputs and outputs. In response, they can create buffers on both the input and output boundaries with the environment. Buffering creates supplies of excess resources to meet unpredictable needs. On the input side, organizations establish relationships with employment agencies to hire part-time and temporary help during rush periods when labor demand is difficult to predict. In the U.S. labor force, these workers, known as contingent workers, include independent contractors, standard part-time workers, on-call workers, and temporary-help agency workers, suggesting widespread use of this approach to buffering labor input uncertainties.[79] On the output side of the system, most organizations use some type of ending inventories, keeping merchandise on hand in case a rush of customers decides to buy their products. Auto dealers are a common example of this practice; other companies that use buffer inventories include fast-food restaurants, bookstores, shoe companies, and even real estate agencies.[80]

In addition to buffering, organizations may try smoothing or leveling normal fluctuations at the boundaries of the environment. For example, during winter months in the north, when automobile sales drop off, dealers commonly cut the price of their in-stock vehicles to increase demand. At the end of each

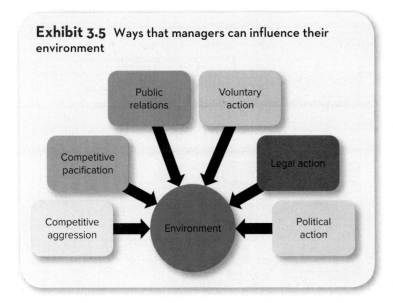

Exhibit 3.5 Ways that managers can influence their environment

Public relations

Voluntary action

Competitive pacification

Legal action

Competitive aggression

Environment

Political action

independent strategies strategies that an organization acting on its own uses to change some aspect of its current environment

cooperative strategies strategies used by two or more organizations working together to manage the external environment

strategic maneuvering an organization's conscious efforts to change the boundaries of its task environment

domain selection entering a new market or industry with existing expertise

beer industry as a whole through Beer-to-Go legislation and by building relationships with other local brewers.[86]

- *Public relations*—establishing and maintaining favorable images in the minds of people in the environment (e.g., sponsoring sporting events). The oil and natural gas industry advertises its role in a country's energy independence.

- *Voluntary action*—voluntary commitment to various interest groups, causes, and social problems (e.g., donating supplies to schools). Fitppl, a health foods brand, sponsors organized volunteer cleanups of waterways and other natural areas.[87]

- *Legal action*—engaging the company in a private legal battle (e.g., lawsuits against illegal music copying). Singer Ariana Grande sued the fashion retailer Forever 21 for using unlicensed images from her music videos and using a look-alike model in its promotional Instagram account.[88]

- *Political action*—efforts to influence elected representatives to create a more favorable business environment or limit competition (e.g., issue advertising or lobbying at state and national levels). In 2019, the top 20 special interest groups, like companies, labor unions, and other organizations, spent more than $13 billion in efforts to influence elected officials and candidates in the United States.[89]

Each of these examples shows how organizations—on their own—can have an impact on the environment.

Cooperative Action In some situations, two or more organizations work together using cooperative strategies to influence the environment.[90] Several types of cooperative strategies are common:[91]

- *Contracts*—negotiating an agreement between the organization and another group to exchange goods, services, information, patents, and so on. Suppliers and customers, or managers and labor unions, may sign formal agreements about the terms and conditions of their future relationships. These contracts are explicit attempts to make their future relationship predictable.

- *Cooptation*—absorbing new elements into the organization's leadership structure to avert threats to its stability or existence. Many universities invite wealthy alumni to join their boards of directors.

- *Coalition*—groups that act jointly on political initiatives. Local businesses may band together to curb the rise of employee health care costs, and organizations in some industries have formed industry associations and special interest groups.

Firms establish strategic alliances, partnerships, joint ventures, and mergers with competitors to deal with environmental uncertainties. Cooperative strategies such as these make the most sense when two conditions exist:

1. Taking joint action will reduce the organizations' costs and risks.

2. Cooperation will increase their power (their ability to successfully accomplish the changes they desire).

4.3 | Change the Boundaries of the Environment

Besides changing themselves (environmental adaptation) or their environment, organizations can redefine or change which environment they are in. This last category is strategic maneuvering. By making a conscious effort to change the boundaries of its competitive environment, a firm can maneuver around potential threats and capitalize on opportunities.[93] Managers can use several strategic maneuvers, including domain selection, diversification, merger and acquisition, and divestiture.[94]

Domain selection is the entrance by a company into another suitable market or industry. For instance, the market may have limited competition or regulation, ample suppliers and customers, or high growth. For example, Anheuser-Busch recently entered the fast-growing hard seltzer market by acquiring Bob & Viv's

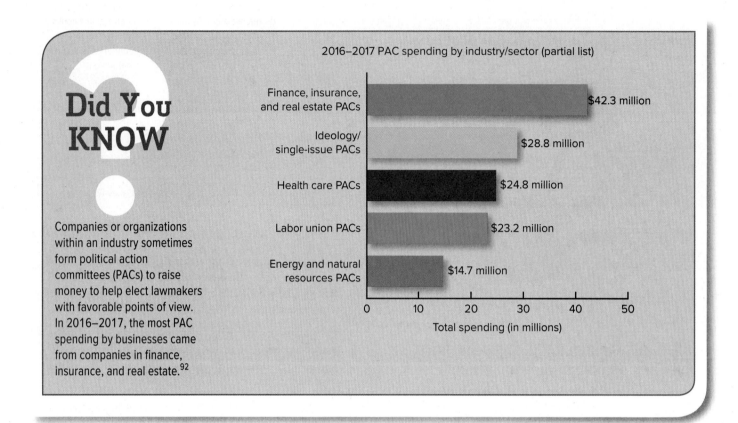
Spiked Seltzer.[95] Using its brewing tanks, the beverage company can make both beer and seltzer to broaden its offered goods.

Diversification occurs when a firm invests in different types of businesses or products or when it expands geographically to reduce its dependence on a single market or technology. Google, which earns the bulk of its revenues from advertising on its ubiquitous search engine, has changed its name to Alphabet (and changed its structure) in order to better manage its growing diversification. In addition to Google, Alphabet owns more than 200 businesses including Nest (smart home devices), Waymo (self-driving cars), and Sidewalk Labs (urban innovation through technology).[96]

A **merger** or **acquisition** takes place when two or more firms combine, or one firm buys another, to form a single company. Mergers and acquisitions can offer greater efficiency from combined operations or give companies relatively quick access to new markets or industries. For example, Swedish automaker Volvo was acquired by Geely Holding Group in China.[97] Geely wanted to work with Volvo on electrification, connectivity, and driverless vehicles; the companies plan to collaborate in China.[98]

Divestiture occurs when a company sells one or more businesses. In 2016, Alaska Airlines purchased Virgin Airlines for $2.6 billion.[99] Alaska Airlines paid off the debt and is updating the 71-aircraft fleet.[100]

Organizations engage in strategic maneuvering when they move into different environments. **Prospectors** are the companies most likely to engage in strategic maneuvering.[101] Aggressive companies like Apple, Microsoft, and Marriott International continuously change the boundaries of their competitive environments by seeking new products and markets, diversifying, and merging or acquiring new enterprises.

● Alphabet Inc. is an American multinational conglomerate created through a corporate restructuring of Google on October 2, 2015. Its portfolio encompasses industries such as technology, life sciences, investment capital, and research.
Stanislau Palaukou/Shutterstock

In these and other ways, corporations put their competitors on the defensive and force them to react. Defenders, in contrast, stay within a more limited, stable product domain.

4.4 | Three Criteria Help You Choose the Best Approach

Three general considerations help guide management's response to the environment:

1. *Managers need to change what matters and can be changed.* Environmental responses are most useful when aimed at elements of the environment that cause the company problems, provide opportunities, and allow the company to change successfully. Thus, Nintendo recognized that its game console would have difficulty competing on superior graphics, so it addressed underserved segments of the market, where customers and favorable publicity made the Wii successful.

2. *Managers should use the most appropriate response.* If a company wants to better manage its competitive environment, competitive aggression and pacification are viable. Political action influences the legal environment, and contracting helps manage customers and suppliers. No business likes bad press, but if it occurs, managers must choose a response. They can ignore the negative publicity or address it in such a way that the incident is viewed as neutral, or even positive.

3. *Managers should choose responses that offer the most benefit at the lowest cost.* Return-on-investment calculations should incorporate short-term financial considerations and long-term impact.

Proactive managers who consider these factors carefully will more effectively guide their organizations to competitive advantage.

Effective managers also look to their *internal* environment for ways to respond to *external* environmental changes. For this, we turn to the organization's culture as a vital managerial priority.

> **LO5** Discuss how to use organizational cultures to overcome challenges in the external environment.

5 | YOUR ORGANIZATION'S INTERNAL ENVIRONMENT AND CULTURE

An organization's internal environment refers to all relevant forces inside a firm's boundaries, such as its managers, employees, resources, and organizational culture.

---

diversification a firm's investment in a different product, business, or geographic area

merger one or more companies combining with another

acquisition one firm buying another

divestiture a firm selling one or more businesses

prospectors companies that continuously change the boundaries for their task environments by seeking new products and markets, diversifying, and merging or acquiring new enterprises

defenders companies that stay within a stable product domain as a strategic maneuver

internal environment all relevant forces inside a firm's boundaries, such as its managers, employees, resources, and organizational culture

organizational culture the set of assumptions that members of an organization share to create internal cohesion and adapt to the external environment

visible artifacts the components of an organization that can be seen and heard, such as office layout, dress, orientation, stories, and written material

values the underlying qualities and desirable behaviors that are important to the organization

unconscious assumptions strongly held and taken-for-granted beliefs that influence behavior in the firm

---

As you know, an organization's managers serve a critical role in scanning and responding to threats and opportunities in the external environment. One of the most important factors influencing how an organization responds to its external environment is its culture.

5.1 | What Is Organizational Culture?

Organizational culture is the set of assumptions about the organization and its goals and practices that members of the company share.[102] It is a system of shared values about what is important and beliefs about how the world works. It provides a framework that organizes and directs people's behavior on the job.[103]

The culture of an organization may be difficult for an observer to describe easily, yet like an individual's personality, an astute observer can decipher cultural clues over time.

As illustrated in Exhibit 3.6, there are three layers of organizational culture.[104] The first level is like the exposed part of an iceberg and consists of visible artifacts, which are the components of an organization that can be seen and heard such as office layout, dress, orientation, stories, and written material (e.g., annual reports and strategic plans). Though seemingly easy to interpret, these clues to understanding the culture often take time to figure out.

The second level of culture refers to its values, the underlying qualities and desirable behaviors that are important to the organization. Values are akin to that part of the iceberg that is just below the surface of the water. They can't be observed directly, but rather values need to be inferred from the behavior of managers. The third and deepest level of an organization's culture refers to unconscious assumptions, which are strongly held and taken-for-granted beliefs that influence people's behavior in the firm.

Exhibit 3.6 The three levels of organizational culture

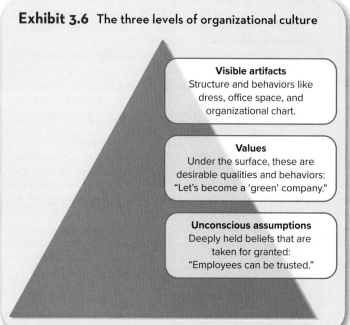

Visible artifacts
Structure and behaviors like dress, office space, and organizational chart.

Values
Under the surface, these are desirable qualities and behaviors: "Let's become a 'green' company."

Unconscious assumptions
Deeply held beliefs that are taken for granted: "Employees can be trusted."

Source: Adapted from E. H. Schein, "Coming to a New Awareness of Organizational Culture," *Sloan Management Review* 25, no. 2 (Winter 1984), pp. 3–16.

Cultures can be strong or weak. *Strong cultures* greatly influence the way people think and behave. A strong culture is one in which people understand and believe in the firm's goals, priorities, and practices. A strong culture can be a real advantage to

● Annie's CEO John Foraker. Annie's culture entails a passion for food, people, and the planet we all share.
Kristopher Skinner/MCT/Newscom

the organization if the behaviors it encourages and facilitates are appropriate. Zappos' culture encourages extraordinary devotion to customer service, the culture at Cirque du Soleil encourages innovation, and the culture at Walmart stresses low cost and frugality. These behaviors are conveyed as "the way we do things around here," rooted in their companies' cultures.

In contrast, a strong culture that encourages inappropriate behaviors can severely hinder an organization's effectiveness, particularly if the environment is undergoing change, as is almost always the case today. A culture that was suitable and even advantageous in a prior era may become counterproductive in a new environment. For instance, a small start-up may have a top-down culture in which the founder makes all the decisions. But this becomes less suitable when the company grows, faces more competition, and requires decisions and input from many specialized employees spread out over many locations.

Google (part of Alphabet) quickly became a role model for its brainy culture of innovation. Software writers and engineers were attracted to Google not just for its famous perks, such as free meals and laundry facilities, but also for a climate in which they were encouraged to let their imaginations roam free, dreaming up ideas that could be crazy but just might be the next big thing on the Internet. During a long-running business boom, that culture served Google well. The best engineers were thrilled to work for a company that let them spend one-fifth of their time on new projects of their own choosing. But when the economy slowed and the stock market nosedived, Google's managers had to cope with a new reality in which money was tight. It could no longer afford its free-spending culture. Managers had to figure out how to maintain the best of the culture while innovating at a more prudent pace. Google's modified culture now values setting priorities. New ideas are still welcome if they are focused on core businesses of search, advertising, and web-based software applications.[105]

Google made another major change when it adjusted its community guidelines that formerly enabled a very open and anything-goes culture. The new guidelines ban name-calling, disruptive political debates, and disclosing Google information to the public. The guidelines said that "sharing information and ideas" helps build a sense of community, while disruptive and aggressive political debates distract from work and create rifts between coworkers.[106]

In contrast, at a company with a *weak culture,* different people hold different values, there is confusion about corporate goals, and it is not clear from one day to the next what principles should guide decisions. Some managers may pay lip service to some aspects of the culture ("we would never cheat a customer") but behave very differently ("don't tell him about the flaw"). As you can guess, such a culture fosters confusion, conflict, and poor performance.

Most managers want a strong culture that encourages and supports goals and useful behaviors that will make the company more effective. In other words, they want to create a culture that works well because it is well suited to the organization's competitive environment.[107]

Take Charge of Your Career

Assess the organizational culture—and yourself

Starting a new job or career is never easy. One of the biggest challenges is figuring out where you fit into a company's processes and culture. Ideally, you would have a sense of this *before* accepting a job offer. For most new hires, though, this process takes time. Fortunately, there are steps you can take to better prepare yourself for such a transition.

One obvious step is to read everything you can about the organization you're interested in. Start with the organization's website, but don't stop there. Look for recent articles about the organization and try to find feedback from current or former employees, such as that on sites like Glassdoor. Getting facts and opinions from diverse sources will give you a more complete picture of the organization.

Second, use your social and professional networks. Reach out to people who might have connections to the organization. Perhaps they have a friend, or a friend of a friend, who has worked there. Getting firsthand knowledge of the organizational culture can be helpful and empowering.

While looking outward is useful, it's also important to look *inward*. Sometimes we spend so much time examining the culture and priorities of an organization that we forget the most important thing: our own values and interests. Businesses and hiring managers are increasingly turning to personality and workplace assessments of prospective employees to better determine degree of organizational fit during the hiring process. Conducting such assessments makes sense for businesses because it can potentially save them time, money, and resources to replace new hires who don't work out. The same logic applies in reverse: Take time to assess your values and interests to ensure that organizations align with what matters most to you.

There are many self-assessments you can take, many of which you can access for free online. You can take these inventories to get a better sense of your overall personality, values, occupational interests, emotional intelligence, work preferences, and skills, just to name a few. Are you more introverted or extroverted? Do you prefer working alone or in teams? How important is work–life balance? Having a clearer sense of who you are allows you to better understand the organizations you're interested in—and how those organizations align with you.

Source: D. Meinert, "What Do Personality Tests Really Reveal?" SHRM, June 1, 2015, https://www.shrm.org/hr-today/news/hr-magazine/pages/0615-personality-tests.aspx.

5.2 | Companies Give Clues About Their Culture

Let's say you want to understand a company's culture. Perhaps you are thinking about working there and you want a good "fit," or perhaps you are working there right now and want to deepen your understanding of the organization and determine whether its culture matches the challenges it faces. How would you go about making the diagnosis? As the "Take Charge of Your Career" feature discusses, a variety of things will give you useful clues about culture:

- *Corporate mission statements and official goals* provide a starting point by telling you the firm's desired public image. Most companies have mission statements, but are they a true expression of culture? Mission statements sometimes are just publicity tools on a web page, but written and followed properly they can guide a company to success. Jeff Bezos reinforces Amazon's mission to be "Earth's most customer-centric company" by fostering a customer-obsessed culture and creating more shareholder value than any other working CEO.[108]

- *Business practices* can be observed. How a company responds to problems, makes strategic decisions, and treats employees and customers tells a lot about what top management really values. When an unknown person(s) laced some Extra Strength Tylenol capsules with cyanide in the Chicago area back in the early 1980s, Jim Burke and the other leaders of Johnson & Johnson reacted to the crisis by recalling all related products throughout the United States. This decisive move, though not good for short-term profitability, was respected throughout the company and community and remains revered to this day.

- *Symbols, rites, and ceremonies* give further clues about culture. For instance, status symbols can give you a feel for how rigid the hierarchy is and for the nature of relationships between lower and higher levels. Who is hired and fired—and why—and the activities that are rewarded indicate the firm's real values.

- *The stories people tell* carry a lot of information about the company's culture. Every company has its myths, legends, and true stories about important past decisions and actions that convey the company's main values. The stories often feature the company's heroes: people who made decisions and acted in ways that the culture values and who serve as models for others about how to behave.

A strong culture displays these indicators consistently. The Chevron Way is the firm's mission, vision, and goals infused in the organizational culture. The company lives the "Way" by tying executive pay to meeting greenhouse gas reduction targets;[109] creating partnerships that advance workplace gender diversity—like the $5 million collaboration with Catalyst's "Men Advocating Real Change" program;[110] and by caring about employees' health—Chevron offers on-site personal training, massages, and fitness centers and requires employees to take regular breaks.[111]

5.3 | Four Types of Organizational Cultures

Cultures can be categorized according to whether they emphasize flexibility versus control and whether their focus is internal or external to the organization.

Managers should discuss culture with one another to compare notes on how the culture is evolving and its strengths and weaknesses relative to the demands of the external environment. Juxtaposing these two dimensions reveals four types of organizational cultures, depicted in Exhibit 3.7:

- *Clan culture.* The New Belgium Brewery in Fort Collins, Colorado, is an example of a group culture that is internally oriented and flexible. The employees (organizational members) comply with organizational directives that flow from

trust, tradition, and long-term commitment. Their culture emphasizes member development and values participation in decision making. The strategic orientation associated with this cultural type is one of implementation through consensus building. Its leaders tend to act as mentors and facilitators.

- *Hierarchical culture.* The U.S. armed forces are based on a hierarchical culture that is internally oriented by more focus on control and stability. It has the values and norms associated with a bureaucracy. It values stability and assumes that individuals will comply with organizational mandates when roles are stated formally and enforced through rules and procedures.

- *Market culture.* Oil and natural gas companies tend to have rational cultures that are externally oriented and focused on control. This type of culture's primary objectives are productivity, planning, and efficiency. Organizational members are motivated by the belief that performance that leads to the desired organizational objectives will be rewarded.

Exhibit 3.7 Competing-values model of culture

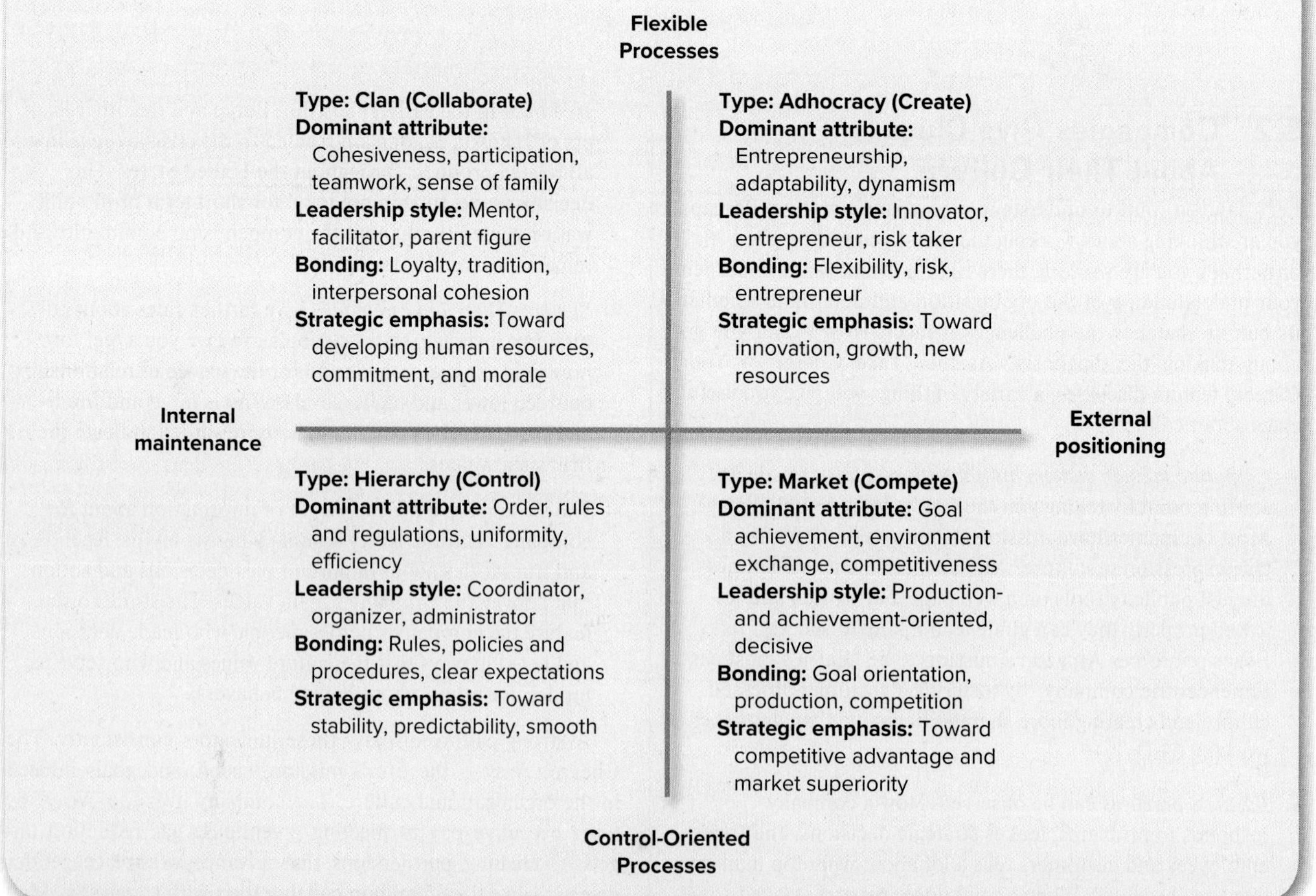

Flexible Processes

Type: Clan (Collaborate)
Dominant attribute: Cohesiveness, participation, teamwork, sense of family
Leadership style: Mentor, facilitator, parent figure
Bonding: Loyalty, tradition, interpersonal cohesion
Strategic emphasis: Toward developing human resources, commitment, and morale

Type: Adhocracy (Create)
Dominant attribute: Entrepreneurship, adaptability, dynamism
Leadership style: Innovator, entrepreneur, risk taker
Bonding: Flexibility, risk, entrepreneur
Strategic emphasis: Toward innovation, growth, new resources

Internal maintenance — External positioning

Type: Hierarchy (Control)
Dominant attribute: Order, rules and regulations, uniformity, efficiency
Leadership style: Coordinator, organizer, administrator
Bonding: Rules, policies and procedures, clear expectations
Strategic emphasis: Toward stability, predictability, smooth

Type: Market (Compete)
Dominant attribute: Goal achievement, environment exchange, competitiveness
Leadership style: Production- and achievement-oriented, decisive
Bonding: Goal orientation, production, competition
Strategic emphasis: Toward competitive advantage and market superiority

Control-Oriented Processes

Source: Adapted from K. S. Cameron and R. E. Quinn, *Diagnosing and Changing Organizational Culture,* 3rd ed. (Jossey-Bass, 2011).

- *Adhocracy.* Google is an adhocracy that is externally oriented and flexible. This culture type emphasizes growth, change, and innovation. Organizational members are motivated by the importance or ideological appeal of the work. Leaders tend to be entrepreneurial and risk takers. Other members tend to have these characteristics as well.[112]

This type of diagnosis is important when two companies are considering combining operations, as in a merger, acquisition, or joint venture, because cultural differences can sink these arrangements. Organizations sometimes benefit from setting up a "clean team" of third-party experts who investigate each company's culture. The clean team can identify for the organizations' leaders the types of issues they will have to resolve and the values they must choose among as they try to establish a combined culture.[113]

to accomplish in order to continue achieving sustainable, quality growth.

- **People:** *Be a great place to work where people are inspired to be the best they can be.*

- **Portfolio:** *Bring to the world a portfolio of quality beverage brands that anticipate and satisfy people's desires and needs.*

- **Partners:** *Nurture a winning network of customers and suppliers; together we create mutual, enduring value.*

- **Planet:** *Be a responsible citizen that makes a difference by helping build and support sustainable communities.*

- **Profit:** *Maximize long-term return to shareowners while being mindful of our overall responsibilities.*

- **Productivity:** *Be a highly effective, lean, and fast-moving organization.*[114]

> ## "The stronger the culture, the less corporate process a company needs. When the culture is strong, you can trust [people] to do the right thing."
>
> —Brian Chesky, cofounder of Airbnb

What type of company culture is important to you in your career? Do you prefer to work in a culture focused on teamwork, efficiency, creativity, or competitiveness?

5.4 | Managers Can Leverage Culture to Meet External Challenges

Effective managers can take several approaches to managing culture:

- Craft an inspirational vision of "what can be" for the organizational culture.

- "Walk the talk"—actually do the things you want others to do—and show that you are serious about and committed to long-term change.

- Celebrate and reward members who behave in ways that exemplify the desired culture.

First, effective managers should espouse appropriate ideals and visions that will inspire organization members. The vision should be repeated until it becomes a tangible presence throughout the organization. For example, Coca-Cola's vision statement provides a clear idea of what the company stands for:

Our vision serves as the framework for our roadmap and guides every aspect of our business by describing what we need

Second, executives need to "walk the talk" of the new organizational direction by communicating regularly, being visible and active throughout the company, and setting examples. The CEO and other managers not only should talk about the vision but also should embody it day in and day out. This makes managers' pronouncements credible, creates a personal example others can emulate, and builds trust that the organization's progress toward the vision will continue over time.

Important here are the moments of truth requiring hard choices. Imagine top management trumpeting a culture that emphasizes quality and then discovering that a part used in a batch of assembled products is defective. Whether you replace the part at great expense in the interest of quality or ship the defective part to save time and money is a decision that people will talk about; it will strengthen or undermine a quality-oriented culture. To reinforce the organization's culture, the CEO and other managers should routinely celebrate and reward decisions and actions that exemplify the new values.

Managing culture also involves hiring, socializing newcomers, and promoting employees on the basis of the new corporate values. In this way, the new culture will begin to permeate the organization. While this may seem like a time-consuming approach to building a new culture, the rewards of that effort will be an organization much more effective and responsive to its environmental challenges and opportunities.

Notes

1. K. Strauss, "How Gordon Logan Reinvented the Barber Shop and Made Sport Clips One of America's Best Franchises," *Forbes,* June 1, 2018, www.forbes.com.

2. "Franchise 500 Top Low-Cost Franchise 2020," *Entrepreneur,* https://www.entrepreneur.com/business-opportunities/197937, accessed March 2, 2020.

3. K. Strauss, "How Gordon Logan Reinvented the Barber Shop and Made Sport Clips One of America's Best Franchises," *Forbes,* June 1, 2018, www.forbes.com; B. Shoot, "To Compete against Other Salons, Sport Clips Made It Easier for Franchisees to Run Their Businesses," *Entrepreneur,* February 16, 2018, www.entrepreneur.com.

4. "IFA's Highest Honor, the Hall of Fame Award Recognizes a Lifetime of Achievement in Franchising," Sport Clips press release,https://sportclips.com/about-us/press-box, accessed March 5, 2020.

5. "IFA's Highest Honor, the Hall of Fame Award Recognizes a Lifetime of Achievement in Franchising," Sport Clips press release,https://sportclips.com/about-us/press-box, accessed March 5, 2020.

6. K. Kranhold, "Twice as Many Companies Paying Zero Taxes under Trump Tax Plan," *NBC News,* April 11, 2019, www.nbcnews.com.

7. K. Kranhold, "Twice as Many Companies Paying Zero Taxes under Trump Tax Plan," *NBC News,* April 11, 2019, www.nbcnews.com.

8. See www.justice.gov/criminal/fraud/fcpa/.

9. "SEC Charges Microsoft with FCPA Violations," U.S. Securities and Exchange Commission press release, July 22, 2019, www.sec.gov.

10. See www.sec.gov, "SEC Enforcement Actions: FCPA Cases," accessed August 25, 2019.

11. "Wage and Hour Division Questions and Answers," U.S. Department of Labor, www.dol.gov, accessed August 25, 2019.

12. S. Sjolin, "Dow Ends above 25,000; S&P, Nasdaq Close at Records," *MarketWatch,* January 4, 2018, www.marketwatch.com.

13. A. Tappe, "Stocks Post Worst Week Since the Financial Crisis," *CNN,* February 28, 2020, www.cnn.com.

14. J. Fuller and M. C. Jensen, "Just Say No to Wall Street," *Journal of Applied Corporate Financ*e 14, no. 4 (Winter 2002), pp. 41–46.

15. S. Perez, "App Stores Saw Record 204 Billion App Downloads in 2019, Consumer Spend of $120 Billion," *TechCrunch,* January 15, 2020, www.techcrunch.com.

16. See company website, www.gusto.com.

17. See company website, www.slack.com.

18. See company website, www.slack.com.

19. Y. Ellis, B. Daniels, and A. Jauregui, "The Effects of Multitasking on the Grade Performance of Business Students," *Research in Higher Education Journal* 8 (August 2010), pp. 1–10.

20. "Civilian Labor Force Participation Rate," Bureau of Labor Statistics, www.bls.gov, accessed August 26, 2019.

21. G. Heeb, "The US Has Added Jobs for a Record 105 Straight Months. But a Commonly Overlooked Measure Paints a Far Less Rosy Picture of the Labor Market," *Business Insider,* July 24, 2019, www.markets.businessinsider.com.

22. M. Toosi, "Labor Force Projections to 2024: The Labor Force Is Growing, but Slowly," *Monthly Labor Review,* U.S. Bureau of Labor Statistics, December 2015, www.bls.gov.

23. M. Toosi, "Labor Force Projections to 2024: The Labor Force Is Growing, but Slowly," *Monthly Labor Review,* U.S. Bureau of Labor Statistics, December 2015, www.bls.gov.

24. B. Pisani, "Baby Boomers Face Retirement Crisis—Little Savings, High Health Costs and Unrealistic Expectations," *CNBC,* April 9, 2019, www.cnbc.com.

25. V. Brundage Jr, "Educational Attainment Rises over the Last 24 Years," Bureau of Labor Statistics, August 2017, www.bls.gov.

26. P. Hull, "Four Acres–Unilever's Heart of Leadership Development," LinkedIn, June 11, 2018, www.linkedin.com; and P. Kolo, R. Strack, P. Cavat, R. Torres, and V. Bhalla, "Corporate Universities: An Engine for Human Capital," The Boston Consulting Group, July 2013, www.bcg.com.

27. B. Arnoldy, "Too Prosperous, Massachusetts Is Losing Its Labor Force," *Christian Science Monitor,* January 9, 2007, www.csmonitor.com; and J. Fuller, "Whose Responsibility Is It to Erase America's Shortage of Skilled Workers?" *The Atlantic,* September 22, 2015, www.theatlantic.com.

28. "Job Openings and Labor Turnover Summary," *Economic News Release,* August 6, 2019, U.S. Bureau of Labor Statistics, www.bls.gov.

29. W. Pfeiffer, "There Are 700,000 Open Tech Jobs in the US. Here Is How Companies Can Fill Them," *CNBC,* June 18, 2019, www.cnbc.com.

30. "Labor Force Characteristics of Foreign-Born Workers Summary," *Economic News Release,* May 16, 2019, U.S. Bureau of Labor Statistics, www.bls.gov.

31. J. Radford, "Key Findings about U.S. Immigrants," Pew Research Center, June 17, 2019, www.pewresearch.org.

32. See U.S. Department of Homeland Security website, www.uscis.gov/e-verify; and M. J. Kim, "Is Supreme Court Right to OK Arizona's 'Business Death Penalty?'" *U.S. News & World Report,* May 26, 2011, www.usnews.com.

33. "Labor Force Rate of Women, 1950 to 2015 and Projected to 2024," *Economic News Release,* September 15, 2017, U.S. Bureau of Labor Statistics, www.bls.gov.

34. B. Frankel, "How the 2018 Top 10 Companies Support Working Families," *Working Mother,* September 19, 2018, www.workingmother.com.

35. B. Frankel, "How the 2018 Top 10 Companies Support Working Families," *Working Mother,* September 19, 2018, www.workingmother.com.

36. E. Hinchliffe, "Trump Offshore Drilling Plan Opens Almost Entire U.S. Coastline to Oil and Gas Companies," *Fortune,* January 4, 2018, www.fortune.com.

37. S. Hoalst, "Top 15 Best VR Fitness Games for a Total Body Workout," VR Fitness Insider, January 30, 2018, https://www.vrfitnessinsider.com/.

38. See company website, www.blackbox-vr.com.

39. M. E. Porter, "How Competitive Forces Shape Strategy," *Harvard Business Review* 57, no. 2 (March/April 1979), pp. 137–45.

40. "US Smartphone Market Share: By Quarter," Counterpoint Research, June 7, 2019, www.counterpointresearch.com.

41. D. Pierce and L. Goode, "The WIRED Guide to the iPhone," *WIRED,* December 7, 2018, www.wired.com.

42. A. Swanson and J. Tankersly, "Trump Just Signed the U.S.M.C.A. Here's What's in the New NAFTA," *The New York Times,* January 29, 2020, www.nytimes.com.

43. A. Swanson and J. Tankersly, "Trump Just Signed the U.S.M.C.A. Here's What's in the New NAFTA," *The New York Times,* January 29, 2020, www.nytimes.com.

44. "50 Greatest Business Rivalries of All Time," *CNNMoney,* March 21, 2013, www.money.cnn.com.

45. "NIKE, Inc. Reports Fiscal 2019 Fourth Quarter and Full Year Results," Nike News, June 27, 2019, www.news.nike.com.

46. D. J. Collis and C. A. Montgomery, *Corporate Strategy: Resources and Scope of the Firm* (New York: McGraw-Hill/Irwin, 1997).

47. A. Nusca, "The Most Popular Google Android and Apple iOS Apps in 2017," *Fortune,* December 29, 2017, www.fortune.com.

48. M. Herper, "Can Merck Really Revive Itself by Jettisoning Employees?" *Forbes,* October 7, 2013, www.forbes.com.

49. P. Sanders and D. Michaels, "Boeing Courts American with Upgraded 737," *The Wall Street Journal,* July 20, 2011, www.wsj.com.

50. A. Krants, "Alphabet Is the New Google," *USA Today,* October 5, 2015, www.usatoday.com.

51. "Personalized 8 fl Oz. Glass Bottle of Coca-Cola," Coca Cola Store, accessed August 30, 2019, www.cokestore.com.

52. See company website, www.chacos.com/US.

53. See company website, www.stitchfix.com.

54. P. Suciu, "Social Media's 'Callout Culture' Continues to Improve Customer Service," *Forbes,* January 8, 2020, www.forbes.com.

55. T. Smith, "Backlash Erupts after Gillette Launches a New #MeToo-Inspired Ad Campaign," National Public Radio, January 17, 2019, www.npr.org.

56. T. Smith, "Backlash Erupts after Gillette Launches a New #MeToo-Inspired Ad Campaign," National Public Radio, January 17, 2019, www.npr.org.

57. P. Kotler, *Marketing Management: Analysis, Planning, Implementation and Control,* 9th ed. (Engelwood Cliffs, NJ: Prentice Hall, 1990).

58. D. Blankenhorn, "Amazon's Whole Foods Experiment Will Render Kroger Obsolete," Yahoo! Finance, April 3, 2019, www.finance.yahoo.com.

59. L. Painter, "Apple iCar Release Date Rumours, Features, and Images," *Macworld* (blog), January 26, 2018, www.macworld.com.

60. T. Krazit, "Intel Looks to Maintain Its Data Center Dominance with Powerful New Server Chips," *Geekwire,* July 11, 2017, www.geekwire.com.

61. T. Krazit, "Intel Looks to Maintain Its Data Center Dominance with Powerful New Server Chips," *Geekwire,* July 11, 2017, www.geekwire.com.

62. Adapted from H. L. Lee and C. Billington, "The Evolution of Supply-Chain-Management Models and Practice at Hewlett-Packard," *Interfaces* 25, no. 5 (September–October 1995), pp. 42-63.

63. R. Premack, "Uber Freight Is Helping Combat a $1.3 Billion Problem That the Trucking Industry Has Ignored for Years," *Business Insider,* January 31, 2019, www.businessinsider.com.

64. D. Busvine, "Uber Freight Launches in Germany, Taking On Local Competition," Reuters, July 23, 2019, www.reuters.com.

65. A. A. Buchko, "Conceptualization and Measurement of Environmental Uncertainty: An Assessment of the Miles and Snow Perceived Environmental Uncertainty Scale," *Academy of Management Journal* 37, no. 2 (April 1994), pp. 410-25.

66. S. Ghoshal, "Building Effective Intelligence Systems for Competitive Advantage," *Sloan Management Review* 28, no. 1 (Fall 1986), pp. 49-58; and K. D. Cory, "Can Competitive Intelligence Lead to a Sustainable Competitive Advantage?" *Competitive Intelligence Review* 7, no. 3 (Fall 1996), pp. 45-55.

67. S. Ghoshal, "Building Effective Intelligence Systems for Competitive Advantage," *Sloan Management Review* 28, no. 1 (Fall 1986), pp. 49-58; and K. D. Cory, "Can Competitive Intelligence Lead to a Sustainable Competitive Advantage?"*Competitive Intelligence Review* 7, no. 3 (Fall 1996), pp. 45-55.

68. L. Chen, "The Most Profitable Industries in 2015," *Forbes,* September 23, 2015, www.forbes.com.

69. L. Chen, "The Most Profitable Industries in 2015," *Forbes,* September 23, 2015, www.forbes.com.

70. P. S. Adler, "Alternative Economic Futures: A Research Agenda for Progressive Management Scholarship," *Academy of Management Perspectives* 30 (2016), pp. 123-28.

71. J. Cachila, "How Are Apple's iPads Faring Amid Shrinking Tablet Market?" *International Business Times,* August 7, 2019, www.ibtimes.com.

72. S. K. Evans, "Connecting Adaptation and Strategy: The Role of Evolutionary Theory in Scenario Planning," *Futures* 43, no. 4 (May 2011), pp. 460-68.

73. K. Naughton and D. Welch, "Lincoln and Cadillac Are Still Cool Cars in China," *Bloomberg Businessweek,* August 7, 2019, www.bloomberg.com.

74. K. Naughton and D. Welch, "Lincoln and Cadillac Are Still Cool Cars in China," *Bloomberg Businessweek,* August 7, 2019, www.bloomberg.com.

75. P. J. H. Schoemaker, "Multiple Scenario Development: Its Conceptual and Behavioral Foundation," *Strategic Management Journal* 14, no. 3 (March 1993), pp. 193-213.

76. "Per Scholas Recipient of National Youth Opportunity Fund to Connect Low-Income Young Adults in New York City to Career Opportunities," press release, August 26, 2015, www.perscholas.org; and M. Sledge, "Per Scholas, Bronx Job-Training Non-Profit with Record of Success, Expands to Ohio," *Huffington Post,* August 5, 2012, www.huffingtonpost.com.

77. See www.perscholas.org.

78. See www.cognizant.com; "Platform by Per Scholas Launches First Software Support Course in Dallas Partnered with Cognizant," Per Scholas, March 7, 2018, www.perscholas.org.

79. E. Pofeldt, "Shocker: 40% of Workers Now Have 'Contingent' Jobs, Says U.S. Government," *Forbes,* May 25, 2015, www.forbes.com.

80. M. Gupta and J. F. Fox, "Build to Buffer," *APICS Magazine,* July/August 2012, www.apics.org; and M. B. Meznar, "Buffer or Bridge? Environmental and Organizational Determinants of Public Affairs Activities in American Firms," *Academy of Management Journal* 38, no. 4 (August 1995), pp. 975–96.

81. "A Tough Performance to Follow: Explore 2019 F-150," www.ford.com, accessed August 31, 2019.

82. D. Lei, "Advanced Manufacturing Technology: Organizational Design and Strategic Flexibility," *Organization Studies* 17, no. 3 (1996), pp. 501–23; and J. W. Dean Jr. and S. A. Snell, "The Strategic Use of Integrated Manufacturing: An Empirical Examination," *Strategic Management Journal* 17, no. 6 (June 1996), pp. 459–80.

83. K. Shahabi, "Agility Is Within Reach," *strategy + business,* March 16, 2015, www.strategy-business.com.

84. C. Zeithaml and V. Zeithaml, "Environmental Management: Revising the Marketing Perspective," *Journal of Marketing* 48 (Spring 1984), pp. 46–53.

85. See Climate Reality Project, "Five Major Businesses Powered by Renewable Energy," www.climaterealityproject.org, accessed February 24, 2018.

86. See https://austinbeerworks.com/community.

87. See https://fitppl.com/cleanups/.

88. J. Jacobs, "Ariana Grande Sues Forever 21 over 'Look-Alike Model' in Ads," *The New York Times,* September 3, 2019, www.nytimes.com.

89. Center for Responsive Politics, "Top 20 PAC Contributors to Candidates, 2019–2020," OpenSecrets, www.opensecrets.org, accessed September 6, 2019.

90. W. P. Burgers, "Cooperative Strategy in High Technology Industries," *International Journal of Management* 13, no. 2 (June 1996), pp. 127–34; and J. E. McGee, "Cooperative Strategy and New Venture Performance: The Role of Business Strategy and Management Experience," *Strategic Management Journal* 16, no. 7 (October 1995), pp. 565–80. See company website, "The B Team and Ceres Introduce New Primer for Building Climate Competent Boards," The B Team, May 16, 2018, www.bteam.org.

91. C. Zeithaml and V. Zeithaml, "Environmental Management: Revising the Marketing Perspective," *Journal of Marketing* 48 (Spring 1984), pp. 46–53.

92. Center for Responsive Politics, "PACs by Industry," OpenSecrets, www.opensecrets.org (based on data from the Senate Office of Public Records, accessed January 24, 2018).

93. R. A. D'Aveni, *Hypercompetition—Managing the Dynamics of Strategic Maneuvering* (New York: Free Press, 1994); and M. A. Cusumano, "Strategic Maneuvering and Mass-Market Dynamics: The Triumph of VHS over Beta," *Business History Review* 66, no. 1 (Spring 1992), pp. 51–94.

94. R. A. D'Aveni, *Hypercompetition—Managing the Dynamics of Strategic Maneuvering* (New York: Free Press, 1994).

95. S. Fitzgerald, "Move Over Rosé: Hard Seltzer Is Taking Over Summer," *Fortune,* May 31, 2019, www.fortune.com.

96. K. B. Johnston, "Top 4 Companies Owned by Google," Investopedia, June 25, 2019, www.investopedia.com.

97. N. Shirouzu, "Chinese Begin Volvo Overhaul," *The Wall Street Journal,* June 7, 2011, p .B.1.

98. E. Behrmann, "Volvo Explores Closer Ties with Shareholder Geely in China," *Bloomberg,* April 9, 2019, www.bloomberg.com.

99. M. de la Merced and L. Picker, "Alaska Airlines Poised to Buy Virgin America, Report Says," *The New York Times,* April 4, 2016, www.nytimes.com.

100. J. Bachman, "Virgin America Vanishes along with Branson's U.S. Dream," *Bloomberg,* June 3, 2019, www.bloomberg.com.

101. R. A. D'Aveni, *Hypercompetition—Managing the Dynamics of Strategic Maneuvering* (New York: Free Press, 1994).

102. R. Miles and C. Snow, *Organizational Strategy, Structure, and Process* (New York: McGraw-Hill, 1978); E. H. Schein, "Organizational Psychology Then and Now: Some Observations," *Annual Review of Organizational Psychology and Organizational Behavior 2* (2015), pp. 1–19; S. Giorgi, C. Lockwood, and M.Glynn, "The Many Faces of Culture: Making Sense of 30 Years of Research on Culture in Organization Studies," *Academy of Management Annals* 9 (2015), pp. 1–54.

103. R. H. Kilmann, M. J. Saxton, and R. Serpa, *Gaining Control of the Corporate Culture* (San Francisco: Jossey-Bass, 1985); and K. S. Cameron and R. E. Quinn, *Diagnosing and Changing Organizational Culture: Based on the Competing Values Framework* (Englewood Cliffs, NJ: Addison-Wesley, 1998).

104. E. H. Schein, "Coming to a New Awareness of Organizational Culture," *Sloan Management Review* 25, no. 2 (Winter 1984), pp. 3–16.

105. K. S. Cameron and R. E. Quinn, *Diagnosing and Changing Organizational Culture: Based on the Competing Values Framework* (Englewood Cliffs, NJ: Addison-Wesley, 1998).

106. C. Albert-Deitch, "Google's Newest Major Company Culture Shift: Discouraging Political Debates at Work," *Inc.,* August 26, 2019, www.inc.com.

107. S. Desmidt and A. Heene, "Mission Statement Perception: Are We All on the Same Wavelength? A Case Study in a Flemish Hospital," *Health Care Management Review,* January–March 2007.

108. L. Sherman, "Corporate Mission Statements Don't Really Matter, Unless You Want to Be a Great Leader," *Forbes,* April 3, 2017, www.forbes.com.

109. J. Hiller, "Chevron Ties Executive Pay to Methane and Flaring Reduction Targets," Reuters, February 7, 2019, www.reuters.com.

110. J. Sieving, "Chevron Partners with Catalyst to Advance Gender Equality," Chevron Corp press release, February 26, 2019.

111. S. Patel, "10 Examples of Companies with Fantastic Cultures," *Entrepreneur,* August 5, 2015, www.entrepreneur.com.

112. J. Walton, "You Can Rework Company Culture: Start by Reworking Your Office," *Inc.,* July 25, 2017, www.inc.com.

113. J. Koob, "Early Warnings on Culture Clash," *Mergers & Acquisitions: The Dealmaker's Journal* 41, no. 7 (July 1, 2006).

114. www.coca-colacompany.com/our-company/mission-vision-values.

Design elements: Take Charge of Your Career box photo: ©Tetra Images/Getty Images; Thumbs Up/Thumbs Down icons: McGraw-Hill Education

chapter 4

Ethics and Corporate Responsibility

Learning Objectives

After studying Chapter 4, you should be able to

LO1 Describe how different ethical perspectives guide managerial decision making.

LO2 Identify the ethics-related issues and laws facing managers.

LO3 Explain how managers influence their ethics environment.

LO4 Outline the process for making ethical decisions.

LO5 Summarize the important issues surrounding corporate social responsibility.

LO6 Discuss the growing importance of managing the natural environment.

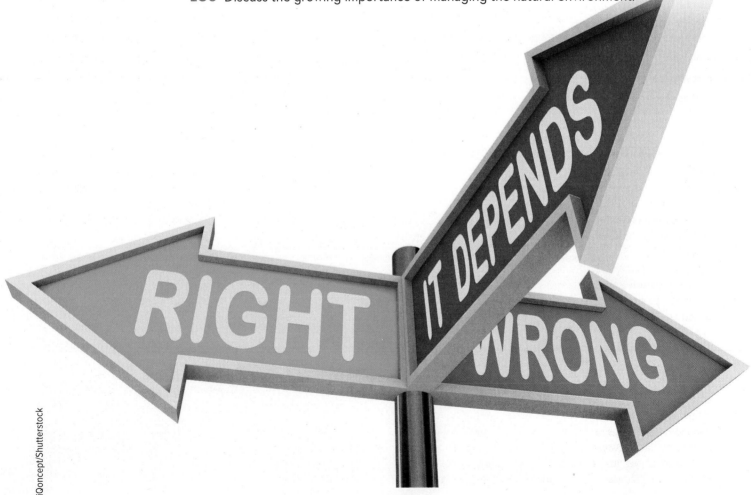

iQoncept/Shutterstock

For most young people, interacting on social media isn't a new way of life; it's simply life. But the intersection of social media and work has created some thorny ethical issues for employees and managers alike. Is it ethical, for example, for a manager, before making an offer to a job applicant, to search the applicant's social media pages? Or to monitor existing employees' social media usage without informing them? Is it ethical for employees to spend company time texting friends or updating their streaks on Snapchat? What about negative posts an employee makes about competing firms outside of work hours?

More than ever, companies need to strike an ethical balance between employee privacy and productivity. As many firms discover, this can be challenging. More than a quarter of employers have fired employees for misuse of company email and a third have fired employees for misusing the Internet.[1] Employers in some states are even asking lawmakers for the right to demand an employee's username and password if they're suspected of online misbehavior, which is part of a growing debate over social media privacy laws. As of 2019, 26 states have enacted laws that prohibit companies from obtaining employees' passwords to social media websites. Currently only two states—Connecticut and Delaware—require employers to inform employees that they are being monitored.[2]

Employers and employees both have to come to terms with what's ethical (and legal) when it comes to using social media at work. According to Natalie C. Rougeux (www.rougeuxpllc.com): "Our employers are struggling more than ever with how to bridge the gap between: (1) the company's need to protect company data; and (2) employees who consider the unfettered use of technology to be essential to their work–life balance. Quite simply, technology, employee/employer expectations, and the law are not in sync on this issue."

As state and federal laws continue to evolve, many businesses are enacting ethical policies that both protect the company and provide transparency for employees. Intel, for example, has a policy centered around "3 Rules of Engagement": disclose, protect, and use common sense. Intel emphasizes that transparency is important for both the organization as well as in individual employee behavior. In addition, it states that its employees should behave in ways that protect themselves and also the company brand. Companies like Coca-Cola, Ford, Best Buy, and Dell have developed similar best practices.[3]

This chapter explores ways of applying ethics, the moral principles and standards that guide the behavior of an individual or group. We do so based on the premise that employees, their organizations, and their communities thrive over the long term when managers apply ethical standards that direct them to act with integrity. In addition, we consider the idea that organizations have a responsibility to meet social obligations beyond earning profits within legal and ethical constraints.

As you study this chapter, consider what kind of manager you want to be. What reputation do you hope to have? How would you like others to describe your behavior as a manager?

It's a Big Issue

It seems ethics-related scandals have become a part of everyday life.[4] Bad behavior can occur anywhere at any time. Recent business-related scandals include Facebook selling users' data to Cambridge Analytica, Google influencing phone manufacturers to preload Google apps on new devices, and WhatsApp being used to circulate fake news about the Brazilian presidential election.[5]

Top colleges are not immune to scandal. The Justice Department accused 50 people, including celebrities and business leaders, of taking part in a college admissions scandal. Celebrities like Lori Loughlin of *Full House* and Felicity Huffman of *Desperate Housewives* were convicted of bribing college officials and manipulating information to get their children admitted into top colleges. This is the largest college admissions scandal ever prosecuted by the Justice Department.[6]

marekuliasz/Shutterstock

> ## "In matters of style, swim with the current. In matters of principle, stand like a rock."
>
> —Thomas Jefferson

What other news disturbs you about managers' behavior? Tainted products in the food supply . . . damage to the environment . . . price fixing . . . Internet scams . . . employees pressured to meet lofty sales or production targets by any means? The list goes on, and the public becomes cynical. In a survey by public relations firm Edelman, just 56 percent of Americans trusted business in 2019.[7]

Unethical behavior can happen anywhere, not just in business. It occurs when police officers take care of parking tickets so friends and family members do not have to pay fines.[8] This may seem minor, but it is an unfair practice and an abuse of power. Prosecutors charged members of New York City's Patrolmen's Benevolent Association, a powerful police union, with ticket fixing.[9]

Sports see their share of unethical behavior. For example, a district court judge sentenced three Adidas employees to federal prison time.[10] The three men bribed high-profile college basketball recruits to ensure they signed with Adidas and certain business managers and financial planners if they turned pro.[11]

The list of bad behavior goes on. Dr. Larry Nassar, former USA Gymnastics team doctor, was convicted and sent to jail for molesting 265 girls and young women over a 20-year period.[12] Nassar was sentenced to up to 175 years for the molestation charges.[13] His employer, Michigan State University, paid a $4.5 million fine for failing to address Nassar's actions in an effective and timely manner.[14]

Simply talking about famous examples of poor ethics does not get at the heart of the problem. Saying "I would never do anything like that" or "I would have reported it if it were me" is too easy. The fact is that temptations and levels of silence exist in all organizations. A recent survey of U.S. adults reported that nearly one-third said they reported seeing unethical conduct at work.[15]

Another survey found that the top justification given for unethical behavior was "pressure to meet unrealistic goals and deadlines."[16] Many decisions you will face as a manager will pose ethical dilemmas, and the right thing to do is not always clear.

It's a Personal Issue

"Answer true or false: 'I am an ethical manager.' If you answered 'true,' here's an uncomfortable fact: You're probably not."[17] These sentences are the first in a *Harvard Business Review* article called "How (Un)Ethical Are You?" The point is that most of us think we are good decision makers, ethical, and unbiased. But the fact is, most people have unconscious biases that favor themselves and their own group. For example, managers often hire people who are like them, think they are immune to conflicts of

● Larry Nassar is an American convicted serial child molester who was the USA Gymnastics national team doctor and an osteopathic physician at Michigan State University. Rena Laverty/EPA-EFE/Shutterstock

interest, take more credit than they deserve, and blame others when they deserve some blame themselves.

Knowing that you have biases may help you try to overcome them, but usually that's not enough. Consider the basic ethical issue of telling a lie. Many people lie—some more than others, and in part depending on the situation, usually presuming that they will benefit from the lie.[18] At a basic level, we all can make ethical arguments against lying and in favor of honesty. People often lie or commit other ethical transgressions somewhat mindlessly, without realizing the full array of negative personal consequences.

Ethics issues are not easy, and they are not faced only by top corporate executives and CEOs. You will face them; no doubt, you already have. You've got your own examples, but consider this one: If your employer pays for the computer and the time you spend sitting in front of it, is it ethical for you to use the computer to do tasks unrelated to your work? Would you bend the rules for certain activities or certain amounts of time? Maybe you think it's OK to do a little online shopping during your lunch hour or to check scores during March Madness. But what if you stream video of the games or take a two-hour lunch to locate the best deal on a flat-panel TV?

Besides lost productivity, employers are most concerned about computer users introducing viruses, leaking confidential information, and creating a hostile work environment by downloading inappropriate content.

Sometimes employees write blogs or post comments online about their company and its products. Companies do not want their employees to say bad things about them. Some companies are concerned about employees who plug their companies and products on comments pages without disclosing their relationship with their company. Another practice considered deceptive is when companies create fictional blogs as a marketing tactic without disclosing their sponsorship.

And in a practice known as Astroturfing—because the "grassroots" interest it builds is fake—businesses pay bloggers to write positive comments about them. Instagram influencers promote everything from makeup to coffee to cleaning products to their thousands of followers. Kim Kardashian, a top celebrity influencer, has more than 140 million followers and gets paid $1 million per post.[19]

How credible are these promotions when the influencer is paid to promote the product? The Federal Trade Commission requires influencers to disclose influencer–company connections. The disclosure is intended to make consumers aware of the influencer's motives and allow them judge the motivation behind the endorsement.[20]

Are these examples too small to worry about? What do you do that has potential ethical ramifications? This chapter will help you think through decisions with ethical implications.

> **LO1** Describe how different ethical perspectives guide managerial decision making.

1 | YOUR PERSPECTIVES SHAPE YOUR ETHICS

The aim of ethics is to identify both the rules that should govern people's behavior and the "goods" that are worth seeking. Ethical decisions are guided by the underlying values of the individual. Values are principles of conduct such as caring, being honest, keeping promises, pursuing excellence, showing loyalty,

being fair, acting with integrity, respecting others, and being a responsible citizen.[21]

Most people would agree that all of these values are admirable guidelines for behavior. However, ethics becomes a more complicated issue when a situation dictates that one value overrules others. An ethical issue is a situation, problem, or opportunity in which one must choose among several actions that must be evaluated as morally right or wrong.[22]

Ethical issues arise in every facet of life; we concern ourselves here with business ethics in particular. **Business ethics** comprises the moral principles and standards that guide behavior in the world of business.[23]

Moral philosophy refers to the principles, rules, and values people use in deciding what is right or wrong. This seems to be a simple definition but often becomes terribly complex and difficult when facing real choices. How do you decide what is right and wrong? Do you know what criteria you apply and how you apply them?

Ethics scholars point to various major ethical systems as guides.[24] We will consider five of these:

1. Universalism.
2. Egoism.
3. Utilitarianism.
4. Relativism.
5. Virtue ethics.

These major ethical systems underlie personal moral choices and ethical decisions in business.

1.1 | Universalism

According to **universalism**, all people should uphold certain values that society needs to function. Universal values are principles so fundamental to human existence that they are important in all societies—for example, rules against murder, deceit, torture, and oppression.

Some efforts have been made to establish global, universal ethical principles for business. The Caux Round Table, a group of international executives based in Caux, Switzerland, worked with business leaders from Japan, Europe, and the United States to create the Caux Principles for Business.[25] Two basic ethical ideals underpin the Caux Principles: *kyosei* and human dignity. *Kyosei* means living and working together for the common good, allowing cooperation and mutual prosperity to coexist with healthy and fair competition. Human dignity concerns the value of each

ethical issue a situation, problem, or opportunity in which one must choose among several actions that must be evaluated as morally right or wrong

business ethics the moral principles and standards that guide behavior in the world of business

moral philosophy the principles, rules, and values people use in deciding what is right or wrong

universalism the ethical system stating that all people should uphold certain values that society needs to function

egoism an ethical principle holding that individual self-interest is the actual motive of all conscious action

utilitarianism an ethical system stating that the greatest good for the greatest number should be the overriding concern of decision makers

person as an end, not a means to the fulfillment of others' purposes. Research conducted by the Institute for Global Ethics identified five core ethical values that are found in all human cultures, including truthfulness, responsibility, fairness, respectfulness, and compassion.[26]

Universal principles can be powerful and useful, but what people say, hope, or think they would do is often different from what they *really* do, faced with conflicting demands in real situations. Before we describe other ethical systems, consider the following example, and think about how you or others would resolve it.

Suppose that Sam Colt, a sales representative, is preparing a sales presentation on behalf of his firm, Midwest Hardware, which manufactures nuts and bolts. Colt hopes to obtain a large sale from a construction firm that is building a bridge across the Missouri River near St. Louis. The bolts manufactured by Midwest Hardware have a 3 percent defect rate, which, although acceptable in the industry, makes them unsuitable for use in certain types of projects, such as those that might be subject to sudden, severe stress. The new bridge will be located near the New Madrid fault line, the source of a major earthquake in 1811. The epicenter of that earthquake, which caused extensive damage and altered the flow of the Missouri, is about 190 miles from the new bridge site.

Bridge construction in the area is not regulated by earthquake codes. If Colt wins the sale, he will earn a commission of $25,000 on top of his regular salary. But if he tells the contractors about the defect rate, Midwest may lose the sale to a competitor whose bolts are slightly more reliable. Thus Colt's ethical issue is whether to point out to the bridge contractor that in the event of an earthquake, some Midwest bolts could fail.[28]

1.2 | Egoism

According to **egoism**, individual self-interest is the actual motive of all conscious action. "Doing the right thing," the focus of moral philosophy, is defined by egoism as "do the act that promotes the greatest good for oneself." If everyone follows this system, according to its proponents, the well-being of society as a whole should increase. This notion is similar to Adam Smith's concept of the invisible hand in business. Smith argued that if every organization follows its own economic self-interest, the total wealth of society will be maximized.

An example of egoism is how individual self-interest may have contributed to the subprime mortgage crisis. According to Adam

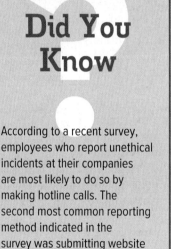

Did You Know

According to a recent survey, employees who report unethical incidents at their companies are most likely to do so by making hotline calls. The second most common reporting method indicated in the survey was submitting website forms, followed by open door reports to their manager, their manager's manager, or the HR department.[27]

Smith, individual financial and mortgage professionals should have acted in their own best interest, and ultimately the invisible hand of the mortgage and financial markets would be the best control mechanism to ensure the greater good. If that were the case, why did the housing market reach an unsustainable level that could not be maintained? Did opportunism and the deceptive use of information play a role? Stated differently, did unethical managerial behavior contribute to the subprime mortgage crisis?

Some financial and mortgage experts encouraged prospective home buyers to purchase homes that they could not afford by applying for adjustable-rate mortgages (ARMs). ARMs allow home buyers to pay a low introductory monthly payment for a few years; after this period expires, the monthly payment increases significantly.[29] The experts convinced many home buyers to assume this risk by pointing out that as long as the value of their homes continued to rise, their wealth would increase. Homeowners were also told they could manage their risk by selling their homes anytime they wanted for a profit.

How did these financial and mortgage professionals benefit? They received commissions and other fees from the loans they sold. Higher compensation became a driving force for these managers to continue pushing high-risk loans. Others in the financial industry also profited, including banks, mortgage firms, and investment companies.[30]

The housing bubble burst when the economy went into a recession and homeowners began to struggle to pay their "adjusted" mortgage payments. The large number of foreclosures and defaults contributed to a historic shake-up of the financial industry, including the collapse of Lehman Brothers; huge losses at Morgan Stanley, Citigroup, and Merrill Lynch; and unprecedented governmental intervention to help firms like JPMorgan to purchase Bear Stearns.[31] It is useful to ask yourself the following questions: To what degree did egoism motivate individuals in the mortgage and financial markets to make and sell loans that became toxic assets? Is there an alternative explanation for what caused the subprime mortgage crisis?

1.3 | Utilitarianism

Unlike egoism, **utilitarianism** directly seeks the greatest good for the greatest number of people. Refer back to the subprime mortgage crisis that was just discussed. Certain utilitarian policies and practices implemented after 9/11/2001 and the dot-com meltdown inadvertently contributed to the subprime mortgage crisis. In an effort to do the greatest good for the greatest number of people, the Federal Reserve slashed the federal funds rate from 6.5 percent in May 2000 to 1.75 percent in December 2001. In 2004, the Fed lowered the rate to 1.0 percent.[32] The period from 2001 to 2004 became known as the "credit boom"

Real estate signs at foreclosed properties. moodboard/Getty Images

when mortgages, bank loans, and credit cards were easily obtained at low interest rates.[33] The goal of these rate cuts was to spur the economy and job creation while also encouraging people to buy homes. This low interest rate policy made home ownership available to higher-risk borrowers.

While some subprime loans were properly documented and executed, many lacked supervision.[34] This allowed opportunistic financial and mortgage experts to convince borrowers to assume subprime mortgages that had "teaser" introductory interest rates for a couple of years before automatically adjusting upward.

Adding to the rapid growth of the subprime market were the Federal National Mortgage Association (Fannie Mae) and the Federal Home Loan Mortgage Corporation (Freddie Mac), two government-sponsored entities that bought many of these high-risk loans from banks and then packaged and sold them (as a way to diversify the risk of the loans) to U.S. and foreign investors. These two companies ran afoul of U.S. regulators. Freddie Mac admitted that it "underreported earnings by over $5 billion," and in 2004, Fannie Mae was investigated for committing widespread accounting errors.[35] Several former executives from these firms face civil charges ranging from manipulating earnings to fraud.[36]

In 2006, the housing market began to weaken as prices started to decline and inflation started to increase. Contributing to the decline was the Federal Reserve's decision to raise interest rates in order to decrease inflation. This move led banks to tighten credit and require borrowers to make larger down payments on homes,

Did You Know

The United States came in 23rd (tied with France) in a 2019 survey ranking 180 nations from most to least honest. The top honesty ratings went to New Zealand, Denmark, Finland, Singapore, Sweden, and Switzerland. The bottom-ranked nations—including Somalia, South Sudan, and Syria—tended to be among the poorest. Sadly, the combination of corruption and poverty in these nations can literally amount to a death sentence for many of their citizens.[41]

while many subprime mortgage owners saw their adjustable-rate mortgages increase to unexpectedly high levels. The net effect was that many homeowners could not make their mortgage payments and defaulted on their loans.[37]

In determining whether decisions made at the Federal Reserve, Fannie Mae, and Freddie Mac, and other institutions achieved utilitarian outcomes, we need to ask: Did these decisions result in the greatest good for the greatest number of homeowners? Were the decisions completely rational, or did subjectivity lead to a suboptimal set of consequences? Was it egoism on the part of individuals or utilitarianism on the part of institutions that ultimately caused the subprime mortgage meltdown?

1.4 | Relativism

It may seem that an individual makes ethical choices by applying personal perspectives. But this view is not necessarily true. Relativism defines ethical behavior based on the opinions and behaviors of relevant other people.

Relativism acknowledges the existence of different ethical viewpoints. It defines ethical behavior according to how others behave. For example, *norms,* or standards of expected and acceptable behavior, vary from one culture to another. The perceived effectiveness of *whistleblowing*—telling others, inside and outside the organization, about wrongdoing—differs across cultures.[38] While U.S. managers believe that whistleblower hotlines are effective at reducing unethical behaviors, managers in the Far East and Central Europe do not believe they are effective. For example, Chinese employees are less likely to report that their superiors have engaged in fraud or corruption.

The Chinese government considers this a major problem. It is believed that *guanxi,* a Chinese term for personal relationships, prevents many Chinese employees from acting in an independent manner when it comes to blowing the whistle on unethical managers.[39] However, Chinese workers are more inclined to report wrongdoing if they have a trustworthy leader and supportive team.[40]

1.5 | Virtue Ethics

The moral philosophies just described apply different types of rules and reasoning. Virtue ethics is a perspective that goes beyond the conventional rules of society by suggesting that what is moral must also come from what a mature person with good "moral character" would deem right. Society's rules provide a moral minimum; moral individuals transcend rules by applying their personal virtues such as faith, honesty, and integrity.

Individuals differ in their moral development. As illustrated in Exhibit 4.1, Kohlberg's model of cognitive moral development classifies people into categories based on their level of moral judgment.[42] People in the *preconventional* stage make decisions based on concrete rewards and punishments and immediate self-interest. People in the *conventional* stage conform to the expectations of ethical behavior held by groups or institutions such as society, family, or peers. People in the *principled* stage see beyond authority, laws, and norms and follow their self-chosen ethical principles.[43] Some people forever reside in the preconventional stage, some move into the conventional stage, and some develop even further into the principled stage. Over time, and through education and experience, people may change their values and ethical behavior.

Returning to the bolts-in-the-bridge example, *egoism* would result in keeping quiet about the bolts' defect rate. *Utilitarianism* would dictate a more thorough cost–benefit analysis and possibly the conclusion that the probability of a bridge collapse is so low compared to the utility of jobs, economic growth, and company growth that the defect rate is not worth mentioning. The *relativist* perspective might prompt the salesperson to look at company policy and general industry practice and to seek opinions from colleagues and perhaps trade journals and ethics codes. Whatever is then perceived to be a consensus or normal practice would dictate action.

Finally, virtue ethics, applied by people in the principled stage of moral development, would likely lead to full disclosure about the product and risks and perhaps suggestions for alternatives that would reduce the risk.[44]

Exhibit 4.1	Kohlberg's stages of moral development
Preconventional stage	• Make decisions based on immediate self-interest. • Example: You take some office supplies home from work because you need them and do not want to pay for them.
Conventional stage	• Make decisions that conform to expectations of groups and institutions like family, peers, and society. • Example: You think about taking the office supplies home, but decide against it because it would not look right.
Principled stage	• Make decisions based on self-chosen ethical principles. • Example: You do not consider taking the office supplies from work because you believe that would be wrong.

Source: Adapted from L. Kohlberg, "Moral Stages and Moralization: The Cognitive-Development Approach," in T. Lickona (ed.), *Moral Development and Behavior Theory, Research, and Social Issues* (New York: Holt, Rinehart & Winston, 1976), pp. 31–53.

2 | BUSINESS ETHICS MATTER

Insider trading, illegal campaign contributions, bribery and kickbacks, famous court cases, and other scandals have created a perception that business leaders use illegal means to gain competitive advantage, increase profits, or improve their personal positions. Neither young managers nor consumers believe top executives are doing a good job of establishing high ethical standards.[45] Some even joke that *business ethics* has become a contradiction in terms.

It gets worse. A national study in 2018 found the rate of retaliation against employees who report unethical behavior tripled over a recent 10-year period.

If unethical behavior goes unchecked, it may spread to other managers, creating a toxic work environment where those in power are abusive, narcissistic, and unfair.[46] These negative workplace behaviors affect the entire organization and encourage similar behaviors among other employees.[47]

2.1 | Ethical Dilemmas

Most business leaders believe they uphold ethical standards in business practices.[48] But many managers and their organizations frequently must deal with ethical dilemmas, and the issues are becoming increasingly complex. Here are just a few of the dilemmas challenging managers and employees:[49]

- *Brands*—In-your-face marketing campaigns have sparked anti-brand attitudes among people who see tactics as manipulative and deceptive.

- *CEO pay*—Nearly three-fourths of Americans say executives' pay packages are excessive.

- *Commercialism in schools*—Parent groups in hundreds of communities have battled advertising in the public schools.

- *Religion at work*—Many people seek spiritual renewal in the workplace, in part reflecting a broader religious awakening in America, while others argue that this trend violates religious freedom and the separation of church and boardroom.

- *Sweatshops*—At many colleges, students have formed anti-sweatshop groups, which picket clothing manufacturers, toy makers, and retailers.

- *Wages*—More than half of workers feel they are underpaid, especially because wages since 1992 have not grown as fast as productivity levels.

Despite the fact the United States pulled out of the Paris climate accord, more than 2,200 leaders of American companies—including Apple, Facebook, Google, Intel, and Ingersoll Rand—declared they would remain committed to the accord's goal of limiting greenhouse gas emissions and climate change.[50] These "we are still in" companies are committed to making significant investments in renewable energy.[51] For example, Budweiser committed to brewing beer with 100 percent renewable energy by 2025.[52]

2.2 | Ethics and the Law

Responding to a series of corporate scandals—particularly the high-profile cases of Enron and WorldCom—Congress passed the Sarbanes-Oxley (SOX) Act in 2002 to improve and maintain investor confidence. Violations could result in heavy fines and criminal prosecution. The law requires companies to do the following:

- Have more independent board directors, not just company insiders.

- Adhere strictly to accounting rules.

- Have senior managers personally sign off on financial results.

One of the biggest impacts of the law is the requirement for companies and their auditors to provide reports to financial statement users about the effectiveness of internal controls over the financial reporting process.

Companies that make the effort to meet or exceed these requirements can reduce their risks by lowering the likelihood of misdeeds and the consequences if an employee does break the law. Organizations convicted of federal criminal laws may receive more lenient sentences if they have an effective compliance and ethics program. See Exhibit 4.2 for ways that organizations can meet the requirements of these guidelines.

Exhibit 4.2 Steps organizations can take to meet SOX guidelines

Establish written standards of ethical conduct and controls for enforcing them.
Assign responsibility to top managers to ensure that the program is working as intended.
Exclude anyone who violates the standards from holding management positions.
Provide training in ethics to all employees and monitor compliance.
Give employees incentives for complying and consequences for violating the standards.
Respond with consequences and more preventive measures if criminal conduct occurs.

Sources: "Staying on Course: A Guide for Audit Committees," Ernst & Young Center for Board Matters, www.ey.com, accessed April 15, 2016; "2010 Report to the Nations on Occupational Fraud and Abuse," Association of Certified Fraud Examiners, www.acfe.com/.

Some executives say SOX distracts from their real work and makes them more risk-averse. Some complain about the time and money needed to comply with the internal control reporting—reportedly spending millions of dollars for technology. Others point out that unethical behavior has negative consequences, especially when it includes illegal actions that later come to light. Fraud hurts both the customer and the company itself when employees find ways to steal. Companies around the globe lose about 5 percent of their annual sales to fraud, but the losses are less than half those at organizations with a mechanism for reporting misconduct.[53] Regardless of managers' attitudes toward SOX, it creates legal requirements intended to improve ethical behavior.

> **Sarbanes-Oxley (SOX) Act** an act that established strict accounting and reporting rules to make senior managers more accountable and to improve and maintain investor confidence

> **ethical climate** in an organization, the processes by which decisions are evaluated and made on the basis of right and wrong

2.3 | The Ethical Climate Influences Employees

Ethics are shaped not only by laws and personal virtue but also by the company's work environment. The ethical climate of an organization refers to the processes by which decisions are evaluated and made on the basis of right and wrong.[54]

For example, Chick-fil-A fosters its signature culture by hiring employees who are respectful, honest, and kind.[55] One manager tests applicants by leaving a piece of trash on the floor and seeing if they pick it up. Those who do are seen as caring about the work environment, an indicator that they will fit within the company's culture.[56] When it comes to performance reviews and expectations, Chick-fil-A values honesty by telling employees the truth so they can learn and grow.[57]

When people make decisions, certain questions always seem to get asked: Why did she do it? Good motives or bad ones? So often, responsibility for unethical acts is placed squarely on the individual who commits them. But the work environment has a profound influence as well. When employees feel pressured to meet unreasonable goals or deadlines, they may act unethically; but managers are in part responsible for setting the right standards, selecting employees with the ability to meet standards, and providing employees with the resources required for success. Managers also need to keep the lines of communication open so that employees will discuss problems in meeting goals, rather than resorting to unethical and possibly illegal behavior.

Unethical corporate behavior may be the responsibility of a misbehaving individual, but it often also reveals a company culture that is ethically lax.[58] Maintaining a positive ethical climate is always challenging, but it is especially complex for organizations with international activities. Different cultures and countries may have different standards of behavior, and managers have to decide when relativism is appropriate, rather than adherence to firm standards.

Take Charge of Your Career

Want to find an ethical employer?

As we're seeing in this chapter, business ethics matter. Strong ethical values are the foundation for an organization's productivity and success. Each year the Ethisphere Institute, a global leader in defining and advancing ethical business practices, releases its list of most ethical companies from around the world. Organizations are evaluated on five criteria: corporate citizenship and responsibility, governance, leadership and reputation, ethics and compliance programs, and culture of ethics.

In 2020, American companies from a diverse range of industries comprised nearly 75 percent of the 132 honorees. Prudential and Voya are two firms that made the list in financial services, while General Motors was listed in the automotive category. For the seventh year in a row, 3M made the list for industrial manufacturing, and Lilly was the only pharmaceutical company in the world to be honored. For the full list, check out the Ethisphere website.

Over the past five years, organizations that made the Ethisphere list outperformed large capital market competitors by over 13 percent, showing once again that being ethical is both right and good for business. In a job market that is tighter than it has been in decades, seeking out firms that have a proven track record of high ethical standards may not only be an ethical choice, but also a wise one for job security and individual success.

Sources: "Ethisphere Announces 132 World's Most Ethical Companies for 2020," https://www.worldsmostethicalcompanies.com/, accessed March 11, 2020; "3M Named One of the 2020 World's Most Ethical Companies for the 7th Year in a Row," February 25, 2020, https://news.3m.com/blog/3m-stories/3m-named-one-worlds-most-ethical-companies-7th-year-row; "The 2020 World's Most Ethical Companies Honoree List." https://www.worldsmostethicalcompanies.com/honorees/, accessed March 11, 2020; and E. Morath and L. Weber, "Inside the Hottest Job Market in Half a Century," *The Wall Street Journal*, March 1, 2019, https://www.wsj.com/articles/inside-the-hottest-job-market-in-half-a-century-11551436201.

Digital Vision/Getty Images

Cognizant Technology Solutions paid $25 million to the U.S. government to settle a civil case concerning attempted bribery.[59] Two executives allegedly authorized a $2 million payment to Indian government officials to secure permits to build a new corporate campus. They were caught after talking about the bribery scheme during a video conference call.[60]

2.4 | Danger Signs

Maintaining consistent ethical behavior by all employees is an ongoing challenge. What are some danger signs that an organization may be allowing or even encouraging unethical behavior? Many factors, including the following, create a climate conducive to unethical behavior:

- Excessive emphasis on short-term revenues over longer-term considerations.

- Failure to establish a written code of ethics.

- Desire for simple, "quick fix" solutions to ethical problems.

- Unwillingness to take an ethical stand that may impose financial costs.

- The view that ethics is solely a legal issue or a public relations tool.

- Lack of clear procedures for handling ethical problems.

- Response to the demands of shareholders at the expense of other constituencies.[61]

> "It takes many good deeds to build a good reputation, and only one bad one to lose it."
>
> —Benjamin Franklin

To understand your organization's ethics climate, think about issues from the employees' perspective. What do people think is required to succeed? Do they think that ethical people "finish last" and that the "bad guys win"? Or vice versa, that the company rewards ethical behavior and won't tolerate unethical behavior?[62] Lynn Brewer, who brought to light the financial misdeeds at Enron, heard Enron's management advocate values such as respect and integrity, but she later determined that these messages were just "window dressing" and that people would undermine one another as they looked out for their self-interests. She eventually concluded that "no one cared" about unethical and illegal behavior.[63]

> **LO3** Explain how managers influence their ethics environment.

3 | MANAGERS SHAPE (UN)ETHICAL BEHAVIOR

People often give in to what they perceive to be the pressures or preferences of powerful others. In the workplace, that means managers influence their employees for good or for ill. As we'll see in the discussions of leadership and motivation later, managers formally and informally shape employees' behavior with money, approval, good job assignments, a positive work environment, and in many other ways.

To create a culture that encourages ethical behavior, managers must be more than ethical people. They also should lead others to behave ethically.[64] Sharon Allen, former chair of the board of the accounting and taxation firm Deloitte LLP, is convinced that being ethical can give organizations a competitive advantage. She believes that "the shared language of ethical values that enables people to conduct business with each other, where a deal can be sealed with a handshake and your word is your bond" is essential.

Ethical leadership is also important when it comes to retaining employees. According to a global survey by LinkedIn, one of the top reasons why employees leave their organizations is due to dissatisfaction with leadership.[65] Managers can boost employee retention by acting in an ethical, consistent, and fair manner.

3.1 | Ethical Leadership

It's been said that your reputation is your most precious asset. Here's a suggestion: Set a goal for yourself to be seen by others as both a "moral person" and also as a "moral manager," someone who influences others to behave ethically. When you are both personally moral and a moral manager, you will truly be an **ethical leader**.[66] You can have strong personal character, but if you pay more attention to other things, and ethics is "managed" by "benign neglect," you won't have a reputation as an ethical leader.

In 2019, Ethisphere Institute honored 128 companies from 21 countries for making a positive impact on global society.[67] The honorees included Hilton (United States), H&M (Sweden), illy (Italy), L'Oréal (France), and Grupo Bimbo (Mexico).[68]

In Asia, anxiety about losing face often makes executives resign immediately if they are caught in ethical transgressions or if their companies are embarrassed by revelations in the press. By contrast, in the United States, exposed executives might respond with indignation, intransigence, pleading the Fifth Amendment, stonewalling, an everyone-else-does-it self-defense, or by not admitting wrongdoing. Partly because of legal tradition, the attitude often is never explain, never apologize, don't admit the mistake, and do not resign—even if the entire world knows exactly what happened.[69]

3.2 | Ethics Codes

The Sarbanes-Oxley Act, described earlier, requires that public companies periodically disclose whether they have adopted a code of ethics for senior financial officers—and if not, why not. Often, the statements are just for show, but when implemented well, they can change a company's ethical climate for the better and truly encourage ethical behavior. Executives say they pay most attention to their company's code of ethics when they feel that stakeholders (customers, investors, lenders, and suppliers) try to influence them to create a strong ethical culture and promote a positive image.[70]

Ethics codes must be carefully written and tailored to individual companies' philosophies. For example, Aetna Life & Casualty believes that tending to the broader needs of society is essential to fulfilling its economic role. Coca-Cola's 44-page code of business conduct covers a variety of topics, from when written approval is necessary to how to prevent conflict of interest.[71]

Most ethics codes address subjects such as employee conduct, community and environment, shareholders, customers, suppliers and contractors, political activity, and technology. Often, the codes are drawn up by the organizations' legal departments and begin with research into other companies' codes. The Ethics Resource Center in Arlington, Virginia, assists companies interested in establishing a corporate code of ethics.[72]

To make an ethics code effective, apply the following principles:

- Involve those who live with the code in writing it.

- Focus on real-life situations that employees can relate to.

- Keep it short and simple, so it is easy to understand and remember.

- Write about values and shared beliefs that are important and that people can really believe in.

- Set the tone at the top, having executives talk about and live up to the statement.[73]

When reality differs from the statement—as when a motto says people are our most precious asset or a product is the finest in the world, but in fact people are treated poorly or product quality is weak—the statement becomes a joke to employees rather than a guiding light.

3.3 | Ethics Programs

Corporate ethics programs commonly include formal ethics codes that articulate the company's expectations regarding ethics; ethics committees that develop policies, evaluate actions, and investigate violations; ethics communication systems that give employees a means of reporting problems or getting guidance; ethics officers or ombudspersons who investigate allegations and provide education; ethics training programs; and disciplinary processes for addressing unethical behavior.[74]

Programs can range from compliance-based to integrity-based.[75] **Compliance-based ethics programs** are designed by corporate counsel to prevent, detect, and punish legal violations. Compliance-based programs increase surveillance and controls on people and impose punishments on wrongdoers.

Integrity-based ethics programs go beyond the mere avoidance of illegality; they are concerned with the law but also with instilling in people a personal responsibility for ethical behavior. With such a program, individuals govern themselves through a set of guiding principles that they embrace.

For example, the Americans with Disabilities Act Amendments Act (ADAAA) requires companies to change the physical work environment to allow people with disabilities to function on the job. Mere compliance would involve making the changes necessary to avoid legal problems. Integrity-based programs go further by training people to understand and perhaps change attitudes toward people with disabilities and sending clear signals that people with disabilities have valued abilities. This effort goes far beyond taking action to stay out of trouble with the law.

When top management is committed to ethical behavior, it becomes better integrated into operations, thinking, and behavior. However, if management doesn't emphasize ethical standards, they might empower employee wrongdoing.[76] Some companies base a percentage of managers' pay raises on how well they carry out the company's ethical ideals. Their ethical behavior is assessed by superiors, peers, and subordinates—thus making ethics an integral part of how the company does business.

Acting with integrity is important not only to managers but also to MBA students. More than 400 graduating students of the Harvard Business School's MBA program took an oath stating that as future managers they would "act with the utmost integrity."[77] Created by then-MBA student Max Anderson with encouragement from a few faculty members, the oath signals

JODI HILTON/The New York Times/Redux

that graduating MBA students are committed to applying ethics and integrity in all of their future managerial and leadership endeavors. Since its creation, the MBA Oath has been signed by more than 10,000 students and graduates representing 300 institutions around the globe.[78]

LO4 Outline the process for making ethical decisions.

4 | YOU CAN LEARN TO MAKE ETHICAL DECISIONS

We've said it's not easy to make ethical decisions. Such decisions are complex.[79] For starters, you may face pressures that are difficult to resist. It's not always clear that a problem has ethical dimensions; they don't hold up signs that say, "Hey, I'm an ethical issue, so think about me in moral terms!"[80] Making ethical decisions takes three things:

1. *Moral awareness*—realizing the issue has ethical implications.

2. *Moral judgment*—knowing what actions are morally defensible.

3. *Moral character*—having the strength and persistence to act in accordance with your ethics despite the challenges.[81]

Moral awareness begins with considering whether a decision has ramifications that disadvantage employees, the environment, or other stakeholders. Then the challenge is to apply moral judgment.

The philosopher John Rawls created a thought experiment based on the "veil of ignorance."[82] Imagine you are making a decision about a policy that will benefit or disadvantage some groups more than others. For example, a policy might provide extra vacation time for all employees but eliminate flex time, which allows parents of young children to balance their work and family responsibilities. Or you're a university president considering raising tuition or cutting financial support for study abroad.

Now pretend that you belong to one of the affected groups, but you don't know which one—for instance, those who can afford to study abroad or those who can't, or a young parent or a young single person. You won't find out until after the decision is made. How would you decide? Would you be willing to risk being in the disadvantaged group? Would your decision be different if you were in a group other than your own? Rawls maintained that only a person ignorant of his or her own identity can make a truly ethical decision. A decision maker can apply the veil of ignorance to help minimize personal bias.

4.1 | The Ethical Decision-Making Process

To resolve ethical problems, you can use the process illustrated in Exhibit 4.3. Understand the various moral standards (universalism, relativism, etc.), as described earlier in the chapter. Begin to follow a formal decision-making process. As you identify and diagnose your problem, generate and evaluate each alternative. Your evaluation should recognize the impacts of your alternatives: Which people do they benefit and harm, which are able to exercise their rights, and whose rights are denied? You now know the full scope of the moral problem.

As you define the problem, it's easy to find excuses for unethical behavior. People can rationalize unethical behavior by denying responsibility ("What can I do? They're twisting my arm"), denying injury ("No one was badly hurt; it could have been worse"), denying the victim ("They deserved it"), social weighting ("Those people are worse than we are"), and appealing to higher loyalties ("I'm too loyal to my boss to report it").[83]

Only days after the U.S. government had posted $85 billion to keep insurance giant American International Group (AIG) from collapsing, AIG sent executives on a luxurious retreat. When asked to justify this, executives initially argued that the $440,000 spent was far, far less than the amount of the government bailout, and the executives who participated in the retreat did not work in the AIG division where the company's financial problems had originated. Eventually they had to concede that these responses did not really address the question of whether the retreat was an ethical use of company money at a time when the company—along with many of the taxpayers whose money was bailing out AIG—was in economic crisis.[84]

4.2 | Outcomes of Unethical Decisions

You must consider legal requirements to ensure full compliance and the economic outcomes of your options, including costs and potential profits. Exhibit 4.4 shows some of the costs associated with unethical behavior.[86] Some are obvious: fines and penalties. Others, like administrative costs and corrective actions, are less obvious. Ultimately, the effects on customers and employees and the government reactions can be huge. Being fully aware of the potential costs can help prevent people from straying into unethical terrain.

Evaluating your ethical duties requires looking for actions that meet the following criteria:

- You would be proud to see the action widely reported in newspapers.

- It would build a sense of community among those involved.

- It would generate the greatest social good.

- You would be willing to see others take the same action when you might be the victim.

- It doesn't harm the "least among us."

- It doesn't interfere with the right of others to develop their skills to the fullest.[87]

As you can see, making ethical decisions is complex, but considering all these factors will help you develop the most convincing moral solution.

Exhibit 4.3 A process for ethical decision making

Understand all the moral standards.

Recognize all moral impacts:
—Benefits to some.
—Harms to others.
—Rights exercised.
—Rights denied.

Define the complete moral problem.

Determine the economic outcomes.

Consider the legal requirements.

Evaluate the ethical duties.

Propose a convincing moral solution.

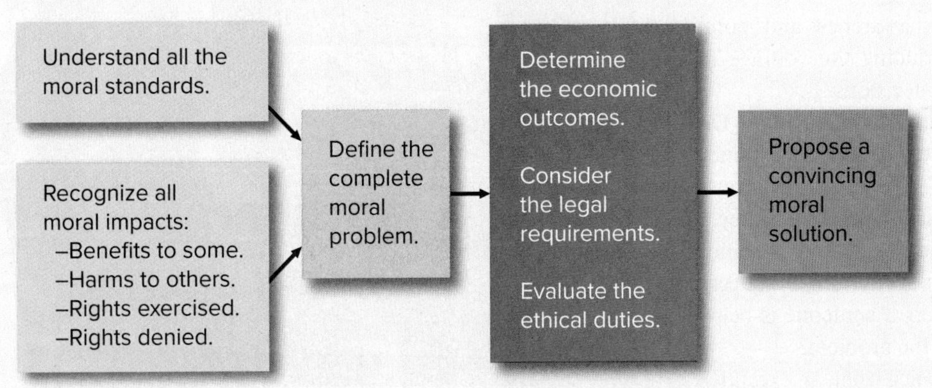

Source: L. T. Hosmer, *The Ethics of Management,* 4th ed. (New York: McGraw-Hill/Irwin, 2003), p. 32.

According to a report by the Association of Certified Fraud Examiners, 30 percent of fraud cases in 2016 occurred in small businesses (with fewer than 100 employees) and the average loss per case from workplace fraud was about $150,000.[85]

Exhibit 4.4 The business costs of ethical failures

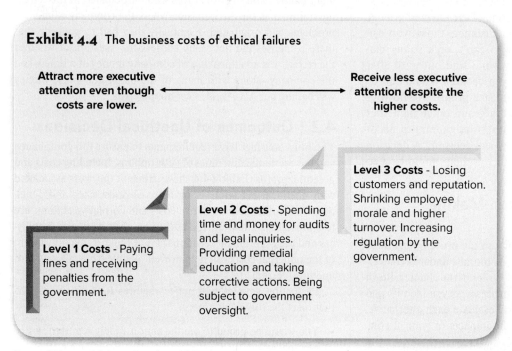

Attract more executive attention even though costs are lower. ←——————→ Receive less executive attention despite the higher costs.

Level 3 Costs - Losing customers and reputation. Shrinking employee morale and higher turnover. Increasing regulation by the government.

Level 2 Costs - Spending time and money for audits and legal inquiries. Providing remedial education and taking corrective actions. Being subject to government oversight.

Level 1 Costs - Paying fines and receiving penalties from the government.

Source: T. Thomas, J. Schermerhorn Jr., and J. Dienhart, "Strategic Leadership of Ethical Behavior in Business," *Academy of Management Executive,* May 2004, p. 58.

Pepsi's managers notified Coca-Cola. There, management fired the secretary and contacted the FBI. Eventually, the secretary and two acquaintances were convicted of conspiring to steal trade secrets.[89] PepsiCo still doesn't have the secret recipe for Coke, but it did maintain its reputation as a competitor with integrity. Choosing integrity over short-term business gain took courage.

Companies with high-quality ethics and compliance initiatives report fewer ethical violations than companies with lower-quality programs.[90] Employees working for ethical companies are three times more likely to report ethics violations.[91]

4.3 | Ethics Requires Courage

Behaving ethically requires not just moral awareness and moral judgment but also moral character, including the courage to take actions consistent with your ethical decisions.

Think about how hard it can be to do the right thing.[88] On the job, how hard would it be to walk away from lots of money in order to "stick to your ethics"? To tell colleagues or your boss that you believe they've crossed an ethical line? To disobey a boss's order? To go over your boss's head to someone in senior management with your suspicions about accounting practices? To go outside the company to alert others if someone is being hurt and management refuses to correct the problem?

PepsiCo managers faced a difficult choice when an executive secretary from Coca-Cola Company's headquarters contacted them to offer confidential documents and product samples for a price. Rather than seek an unethical (and illegal) advantage,

● PepsiCo managers made an ethical decision by reporting an executive secretary from Coca-Cola Company who offered them confidential documents. monticello/Shutterstock

Besides online reporting systems, such as e-mail and web-based tools, companies can use drop boxes and telephone hotlines. Often, these channels of communication are administered by third-party organizations, whose employees protect whistleblowers' identity and have procedures to follow if the complaint involves higher-level executives.[92] Under the Dodd-Frank Act, reporting systems should give access to customers, suppliers, shareholders, associates of employees, and others who could potentially report ethical violations.[93]

> **LO5 Summarize the important issues surrounding corporate social responsibility.**

5 | CORPORATE SOCIAL RESPONSIBILITY

Should a business be responsible for social concerns beyond its own economic well-being? Do social concerns affect a corporation's financial performance? The extent of a business's responsibility for noneconomic concerns has been hotly debated for years. In the 1960s and 1970s, the political and social environment became more important to U.S. corporations as society focused on issues like equal opportunity, pollution control, energy and natural resource conservation, and consumer and worker protection.[94] Public debate addressed these issues and the ways business should respond. This controversy focused on the concept of corporate social responsibility—the obligation toward society assumed by business.[95]

corporate social responsibility obligation toward society assumed by business

economic responsibilities to produce goods and services that society wants at a price that perpetuates the business and satisfies

its obligations to investors

legal responsibilities to obey local, state, federal, and relevant international laws

ethical responsibilities meeting other social expectations, not written as law

5.1 | Levels of Corporate Social Responsibility

Social responsibilities can be categorized more specifically,[96] as shown in Exhibit 4.5. The economic responsibilities of business are to produce goods and services that society wants at a price that perpetuates the business and satisfies its obligations to investors. For Smithfield Foods, the largest pork producer in the United States, this means selling bacon, deli meat, sausage, ham, and other products to customers at prices that maximize Smithfield's profits and keep the company growing over the long term.[97] Economic responsibility might offer certain products to in-need consumers at a reduced price.

Legal responsibilities are to obey local, state, federal, and relevant international laws. Laws affecting Smithfield cover a wide range of requirements, from filing tax returns to meeting worker safety standards. Ethical responsibilities include meeting other societal expectations, not written as law. Smithfield took on this level of responsibility when it responded to requests by major customers, including McDonald's, Target, and Campbell Soup, that it discontinue using gestation crates. The customers were reacting to pressure from animal rights advocates who consider it cruel for sows to live in the two-foot by seven-foot crates during their entire gestation period, which means they cannot walk, turn around, or stretch their legs for months at a time.

Smithfield asked its suppliers to phase out by 2022 the use of small crates in favor of roomier "group housing," which allows the animals to socialize, even though group housing costs more.[98] Smithfield is not legally

Exhibit 4.5 Pyramid of global corporate social responsibility and performance

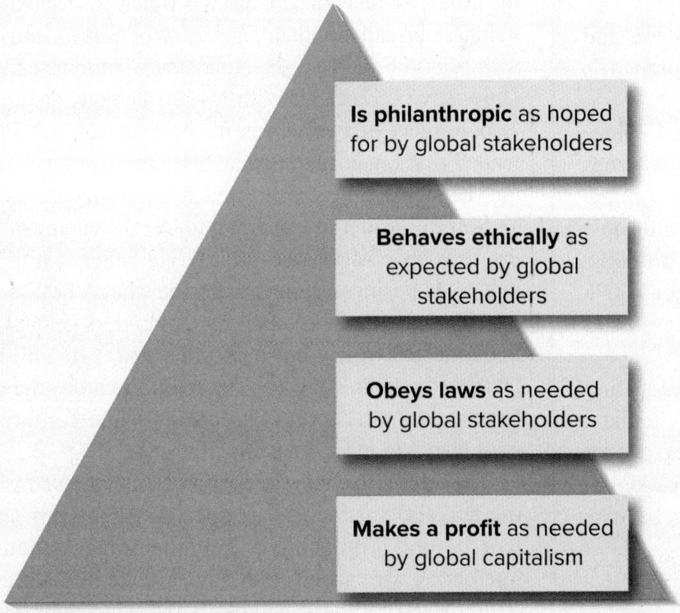

Is philanthropic as hoped for by global stakeholders

Behaves ethically as expected by global stakeholders

Obeys laws as needed by global stakeholders

Makes a profit as needed by global capitalism

Source: A. Carroll, "Managing Ethically with Global Stakeholders: A Present and Future Challenge," *Academy of Management Executive,* May 2004, pp. 116, 114–20.

Traditional Thinking

Businesses see environmental issues as a win/lose situation: Either you help the environment and hurt your business, or vice versa.

The Best Managers Today

Incorporate environmental values into the design and manufacture of their products; this helps achieve competitive advantage, build brand value, and reduce costs.

Source: C. Holliday, "Sustainable Growth, the DuPont Way," *Harvard Business Review,* September 2001, pp. 129–34.

---

philanthropic responsibilities additional behaviors and activities that society finds desirable and that the values of the business support

transcendent education an education with five higher goals that balance self-interest with responsibility to others

shareholder model theory of corporate social responsibility that holds that managers are agents of shareholders whose primary objective is to maximize profits

stakeholder model theory of corporate social responsibility that suggests that managers are obliged to look beyond profitability to help their organizations succeed by interacting with groups that have a stake in the organization

required to make the change (except in specific states), and the arrangement may not maximize profits, but the company's actions help customer relationships and public image.

Finally, philanthropic responsibilities are additional behaviors and activities that society finds desirable and that the values of the business support. Examples include supporting community projects and making charitable contributions. Philanthropic activities can be more than mere altruism; managed properly, "strategic philanthropy" can become not an oxymoron but a way to build goodwill in a variety of stakeholders and even add to shareholder wealth.[99]

Robert Giacalone believes that a 21st-century education must help students think beyond self-interest and profitability. A real education, he says, teaches students to leave a legacy that extends beyond the bottom line—a transcendent education.[100] A transcendent education has five higher goals that balance self-interest with responsibility to others:

1. *Empathy*—feeling your decisions as potential victims might feel them, to gain wisdom.

2. *Generativity*—learning how to give as well as take, to others in the present as well as to future generations.

3. *Mutuality*—viewing success not merely as personal gain, but a common victory.

4. *Civil aspiration*—thinking not just in terms of "don'ts" (lie, cheat, steal, kill), but also in terms of positive contributions.

5. *Intolerance of ineffective humanity*—speaking out against unethical actions.

5.2 | Do Businesses Really Have a Social Responsibility?

Two basic and contrasting views describe principles that should guide managerial responsibility. The first, known as the shareholder model, holds that managers act as agents for shareholders and, as such, are obligated to maximize the present value of the firm. This tenet of capitalism is widely associated with the early writings of Adam Smith in *The Wealth of Nations,* and more recently with Milton Friedman, the Nobel Prize–winning economist of the University of Chicago. With his now-famous dictum "The social responsibility of business is to increase profits," Friedman contended that organizations may help improve the quality of life as long as such actions are directed at increasing profits.

Some considered Friedman to be "the enemy of business ethics," but his position was ethical: He believed it is unethical for unelected business leaders to decide what is best for society, and unethical for them to spend shareholders' money on projects unconnected to key business interests.[101] In addition, the context of Friedman's famous statement includes the qualifier that business should increase its profits while conforming to society's laws and ethical customs.

The alternative view of corporate social responsibility, called the stakeholder model, assumes that managers are obliged to look beyond profitability to help their organizations succeed by interacting with groups that have a stake in the organization.[102] A firm's stakeholders include shareholders, employees, customers, suppliers, competitors, society, and the government.[103] As members of society, organizations should actively and responsibly participate in the community and in the larger environment.

> ## "Every one of us is responsible for the future of all of us."
>
> —Dr. Gro Harlem Brundtland, former prime minister of Norway[113]

After Hurricane Harvey devastated more than 300,000 homes and businesses in Houston, Texas, in 2017, Wells Fargo stepped up to help its customers.[104] The financial institution allowed its mortgage customers to postpone payments without penalty. Wells Fargo also postponed negative credit reporting and foreclosure procedures for a period after the hurricane.[105] Wells Fargo helped preserve its customers' credit scores and finances while they addressed flood damage to their homes. Unfortunately, many headlines about the infamous Wells Fargo scandal of 2016 have overshadowed this fine example of socially responsible action.

Do companies that operate internationally have a social responsibility to insist on better working conditions?[106] Walmart and other companies that buy products made in China have written codes of conduct and perform onsite audits. Unfortunately, some factories hide violations instead of correcting them. For example, many Chinese employees live on company campuses and work over 100 overtime hours per month, often subjected to unsanitary and bleak living conditions.[107]

Still, as demand for Chinese-made products and pressure from multinational corporations intensify, observers say pay and working conditions in China are improving somewhat.[108]

5.3 | You Can Do Good and Do Well

Profit maximization and corporate social responsibility used to be regarded as leading to opposing policies. But in today's business climate, which emphasizes both doing good and doing well, the two views can converge.[109] New Belgium Brewery, the Colorado-based maker of Fat Tire, has a long and successful history of blending an employee-centric culture with sustainability and profit making. The company, which is 100 percent employee-owned and the third largest craft brewer in the United States, practices being a "force for good in the world."[110] Following are some of the practices that make this brewer unique: (1) it recycles 99.9 percent of its waste, (2) it generates nearly 18 percent of the operation's electricity onsite with solar and biogas, and (3) it set a goal to reduce greenhouse gas emissions by 50 percent by 2050.[111]

Earlier attention to corporate social responsibility focused on alleged wrongdoing and how to control it. Attention also centers on the possible competitive advantage of socially responsible actions. LEGO incorporates care for the environment into its business to get ahead of the competition. The company created LEGO's Sustainable Materials Center to identify sustainable alternatives for production materials such as LEGO bricks and product packaging.[112] Sustainable goods are expected to be

● Barclays Cycle Hire scheme (or Boris Bikes) is part of a green initiative by Transport for London. Global Warming Images/REX/Shutterstock

a $150 billion market, and LEGO is working to be a leader in environmentally friendly products for children.[114]

The real relationship between corporate social performance and corporate financial performance is highly complex; socially responsible organizations do not necessarily become more or less successful in financial terms.[115] Some advantages are clear, however. Socially responsible actions can have long-term benefits. Companies can avoid unnecessary and costly regulation if they are socially responsible. Honesty and fairness may pay great dividends to the conscience, to personal reputation, and to the public image of the company as well as in the market response.[116]

In addition, society's problems can offer business opportunities and profits. Firms can perform a cost–benefit analysis to identify actions that will maximize profits while satisfying the demand for corporate social responsibility from multiple stakeholders.[117] In other words, managers can treat corporate social responsibility as they would treat all investment decisions. This has been the case as firms attempt to reconcile their business practices with their effect on the natural environment.

For a clearer link between social and business goals, companies can benefit from integrating social responsibility with corporate strategy—and society can benefit as well. Applying the principles of strategic planning can identify areas in which they can capitalize on their strengths to neutralize threats and benefit from opportunities that result from serving the society of which they are a part.[118]

ecocentric management
creates sustainable economic development and improves quality of life worldwide for all organizational stakeholders

sustainable growth
economic growth and development that meet present needs without harming the needs of future generations

life cycle analysis (LCA) a process of analyzing all inputs and outputs, through the entire "cradle-to-grave" life of a product, to determine total environmental impact

For example, suppose a company is interested in exercising social responsibility for the environment by reducing its carbon emissions. The extent to which this choice is strategic varies from one company to another. Reducing carbon emissions would be a good deed for Nintendo, but doing so is not directly related to its strategy except to the extent it might lower its operating costs. For Southwest Airlines, reducing carbon emissions would directly affect its day-to-day activities but still might not give the company a competitive advantage. For Honda, reducing carbon emissions—say, by leading in the development and marketing of hybrid technology as well as by operating more efficiently—can be a significant competitive advantage.

> **LO6** Discuss the growing importance of managing the natural environment.

6 | THE NATURAL ENVIRONMENT

Most large corporations developed in an era of abundant raw materials, cheap energy, and unconstrained waste disposal.[119] But many of the technologies developed during that era contributed to the destruction of ecosystems. Industrial age systems follow a linear flow of extract, produce, sell, use, and discard—what some call a "take-make-waste" approach.[120] But perhaps no time in history has offered greater possibilities for a change in business thinking than the 21st century.

Business used to look at environmental issues as a no-win situation: Either you help the environment and hurt your business, or you help your business at a cost to the environment. But now companies deliberately incorporate environmental values into competitive strategies and into the design and manufacturing of products.[121] Why? In addition to philosophical reasons, companies "go green" to satisfy consumer demand, react to competitor actions, meet requests from customers or suppliers, comply with guidelines, and create competitive advantages.

Mike Bloomberg, CEO of his namesake company and former mayor of New York, sees environmentalism as not just an investment in the future, but as something that brings immediate economic and public health benefits.[122] Bloomberg Philanthropies brings together mayors, activists, business leaders, and scientists from across the country to identify ways to replace coal with clean energy, protect the oceans, reduce pollution, and more.[123] Bloomberg also launched America's Pledge, which includes a consortium of states, cities, universities, and businesses to address the goals of the Paris Climate Accord.[124]

6.1 | Economic Activity Has Environmental Consequences

We live in a risk society. That is, the creation and distribution of wealth generate by-products that can cause injury, loss, or danger to people and the environment. The fundamental sources of risk in modern society are the excessive production of hazards and ecologically unsustainable consumption of natural resources.[125] Risk has proliferated through population explosion, industrial pollution, and environmental degradation.[126]

Industrial pollution risks include air pollution, global warming, ozone depletion, acid rain, toxic waste sites, nuclear hazards, obsolete weapons arsenals, industrial accidents, and hazardous products. The situation is far worse in other parts of the world. The pattern for toxic waste and many other risks is one of accumulating risks and inadequate remedies.

6.2 | Development Can Be Sustainable

Ecocentric management has as its goal the creation of sustainable economic development and improvement of quality of life worldwide for all organizational stakeholders.[127] **Sustainable growth** is economic growth and development that meet the organization's present needs without harming the ability of future generations to meet their needs.[128] Sustainability is fully compatible with the natural ecosystems that generate and preserve life.

The concept of sustainable growth can be applied in several ways:

- As a framework for organizations to use in communicating to all stakeholders.

- As a planning and strategy guide.

- As a tool for evaluating and improving the ability to compete.[129]

The principle can begin at the highest organizational levels and be made explicit in performance appraisals and reward systems.

With two-thirds of the world's population expected to experience water scarcity by 2025, businesses are concerned about this essential natural resource. If you haven't experienced a water shortage, water usage might not seem to be an obvious area of concern, but it should be.

Brewer SABMiller is a leader in making water conservation part of its strategy. It takes seven gallons of water to make one gallon of beer. The brewer set a goal to reduce this ratio to just under 3 gallons of water per gallon of beer by 2025.[130] Miller also works with its barley suppliers to conserve water used on farms; agricultural production constitutes 90 percent of Miller's "water footprint."[131]

Firms often look at the total environmental impact throughout the life cycle of their products.[132] **Life cycle analysis (LCA)** is a process of analyzing all inputs and outputs, through the entire "cradle-to-grave" life of a product, to determine the total

Sustaining for Tomorrow

A College Built by and for the Poor

Sanjit "Bunker" Roy came from a wealthy Indian family, but in his 20s he decided to try living on $1 a day. Based on that experience, in 1972 he created Barefoot College, which he calls "the only college where the teacher is the learner and the learner the teacher." Barefoot College now operates in 1,300 villages across 93 of the world's least-developed countries in Asia, Africa, the Pacific Islands, and South America. Its mission is to improve rural lives and communities through learning-by-doing training programs in health care, women's empowerment, solar energy, water, and land development that are designed and built by and for the poor.

Barefoot College is based on the guiding principles of service and sustainability espoused by Mahatma Gandhi, along with a commitment to equality, shared decision making, and self-reliance. Its projects have brought artificial light to more than half a million people and provided clean water and solar energy for cooking and heating to thousands of communities. Its Enriche program is dedicated to using simple methods to empower rural women, even if illiterate, with the scientific and engineering skills they need to undertake environmental stewardship, manage solar energy, and protect women's reproductive health. Its four building blocks are "enhance, enable, engage, establish."

Each woman in the program is trained to teach others. For example, those trained in the six-month solar energy program in Tilonia, India, a campus powered by an off-grid solar system, come from around the world. They receive fellowship grants from the Indian government while enrolled and leave with a stipend for starting their own business.

Roy has been honored by *Time* magazine for his "grassroots social entrepreneurship" and was a past recipient of *Business Standard*'s Social Entrepreneur of the Year award. Roy's ambitious plans for Barefoot College's future are to help the world meet its sustainability goals by 2030. Barefoot is offering solutions for 14 of the 17 sustainability goals outlined by the United Nations. These are ambitious targets, but Roy and the Barefoot approach have a proven track record of making the world a better place.

Discussion Questions

- In what ways do you think Barefoot College's mission and goals are characteristic of a sustainable enterprise?

- Which of Barefoot College's guiding principles have you observed where you have worked or volunteered? Choose a principle you might not have observed and explain how you would go about incorporating it into a workplace.

Sources: Barefoot College website, www.barefootcollege.org and www.barefootcollege.org/the-right-tools-for-women-to-lead/, and https://www.barefootcollege.org/solutions/, accessed March 11, 2020; Sraisth, "Philips, Orb Energy Lighten Barefoot College in Rajasthan," *PV Magazine*, February 13, 2018, www.pv-magazine-india.com/2018/02/13/philips-orb-energy-lighten-barefoot-college-in-rajasthan/; and S. Dey, "Social Entrepreneur of the Year: A Place for Learning and Unlearning," *Business Standard*, March 8, 2017, www.business-standard.com/article/companies/social-entrepreneur-of-the-year-a-place-for-learning-unlearning-117030800010_1.html.

---

environmental impact of its production and use. LCA quantifies the total use of resources and the releases into the air, water, and land.

LCA considers the extraction of raw materials, product packaging, transportation, and disposal. Consider packaging alone. Goods make the journey from manufacturer to wholesaler to retailer to customer; then they are recycled back to the manufacturer. They may be packaged and repackaged several times, from bulk transport, to large crates, to cardboard boxes, to individual consumer sizes. Repackaging not only creates waste, but also costs time. The design of initial packaging in sizes and formats adaptable to the final customer can minimize the need for repackaging, cut waste, and realize financial benefits.

Profitability need not suffer and may be increased by eco-centric philosophies and practices. Some, but not all, research has shown a positive relationship between corporate environmental performance and profitability.[133] Of course, whether the relationship is positive, negative, or neutral depends on the strategies chosen and the effectiveness of implementation. And managers of profitable companies may feel more comfortable turning their attention to the environment than managers of companies in financial difficulty.

6.3 | Some Organizations Set Environmental Agendas

In the past, most companies were oblivious to their negative environmental impact. More recently, many began striving for low impact. Now some strive for positive impact, eager to sell solutions to the world's problems.

Ben & Jerry's will no longer use ingredients dried with the harmful herbicide glyphosate.[134] Furniture maker IKEA is working toward using 100% renewable energy and sourcing wood from only sustainable sources.[135]

Google announced it is "100 percent renewable," meaning that its global data centers and offices run exclusively on solar and wind power. Company engineers made the data centers 50 percent more energy efficient than the industry average. That gain, combined with the lower costs of renewable energies, made Google the "largest corporate renewable energy purchaser on the planet."[136]

An important development is the **circular economy**, a regenerative, collaborative economic system that contrasts with the linear economy by minimizing input waste, emissions, and energy leakage. Webs of companies with a common ecological vision can combine their efforts into high-leverage, impactful action.[137] In Kalundborg, Denmark, such a collaborative alliance exists among an electric power generating plant, an oil refiner, a biotech production plant, a plasterboard factory, cement producers, heating utilities, a sulfuric acid producer, and local agriculture and horticulture. Chemicals, energy (for heating and cooling), water, and organic materials flow among companies. Resources are conserved; "waste" materials generate revenues; and water, air, and ground pollution all are reduced.

Companies not only have the *ability* to solve environmental problems; they are coming to see and acquire the *motivation* as well. Solving environmental problems, including preparing for and adapting to climate change, may be one of the biggest opportunities in the history of commerce.[138]

Notes

1. AMA Staff, "The Latest on Workplace Monitoring and Surveillance," American Management Association, April 8, 2019, https://www.amanet.org/articles/the-latest-on-workplace-monitoring-and-surveillance/.

2. "Twelve Most Asked Questions on US Employee Monitoring Laws," WorkTime, January 27, 2020, https://www.worktime.com/what-are-the-u-s-employee-monitoring-laws-get-updated-in-2020; and "State Social Media Privacy Laws," National Conference of State Legislatures, January 2, 2018, www.ncsl.org, accessed March 1, 2018.

3. J. Bouman, "Need Social Media Policy Examples? Here Are 7 Terrific Social Policies to Inspire Yours," EveryoneSocial, March 15, 2019, https://everyonesocial.com/blog/need-sample-social-media-policies-here-are-7-to-inspire-yours/.

4. D. Welch, "GM Doubles Profit in North America to Record on Truck Surge," *Bloomberg Business,* July 23, 2015, http://www.bloomberg. com; S. Terlep, "GM Caps Profitable Year," *The Wall Street Journal,* February 24, 2011, http://online.wsj.com; B. Cox, "For Big Three Automakers, an Unlikely Time for a Turnaround," *Fort Worth Star-Telegram,* April 15, 2011, http://www.star-telegram.com; D. Barkholz, "Dealers: We Want More Cars!" *Automotive News,* August 23, 2010, Business & Company Resource Center, http://galenet.galegroup.com.

5. P. Leskin and N. Bastone, "The 18 Biggest Tech Scandals of 2018," *Business Insider,* December 29, 2018, www.businessinsider.com.

6. J. Medina, K. Benner, and K. Taylor, "Actresses, Business Leaders and Other Wealthy Parents Charged in U.S. College Entry Fraud," *The New York Times,* March 12, 2019, www.nytimes.com.

7. "2019 Edelman Trust Barometer Reveals 'My Employer' Is the Most Trusted Institution," Edelman, January 20, 2019, www.edelman.com.

8. T. Hays, "Prosecutors Take On Powerful NYC Police Union," *Bloomberg Businessweek,* October 28, 2011, www.bloomberg.com/businessweek.

9. T. Hays, "Prosecutors Take On Powerful NYC Police Union," *Bloomberg Businessweek,* October 28, 2011, www.bloomberg.com/businessweek.

10. M. Schlabach, "Three Sentenced in Adidas Recruiting Scandal," ESPN, March 5, 2019, www.espn.com.

11. M. Schlabach, "Three Sentenced in Adidas Recruiting Scandal," ESPN, March 5, 2019, www.espn.com.

12. K. Johnson, "Congress Opens Second Investigation into USA Gymnastics Sex Abuse Scandal," Reuters, February 8, 2018, www.reuters.com.

13. C. Dwyer, "Michigan State University to Pay $4.5 Million Fine over Larry Nassar Scandal," NPR, September 5, 2019, www.npr.org.

14. C. Dwyer, "Michigan State University to Pay $4.5 Million Fine over Larry Nassar Scandal," NPR, September 5, 2019, www.npr.org.

15. "2018 Global Benchmark on Workplace Ethics," Ethics & Compliance Initiative, accessed September 13, 2019, www.ethics.org.

16. T. Zucco, "Ethics Issues? Check Goals," *Tampa Bay Times,* January 28, 2006.

17. M. Banaji, M. Bazerman, and D. Chugh, "How (Un)Ethical Are You?" *Harvard Business Review,* December 2003, pp. 56–64.

18. Company website, "2018 Annual Report," http://www.novonodisk-us.com, accessed March 13, 2020; K. Leavitt and D. Sluss, "Lying for Who We Are: An Identity-Based Model of Workplace Dishonesty," *Academy of Management Review* 40 (2015), pp. 587–610.

19. J. Garsd, "Instagram Advertising: Do You Know It, When You See It?" NPR, June 24, 2019, www.npr.org.

20. L. Fair, "FTC-FDA Warning Letters: Influential to Influencers and Marketers," Federal Trade Commission, June 7, 2019, www.ftc.gov.

21. M. E. Guy, *Ethical Decision Making in Everyday Work Situations* (New York: Quorum Books, 1990).

22. O. C. Ferrell, J. Fraedrich, and L. Ferrell, *Business Ethics: Ethical Decision Making and Cases,* 8th ed. (Cincinnati, OH: South-Western College Publishing, 2010).

23. O. C. Ferrell, J. Fraedrich, and L. Ferrell, *Business Ethics: Ethical Decision Making and Cases,* 8th ed. (Cincinnati, OH: South-Western College Publishing, 2010).

24. M. E. Guy, *Ethical Decision Making in Everyday Work Situations* (New York: Quorum Books, 1990).

25. Caux Round Table, "Principles for Business," www.cauxroundtable.org/index.cfm?&menuid58.PDF, adopted 1994.

26. See www.globalethics.org.

27. "2017 Ethics and Compliance Survey," Ethisphere and Convercent, https://www.convercent.com/resource/2017-ethics-and-compliance-survey.pdf.

28. O. C. Ferrell and J. Fraedrich, *Business Ethics: Ethical Decision Making and Cases,* 3rd ed. (Boston: Houghton Mifflin, 1997).

29. J. B. Kau, D. C. Keenan, C. Lyubinov, and V. C. Slawson, "Subprime Mortgage Default," *Journal of Urban Economics* 70, no. 2–3 (September–November 2011), pp. 75–86.

30. S. N. Robinson and D. P. Nantz, "Lessons to Be Learned from the Financial Crisis," *Journal of Private Enterprise* 25, no. 1 (Fall 2009), pp. 5–23.

31. O. C. Ferrell, J. Fraedrich, and L. Ferrell, *Business Ethics: Ethical Decision Making and Cases 2009 Update,* 7th ed. (Mason, OH: South-Western Cengage Learning, 2010), p. vii.

32. M. I. Mazumder and N. Ahmad, "Greed, Financial Innovation or Laxity of Regulation? A Close Look into the 2007–2009 Financial Crisis and Stock Market Volatility," *Studies in Economics and Finance* 27, no. 2 (2010), pp. 110–44.

33. M. I. Mazumder and N. Ahmad, "Greed, Financial Innovation or Laxity of Regulation? A Close Look into the 2007–2009 Financial Crisis and Stock Market Volatility," *Studies in Economics and Finance* 27, no. 2 (2010), pp. 110–44.

34. M. I. Mazumder and N. Ahmad, "Greed, Financial Innovation or Laxity of Regulation? A Close Look into the 2007–2009 Financial Crisis and Stock Market Volatility," *Studies in Economics and Finance* 27, no. 2 (2010), p. 116.

35. O. C. Ferrell, J. Fraedrich, and L. Ferrell, *Business Ethics: Ethical Decision Making and Cases 2009 Update,* 7th ed. (Mason, OH: South-Western Cengage Learning, 2010), p. iii.

36. J. Ydstie, "SEC Charges Ex-Fannie Mae, Freddie Mac CEOs," NPR, December 16, 2011, www.npr.org.

37. M. I. Mazumder and N. Ahmad, "Greed, Financial Innovation or Laxity of Regulation? A Close Look into the 2007–2009 Financial Crisis and Stock Market Volatility," *Studies in Economics and Finance* 27, no. 2 (2010), pp. 110–44.

38. J. A. Andrade, "Reconceptualising Whistleblowing in a Complex World," *Journal of Business Ethics* 128 (2015), pp. 321–35.

39. J. L. Bierstaker, "Differences in Attitudes about Fraud and Corruption Across Cultures: Theories, Examples and Recommendations," *Cross Cultural Management* 16, no. 3 (2009), pp. 241–50.

40. S. Liu, J. Liao, and H. Wei, "Leadership and Whistleblowing: Mediating Roles of Psychological Safety and Personal Identification," *Journal of Business Ethics* 131 (2015), pp. 107–19.

41. Transparency International, "Corruption Perceptions Index 2019 Results," www.transparency.org/files/content/pages/2019_CPI_Report_EN.pdf.

42. L. Kohlberg and D. Candee, "The Relationship of Moral Judgment to Moral Action," in *Morality, Moral Behavior, and Moral Development,* eds. W. M. Kurtines and J. L. Gerwitz (New York: Wiley, 1984).

43. L. Kohlberg and D. Candee, "The Relationship of Moral Judgment to Moral Action," in *Morality, Moral Behavior, and Moral Development,* eds. W. M. Kurtines and J. L. Gerwitz (New York: Wiley, 1984); J. O. Y. Chung and S. H. Hsu, "The Effect of Cognitive Moral Development on Honesty in Managerial Reporting," *Journal of Business Ethics* 145 (2017), pp. 563–75; L. K. Trevino, "Ethical Decision Making in Organizations: A Person–Situation Interactionist Model," *Academy of Management Review* 11, no. 3 (July 1986), pp. 601–17.

44. O. C. Ferrell and J. Fraedrich, *Business Ethics: Ethical Decision Making and Cases,* 3rd ed. (Boston: Houghton Mifflin, 1997).

45. J. Badarocco Jr. and A. Webb, "Business Ethics: A View from the Trenches," *California Management Review,* Winter 1995, pp. 8–28; and G. Laczniak, M. Berkowitz, R. Brookes, and J. Hale, "The Business of Ethics: Improving or Deteriorating?" *Business Horizons,* January–February 1995, pp. 39–47.

46. K. Lawrence, "How to Cleanse a Toxic Workplace," UNC Kenan-Flagler Business School–Executive Development (2014), www.kenan-flagler.unc.edu.

47. "Is Your Workplace Tough—Or Is It Toxic?" Knowledge@ Wharton, August 12, 2015, www.knowledge.wharton.upenn.edu.

48. D. Meinert, "Creating an Ethical Culture," *HRMagazine* 59, no. 4 (April 2014), pp. 22–27; and M. Gunther, "God and Business," *Fortune,* July 9, 2001, pp. 58–80.

49. V. Anand, B. Ashworth, and M. Joshi, "Business as Usual," *Academy of Management Executive* 18, no. 2 (2004), pp. 39–53; and A. Bernstein, "Too Much Corporate Power?" *BusinessWeek,* September 11, 2000, pp. 146–47.

50. "Leaders in U.S. Economy Say 'We Are Still In' on Paris Climate Agreement," We Are Still In, www.wearestillin.com, accessed September 14, 2019.

51. "Leaders in U.S. Economy Say 'We Are Still In' on Paris Climate Agreement," We Are Still In, www.wearestillin.com, accessed September 14, 2019.

52. "Budweiser Puts 100% Renewable Electricity Message at the Heart of Super Bowl Commercial," The Climate Group, February 1, 2019, www.theclimategroup.com.

53. "Report to the Nations, 2018 Global Study on Occupational Fraud and Abuse," Association of Certified Fraud Examiners, www.acfe.com, accessed September 13, 2019.

54. D. M. Thorne, O. C. Ferrell, and L. Ferrell, *Business & Society,* 4th ed. (Cincinnati, OH: South-Western College Publishing, 2011); and R. T. De George, *Business Ethics,* 3rd ed. (New York: Macmillan, 1990).

55. K. Kruse, "How Chick-fil-A Created a Culture That Lasts," *Forbes,* December 8, 2015, www.forbes.com.

56. H. Peterson, "Chick-fil-A Manager Reveals One Test Workers Need to Pass to Get Hired," *Business Insider,* March 24, 2016, www.businessinsider.com.

57. K. Kruse, "How Chick-fil-A Created a Culture That Lasts," *Forbes,* December 8, 2015, www.forbes.com.

58. R. E. Allinson, "A Call for Ethically Centered Management," *Academy of Management Executive,* February 1995, pp. 73–76.

59. J. Stempel, "U.S. Fines Cognizant, Charges 2 Former Top Execs in India Bribery Case," Reuters, February 15, 2019, www.reuters.com.

60. "Cognizant Execs Allegedly Discussed Bribery Scheme during Video Conference Calls," Governance, Risk & Compliance Monitor Worldwide, Yahoo Finance, February 19, 2019, www.finance.yahoo.com.

61. R. A. Cooke, "Danger Signs of Unethical Behavior: How to Determine If Your Firm Is at Ethical Risk," *Journal of Business Ethics,* April 1991, pp. 249–53.

62. L. K. Trevino and M. Brown, "Managing to Be Ethical: Debunking Five Business Ethics Myths," *Academy of Management Executive,* May 2004, pp. 69–81.

63. L. Brewer, "Decisions: Lynn Brewer, Enron Whistleblower," *Management Today,* August 2006.

64. L. K. Trevino and M. Brown, "Managing to Be Ethical: Debunking Five Business Ethics Myths," *Academy of Management Executive,* May 2004, pp. 69–81.

65. R. Maurer, "People Are Changing Jobs, and How to Recruit and Retain Them," Society for Human Resource Management, August 5, 2015, www.shrm.org.

66. L. K. Trevino and M. Brown, "Managing to Be Ethical: Debunking Five Business Ethics Myths," *Academy of Management Executive,* May 2004, pp. 69–81.

67. C. Nabozny, "Ethisphere Recognizes 128 World's Most Ethical Companies for 2019," Ethisphere Institute, February 26, 2019, www.ethisphere.com.

68. C. Nabozny, "Ethisphere Recognizes 128 World's Most Ethical Companies for 2019," Ethisphere Institute, February 26, 2019, www.ethisphere.com.

69. C. Handy, *Beyond Uncertainty: The Changing Worlds of Organizations* (Boston: Harvard Business School Press, 1996).

70. J. Stevens, H. Steensma, D. Harrison, and P. Cochran, "Symbolic or Substantive Document? The Influence of Ethics Codes on Financial Executives' Decisions," *Strategic Management Journal* 26 (2005), pp. 181-95; and J. Weber, "Does It Take an Economic Village to Raise an Ethical Company?" *Academy of Management Executive* 19 (May 2005), pp. 158-59.

71. See www.coca-colacompany.com/investors/code-of-business-conduct.

72. See www.ethics.org.

73. "Code Construction and Content," The Ethics Resource Center Toolkit, www.ethics.org; and "Ten Style Tips for Writing an Effective Code of Conduct," The Ethics Resource Center Toolkit, www.ethics.org.

74. G. R. Weaver, L. K. Trevino, and P. L. Cochran, "Corporate Ethics Programs as Control Systems: Influences of Executive Commitment and Environmental Factors," *Academy of Management Journal* 42 (1999), pp. 41-57.

75. L. S. Paine, "Managing for Organizational Integrity," *Harvard Business Review,* March–April 1994, pp. 106-17.

76. "Shaping an Ethical Workplace Culture," SHRM Foundation's Effective Practice Guidelines Series, Society for Human Resource Management, www.shrm.org, accessed March 10, 2020.

77. "A Voluntary Pledge by MBAs to Create Value Responsibly and Ethically," The MBA Oath, www.mbaoath.org, accessed September 14, 2019.

78. See the MBA Oath website, www.mbaoath.org/list-of-oath-signers/.

79. C. Moore and F. Gino, "Approach, Ability, Aftermath: A Psychological Process Framework for Unethical Behavior at Work," *Academy of Management Annals* 9 (2015), pp. 235-89.

80. L. K. Trevino and M. Brown, "Managing to Be Ethical: Debunking Five Business Ethics Myths," *Academy of Management Executive,* May 2004, p. 70.

81. L. K. Trevino and M. Brown, "Managing to Be Ethical: Debunking Five Business Ethics Myths," *Academy of Management Executive,* May 2004, pp. 69-81.

82. M. Banaji, M. Bazerman, and D. Chugh, "How (Un)Ethical Are You?" *Harvard Business Review,* December 2003, pp. 56-64.

83. V. Anand, B. Ashworth, and M. Joshi, "Business as Usual," *Academy of Management Executive* 18, no. 2 (2004), pp. 39-53.

84. A. Taylor, "Execs' Posh Retreat after Bailout Angers Lawmakers," *Yahoo News,* October 7, 2008, www.yahoo.com/news.

85. "2016 Report Fraud in Small Business," Association of Certified Fraud Examiners, www.acfe.com.

86. T. Thomas, J. Schermerhorn Jr., and J. Dienhart, "Strategic Leadership of Ethical Behavior in Business," *Academy of Management Executive,* May 2004, pp. 56-66.

87. L. T. Hosmer, *The Ethics of Management,* 4th ed. (New York: McGraw-Hill/Irwin, 2003).

88. L. K. Trevino and M. Brown, "Managing to Be Ethical: Debunking Five Business Ethics Myths," *Academy of Management Executive,* May 2004, pp. 69-81; and D. Comer and L. Sekerka, "Keep Calm and Carry On (Ethically): Durable Moral Courage in the Workplace," *Human Resource Management Review* 28 (2018), pp. 116-30.

89. "Ex-Aide at Coke Is Guilty in Plot to Steal Secrets," *The Wall Street Journal,* February 5, 2007, www.wsj.com.

90. "State of Ethics in Large Companies," Ethics & Compliance Initiative, www.ethics.org, accessed September 14, 2019.

91. "State of Ethics in Large Companies," Ethics & Compliance Initiative, www.ethics.org, accessed September 14, 2019.

92. M. E. Schreiber and D. R. Marshall, "Reducing the Risk of Whistleblower Complaints," *Risk Management* 53, no. 11 (November 2006).

93. A. Lendez and N. Sliger, "Listen Closely: Is That a Whistle Blowing or a Slot Machine Ringing?" *Directorship* 36, no. 6 (December 2010-January 2011), pp. 64-68.

94. L. Preston and J. Post, eds., *Private Management and Public Policy* (Englewood Cliffs, NJ: Prentice-Hall, 1975).

95. S. Mena, J. Rintamaki, P. Fleming, et al., "On the Forgetting of Corporate Irresponsibility," *Academy of Management Review* 41 (2016), pp. 720-38; J. Schrempf-Stirling, G. Palazzo, and R. Phillips, "Historic Corporate Social Responsibility," *Academy of Management Review* 41 (2016), pp. 700-19; M. Nalick, M. Josefy, A. Zardkoohi, et al., "Corporate Sociopolitical Involvement: A Reflection of Whose Preferences?" *Academy of Management Perspectives* 30 (2016), pp. 384-403; M. Westermann-Behaylo, K. Rehbein, and T. Fort, "Enhancing the Concept of Corporate Diplomacy: Encompassing Political Corporate Social Responsibility, International Relations, and Peace through Commerce," *Academy of Management Perspectives* 29 (2015), pp. 387-404; A. Simha and J. Cullen, "Ethical Climates and Their Effects on Organizational Outcomes: Implications from the Past and Prophecies for the Future," *Academy of Management Perspectives* 26 (2012), pp. 20-34; and O. C. Ferrell and J. Fraedrich, *Business Ethics: Ethical Decision Making and Cases,* 3rd ed. (Boston: Houghton Mifflin, 1997).

96. A. Carroll, "Managing Ethically with Global Stakeholders: A Present and Future Challenge," *Academy of Management Executive,* May 2004, pp. 114-20.

97. See Smithfield's company website, www.smithfieldfoods.com/trusted-brands.

98. C. Doering, "Smithfield Urges Farmers to End Use of Gestation Crates," *USA Today,* January 7, 2014, www.usatoday.com.

99. P. C. Godfrey, "The Relationship between Corporate Philanthropy and Shareholder Wealth: A Risk Management Perspective," *Academy of Management Review* 30 (2005), pp. 777-98.

100. R. Giacalone, "A Transcendent Business Education for the 21st Century," *Academy of Management Learning & Education,* 2004, pp. 415-20.

101. M. Witzel, "Not for Wealth Alone: The Rise of Business Ethics," *Financial Times Mastering Management Review,* November 1999, pp. 14-19.

102. Y. Fassin, "The Stakeholder Model Refined," *Journal of Business Ethics,* no. 84 (2009), pp. 113-35; R. K. Mitchell, B. R. Agle, and D. J. Wood, "Toward a Theory of Stakeholder Identification and Salience: Defining the Principle of Who and What Really Counts," *Academy of Management Review* 4, no. 22 (1997),

pp. 853–86; and R. E. Freeman, *Strategic Management: A Stakeholder Approach* (Boston: Pittman), 1984.

103. R. E. Freeman, *Strategic Management: A Stakeholder Approach* (Boston: Pittman), 1984.

104. J. A. Lozano and M. Hoyer, "Harvey's Devastating Flooding Boosts Insurance in Texas," AP News, July 30, 2018, www.apnews.com.

105. B. Condon and K. Sweet, "About 80% of Hurricane Harvey Victims Do Not Have Flood Insurance, Face Big Bills," *USA Today,* August 30, 2017, www.usatoday.com.

106. E. Segran, "Escalating Sweatshop Protests Keep Nike Sweating," *Fast Company,* July 28, 2017, www.fastcompany.com.

107. C. Taylor, "'Nightmare' Conditions at Chinese Factories Where Hasbro and Disney Toys Are Made," *CNBC,* December 11, 2018, www.cnbc.com.

108. S. Clifford and S. Greenhouse, "Fast and Flawed Inspections of Factories Abroad," *The New York Times,* www.nytimes.com, accessed April 16, 2016.

109. C. Farrell, "'Social Finance': Doing Good by Doing Well," *Bloomberg,* April 1, 2014, www.bloomberg.com; and D. Quinn and T. Jones, "An Agent Morality View of Business Policy," *Academy of Management Review* 20 (1995), pp. 22–42.

110. "Brewery Workers Pour Their Hearts into Business When Given a Stake," *PBS NewsHour,* October 22, 2015, www.pbs.org; and S. Parrish, "Three Companies Doing Well by Doing Good," *Forbes,* December 15, 2014, www.forbes.com.

111. See company website, www.newbelgium.com/sustainability.

112. S. Mainwaring, "How Lego Rebuilt Itself as a Purposeful and Sustainable Brand," *Forbes,* August 11, 2016, www.forbes.com.

113. "Social Good Summit 2015," Mashable, www.mashable.com.

114. M. Pflum, "As Millennial Parents Demand Sustainable Toys, Lego Is Perfecting Plant-Based Bricks," NBC News, August 2, 2019, www.nbcnews.com.

115. M. Delmas, D. Etzion, and N. Nairn-Birch, "Triangulating Environmental Performance: What Do Corporate Social Responsibility Ratings Really Capture?" *Academy of Management Perspectives* 27 (2013), pp. 255–67; J. A. Aragon-Correa, A. Marcus, and N. Hurtado-Torres, "The Natural Environmental Strategies of International Firms: Old Controversies and New Evidence on Performance and Disclosure," *Academy of Management Perspectives* 30 (2016), pp. 24–39; D. Schuler and M. Cording, "A Corporate Social Performance–Corporate Financial Performance Behavioral Model for Consumers," *Academy of Management Review* 31 (2006), pp. 540–58; K. Kim, M. Kim, and C. Qian, "Effects of Corporate Social Responsibility on Corporate Financial Performance: A Competitive-Action Perspective," *Journal of Management* 44 (2018), pp. 1097–1118; D. Turban and D. Greening, "Corporate Social Performance and Organizational Attractiveness to Prospective Employees," *Academy of Management Journal* 40 (1997), pp. 658–72; and M. Turner, T. McIntosh, and S. Reid, "Corporate Implementation of Socially Controversial CSR Initiatives: Implications for Human Resource Management," *Human Resource Management Review* 19 (2019), pp. 125–36.

116. D. Turban and D. Greening, "Corporate Social Performance and Organizational Attractiveness to Prospective Employees," *Academy of Management Journal* 40 (1997), pp. 658–72.

117. A. McWilliams and D. Siegel, "Corporate Social Responsibility: A Theory of the Firm Perspective," *Academy of Management Review* 26 (2001), pp. 117–27.

118. M. E. Porter and M. R. Kramer, "Strategy and Society: The Link between Competitive Advantage and Corporate Social Responsibility," *Harvard Business Review,* December 2006, pp. 78–92.

119. S. L. Hart and M. B. Milstein, "Global Sustainability and the Creative Destructions of Industries," *Sloan Management Review,* Fall 1999, pp. 23–33.

120. P. M. Senge and G. Carstedt, "Innovating Our Way to the Next Industrial Revolution," *Sloan Management Review,* Winter 2001, pp. 24–38.

121. C. Holliday, "Sustainable Growth, the DuPont Way," *Harvard Business Review,* September 2001, pp. 129–34.

122. See Mike Bloomberg's personal website, mikebloomberg.com/global-impact/environment.

123. Annual Report 2019, Bloomberg Philanthropies, www.annualreport.bloomberg.org.

124. Annual Report 2019, Bloomberg Philanthropies, www.annualreport.bloomberg.org.

125. P. Shrivastava, "Ecocentric Management for a Risk Society," *Academy of Management Review* 20 (1995), pp. 118–37; G. George, S. Schillebeeckx, and T. Liak, "The Management of Natural Resources: An Overview and Research Agenda," *Academy of Management Review* 58 (2015), pp. 1595–1613.

126. P. Shrivastava, "Ecocentric Management for a Risk Society," *Academy of Management Review* 20 (1995), pp. 118–37.

127. P. Shrivastava, "Ecocentric Management for a Risk Society," *Academy of Management Review* 20 (1995), pp. 118–37.

128. M. Gunther, "Green Is Good," *Fortune* 155 (April 2, 2007), pp. 42–44.

129. J. O'Toole, "Do Good, Do Well: The Business Enterprise Trust Awards," *California Management Review* (Spring 1991), pp. 9–24.

130. M. Agnew, "The Thirsty Business of Beer: How Breweries Are Confronting the Industry's Water Problem," *The Growler,* March 2, 2016, www.growlermag.com.

131. See MillerCoors' company website, millercoors.com/sustainability.

132. P. Shrivastava, "Ecocentric Management for a Risk Society," *Academy of Management Review* 20 (1995), pp. 118–37.

133. M. Russo and P. Fouts, "A Resource-Based Perspective on Corporate Environmental Performance and Profitability," *Academy of Management Journal* 40 (1997), pp. 534–59; and R. D. Klassen and D. Clay Whybark, "The Impact of Environmental Technologies on Manufacturing Performance," *Academy of Management Journal* 42 (1999), pp. 599–615.

134. "Towards a Vision of Sustainable Agriculture," Ben & Jerry's, www.benjerry.com, accessed September 15, 2019.

135. "People & Planet," IKEA, www.ikea.com, accessed September 15, 2019.

136. See Environment, Google, Inc., www.sustainability.google/projects/announcement-100.

137. G. Pinchot and E. Pinchot, *The Intelligent Organization* (San Francisco: Berrett-Koehler, 1996).

138. S. L. Hart, "Beyond Greening: Strategies for a Sustainable World," *Harvard Business Review,* January–February 1997, pp. 66–76.

Planning and Decision Making

Learning Objectives

After studying Chapter 5, you should be able to

LO1 Summarize the basic steps in any planning process.

LO2 Discuss how strategic planning should be integrated with tactical and operational planning.

LO3 Describe the strategic management process and the importance of SWOT analysis in strategy formulation.

LO4 Analyze how companies can achieve competitive advantage through business strategy.

LO5 Identify the keys to effective strategy implementation.

LO6 Explain how to make effective decisions as a manager.

LO7 Describe some personal obstacles to rational decision making.

LO8 Summarize principles for group decision making.

In December 2019, the first cases of a new strain of coronavirus, later known as COVID-19, appeared in China. In early January 2020, China reported its first death. The virus spread rapidly to other countries, with the first case being reported in the United States on January 20.[1] By March, over 100,000 cases and over 4,000 deaths had been reported worldwide. The effects of the virus were felt in the financial markets and global business supply chains. Oil and stock markets plummeted; sporting events, concerts, and political rallies were canceled; and schools closed. People had to adapt, and so did business.

Smart, strategic management is critical to the success of organizations even in the best of times, but it is perhaps even more essential during crises. Important decisions about how organizations would adapt to the growing crisis needed to be made on multiple fronts quickly and simultaneously. "Every CEO that I know has got to manage an employee dimension, supply-chain dimension, in many cases a revenue dimension," said Mike White, who sits on the board of a number of *Fortune* 500 companies.[2]

Tech companies such as Apple, Google, and Microsoft, located on the West Coast of the United States where COVID-19 hit first, implemented telecommuting policies to minimize its spread. Fearing a sharp economic downturn, airlines such as United, American, and Southwest trimmed

In an effort to keep its employees and customers safe during the COVID-19 pandemic, Costco required everyone in their stores to wear protective face coverings. Ron Adar/Shutterstock

capacity to reduce costs. The CEOs for United and Southwest even announced they would be taking pay cuts.[3]

Unfortunately, because of the increasing interconnectedness of our world, pandemics such as COVID-19 are likely to become more frequent.[4] Organizations will therefore need to incorporate these and other kinds of risks into their strategic planning and decision making.

This chapter examines the most important concepts and processes involved in planning and strategic management. By learning these concepts and reviewing the steps outlined, you will be on your way to understanding approaches to strategically managing today's organizations through any conditions. Whether or not you engage directly in strategic planning for your firm, you will make key decisions that contribute to strategy implementation. The chapter explores the types of decisions managers face, the ways they are made, and the ways they *should* be made.

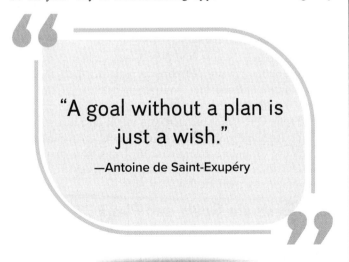

> "A goal without a plan is just a wish."
>
> —Antoine de Saint-Exupéry

LO1 Summarize the basic steps in any planning process.

1 | THE PLANNING PROCESS

Planning is the conscious, systematic process of making decisions about goals and activities that an individual, group, work unit, or organization will pursue in the future. Planning is not an informal or haphazard response to a crisis; it is a purposeful effort that is directed and controlled by managers. Sometimes it draws on the knowledge and experience of employees at all levels.

Planning is one of the most common management practices but typically is not done very well; most firms do not come close to realizing its potential benefits.[5] Exhibit 5.1 shows the steps in an effective planning process. Notice that planning moves in a *cycle.* The outcomes of plans are evaluated and, if necessary, revised.

Planning gives individuals and work units a clear map to follow in their future activities, yet is flexible enough to allow for unique circumstances and changing conditions. Next, we describe the basic planning process in more detail. Later in this chapter, we discuss how managerial decisions and plans fit into the larger purposes of the organization—its ultimate strategy, mission, vision, and goals.

1.1 | Analyze the Situation

Planning begins with a situational analysis. Within their time and resource constraints, planners should gather, interpret,

and summarize all information relevant to the planning issue in question. They study past events, examine current conditions, and try to forecast future trends. The analysis focuses on the internal forces at work in the organization or work unit and, consistent with the open-systems approach (Chapter 3), examines influences from the external environment. The outcome of this step is the identification and diagnosis of planning assumptions, issues, and problems.

A thorough situational analysis will provide information about the planning decisions you need to make. For example, if you are a manager of an online jewelry company considering the launch of a new product line for the female teen market, your analysis will include such factors as the number of female teens who order jewelry online, the appeal of the female teen market to advertisers, your firm's ability to serve this market effectively, current economic conditions, the level of female teen interest in jewelry, and online jewelry retailers already serving this market and their current sales. Such an analysis will help you decide whether to proceed with the next step in your product line launch.

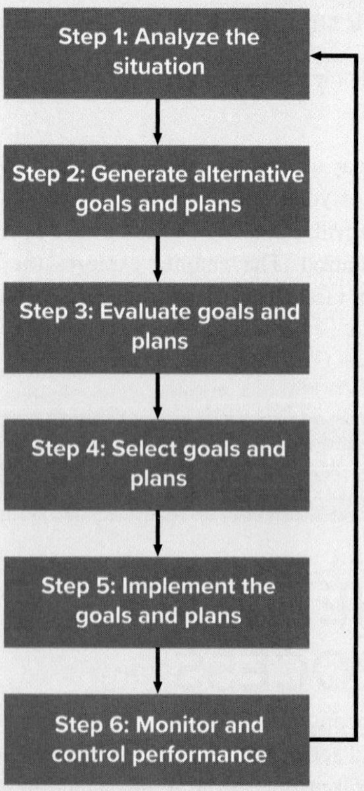

1.2 | Generate Alternative Goals and Plans

Based on the findings from situational analysis, the planning process should generate alternative goals that could be pursued and alternative plans for achieving those goals. This step should stress creativity and encourage managers and employees to think broadly and develop a variety of options. Continuing with the new jewelry product line for female teens, you could identify multiple markets to target, for instance online customers in certain regions of the United States, the entire country, or multiple countries.

Goals are the targets or ends the manager wants to reach. In your jewelry product line, you might set a goal to sell 10,000 necklaces ($150,000 in gross sales) within the first year of the launch.

Plans are the actions or means the manager intends to use to achieve goals. Three types of plans are common (see Exhibit 5.2). At a minimum, planning should outline alternative actions that may lead to the attainment of each goal, the resources required to reach the goal, and the obstacles that may develop. For your online jewelry company to reach its first-year sales goals, you would consider contracting with a jewelry supplier, a website designer, a marketing professional, and some salespeople. One major obstacle you might face is a shortage of funds for the product launch. You could try to finance it through crowdfunding, microloans, or loans from family and friends.[6]

1.3 | Evaluate Goals and Plans

Next, a good planning process evaluates the advantages, disadvantages, and potential effects of each alternative goal and plan. Managers must prioritize the goals, evaluate how well

Exhibit 5.1 Formal planning steps

Step 1: Analyze the situation

Step 2: Generate alternative goals and plans

Step 3: Evaluate goals and plans

Step 4: Select goals and plans

Step 5: Implement the goals and plans

Step 6: Monitor and control performance

scenario a narrative that describes a particular set of future conditions

Exhibit 5.2 Three common plans used by organizations

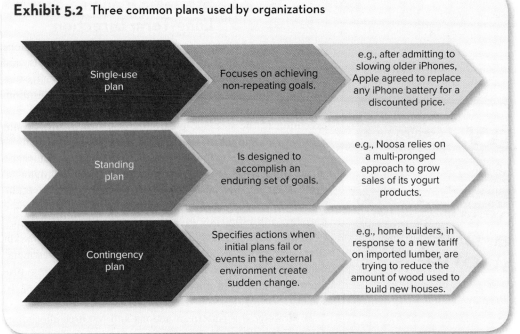

| Single-use plan | Focuses on achieving non-repeating goals. | e.g., after admitting to slowing older iPhones, Apple agreed to replace any iPhone battery for a discounted price. |

| Standing plan | Is designed to accomplish an enduring set of goals. | e.g., Noosa relies on a multi-pronged approach to grow sales of its yogurt products. |

| Contingency plan | Specifies actions when initial plans fail or events in the external environment create sudden change. | e.g., home builders, in response to a new tariff on imported lumber, are trying to reduce the amount of wood used to build new houses. |

Sources: M. Snider, "Apple Said to Replace iPhone Batteries at Discount Regardless of Diagnostic Test," *USA Today,* January 2, 2018, www.usatoday.com; J. Skerrit, "Timber Tariffs Are Hammering U.S. Builders," *Bloomberg Businessweek,* March 12, 2018, www.bloomberg.com; and J. Feifer, "Landing on the Wrong Shelves," *Entrepreneur* 46, no. 1 (January–February 2018), p. 20.

alternative plans meet high-priority goals, and consider the cost and likely investment return of each. In our online jewelry company example, your evaluation might determine that necklace sales alone wouldn't be profitable enough to justify the launch. Perhaps you could improve profits by adding earrings and rings to the product offerings.

1.4 | Select Goals and Plans

The evaluation process identifies priorities and trade-offs among the goals and plans. Now it's time to select the most appropriate and feasible alternatives. Assume that you were able to raise about $20,000 to launch the new product line. You then must decide which priorities to fund initially, most likely the jewelry supplier and website designer. You then may need to lead the sales effort until the company generates additional cash to hire more salespeople. You have to choose which ones to go with. Experienced judgment plays an important role in this process. As you will discover later in the chapter, however, relying on judgment alone may not be the best way to proceed.

Sometimes the alternative generation, evaluation, and selection steps reveal several different future scenarios. A different contingency plan is attached to each scenario. Managers pursue the goals and implement the plans associated with the most likely scenario. However, the manager should also be prepared to switch to another set of plans if the situation changes and another scenario becomes relevant.

This approach helps the firm anticipate and manage crises and allows greater flexibility and responsiveness.

As the manager of the online jewelry company, you might develop a few scenarios linked to sales growth. For example, you might plan to hire a second salesperson when company sales revenue tops $75,000 or contract with a blogger who can influence female teens to purchase your jewelry.

1.5 | Implement the Goals and Plans

Once managers have selected the goals and plans, they must pursue and implement them. Proper implementation is key to achieving goals. Managers and employees must understand the plan, have the resources to implement it, and be motivated to do so.

Including employees in the previous steps of the planning process paves the way for the implementation phase. Employees usually are better informed, more committed, and more highly motivated when a goal or plan is one that they helped develop.

While developing the business plan and sales goals for the online jewelry company, you would likely seek feedback about their feasibility from the owner(s), web designer, supplier, and new salesperson. Incorporating some of their ideas into the plan and goals will build their commitment to the project.

Linking the plan to other systems in the organization, particularly the budget and reward systems, helps ensure its successful implementation. If the manager does not have or cannot find the financial resources to execute the plan, the plan is probably doomed. Similarly, linking goal achievement to the organization's reward system, such as bonuses or promotions, encourages employees to achieve goals and to implement plans properly.

1.6 | Monitor and Control Performance

Although it is sometimes ignored, the sixth step in the formal planning process—monitoring and controlling—is essential. Without it, you won't know whether your plan is working.

Ivelin Radkov/Shutterstock

As we mentioned earlier, planning works in a cycle. Managers must continually monitor the actual performance of their work units against the units' goals and plans. They also need to develop control systems to measure that performance and allow them to take corrective action when plans are implemented improperly or the situation changes. As the manager of the online jewelry company, you would want to monitor necklace sales on a daily, weekly, and annual basis. A good manager would also keep an eye on other key metrics like shipping costs, delivery time, number of visits to the company website, and customer satisfaction. We elaborate on control systems later in the book.

LO2 Discuss how strategic planning should be integrated with tactical and operational planning.

2 | LEVELS OF PLANNING

Managers plan at all levels[7] described in Chapter 1: top-level (*strategic* managers), middle-level (*tactical* managers), frontline (*operational* managers), and team leaders. However, the scope and activities of the planning process tend to differ at each level.

2.1 | Strategic Planning Sets a Long-Term Direction

Strategic planning involves making decisions about the organization's long-term goals and strategies. Strategic plans have a strong external orientation and cover major portions of the organization. Senior executives are responsible for the development and execution of the strategic plan, although they usually do not formulate or implement the entire plan personally.

Strategic goals are major targets or end results that relate to the long-term survival, value, and growth of the organization. Strategic managers—top-level managers—usually establish goals aimed at effectiveness (providing appropriate outputs) and efficiency (a high ratio of outputs to inputs). Common strategic goals include growing, increasing market share, improving profitability, boosting return on investment, fostering quantity and quality of outputs, increasing productivity, improving customer service, and contributing to society.

A strategy is a pattern of actions and resource allocations designed to achieve the organization's goals. An effective strategy provides a basis for answering five broad questions about how the organization will meet its objectives:

1. Where will we be active?

2. How will we get there (e.g., by increasing sales or acquiring another company)?

3. How will we win in the marketplace (e.g., by keeping prices low or offering the best service)?

4. How fast will we move, and in what sequence will we make changes?

5. How will we obtain financial returns (low costs or premium prices)?[8]

Later in this chapter, we discuss how managers try to craft a strategy by matching the organization's skills and resources to the opportunities found in the external environment.

2.2 | Tactical and Operational Planning Support the Strategy

The organization's strategic goals and plans serve as the foundation for planning by middle-level and frontline managers. Exhibit 5.3 shows that as goals and plans move from the strategic level to the tactical level and then to the operational level, they become more specific and involve shorter time periods. A strategic plan typically has a time horizon of three to seven years, but sometimes it spans decades, as with the successful plan to land a probe on Titan, Saturn's moon. Tactical plans may have a time horizon of a year or two, and operational plans may cover several months.

Level of planning	Who develops the plan?	How detailed is it?	How long is the plan?
Strategic	Top-level managers	Low	Long (3–7 years)
Tactical	Middle managers	Medium	Medium (1–2 years)
Operational	Frontline managers	High	Short (< 1 year)

Exhibit 5.3 Three levels of planning in organizations

tactical planning a set of procedures for translating broad strategic goals and plans into specific goals and plans that are relevant to a particular portion of the organization, such as a functional area like marketing

operational planning the process of identifying the specific procedures and processes required at lower levels of the organization

study tip 5

Study strategically for exams

Have you ever had to take two or three exams on the same day or within a day of each other? A good study strategy will help in these situations. Here is a sample strategy you might consider trying. *One week before the next exam,* make it a point to have finished reading and outlining the chapters, making vocabulary flashcards, reviewing the online materials, and completing anything else you will need to know for the upcoming exams. This should leave you plenty of time to review the study materials and those of your other courses before the exams hit.

into more specific goals and plans and an ever-more-limited timetable. But in today's complex organizations, planning also needs to be dynamic and flexible. Managers throughout an organization may be involved in developing the strategic plan and contributing critical elements. Also, in practice, lower-level managers may make decisions that shape strategy, whether or not top executives realize it.

When Intel's former CEO Andy Grove suggested that the company exit the computer memory business, Intel was directing about one-third of its research dollars to memory-related projects. Yet on a practical level, the company had already been exiting the business; only 4 percent of its total sales were for computer memory products. Why was this occurring, if it wasn't a defined strategy? Finance executives had directed manufacturing managers to set up factories in a way that would generate the biggest margins (revenues minus costs) per square inch of microchips produced. As computer memory became a money-losing commodity, manufacturing made fewer of those products. So when Intel announced it would get out of the memory business, its strategy was catching up with its operational planning, which had been driven by tactical plans.[9] The lesson for top managers is to make sure they are communicating strategy

> "If you don't know where you are going, you'll end up someplace else."
>
> —Yogi Berra

Tactical planning translates broad strategic goals and plans into specific goals and plans relevant to particular organizational units, often functional areas such as marketing or human resources. Tactical plans focus on the major actions a unit must take to fulfill its part of the strategic plan. Suppose a strategy calls for the rollout of a new product line. The tactical plan for the manufacturing unit might involve the design, testing, and installation of the equipment needed to produce the new line.

Operational planning identifies the specific procedures and processes required at lower levels of the organization. Frontline managers usually focus on routine tasks such as production runs, delivery schedules, and human resource requirements.

The formal planning model is hierarchical, with top-level strategies flowing down through the levels of the organization

to all levels of the organization and paying attention to what is happening at all levels in the organization.

2.3 | All Levels of Planning Should Be Aligned

To be fully effective, the organization's strategic, tactical, and operational goals and plans must be *aligned*—that is, they must be consistent, mutually supportive, and focused on achieving the common purpose and direction. Whole Foods Market (owned by Amazon), for example, links its tactical and operational planning directly to its strategic planning. A strategic goal of Whole Foods is "to sell the highest-quality products that also offer high value for our customers." Its operational goals

● Whole Foods Market's vision has guided the company's growth into one of the biggest health food store chains in the United States.
NYCStock/Shutterstock

focus on ingredients, freshness, taste, nutritional value, safety, and appearance that meet or exceed its customers' expectations, including guaranteeing product satisfaction. Tactical goals include store environments that are safe and inviting for employees and "inviting, fun, unique, comfortable, attractive, nurturing, and educational" for customers.[10]

Even the best strategies rely on managers' ability to set tactical and operational priorities, allocate resources, analyze market conditions, and ensure proper implementation. The next section discusses six steps that managers can follow to convert strategic ideas into successful outcomes like higher profits, new products, and greater efficiencies.

> **LO3 Describe the strategic management process and the importance of SWOT analysis in strategy formulation.**

3 | STRATEGIC PLANNING PROCESS

Traditionally, strategic planning flowed from the top. Senior executives and specialized planning units developed goals and plans for the entire organization. Tactical and operational managers received those goals and plans and then simply prepared procedures and budgets for their units. Now, however, senior executives are more likely to involve managers throughout the organization in strategy formulation.[11] In a highly competitive and rapidly changing environment, executives need to look for ideas from all levels of the organization. Although top managers continue to furnish the organization's strategic direction, or "vision," tactical and operational managers provide valuable inputs to the organization's strategic plan. These managers may formulate or change their own plans, making the organization more flexible and responsive.

Because of this trend, a new term for the strategic planning process has emerged: "strategic management." **Strategic management** involves managers from all parts of the organization in formulating and implementing strategic goals and strategies. It integrates strategic planning and management into a single process. Strategic planning becomes an ongoing activity in which all managers are encouraged to think strategically and focus on long-term, externally oriented issues as well as short-term tactical and operational issues.

As shown in Exhibit 5.4, the strategic management process has six elements: (1) establishing mission, vision, and goals; (2) analyzing external opportunities and threats; (3) analyzing internal strengths and weaknesses; (4) SWOT analysis and strategy formulation; (5) strategy implementation; and (6) strategic control. This planning and decision process resembles the planning framework discussed earlier, and we elaborate on them in the next few sections.

3.1 | Establish a Mission, Vision, and Goals

The first step in strategic planning is establishing a mission, a vision, and goals for the organization. The **mission** is a clear and concise expression of the organization's basic purpose. It describes what the organization does and for whom, its basic good or service, and its values. Increasingly, organizations recognize that they are "mission driven," focusing on a purpose beyond themselves. Such missions are important nowadays given that employees want a "reason to believe."

Following are some mission statements from firms you might recognize:

Life is Good: "To spread the power of optimism."[12]

Patagonia: "Build the best product, cause no unnecessary harm, use business to inspire and implement solutions to the environmental crisis."[13]

Honest Tea: "To create and promote great-tasting, healthy, organic beverages."[14]

The mission describes the organization as it currently operates. The **strategic vision** points to the future; it provides a perspective on where the organization is headed and what it can become. Here are some actual vision statements:

Creative Commons: "Realizing the full potential of the Internet—universal access to research and education, full participation

Exhibit 5.4 The strategic management process

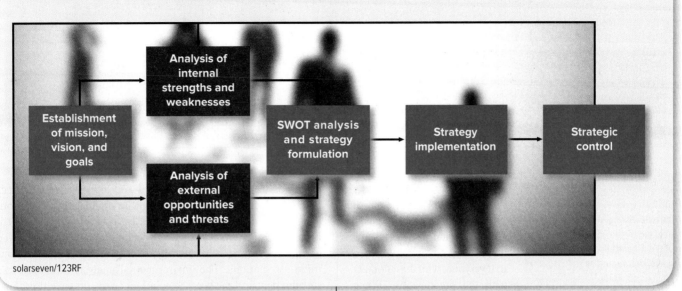

solarseven/123RF

in culture—to drive a new era of development, growth, and productivity."[15]

Alzheimer's Association: "A world without Alzheimer's disease."[16]

Hilton: "To fill the earth with the light and warmth of hospitality."[17]

The most effective vision statements inspire organization members. They offer a worthwhile target for the entire organization to work together to achieve. Often, these statements are not strictly financial because financial targets alone may not motivate all organization members. Thus, Creative Commons' vision refers to giving its users universal access while driving a new era of development.[18] This vision inspires user cooperation to change the way things have been done in the past, which in turn inspires creators and users to share their products and ideas in the Creative Commons.

- Embrace the challenges of becoming more sustainable to protect the natural ecosystem.[19]

Different city departments contribute to various aspects of this vision in the way they carry out their operational plans with an emphasis on collaborating with local businesses and residents.

Lofty words in a vision and mission statement mean little without strong leadership support. At McDonald's, the commitment of past and present CEOs has played a large role in the success of the company's strategy implementation. Several years ago, the company floundered as it lost sight of its commitment to quality, value, speed, and convenience. Under the leadership of James Cantalupo, the company created a customer-focused mission statement: "To be our customers' favorite place and way to eat." When Steve Easterbrook took over as CEO in 2015,

> ## "Leadership is the capacity to translate vision into reality."
> —Warren G. Bennis

Strategic goals evolve from the organization's mission and vision. For example, in support of its mission to sustainably create the best products with the least amount of harm, Patagonia established the following goals:

- Create products that are durable, functional, and repairable.
- Create products that will last for generations.
- Improve our business processes to do less harm to the environment.

he enthusiastically backed the mission statement and initiated several positive changes, including offering breakfast items all day long. Other positive changes included renovating 4,000 restaurants, many with modern furniture, self-serve kiosks, and table service. These changes seemed to help the fast-food giant improve its performance. In 2019, McDonald's started using fresh beef for its Quarter Pounder and sales increased 30 percent.[20] In that same year, McDonald's reported a healthy 6.5 percent increase in global sales.[21]

Traditional Thinking

Strategic decisions are based on intuition and past experiences.

Source: Adapted from D. Meinert, "Top Performers Boast Analytics over Intuition," *HRMagazine* 56, no. 2 (February 2011), pp. 18–19.

The Best Managers Today

Use analytics and data to gain insights and formulate strategic plans.

---

stakeholders groups and individuals who affect and are affected by the achievement of the organization's mission, goals, and strategies

Large firms generally create formal public statements of their missions, visions, goals, and even values. These statements can be communicated to everyone who has contact with the organization. When you seek employment with a firm, review the firm's statements of mission, vision, and goals; they can help you determine whether the firm's purposes and values are compatible with your own.

3.2 | Analyze External Opportunities and Threats

The mission and vision drive the second component of the strategic management process: analysis of the external environment. Successful strategic management depends on accurate and thorough evaluation of the competitive environment and macroenvironment, described in Chapter 3.

As illustrated in Exhibit 5.5, an environmental analysis includes many elements. The analysis begins with an examination of the industry. Next, organizational stakeholders are examined. Stakeholders are groups and individuals who affect and are affected by achievement of the organization's mission, goals, and strategies. They include buyers, suppliers, competitors, government and regulatory agencies, unions and employee groups, the financial community, owners and shareholders, and trade associations. The environmental analysis assesses these stakeholders and the ways they influence the organization.[22]

Learning from leaders of noncompeting organizations can help a top management team successfully develop and implement their strategic plan. At software company Intuit (of QuickBooks and Quicken Loans fame), former chair and CEO Brad Smith and his leadership team spent a day shadowing CEOs of successful product companies. They were especially interested in learning how these individuals encouraged their teams to develop new products.

As a result of shadowing CEOs who were skilled stewards of new-product development processes, Smith and his leadership team gained insights that helped them establish priorities for Intuit's strategy. One strategic outcome led to the overhaul of QuickBooks accounting and TurboTax software for small and medium-sized businesses. Another was to shift customers from software purchases in retail stores to cloud-based subscriptions, which yield a more consistent revenue stream. In 2018, the company reported a record 2.8 million worldwide subscribers of QuickBooks Online.[23]

The environmental analysis also should examine other forces in the environment, such as economic conditions and technological factors. One critical task in environmental analysis is forecasting future trends. As noted in Chapter 3, forecasting techniques range from simple judgment to complex mathematical models that examine systematic relationships among many variables. Because of biases and

Exhibit 5.5	Elements of an environmental analysis
Industry growth	Growth rates for the entire industry and key market segments, and projected changes in patterns and determinants of growth.
Industry forces	Threat of new industry entrants, threat of substitutes, economic power of buyers/customers, economic power of suppliers, and internal industry rivalry.
Competitor analysis	Goals, strategies, strengths, and weaknesses of each major competitor.
Legal trends	Legislation and regulatory activities and their effects on the industry.
Political activity	The level of political activity undertaken by organizations and associations within the industry.
Social issues	Current and potential social issues and their effects on the industry.
Social interest groups	Social interest groups: consumer, environmental, and other activist groups that try to influence the industry.
Labor issues	Key labor needs, shortages, opportunities, and problems confronting the industry.
Macroeconomic conditions	Economic factors that affect supply, demand, growth, competition, and profitability within the industry.
Technological factors	Scientific or technical methods that affect the industry, particularly recent and potential innovations.

limits on human thinking, even simple quantitative techniques can outperform the intuitive assessments of experts.

The difference between an opportunity and a threat depends in part on how a company positions itself strategically. For example, some states have required that electric utilities get a certain share of their power from renewable sources, such as wind and solar energy, rather than from fossil fuels, including coal, oil, and natural gas. This requirement poses a threat to utilities because the costs of fossil fuel energy are less, and customers demand low prices. However, some companies see strategic opportunities in renewable power. Florida Power & Light was a traditional utilities company that invested in nuclear, wind, and solar-powered energy. The company rebranded to NextEra Energy to show its intention to lead the country in renewable energy creation and is now one of the largest nuclear power generators in the United States.[24]

Solar energy organizations aren't the only renewable energy firms making headway in the market. Denmark's Orsted, the world's largest operator of offshore wind turbines, expanded globally to promote renewable energy consumption.[25] Partnering with GE Renewable Energy, Orsted is building offshore wind farms off the coast of Maryland and New Jersey to be completed by 2024.[26]

3.3 | Analyze Internal Strengths and Weaknesses

As managers conduct an external analysis, they should also assess the strengths and weaknesses of major functional areas inside their organization. This internal resource analysis has several components:

- *Financial analysis*—Examines financial strengths and weaknesses through financial statements such as a balance sheet and an income statement and compares trends to historical and industry figures.

- *Human resources assessment*—Examines strengths and weaknesses of all levels of managers and employees and focuses on key human resources activities, including recruitment, selection, placement, training, labor (union) relationships, compensation, promotion, appraisal, quality of work life, and human resources planning.

- *Marketing audit*—Examines strengths and weaknesses of major marketing activities and identifies markets, key market segments, and the organization's competitive position (market share) within key markets.

- *Operations analysis*—Examines the strengths and weaknesses of the organization's manufacturing, production, or service delivery activities.

- *Other internal resource analyses*—Examine, as appropriate, the strengths and weaknesses of other organizational activities, such as research and development (product and process), management information systems, engineering, and purchasing.

resources inputs to a system that can enhance performance

Is your firm strong enough financially to invest in new projects, and can your existing staff carry out the plan? Is your firm's image compatible with its strategy, or will it have to persuade key stakeholders that a change in direction makes sense? Internal analysis provides an inventory of the organization's existing functions, skills, and resources as well as its overall performance level. Many of your other business courses will prepare you to conduct internal analyses.

Resources and Core Capabilities Strategic planning has been strongly influenced in recent years by a focus on internal resources. Resources are inputs to production (recall systems theory) that can be accumulated over time to enhance the performance of a firm. Resources can take many forms, but they tend to fall into two broad categories:

1. *Tangible assets* such as real estate, production facilities, raw materials, and so on.

2. *Intangible assets* such as company reputation, culture, technical knowledge, and patents, as well as accumulated learning and experience.

Anheuser-Busch InBev, for example, develops its strategic plan based on combinations of tangible assets (including factories and breweries) and intangible assets (brand recognition, patents and recipes, and national craft beer brands).[27]

Internal analysis provides a clearer understanding of how a company can compete through its resources. Resources provide competitive advantage only under certain circumstances:

- The resources are instrumental in creating customer *value,* increasing the benefits customers derive from a good or service relative to the costs they incur.[28] For example, Amazon's powerful search technology, ability to track customer preferences and offer personalized recommendations, and quick product delivery are valuable resources.

- The resources are *rare* and not equally available to all competitors. IBM's patented technologies represent rare resources. IBM received nearly 10,000 patents in 2018—the most granted to a single company.[29]

- The resources are *difficult to imitate.* SolarCity, a renewable energy company working to lower the cost of solar energy, has developed a strong, mission-driven corporate culture. With a reputation for hiring military veterans and college students who are dedicated to reversing climate change, SolarCity's employee commitment is hard to imitate and could give the company a competitive advantage in the renewable energy sector.[30]

- The resources are well *organized.* For example, IBM organized its staff and systems to efficiently produce a consolidated technology product for its corporate clients' hardware, software, and service in one package. IBM created a blockchain-based health care network, featuring notable providers Aetna and Cigna, to improve how they use data to serve customers.[31]

● SolarCity, a subsidiary of Tesla, Inc., is a renewable energy company with a purpose: to make a big difference in the fight against climate change. Patrick T. Fallon/Bloomberg/Getty Images

Resources that are valuable, rare, inimitable, and organized are a company's core capabilities. Simply stated, a **core capability** is something a company does especially well relative to its competitors. Jimmy John's core capability is fast sandwich production and delivery, and Apple is creating a core capability in creating user-friendly interfaces and appealing product designs. As in these examples, a core capability typically refers to a set of skills or expertise in some activity, rather than physical or financial assets.

IBM continues to expand its "Smarter Planet" initiative, which focuses on the company's core capabilities in business analytics, e-commerce, and cloud computing. "Smarter Planet" is a platform that creates an "intelligent, instrumented and interconnected world."[32] Whether it's working with doctors to train IBM Watson to create customized treatments to fight cancer cells or helping cities save money and run more efficiently through the Smarter Cities campaign, IBM stays ahead of the competition by creating value that is unique and difficult to imitate.[33]

Benchmarking As introduced earlier in the book, some companies use benchmarking, the process of assessing how well one company's basic functions and skills compare with those of another company or set of companies. The goal of benchmarking is to thoroughly understand the "best practices" of other firms and to undertake actions to achieve better performance and lower costs. Benchmarking programs have helped In-N-Out

Exhibit 5.6	Overall service quality of six fast-food restaurants		
Criteria	**1st Place**	**2nd Place**	**3rd Place**
Cleanliness	Subway	McDonald's	Wendy's
Service response time	McDonald's	Wendy's	Burger King
Employee courtesy	Subway	Arby's	McDonald's
Healthful food	Subway	Wendy's	Arby's
Taste of food	Subway	Wendy's	Arby's
Competitive price	McDonald's	Wendy's	Burger King
Proximity to customer	McDonald's	Wendy's	Subway

Burger, Walmart, Honda, and many other companies eliminate inefficiencies and improve competitiveness.

A recent benchmarking study compared the overall service quality of six popular fast-food restaurant chains in the United States.[34] Exhibit 5.6 shows how the restaurant rankings vary across different criteria.

Managers at McDonald's no doubt were pleased to learn their restaurant was ranked first in service response time, proximity to customer's home, and price, but they also learned that the chain ranked below some of its competitors in other important service dimensions. Customers liked Subway for its cleanliness, employee courtesy, and taste; however, the chain failed to make the top three for response time and price. As a result of such benchmarking, managers at Subway may have looked for ways to serve customers faster. The chains with no top-three finishes may have used this information to think hard about what and how to change. How are they doing now?

Strategic management aims not to match but to surpass competitors. In addition to benchmarking against leading organizations in other industries, companies engage in internal benchmarking, measuring internal operations and units against one another to spread the company's best practices throughout the organization and add to its competitive advantage.

British Retail Photography/Alamy Stock Photo

3.4 | Conduct a SWOT Analysis and Formulate Strategy

Once managers have analyzed the external environment and the organization's internal resources, they have the information needed for a **SWOT analysis**: an assessment of the organization's strengths, weaknesses, opportunities, and threats.

Strengths and weaknesses refer to internal resources. An organization's *strengths* might include skilled management, positive cash flow, and well-known and highly regarded brands. *Weaknesses* might be lack of spare production capacity and the absence of reliable suppliers.

Opportunities and threats arise in the macroenvironment and competitive environment. Examples of *opportunities* are a new technology that could make the supply chain more efficient and a market niche that is currently underserved. *Threats* might include the possibility that competitors will enter the underserved niche once it has been shown to be profitable.

SWOT analysis helps managers summarize the relevant, important facts from their external and internal analyses. Based on this summary, they can identify the primary and secondary strategic issues their organization faces. The managers then formulate a strategy that will build on the SWOT analysis to take advantage of available opportunities by capitalizing on the organization's strengths, neutralizing its weaknesses, and countering potential threats.

As an example, consider how SWOT analysis might be conducted at Sony (see Exhibit 5.7). The company's size—$67.9 billion in sales and over 128,000 employees worldwide (in 2017)—is an obvious strength. Also, the firm sells more than 2,000 diversified products, from headphones and printers to movies and televisions. Sony has a history of "hit products" such as the Walkman, Trinitron television, the *Spider-Man* movie franchise, Xperia smartphones and tablets, and VAIO personal computers.

And don't forget sales of the PlayStation 4 video console surpassed 108 million units in early 2020.[35] As for weaknesses, the company's separate divisions prefer to act independently and resist change that might hurt their profitability. Several recent leaders have tried unsuccessfully to transform the company into one that is more adaptive and aligned with consumer interests. Sony's organizational culture has traditionally placed more value on hardware than on content like songs and movies.

Beyond internal strengths and weaknesses, the firm's macroenvironment presents several opportunities. The Internet age ushered in consumer demand for connectivity. To tap this demand, Sony connected all of its devices with all of its content, including Sony's 81 million PlayStation users, via a new Sony entertainment network (called PlayStation Plus). This network allows a PlayStation user to download music or movies onto a Sony tablet or smartphone. Another opportunity is to continue to offer financial services like life and automobile insurance; surprisingly, this area has been Sony's most profitable business over the past several years.

Sony faces many threats from its macroenvironment, including low-priced televisions from competitors Samsung and Vizio. This is making it very difficult for Sony to compete profitably in the product category that it once dominated.

Unpredictable natural disasters, like the tsunami and earthquake that rocked eastern Japan and floods in Thailand, led to temporary closings of several of both Sony's and its suppliers' plants. These supply chain disruptions contributed to a net loss of $3.1 billion.

Exhibit 5.7 SWOT analysis at Sony

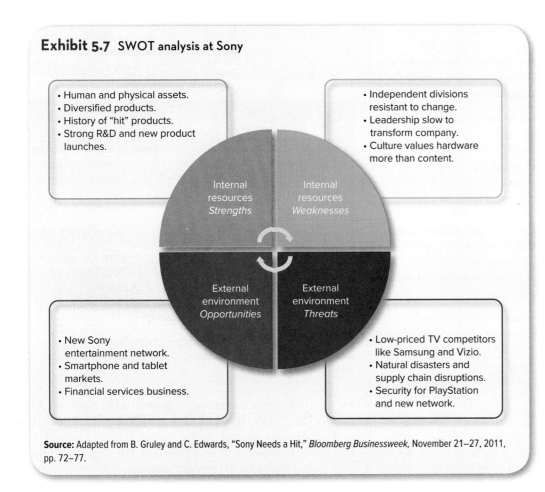

- Human and physical assets.
- Diversified products.
- History of "hit" products.
- Strong R&D and new product launches.

Internal resources Strengths

Internal resources Weaknesses

- Independent divisions resistant to change.
- Leadership slow to transform company.
- Culture values hardware more than content.

External environment Opportunities

External environment Threats

- New Sony entertainment network.
- Smartphone and tablet markets.
- Financial services business.

- Low-priced TV competitors like Samsung and Vizio.
- Natural disasters and supply chain disruptions.
- Security for PlayStation and new network.

Source: Adapted from B. Gruley and C. Edwards, "Sony Needs a Hit," *Bloomberg Businessweek,* November 21–27, 2011, pp. 72–77.

Other unforeseen factors that hurt the company's profitability were the burning of a CD and DVD warehouse in London by a rioting mob and a hacker attack that shut down the PlayStation network.[36]

Corporate Strategy A corporate strategy identifies the set of businesses, markets, or industries in which the organization competes and the distribution of resources among those businesses. The four basic alternatives for a corporate strategy range from very specialized to highly diverse:

1. Concentration—focusing on a single business competing in a single industry. Companies pursue concentration strategies to gain entry into a growing industry or when the company has a narrow range of competencies. Five Guys pursues a concentration strategy by focusing on making only the best fresh-cut fries and never-frozen burgers on house-baked buns, resulting in explosive growth since 1986.[37]

2. Vertical integration—expanding the organization's domain into supply channels or to distributors to eliminate uncertainties and reduce costs associated with suppliers or distributors. Henry Ford fully integrated his company from the ore mines needed to make steel all the way to the showrooms where his cars were sold.

3. Related diversification—moving into new businesses related to the company's original core business. Since its beginnings as a cartoon studio in the 1920s, Disney expanded into a global firm known for its broadcast and cable television networks, movies and movie studios, books, TV shows, retail stores, theme parks, music, cruise lines, and more.[38] Each of these businesses within the entertainment industry is related in terms of the goods and services it provides and the customers it attracts. Related diversification applies strengths in one business to gain advantage in another. Success requires adequate management and other resources for operating more than one business.

4. Unrelated diversification—expansion into unrelated businesses, typically to minimize risks due to market fluctuations in one industry. Procter & Gamble diversified from its original base in soap and candles to a wide range of home goods from diapers and laundry detergents to paper towels and dental care.[39]

The diversified businesses of an organization comprise its business *portfolio*. A popular technique for analyzing a corporation's strategy for managing its portfolio is the BCG matrix, developed by the Boston Consulting Group and shown in Exhibit 5.8.

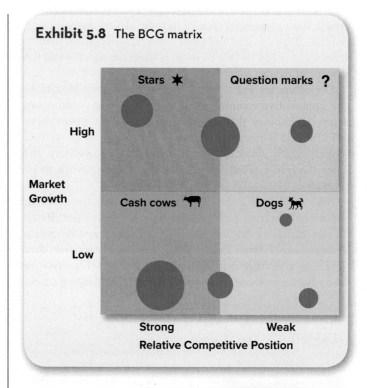

Exhibit 5.8 The BCG matrix

● Sony Corporation's diversified business includes consumer and professional electronics, gaming, entertainment, and financial services. charnsitr/Shutterstock

Each business in the corporation is plotted on the matrix on the basis of the growth rate of its market and the relative strength of its competitive position in that market (market share). The business is represented by a circle whose size depends on the business's contribution to corporate revenues.

The four categories of businesses in the BCG matrix are:

- *Question marks*—These high-growth, weak-competitive-position businesses require substantial investment to improve their position, or else they should be divested.

- *Stars*—Businesses with high growth and a strong competitive position require heavy investment, but their strong position lets them generate the needed revenues.

- *Cash cows*—These low-growth businesses with a strong competitive position generate revenues in excess of their investment needs, so they fund other businesses.

- *Dogs*—These low-growth, weak-competitive-position businesses should be divested after their remaining revenues are realized.

The BCG matrix alone is not a substitute for management judgment, creativity, insight, or leadership. But along with other techniques, it can help managers evaluate their strategy alternatives.[40] This type of thinking transformed the ubiquitous UK company, Boots. After record-low profits, Boots realized its star business faced the possibility of becoming a question mark or worse. The company scheduled 200 store closures, redesigned its interior layout (specifically the beauty section), and introduced new brands like Rihanna's Fenty Beauty.[41]

> **LO4 Analyze how companies can achieve competitive advantage through business strategy.**

4 | BUSINESS STRATEGY

After the top management team and board make the corporate strategic decisions, executives must determine how to compete in each business area. Business strategy defines the major actions by which an organization builds and strengthens its competitive position in the marketplace. A competitive advantage typically results from business strategies based on either keeping costs low or offering products that are unique and highly valued.[42]

Businesses using a low-cost strategy try to be efficient and offer a standard, no-frills product. In the furniture industry, IKEA offers a large selection of items for the home at affordable prices. Lower prices haven't kept this behemoth furniture company from becoming one of the largest in the world. Founded in 1943, the Swedish retailer currently operates 313 stores in 38 countries with sales of approximately $1 billion.[43]

Companies that succeed with a low-cost strategy often are large and take advantage of economies of scale—reductions in unit cost from large purchases or manufacturing runs—in production or distribution. Their scale may allow them to buy and sell goods and services at a lower price, which leads to higher market share, volume, and ultimately profits. To succeed, an organization using this strategy generally must be the cost leader in its industry or market segment. However, even a cost leader must offer a product that is acceptable to customers.

With a differentiation strategy, a company tries to be unique in its industry or market segment along dimensions that customers value. This unique or differentiated position within the industry often is based on high product quality, excellent marketing and distribution, or superior service. Tieks' commitment to providing customers with an outstanding experience is an excellent example of a differentiation strategy. While other online retailers often skimp on this part of their businesses, Tieks makes handwritten thank-you cards, colorful high-quality packaging, and personalized service important parts of its strategy.[44]

Innovation is another ingredient of many differentiation strategies. In the market for dairy alternatives, Swedish company Oatly used exclusivity to drive demand for its unique product. Its oat milk is high in fiber and able to foam.[45] Baristas, who liked the product's flavor and foam-ability, spread the word about its quality.[46] Oatly expanded from 1,500 to 5,000 grocery stores in 2019 and was expected to double its revenue.[47]

New technology can support either of these strategies. It can give the business a cost advantage through pioneering lower-cost product designs and low-cost ways to operate, or it can support differentiation with unique goods or services that increase buyer value and thus command premium prices.

Industry leaders such as Xerox, 3M, Google (part of Alphabet), Sony, and Apple built and now maintain their competitive positions through early development and application of new technologies. As illustrated in Exhibit 5.9, however, technology leadership also imposes costs and risks:[48]

business strategy
the major actions by which an organization competes in a particular industry or market

low-cost strategy
a strategy an organization uses to build competitive advantage by being efficient and offering a standard, no-frills product

differentiation strategy
a strategy an organization uses to build competitive advantage by being unique in its industry or market segment along one or more dimensions

Exhibit 5.9	Advantages and disadvantages of industry leadership

Advantages	Disadvantages
First-mover advantage	Greater risks
Little or no competition	Cost of technology development
Greater efficiency	Cost of market development
Higher profit margins	Cost of customer education
Sustainability advantage	Infrastructure costs
Reputation for innovation	Cost of learning and eliminating defects
Establishment of entry barriers	Possible cannibalization of existing products
Occupation of best market niches	
Opportunities to learn	

Sustaining for Tomorrow

The Green Cities Movement

More than half the people on Earth today live in cities, and by 2050 that number could increase to nearly 70 percent. This means urban areas have a tremendous impact on the environment. City dwellers' use of energy, treatment of waste and sewage, attitude toward plastics and harmful emissions, and use of water can all help bring urban environments into a more sustainable future—or leave vulnerable areas to suffer from the effects of climate change.

Earth Day Network is one organization calling for cities to become green and sustainable, in this case to be 100 percent renewable within a generation. Earth Day Network hopes to promote the use of self-driving electric cars with no carbon dioxide emissions; buildings that adapt heating, cooling, and ventilation to real-time needs; and sustainable and efficient public transportation systems. The group is reaching out to city governments around the world and asking them to adopt its renewable goals.

For example, the center of Curitiba, Brazil, is a car-free zone almost a mile across, outside of which a high-tech, low-pollution bus system serves three-quarters of the city's people every day. Sixteen parks and 14 forests within the city provide about 600 square feet of green space per person, and 1.5 million new trees line the city's streets. And in Reykjavik, Iceland, buses are powered by hydrogen, a clean energy source, while heat and electricity come from renewable geothermal and hydropower sources.

After the U.S. withdrawal from the 2015 Paris Climate Accord, more than 110 U.S. cities, making what they called "America's Pledge," committed to meeting the goals of the global accord. In 2019, this coalition announced an even more ambitious set of goals, called "Accelerating America's Pledge." The pledge calls for increased efforts to reduce cities' carbon footprints and to get closer to being carbon neutral. The pledge has three guiding principles: focus on clean electricity and energy supplies; decarbonize buildings, transportation, and industry; and enhance ecosystems.

The "green cities" movement encompasses thousands of urban areas around the world and focuses on reducing waste, recycling more, cutting emissions, increasing housing density while expanding open space, and encouraging the development of sustainable local businesses.

Jon Bilous/Shutterstock

Discussion Questions

- Reykjavik hopes to become the world's first carbon-neutral urban area by 2040. What are the strategic risks and benefits for a city trying to be a first mover in renewable energy?

- How hopeful are you that Accelerating America's Pledge will yield results? If you were managing this plan in a city, which of the three principles would you focus on most? Why?

Sources: "68% of the World Population Projected to Live in Urban Areas by 2050, Says UN," United Nations, May 16, 2018, https://www.un.org/development/desa/en/news/population/2018-revision-of-world-urbanization-prospects.html; Earth Day website, "Green Cities and Local Governments," https://www.earthday.org/campaign/green-cities/, accessed March 12, 2020; "Green City: Bus System and Urban Planning in Curitiba," Green City Times, www.greencitytimes.com/Sustainable-Cities/curtiba.html; M. D. Regan, "U.S. Cities, States Pledge Support for Climate Accord," *PBS NewsHour,* November 11, 2017, www.pbs.org/newshour/nation/u-s-cities-states-pledge-support-for-climate-accord; S. Boztas, "Reykjavik: The Geothermal City That Aims to Go Carbon Neutral," *The Guardian,* October 3, 2016, www.theguardian.com/sustainable-business/2016/oct/03/reykjavik-geothermal-city-carbon-neutral-climate; "Accelerating America's Pledge 2019, Executive Summary," retrieved from https://www.bbhub.io/dotorg/sites/28/2019/12/Accelerating-Americas-Pledge-Executive-Summary-.pdf.

For example, being a "first mover"—first to market with a new technology—may allow a company to charge a premium price because it faces no competition. Higher prices and greater profits can defray the costs of developing new technologies. This one-time advantage of being the technology leader can be turned into a sustainable advantage if competitors cannot duplicate the technology and the organization can keep building on the lead quickly enough to outpace competitors. Patents and scientific expertise can keep an organization in the lead for years.

However, being the first to develop or adopt a new technology does not always lead to immediate advantage and high profits. Technology leadership imposes high costs and risks that followers do not have to bear.

Interestingly, technology followership can support both low-cost and differentiation strategies. If the follower learns from the leader's experience, it can avoid the costs and risks of technology leadership, thereby establishing a low-cost position. Generic drug makers use this strategy.

Followership can also support differentiation. By learning from the leader, the follower can adapt the products or delivery systems to fit buyers' needs more closely. Microsoft is famous for having built a successful company on this type of followership. The company purchased its original operating system, MS-DOS, for $50,000 from Seattle Computer Works to compete with the industry's first desktop operating system, CP/M, sold by Digital Research. Marketing strength, combined with incremental product innovations, helped Microsoft take the lead in software categories (Excel's spreadsheet program beat Lotus 1-2-3, which had taken share from the first mover, VisiCalc).[49] Microsoft launched many products, including Cortana (the Windows 10 personal assistant), the Xbox video game system, and the Bing search engine, after other technology leaders paved the way.

Whatever strategy managers adopt, *the most effective strategy is one that competitors are unwilling or unable to imitate.* If the organization's strategic plan is one that can easily be adopted by industry competitors, it will not be sufficiently distinctive or, in the long run, contribute significantly to the organization's competitiveness. In some industries, technology advances so fast that the first company to provide a new product is quickly challenged by later entrants offering new, superior products.[50]

Functional Strategy The final step in strategy formulation is to establish the major functional strategies. Functional strategies are implemented by each functional area of the organization to support the business strategy. Major functional areas include production, human resources, marketing, research and development, finance, and distribution.

At Wells Fargo, the strategy to grow through cross-selling required functional strategies for advertising, training employees to cross-sell, and developing systems for sharing information across department boundaries.[51] This strategy helped boost the bank's sales revenue. However, the strong sales culture at the bank may have become too strong. Governmental regulators in California concluded that Wells Fargo pushed its employees too hard to meet sales quotas without preventing questionable behavior.[52] The bank paid $575 million as part of a settlement agreement for creating fake customer accounts and violating other consumer protection laws.[53]

Functional managers develop strategies with input of and approval from the executives responsible for business strategy. Senior strategic decision makers review the functional strategies to ensure that each function is operating consistently with the organization's business strategies. For example, automated production techniques—even if they save money—would not be appropriate for a piano company like Steinway, whose products are strategically positioned (and priced) as high-quality and handcrafted.

At companies that compete based on product innovation, research and development strategies are especially critical. In the late 1970s, companies spent about as much on R&D as they did on advertising; today companies spend 10 times more on R&D.[54] This trend shows companies shifting focus from marketing toward innovation, engineering, and technology. Companies that spend heavily on R&D include Amazon, Alphabet, and Volkswagen.[55]

functional strategies strategies implemented by each functional area of the organization to support the organization's business strategy

LO5 Identify the keys to effective strategy implementation.

5 | IMPLEMENT THE STRATEGY

As with any plan, simply formulating a good strategy is not enough. Strategic managers also must ensure that the new strategies are implemented effectively and efficiently. The best corporations and strategy consultants realize that clever techniques and a good plan do not guarantee success.

The best, therefore, adopt a comprehensive view of implementation. The organizational structure, technology, human resources, employee reward systems, information systems, organizational culture, and leadership style must all support the strategy. Just as strategy must match the external environment, so must it also fit the multiple factors through which it is implemented.

Employees at all levels implement strategies. Senior executives still oversee the implementation process, but they place greater responsibility and authority in the hands of others.

In general, strategy implementation involves four related steps:

1. *Define strategic tasks.* Articulate in simple language what a business must do to create or sustain competitive advantage. Help employees understand how they contribute to the strategy.

"Competitive strategy is about being different. It means deliberately choosing a different set of activities to deliver a unique mix of value."

—Michael Porter

2. *Assess organization capabilities.* Evaluate the organization's ability to implement the strategic tasks. Task forces can interview employees and managers to identify issues that help or hinder implementation and then summarize the results for top management.

3. *Develop an implementation agenda.* Management decides how it will change its own activities and procedures, deal with critical interdependencies, assign people to key roles, and provide structures, measures, training, information, and rewards to support the needed behaviors.

4. *Create an implementation plan.* The top management team, employee task force, and others develop the implementation plan. The top management team monitors progress. The task force provides feedback about how people are responding to the changes.

This process, though straightforward, does not always go smoothly.[56] To prevent problems, top managers need to be actively involved, developing a statement of strategy and priorities that employees will accept. Communication is essential, including information sharing by top management with all levels of the organization. Managers should ensure that various groups are coordinating their work rather than working at cross-purposes. Furthermore, lower-level managers need coaching and training to help them lead their groups effectively. People who don't adapt to the needed changes may have to be replaced. Paying close attention to implementation helps executives, managers, and employees ensure that strategic plans have a fighting chance to achieve their potential.[57]

● The GE Honda HF120 engine program was launched over 10 years ago and was selected to power Honda Aircraft Company's advanced light jet, the HondaJet.
Copyright, 2016 Honda Motor Co., Ltd. and its subsidiaries and affiliates. All Rights Reserved.
YOSHIKAZU TSUNO/AFP/Getty Images

The final component of the strategic management process is strategic control. A strategic control system supports managers in evaluating progress with strategy and, when discrepancies exist, taking corrective action. The system must encourage efficient operations that are consistent with the plan while allowing flexibility to adapt to changing conditions. As with all control systems, managers must develop performance indicators, an information system, and specific mechanisms to monitor progress. More than 20 years in development, the HondaJet had to pass a series of performance milestones before it could be certified as ready for commercial use.[58]

Most strategic control systems include a budget to monitor and control major financial expenditures. As a first-time manager, you will most likely work with your work unit's budget—a key aspect of your organization's strategic plan. Your executive team may give you budget assumptions and targets for your area, reflecting your part in the overall plan, and ask you to revise your budget after reviewing all units' budgets.

A control system's dual responsibilities—efficiency and flexibility—often seem contradictory. The budget usually establishes spending limits, but changing conditions or the need for innovation may require changing financial commitments. To solve this dilemma, some companies create two budgets: strategic and operational. For example, at Texas Instruments, the strategic budget creates and maintains long-term effectiveness and the operational budget promotes short-term efficiency. You will learn more about control generally, and budgets in particular, in Chapter 14.

LO6 Explain how to make effective decisions as a manager.

6 | MANAGERIAL DECISION MAKING

Managers constantly face problems and opportunities, ranging from simple and routine decisions to problems requiring months of analysis. However, managers often ignore problems because they are unsure how much trouble will be involved in solving the problems, they are concerned about the consequences if they fail, and many management problems are so much more complex than routine tasks.[59] For these reasons, managers may lack the insight, courage, or will to act.

Why is decision making so challenging? Most managerial decisions lack structure and entail risk, uncertainty, and conflict.

Lack of structure is typical of managerial decisions.[60] Usually there is no automatic procedure to follow. Problems are novel and unstructured, leaving the decision maker uncertain about how to proceed. In other words, a manager's decisions most often have the characteristics of nonprogrammed decisions (see Exhibit 5.10).[61]

Exhibit 5.10 — Two types of decisions

Programmed	Nonprogrammed
Problem is frequent, repetitive, and routine, with much certainty regarding cause-and-effect relationships.	Problem is novel and unstructured, with much uncertainty regarding cause-and-effect relationships.
Decision procedure depends on policies, rules, and definite procedures.	Decision procedure needs creativity, intuition, tolerance for ambiguity, and creative problem solving.
Examples: periodic reorders of inventory; procedure for admitting patients.	Examples: diversification into new products and markets; purchase of experimental equipment; reorganization of departments.

With nonprogrammed decisions, *risk and uncertainty* are the rule. If you have all the information you need, and can predict precisely the consequences of your actions, you are operating under a condition of certainty.[62] But perfect certainty is rare. More often managers face uncertainty, meaning they have insufficient information to know the consequences of different actions. Decision makers may have strong opinions—they may feel sure of themselves—but they are still operating under uncertainty if they lack pertinent information and cannot estimate accurately the likelihood of different results.

When you can estimate the likelihood of various consequences but still do not know with certainty what will happen, you are facing risk.

Risk exists when the probability of an action succeeding is less than 100 percent and losses may occur. If the decision is the wrong one, you may lose money, time, reputation, or other important assets. Risk as a quality of managerial decision making differs from *taking* a risk. Although it sometimes seems as

● Created by Amazon, Echo smart speakers connect via Wi-Fi with Alexa, the company's voice-controlled intelligent personal assistant.
James W Copeland/Shutterstock

though risk takers are admired and that entrepreneurs and investors thrive on taking risks, good decision makers prefer to *manage* risk. Knowing that their decisions entail risk, they anticipate the risk, minimize it, and try to control it.

For example, Amazon took a risk when it created the Echo speaker. At the time it came out, there was little demand for a voice-activated Internet-connected speaker[63] and Amazon's recently launched smartphone, the Fire Phone, was bombing.[64] The speaker was met with some initial criticism but proved to be a quick success. In the past five years, over 100 million Echo speakers with Alexa voice activation have been sold.[65] Was Amazon's decision to create Echo made under conditions of uncertainty or risk or both?

Faced with these challenges, how can you make good decisions? The ideal decision-making process includes these phases:

1. Identify and diagnose the problem.

2. Generate alternative solutions.

3. Evaluate alternatives.

4. Make the choice.

5. Implement the decision.

6. Evaluate the decision.

You will notice the similarity to the planning process you've already learned about. Here, we will be making new and different points with this broad decision-making framework.

6.1 | Identifying and Diagnosing the Problem

The decision-making process begins with recognition that a problem (or opportunity) exists and must be solved (or should be pursued). Typically a manager realizes some discrepancy between the current state (the way things are) and a desired state (the way things ought to be). To detect such discrepancies, managers compare current performance against (1) *past* performance, (2) the *current* performance of other organizations or units, or (3) *future* expected performance as determined by plans and forecasts.[66] Larry Cohen, who founded Accurate Perforating with his father, knew his company was having difficulty making a profit because costs at the metal company were rising while the prices customers were willing to pay remained unchanged. However, when the company's bank demanded immediate payment of its $1.5 million loan, Cohen realized the problem had to be solved or the company would have to sell off all its assets and close.[67] You will learn more about how Cohen solved this problem as we look at the subsequent stages of the decision process.

certainty the state that exists when decision makers have accurate and comprehensive information

uncertainty the state that exists when decision makers have insufficient information

risk the state that exists when the probability of success is less than 100 percent and losses may occur

The "problem" may actually be an opportunity that needs to be exploited—a gap between what the organization is doing now and what it can do to create a more positive future. In that case, decisions involve choosing how to seize the opportunity. To recognize important opportunities as a manager, you will need to understand your company's macro and competitive environments (described in Chapter 3), including the opportunities offered by technological developments. According to a study by McKinsey, the Internet of Things will save businesses about $11 trillion annually, while other studies suggest that it will boost corporate profits up to 22 percent by 2022.[68]

Recognizing that a problem or opportunity exists is only the beginning of this stage. The decision maker also must want to do something about it and must believe that the resources and abilities necessary for solving the problem exist.[69] Then the decision maker must dig in deeper and attempt to *diagnose* the true cause of the situation. Asking why, of yourself and others, is essential. Unfortunately, in the earlier example of Accurate Perforating, Larry Cohen did not ask why profits were declining; he simply assumed that the company's costs were too high.[70] A more thorough approach would include questions such as these:[71]

- Is there a difference between what is actually happening and what should be happening?

- How can you describe the deviation, as specifically as possible?

- What is/are the cause(s) of the deviation?

- What specific goals should be met?

- Which of these goals are absolutely critical to the success of the decision?

6.2 | Generating Alternative Solutions

The second stage of decision making links problem diagnosis to the development of alternative courses of action aimed at solving the problem. Managers generate at least some alternative solutions based on past experiences.[72]

Solutions range from ready-made to custom-made.[73] Decision makers who search for **ready-made solutions** use ideas they have tried before or follow the advice of others who have faced similar problems. **Custom-made solutions**, by contrast, must be designed for specific problems. This technique often combines ideas into new, creative solutions. Potentially, custom-made solutions can be devised for any challenge.

Often, many more alternatives are available than managers realize. For example, what would you do if one of your competitors reduced prices? An obvious choice would be to reduce your own prices, but the only sure outcome of a price cut is lower profits. Fortunately, cutting prices is not the only alternative. If one of your competitors cuts prices, you should generate multiple options and thoroughly forecast the consequences of each option. Options include emphasizing consumer risks to low-priced products, building awareness of your products' features and overall quality, and communicating your cost advantage to your competitors so they realize that they can't win a price war. If you do decide to cut your price as a last resort, do it fast—if you do it slowly, your competitors will gain sales in the meantime, which may embolden them to employ the same tactic again in the future.[74]

The example of Accurate Perforating illustrates the importance of looking for every alternative. The company had become successful by purchasing metal from steel mills, punching many holes in it to make screenlike sheets, and selling this material in bulk to distributors, who sold it to metal workshops, which used it to make custom products. Cohen admits, "We wound up in a very competitive situation where the only thing we were selling was price." Management cut costs wherever possible, avoiding investment in new machinery or processes. The result was an out-of-date factory managed by people accustomed to resisting change. Only after the bank called in its loan did Cohen begin to see alternatives. The bank offered one painful idea: Liquidate the company. It also suggested a management consultant, who advised renegotiating payment schedules with the company's suppliers. Cohen also received advice from managers of a company Accurate had purchased a year before. That company, Semrow Perforated & Expanded Metals, sold more sophisticated products directly to manufacturers, and Semrow's managers urged Cohen to invest more in finished metal products such as theirs.[75]

6.3 | Evaluating Alternatives

The third stage of decision making involves determining the value or adequacy of the alternatives that were generated. In other words, which solution will be the best?

Too often, managers evaluate options with insufficient thought or logic. At Accurate Perforating, Cohen made changes to cut costs but dismissed the idea to invest in marketing finished metal products, even though these product lines were more profitable. Accurate's general manager, Aaron Kamins (also Cohen's nephew), counseled that money spent on finished metal products would be a distraction from Accurate's core business. That reasoning persuaded Cohen, even though it meant focusing on unprofitable product lines.[76]

Obviously, managers should evaluate their alternatives more carefully. The process requires trying to predict the consequences that will occur if the various options are put into effect. Managers should consider several types of consequences, including quantitative measures of success such as lower costs, higher sales, lower employee turnover, and higher profits.

Also, the decisions made at all levels of the organization should contribute to, and not interfere with, achieving the company's overall strategies. Business professors Joseph Bower and Clark Gilbert say that when investing in new projects, managers focus on whether alternatives generate the most sales or savings without asking the more basic question: In light of

Take Charge of Your Career

Strategically manage your job search

The focus in this chapter is on strategic planning and decision making once you're *in* a career. But these skills can also be vital to getting the career you want in the first place. Here are some ways you can manage your job search to remove variables, inefficiencies, and stress to help you take charge of your career.

First and foremost, it is important to stay focused on your values, interests, and core career goals. The stress of finding a job can sometimes lead people to stray from those important considerations. Once you know what you want, you can organize around achieving your vision. Having a plan is key.

Many tools are available that can help you organize your search. Create a spreadsheet with relevant data, including company name, points of contact, dates you applied, follow-ups from interviews, and so on. Rather than continually checking for openings with employers you're interested in, set up job alerts for those companies on Twitter. This lets recruiters and companies do the work for you. There are also job search management sites, such as JibberJobber, that help you manage and put together a framework for your search.

Equally vital is networking, which is always important, whether you are in a job or trying to find one. One common mistake job seekers make is trying to find new contacts while overlooking the contacts they already have. To keep yourself top of mind for valuable contacts in your network, you can use tools like Contactually, a service that reminds you to reach out to people who can help in your career search. It's also important to update your profile on LinkedIn and any job networking sites you belong to.

Finally, stay positive if—actually, when—things don't go the way you wanted. A job search usually takes longer than expected, so it's important to be patient and proactive, and to stay true to who you are and what you want. If you need to take a job that's not ideal, know that it doesn't need to lock you in forever. Any position you take can lead to better opportunities as well as help you learn more about yourself.

Sources: C. Burns, "How to Organize Your Job Search," Glassdoor, January 4, 2019, https://www.glassdoor.com/blog/organizing-your-job-search/; A. Doyle, "10 Easy Ways to Organize Your Job Search," The Balance, March 3, 2020, https://www.thebalancecareers.com/organize-your-job-search-2060710; A. Runyan, "10 Job Hunting Tools, Tips, and Tricks That Will Turn Your Search Around," The Muse, accessed from https://www.themuse.com/advice/10-job-search-tricks-that-will-change-everything-youve-been-doing, March 12, 2020; M. Buj, "14 Quick Tips for Finding a New Job," LiveCareer, accessed from https://www.livecareer.com/resources/jobs/search/14-job-hunting-tips, March 12, 2020.

our strategy, is this investment an idea we should support at all?[77] When the 2008–2010 downturn in the U.S. economy required cutbacks, organizations as diverse as the University of California system, the State of North Carolina, American Airlines, and United Parcel Service evaluated the alternatives of layoffs (permanent job cuts) versus furloughs (requiring employees to take some unpaid time off until demand picks up again). The number of furloughed employees in the United States reached 6.5 million.[78] While layoffs save more money per employee because the company doesn't have to continue paying for benefits, furloughs maintain relationships with talented employees, who are more likely than laid-off workers to return when the company needs them again. Furloughs may seem kinder to employees, who can hope to return to work eventually, but workers may not be eligible for unemployment compensation during the furlough period.[79]

To evaluate alternatives, refer to your original goals, defined in the first stage. Which goals does each alternative meet and fail to meet? Which alternatives are most acceptable to you and to other important stakeholders? If several alternatives may solve

Did You KNOW ?

A scenario may use numbers that sound reasonable, but you should look at the data in different ways to check your assumptions. As Dean Kamen's company developed the Segway scooter, Kamen decided that each year Segway could capture 0.1 percent of the world's population. That percentage might sound conservative, but consider that 0.1 percent of 6 billion people is 6 million Segways a year! Kamen decided to build a factory that could produce 40,000 units a month; five years later, sales had reached fewer than 25,000.[81]

the problem, which can be implemented at the lowest cost or greatest profit? If no alternative achieves all your goals, perhaps you can combine two or more of the best ones. Before selecting any alternative, it may be helpful to ask:[80]

- Is our information about alternatives complete and current? If not, can we get more and better information?

- Does the alternative meet our primary objectives?

- What problems could we have if we implement the alternative?

6.4 | Making the Choice

Once you have considered the possible consequences of your options, it is time to make your decision. Some managers are more comfortable with the analysis stage but then have trouble making the actual decision. Especially with all the advanced technology that is available, quantitatively inclined people can easily tweak the assumptions behind every scenario in countless ways. But the temptation to do so can lead to "paralysis by analysis"—that is, indecisiveness caused by too much analysis rather than the kind of active, assertive decision making that is essential for seizing new opportunities or thwarting challenges. Managers can apply the following types of thinking or criteria as they make decisions:[82]

- **Maximizing** is achieving the best possible outcome, the one that realizes the greatest positive consequences and the fewest negative consequences. In other words, maximizing results in the greatest benefit at the lowest cost, with the largest expected total return.

  Maximizing requires searching thoroughly for a complete range of alternatives, carefully assessing each alternative, comparing one to another, and then choosing or creating the very best. As a manager, you won't always have time to maximize; many decisions require quick responses, not exhaustive analysis. The necessary analysis requires money as well as time. But for decisions with major consequences, such as determining the company's strategy, maximizing is worthwhile—even essential.

- **Satisficing** is choosing the first option that is minimally acceptable or adequate; the choice appears to meet a targeted goal or criterion. When you satisfice, you compare your choice against your goal, not against other options, and you end your search for alternatives at the first one that is okay. When the consequences are not huge, satisficing can actually be the ideal approach.

  But when managers satisfice, they may fail to consider important options. For example, if you need a new sales manager and your goal is to get this person hired within two weeks, you are satisficing if you hire the first adequate candidate you interview. By not interviewing more candidates, you will miss out on other, potentially better-qualified people.

- **Optimizing** means achieving the best possible balance among several goals. Perhaps, in purchasing equipment, you are interested in quality and durability as well as price. Instead of buying the cheapest piece of equipment that works, you buy the one with the best combination of attributes, even though some options may be better on the price criterion and others may offer better quality and durability. Likewise, for achieving business goals, one marketing strategy could maximize sales while a different strategy maximizes profit. An optimizing strategy achieves the best balance among multiple goals.

6.5 | Implementing the Decision

As you know, the chosen alternative must be implemented. Sometimes the people involved in making the choice put it into effect. At other times, they delegate the responsibility for implementation, as when a top management team changes a policy or operating procedure and has operational managers carry out the change.

Unfortunately, managers sometimes make decisions but don't take action. Implementing may fail to occur when talking a lot is mistaken for doing a lot; when people just assume that a decision will "happen"; when people forget that merely making a decision changes nothing; when meetings, plans, and reports are seen as "actions," even if they don't affect what people actually do; and if managers don't check to ensure that what was decided was actually done.[83]

Those who implement the decision should *understand* why it was made. They also must be *committed* to its successful implementation. These needs can be met by involving those people in the early stages of the decision process. At Finland-based game developer Supercell, employees are organized into "cells" (teams) and allowed to make decisions and give input into what's being produced.[84] Once management gives the go-ahead, the team runs it and is held accountable for its successful completion. They can stop working on a game if the team concludes it won't succeed. Supercell believes the best teams make the best games.[85]

Managers should plan implementation carefully by taking several steps:[86]

1. Determine how things will look when the decision is fully operational.

2. Chronologically order, perhaps with a flow diagram, the steps necessary to achieve a fully operational decision.

3. List the resources and activities required to implement each step.

4. Estimate the time needed for each step.

5. Assign responsibility for each step to specific individuals.

Decision makers should presume that implementation will *not* go smoothly. It is very useful to take a little extra time to *identify potential problems* and *identify potential opportunities* associated with implementation. Then you can take actions to prevent problems and also be ready to seize unexpected opportunities.

Many of the chapters in this book address implementation issues: how to allocate resources, organize for results, lead and motivate people, manage change, and so on. View the chapters from this perspective, and learn as much as you can about how to implement properly.

6.6 | Evaluating the Decision

The final stage in the decision-making process is evaluating the decision. It involves collecting information on how well the decision is working. If you set quantifiable goals—a 20 percent increase in sales, a 95 percent reduction in accidents, 100 percent on-time deliveries—before implementation of the solution, you can gather objective data for accurately determining the decision's success or failure.

Decision evaluation is useful whether the conclusion is positive or negative. Feedback that suggests the decision is working implies that the decision should be continued and perhaps applied elsewhere in the organization. Negative feedback means one of two things:

1. Implementation will require more time, resources, effort, or thought.

2. The decision was not a good one.

If the decision was inadequate, it's back to the drawing board. Then the process cycles back to the first stage: definition of the problem. The decision-making process begins anew, preferably with more information, new suggestions, and an approach that attempts to eliminate the mistakes made the first time around.

This is the stage where Accurate Perforating finally began to see hope. When cost-cutting efforts could not keep the company ahead of the competition or in favor with the bank, Larry Cohen turned the problem over to his general manager, Aaron Kamins. He gave Kamins 90 days to show that he could keep the business from going under. Kamins hired a consultant to help him identify more alternatives and make more professional decisions about investment and marketing. This stage of the implementation showed Kamins that the company needed better-educated management, and he began taking courses in an executive education program. With what he learned in school and from his consultant, Kamins realized that the advice he had received from the managers at the Semrow subsidiary—to invest in producing finished metal products—was wiser than he had realized. He arranged new financing to purchase modern equipment, hired salespeople, developed a website, and finally began to see profits from his improved decision making.[87]

> **LO7 Describe some personal obstacles to rational decision making.**

7 | HUMAN NATURE ERECTS BARRIERS TO GOOD DECISIONS

Full and careful execution of the decision-making process is the exception rather than the rule. But when managers use such rational processes, better decisions result.[88] Managers who make sure they engage in these processes are more effective.

In his book *Thinking, Fast and Slow*, Nobel Prize–winning economist Daniel Kahneman decribes how people use two very different modes of thought.[89] The first, known as System 1, is fast, automatic, and emotional in nature. The second, System 2, is slow, deliberate, and logical. Kahneman argues that decision making is often driven by the intuitive, efficiency-based System 1 with little input from System 2.[90] This mental shortcut in decision making helps explain why managers and employees sometimes take actions and say things without thinking carefully beforehand.

Why don't people automatically invoke rational processes? It is easy to neglect or improperly execute these processes, and decisions are influenced by subjective psychological biases, time pressures, and social realities.

7.1 | Psychological Biases

Decision makers are far from objective in the way they gather, evaluate, and apply information in making their choices. People have biases that interfere with objective rationality. Here are just a few of the many documented subjective biases:[91]

- **Illusion of control**: a belief that you can influence events even when you have no control over what will happen. Such overconfidence can lead to failure because you ignore risks and fail to evaluate the odds of success objectively. You might believe you can do no wrong, or you might hold a general optimism about the future and believe you are immune to risk and failure.[92]

  Managers also may overrate the value of their experience. They may believe that a previous project met its goals because of their decisions, so they can succeed by doing everything the same way on the next project. Managers can correct for this by developing a realistic picture of their strengths and weaknesses and seeking advisers who can point out consequences they may not have considered.

- **Framing effects**: phrasing or presenting problems or decision alternatives in a way that lets subjective influences override objective facts. In one example, managers indicated a desire to invest more money in a course of action that was reported to have a 70 percent chance of profit than in one said to have a 30 percent chance of loss.[93] The choices had equivalent chances of success; the way the options were expressed determined the managers' choices.

  Managers also may frame a problem as similar to problems they have already handled, so they don't search for new alternatives. Reed Hastings offered to sell Netflix, his DVD mailing company, to Blockbuster in 2000 for $50 million.[94] Blockbuster's CEO at the time was John Antioco, who turned down the deal out of concern that Netflix served only a niche market.[95]

- **Discounting the future**: in evaluating alternatives, weighing short-term costs and benefits more heavily than longer-term

illusion of control people's belief that they can influence events, even when they have no control over what will happen

framing effects a decision bias influenced by the way in which a problem or decision alternative is phrased or presented

discounting the future a bias weighting short-term costs and benefits more heavily than longer-term costs and benefits

● Flint, Michigan endured a years-long water crisis due to high lead levels in its water supply. Brett Carlsen/Getty Images

costs and benefits. This bias applies to students who don't study, workers who take the afternoon off to play golf when they really need to work, and managers who hesitate to invest funds in research and development programs that may not pay off until far into the future. In all these cases, avoiding short-term costs or seeking short-term rewards yields problems in the long term. Discounting the future partly explains government budget deficits, environmental destruction, and decaying urban infrastructure.[96]

7.2 | Time Pressures

As you know, in today's rapidly changing business environment, the premium is on acting quickly and keeping pace. The most conscientiously made business decisions can become irrelevant and even disastrous if managers take too long to make them.

To make decisions quickly, many managers rely on simple rule-of-thumb techniques that have worked in the past and in so doing, reduce the amount of time they spend analyzing the decision.[97] These strategies may speed up decision making, but they reduce decision *quality.*

Can managers under time pressure make decisions that are timely and high quality? A study of decision-making processes in technology firms showed some important differences between fast-acting and slower firms.[98] The fast-acting firms realized significant competitive advantage without sacrificing the quality of their decisions. They used three important tactics:

1. Instead of relying on old data, long-range planning, and futuristic forecasts, they focus on *real-time information:*

current information obtained with little or no time delay. For example, they constantly monitor daily operating measures like work in process rather than periodically checking traditional accounting-based indicators such as profitability.

2. They *involve people more effectively and efficiently* in the decision-making process. They rely heavily on trusted experts, and this yields both good advice and the confidence to act quickly despite uncertainty.

3. They take a *realistic view of conflict:* they value differing opinions, but they know that if disagreements are not resolved, the top executive must make the final choice in the end. Slow-moving firms, in contrast, are stymied by conflict. Like the fast-moving firms, they seek consensus, but when disagreements persist, they fail to come to a decision.

7.3 | Social Realities

Many decisions are made by a group rather than by an individual manager. In slow-moving firms, interpersonal factors decrease decision-making effectiveness. Even the manager acting alone is accountable to the boss and to others and must consider the preferences and reactions of many people. Important managerial decisions are marked by conflict among interested parties. Therefore, many decisions are the result of intensive social interactions, bargaining, and politicking.

It won't surprise you that one social reality is that managers often make decisions in groups; this is where we now turn our attention.

8 | GROUP PROCESS AFFECTS DECISION QUALITY

Sometimes a manager convenes a group of people to make an important decision. Some advise that in today's complex business environment, significant problems should *always* be tackled by groups.[99] As a result, managers must understand how groups operate and how to use them to improve decision making.

8.1 | Groups Can Help

The basic philosophy behind using a group to make decisions is captured by the adage "Two heads are better than one." But is this statement really valid? Yes, it is—potentially. If enough time is available, groups usually make higher-quality decisions than most individuals acting alone. However, groups often are inferior to the *best* individual.[100]

How well the group performs depends on how effectively it capitalizes on the potential advantages and minimizes the potential problems. Using groups to make a decision offers at least five potential advantages:[101]

- More *information* is available when several people are making the decision. If one member doesn't have all the facts or needed expertise, another member might.

- A greater number of *perspectives* on the issues, or different *approaches* to solving the problem, are available. The problem may be new to one group member but familiar to another. Or the group may need to consider several viewpoints—financial, legal, marketing, human resources, and so on—to achieve an optimal solution.

- Group discussion provides *intellectual stimulation*. It can get people thinking and unleash their creativity to a far greater extent than would be possible with individual decision making.

- People who participate in a group discussion are more likely to *understand* why the decision was made. They will have heard the relevant arguments both for the chosen alternative and against the rejected alternatives.

- Group discussion typically leads to a higher level of *commitment* to the decision. Buying into the proposed solution translates into high motivation to ensure that it is executed well.

The first three potential advantages of using a group suggest that better-informed, higher-quality decisions result when managers involve people with different backgrounds, perspectives, and access to information. The last two advantages imply that decisions will be implemented more successfully when managers involve the people who will implement the decision as early in the deliberations as possible.

Some groups reach a high level of performance. Over time, effective groups like surgical teams and flight crews develop "transactive memory" in which members learn each other's strengths, weaknesses, and preferences.[102] This shared memory helps the group to work at an expert level with minimal communication.[103] In essence, the group thinks and acts like a unit.

8.2 | Groups Can Hurt

Things *can* go wrong when groups make decisions. Most potential problems concern the processes through which group members interact with one another:[104]

- Sometimes, one group member *dominates* the discussion. When this occurs—as when a strong leader makes his or her preferences clear—the result is the same as it would have been if the dominant individual had made the decision alone. However, the dominant person does not necessarily have the most valid opinions, and even if that person leads the group

to a good decision, the process may have wasted everyone else's time.

- *Satisficing* is more likely with groups. Most people don't like meetings and will do what they can to end them. This may include criticizing members who want to continue exploring new and better alternatives. The result is a satisficing, not an optimizing or maximizing, decision.

- *Pressure to avoid disagreement* can lead to a phenomenon called *groupthink*. **Groupthink** occurs when people choose not to disagree or raise objections because they don't want to break up a positive team spirit. Some groups want to think as one, tolerate no dissension, and strive to remain cordial. Such groups are overconfident, complacent, and perhaps too willing to take risks. Pressure to go along with the group's preferred solution stifles creativity and other behaviors characteristic of vigilant decision making.

- *Goal displacement* often occurs in groups. Group members' goal should be to come up with the best possible solution. With **goal displacement**, new goals emerge to replace the original

groupthink a phenomenon that occurs in decision making when group members avoid disagreement as they strive for consensus

goal displacement a condition that occurs when a decision-making group loses sight of its original goal and a new, less important goal emerges

● Groups spur creative thinking, effective problem solving, and goal commitment. However, not all groups perform to their full potential.
Radius Images/Alamy Stock Photo

devil's advocate a person who has the job of criticizing ideas to ensure that their downsides are fully explored

dialectic a structured debate comparing two conflicting courses of action

brainstorming a process in which group members generate as many ideas about a problem as they can; criticism is withheld until all ideas have been proposed

design thinking a human-centered approach to innovation that integrates customer needs, the potential of technology, and the requirements for business success

ones. When group members have different opinions, attempts at rational persuasion might become a heated disagreement, and then winning the argument becomes the new goal.

8.3 | Groups Must Be Well Led

Effective managers pay close attention to the group process; they manage it carefully. Effectively leading group decision making requires:

1. *Appropriate leadership style:* The group leader must try to keep process-related problems to a minimum by ensuring that everyone has a chance to participate, not allowing the group to pressure individuals to conform, and keeping everyone focused on the decision-making objective.

2. *Constructive conflict:* Total and consistent agreement among group members can be destructive, leading to groupthink, uncreative solutions, and a waste of the knowledge and diverse viewpoints that individuals bring to the group. A certain amount of *constructive* conflict should exist.[105] Conflict should be task-related, involving differences in ideas and viewpoints, rather than personal.[106]

    Still, even task-related conflict can hurt performance;[107] disagreement is good only when managed properly. Managers can increase the likelihood of constructive conflict by assembling teams of different types of people, creating frequent interactions and active debates, and encouraging multiple alternatives from a variety of perspectives.[108] Methods for encouraging different views include assigning someone the role of devil's advocate—the job of criticizing ideas. Or the leader may use a process called dialectic, a structured debate between two conflicting courses of action.[109] Structured debates between plans and counterplans can be useful before making a strategic decision—one team might present the case for acquiring a firm while another team advocates not making the acquisition.

3. *Creativity:* To "get" creativity out of other people, give creative efforts the credit they are due, and don't punish creative failures.[110] Avoid extreme time pressure if possible.[111] Support some innovative ideas without heeding projected returns. Stimulate and challenge people intellectually, and give people some creative freedom. Listen to employees' ideas, and allow enough time to explore different ideas. Be aware that creativity emerges from conversations.

Put together groups of people with different styles of thinking and behaving. Get your people in touch with customers, and let them bounce ideas around. Protect your people from managers who demand immediate payoffs, don't understand the importance of creative contributions, or try to take credit for others' successes.

People are likely to be more creative if they believe they are capable, know that their coworkers expect creativity, and believe that their employer values creativity.[112] A common technique for eliciting creative ideas, brainstorming, asks group members to generate as many ideas about a problem as they can. As the ideas are presented, they are posted so everyone can read them and use the ideas as building blocks. The group is encouraged to say anything that comes to mind, except for criticizing other people or their ideas.

8.4 | Groups Can Drive Innovation

Many organizations now use design thinking, a human-centered approach to innovation that integrates customer needs, the potential of technology, and the requirements for business success.[113] Design thinking relies on "close, almost anthropological observation of people to gain insight into problems that may not be articulated yet."[114]

IDEO, the global design firm that uses design thinking with clients, views the process as a "system of overlapping spaces rather than a sequence of orderly steps."[115] The company defines the three interrelated spaces this way: (1) *inspiration* is the motivating problem or solution; (2) *ideation* is the process of generating, developing, and testing ideas, and (3) *implementation* is the path that leads from the project stage into customers' lives. The problem-solving process is not linear but rather moves iteratively, in and out of these spaces.

Traditionally, when a company wanted to redesign or create a new product, it would use customer focus groups to provide

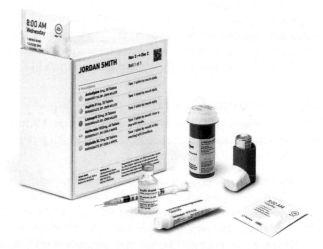

feedback on projects already under development.[116] Design thinking differs by starting with developing a thorough understanding (through direct observation) of current and potential customers. Design teams, consisting of people with diverse expertise (engineering, anthropology, design, marketing, and so forth), work together to identify "what people want and need in their lives and what they like or dislike about the way particular products are made, packaged, marketed, sold, and supported."[117]

PillPack, a prescription home delivery company, used design thinking to improve how people obtain and keep their medicines organized. In a three-month residency with IDEO, the PillPack founders and a design team made the prescription process "straightforward and reassuring." They redesigned the firm's website, customer dashboard, and its physical products. The final product delivered 14-day supplies of pills in personalized and presorted packets, labeled with the day and time to take them, and different dispensers to keep at home or take on the go. The company was named one of *TIME* magazine's best inventions of 2014 and was bought by Amazon for $1 billion in 2018.[118]

Notes

1. M. L. Holshue, et al., "First Case of 2019 Novel Coronavirus in the United States," *New England Journal of Medicine*, March 5, 2020, https://www.nejm.org/doi/full/10.1056/NEJMoa2001191.

2. T. Gryta and R. Adams, "Coronavirus Is Different. It's Rapidly Hitting Supply and Demand," *The Wall Street Journal*, March 1, 2020, www.wsj.com.

3. A. Sider, "Airlines Trim Capacity over Coronavirus Spread; Some Executives Take Pay Cuts," *The Wall Street Journal*, March 10, 2020, https://www.wsj.com/articles/southwest-ceo-to-cut-his-pay-by-10-as-coronavirus-chills-bookings-11583840287; J. Lee and J. Swartz, "Coronavirus Has Prompted These Tech Companies to Ask Employees to Work from Home," MarketWatch, March 10, 2020, https://www.marketwatch.com/story/coronavirus-has-prompted-these-tech-companies-to-ask-employees-to-work-from-home-2020-03-05.

4. K. Whiting, "Coronavirus Isn't an Outlier, It's Part of Our Interconnected Viral Age," World Economic Forum, March 4, 2020, https://www.weforum.org/agenda/2020/03/coronavirus-global-epidemics-health-pandemic-covid-19/.

5. C. Wolf and S. W. Floyd, "Strategic Planning Research: Toward a Theory-Driven Agenda," *Journal of Management* 43 (2017), pp. 1754–88.

6. "10 Ways to Finance Your Business," *Inc.*, www.inc.com, accessed March 11, 2018.

7. Wolf, C. and Floyd, S.W. (2017). "Strategic Planning Research: Toward a Theory-Driven Agenda," Journal of Management, 43, pp. 1754–88.

8. D. C. Hambrick and J. W. Fredrickson, "Are You Sure You Have a Strategy?" *Academy of Management Executive* 19, no. 4 (2005), pp. 51–62.

9. J. L. Bower and C. G. Gilbert, "How Managers' Everyday Decisions Create or Destroy Your Company's Strategy," *Harvard Business Review*, February 2007, pp. 72–79.

10. See Whole Foods' company website, www.wholefoodsmarket.com, accessed September 16, 2019.

11. A. M. Raes, M. G. Heijltjes, U. Glunk, and R. A. Roe, "The Interface of the Top Management Team and Middle Managers: A Process Model," *Academy of Management Review* 36, no. 1 (2011), pp. 102–26; and S. W. Floyd and P. J. Lane, "Strategizing throughout the Organization: Management Role Conflict in Strategic Renewal," *Academy of Management Review* 25, no. 1 (January 2000), pp. 154–77.

12. See Life is Good company website, content.lifeisgood.com/purpose.

13. A. Vetter, "Here's the Secret to Creating a Mission Statement That Works (and How to Get Started)," *Inc.*, January 31, 2018, www.inc.com.

14. See Honest Tea's company website, www.honesttea.com/our-mission/.

15. See Creative Commons' company website, www.creativecommons.org/about/mission-and-vision/.

16. See the Alzheimer's Association's website, www.alz.org/about/strategic-plan.

17. See Hilton's company website, www.hilton.com.

18. See Creative Commons' company website, www.creativecommons.org/about/mission-and-vision/.

19. See Patagonia's company website, patagonia.com/company-info.html.

20. A. Kelso, "'Customers Are Noticing' McDonald's Significant Supply Chain Changes," *Forbes*, July 9, 2019, www.forbes.com.

21. "McDonald's Reports Second Quarter 2019 Results," McDonald's Financial News, July 26, 2019, https://www.prnewswire.com/news-releases/mcdonalds-reports-second-quarter-2019-results-300891499.html.

22. A. A. Thompson and A. J. Strickland III, *Strategic Management: Concepts and Cases*, 8th ed. (Burr Ridge, IL: Richard D. Irwin, 1995), p. 23.

23. "Become Master of Your Financial Domain with QuickBooks," *Entrepreneur*, September 3, 2019, www.entrepreneur.com.

24. "Our History," NextEra Energy, www.nexteraenergy.com, accessed September 22, 2019.

25. C. Wienberg and F. Schwartzkopff, "Orsted Enters $3.2 Billion Deal to Sell Assets to SEAS-NVE," *Bloomberg,* September 18, 2019, www.bloomberg.com.

26. A. Frangoul, "Orsted Set to Use a Massive Turbine to Power Two of Its Offshore Wind Farms in the US," *CNBC News,* September 19, 2019, www.cnbc.com.

27. See Anheuser-Busch InBev's company website, https://www.ab-inbev.com/.

28. R. L. Priem, "A Consumer Perspective on Value Creation," *Academy of Management Review* 32, no. 1 (2007), pp. 219-35.

29. N. McCarthy, "The U.S. Companies Granted the Most Patents in 2018," *Forbes,* August 13, 2019, www.forbes.com.

30. W. Arruda, "5 Great Companies That Get Corporate Culture Right," *Forbes,* August 17, 2017, www.forbes.com.

31. R. Wolfson, "Cigna and Sentara Healthcare Join IBM's Blockchain Health Utility Network to Improve Data Sharing," *Forbes,* February 16, 2019, www.forbes.com.

32. "IBM Builds a Smarter Planet," IBM, www.ibm.com, accessed September 20, 2019.

33. "IBM Builds a Smarter Planet," IBM, www.ibm.com, accessed September 20, 2019.

34. H. Min and H. Min, "Benchmarking the Service Quality of Fast-Food Restaurant Franchises in the USA," *Benchmarking* 18, no. 2 (2011), pp. 282-300.

35. C. Gough, "Global Unit Sales of Sony PlayStation 4 Consoles 2014-2020," Statista, April 21, 2020, www.statista.com.

36. See www.sony.com/SCA/bios/stringer.shtml; and B. Gruley and C. Edwards, "Sony Needs a Hit," *Bloomberg Businessweek,* November 21-27, 2011, pp. 72-77.

37. "The Five Guys Story," see Five Guys' company website, www.fiveguys.com.

38. J. W. Carpenter, "Top 5 Companies Owned by Disney," Investopedia, February 11, 2019, www.investopedia.com.

39. See Procter & Gamble's company website, us.pg.com/brands.

40. P. C. Haspeslagh, "Portfolio Planning: Uses and Limits," *Harvard Business Review* 60, no. 1 (1982), pp. 58-67; R. Hamermesh, *Making Strategy Work* (New York: Wiley, 1986); and R. A. Proctor, "Toward a New Model for Product Portfolio Analysis," *Management Decision* 28, no. 3 (1990), pp. 14-17.

41. J. Eley, "Boots Prepares for Makeover as Challenges Mount," *Financial Times,* August 31, 2019, www.ft.com.

42. M. Porter, *Competitive Advantage* (New York: Free Press, 1985), pp. 11-14.

43. "About the IKEA Group," IKEA, accessed September 20, 2019, www.ikea.com.

44. See Tieks' company website, www.tieks.com.

45. C. G. Weissman, "How Swedish Oat Milk Exploded into a $15 Million Business Last Year," *Fast Company,* February 19, 2019, www.fastcompany.com.

46. C. G. Weissman, "How Swedish Oat Milk Exploded into a $15 Million Business Last Year," *Fast Company,* February 19, 2019, www.fastcompany.com.

47. S. Pham, "This Swedish Company Made Oat Milk Cool in the US. Now It's Eyeing China," *CNN Business,* April 12, 2019, www.cnn.com.

48. A. M. Franco, M. B. Sarkar, R. Agarwal, and R. Echambadi, "Swift and Smart: The Moderating Effects of Technological Capabilities on the Market Pioneering-Firm Survival Relationship," *Management Science* 55, no. 11 (November 2009), pp. 1842-61; S. A. Zahra, S. Nash, and D. J. Bickford, "Transforming Technological Pioneering in Competitive Advantage," *Academy of Management Executive* 9, no. 1 (1995), pp. 17-31; and M. Sadowski and A. Roth, "Technology Leadership Can Pay Off," *Research Technology Management* 42, no. 6 (November–December 1999), pp. 32-33.

49. A. G. Shilling, "First-Mover Disadvantage," *Forbes,* June 18, 2007.

50. F. F. Suarez and G. Lanzolla, "The Role of Environmental Dynamics in Building a First Mover Advantage Theory," *Academy of Management Review* 32, no. 2 (2007), pp. 377-92.

51. B. Tayan, "The Wells Fargo Cross-Selling Scandal," Stanford Closer Look Series, December 2, 2016, www.gsb.stanford.edu.

52. M. Egan, "Wells Fargo Dumps Toxic 'Cross-Selling' Metric," *CNNMoney,* January 13, 2017, www.money.cnn.com; K. Berry, "Wells Fargo's Cross-Selling Prowess May Be Backfiring," *American Banker,* January 20, 2016, www.americanbanker.com; and E. Glazer, "At Wells Fargo, How Far Did Bank's Sales Culture Go?" *The Wall Street Journal,* November 30, 2015, www.wsj.com.

53. B. Rodriguez, "Wells Fargo Agrees to $575 Million Settlement Affecting All 50 States in Wake of Fake Accounts," *USA Today,* December 28, 2018, www.usatoday.com.

54. V. Govindarajan, S. Rajgopal, A. Srivastava, and Y. Wang, "R&D Spending Has Dramatically Surpassed Advertising Spending," *Harvard Business Review,* May 20, 2019, www.hbr.org.

55. "The 2018 Global Innovation 1000 Study," *strategy&,* accessed September 22, 2019, strategyand.pwc.com.

56. B. Smith, "Maybe I Will, Maybe I Won't: What the Connected Perspectives of Motivation Theory and Organisational Commitment May Contribute to Our Understanding of Strategy Implementation," *Journal of Strategic Marketing* 17, no. 6 (2009), pp. 473-85; and M. Beer and R. A. Eisenstat, "The Silent Killers of Strategy Implementation and Learning," *MIT Sloan Management Review* 4 (Summer 2000), pp. 29-40.

57. L. Hrebiniak, "Obstacles to Effective Strategy Implementation," *Organizational Dynamics* 35, no. 1 (2006), pp. 12-31; and R. A. Eisenstat, "Implementing Strategy: Developing a Partnership for Change," *Planning Review,* September–October 1993, pp. 33-36.

58. J. Bogaisky, "Honda's Jet Business Clears the Trees, but Flight Path Is in Question," *Forbes,* December 19, 2018, www.forbes.com.

59. M. Magasin and F. L. Gehlen, "Unwise Decisions and Unanticipated Consequences," *Sloan Management Review* 41 (1999), pp. 47-60; M. McCall and R. Kaplan, *Whatever It Takes: Decision Makers at Work* (Englewood Cliffs, NJ: Prentice-Hall, 1985); and L. Kopeikina, "The Elements of a Clear Decision," *MIT Sloan Management Review* 47 (Winter 2006), pp. 19-20.

60. B. Bass, *Organizational Decision Making* (Homewood, IL: Richard D. Irwin, 1983).

61. J. Gibson, J. Ivancevich, J. Donnelly Jr., and R. Konopaske, *Organizations: Behavior, Structure, Processes,* 14th ed. (Burr

Ridge, IL: McGraw-Hill, 2012), p. 464. Copyright 2012 by The McGraw-Hill Companies. Reproduced with permission of The McGraw-Hill Companies.

62. J. March, "Bounded Rationality, Ambiguity, and the Engineering of Choice," *Bell Journal of Economics* 9 (1978), pp. 587–608.

63. B. Gilbert, "Jeff Bezos Explains How Creating the Echo Was a Huge Risk for Amazon That Was Worth Taking," *Business Insider,* April 11, 2019, www.businessinsider.com.

64. J. Brustein, "The Real Story of How Amazon Built the Echo," *Bloomberg,* April 19, 2016, www.bloomberg.com.

65. B. Gilbert, "Jeff Bezos Explains How Creating the Echo Was a Huge Risk for Amazon That Was Worth Taking," *Business Insider,* April 11, 2019, www.businessinsider.com.

66. M. McCall and R. Kaplan, *Whatever It Takes: Decision Makers at Work* (Englewood Cliffs, NJ: Prentice-Hall, 1985).

67. M. Chafkin, "Case Study: When the Bank Called In a Loan, Larry Cohen Had to Act Fast to Save the Family Business," *Inc.,* June 2006, pp. 58–60.

68. A. L. Wolmer, "Is Your Business Ready for the Internet of Things?" *Entrepreneur,* March 14, 2019, www.entrepreneur.com.

69. K. MacCrimmon and R. Taylor, "Decision Making and Problem Solving," in *Handbook of Industrial and Organizational Psychology,* ed. M. D. Dunnette (Chicago: Rand McNally, 1976).

70. M. Chafkin, "Case Study: When the Bank Called In a Loan, Larry Cohen Had to Act Fast to Save the Family Business," *Inc.,* June 2006, pp. 58–60.

71. Q. Spitzer and R. Evans, *Heads, You Win! How the Best Companies Think* (New York: Simon & Schuster, 1997).

72. C. Gettys and S. Fisher, "Hypothesis Plausibility and Hypothesis Generation," *Organizational Behavior and Human Performance* 24 (1979), pp. 93–110.

73. E. R. Alexander, "The Design of Alternatives in Organizational Contexts: A Pilot Study," *Administrative Science Quarterly* 24 (1979), pp. 382–404.

74. A. R. Rao, M. E. Bergen, and S. Davis, "How to Fight a Price War," *Harvard Business Review,* March–April 2000, pp. 107–16.

75. M. Chafkin, "Case Study: When the Bank Called In a Loan, Larry Cohen Had to Act Fast to Save the Family Business," *Inc.,* June 2006, pp. 58–60.

76. M. Chafkin, "Case Study: When the Bank Called In a Loan, Larry Cohen Had to Act Fast to Save the Family Business," *Inc.,* June 2006, pp. 58–60.

77. J. L. Bower and C. G. Gilbert, "How Managers' Everyday Decisions Create or Destroy Your Company's Strategy," *Harvard Business Review,* February 2007, pp. 72–79.

78. A. Fox, "Avoiding Furlough Fallout," *HRMagazine* 54, no. 9 (September 2009), pp. 37–41.

79. D. Mattioli and S. Murray, "Employers Hit Salaried Staff with Furloughs," *The Wall Street Journal,* February 24, 2009, www.wsj.com.

80. Q. Spitzer and R. Evans, *Heads, You Win! How the Best Companies Think* (New York: Simon & Schuster, 1997).

81. "Is Executive Hubris Ruining Companies?" *IndustryWeek,* January 26, 2007, www.industryweek.com.

82. M. McCall and R. Kaplan, *Whatever It Takes: Decision Makers at Work* (Englewood Cliffs, NJ: Prentice-Hall, 1985).

83. J. Pfeffer and R. Sutton, *The Knowing-Doing Gap* (Boston: Harvard Business School Press, 2000).

84. D. Takahashi, "Supercell CEO Thrives on Trusting the Instincts of Game Developers," VentureBeat, March 29, 2019, www.venturebeat.com.

85. "The Best Teams Make the Best Games," Supercell, www.supercell.com, accessed September 22, 2019.

86. D. Siebold, "Making Meetings More Successful," *Journal of Business Communication* 16 (Summer 1979), pp. 3–20.

87. M. Chafkin, "Case Study: When the Bank Called In a Loan, Larry Cohen Had to Act Fast to Save the Family Business," *Inc.,* June 2006, pp. 58–60.

88. J. W. Dean Jr. and M. Sharfman, "Does Decision Process Matter? A Study of Strategic Decision-Making Effectiveness," *Academy of Management Journal* 39 (1996), pp. 368–96.

89. D. Kahneman, *Thinking, Fast and Slow* (London: Macmillan, 2011).

90. D. Kahneman, *Thinking, Fast and Slow* (London: Macmillan, 2011).

91. R. Nisbett and L. Ross, *Human Inference: Strategies and Shortcomings* (Englewood Cliffs, NJ: Prentice-Hall, 1980).

92. D. Messick and M. Bazerman, "Ethical Leadership and the Psychology of Decision Making," *Sloan Management Review,* Winter 1996, pp. 9–22.

93. T. Bateman and C. Zeithaml, "The Psychological Context of Strategic Decisions: A Model and Convergent Experimental Findings," *Strategic Management Journal* 10 (1989), pp. 59–74.

94. C. Chong, "Blockbuster's CEO Once Passed Up a Chance to Buy Netflix for Only $50 Million," *Business Insider,* July 17, 2015, www.businessinsider.com.

95. C. Chong, "Blockbuster's CEO Once Passed Up a Chance to Buy Netflix for Only $50 Million," *Business Insider,* July 17, 2015, www.businessinsider.com.

96. D. Messick and M. Bazerman, "Ethical Leadership and the Psychology of Decision Making," *Sloan Management Review,* Winter 1996, pp. 9–22.

97. P. A. F. Fraser-Mackenzie and I. E. Dror, "Dynamic Reasoning and Time Pressure: Transition from Analytical Operations to Experiential Responses," *Theory and Decision* 71, no. 2 (August 2011), pp. 211–25; and D. Malhotra, G. Ku, and J. K. Murnigham, "When Winning Is Everything," *Harvard Business Review* 86, no. 5 (May 2008), pp. 78–86.

98. K. M. Eisenhardt, "Speed and Strategic Choice: How Managers Accelerate Decision Making," *California Management Review* 32 (Spring 1990), pp. 39–54.

99. Q. Spitzer and R. Evans, "New Problems in Problem Solving," *Across the Board,* April 1997, pp. 36–40.

100. G. W. Hill, "Group versus Individual Performance: Are N + 1 Heads Better Than 1?" *Psychological Bulletin* 91 (1982), pp. 517–39.

101. N. R. F. Maier, "Assets and Liabilities in Group Problem Solving: The Need for an Integrative Function," *Psychological Review* 74 (1967), pp. 239–49.

102. R. L. Moreland, "Transactive Memory: Learning Who Knows What in Work Groups and Organizations," in *Shared Cognition in Organizations: The Management of Knowledge,* eds. L. Thompson, D. Messick and J. Levine (Hillsdale, NJ: Erlbaum, 2000), pp. 3-31.

103. J. A. Cannon-Bowers and E. Salas, "Reflections on Shared Cognition," *Journal of Organizational Behavior* 22 (2001), pp. 195-202.

104. J. A. Cannon-Bowers and E. Salas, "Reflections on Shared Cognition," *Journal of Organizational Behavior* 22 (2001), pp. 195-202.

105. A. Vollmer, "Conflicts in Innovation and How to Approach the 'Last Mile' of Conflict Management Research—A Literature Review," *International Journal of Conflict Management* 26, no. 2 (2015), pp. 192-213; and D. A. Garvin and M. A. Roberto, "What You Don't Know about Making Decisions," *Harvard Business Review,* September 2001, pp. 108-16.

106. A. C. Amason, "Distinguishing the Effects of Functional and Dysfunctional Conflict on Strategic Decision Making: Resolving a Paradox for Top Management Teams," *Academy of Management Journal* 39 (1996), pp. 123-48; and R. S. Dooley and G. E. Fryxell, "Attaining Decision Quality and Commitment from Dissent: The Moderating Effects of Loyalty and Competence in Strategic Decision-Making Teams," *Academy of Management Journal,* August 1999, pp. 389-402.

107. C. De Dreu and L. Weingart, "Task versus Relationship Conflict, Team Performance, and Team Member Satisfaction: A Meta-Analysis," *Journal of Applied Psychology* 88 (2003), pp. 741-49.

108. K. Eisenhardt, J. Kahwajy, and L. J. Bourgeois III, "Conflict and Strategic Choice: How Top Management Teams Disagree," *California Management Review,* Winter 1997, pp. 42-62.

109. K. Eisenhardt, J. Kahwajy, and L. J. Bourgeois III, "Conflict and Strategic Choice: How Top Management Teams Disagree," *California Management Review,* Winter 1997, pp. 42-62.

110. "Innovation from the Ground Up," *IndustryWeek,* March 7, 2007, www.industryweek.com (interview of Erika Andersen); A. Farnham, "How to Nurture Creative Sparks," *Fortune,* January 10, 1994, pp. 94-100; and T. M. Amabile, "A Model of Creativity and Innovation in Organizations," in *Research in Organizational Behavior,* eds. B. Straw and L. Cummings, vol. 10 (Greenwich, CT: JAI Press, 1988), pp. 123-68; and S. Finkelstein, "What Stan Lee Knew about Managing Creative People," *Harvard Business Review,* November 13, 2018, www.hbr.org, pp. 123-68.

111. T. Amabile, C. Hadley, and S. Kramer, "Creativity under the Gun," *Harvard Business Review,* August 2002, pp. 52-61.

112. S. Farmer, P. Tierney, and K. Kung-McIntyre, "Employee Creativity in Taiwan: An Application of Role Identity Theory," *Academy of Management Journal* 46 (2003), pp. 618-30.

113. T. Brown, "Design Thinking," *Harvard Business Review* 86, no. 6 (June 2008), pp. 84-92.

114. M. Korn and R. Silverman, "Business Education: Forget B-School, D-School Is Hot," *The Wall Street Journal,* June 7, 2012, www.wsj.com.

115. IDEO website, "About IDEO," www.ideo.com, accessed July 5, 2015.

116. M. Korn and R. Silverman, "Business Education: Forget B-School, D-School Is Hot," *The Wall Street Journal,* June 7, 2012, www.wsj.com.

117. T. Brown, "Design Thinking," *Harvard Business Review* 86, no. 6 (June 2008), pp. 84-92.

118. "This Startup Revolutionized an Industry through Design," IDEO, www.ideo.com, accessed September 23, 2019.

Entrepreneurship

Learning Objectives

After studying Chapter 6, you should be able to

LO1 Describe why people become entrepreneurs and what it takes, personally.

LO2 Summarize how to assess opportunities to start new businesses.

LO3 Identify common causes of success and failure.

LO4 Discuss common management challenges.

LO5 Explain how to increase your chances of success, including good business planning.

LO6 Describe how managers of large companies can foster entrepreneurship.

Matt Winkelmeyer/WIRED25/Getty Images

Many extraordinary individuals founded companies that became famously successful. Some, like Oprah Winfrey, Richard Branson, Martha Stewart, and Elon Musk, have become household names. But the fame bestowed on these iconic entrepreneurs doesn't convey the true story of entrepreneurship. Entrepreneurs aren't exceptions in business; they are the lifeblood of business. Entrepreneurs push the status quo, take risks, and drive innovation. They don't go with the flow, they chart the course for business—and they often do so without great fanfare and fame.

Take Anne Wojcicki, the cofounder and CEO of 23andMe, which offers the only direct-to-consumer genetics test available to the public. Like most entrepreneurs, Wojcicki's path to success wasn't a linear one. She started out as a Wall Street analyst but left to enter medical school. In 2006, she formulated a plan to take advantage of both of these experiences, using her knowledge of medicine and private markets to form 23andMe. As she said in a recent interview, it's important for young people to "enjoy the uncertainty and take advantage of every opportunity that comes your way. You never know what opportunities will be meaningful in your life, and you cannot predict how life will evolve."[1]

What's evolved for Wojcicki is a company valued at $1.8 billion that is changing the face of how we understand our heritage, our health, and ourselves. As with almost any entrepreneurial endeavor, there were hiccups along the way, as in 2013 when the FDA declared that the vial used to capture clients' saliva for testing was an "unapproved medical device."[2] But Wojcicki worked through this problem and is now hoping to shift the company's focus from helping people identify genetic health risks to helping solve them.[3]

As Wojcicki and others have demonstrated, great opportunity is available to talented people who are willing to work hard to achieve their dreams. Entrepreneurship occurs when an enterprising individual pursues a lucrative opportunity under conditions of uncertainty.[4] To be an entrepreneur is to initiate and build an organization, rather than being only a passive part of one.[5] It involves creating *new* systems, resources, or processes to produce *new* goods or services and/or serve *new* markets.[6]

Sir Richard Branson is a perfect example. He was only a teenager when he started his first company, a magazine called *Student,* in the mid-1960s. Branson launched his next enterprise in 1970, the iconic Virgin Records, which generated his first fortune. Since then, Branson has built 300 other businesses, all under the Virgin umbrella, including a space travel venture; a global airline; a mobile phone enterprise; and companies in financial services, leisure, publishing, and retailing.

Today, the Virgin empire has nearly 70,000 employees across the globe and earns over $20 billion in annual revenue; it reports more than 37 million social media followers.[7] Branson has a mind-boggling net worth of more than $4 billion and was knighted by Queen Elizabeth.[8]

Entrepreneurs differ from managers generally. An entrepreneur *is* a manager but engages in additional activities that not all managers do.[9] Traditionally, managers operate in a formal management hierarchy with well-defined authority and responsibility. In contrast, entrepreneurs use networks of contacts more than formal authority. And although managers usually prefer to own assets, entrepreneurs often rent or use assets on a temporary basis. Some say that managers often are slower to act and tend to avoid risk, whereas entrepreneurs are quicker to act and actively manage risk.

An entrepreneur's organization may be small, but it differs from a typical small business:[10]

- Though it can vary from a one- or two-person start-up to a 500-employee company, a small business makes less than $7.5 million in average annual revenue, is independently owned and operated, is not dominant in its field, and is not characterized by many innovative practices.[11] Small business owners tend not to manage particularly aggressively, and they

"Entrepreneurship is neither a science nor an art. It is a practice."

—Peter Drucker

entrepreneurial venture a new business having growth and high profitability as primary objectives

entrepreneur an individual who establishes a new organization without the benefit of corporate sponsorship

intrapreneurs new venture creators working inside big companies

expect normal, moderate sales, profits, and growth.

- An **entrepreneurial venture** has growth and high profitability as its primary objectives. Entrepreneurs manage aggressively and develop innovative strategies, practices, and products. By definition, they and their financial backers usually seek rapid growth, immediate and high profits, and sometimes a quick sellout with large capital gains.

Entrepreneurship Excitement

Consider these words from Jeffry Timmons, a leading entrepreneurship scholar and author: "America has unleashed the most revolutionary generation the nation has experienced since its founding in 1776. This new generation of entrepreneurs has altered permanently the economic and social structure of this nation and the world. . . . It will determine more than any other single impetus how the nation and the world will live, work, learn, and lead in this century and beyond."[12]

Overhype? Sounds like it could be, but it's not. Entrepreneurship transforms economies all over the world, and the global economy in general. It has been estimated that since World War II, small entrepreneurial firms have generated 95 percent of all radical innovation in the United States. Start-ups are good for the economy, as they contribute to "higher productivity, wage growth and quality of life."[13] In 2018, about one-third of adults started businesses,[14] with Texas, Utah, California, and Colorado being top states in which to start a business.[15]

Start-ups come in all shapes and sizes. Cindy Mi, CEO of VIPKID, developed a platform connecting North Americans to teach English to students from China and other countries. The company has over half a million Chinese students and reports a 95 percent retention rate.[16]

The self-employed love the entrepreneurial process, and they report the highest levels of pride, satisfaction, and income. Importantly, entrepreneurship is not about the privileged descendants of the Rockefellers and the Vanderbilts; instead it provides opportunity and upward mobility for anyone who performs well.[17]

Myths About Entrepreneurship
Simply put, entrepreneurs generate new ideas and turn them into business ventures.[18] But entrepreneurship is not simple, and it is frequently misunderstood.[19] Exhibit 6.1 describes 12 myths and realities regarding entrepreneurship.[20]

Here is another myth: Being an entrepreneur is great because you can "get rich quick" and enjoy a lot of leisure time while

● Estee Lauder, founder of her iconic cosmetics company, pioneered an innovative marketing strategy of giving away samples at fashion shows and through mailings. Rawpixel.com/Shutterstock

your employees run the company. But the reality is much more difficult. During the start-up period, you are likely to have a lot of bad days. It's stressful—usually[21]—and exhausting. Even if you don't have employees, you should expect communication breakdowns and other "people problems" with agents, vendors, distributors, family, subcontractors, lenders, and so on. Dan Bricklin, the founder of VisiCalc (an early electronic spreadsheet software program), advises that the most important thing to remember is this: "You are not your business. On those darkest days when things aren't going so well—and trust me, you will have them—try to remember that your company's failures don't make you an awful person. Likewise, your company's successes don't make you a genius or superhuman."[22]

As you read this chapter, you will learn about two primary sources of new venture creation:

1. Independent **entrepreneurs** are individuals who establish a new organization without the benefit of corporate support.

2. **Intrapreneurs** are new venture creators working inside big companies; they are corporate entrepreneurs, using their company's resources to build a profitable line of business based on a fresh new idea.[23]

Exhibit 6.1 Myths and realities about entrepreneurship

Myths	Realities
1. "Anyone can start a business."	Starting is easy. The hard part is building and sustaining a successful venture.
2. "Entrepreneurs are gamblers."	They take careful, calculated risks and are not afraid to act on those decisions.
3. "Entrepreneurs want the whole show to themselves."	Higher-potential entrepreneurs build a team, an organization, and a company.
4. "Entrepreneurs are their own bosses and independent."	They have to answer to many stakeholders, including partners, investors, customers, suppliers, creditors, employees, and families.
5. "Entrepreneurs work harder than managers in big firms."	There is no evidence to support this claim. Some work more, some less.
6. "Entrepreneurs experience a great deal of stress."	Entrepreneurs experience stress, but they also have high job satisfaction. They tend to be healthier and less likely to retire than those who work for others.
7. "Entrepreneurs are motivated solely by the quest for the dollar."	More are driven by building high-potential ventures and realizing long-term capital gains than instant gratification from high salaries. Feeling in control of their own destinies and realizing vision and dreams are powerful motivators.
8. "Entrepreneurs seek power and control over others."	Many are driven by responsibility, achievement, and results. Successful entrepreneurs may become powerful and influential, but these are by-products.
9. "If an entrepreneur is talented, then success will happen quickly."	Actually, many new businesses take three to four years to solidify. A saying from venture capitalists sums it up: "The lemons ripen in two and a half years, but the pearls take seven or eight."
10. "Any entrepreneur with a good idea can raise venture capital."	In practice, only 1 to 3 (out of 100) ventures are funded.
11. "If an entrepreneur has enough start-up capital, s/he can't miss."	Too much money at the beginning often leads to impulsive or undisciplined spending that usually results in serious problems or failure.
12. "Unless you attained a high score on your SATs or GMATs, you'll never be a successful entrepreneur."	Entrepreneurial IQ is actually a unique combination of creativity, motivation, integrity, leadership, team building, analytical ability, and ability to deal with ambiguity and adversity.

John Lund/Blend Images LLC

Source: Adapted from J. A. Timmons and S. Spinelli, *New Venture Creation*, 6th ed., pp. 67–68.

LO1 Describe why people become entrepreneurs and what it takes, personally.

1 | ENTREPRENEURSHIP

Emily Weiss started a beauty blog called *Into the Gloss* while working as a fashion assistant at *Vogue*. This led to Weiss launching Glossier, a makeup and skin care company. Needing capital, she pitched to over 10 venture capital firms before one agreed to fund her start-up. Glossier's valuation recently surpassed $1 billion, and the company added more than 1 million new customers in 2018.[24]

Exceptional though Weiss' story may be, the real, more complete story of entrepreneurship is about people you've probably never heard of. They have built companies, thrived personally, created jobs, and contributed to their communities through their businesses.

Or they're just starting out. Consider Shama Hyder, who in her 20s went from graduate student to social media millionaire. An early proponent of using social media to market firms' products and services, Hyder wrote her master's thesis on "why people use Twitter and other social networking sites." After applying and being rejected for jobs at large management consulting firms, she decided to trust her own entrepreneurial instincts and founded a web marketing company, Zen Media (formerly The Marketing Zen Group). Since founding her company in 2009, Hyder has grown the company to over $2.0 million in revenue.[25]

For the past three years, Hyder has been named one of the "Top Voices" in social media and marketing on LinkedIn. As the Zen CEO, Hyder has worked with notable brands such as Mary Kay, Tupperware, and even the U.S. Navy.

1.1 | Why Become an Entrepreneur?

Bill Gross has helped start more than 150 companies. When he was a boy, he devised homemade electronic games and sold candy for a profit to friends. In college, he built and sold plans for a solar heating device, started a stereo equipment company, and sold a software product to Lotus. Then, he started Idealab, which hatched dozens of Internet start-ups. Recent Idealab start-ups include one that helps hourly-wage employees manage finances and another that sells candy-box subscriptions.[26]

Why do Bill Gross and other entrepreneurs do what they do? Entrepreneurs start their own firms because of the challenge, profit potential, and enormous satisfaction they hope lies ahead. People starting their own businesses are seeking a better quality of life than they might have at big companies. They seek independence and a feeling that they are part of the action. They get tremendous satisfaction from building something from nothing, seeing it succeed, and watching the market embrace their ideas and products.

People also start their own companies when they see their progress or ideas blocked at big corporations. When people are laid off, believe they will not receive a promotion, or are frustrated by bureaucracy or other features of corporate life, they may become entrepreneurs. Well worth considering is the hybrid path: starting a business while retaining your "day job."[27]

To migrate is to move within or across meaningful social or political boundaries, both intra- and internationally.[28] Immigrants may find conventional paths to economic success closed to them and turn to entrepreneurship.[29] Immigrants are almost twice as likely to start a business in the United States than native-born Americans.[30] A recent study found that immigrants or their children founded almost half of *Fortune* 500 companies, which earned a combined $6 trillion in 2018.[31]

Born Josephine Esther Mentzer, the beauty company entrepreneur Estée Lauder was raised in Queens, New York, by her Hungarian mother and Czech father. Living on the floor above her father's hardware store, Lauder was always interested in beauty. In 1946, Lauder's chemist uncle created skin creams that she began selling to beauty salons and hotels. Two years after starting her business, she expanded her enterprise by convincing the managers at New York City department stores to give her counter space to sell her beauty products. Holding strong to the belief that "every woman can be beautiful," Lauder developed and perfected personal selling techniques that included advising customers and working with beauty advisers.

Lauder had a keen sense for marketing. At a time when her competitors were selling French perfumes to be applied in drops behind women's ears, Lauder launched *Youth Dew,* a combination bath oil and perfume that people consumed much faster as they poured it into their bathwater. Such business instincts, combined with strong selling and leadership skills, earned Estée Lauder the United States' Presidential Medal of Freedom and France's Legion of Honor.

Estée Lauder left a legacy of success. The company sells products in more than 150 countries under brand names such as Estée Lauder, La Mer, Bumble, and Clinique. As of 2018, the company reported nearly $14 billion in revenue and continues to be a leader in skin care, makeup, fragrance, and hair care products.[32]

1.2 | What Does It Take to Succeed?

What can we learn from the people who start their own companies and succeed? Let's start with the example of Ken Hendricks, former founder of ABC Supply.[33] As he acquired buildings and businesses, he saw opportunities where others saw problems. Several years after the town's largest employer, Beloit Corporation, closed its doors, Hendricks bought its property,

● Idealab's Migo app combines multiple transportation and ride-share options under one umbrella. People can compare prices and arrival times and contact and pay for their ride in a single app. Ringo Chiu/ZUMA Wire/Alamy Stock Photo

● The Estée Lauder Companies Inc. launched the Jo Malone London brand in Bejing, China. The brand is now available in 34 countries worldwide and inspires a loyal following. withGod/Shutterstock

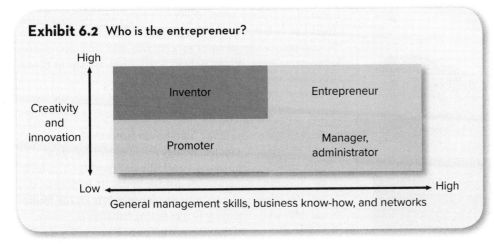

Exhibit 6.2 Who is the entrepreneur?

Creativity and innovation (High / Low)

| Inventor | Entrepreneur |
| Promoter | Manager, administrator |

General management skills, business know-how, and networks (Low → High)

Source: J. A. Timmons and S. Spinelli, *New Venture Creation,* 6th ed. (McGraw-Hill Education, 2004), p. 65.

where he discovered almost a half million patterns (wooden molds) used to make a variety of machine parts. Although a bankruptcy court ordered that he be paid to move the patterns to the dump, Hendricks called on a friend, artist Jack De Munnik, and offered him the patterns as free material to create art. De Munnik fashioned them into tables, clocks, sculptures, and other pieces. Hendricks calculated, "Even if we only got $50 apiece for them, 50 times 500,000 is $25 million," and he noted that that amount could have "taken the Beloit Corporation out of bankruptcy."[34]

This example shows how Hendricks viewed business success: Problems can be fixed. "It's how you look at something and how it's managed that make the difference."[35]

Ken Hendricks possessed the talents that enable entrepreneurs to succeed. We express these talents in general terms with Exhibit 6.2. Successful entrepreneurs are innovators who also have good knowledge and skills in management, business, and networking.[36] In contrast, inventors are creative but may lack the skills to turn their ideas into a successful business. Manager–administrators may be great at ensuring efficient operations but aren't necessarily innovators. Promoters have a different set of marketing and selling skills that are useful for entrepreneurs, but those skills can be hired. Innovativeness and business management skills remain the essential combination for successful entrepreneurs.

LO2 Summarize how to assess opportunities to start new businesses.

2 | WHAT BUSINESS SHOULD YOU START?

You need a good idea, and you need to find or create the right opportunity. The following discussion offers some general considerations for choosing a type of business. For guidance on how your start-up can create innovative products or services that fit customers' needs, refer to *The Lean Startup* by Eric Ries.[37]

2.1 | The Idea

Many entrepreneurs and observers say that in contemplating your business, you must start with a great idea. A great product, a viable market, and good timing are essential ingredients in any recipe for success. For example, Tom Stemberg knew that the growing number of small businesses in the 1980s had no one dedicated to selling them office supplies. He saw his opportunity, so he opened his first Staples store, the first step toward a nationwide chain. Staples' sales reached $16 billion in 2018.[38]

Some of the best ideas start off as simple ideas. In 1999, Leon Chen and Tiffany Taylor started a hot-cookie delivery service from Chen's apartment in Austin, Texas. One year later, Tiff's Treats relocated to a brick-and-mortar location near the University of Texas. The chain expanded to Dallas, Houston, Atlanta, and Nashville and offers traditional cookies, as well as ice cream, milk, and brownies. As of 2020, Tiff's Treats has 51 stores and over 1,000 employees.[39]

Many great organizations were built on a different kind of idea: the founder's desire to build a great organization, rather than offering a particular product or product line.[40] Examples abound. Bill Hewlett and David Packard decided to start a company and then figured out what to make. J. Willard Marriott knew he wanted to be in business for himself but didn't have a product in mind until he opened an A&W Root Beer stand. Anita Roddick, the founder of The Body Shop, wanted to create natural products that would appeal to customers' environmental concern and used "low-key marketing, consumer education and social activism" to promote the products.[41]

Many now-great companies had early failures. But the founders persisted; they believed in themselves and in their dreams of building great organizations. Although the conventional logic is to see the company as a vehicle for your products, the alternative perspective sees the products as a vehicle for your company. Be prepared to kill or revise an idea, but never give up on your company—this has been a prescription for success for many great entrepreneurs and business leaders. At organizations including Disney, Procter & Gamble, Estée Lauder, Facebook, and Walmart, the founders' greatest achievements—their greatest ideas—were their organizations.[42]

2.2 | The Opportunity

Entrepreneurs spot, create, and exploit opportunities in a variety of ways.[43] Entrepreneurial companies can explore domains that big companies avoid and introduce goods or services that

● Shayne McQuade is the founder of sustainable products company Voltaic Systems. Jae C. Hong/AP Photo

capture the market because they are simpler, cheaper, more accessible, or more convenient.

Twenty failed start-ups didn't stop Apoorva Mehta. While living without a car in San Francisco, Mehta was frustrated by the limited grocery options in his neighborhood. So he created Instacart, a grocery home delivery service, and partnered with stores like H-E-B, Costco, Kroger, and Publix.[44] Customers use the company's app to enter grocery lists and time preferences for home delivery. Within only six years, Instacart was in 15,000 stores and was valued at almost $8 billion.[45]

To spot opportunities, think carefully about events and trends as they unfold. Consider, for example, the following possibilities:

- *Technological discoveries.* Start-ups in biotechnology, micro-computers, and nanotechnology followed technological advances. Scotland-based Touch Bionics provides high-tech prosthetics to patients with missing limbs. Its leading product, the *i-limb,* responds to muscular signals from the residual limb while featuring longer-lasting batteries and more power-efficient microprocessors. Touch Bionics also developed functioning prototypes of artificial organs to replace one's spleen, pancreas, or lungs.[46]

- *Demographic changes.* As the population ages, many organizations have sprung up to serve the older demographic, from specially designed tablet and smartphone apps for seniors to assisted-living facilities. Apple and IBM teamed up to provide iPads with apps tailored for the aging population. Connecting older users with their families, the apps monitor health, provide reminders about medications and doctors' appointments, and communicate with home care service providers.[47]

- *Lifestyle and taste changes.* Many consumers want to help take care of the environment, and more businesses are concerned about showing consumers that they care, too. This trend opened a niche for Affordable Internet Services Online. Featured in *Inc.* magazine's Top 50 Green Companies, the web-hosting company, based in Romoland, California, is powered by 120 solar panels. Clients' websites can boast, "Site hosted with 100% solar energy."[48]

- *Economic dislocations,* such as booms or failures. The environmental and health-damaging effects of coal mines spurred the development of alternative energy. Chris Riley, cofounder of Guzman Energy, came from a long line of coal miners and grew up in a mining town. Guzman Energy provides affordable renewable energy to communities in the western United States.[49] Says Riley: "We want to pave the way toward a better future for generations to come—both on and off the energy grid."[50]

"What good is an idea if it remains an idea?
Try. Experiment. Iterate. Fail.
Try again. Change the world."

—Simon Sinek

Take Charge of Your Career

You don't have to wait! You can be an entrepreneur while still in school

Most of us are familiar with famous people who started businesses while still in college, like Tom Szaky of TerraCycle and Evan Spiegel and Robert Murphy of Snapchat. Less well known are the growing number of college student entrepreneurs who are busy launching businesses while taking courses. Anais Tadlaoui, while a student at UCLA, founded Ezkie. This two-year-old start-up is a home-sharing service—like an "Airbnb for university students" who want to rent a room in a house shared with other students. Reasons vary for students to change their living arrangements, from temporary jobs and internships to international study abroad programs. Ezkie hopes to change the way college students travel, live, and connect internationally.

Entrepreneurship doesn't have to be something you undertake only once you graduate from school. A growing number of students are busy launching businesses while taking courses. The first winners of a $5,000 grant from GenFKD, a nonprofit supporting young U.S. adults' entrepreneurial ventures, were a pair of students from Purchase College, State University of New York. Sheldon Pearce and Derick Ansah founded Flynance, an organization aimed at providing young athletes with the financial literacy skills they need to help them achieve financial stability. To win the grant money, the pair aced a competition based on the TV show *Shark Tank*.

Other college entrepreneurs are venturing into the food industry. Rip Pruisken and Marco De Leon of Brown University created a Dutch cookie not readily available in the United States. They named them Rip Van Wafels and began selling them person-to-person on the university campus. They now distribute nationwide, including to thousands of Starbucks stores.

Not all college entrepreneurial ventures will achieve such success, of course, but that's no reason to avoid taking the leap. Trying to execute a vision can be an invaluable experience. While still in school, you get to learn from mistakes in an environment that is more forgiving than the environment when you get out of school. And showing industry and initiative will be an asset whether you're trying to acquire investors for a new idea or interviewing for a job. Don't be afraid to take that first step and try out your ideas.

There are countless other examples of college students who turned into entrepreneurs while still in school. Talk to your family, friends, professors, current entrepreneurs, and other people who are willing to listen to your ideas and serve as sounding boards. Most important is to not be afraid to take that first step and try out your cool idea.

Sources: "Purchase College Student Entrepreneurs Win Prize Funding for Startup Ventures," PR Newswire, December 4, 2017, www.prnewswire.com/news-releases/purchase-college-student-entrepreneurs-win-prize-funding-for-startup-ventures-300566050.html; E. Rosen, "Dorm to Table: College Start-ups Take Aim at Food Industry," *The New York Times*, August 26, 2019, https://www.nytimes.com/2019/08/26/business/college-food-entrepreneurs.html; The College Investor, "4 Lessons That Every College Entrepreneur Should Know," October 16, 2019, https://thecollegeinvestor.com/17479/4-lessons-that-every-college-entrepreneur-should-know/; and www.ezkie.com.

- *Calamities* such as wars and natural disasters. Following the landfall of Hurricane Dorian in the Bahamas in 2019, Team Rubicon sent a three-person team to coordinate with the local officials and then launched a "large-scale response operation" to help those in need.[51] Team Rubicon's mission

> **franchising** an entrepreneurial alliance between a franchisor (an innovator who has created at least one successful store and wants to grow) and a franchisee (a partner who manages a new store of the same type in a new location)

is to connect military veterans with first responders to rapidly deploy emergency response teams to disasters around the world.[52]

- *Government initiatives and rule changes.* Deregulation spawned new airlines and trucking companies. Whenever the government tightens energy efficiency requirements, opportunities become available for entrepreneurs developing ideas for cutting energy use.

2.3 | Franchises

One important type of opportunity is the franchise. You may know intuitively what franchising is, or at least you can name some prominent franchises: Jimmy John's Sandwiches, Anytime Fitness, The UPS Store, and Jiffy Lube. **Franchising** is an entrepreneurial alliance between two parties:[53]

Prince Harry of Wales volunteers with Team Rubicon, an American nongovernmental organization. Becky Maynard/Team Rubicon UK/Getty Images

The Dallas Morning News/MCT/Getty Images

People often assume that buying a franchise is less risky than starting a business from scratch, but the evidence is mixed. A study that followed businesses for six years found the opposite of the popular assumption: 65 percent of the franchises studied were operating at the end of the period, while 72 percent of independent businesses were still operating. One reason may be that the franchises in the study were in just a few, possibly riskier industries.

If you are contemplating a franchise, consider its market presence (local, regional, or national); market share and profit margins; national programs for marketing and purchasing; the nature of the business, including required training and degree of field support; terms of the license agreement (e.g., 20 years with automatic renewal versus less than 10 years or no renewal); capital required; and franchise fees and royalties.[56] You can learn more from plenty of useful sources, including these:

- International Franchise Association (www.franchise.org).
- The Small Business Administration (www.sba.gov).
- Franchise & Business Opportunity Directory (www.franchise.com).
- FTC Consumer's Guide to Buying a Franchise (www.ftc.gov).

In addition, the Federal Trade Commission investigates complaints of deceptive claims by franchisors and publishes information about those cases.

2.4 | The Internet

The Internet is a business frontier that continues to expand. With e-commerce, as with any start-up, entrepreneurs need sound business models and practices. You need to

1. The *franchisor*–an innovator who has created at least one successful store and seeks partners to operate the same concept in other local markets.

2. The *franchisee*–the operator of one or more stores according to the terms of the alliance.

For the franchisee, the opportunity is wealth creation via a proven–but not failure-proof–business concept, with the added advantage of the franchisor's expertise. For the franchisor, the opportunity is wealth creation through growth. The partnership is manifest in a trademark or brand, and together the partners' mission is to maintain and build the brand.

Krispy Kreme started in 1937 but didn't expand nationally with franchising until the 1990s. It now has over 1,000 stores around the world.[55]

Did You KNOW

More than 733,000 franchised businesses in the United States provide nearly 8 million jobs. Franchises contribute hundreds of billions to the economy, most of which stays in local communities.[54]

 Traditional Thinking

Facebook, Twitter, and LinkedIn help entrepreneurs market their goods and services to "friends."

Source: Adapted from S. E. Needleman and A. Loten, "When 'Friending' Becomes a Source of Start-up Funds," *The Wall Street Journal*, November 1, 2011, p. B1.

The Best Managers Today

Raise capital by issuing securities to micro-investors through crowdfunding websites like Kickstarter and Indiegogo.

Source: H. Morton, "Crowdfunding State Laws," National Conference of State Legislators, April 12, 2016, www.ncls.org.

Kristoffer Tripplaar/Alamy Stock Photo.

watch costs carefully, and you want to achieve profitability as soon as possible.[57]

At least five successful business models have proven successful for e-commerce:[58]

1. Transaction fee model—Companies charge a fee for goods or services. Amazon.com and online travel agents are prime examples.

2. Advertising support model—Advertisers pay the site operator to gain access to the demographic group that visits the site. In 2018, online advertising expenditures surpassed $108 billion, with Google and Facebook accounting for the bulk of the spending.[59]

3. Intermediary model—A website brings buyers and sellers together and charges a commission for each sale. The premier example is eBay.

4. Affiliate model—Sites pay commissions to other sites to drive business to their own sites. Society6.com sells more than 30 custom-decorated, premium consumer goods such as T-shirts, shower curtains, and art prints.[60] Designer affiliates choose basic, undecorated products (such as a plain sweatshirt) and add their own designs. Society6 sets the basic price, and the designer gets about 10 percent.[61]

5. Subscription model—The website charges a monthly or annual fee for site visits or access to site content. Newspapers and magazines are good examples.

2.5 | Next Frontiers

The next frontiers for entrepreneurship—where do they lie? The powerful potential of big data to improve decision making is opening up tremendous opportunities for businesses that can help their clients collect, store, manage, and analyze data.

Other entrepreneurial frontiers include education, virtual reality (e.g., HTC), cryptocurrency (e.g., Bitcoin), green energy (e.g., wind, solar, and hydro energy),[62] and robots powered by artificial intelligence, which has far-reaching implications for business, government, and society.[63]

One fascinating opportunity for entrepreneurs is space travel. With increasing demand for satellite launches and interest in space tourism, smaller entrepreneurs are entering the field. SpaceX has been transporting cargo to the International Space Station for NASA and is developing the capability to transport astronaut crews. NASA also has granted a cargo-shuttling contract to Orbital Sciences Corporation.

Another emerging market is powerful Earth-observation satellites. Farmers, scientists, and first responders need high-resolution images to understand climate patterns, perform research, and plan emergency responses.[64] Capella Space plans to launch seven satellites in 2020 that will monitor the entire surface of the planet every six hours. Using a new technology, Capella's satellites can detect changes to Earth's surface less than a meter in size. The company signed multimillion-dollar contracts with several U.S. government agencies, including the Air Force.[65]

Changes are happening fast in the health care sector in the United States. Health care providers are digitizing their data for patient care, medication management, and treatment outcomes—offering opportunities for hardware and software businesses that cut costs or understand client needs. New apps keep appearing and appealing to insurance companies, employers, and consumers.

2.6 | Social Entrepreneurship

Social entrepreneurship, which has been around for decades, is surging in popularity and impact.[66] Social entrepreneurship has been defined in many ways, but most fundamentally it refers to leveraging resources to address social problems.[67]

It does so by using market-based methods.[68] Organizations that do this are social enterprises.[69] Social entrepreneurship creates social value by stimulating social change or meeting social needs.[70]

Such enterprises can advance societal well-being in one or more broad domains, including: (1) the environment—for example, energy conservation, responsible consumption, and habitat conservation; (2) social and economic inclusion—for example, empowering marginalized groups, revitalized neighborhoods,

transaction fee model charging fees for goods and services

advertising support model charging fees to advertise on a site

intermediary model charging fees to bring buyers and sellers together

affiliate model charging fees to direct site visitors to other companies' sites

subscription model charging fees for site visits

social entrepreneurship leveraging resources to address social problems

social enterprise organization that applies business models and leverages resources in ways that address social problems

> "To launch a business means successfully solving problems. Solving problems means listening."
>
> —Richard Branson, CEO, Virgin Group[74]

side street effect
as you head down a road, unexpected opportunities begin to appear

improving educational attainment, and reducing community violence; (3) health and well-being—for example, preventing and reducing health risk behaviors and improving access to health care; and (4) civic engagement, such as community volunteering, charitable giving, and responsible investing.[71]

Combining social and commercial goals isn't new; consider hospitals, universities, and arts organizations.[72] And not all social problems have entrepreneurial solutions. But pursuing the dual goal of both economic and social value may be developing as a new norm, with positive social outcomes as key to long-term success.

● Mario, Nintendo's iconic video game character, floats with ZERO-G coaches in zero-gravity atmosphere to train for "Super Mario Galaxy." Denise Truscello/Getty Images

Pierre Omidyar, founder of eBay, states: "You really can make the world better in any sector—in nonprofits, in business, or in government. It's not a question of one sector's struggling against another, or of 'giving back' versus 'taking away.' That's old thinking. A true philanthropist will use every tool he can to make an impact. Today business is a key part of the equation, and the sectors are learning to work together."[73]

2.7 | Side Streets

Trial and error also can be useful in starting new businesses. Some entrepreneurs start their enterprises and then let the market decide whether it likes their ideas. This method is risky, of course, and should be done only if you can afford the risks. But even if the original idea doesn't work, you may be able to capitalize on the side street effect.[75] As you head down a road, you come to unknown places, and unexpected opportunities begin to appear. And while you are looking, *prepare* so you can act quickly and effectively on any opportunity that presents itself.

LO3 Identify common causes of success and failure.

3 | WHAT DOES IT TAKE, PERSONALLY?

Many people assume that there is an "entrepreneurial personality." No single personality type predicts entrepreneurial success, but you are more likely to succeed as an entrepreneur if you apply:[76]

1. *Commitment and determination:* Successful entrepreneurs are decisive, tenacious, disciplined, willing to sacrifice, and able to immerse themselves totally in their enterprises.

2. *Leadership:* They are self-starters, team builders, superior learners, and teachers. Communicating a vision for the future of the company—an essential component of leadership—has a direct impact on venture growth.[77]

3. *Opportunity obsession:* They have an intimate knowledge of customers' needs, are market driven, and are obsessed with value creation and enhancement.

4. *Tolerance of risk, ambiguity, and uncertainty:* They are calculated risk takers and risk managers, tolerant of stress, and able to resolve problems.

5. *Creativity, self-reliance, and ability to adapt:* They are open-minded, restless with the status quo, able to learn quickly, highly adaptable, creative, skilled at conceptualizing, and attentive to details.

6. *Motivation to excel:* They have a clear results orientation, set high but realistic goals, have a strong drive to achieve, know their own weaknesses and strengths, and focus on what can be done rather than on the reasons why things can't be done.

Bill Gross—whom you met in our earlier discussion of "Why become an entrepreneur?"—exemplifies many of these things. He persevered even after his brainchild, Idealab, apparently crashed and burned. He launched the company in the mid-1990s to nurture Internet start-ups as they were being formed left and right. Companies that Idealab invested in included eToys, Eve.com, and Pets.com. If you haven't heard of them, it's probably because they went out of business when sales couldn't keep up with the hype and the hopes. Gross explains that he hadn't intended for Idealab to help exclusively dot-com businesses, but that's what entrepreneurs were all starting in the 1990s. When the Internet boom crashed, Gross laid off employees and shuttered offices, but he maintained his vision of helping entrepreneurs. Instead of giving up, Gross established stricter criteria for funding companies and determined that he would choose companies whose activities make a difference. In two decades, Idealab launched over 150 start-ups.[78]

3.1 | Making Good Choices

Success is a function not only of personal characteristics but also of making good choices about the business you start. Exhibit 6.3 presents a model for conceptualizing entrepreneurial ventures and making the best choices. According to this model, a new venture may involve high or low levels of *innovation,* or the creation of something new and different. It can also be characterized by low or high *risk,* including the probability of major financial loss, as well as psychological risk perceived by the entrepreneur, including risk to reputation and ego.[79] Combining these two variables, we can identify four kinds of new ventures:

1. In the upper left quadrant, innovation is high (ventures are truly novel ideas), and there is little risk. For example, a pioneering product idea from Procter & Gamble might fit here if there are no current competitors and because, for a company of that size, the financial risks of new product investments can seem relatively small.

2. In the upper right quadrant, novel product ideas (high innovation) are accompanied by high risk because the financial investments and competition are great. Virgin Galactic's space tourism venture would likely fall into this category.

3. Most small business ventures are in the lower right, where innovation is low and risk is high. They are fairly conventional entries in well-established fields. New restaurants, retail shops, and commercial outfits involve a sizable investment by the entrepreneur and face direct competition from similar businesses.

4. Finally, the low-innovation/low-risk category includes ventures that require minimal investment and/or face minimal competition for strong market demand. Examples are some service businesses having low start-up costs and those entering small towns if there is no competitor and demand is adequate.

This matrix helps entrepreneurs think about their venture idea and decide whether it suits their particular objectives. It also helps identify effective and ineffective strategies.

You might find one cell more appealing than others. The lower left cell is likely to have relatively low payoffs but provide more security. The possible risks and returns are higher in other cells, especially the upper right. So you might place your new venture idea in the appropriate cell and pursue it only if it is in a cell where you would prefer to operate. If it is not, you can reject the idea or look for a way to move it toward a different cell.

The matrix also can help entrepreneurs remember a useful point: Successful companies do not always require a cutting-edge technology or an exciting new product. Even companies offering the most mundane products—the type that might reside in the lower left cell—can gain competitive advantage by doing basic things better than competitors.

Oprah Winfrey is an award-winning entrepreneur with a long track record of success. From 1986 to 2011, her iconic talk show became the highest-rated talk show in television history. The show spurred nationwide debates on such topics as sexual abuse, discrimination, adoption, and homelessness, and served as a launch pad for several other shows like *Dr. Phil, Rachael Ray,* and *The Dr. Oz Show.* In addition to publishing a monthly magazine,[80] Oprah also acts, produces movies, and

Exhibit 6.3	Entrepreneurial strategy matrix	
	Low Risk	**High Risk**
High Innovation	Subway launches an online service to preorder sandwiches.	Medical researchers try to use 3D printing technology to create organs.
Low Innovation	A college student launches a résumé writing and interviewing tips venture.	An entrepreneur opens a pub in a downtown nightclub area.

Source: Adapted from M. Sonfield and R. Lussier, "The Entrepreneurial Strategy Matrix: A Model for New and Ongoing Ventures," *Business Horizons,* May–June 1997.

● Oprah Winfrey's exclusive, no-holds-barred interview with controversial cyclist Lance Armstrong, "Oprah and Lance Armstrong: The Worldwide Exclusive," aired as a two-night event on OWN: Oprah Winfrey Network.
George Burns/Oprah Winfrey Network/Getty Images

leads philanthropic activities like the Angel Network and the Leadership Academy for Girls in South Africa.

Winfrey launched the Oprah Winfrey Network (OWN) on cable in 2011. While many believed the Oprah brand would translate immediately into success with the new network, this has not been the case. Since its inception, OWN received more than $500 million from its partner, Discovery. This working capital gave Winfrey some breathing room to learn the ins and outs of managing a network.

Her skill and experience as an entrepreneur continue to pay off. On average, the number of prime-time viewers who watch OWN is 465,000, and the network has the top four original series on cable for African-American women.[81]

3.2 | Failure Happens, but You Can Improve the Odds of Success

Success or failure lies ahead for entrepreneurs starting their own companies, as well as for those starting new businesses within bigger corporations. Entrepreneurs succeed or fail in private, public, and not-for-profit sectors, as well as in nations at all stages of development and of all political types.[82]

Start-up failure rates vary. Most estimates indicate that failure is more the rule than the exception.

Start-ups have at least two major liabilities: newness and smallness.[84] New companies are relatively unknown and must learn how to beat established competitors at doing something customers value. The odds of survival improve if the venture grows to at least 10 or 20 people, has revenues of $2 or $3 million, and is pursuing opportunities with growth potential.[85]

Acquiring venture capital is not essential to the success of most start-up businesses; in fact, it is rare. More than three-fourths of start-up companies were financed by entrepreneurs' own assets or family assets. Approximately one-tenth of businesses were financed with the owners' credit cards.[86] Still, in 2018, venture capitalists invested $60 billion in start-ups.[87]

Further factors that influence success and failure include risk, the economic environment, various management-related hazards, and initial public offerings (IPOs) of stock.

Risk It's a given: Starting a new business is risky. Experienced entrepreneurs are especially aware of this. While running his fourth start-up company—an online driver's education website for teens—Blake Mycoskie vacationed in Argentina and liked the local *alpargata* shoe.[88] He took a big risk by entering the saturated shoe market with no experience and attempting to bring a foreign style into the U.S. market. The big risk paid off big time. In 2018, TOMS donated 93 million shoes to children in need, expanded to sell online and in brick-and-mortar stores, and offered new products like eyewear, shoes, and bags.[89]

3.3 | The Role of the Economic Environment

Entrepreneurial activity stems from the economic environment[91] as well as the behavior of individuals. For example, money is a critical resource for all new businesses. Increases in the money supply, bank loan availability, real economic growth, and

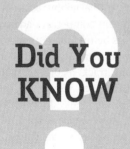

Did You KNOW

What are the best U.S. cities in which to start a new business? WalletHub, a financial website, measured 19 key metrics across 150 cities. They grouped the data into three categories: business environment (e.g., average length of the workweek), access to resources (e.g., ease of obtaining a loan), and business costs (e.g., affordability of office space). Here are WalletHub's top 10 cities for launching a company.[83]

Rank/City	Rank/City
1 Orlando, Florida	6 Charlotte, North Carolina
2 Oklahoma City, Oklahoma	7 Durham, North Carolina
3 Miami, Florida	8 Raleigh, North Carolina
4 Austin, Texas	9 Atlanta, Georgia
5 Tampa, Florida	10 Denver, Colorado

> Bill Gross studied hundreds of start-up companies to identify the factors that contributed most to their success. The top three contributors were timing, team and execution, and uniqueness of the idea.[90]

improved stock market performance lead to improved prospects and increased sources of capital. In turn, the prospects and the capital increase the rate of business formation. Under favorable conditions, many aspiring entrepreneurs find early success. But economic cycles change favorable conditions into downturns. To succeed, entrepreneurs must have the foresight and talent to survive when the environment becomes more hostile.

3.4 | Business Incubators

The need to provide a nurturing environment for fledgling enterprises led to the creation of business incubators. **Business incubators**, often located in industrial parks or abandoned factories, are protected environments for new, small businesses. Incubators offer benefits such as low rents and shared costs. Shared staff costs, such as for receptionists and administrative assistants, avoid the expense of a full-time employee but still provide convenient access to services. The staff manager is usually an experienced businessperson or consultant who advises the new business owners. Incubators often are associated with universities, which provide technical and business services for the new companies.

The heyday of business incubators came in the 1990s, when around 700 of them were financing start-ups, mainly emphasizing technology. Eight out of ten shut down following the collapse of the Internet bubble, but the idea of nurturing new businesses persists. MGE Innovation Center, part of the University of Wisconsin–Madison Research Park, has helped launch more than 70 early-stage companies. The center provides founders of high-tech start-ups with expert advice in product development, seed funding, legal services, and access to relevant networks.[92]

> **LO4 Discuss common management challenges.**

4 | COMMON MANAGEMENT CHALLENGES

As an entrepreneur, you should understand and be prepared to face certain challenges. Then you can manage them more effectively when the time comes. Exhibit 6.4 illustrates eight common management challenges.

> **business incubators**
> protected environments for new small businesses

4.1 | You Might Not Enjoy It

Working for a big company, you might be able to specialize in what you love, whether it's selling or accounting. But entrepreneurs usually have to do it all, at least in the beginning. If you love product design, you also have to sell what you invent. If you love marketing, get ready to manage the money too.

When Will Russell quit his job to launch a digital marketing business to help nonprofits and social enterprises increase their impact, he had no idea what he was getting into. After enduring several ups and downs during his first year as an entrepreneur, Russell had second thoughts about his decision. He persisted despite those doubts. Five years later his company, Russell Marketing, is thriving. He offers these tips to would-be entrepreneurs: (1) Successful people aren't special or extremely talented, but they have courage and perseverance; (2) seek support from a network of mentors, peers, family, and friends; and (3) identify and complete a limited number of key priorities each week while ignoring noncritical tasks.[93]

4.2 | Survival Is Difficult

Zappos cofounder Tony Hsieh says, "We thought about going under every day—until we got a $6 million credit line from Wells Fargo."[94] Companies without much of a track record tend to have trouble lining up lenders, investors, and even customers. When economic conditions cool or competition heats up, a small start-up serving a niche market may have limited options for survival.

Gary Gottenbusch worried when orders slowed at his Servatii Pastry Shop & Deli in Cincinnati. As a recession hit Ohio hard, customers decided that fancy breads and cakes were a luxury they could go without. Servatii might have closed, but Gottenbusch changed his vision. He kept afloat and even added to sales by cultivating new distribution channels (sales in hospitals), new products (distinctive pretzel sticks), and cost-cutting measures (a purchasing association with other bakers in the area).[95]

Failure can be devastating. Pursuing his dream to be a successful food industry entrepreneur, Manoj Tripathi eventually bought several Subway franchises in the East Bay region of

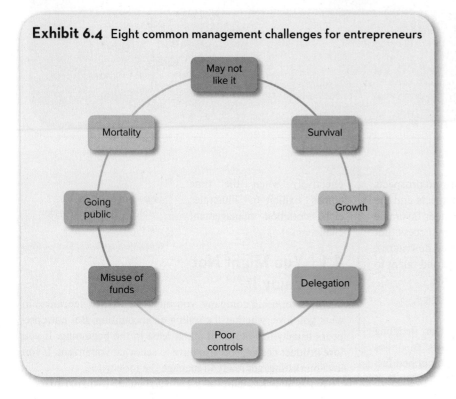

Exhibit 6.4 Eight common management challenges for entrepreneurs

- May not like it
- Survival
- Growth
- Delegation
- Poor controls
- Misuse of funds
- Going public
- Mortality

California.[96] That's when his troubles began. Tripathi claimed that regional management was conducting inspections that identified insignificant infractions, like using the wrong brand of bathroom soap, or a vegetable slice that was too thick—a complaint that his inspector confirmed. A year after the inspections, he lost a franchise.[97]

4.3 | Growth Creates New Challenges

Just one in three *Inc.* 500 companies keeps growing fast enough to make this list of fastest-growing companies two years running. The reason: They are facing bigger challenges, competing with bigger firms, stretching the founders' capacities, and probably burning cash.[98] It's a difficult transition.

The transition is particularly complex for entrepreneurs who quickly consider expanding internationally. Whether a firm should expand internationally soon after it is created or wait until it is better established is an open question. Entering international markets should help a firm grow, but going global creates challenges that can make survival more difficult, especially when the company is young.

When Lou Hoffman decided to expand his public relations (PR) firm to China, he couldn't find anyone familiar with both Chinese business and the creative business culture that had served his agency well. So he hired a Chinese PR staffer who was willing to spend a year at his California headquarters, just absorbing the business culture. That method worked for the Chinese market but flopped when Hoffman tried it for opening a London office; the British employee didn't want to leave the California lifestyle and return home.[99] Of course, the risks tend

to be lower when entrepreneurs (or their company's managers) have experience in serving foreign markets.[100]

Uber's revenue remained flat at $2.3 billion from 2018 to 2019; its bookings doubled, but the rate per ride dropped 4 percent.[101] With ample competition from Lyft rides, Lime scooters, Favor food delivery, and others, Uber launched new services to spur growth. For example, Uber Mobility offers rentable battery-powered bikes on docking stations throughout cities, and Uber Pass is a monthly subscription for unlimited Uber Eats deliveries.[102]

In the beginning, the start-up mentality tends to be "we try harder."[103] Entrepreneurs work long hours at low pay, deliver great service, get good word of mouth, and their business grows. At first, it's "high performance, cheap labor." But with growth comes the need to pay higher wages to hire more people who are less dedicated than the founders. Then it's time to raise prices, establish efficient systems, or accept lower profits.[104]

The founder's talents may not spread to everyone else. You need a unique value proposition that will work as well with 100 employees, because hard work or instincts alone no longer will get the job done. Complicating matters is the continuing growth and change in customers' needs and expectations.[105]

4.4 | It's Hard to Delegate

As the business grows, entrepreneurs often hesitate to delegate work they are used to doing. Leadership deteriorates into micromanagement.[106] Even Sir Richard Branson, the billionaire leader of the Virgin Group, struggled with delegation soon after starting his first business: "If you really want to grow as an entrepreneur, you've got to learn to delegate."[107] Supporting Branson's opinion was a survey reporting that CEOs who delegated effectively achieved greater revenue growth and higher revenues over a three-year period than those who tried to micromanage.[108]

4.5 | Poor Controls

Entrepreneurs, in part because they are so busy, often fail to use formal control systems. One common entrepreneurial malady is an aversion to record keeping. Expenses mount, but records do not keep pace. Pricing decisions are based on intuition without adequate reference to costs. As a result, the company earns inadequate margins to support growth.

Sometimes, an economic slowdown provides a necessary alarm, warning business owners to pay attention to controls. When Servatii Pastry Shop & Deli's sales deteriorated as ingredient prices rose, owner Gary Gottenbusch pushed himself to go "a little out of [his] comfort zone" and consulted with advisers

> "If you want to do a few small things right, do them yourself. If you want to do great things and make a big impact, learn to delegate."
>
> —John C. Maxwell, American author

at the Manufacturing Extension Partnership. Besides encouraging him to innovate, the advisers helped him set goals and monitor progress. One problem Gottenbusch tackled was the price of baking commodities, such as shortening and flour. He partnered with other local bakeries to form a purchasing association that buys in bulk and passes along the savings. Keeping costs down helped Servatii stay profitable when customers were trimming their budgets for baked goods.[109]

Even in high-growth companies, great numbers can mask brewing problems. Blinded by the light of growing sales, many entrepreneurs fail to maintain vigilance over other aspects of the business. In the absence of controls, the business veers out of control.

Don't get overconfident; keep asking critical questions. Is our success based on just one big customer? Is our product just a fad that can fade away? Can other companies enter our domain and hurt our business? Are we losing a technology lead? Do we really understand the numbers, know where they come from, and have any hidden causes for concern?

4.6 | Misuse of Funds

Many unsuccessful entrepreneurs blame their failure on inadequate financial resources. Yet failure due to a lack of financial resources doesn't necessarily indicate a real lack of money; it could mean a failure to use the available money properly. A lot of start-up capital may be wasted—on expensive locations, great furniture, fancy stationery. Entrepreneurs who fail to use their resources wisely usually make one of two mistakes: They apply financial resources to the wrong uses, or they maintain inadequate control over their resources.

This problem may be more likely when a lucky entrepreneur gets a big infusion of cash from a venture capital firm or an initial stock offering. For most start-ups, where the money on the line comes from the entrepreneur's own assets, he or she has more incentive to be careful. Tripp Micou, founder of Practical Computer Applications, says, "If all the money you spend is based on what you're bringing in [through sales], you very quickly focus on the right things to spend it on."[110] Micou, an experienced entrepreneur who expects the company's revenues to double each year for the next few years, believes that this financial limitation is actually a management advantage.

4.7 | Going Public

Sometimes companies reach a point at which the owners want to "go public." Initial public offerings (IPOs) offer a way to raise capital through federally registered and underwritten sales of shares in the company.[111] To go public, you need lawyers and accountants who know current regulations.

initial public offering (IPO) sale to the public, for the first time, of federally registered and underwritten shares of stock in the company

The reasons for going public include raising more capital, reducing debt or improving the balance sheet and enhancing net worth, pursuing otherwise unaffordable opportunities, and improving credibility with customers and other stakeholders—"you're in the big leagues now."

Disadvantages include the expense, time, and effort involved; the tendency to become more interested in the stock price and capital gains than in running the company properly; and the creation of a long-term relationship with an investment banking firm that won't necessarily always be a good one.[112]

Many entrepreneurs prefer to avoid going public, feeling they'll lose control if they do. As Yvon Chouinard of sports and apparel firm Patagonia states, "There's a certain formula in business where you grow the thing and go public. I don't think it has to be that way. Being a closely held company means being able to take risks and try new things—the creative part of business. If I were owned by a bunch of retired teachers, I wouldn't be able to do what I do; I'd have to be solely concerned with the bottom line."[113]

Executing IPOs and other approaches to acquiring capital is complex and beyond the scope of this chapter. Sources for more information include *The Ernst & Young Guide to Raising Capital*, the National Venture Capital Association (www.nvca.org), CB Insights and *The New York Times* Top 100 Venture Capitalists (https://www.cbinsights.com), and *The Entrepreneur's Guide to Venture Capital* (https://blog.hubspot.comsales/venture-capitalist).

4.8 | Mortality

One long-term measure of an entrepreneur's success is the fate of the venture after the founder's death. Founding entrepreneurs have trouble letting go, and often fail to plan for succession.[114]

When death occurs, the lack of a skilled replacement for the founder can lead to business failure.

Management guru Peter Drucker offered the following advice to help family-managed businesses survive and prosper:[115]

- Family members working in the business must be at least as capable and hard-working as other employees.

- At least one key position should be filled by a nonfamily member.

- Someone outside the family and the business should help plan succession.

Family members who are mediocre performers are resented by others; outsiders can be more objective and contribute expertise the family might not have. Issues of management succession are often the most difficult of all, causing serious conflict and possible breakup of the firm.

> **LO5 Explain how to increase your chances of success, including good business planning.**

5 | PLANNING AND RESOURCES HELP YOU SUCCEED

Aside from financial resources, entrepreneurs need to think through their business idea carefully to help ensure its success.[116] This calls for good planning and nonfinancial resources. We discuss these next, in turn.

5.1 | Planning

So you think you have identified a business opportunity and have the potential to make it succeed. Now what? Should you act on your idea? Where should you begin?

The Business Plan Your excitement and intuition may convince you that you are on to something. But they might not convince anyone else. You need more thorough planning and analysis. This effort will help convince others to get on board and help you avoid costly mistakes.

The first formal planning step is to do an opportunity analysis. This includes a description of the good or service, an

assessment of the opportunity, an assessment of the entrepreneur (you), a specification of activities and resources needed to translate your idea into a viable business, and your source(s) of capital.[117] Your opportunity analysis should include the following questions:[118]

- What market need does my idea fill?

- What personal observations have I experienced or recorded with regard to that market need?

- What social condition underlies this market need?

- What market research data can be marshaled to describe this market need?

- What patents might be available to fulfill this need?

- What competition exists in this market? How would I describe the behavior of this competition?

- What does the international market look like?

- What does the international competition look like?

- Where is the money to be made in this activity?

The opportunity analysis, or opportunity assessment plan, focuses on the opportunity, not the entire venture. It provides the basis for deciding whether to act. Then the business plan describes all the elements involved in starting the new venture.[119] The business plan describes the venture and its market, strategies, and future directions. It often has functional plans for marketing, finance, manufacturing, and human resources. Exhibit 6.5 outlines a typical business plan.

The business plan serves several purposes:

- It helps determine the viability of your enterprise.

- It guides you as you plan and organize.

- It helps you obtain financing.

It is read by potential investors, suppliers, customers, and others. Get help in writing a sound plan!

Key Planning Elements Most business plans devote so much attention to financial projections that they neglect other important information—information that matters greatly to astute investors.

In fact, financial projections tend to be overly optimistic. Investors know this and discount the figures.[120] In addition to the numbers, the best plans convey—and make certain that the entrepreneurs have carefully thought through—five key factors:[121]

1. *The people:* The new organization's people should be energetic and have skills and expertise directly relevant to the venture. For many astute investors, the people are the most important element, more important even than the idea. Arthur Rock, a legendary venture capitalist who helped start Intel, Teledyne, and Apple, stated, "I invest in people, not ideas. If you can find good people, if they're wrong about the product, they'll make a switch."[122]

Exhibit 6.5 Outline of a business plan

 I. EXECUTIVE SUMMARY

    A. Description of the Business Concept and the Business.

    B. The Opportunity and Strategy.

    C. The Target Market and Projections.

    D. The Competitive Advantages.

    E. The Economics, Profitability, and Harvest Potential.

    F. The Team.

    G. The Offering.

 II. THE INDUSTRY AND THE COMPANY AND ITS PRODUCT(S) OR SERVICE(S)

    A. The Industry.

    B. The Company and the Concept.

    C. The Product(s) or Service(s).

    D. Entry and Growth Strategy.

 III. MARKET RESEARCH AND ANALYSIS

    A. Customers.

    B. Market Size and Trends.

    C. Competition and Competitive Edges.

    D. Estimated Market Share and Sales.

    E. Ongoing Market Evaluation.

 IV. THE ECONOMICS OF THE BUSINESS

    A. Gross and Operating Margins.

    B. Profit Potential and Durability.

    C. Fixed, Variable, and Semivariable Costs.

    D. Months to Breakeven.

    E. Months to Reach Positive Cash Flow.

 V. MARKETING PLAN

    A. Overall Marketing Strategy.

    B. Pricing.

    C. Sales Tactics.

    D. Service and Warranty Policies.

    E. Advertising and Promotion.

    F. Distribution.

VI. DESIGN AND DEVELOPMENT PLANS

    A. Development Status and Tasks.

    B. Difficulties and Risks.

    C. Product Improvement and New Products.

    D. Costs.

    E. Proprietary Issues.

 VII. MANUFACTURING AND OPERATIONS PLAN

    A. Operating Cycle.

    B. Geographical Location.

    C. Facilities and Improvements.

    D. Strategy and Plans.

    E. Regulatory and Legal Issues.

VIII. MANAGEMENT TEAM

    A. Organization.

    B. Key Management Personnel.

    C. Management Compensation and Ownership.

    D. Other Investors.

    E. Employment and Other Agreements and Stock Option and Bonus Plans.

    F. Board of Directors.

    G. Other Shareholders, Rights, and Restrictions.

    H. Supporting Professional Advisers and Services.

 IX. OVERALL SCHEDULE

 X. CRITICAL RISKS, PROBLEMS, AND ASSUMPTIONS

 XI. THE FINANCIAL PLAN

    A. Actual Income Statements and Balance Sheets.

    B. Pro Forma Income Statements.

    C. Pro Forma Balance Sheets.

    D. Pro Forma Cash Flow Analysis.

    E. Breakeven Chart and Calculation.

    F. Cost Control.

    G. Highlights.

 XII. PROPOSED COMPANY OFFERING

    A. Desired Financing.

    B. Offering.

    C. Capitalization.

    D. Use of Funds.

    E. Investor's Return.

 XIII. APPENDIXES

Source: J. A. Timmons, *New Venture Creation,* 5th ed. (McGraw-Hill Education, 1999), p. 374.

2. *The opportunity:* You need a competitive advantage that can be defended. The focus should be on customers. Who is the customer? How does the customer make decisions? What price will the customer pay? How will the venture reach all customer segments? How much does it cost to acquire and support a customer, and to produce and deliver the product? How easy or difficult is it to retain a customer?

3. *The competition:* The plan must identify current competitors and their strengths and weaknesses, predict how they will respond to the new venture, indicate how the new venture will respond to the competitors' responses, identify future potential competitors, and consider how to collaborate with or face off against actual or potential competitors.

4. *The context:* The environment should be favorable from regulatory and economic perspectives. Such factors as tax policies, rules about raising capital, interest rates, inflation, and exchange rates will affect the viability of the new venture. The context can make it easier or harder to get backing. Importantly, the plan should make clear that you know that the context inevitably will change, forecast how the changes will affect the business, and describe how you will deal with the changes.

5. *Risk and reward:* The risk must be understood and addressed as fully as possible. The future is uncertain, and the elements described in the plan will change. Although you cannot predict the future, you must contemplate head-on the possibilities of key people resigning, interest rates changing, a key customer leaving, or a powerful competitor responding ferociously. Then describe what you will do to prevent, avoid, or cope with such possibilities. You should also speak to the end of the process: how to get money out of the business eventually. Will you go public? Will you sell or liquidate? What are the various possibilities for investors to realize their ultimate gains?[123]

Did You KNOW?

Revolution Foods received the Best for the World (customers category) award from B Lab, a nonprofit organization dedicated to using the power of business as a force for good. Revolution Foods provides over 1.5 million nutritious meals to school children throughout the United States. The meals consist of high-quality, locally sourced ingredients with an emphasis on fresh fruits, vegetables, and whole grains.[124]

Selling the Plan Your goal is to get investors to support the plan. The elements of a great plan, as just described, are essential. Also important is whom you decide to try to convince to back your plan.

Many entrepreneurs want passive investors who will give them money and let them do what they want. Doctors and dentists generally fit this image. Professional venture capitalists do not, as they demand more control and more of the returns. But when a business goes wrong—and chances are, it will—nonprofessional investors are less helpful and less likely to advance more (needed) money. Sophisticated investors have seen sinking ships before and know how to help. They are more likely to solve problems, provide more money, and also navigate financial and legal waters such as going public.[125]

View the plan as a way for you to figure out how to reduce risk and maximize reward, and to convince others that you understand the entire new venture process. Don't put together a plan built on naïveté or overconfidence or one that cleverly hides major flaws. You might not fool others, and you certainly would be fooling yourself.

5.2 | Nonfinancial Resources

Also crucial to the success of a new business are nonfinancial resources, including legitimacy in the minds of the public and how other people can help.

Legitimacy An important resource for the new venture is legitimacy—people's judgment of a company's acceptance, appropriateness, and desirability.[126] When the market confers legitimacy, it helps overcome the "liability of newness" that creates a high percentage of new venture failure.[127] Legitimacy helps a firm acquire other resources such as top managers, good employees, financial resources, and government support. A company's success at selling products, hiring employees, and attracting investors depends on how skillfully the entrepreneur demonstrates its legitimacy.[128]

A business is legitimate if its goals and methods are consistent with societal values. You can generate legitimacy by visibly conforming to rules and expectations created by governments, credentialing associations, and professional organizations; by visibly endorsing widely held values; and by visibly practicing widely held beliefs.[129]

Networks The entrepreneur is aided greatly by having a strong network of people. Social capital—being part of a social network and having a good reputation—helps entrepreneurs gain access to useful information, win trust and cooperation from others, recruit employees, form successful business alliances, receive funding from venture capitalists, and become more successful.[130] Social capital provides a lasting source of competitive advantage.[131]

To see just some of the ways social capital can help entrepreneurs, consider these examples. An early-stage venture capital fund, NextGen Ventures, has over 600 venture partners who volunteer several hours a month to advise and work with start-up CEOs. NextGen provides its clients these invaluable expert networking and mentoring opportunities.[132]

A second example of the benefits of a strong network can be seen in Victoria Colligan's Ladies Who Launch, a media firm that provides resources and connections to female entrepreneurs. Members receive advice about promoting and growing their new businesses, network with several other women entrepreneurs, and are teamed up with expert business coaches.[133] Ladies Who Launch has connected more than 100,000 women from San Francisco to Dublin through its free events, workshops, and networking website.[134]

Top Management Teams Your top management team (TMT) is another crucial resource. TMTs typically include seasoned entrepreneurs who have launched successful companies in similar market spaces and industries.[135] Also, a good TMT and board of directors improve the firm's image, help develop longer-term plans, can support day-to-day activities, and offer a network of information sources.

Advisory Boards Whether or not the company has a formal board of directors, entrepreneurs can assemble a group of people willing to serve as an advisory board. Board members with business experience can help an entrepreneur learn basics like how to do cash flow analysis, identify needed strategic changes, and build relationships with bankers, accountants, and attorneys. Karen Usher attributes the success of her human resources outsourcing firm TPO to her advisory board of three veteran executives, who gave management and investment advice and made introductions to potential clients.[136]

Partners Often, two or more people go into business together as partners. Partners can help one another access capital, spread the workload, share the risk, and share expertise.

While some partnerships fall apart over time, others endure and succeed. Some examples of high-performance business partnerships include Twitter's Evan Williams, Biz Stone, and Jack Dorsey; Microsoft's Bill Gates and Paul Allen; Imagine Entertainment's Brian Grazer and Ron Howard; the New York Yankees baseball franchise's Joe Torre and the late Don Zimmer; Rent the Runway's Jenny Fleiss and Jenn Hyman; and Google's Sergei Brin and Larry Page.

What factors contribute to successful, long-lasting business relationships? The answer includes trust, mutual respect, shared vision and values, and honest and open communication.[137] For example, Berkshire Hathaway CEO Warren Buffett's vice chair, Charlie Munger, plays devil's advocate by looking at "every possible business deal skeptically, always

Berkshire Hathaway Inc. chair Warren Buffett (right) talks to Microsoft Corp. chair Bill Gates at the Berkshire Hathaway annual meeting. Chris Machian/Bloomberg/Getty Images

looking for a reason to say no." Meanwhile, Buffett uses every argument possible to obtain Munger's support.[138] After these discussions, the partners decide whether to invest or not. This strategy helped Berkshire Hathaway become an extremely influential investment company, reporting total revenue of nearly $248 billion in 2019.[139]

LO6 Describe how managers of large companies can foster entrepreneurship.

6 | CORPORATE ENTREPRENEURSHIP

Large corporations are more than passive bystanders in the entrepreneurship arena. Some famous examples of successful products that were developed inside large companies include Gmail (Google), iPhone (Apple), Elixir guitar strings (W. L. Gore & Associates), and PlayStation (Sony).[140]

Even established companies try to find and pursue profitable new ideas—and they need in-house entrepreneurs (often called intrapreneurs) to do so. If you work in a company and are considering launching a new business venture, Exhibit 6.6 can help you decide whether to pursue it.

skunkworks
a project team designated to produce a new, innovative product

bootlegging informal work on projects, other than those officially assigned, of employees' own choosing and initiative

6.1 | Build Support for Your Ideas

A manager with an idea to capitalize on a market opportunity will need to get others in the organization to buy in or sign on. In other words, you need to build a network of allies who support and will help implement the idea.

The first step involves *clearing the investment* with your immediate boss or bosses.[141] At this stage, you explain the idea and seek approval to look for wider support.

Higher executives often want evidence that the project is backed by your peers before committing to it. This involves *making cheerleaders*—people who will support the manager before formal approval from higher levels.

Next, *horse trading* begins. You can offer promises of payoffs from the project in return for support, time, money, and other resources that peers and others contribute.

Finally, you should *get the blessing* of relevant higher-level officials. This usually requires a formal presentation. You will need to guarantee the project's technical and political feasibility. Higher management's endorsement of the project and promises of resources help convert potential supporters into an enthusiastic team. At this point, you can go back to your boss and make specific plans for going ahead with the project.

Along the way, expect resistance and frustration—and use your passion and enthusiasm, as well as business logic, to persuade others to get on board.

6.2 | Build Intrapreneurship in Your Organization

Since taking over as CEO of Google (part of Alphabet), Larry Page has been busy reviving the organization's entrepreneurial culture. He sped up the pace of change, restructured the company, advanced the development and application of artificial intelligence, and collaborated with others to enhance the user experience on the mobile web.[142]

Two common approaches used to stimulate intrapreneurial activity are skunkworks and bootlegging. Skunkworks are project teams designated to produce a new product. The team has a specific goal to be achieved within a specified time frame and a respected manager leading the project. In this approach to corporate innovation, risk takers are not punished if they fail—they keep their former jobs. They also have the opportunity to earn large rewards. Adam Gryglak, chief engineer at Ford Motor Company, led a skunkworks team to develop an all-new Ford diesel engine in a record-setting 36 months.[143]

Bootlegging refers to informal efforts—as opposed to official job assignments—in which employees work to create new products and processes of their own choosing and initiative. Informal can mean secretive, such as when a bootlegger believes the company or the boss will frown on those activities. But some companies tolerate bootlegging, and even encourage it. To a limited extent, they allow people freedom to pursue pet projects without asking what they are or monitoring progress; they figure bootlegging will lead to some lost time but also to learning and to some profitable innovations.

W. L. Gore, maker of GoreTex and several other products, encourages its associates to pursue innovative ideas by self-organizing into small teams. The associates spend up to 10 percent of their workweek developing these side projects. If an idea gets traction, then it can be presented to company leadership who will consider funding the new project. This was the process used by a small group of Gore associates who spent a few years developing and perfecting Elixir guitar strings, which have become a popular choice among guitarists.[144]

6.3 | Managing the Risks

Organizations that encourage intrapreneurship face an obvious risk: The effort can fail.[145] However, this risk is manageable. In fact, failing to foster intrapreneurship may represent a subtler but greater risk than encouraging it. The organization that resists entrepreneurial initiative may lose its ability to adapt when conditions require innovation.

The most dangerous risk in intrapreneurship is the risk of overrelying on a

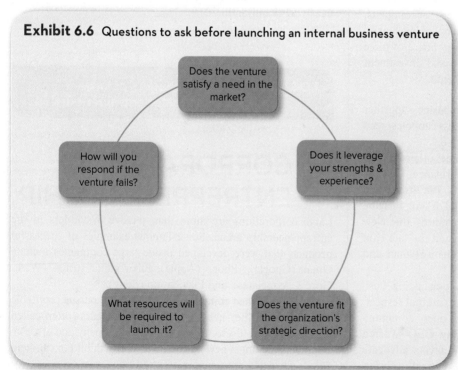

Exhibit 6.6 Questions to ask before launching an internal business venture

- Does the venture satisfy a need in the market?
- Does it leverage your strengths & experience?
- Does the venture fit the organization's strategic direction?
- What resources will be required to launch it?
- How will you respond if the venture fails?

Source: Adapted from G. Pinchot III, *Intrapreneuring.*

single project. Many companies fail while awaiting the completion of one large, innovative project.[146] The successful intrapreneurial organization avoids overcommitment to a single project and relies on its entrepreneurial spirit to produce at least one winner from among several projects.

Organizations also court failure when they spread their entrepreneurial efforts over too many projects.[147] If there are many projects, each effort may be too small in scale. Managers will consider the projects unattractive because of their small size. And, those recruited to manage the projects may have difficulty building power and status within the organization.

6.4 | An Entrepreneurial Orientation Encourages New Ideas

Just as we can distinguish characteristics of individual entrepreneurs, we can do the same for companies. Companies that are highly entrepreneurial differ from those that are not. CEOs play a crucial role in promoting entrepreneurship within large corporations.[148]

Entrepreneurial orientation is the tendency of an organization to engage in activities designed to identify and capitalize successfully on opportunities to launch new ventures by entering new or established markets with new or existing goods or services.[149] Entrepreneurial orientation is determined by five tendencies:

1. *Independent action*—The organization grants individuals and teams the freedom to exercise their creativity, champion promising ideas, and carry them through to completion.

2. *Innovativeness*—The firm supports new ideas, experimentation, and creative processes that can lead to new products or processes; it is willing to depart from existing practices and venture beyond the status quo.

3. *Risk taking*—The organization is willing to commit significant resources and perhaps borrow heavily to venture into the unknown. This tendency can be assessed by considering whether people are bold or cautious, whether they require high levels of certainty before taking or allowing action, and whether they tend to follow tried-and-true paths.

4. *Proactiveness*—The organization acts in anticipation of future problems and opportunities. A proactive firm changes the competitive landscape; other firms merely react. Proactive firms, like proactive individuals, are forward-thinking and take the lead with new initiatives.[150] Proactive firms encourage and allow individuals and teams to *be* proactive.

5. *Competitive aggressiveness*—The firm tends to challenge competitors directly and intensely to achieve entry or improve its position. In other words, it competes energetically to outperform its rivals in the marketplace. This might involve striking fast to beat competitors to the punch, tackle them head-to-head, and analyze and target competitors' weaknesses.

Entrepreneurial orientation should enhance the likelihood of success and may be particularly important for conducting business internationally.[151]

Thus an "entrepreneurial" firm engages in an effective combination of independent action, innovativeness, risk taking, proactiveness, and competitive aggressiveness.[152] The relationship between these factors and the performance of the firm is complicated and depends on many things. Still, you can imagine how the opposite profile—too many constraints on action, business as usual, extreme caution, passivity, and a lack of competitive fire—will undermine entrepreneurial activities. And without entrepreneurship, how would firms survive and thrive in a constantly changing competitive environment?

Thus management can create environments that foster entrepreneurship. If your bosses are not doing this, consider trying some entrepreneurial experiments on your own.[154] Seek out others with an entrepreneurial bent. What can you learn from them, and what can you teach others? Sometimes it takes individuals and teams of experimenters to show the possibilities to those at the top. Ask yourself, and ask others: Between the bureaucrats and the entrepreneurs, who is having a more positive impact? And who is having more fun?

> **entrepreneurial orientation** the tendency of an organization to identify and capitalize successfully on opportunities to launch new ventures by entering new or established markets with new or existing goods or services

---

"I had to make my own living and my own opportunity! But I made it! Don't sit down and wait for the opportunities to come. Get up and make them."

—Madam C. J. Walker, legendary entrepreneur and founder of Walker cosmetics line[153]

Sustaining for Tomorrow

Ashoka's Bill Drayton, Pioneering Social Entrepreneur

Can a company do well and do good at the same time? The idea that business success and positive social change should happen together is the driving force behind social entrepreneurship. Social entrepreneurs are change agents, managers who use management functions to create not only private value in the form of profit, but also social value in the form of innovation, sustainability, and environmental responsibility.

A leading force behind the growing strength of social enterprise is Ashoka, a worldwide organization founded by Bill Drayton in 1981 as a group of Fellows, or social entrepreneurs, then mostly in developing countries. The group has since grown to more than 3,500 social entrepreneurs, or "changemakers," in 92 countries. Among other achievements, it has helped make social enterprise programs available in business schools and public policy schools around the world and has supported business, social, and financial systems to encourage even more social innovation.

The idea of social entrepreneurship may have started with Bill Drayton, but it has evolved to influence thousands of people since. In fact, social entrepreneurship, once a peripheral endeavor, is now becoming more mainstream, with a third of all new start-ups focusing on performing a social good. Jazzmine Raine, for example, is cofounder of Hara House, the first zero-waste guesthouse in North India. She donates 20 percent of her profits to environmental action and education for local youth. Dave Mauro is the founder of Mauro Seed Company, whose mission is to fight hunger with sustainable agriculture. These social entrepreneurs, and thousands more like them, are trying to change the world for the better one business at a time.

Bill Drayton founded Ashoka, an organization that builds and cultivates a community of change leaders focusing on critical issues from health to justice to the environment. They believe that to create change, everyone needs to be a changemaker. The Washington Times/ZUMAPREss.com/Newscom

Discussion Questions

- Do you think every manager should have the responsibility to do good and to do well? Why or why not?

- Besides the efforts of those noted here, what other means to create sustainability do you think can be effective?

Sources: "About Ashoka," www.ashoka.org/en/about-ashoka, accessed March 13, 2020; B. Groom, "A Third of Start-ups Aim for Social Good," *Financial Times,* June 14, 2018, https://www.ft.com/content/d8b6d9fa-4eb8-11e8-ac41-759eee1efb74; G. Trahant, "The 35 Social Entrepreneurs to Watch for in 2019," Cause Artist, https://www.causeartist.com/social-entrepreneurs-to-watch-for-2019/, accessed March 13, 2020.

Notes

1. "25 Women Changing the Future." Marie Claire, September 24, 2019. Retrieved from https://www.marieclaire.com/celebrity/a28967312/women-changing-future/.

2. P. Schrodt, "Meet the Sisters Who Run YouTube and 23andMe—and Have a Collective Net Worth of Nearly $1 Billion," *Money,* August 30, 2018, https://money.com/youtube-23and-me-susan-anne-wojcicki/.

3. Ryan, Kevin. "23andMe Knows What Diseases Are in Your DNA. Now, It's Looking for the Cures." Inc., accessed from https://www.inc.com/kevin-j-ryan/23andme-2018-company-of-the-year-nominee.html, March 13, 2020.

4. D. Harper, "Towards a Theory of Entrepreneurial Teams," *Journal of Business Venturing* 23, no. 6 (2008), pp. 613–26; and S. Shane and S. Venkataraman, "The Promise of Entrepreneurship as a Field of Research," *Academy of Management Review* 25 (2000), pp. 217–26.

5. J. A. Timmons, *New Venture Creation* (Burr Ridge, IL: Richard D. Irwin, 1994).

6. G. T. Lumpkin and G. G. Dess, "Clarifying the Entrepreneurial Orientation Construct and Linking It to Performance," *Academy of Management Review* 21 (1996), pp. 135–72.

7. See Virgin's company website, https://www.virgin.com/virgin group/virgingroup/content/about-us, accessed September 25, 2019.

8. "Forbes List of Billionaires 2019," https://www.forbes.com/ profile/richard-branson; and "Richard Branson Biography," June 25, 2019, www.biography.com.

9. R. W. Smilor, "Entrepreneurship: Reflections on a Subversive Activity," *Journal of Business Venturing* 12 (1997), pp. 341–46.

10. W. Megginson, M. J. Byrd, S. R. Scott Jr., and L. Megginson, *Small Business Management: An Entrepreneur's Guide to Success,* 2nd ed. (Boston: Irwin/McGraw-Hill, 1997).

11. "Summary of Size Standards by Industry Sector," U.S. Small Business Administration, February 26, 2016, www.sba.gov.

12. J. Timmons and S. Spinelli, *New Venture Creation: Entrepreneurship for the 21st Century,* 6th ed. (New York: McGraw-Hill/Irwin, 2004), p. 3.

13. Kauffman Foundation, "Startup Activity Swings Upward for Third Consecutive Year, Annual Kauffman Index Reports," press release, May 18, 2017, www.kauffman.org.

14. "2018 National Report on Early-Stage Entrepreneurship," Kauffman Indicators of Entrepreneurship, September 2019, www. indicators.kauffman.org.

15. T. Huddleston Jr., "10 Best States for Starting a New Business in America," *CNBC Make It,* July 9, 2019, www.cnbc.com.

16. "The World's Most Innovative Companies 2019," *Fast Company,* www.fastcompany.com, accessed September 25, 2019.

17. J. Timmons and S. Spinelli, *New Venture Creation: Entrepreneurship for the 21st Century,* 6th ed. (New York: McGraw-Hill/Irwin, 2004).

18. J. Timmons and S. Spinelli, *New Venture Creation: Entrepreneurship for the 21st Century,* 6th ed. (New York: McGraw-Hill/Irwin, 2004).

19. R. Arend, H. Sarooghi, and A. Burkemper, "Effectuation as Ineffectual? Applying the 3E Theory-Assessment Framework to a Proposed New Theory of Entrepreneurship," *Academy of Management Review* 40 (2015), pp. 630–51.

20. Adapted from J. A. Timmons and S. Spinelli, *New Venture Creation,* 6th ed., pp. 67–68. Copyright 2004. Reproduced with permission of the authors.

21. R. Baron, R. Franklin, and K. Hmieleski, "Why Entrepreneurs Often Experience Low, Not High, Levels of Stress: The Joint Effects of Selection and Psychological Capital," *Journal of Management* 42 (2016), pp. 742–68.

22. K. Hellman and R. S. Siegel, "Achieving Entrepreneurial Success," *Marketing Management* 20, no. 2 (2011), pp. 24–37; and D. Bricklin, "Natural-Born Entrepreneur," *Harvard Business Review,* September 2001, pp. 53–59, quoting p. 58.

23. A. Levit, "'Insider' Entrepreneurs," *The Wall Street Journal,* April 6, 2009, www.wsj.com; and S. Ramoglou and E. W. K. Tsang, "A Realist Perspective of Entrepreneurship: Opportunities as Propensities," *Academy of Management Review* 41 (2016), p. 410.

24. S. Berger, "Glossier: How This 33-Year-Old Turned Her Beauty Blog to a $1 Billion Brand," *CNBC Make It,* March 20, 2019, www.cnbc.com.

25. "Shama Hyder, CEO of Marketing Zen, Named to Forbes 30 Under 30 List," Marketing Zen, January 7, 2015, zenmedia.com.

26. See Idealab's company website, www.idealab.com, accessed September 28, 2019; and "Announcing UberAds: Deriving Consumer Intent from Social Signals and Tripling Ad Performance," *Marketing Weekly News,* June 8, 2013, p. 26.

27. J. Raffiee and J. Feng, "Should I Quit My Day Job?" *Academy of Management Journal* 57 (2014), pp. 936–63.

28. R. Waldinger, "A Cross-Border Perspective on Migration: Beyond the Assimilation/Transnationalism Debate," *Journal of Ethnic and Migration Studies* 43, no. 1 (2016), pp. 3–17.

29. H. Aldrich, *Ethnic Entrepreneurs: Immigrant Business in Industrial Societies* (Newbury Park, CA: Sage, 1990).

30. R. Pennington, "5 Important Lessons from Immigrant Entrepreneurs," *Entrepreneur,* December 13, 2018, www.entrepreneur.com.

31. B. Fearnow, "Nearly Half of All Fortune 500 Companies Were Founded by Immigrants or Their Children, Study Finds," *Newsweek,* July 22, 2019, www.newsweek.com.

32. See company website, "2018 Year in Review," Estée Lauder Companies, www.elcompanies.com, accessed September 26, 2019; www.elcompanies.com; www.esteelauder.com; and www. thebiographychannel.com.uk/biographies/estee-lauder.com.

33. L. Buchanan, "Create Jobs, Eliminate Waste, Preserve Value," *Inc.,* December 2006, pp. 94–106.

34. L. Buchanan, "Create Jobs, Eliminate Waste, Preserve Value," *Inc.,* December 2006, pp. 94–106.

35. L. Buchanan, "Create Jobs, Eliminate Waste, Preserve Value," *Inc.,* December 2006, pp. 99–100.

36. J. Timmons and S. Spinelli, *New Venture Creation: Entrepreneurship for the 21st Century,* 6th ed. (New York: McGraw-Hill/Irwin, 2004).

37. E. Ries, *The Lean Startup: How Today's Entrepreneurs Use Continuous Innovation to Create Radically Successful Businesses* (New York: Random House, 2011).

38. "Staples," *Forbes,* www.forbes.com, accessed September 26, 2019.

39. See company website, "Our Story," Tiff's Treats, www.cookie delivery.com, accessed September 26, 2019.

40. J. Collins and J. Porras, *Built to Last* (London: Century, 1996).

41. "Anita Roddick, Growth Strategies," *Entrepreneur,* October 10, 2008, www.entrepreneur.com.

42. J. Collins and J. Porras, *Built to Last* (London: Century, 1996); www.esteelauder.com; and www.facebook.com.

43. J. de Jong, "The Decision to Exploit Opportunities for Innovation: A Study of High-Tech Small-Business Owners," *Entrepreneurship Theory and Practice* 37, no. 2 (March 2013), pp. 281–301; K. H. Vesper, *New Venture Mechanics* (Englewood Cliffs, NJ: Prentice Hall, 1993); C. Navis and O. V. Ozbek, "The Right People in the Wrong Places: The Paradox of Entrepreneurial Entry and Successful Opportunity Realization," *Academy of Management Review* 41 (2016), pp. 109–29; D. Shepherd, T. Williams, and H. Patzelt, "Thinking about Entrepreneurial Decision Making: Review and Research Agenda," *Journal of Management* 41 (2015), pp. 11–46; D. Williams and M. Wood, "Rule-Based Reasoning for Understanding Opportunity Evaluation," *Academy of Management Perspectives* 29 (2015), pp. 218–36; and B. Mathias and B. Williams,

chapter 7

Organizing for Success

Learning Objectives

After studying Chapter 7, you should be able to

LO1 Define the fundamental characteristics of organizational structure.

LO2 Distinguish among the four dimensions of an organization's vertical structure.

LO3 Give examples of four basic forms of horizontal structures of organizations.

LO4 Describe important mechanisms used to coordinate work.

LO5 Discuss how organizations can improve their agility through strategy, commitment to customers, and use of technology.

Singkham/Shutterstock

ctivision Blizzard (maker of the *Call of Duty* and *World of Warcraft* franchises) underwent a major restructuring in 2016 when it purchased King Digital, publisher of the *Candy Crush* mobile game.

The goal? For Activision to extend its gaming reach in the mobile market. The price? Nearly $6 billion.

Many analysts thought the price was too high for a game that was past its prime, and in a mobile gaming market that was notoriously unpredictable. Bobby Kotick, CEO of Activision Blizzard, was unfazed: "We are really good at prioritizing opportunities. We have now gotten to a place where we've seen mobile as an opportunity."[1]

So who was right? Did Activision's restructuring work out the way it had hoped?

In 2019, the global gaming market was estimated at $152 billion, with nearly half of that revenue coming from mobile games. Few games sold like *Candy Crush*, which ranked third for consumer spending.[2] Since restructuring, Activision has been able to improve the ways that King Digital's games can make money. In addition, the strength and experience of King Digital's management team has helped Activision launch *Call of Duty* to mobile, with strong initial market results.[3]

Five years later, observers are saying that buying King Digital was a great move.

―――――――――――

A company's success often depends on the way work and responsibilities are organized. Ideally, managers make decisions that align their company's structure with its strategy, so employees have the authority, skills, resources, and motivation to focus on the activities whereby they can contribute most. Activision seems to have aligned management and strategic goals with its purchase of King Digital.

This chapter describes important components of organizational structure. We begin by describing *differentiation* and *integration*. Next we discuss the vertical and horizontal structure and illustrate how organizations can integrate their activities. Finally, we focus on the importance of organizational flexibility and responsiveness―the organization's ability to adapt.

Ilya S. Savenok/King Games/Getty Images

1 | FUNDAMENTALS OF ORGANIZING

Managers often describe a firm's structure by looking at its organization chart. The **organization chart** depicts the positions in the firm and the way they are arranged. The chart provides a picture of the reporting structure (who reports to whom) and the various activities that are carried out in different jobs. Most companies have official organization charts drawn up to give people this information.

> **organization chart** the reporting structure and division of labor in an organization

Exhibit 7.1 shows a traditional organization chart. Note the various types of information, conveyed in simple ways:

- The boxes represent different work.

- The titles in the boxes show the work performed by each unit.

- Solid lines indicate reporting and authority connections and superior–subordinate relationships.

- The horizontal layers indicate levels of management. All persons or units of the same rank and reporting to the same person are on one level.

mechanistic organization a form of organization that seeks to maximize internal efficiency

organic structure an organizational form that emphasizes flexibility

differentiation an aspect of the organization's internal environment created by job specialization and the division of labor

integration the degree to which differentiated work units work together and coordinate their efforts

division of labor the assignment of different tasks to different people or groups

specialization a process in which different individuals and units perform different tasks

Exhibit 7.1 resembles the structure of organizations that German sociologist Max Weber addressed when he wrote about bureaucracy at the beginning of the 20th century. Many years later, two British management scholars (Burns and Stalker) described this as a mechanistic organization, a formal structure intended to promote internal efficiency.[4] But they went on to suggest the modern corporation has another option: the organic structure, which is much less rigid and emphasizes flexibility. Differences between these two types of structures are shown in Exhibit 7.2.

An organic organization depends heavily on an informal structure of employee networks. Astute managers are keenly aware of these interactions, and they encourage employees to work more as teammates than as subordinates who take orders from the boss.[5] As we discuss later in this chapter, the more organic a firm is, the more responsive it is to changing competitive demands and market realities.

Besides differing in their reliance on informal networks and formal organization charts, company structures can vary in terms of their differentiation and integration:

- Differentiation means the organization is composed of different units that work on different kinds of tasks, using different skills and work methods.

- Integration means these differentiated units work together so that work is coordinated into an overall product.[6]

1.1 | Differentiation Creates Specialized Jobs

Within an organization's structure, differentiation is created through division of labor and job specialization. Division of labor means the work of the organization is subdivided into smaller tasks to be performed by individuals and units throughout the organization. Specialization means different people or groups perform specific parts of the larger task.

The two concepts are closely related. Administrative assistants and accountants specialize in, and perform, different jobs; similarly, marketing, finance, and human resources tasks are divided among their respective departments.

Specialization and division of labor are necessary because of the many tasks that must be carried out in an organization. The overall work of the organization would be too complex for any individual.[7]

Differentiation is high when an organization has many subunits and many specialists who think differently. Harvard professors Lawrence and Lorsch famously found that organizations in complex, dynamic environments developed a high degree of differentiation to cope with the challenges. Companies in simple, stable environments had low levels of differentiation. Companies in an intermediate environment had intermediate differentiation.[8]

1.2 | Integration Coordinates Employees' Efforts

As organizations differentiate their structures, managers must figure out how to integrate the various activities. The specialized tasks in an organization cannot be performed completely

coordination the procedures that link the various parts of an organization to achieve the organization's overall mission

Exhibit 7.1 A conventional organization chart

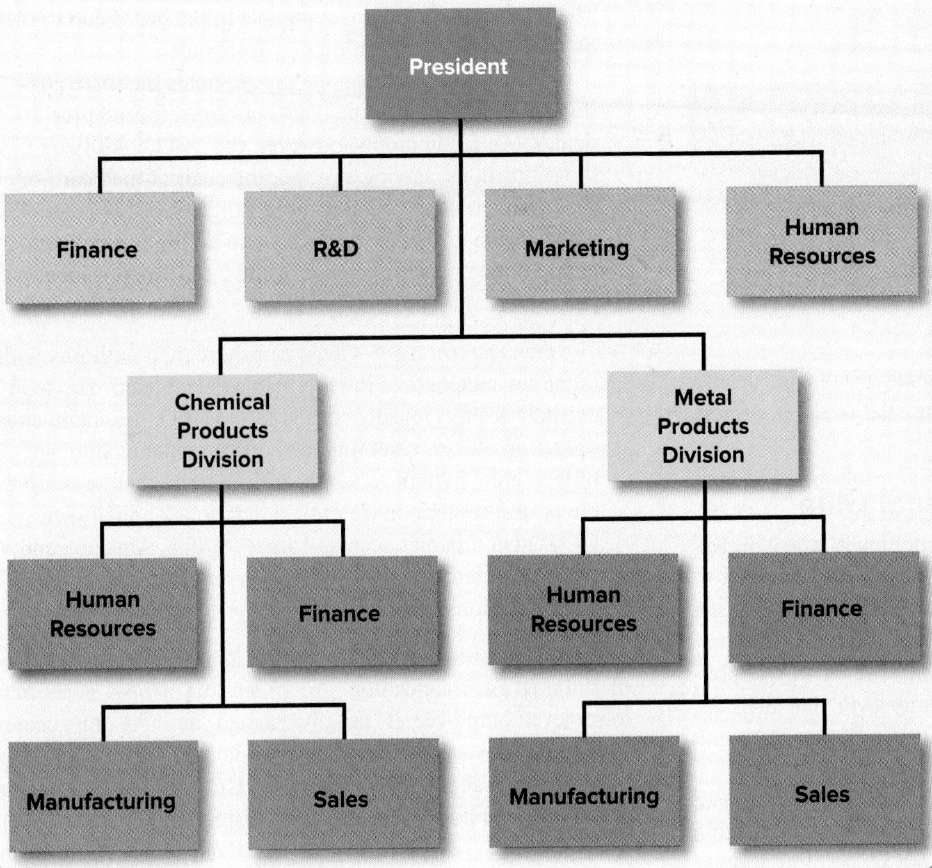

work units performs an integrative function. The more highly differentiated the firm, the greater the need for integration among its units.

Lawrence and Lorsch found that highly differentiated firms were successful if they also had high levels of integration and were more likely to fail if they operated in complex environments but failed to integrate their activities adequately.[9] However, focusing on integration may slow innovation, at least for a while.

These concepts permeate the rest of the chapter. First we discuss *vertical differentiation* within an organization's structure—top-down authority within an organization, the board of directors, the chief executive officer, and hierarchical levels, plus processes of delegation and decentralization. Next we turn to *horizontal differentiation,* exploring different approaches to departmentalization that create functional, divisional, and matrix organizations. Then we cover structural integration, including coordination, organizational roles, interdependence, and boundary spanning. Finally we look at how these issues help organizations seeking greater agility.

independently; they require communication and cooperation. Integration and its related concept, coordination, refer to the procedures that link the various parts of the organization to achieve the organization's overall mission.

Integration occurs through structural mechanisms that enhance collaboration and coordination. Any activity that links

Exhibit 7.2	Comparison of mechanistic and organic organizations	
Characteristic	**Mechanistic**	**Organic**
Degree of formality	Formal	Informal
Primary emphasis	Efficiency	Flexibility
Job responsibilities	Narrowly defined	Broad and evolving
Communication	Orders and instructions	Advice and information
Decision making	Centralized	Decentralized
Expression of commitment	Obedience to authority	Commitment to organization
Source of guidance	Rules	Personal judgment
Employee interdependence	Limited, when necessary	Employees feel interconnected

Source: Adapted from T. Burns and G. Stalker, *The Management of Innovation* (London: Tavistock, 1961).

authority the legitimate
right to make decisions and to
tell other people what to do

2 | THE VERTICAL STRUCTURE

A firm's vertical structure—authority, span of control, delegation, and centralization—shapes reporting relationships, responsibility, and accountability.

2.1 | Authority Is the Vertical Glue

At the most fundamental level, the functioning of every organization depends on the use of authority, the legitimate right to make decisions and tell other people what to do. A boss has the authority to give an order to a subordinate. Traditionally authority resides in *positions* rather than in people. The job of vice president of a particular division has authority over that division, regardless of how many people come and go in that position and who currently holds it.

In private business enterprises, the owners have ultimate authority. In most small, simply structured companies, the owner also acts as manager. Sometimes, the owner hires another person to manage the business and its employees. The owner gives this manager some authority to oversee the operations, but the manager is accountable to—that is, reports and defers to—the owner, who retains the ultimate authority.

In larger companies the principle is the same, but the structure of top management has several components:

- *Board of directors*—In corporations, the owners are the stockholders. But because there are many stockholders and they generally lack timely information, few are directly involved in managing the company. Stockholders elect a board of directors to oversee it.

  The board, led by the chairperson, makes major decisions, subject to corporate charter and bylaw provisions. Boards select, assess, reward, and perhaps replace the CEO; determine the firm's strategic direction and review financial performance; and ensure ethical, socially responsible, and legal conduct.[10]

  The board's membership usually includes some top executives—called *inside directors*. Outside members of the board typically are executives at other companies. Successful boards are active, critical participants in determining company strategies. Diverse boards help their companies achieve higher financial returns than those with less diverse boards.[11]

- *Chief executive officer*—The authority officially vested in the board of directors is assigned to a chief executive officer (CEO), who occupies the top of the corporate hierarchy. The CEO is personally accountable to the board and to the owners for the organization's performance.

  In some corporations, one person holds the three positions of CEO, chair of the board of directors, and president.[12] More commonly, however, the CEO holds two of those positions, serving as either the chair of the board or the president of the organization. When the CEO is president, the chair may be honorary and do little more than conduct meetings. If the chair is the CEO, the president is second in command.

- *Top management team*—CEOs can share their authority with other key members of the top management team. Top management teams typically consist of the CEO, president, chief operating officer, chief financial officer, chief technology officer, chief human resources officer, and other key executives. Rather than make critical decisions on their own, CEOs at companies such as Target, Airbnb, Amazon, and Nepris regularly meet with their top management teams to make decisions as a unit.[13]

Formal position authority is generally the primary means of running an organization. An order that a boss gives to a lower-level employee is usually carried out. As this occurs throughout the organization day after day, the organization can move forward and achieve its goals.[14] However, authority in an organization is not always position-dependent. People with particular expertise, experience, or personal qualities may have considerable *informal* authority—scientists in research companies, for example, or employees who are computer savvy.

Authority relates directly to the three broad levels of the organizational pyramid, or hierarchy, as described in Chapter 1. An authority structure is the glue that holds these levels together.

U.S. businesses over the past few decades have reduced the number of hierarchical layers. Elon Musk flattened Tesla's management structure to improve communication and trim areas that weren't considered "vital to the success" of Tesla's mission.[15] Most executives today believe that fewer layers create a more efficient, fast-acting, and cost-effective organization.[16] Flatter organizations work best when the environment changes rapidly, innovation is the core focus, and people have a strong sense of organizational purpose.[17]

This trend might seem to suggest that hierarchy is a bad thing, but entrepreneur Joel Spolsky learned the hard way that a completely flat structure is less than ideal. When Spolsky and Michael Pryor started Fog Creek Software, they decided to empower employees by having everyone report to the two owners. The system worked fine for a while until Fog Creek grew to 17 full-time employees. At that size, the company was no longer one small, happy family; employees had concerns and were finding it difficult to approach the partners and set up three-way meetings with them. So Spolsky and Pryor tapped two of the employees to serve as leaders of programming teams. Employees found it easier to talk to their team leader, and this "middle management" layer helped the company run more smoothly.[18]

2.2 | Span of Control and Layers Influence a Manager's Authority

The number of subordinates who report directly to an executive or supervisor is called the span of control. Differences in the span of control affect the shape of an organization. Holding size constant, narrow spans build a *tall* organization with many reporting levels. Wide spans create a *flat* organization with fewer reporting levels.

The span of control can be too narrow or too wide. The optimal span of control maximizes effectiveness by balancing two considerations as shown in Exhibit 7.3.

The optimal span of control depends on a number of factors.[19] The span should be wide under the following conditions:

- The work is clearly defined and unambiguous.
- Subordinates are highly trained and have access to information.
- The manager is highly capable and supportive.
- Jobs are similar, and performance measures are comparable.
- Subordinates prefer autonomy to close supervisory control.

If the opposite conditions exist, a narrow span of control is more appropriate.[20]

Whatever the span, if managers continue to make most decisions, they may become so engrossed in tactical issues that they may neglect more strategic activities.[21] This is where delegation comes into play.

2.3 | Delegation Is How Managers Use Others' Talents

As we recognize that authority in organizations is spread out over various levels and spans of control, we see the importance of delegation, the assignment of authority and responsibility to someone at a lower level. Delegation often requires a subordinate to report back to his or her boss about how effectively the assignment was carried out.

Delegation is perhaps the most fundamental process of management at all levels because it entails getting work done through others. The process can occur between any two individuals in any type of structure with regard to any task. Some managers

> **span of control** the number of subordinates who report directly to an executive or supervisor

> **delegation** the assignment of new or additional responsibilities to a subordinate

"Every company has two organizational structures: The formal one is written in charts; the other is the everyday relationship of the men and women in the organization."

—Harold S. Geneen

Exhibit 7.3 The optimal span of control is a balancing act

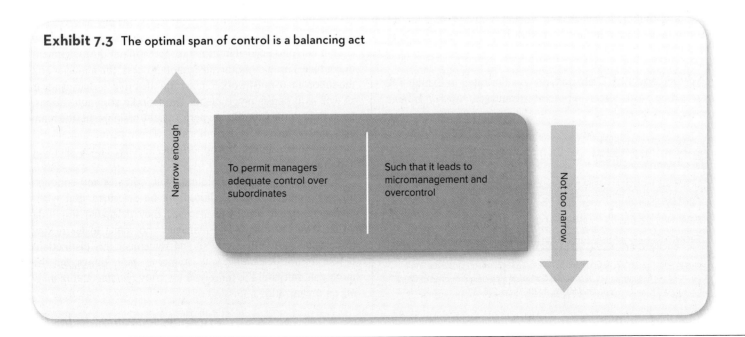

Narrow enough

To permit managers adequate control over subordinates

Such that it leads to micromanagement and overcontrol

Not too narrow

responsibility the assignment of a task that an employee is supposed to carry out

accountability the expectation that employees will perform a job, take corrective action when necessary, and report upward on the status and quality of their performance

are comfortable delegating an assignment to subordinates; others are not.[22]

Here's a personal question for you: How comfortable are you delegating work to others? Here's another: Do you know how to do it well? Read on.

Responsibility, Authority, and Accountability

When delegating work, it helps to distinguish among the concepts of authority, responsibility, and accountability. **Responsibility** means that a person is assigned a task to carry out. When delegating work responsibilities, the manager can also delegate to the subordinate enough authority to get the job done. *Authority* means that the person has the power and the right to make decisions, give orders, draw on resources, and do whatever else is necessary to fulfill the responsibility. Ironically, people often have more responsibility than authority; they must perform as well as they can through informal influence tactics instead of relying on authority.

As the manager delegates responsibilities, subordinates are held accountable for achieving results. **Accountability** means the subordinate's manager has the right to expect the subordinate to perform the job, and the right to take corrective action if the subordinate fails to do so. The subordinate must report upward on the status and quality of his or her performance.

However, the ultimate responsibility—accountability to higher-ups—lies with the manager doing the delegating. Managers remain responsible and accountable not only for their own actions but also for the actions of their subordinates. Managers should not use delegation to escape their own responsibilities; however, sometimes managers refuse to accept responsibility for subordinates' actions. They "pass the buck" or take other evasive action to ensure they are not held accountable for mistakes.[23] Ideally, empowering employees to make decisions or take action results in an increase in employee responsibility.

Advantages of Delegation As illustrated in Exhibit 7.4, delegating work offers important advantages, *when it is done*

properly. Effective delegation leverages the manager's talents and those of his or her subordinates. It lets managers accomplish much more than they could do on their own. Conversely, lack of or ineffective delegation sharply reduces what a manager can achieve. Delegation also conserves one of the manager's most valuable assets—his or her time. It frees the manager to devote energy to important, higher-level activities such as strategic planning and leading.

A big advantage of delegation is that it helps people develop new skills. Delegation essentially gives the subordinate a more important job, plus an opportunity to demonstrate potential for additional responsibilities and perhaps promotion—in effect, a vital form of on-the-job training that may pay off in the future. In addition, at least for some employees, delegation promotes a sense of being an important member of the organization, so people feel stronger commitment, perform better, and innovate more.[24]

Delegation done well benefits not just people but also organizations.[25] When managers can devote more time to important managerial functions while lower-level employees carry out assignments, jobs are done more efficiently and cost-effectively. As subordinates develop and grow in their own jobs, they contribute more.

How Should Managers Delegate?

Managers wanting to realize delegation's potential must delegate properly. As Exhibit 7.5 shows, effective delegation requires certain steps.[26]

The first step in the delegation process, defining the goal, requires a manager to clearly understand the outcome he or she wants. Then the manager should select a person who is capable of performing the task. Delegation is especially beneficial when you can identify an employee who would benefit from the experience of taking on the additional responsibility.

The person who receives the assignment should be given the authority, time, and resources to carry out the task successfully. The required resources usually involve people, money, and equipment, plus needed information that will put the assignment in context. Throughout the delegation process, the manager and the subordinate must work together on the project, sharing ideas as well as progress or problems, via periodic communications. Even though the subordinate performs the assignment, the manager stays aware of its current status. These periodic checkups also provide an important opportunity to offer encouragement and praise.

Some tasks, such as disciplining subordinates and conducting performance reviews, should not be delegated. But when managers err, it usually is because they delegated too little rather than too much. The manager who wants to learn how to delegate more effectively should remember this distinction: If you are not delegating, you are merely *doing* things; but the more you delegate, the more you are truly *building* and *managing* an organization.[27]

Exhibit 7.4	Advantages of delegation

LEVERAGES managers' time and employees' talent.

CONSERVES managers' most valuable asset: time.

DEVELOPS subordinates' managerial skills and knowledge.

PROMOTES subordinates' sense of importance and commitment.

Source: Adapted from Z. X. Chen and S. Aryee, "Delegation and Employee Work Outcomes: An Examination of the Cultural Context of Mediating Processes in China," *Academy of Management Journal* 50, no. 1 (2007), pp. 226–38.

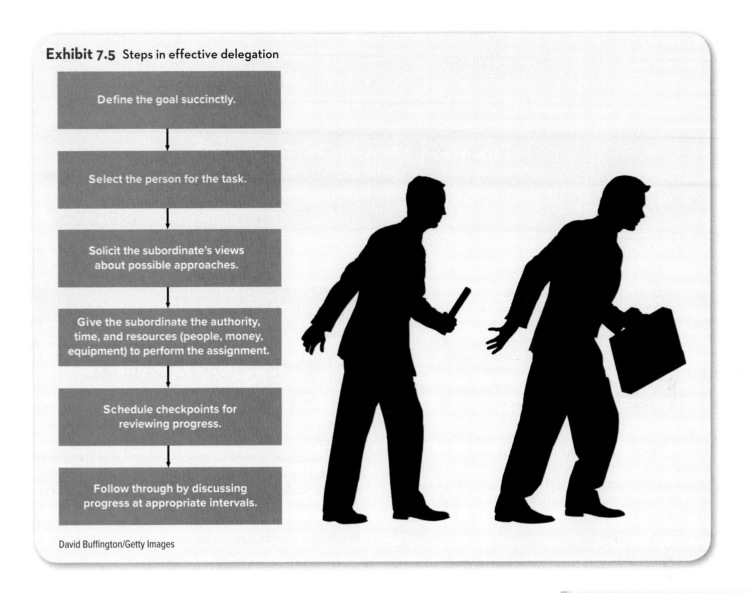

Exhibit 7.5 Steps in effective delegation

- Define the goal succinctly.
- Select the person for the task.
- Solicit the subordinate's views about possible approaches.
- Give the subordinate the authority, time, and resources (people, money, equipment) to perform the assignment.
- Schedule checkpoints for reviewing progress.
- Follow through by discussing progress at appropriate intervals.

David Buffington/Getty Images

2.4 | Decentralizing Spreads Decision-Making Power

Delegating responsibility and authority *decentralizes* decision making.[28] In a centralized organization, important decisions usually are made at the top. In decentralized organizations, more decisions are made at lower levels. Ideally decision making occurs at the level of the people who are most directly affected and have the most intimate knowledge about the work. This is particularly important when the business environment is fast-changing and decisions must be made quickly and well.

Sometimes organizations change their degree of centralization. Tougher times often cause senior management to take charge, whereas in times of rapid growth, they push decisions farther down the chain of command. When Jeff Harvey took over Burgerville, a 39-unit restaurant chain in Vancouver, Washington, he needed to stop sales from declining. His solution was to give more freedom and autonomy to restaurant managers and employees. To do so, he eliminated the regional manager position; some of those managers had "micromanaged" the general managers. Employees responded well, suggesting initiatives that the company chose to implement, including 100 percent wind power; health insurance for both full- and part-time employees; drive-through lanes for cars and bicyclists; and new limited-time-only products.[29] Burgerville provides a Pacific Northwest–style fast-food experience, with local and seasonally grown produce, oil that is recycled into biofuel, and 100 percent renewable energy powered with wind-power energy credits.[30]

Most executives today understand the advantages of pushing decision-making authority down to the point of the action. The

centralized organization an organization in which high-level executives make most decisions and pass them to lower levels for implementation

decentralized organization an organization in which lower-level managers make important decisions

line departments units that deal directly with the organization's primary goods and services

staff departments units that support line departments

level that deals directly with problems and opportunities has the most relevant information and can best foresee the consequences of decisions. Executives also see how the decentralized approach allows people to take timelier action.[31]

According to Raj Gupta, executive chair of Environmental Systems Design (ESD), the engineering design firm decentralized as a necessary response to growth.[32] A traditional "command-and-control" approach to management worked fine when the company was starting out, but now with 275 engineering and design professionals designing for diverse clients working on commercial, transportation, residential, manufacturing, energy, and other projects, it is impossible for a few people at the top to dictate solutions.[33] In fact, it isn't even desirable, given the diverse expertise of its employees.

● Burgerville was founded in 1961 by George Propstra in Vancouver, Washington. Burgerville is known for its progressive business practices and commitment to local resources. Don Ryan/AP Photo

3 | THE HORIZONTAL STRUCTURE

As work becomes ever more complex, the organization inevitably must subdivide—that is, *departmentalize*. Line departments are those that have responsibility for the principal activities of the firm. Line units deal directly with the organization's primary goods or services; they make things, sell things, or provide customer service. At General Motors, line departments include product design, fabrication, assembly, distribution, and the like. Line managers typically have much authority and power in the organization, and they have the ultimate responsibility for making major operating decisions. They are accountable for the "bottom-line" results of their units.

Staff departments provide specialized skills or professional expertise that support line departments. They include research, legal, accounting, public relations, and human resources departments. In large companies, each of these specialized units may have its own vice president, some of whom are vested with a great deal of authority, as when accounting or finance groups approve and monitor budgetary activities.

In traditionally structured organizations, conflicts arise between line and staff departments. One reason is that career paths and success in staff functions depend on functional expertise, whereas success in line functions is based more on achieving bottom-line results. So while line managers might be eager to pursue new products and customers, staff managers might seem to stifle these ideas with a focus on functional requirements and procedures. Line managers might want to take risks for the sake of growth, while staff managers focus on protecting the company from risks.

But in today's organizations, staff units are often less focused on monitoring and controlling performance and more interested in providing strategic support and advice.[34] For example,

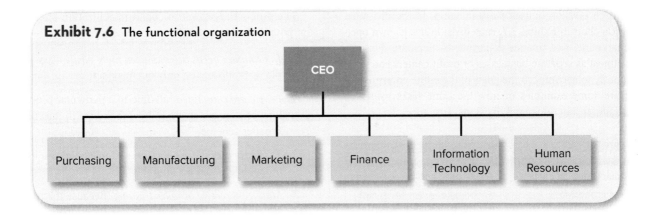

Exhibit 7.6 The functional organization

human resources managers have broadened their focus from merely creating procedures that meet legal requirements to helping organizations plan for, recruit, develop, and keep the kinds of employees who will give the company a long-term competitive advantage. This type of strategic thinking not only makes staff managers more valuable but also can reduce the conflict between line and staff departments.[35]

As organizations divide work into different units, the three basic approaches to departmentalization are functional, divisional, and matrix.

3.1 | Functional Organizations Foster Efficient Experts

In a functional organization, jobs (and departments) are specialized and grouped according to *business functions* and the skills they require: production, marketing, human resources, research and development, finance, accounting, and so forth. Exhibit 7.6 is a basic functional organization chart.

The traditional functional approach to departmentalization has a number of potential advantages:[36]

1. *Economies of scale can be realized.* When people with similar skills are grouped, the company can buy more efficient equipment and obtain discounts for large purchases.

2. *Monitoring of the environment* is more effective. Each functional group is more closely attuned to developments in its own field, so it can adapt more readily.

3. *Performance standards* are better maintained. People with similar training and interests can develop a shared concern for performance in their jobs.

4. People have more opportunity for *specialized training* and *in-depth skill development.*

5. Technical specialists are relatively *free of administrative work.*

6. *Decision making* and *lines of communication* are simple and clearly understood.

The functional form does have disadvantages, however. People may care more about their own function than about the company as a whole, and their attention to functional tasks may reduce their focus on overall product quality and customer satisfaction. Managers develop functional expertise but lack knowledge of the other areas of the business; they become specialists, not generalists. Between functions, conflicts arise, and communication and coordination fall off. In short, this structure may promote functional differentiation but not *functional integration.*

As a consequence, the functional structure is most appropriate in simple, stable environments. If the organization becomes fragmented (or *dis*integrated), it will have difficulty developing and bringing new products to market and responding quickly to customer demands and other changes. Particularly when companies are growing and business environments are changing, they need to integrate more. Other forms of departmentalization can be more flexible and responsive than the functional structure.

High demand for total quality, customer service, innovation, and speed reveal the shortcomings of the functional form. The functional organization will not disappear, in part because functional specialists will always be needed; but functional managers will make fewer decisions. The more important units will be cross-functional teams with integrative responsibilities for products, processes, or customers.[37]

3.2 | Divisional Organizations Increase Customer Focus

As organizations grow and become increasingly diversified, their functional departments have difficulty managing a wide variety of products, customers, and geographic regions. In this case, organizations may restructure by creating a divisional organization,

departmentalization
subdividing an organization into smaller subunits

functional organization
departmentalization around specialized activities such as production, marketing, and human resources

divisional organization
departmentalization that groups units around products, customers, or geographic regions

in which each division houses every function. In the divisional organization chart in Exhibit 7.7, each division has its own operations, marketing, and finance departments. Separate divisions may act almost as separate businesses or profit centers and work autonomously to accomplish the goals of the entire enterprise.

Here are some examples of how the same tasks would be organized under functional and divisional structures:[38]

Functional Organization	Divisional Organization
A central purchasing department	A purchasing unit for each division
Separate companywide marketing, production, design, and engineering departments	Each product group has its own experts in marketing, design, production, and engineering
A central city health department	Separate health units for the school district and the prison
Plantwide inspection, maintenance, and supply departments	Inspection, maintenance, and supply conducted by each production team

Organizations can form divisions around products, customers, or geography.

- *Product divisions*—All functions that contribute to a given product are organized under one product manager. Unilever has four product divisions and more than 100 independent company divisions around the globe,[39] many of which are responsible for particular product lines. One of its companies, Dove, sells soap and lotion, while Ben & Jerry's develops and markets ice cream flavors.

The product approach to departmentalization offers important potential advantages.[40]

1. *Information needs are managed more easily* because people work closely on only one product.

2. *People are committed* full-time to a particular product line, so they are aware of how their jobs fit into the broader scheme.

3. *Task responsibilities are clear,* and managers are more independent and accountable.

4. *Managers receive broader training.* Because the product structure is more flexible than the functional structure, it is best suited for unstable environments, when an ability to adapt rapidly to change is important.

The product form does have some disadvantages, however. Coordination across product lines and divisions is difficult. And although managers learn to become generalists, they may not acquire the depth of expertise that develops in the functional structure. Functions are not centralized at headquarters, and the duplication of effort is expensive. And because decision making is decentralized, top management can lose control over decisions made in the divisions. Properly managing the challenges of decentralization and delegation, as discussed earlier, is essential for this structure to be effective.[41]

- *Customer divisions*—Divisions are built around groups of customers. Michael Lazerow, chief technology officer of Salesforce, states: "We are in a world where it's not about

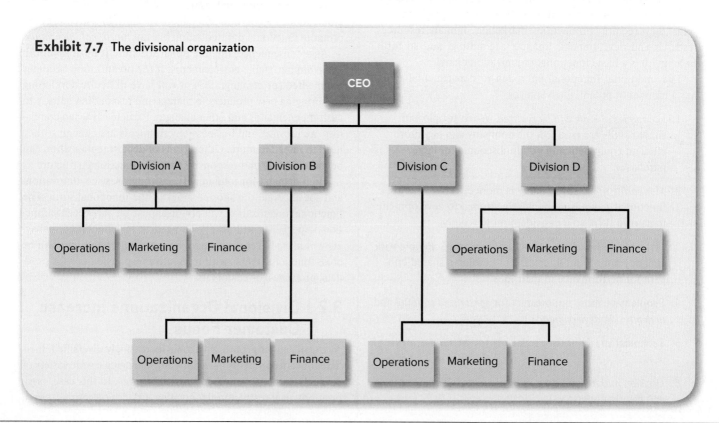

Exhibit 7.7 The divisional organization

the company anymore, it's about the customer."[42] A hospital may organize its services around child, adult, psychiatric, and emergency cases. Bank loan departments commonly have separate groups handling consumer and business needs.

- *Geographic divisions*—Divisions are structured around geographic regions. Geographic distinctions include district, territory, region, and country. Headquartered in Moline, Illinois, John Deere is a well-known manufacturer and supplier of farming equipment. To better serve its customers in Latin America and Europe, the company also maintains regional headquarters in Brazil and Germany.

The primary advantage of the product, customer, and regional approaches to departmentalization is the ability to focus on customer needs and provide faster, better service. But again, duplication of activities across many customer groups and geographic areas is expensive.

3.3 | Matrix Organizations Try to Be the Best of Both Worlds

A matrix organization is a hybrid form in which functional and divisional forms overlap. Managers and staff personnel report to two bosses—a functional manager and a divisional manager—creating a dual line of command. In Exhibit 7.8, each project manager draws employees from each functional area to form a group for the project. The people working on those projects report to the project manager as well as to the manager of their functional area.

For decades, top magazine publisher Time Inc. (owned by Meredith Corporation) used a matrix structure. At major titles like *TIME, Sports Illustrated,* and *Fortune,* production managers sent printed reports to the publisher and editor of each title *and* to a senior corporate executive in charge of production. At the corporate level, Time Inc. achieved enormous economies of scale by buying paper and printing in bulk and by coordinating production activities for the company as a whole. At the same time, production managers ensured that the different needs and schedules of their magazines were met. Similar matrix arrangements were in place for other key managers, like circulation and finance. In this way, the company attempted to benefit from both the divisional and functional organizational structures.

Like other structures, the matrix approach has multiple strengths:[43]

1. *Cross-functional problem solving* leads to better-informed and more creative decisions.

2. *Decision making is decentralized* to a level where information is processed properly and relevant knowledge is applied.

3. *Extensive communications networks* help process large amounts of information.

> **matrix organization** an organization composed of dual reporting relationships in which some managers report to two superiors—a functional manager and a divisional manager

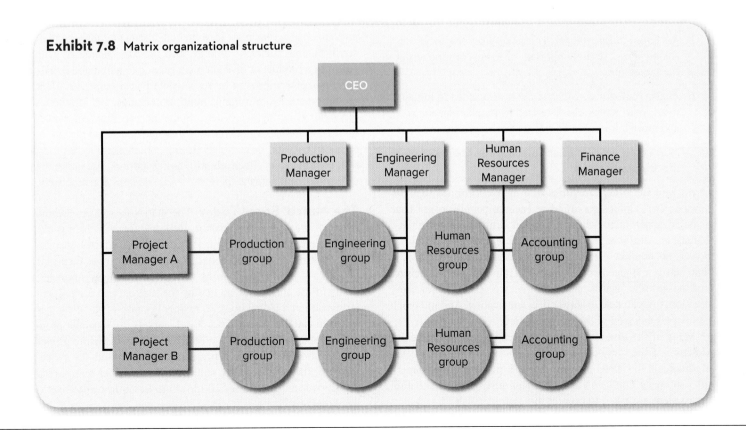

Exhibit 7.8 Matrix organizational structure

Take Charge of Your Career

Land an internship

Internships, whether paid or unpaid, offer great opportunities to gain valuable experience. Through the time you spend working for an organization as an intern, you may find how much you enjoy the industry—or you may decide it's not for you.

What do you need to know to land an internship that will benefit you? Here are a few tips:

1. Apply early. Many undergrads complete an internship in their junior or senior year, but the most competitive internships often require prior internship experience. You can apply as early as freshman year.
2. Tailor your application and résumé to the company for which you're seeking an internship. The more you appear interested and knowledgeable about the organization, the better.
3. Follow the directions for each organization's internship application. Often, failure to do so will disqualify you from competitive applicant pools.
4. Apply for as many internships as you can. These positions are almost always competitive. Restricting yourself to only a few reduces your chances of landing one.

The time and effort you spend in getting an internship will be rewarded when it comes time to find a permanent job. A recent study showed that students who had an internship in college were more likely to receive a job offer upon graduating than those who did not have an internship.

Bottom line: Internships matter. Good luck landing yours!

Sources: A. Doyle, "The Best Time to Apply for an Internship," *The Balance,* January 24, 2018, www.thebalance.com/when-to-apply-for-an-internship-2059852; P. Loretto, "Mistakes to Avoid When Applying for an Internship," *The Balance,* updated August 28, 2017, www.thebalance.com/avoid-mistakes-when-applying-for-internship-1986788; and National Association of Colleges and Employers (NACE), "Job Offers for Class of 2019 Grads Impacted by Internship Experience," May 13, 2019, https://www.naceweb.org/job-market/trends-and-predictions/job-offers-for-class-of-2019-grads-impacted-by-internship-experience.

---

unity-of-command principle a structure in which each worker reports to one boss, who in turn reports to one boss

4. With decisions delegated to appropriate levels, *higher management levels are not overloaded* with operational decisions.

5. *Resource utilization is efficient* because key resources are shared across several important programs or products at the same time.

6. *Employees learn the collaborative skills* needed to function in an environment characterized by frequent meetings and more informal interactions.

7. *More career options* become available, on both sides of the organization.

As with the other structures, the matrix form also has disadvantages.[44] Confusion can arise because people do not have a single superior to whom they feel primary responsibility. Managers who share subordinates are tempted to jockey for power, so conflict can occur. The mistaken belief can arise that matrix management is the same thing as group decision making—in other words, everyone must be consulted for every decision; this can lead to slower decision making. And too much democracy can lead to not enough action.[45]

Many of the disadvantages stem from the matrix's inherent violation of the unity-of-command principle, which states that a person should have only one boss. Reporting to two superiors can create confusion and a difficult interpersonal situation unless steps are taken to prevent these problems.

Matrix Survival Skills To a large degree, problems can be avoided if the key managers learn the behavioral skills demanded in the matrix structure.[46] These skills vary depending on the manager's job. The *top executive* must learn to balance power and emphasis between the product and functional requirements. The middle managers, who are *product* or *division managers* and *functional managers,* must learn to collaborate and manage their conflicts constructively. Finally, the *two-boss managers,* who report to a product or division manager and to a functional manager, must learn how to be responsible to two superiors. This requires maturity, prioritizing multiple demands, and sometimes reconciling conflicting orders. Some people function poorly under this ambiguous circumstance, which can signal the end of their careers with the company. Ideally, others learn to be proactive, communicate effectively with both superiors, rise above the difficulties, and manage these work relationships constructively.

The Matrix Form Today The matrix form has regained some of its earlier popularity. Reasons for this resurgence include pressures to consolidate costs and be faster to market, creating a need for better coordination across functions and across countries for firms with global business strategies. Many of the challenges created by the matrix form are particularly acute in a global context, mainly because of the distances involved and the differences in local markets.[47] Consumer products company Unilever uses a matrix structure to ensure proper coordination among its many subsidiaries around the globe. However, the firm recently reduced the number of matrix relationships it manages from 200 to 32 to be more responsive to local markets.[48]

Sustaining for Tomorrow

Community Solutions' Goal to End Homelessness

Rosanne Haggerty wants to end homelessness in the United States. As the president and CEO of Community Solutions, she has a major challenge to overcome. On any given night in the United States, more than 550,000 individuals are homeless. Perhaps more startling is that approximately one-quarter of this group are children. Though varied and complex, some of the causes of homelessness include poverty, unemployment, mental illness, and high housing costs.

To help empower local communities with the information they need to combat homelessness, Community Solutions captures real-time data and performance metrics to improve decision making and outcomes. Also, it connects communities to one another through an online platform for innovation, knowledge capture, and group problem solving.

Community Solutions has launched many initiatives over the years. The 100,000 Homes Campaign aimed to move chronically homeless individuals—including veterans and those with mental illness—into permanent housing with supportive services. This approach was successful. By mobilizing resources and officials in 186 communities and nationally, Community Solutions announced that it moved more than 105,000 homeless people—including 31,000 veterans—into permanent housing.

After surpassing its goal in the 100,000 Homes Campaign, Community Solutions launched a new initiative called Built for Zero, with a goal to end chronic homelessness. "By ending homelessness," Haggerty says, "we mean getting to a place where it's rare, brief, and it gets solved correctly and quickly when it does happen." This is what Haggerty refers to as "functional zero." So far, 12 communities around the country have reached the goal: 9 for veteran homelessness, and 3 more for chronic homelessness.

Community Solutions is ramping up its program throughout the United States. To date, 82 communities are taking part in the Built for Zero program with a goal of attaining functional zero homelessness.

Discussion Questions

- Do you think it is a good idea for Community Solutions to try to galvanize change through the resources of local communities? Why or why not?

- Do you agree with Haggerty that achieving functional zero homelessness is an achievable goal? Why or why not?

Sources: U.S. Department of Housing and Urban Development, "The 2018 Annual Homeless Assessment Report to Congress," December 2018, https://files.hudexchange.info/resources/documents/2018-AHAR-Part-1.pdf; M. Clendaniel, "10 World-Changing Solutions That Inspired the Most Hope in 2019," *Fast Company,* December 23, 2019, https://www.fastcompany.com/90445669/10-world-changing-solutions-that-inspired-the-most-hope-in-2019; and Community Solutions website, "Built for Zero," https://community.solutions/our-solutions/built-for-zero/, accessed March 20, 2020.

The key to managing today's matrix is not the formal structure itself but the realization that the matrix is a *process.* Many managers who had trouble with the matrix structure failed to change the employee and managerial relationships. Flexible organizations cannot be created merely by changing their structure. To allow information to flow freely as needed, managers must attend also to the norms, values, and attitudes that shape people's behavior.[49]

3.4 | Network Organizations Are Built on Collaboration

Not all firms are traditional hierarchies that include all business functions. A network organization is a collection of independent, mostly single-function firms that collaborate to produce a good or service. As depicted in Exhibit 7.9, the network organization describes not one firm but a web of relationships among many firms. Network organizations are flexible arrangements among designers, suppliers, producers, distributors, and customers in which each firm is able to capitalize more fully on its own distinctive core capability. However, it also must work effectively with other specialized firms in a diverse network. The firm's normal "boundary" becomes blurred or porous as members interact closely with network members outside it. The network as a whole, then, can display the technical specialization of the functional structure, the market responsiveness of the product structure, and the balance and flexibility of the matrix.[50]

A very flexible version of the network organization is the modular network—also called the *virtual network.* It is composed of temporary arrangements among members that can assemble and reassemble to meet changing demands. Contracts stipulate expected results (market mechanisms), rather than hierarchy and authority. Poorly performing firms can be removed and replaced.

> **network organization** a collection of independent, mostly single-function firms that collaborate on a good or service
>
> **modular network** temporary arrangements among partners that can be assembled and reassembled to adapt to the environment; also called *virtual* network

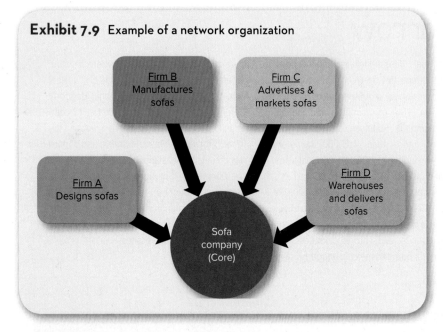

Exhibit 7.9 Example of a network organization

Firm B
Manufactures sofas

Firm C
Advertises & markets sofas

Firm A
Designs sofas

Firm D
Warehouses and delivers sofas

Sofa company (Core)

Networks potentially offer flexibility, innovation, quick responses to threats and opportunities, and reduced costs and risk. But for these arrangements to be successful, several things must occur:

- The firm must choose the right specialty. It must be something (good or service) that the market needs and that the firm is better at providing than other firms—its core capability.

- The firm must choose collaborators that provide complementary strengths and are excellent at what they do.

- The firm must make certain that all parties fully understand the strategic goals of the partnership.

- Each party must be able to trust all the others with strategic information and also trust that each collaborator will deliver quality products even under heavy demands.

broker a person who assembles and coordinates participants in a network

Such arrangements are common in the aerospace, electronics, toy, and apparel industries, each of which creates and sells trendy products at a fast pace. Modular networks also are suited to organizations in which much of the work can be done independently by different experts. For example, Canada-based Bombardier Aerospace makes and sells aircraft (e.g., LearJet) and train systems (e.g., Amtrak Acela Express). Instead of manufacturing everything by itself in Canada, Bombardier uses a virtual network of suppliers to make its products, from cockpits to wings to engines.[51] The strategy appears to be working, as the $16 billion company is now included in the 2019 *Forbes* "Best Employers" lists for America and Canada.[52]

The role of managers shifts in a network from that of command and control to that of a broker. Broker/managers serve several boundary roles that aid network integration and coordination:[53]

- *Designer role:* A *network architect* who envisions a set of groups or firms whose collective expertise could be focused on a particular good or service.

- *Process engineering role:* A *network cooperator* who takes the initiative to lay out the flow of resources and relationships and makes certain that everyone shares the same goals, standards, payments, and the like.

- *Nurturing role:* A *network developer* who nurtures and enhances the network to make certain the relationships are healthy and mutually beneficial.

LO4 Describe important mechanisms used to coordinate work.

4 | ORGANIZATIONAL INTEGRATION

Besides structuring their organization around *differentiation*—different jobs and tasks, and the way they fit on an organization chart—managers also need to consider *integration* and *coordination*—how different parts of the organization work together.

Typically, the more differentiated the organization, the more difficult the integration. Because of specialization and the division of labor, different groups of managers and employees

● Canadian jet manufacturer Bombardier Aerospace relies on a modular network of contractors to supply some of the 12 large components needed to assemble the firm's jets. Patrick Doyle/Bloomberg/Getty Images

develop different orientations. Employees think and act differently depending on whether they are in a functional department or a divisional group, are line or staff, and so on. When they focus on their particular units, it is difficult to integrate all their activities.

Managers can use a variety of approaches to foster coordination among interdependent units and people. Coordination methods include standardization, plans, and mutual adjustment.[54]

4.1 | Standardization Coordinates Work Through Rules and Routines

When organizations coordinate activities with routines and standard operating procedures, work is standardized. Standardization constrains actions and coordinates units by regulating—spelling out—what people do. For example, managers might establish standards for which types of computer equipment the organization will use. This simplifies the purchasing and training processes (everyone is on a common platform) and helps the different work units communicate.

Formalization is the presence of rules and regulations governing how people interact. Simple, often written, policies regarding attendance, dress, and decorum, for example, help eliminate a good deal of uncertainty at work.

An important assumption underlying both standardization and formalization is that the rules and procedures should apply to most (if not all) situations. These approaches, therefore, are most appropriate in stable, unchanging situations. But when situations require flexibility, standardization might not work. Who hasn't experienced a time when rules and procedures became nothing more than red tape that slowed everything down?[55]

4.2 | Plans Set a Common Direction

Specifying exact rules and procedures for integrating is difficult; a more flexible alternative is to establish shared goals and schedules for interdependent units. With coordination by plan,

● Organizations of all types have established routines and standard operating procedures so employees, customers, and other stakeholders know how to act and interact with one another. Randy Faris/Corbis

interdependent units can modify and adapt their actions as long as they meet the deadlines and targets required for working with others.

In writing this textbook, we (the authors) sat down with a publication team that included the editors, the marketing staff, the production group, and support staff. Together we ironed out a two-year schedule for developing the book. That development plan included dates and "deliverables" that specified what everyone needed to accomplish. The plan allowed some flexibility, and the overall approach allowed us to work together effectively, as long as we met deadlines.

4.3 | Mutual Adjustment Allows Flexible Coordination

The simplest and most flexible approach to coordination may just be to have people talk to one another as needed. Coordination by mutual adjustment involves feedback and discussions to jointly figure out how to approach problems and devise solutions that are agreeable to everyone. The popularity of teams today is in part due to the fact that they allow for flexible coordination; teams can operate under the principle of mutual adjustment.

The Chinese motorcycle industry has figured out how to coordinate hundreds of suppliers in the design and manufacturing of motorcycles. Together these small firms collaborate by working from rough blueprints to design, construct, and assemble related components and then deliver them to another plant for final assembly. Because design and assembly are decentralized, suppliers can move quickly to make adjustments, try out new components, and make more changes if necessary before delivering a product for final assembly.

Using this approach, the Chinese motorcycle industry designs and builds new motorcycles faster and less expensively than any other country in the world. And China now is one of the world's largest producers of motorcycles, second only to India.[56]

But the flexibility of mutual adjustment as a coordination device carries some cost. Hashing out every issue takes time and may not be the most expedient approach. Imagine how long it would take to accomplish even the most basic tasks if subunits had to talk through every situation. Still, mutual adjustment is essential when problems are novel and cannot be anticipated by rules, procedures, or plans. Particularly during crises, mutual adjustment is likely to provide the most effective coordination.

standardization establishing common routines and procedures that apply uniformly to everyone

formalization the presence of rules and regulations governing how people in the organization interact

coordination by plan interdependent units create deadlines and objectives that contribute to a common goal

coordination by mutual adjustment units interact with one another to make accommodations in order to achieve flexible coordination

4.4 | Coordination Requires Communication

Business environments tend to be complex, dynamic, and therefore uncertain. Huge amounts of information flow from the external environment to the organization and back. To cope, organizations must acquire, process, and respond to that information. Organizations need to develop structures that process information effectively.

To cope with high uncertainty and heavy information demands, managers can use the two general strategies shown in Exhibit 7.10:[57]

1. *Reduce the need for information.* Managers can do this by creating slack resources. *Slack resources* are extra resources that organizations can rely on in a pinch. For example, a company that carries inventory does not need as much information about sales demand or lead times. Part-time and temporary employees are another type of slack resource because using them helps employers who can't forecast sales peaks perfectly. Creating *self-contained tasks* also helps reduce the need for information. If each unit has the resources it needs to do its work, it has less need to share information across units.

2. *Increase information-processing capability.* An organization can do this by *investing in information systems* or

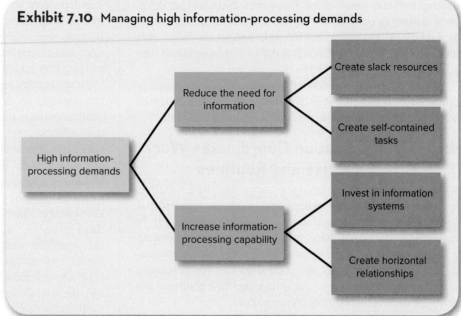

Exhibit 7.10 Managing high information-processing demands

- High information-processing demands
  - Reduce the need for information
    - Create slack resources
    - Create self-contained tasks
  - Increase information-processing capability
    - Invest in information systems
    - Create horizontal relationships

engaging in *knowledge management*—capitalizing on the intellects and experience of the organization's human assets to increase collaboration and effectiveness. Managers can foster knowledge management by creating horizontal relationships. These can be as simple as assigning someone to serve as a *liaison* between groups, or as complex as assembling an interdepartmental task force or team.[58]

> **LO5 Discuss how organizations can improve their agility through strategy, commitment to customers, and use of technology.**

5 | ORGANIZATIONAL AGILITY

Managers today place a premium on *agility*—being able to act fast to meet customer needs and respond to other outside demands. They want to correct mistakes quickly, and to prepare for an uncertain future. They need to respond to threats and capitalize on opportunities when they come along. The best structures for agility depend on the organization's *strategy, customers,* and *technology.*

5.1 | Strategies Promote Organizational Agility

Certain strategies, and the structures, processes, and relationships that accompany them, are especially helpful in terms of improving

● Information sharing is vital at the National Counterterrorism Center. Technology is used to enable the efficient and safe execution of information sharing. PAUL J. RICHARDS/Getty Images

agility. They reflect managers' determination to fully leverage people and assets to make the firm more agile and competitive. These strategies and structures are based on the firm's core capabilities, strategic alliances, and abilities to learn and adapt.

Basecamp is a good example of an agile organization. Founded in 2004 by Jason Fried and David Heinemeier Hansson, Basecamp serves more than 100,000 clients with only 50 employees. The company has never taken venture capital and has been profitable since its beginning. Basecamp runs very differently than most large companies and has a series of benchmarks it uses to maintain its agile, balanced, and anti-workaholic culture.[59] Basecamp works in six-week sprints, and workers' time is split into single hours of uninterrupted work. The company focuses on the short-term future and doesn't set aggressive year-end goals. Employees average 40-hour workweeks and 32-hour weeks in the summer, with 3 scheduled hours per week for office hours. When teams are created, each has no more than three members. Basecamp's principles prioritize "effectiveness over busyness" to keep employees happy and revenues stable.[60]

Organizing Around Core Capabilities
An important perspective on strategy and organization hinges on an organization's *core capability*.[61] As you learned in Chapter 5, a core capability is the ability—knowledge, expertise, skill—that allows the company to compete on the basis of its primary strengths and expertise, not just on what it produces.

Developing a world-class core capability opens the door to a variety of opportunities. To not do so means being foreclosed from many markets. A well-understood, well-developed core capability can enhance a company's responsiveness and competitiveness.

Strategically, companies must commit to excellence and leadership in capabilities and strengthen them; then they can win market share for specific products. Organizationally, the corporation should be viewed as a portfolio of capabilities, not just products and businesses.

Managers therefore:

- Identify existing core capabilities.

- Acquire or build core capabilities that will be important for the future.

- Keep investing in capabilities, so the firm remains world-class and better than competitors.

- Extend capabilities to find new applications and opportunities for the markets of tomorrow.[62]

Keep in mind that it's not enough for an organization to *have* valuable resources that provide capabilities; those resources have to be *managed* in a way that provides advantage.[63] That means managers must:

1. *Accumulate the right resources (such as talented people).* Managers must determine what resources they need; acquire and develop those resources; and eliminate resources that don't provide value.

2. *Combine the resources in ways that give the organization capabilities,* such as researching new products or resolving problems for customers. These combinations may involve knowledge sharing and alliances between departments or with other organizations.

3. *Leverage or exploit their resources.* Managers must identify opportunities where their capabilities deliver value to customers (say, by creating new products or delivering existing products better than competitors) and then coordinate and deploy the resources needed to capitalize.

Strategic Alliances The modern organization has a variety of links with others that are more complex than traditional stakeholder relationships. Even competitors now work together to achieve their strategic goals. Carmaker Hyundai Motor aligned with Uber to develop autonomous "personal air vehicles."[64] The full-scale mock-up of the S-A1 made its debut at the Consumer Electronics Show in early 2020. The electric-powered air vehicle will shuttle up to four passengers at 180 miles per hour for 60 miles; that's enough to commute to and from work or between important business meetings.[65] Uber brings its ride-hailing app and logistics expertise to the partnership, while Hyundai provides capital and manufacturing know-how.[66]

A strategic alliance is a formal relationship created with the purpose of joint pursuit of mutual goals. Different organizations share administrative authority, form social links, and accept joint ownership. Such alliances are blurring firms' boundaries. Alliances occur between companies, competitors, governments, and universities. Such partnering often crosses national and cultural boundaries.

Companies form strategic alliances to develop new technologies, enter new markets, and reduce manufacturing costs through outsourcing. Not only can alliances help companies to move ahead faster and more efficiently, but they also are

> **strategic alliance** a formal relationship created among independent organizations with the purpose of joint pursuit of mutual goals

● Hyundai and Uber have aligned to develop autonomous "personal air vehicles." Shown here at the 2020 Consumer Electronics Show, the electric-powered air vehicle will shuttle up to four passengers at 180 miles per hour for 60 miles. ROBYN BECK/Getty Images

sometimes the only practical way to bring together the variety of specialists needed. Rather than hiring the experts who understand the technology and market segments for each new product, companies can form alliances with partners that already have those experts on board.[67]

Learning Organizations Being responsive requires continually learning new ways to act. Some experts say the only sustainable advantage is learning faster than the competition. A learning organization is an organization skilled at creating, acquiring, and transferring knowledge and modifying its behavior to reflect new knowledge and insights.[68]

Pizza Hut, Microsoft, *USA Today,* and Honeywell are good examples of learning organizations.[69] They are skilled at solving problems, experimenting with new approaches, learning from their own experiences, learning from other organizations, and spreading knowledge quickly and efficiently.

How do firms become true learning organizations? Here are some key ingredients:[70]

- Their people engage in disciplined thinking and attention to details, making decisions based on data and evidence rather than guesswork and assumptions.

- They search constantly for new knowledge and ways to apply it, looking for new horizons and opportunities, not just quick fixes to current problems. The organization values and rewards people who expand their knowledge and skill in useful areas.

- They carefully review successes and failures, looking for lessons and deeper understanding.

- They benchmark—identify and implement the best practices of other organizations, stealing ideas shamelessly.

- They share ideas via reports, information systems, informal discussions, site visits, education, and training. More experienced employees train and mentor others.

High-Involvement Organizations Another increasingly popular way to create agility is participative management. Particularly in high-technology companies facing stiff international competition, the aim is to generate high levels of commitment and involvement as employees and managers work together to achieve organizational goals.

In a high-involvement organization, top management ensures that there is a consensus about the direction in which the business is heading. Leaders seek input from their teams and from lower levels. Task forces, study groups, and other techniques foster participation in important decisions. Participants receive feedback regarding how they are doing compared with the competition and how effectively they are meeting the strategic agenda.

Structurally, this usually means that even lower-level employees have a direct relationship with a customer or supplier and thus receive feedback and are held accountable for their work. The organization has a flat, decentralized structure built around a customer, good, or service. Employee involvement is particularly important when the environment changes rapidly, work is creative, complex activities require coordination, and firms need major breakthroughs in innovation and speed—in other words, when they need to be more responsive.[71]

5.2 | Agile Organizations Focus on Customers

The point of structuring a responsive, agile organization is to meet and exceed the expectations of its customers. Customers are vital, of course: They purchase goods and services, plus their continued relationships[72] with the firm constitute a fundamental driver of sustained, long-term competitiveness and success. One way organizations meet customer needs is by focusing on quality improvement.

Organizing for Quality Improvement Managers can embed quality programs within any organizational structure. Total quality management (TQM) is a way of managing in which everyone is committed to continuous improvement

2014 Mathias Rosenthal/123RF

of his or her part of the operation. TQM is a comprehensive approach to improving product quality and thereby customer satisfaction. It is characterized by a strong orientation toward customers (external and internal) and is a theme for organizing work. Continuous improvement requires mechanisms that facilitate group problem solving, information sharing, and cooperation across business functions. The walls that separate stages and functions of work tend to come down, and the organization operates in a team-oriented manner.[73]

One of the founders of the quality management movement was W. Edwards Deming. As illustrated in Exhibit 7.11, Deming's "14 points" of quality emphasize a holistic approach to management.

TQM uses statistical tools to analyze the causes of product defects, in an approach called *six sigma quality*. Sigma is the Greek letter used to designate the estimated standard deviation or variation in a process. (The higher the "sigma level," the lower the amount of variation.) The product defects analyzed include anything that results in customer dissatisfaction—late delivery, wrong shipment, poor customer service, as well as problems with the product itself. When a defect appears, managers conduct a comprehensive effort to eliminate its causes and reduce it to the lowest practicable level.

At six sigma, a product or process is defect-free 99.99966 percent of the time. Reaching that goal almost always requires managers to restructure their internal processes and relationships with suppliers and customers in fundamental ways. For example, managers may have to create teams throughout the organization to implement process improvements that prevent defects from arising.

The *lean six sigma* approach combines six sigma quality improvement techniques with initiatives that eliminate waste in time, processes, and materials. As a way to be more efficient and

keep budgets under control, city planners in Irving, Texas, used lean six sigma analysis to reduce the time taken on street repairs from an average of 14 weeks to 6 weeks. Instead of maintaining three separate 40-year-old, inefficient community pools (used by about 9,700 residents each year), city planners built a new energy-efficient pool now used by 110,000 visitors annually.[74]

The influence of TQM on the organizing process has become even more acute with the emergence of ISO standards. ISO 9001 is a series of voluntary quality standards developed by a committee working under the International Organization for Standardization (known as ISO), a network of national standards institutions in more than 161 countries. In contrast to most ISO standards, which describe a particular material, product, or process, the ISO 9001 standards apply to management systems at any organization and address eight principles:[75]

1. Customer focus—learning and addressing customer needs and expectations.

2. Leadership—establishing a vision and goals, establishing trust, and providing employees with the resources and inspiration to meet goals.

3. Involvement of people—establishing an environment in which employees understand their contribution, engage in problem solving, and acquire and share knowledge.

4. Process approach—defining the tasks needed to successfully carry out each process and assigning responsibility for them.

5. Systems approach to management—putting processes together into efficient systems that work together effectively.

6. Continual improvement—teaching people how to identify areas for improvement and rewarding them for making improvements.

7. Factual approach to decision making—gathering accurate performance data, sharing the data with employees, and using the data to make decisions.

8. Mutually beneficial supplier relationships—working in a cooperative way with suppliers.

U.S. companies first became interested in ISO 9001 because overseas customers, particularly those in the European Union, embraced it. Hundreds of thousands of companies in

Exhibit 7.11   Deming's 14 points of quality

1. *Create constancy of purpose*—strive for long-term improvement (vs. short-term profit).
2. *Adopt the new philosophy*—don't tolerate delays and mistakes.
3. *Cease dependence on mass inspection*—build quality into the process on the front end.
4. *End the practice of awarding business on price tag alone*—build long-term relationships.
5. *Improve constantly and forever the system of production and service*—at each stage.
6. *Institute training and retraining*—continually update methods and thinking.
7. *Institute leadership*—provide the resources needed for effectiveness.
8. *Drive out fear*—people must believe it is safe to report problems or ask for help.
9. *Break down barriers among departments*—promote teamwork.
10. *Eliminate slogans and arbitrary targets*—supply methods, not buzzwords.
11. *Eliminate numerical quotas*—they are contrary to the idea of continuous improvement.
12. *Remove barriers to pride in work*—allow autonomy and spontaneity.
13. *Institute a vigorous program of education and retraining*—people are assets, not commodities.
14. *Take action to accomplish the transformation*—provide a structure that enables quality.

● Guided by the results of a lean six sigma analysis, city planners in Irving, Texas, built an 11,000-square-foot energy-efficient aquatic center to serve all age groups. Many thousands more people visit the new aquatic center than the three separate inefficient pools that previously served the community.
Cody Duty/AP Photo

technology the systematic application of scientific knowledge to a new product, process, or service

small batch technologies that produce goods and services in low volume

large batch technologies that produce goods and services in high volume

manufacturing and service industries around the world are ISO certified. For example, Minneapolis' Mead Metals, a specialty metal manufacturer, credits ISO 9001 certification with helping it safely create consistent, high-quality products.[76]

5.3 | Technology Can Support Agility

A critical factor affecting an organization's structure and responsiveness is its *technology*. Broadly speaking, technology can be viewed as the methods, processes, systems, and skills used to transform resources (inputs) into products (outputs). We will discuss technology and innovation more fully later; here we highlight important influences technology has on organizational structure.

Technology Configurations Research by Joan Woodward laid the foundation for understanding technology and structure.

According to Woodward, three basic technologies characterize how work is done in service as well as manufacturing companies:[77]

- *Small batch technologies*—When goods or services are provided in very low volume or small batches, a company that does such work is called a *job shop*. For example, PMF Industries, a small custom metalworking company in Williamsport, Pennsylvania, produces stainless steel assemblies for medical and other uses. In the service industry, local restaurants and doctors' offices provide a variety of low-volume, customized services. Structure tends to be organic, with few rules and formal procedures, and decision making tends to be decentralized. The emphasis is on mutual adjustment among people.

- *Large batch technologies*—Companies with higher volumes and lower varieties than a job shop are large batch, or mass production technologies. Examples include the AirPod and Beats headphone assembly operations at Apple, and in the service sector, Panera and In-N-Out Burger. Production runs are standardized, and customers receive similar (if not identical) products. Machines may replace people in the physical execution of work. Structure tends to be mechanistic, with more rules, formal procedures, and centralized decision making. Communication tends to be more formal, and hierarchical authority is more prominent.

- *Continuous process technologies*—At the high-volume end of the scale are companies that use continuous process technologies, which do not stop and start. International Paper and BASF use continuous process technologies to produce a very limited number of products. People are removed from the work itself—which is done by machines and computers—and run the computers that run the machines. Structure can return to a more organic form because less supervision is needed. There are fewer rules and communication tends to be more informal.

Organizing for Flexible Manufacturing Traditionally, volume and variety were seen as trade-offs in a technological sense. Today, organizations try to produce both high-volume and high-variety products at the same time. This is mass customization.[78] Automobiles, clothes, computers, and other products are manufactured to match each customer's taste, specifications, and budget. You can buy clothes cut to your proportions, supplements with the exact blend of the vitamins and minerals you like, streaming music playlists you choose, and textbooks whose chapters are picked by your professor.

How do companies manage customization at low cost? They organize around a dynamic network of relatively independent operating units.[79] Each unit performs a specific process or task—called a *module*—such as making a component, performing a credit check, or performing a particular welding method. Some modules may be performed by outside suppliers or vendors.

Different modules join forces to make the good or provide the service. The unique requests of each customer dictate how and when the various modules interact with one another. The manager's responsibility is to make it easier and less costly for modules to come together, complete their tasks, and recombine to meet the next customer demand. The goal of mass customization is a never-ending campaign to expand the number of ways a company can satisfy customers.

Computer integrated manufacturing (CIM) has helped make mass customization possible. CIM encompasses a host of computerized production efforts, including computer-aided design and computer-aided manufacturing. These systems can produce high-variety and high-volume products at the same time.[80] They also offer greater control and predictability of production processes, reduced waste, faster throughput times, and higher quality.

But managers cannot "buy" their way out of competitive trouble simply by investing in superior technology alone. They must also ensure that their organization has the necessary strategic and people strengths and a well-designed plan for integrating the new technology within the organization.

As the name implies, *flexible factories* provide more production options and a greater variety of products. They differ from traditional factories in three primary ways:[81]

1. The traditional factory has long production runs, generating high volumes of a standardized product. Flexible factories have much shorter production runs, with many different products.

2. Traditional factories move parts down the line from one location in the production sequence to the next. Flexible factories are organized around products, in work cells or teams, so that people work together closely and parts move shorter distances with shorter or no delays.

3. Traditional factories use centralized scheduling, which is time-consuming, inaccurate, and slow to adapt to changes. Flexible factories use local or decentralized scheduling, in which decisions are made on the shop floor by the people doing the work.

Another organizing approach, lean manufacturing, strives for the highest possible productivity and total quality, cost-effectively, by eliminating unnecessary steps in the production process and continually striving for improvement. Rejects are unacceptable, and staff, overhead, and inventory are considered wasteful. The emphasis is on quality, speed, and flexibility more

continuous process a highly automated process with continuous production flow

mass customization the production of varied, individually customized products at the low cost of standardized, mass-produced products

lean manufacturing an operation that strives to achieve the highest possible productivity and total quality, cost-effectively, by eliminating unnecessary steps in the production process and continually striving for improvement

Anyone who has never made a mistake has never tried anything new.

—Albert Einstein

just-in-time (JIT) a system that calls for subassemblies and components to be manufactured in very small lots and delivered to the next stage of the production process just as they are needed

than on cost, efficiency, and hierarchy. Employees who spot problems are authorized to halt the operation and signal for help to correct the problem at its source. Well-managed lean production allows a company to develop, produce, and distribute products with half or less of the human effort, space, tools, time, and overall cost.[82]

LEGO launched the Ideas dashboard aimed at generating new ideas for future products. After 10,000 visitors show support for a new design, the company reviews it and decides whether to manufacture it. This crowdsourcing approach reduces time and costs related to the new-product development process. The dashboard initiative resulted in the launch of The Beatles Yellow Submarine building set.[83] After reading Eric Ries' *The Lean Startup* and blog, Dropbox's Drew Houston released products faster to test the market and get quick feedback on how to improve them. Doing this, Dropbox increased its number of users from about 100,000 to 4 million in less than a year and a half.[84]

Here are some keys for the lean approach to work well:[85]

- People are broadly trained rather than specialized.

- Communication is informal and horizontal among line workers.

- Equipment is general-purpose.

- Work is organized in teams, or cells, that produce a group of similar products.

- Supplier relationships are long-term and cooperative.

- Product development is concurrent, not sequential, and is done by cross-functional teams (see simultaneous engineering in the next section).

Organizing for Speed: Time-Based Competition

Companies worldwide have devoted so much energy to improving product quality that high quality is now the standard attained by all top competitors. Competition has driven quality to such heights that quality products no longer are enough to distinguish one company from another. Time is now a key competitive advantage separating market leaders from also-rans.[86]

One way to compete based on time is **just-in-time (JIT)** operations. JIT manufactures subassemblies and components in very small lots and delivers them to the next stage in the process precisely at the time needed, or "just in time." A customer order triggers a factory order and a production process. The supplying work centers do not produce the next lot of product until the consuming work center requires it. Even external suppliers deliver to the company just in time.

Just-in-time is a companywide philosophy oriented toward eliminating waste and improving materials throughout all operations. This eliminates excess inventory and reduces costs. By making products perfectly, companies eliminate the need for costly and time-consuming inspections. Furthermore, production processes are shortened when they are streamlined so that parts are being worked on every minute they are in production, rather than sitting on a table, waiting for an operator.

Many believe that JIT is realizing only a fraction of its potential, and that its impact will grow as it is applied more to services, distribution, and new-product development.[87] However, it's important to keep in mind that JIT offers efficiency only when the costs of storing items are greater than the costs of frequent delivery.[88]

While JIT concentrates on reducing time in manufacturing, companies use *simultaneous engineering* to speed up research and product development. Traditionally, when R&D completed its part of the project, the work was "passed over the wall" to engineering, which completed its task and passed it over the wall to manufacturing, and so on. In contrast, simultaneous engineering incorporates the issues and perspectives of all the functions—and customers and suppliers—from the beginning of the process.

This team-based approach results in a higher-quality product that is designed for efficient manufacturing *and* customer needs.[89] In the automobile industry, tools such as computer-aided design and computer-aided manufacturing (CAD/CAM) support simultaneous engineering by letting various engineers submit elements and then showing how these submissions affect the overall design and the manufacturing process. With a modern CAD system, automobile engineers enter performance requirements into a spreadsheet and the system identifies a design that meets cost and manufacturing requirements. Automakers slash product development time with this technology.[90] In the realm of computing, some organizations have taken this idea much further, making programming codes for their products available to the public so that anyone at any time can develop new ideas to use with their product. The company can license any ideas that seem to have market potential.

Notes

1. K. Stuart, "Activision CEO Bobby Kotick on the King Deal: 'We Have an Audience of 500 Million,'" *The Guardian,* November 4, 2015, https://www.theguardian.com/technology/2015/nov/04/bobby-kotick-king-deal-activision-blizzard.

2. Kaplan, Omar. "Mobile gaming is a $68.5 billion global business, and investors are buying in." Tech Crunch, August 22, 2019. Retrieved from https://techcrunch.com/2019/08/22/mobile-gaming-mints-money/

3. L. Sanchez, "Why Activision's Deal for King Digital Was a Home Run," *The Motley Fool*, February 20, 2020, https://www.fool.com/investing/2020/02/05/why-activisions-deal-for-king-digital-was-a-home-r.aspx.

4. T. Burns and G. Stalker, *The Management of Innovation* (London: Tavistock, 1961).

5. D. Krackhardt and J. R. Hanson, "Information Networks: The Company behind the Chart," *Harvard Business Review*, July–August 1993, pp. 104–11.

6. R. N. Ashkenas and S. C. Francis, "Integration Managers: Special Leaders for Special Times," *Harvard Business Review* 78, no. 6 (November–December 2000), pp. 108–16.

7. A. West, "The Flute Factory: An Empirical Measurement of the Effect of the Division of Labor on Productivity and Production Cost," *American Economist* 43, no. 1 (Spring 1999), pp. 82–87.

8. P. Lawrence and J. Lorsch, *Organization and Environment* (Homewood, IL: Richard D. Irwin, 1969).

9. P. Lawrence and J. Lorsch, *Organization and Environment* (Homewood, IL: Richard D. Irwin, 1969); B. L. Thompson, *The New Manager's Handbook* (New York: McGraw-Hill, 1994). See also S. Sharifi and K. S. Pawar, "Product Design as a Means of Integrating Differentiation," *Technovation* 16, no. 5 (May 1996), pp. 255–64; and W. B. Stevenson and J. M. Bartunek, "Power, Interaction, Position, and the Generation of Cultural Agreement in Organizations," *Human Relations* 49, no. 1 (January 1996), pp. 75–104.

10. *Corporate Director's Guidebook*, 6th ed. (Washington, DC: American Bar Association, 2012); S. F. Shultz, *Board Book: Making Your Corporate Board a Strategic Force in Your Company's Success* (New York: AMACOM, 2000); and R. D. Ward, *Improving Corporate Boards: The Boardroom Insider Guidebook* (New York: Wiley, 2000).

11. S. H. Jeong and D. A. Harrison, "Glass Breaking, Strategy Making, and Value Creating: Meta-Analytic Outcomes of Women as CEOs and TMT Members," *Academy of Management Journal* 60 (2017), pp. 1219–62; V. Hunt, D. Layton, and S. Prince, "Why Diversity Matters," McKinsey & Company, January 2015, www.mckinsey.com.

12. C. M. Daily and D. R. Dalton, "CEO and Board Chair Roles Held Jointly or Separately: Much Ado about Nothing?" *Academy of Management Executive* 11, no. 3 (August 1997), pp. 11–20.

13. See Target's company website, www.corporate.target.com; Airbnb's company website, www.press.airbnb.com; Amazon's company website, www.aboutamazon.com; and Nepris' company website, www.nepris.com/ourteam.

14. A. Chilcote and S. Reece, "Power Paradox," *Leadership Excellence* 26, no. 6 (June 2009), pp. 8–9; A. J. Ali, R. C. Camp, and M. Gibbs, "The Ten Commandments Perspective on Power and Authority in Organizations," *Journal of Business Ethics* 26, no. 4 (August 2000), pp. 351–61; and R. F. Pearse, "Understanding Organizational Power and Influence Systems," *Compensation & Benefits Management* 16, no. 4 (Autumn 2000), pp. 28–38.

15. T. Higgins, "Tesla CEO Musk Says Company Is 'Flattening Management Structure' in Reorganization," *The Wall Street Journal*, May 14, 2018, www.wsj.com.

16. S. Vickery, C. Droge, and R. Germain, "The Relationship between Product Customization and Organizational Structure," *Journal of Operations Management* 17, no. 4 (June 1999), pp. 377–91.

17. T. Kastelle, "Hierarchy Is Overrated," *Harvard Business Review*, November 20, 2013, www.hbr.com.

18. J. Spolsky, "How Hard Could It Be? How I Learned to Love Middle Managers," *Inc.*, September 2008, www.inc.com.

19. C. Wong, P. Elliott-Miller, H. Laschinger, et al., "Examining the Relationships between Span of Control and Manager Job and Unit Performance Outcomes," *Journal of Nursing Management* 23 (2015), pp. 156–68.

20. P. Jehiel, "Information Aggregation and Communication in Organizations," *Management Science* 45, no. 5 (May 1999), pp. 659–69; and A. Altaffer, "First-Line Managers: Measuring Their Span of Control," *Nursing Management* 29, no. 7 (July 1998), pp. 36–40.

21. Excellence Essentials by HR.com, "Optimizing Spans and Layers."

22. M. Akinola, A. Martin, and K. Phillips, "To Delegate or Not to Delegate: Gender Differences in Affective Associations and Behavioral Responses to Delegation," *Academy of Management Journal* 61 (2018), pp. 1467–91.

23. "Span of Control vs. Span of Support," *Journal for Quality and Participation* 23, no. 4 (Fall 2000), p. 15; J. Gallo and P. R. Thompson, "Goals, Measures, and Beyond: In Search of Accountability in Federal HRM," *Public Personnel Management* 29, no. 2 (Summer 2000), pp. 237–48; and C. O. Longenecker and T. C. Stansfield, "Why Plant Managers Fail: Causes and Consequences," *Industrial Management* 42, no. 1 (January–February 2000), pp. 24–32.

24. Z. X. Chen and S. Aryee, "Delegation and Employee Work Outcomes: An Examination of the Cultural Context of Mediating Processes in China," *Academy of Management Journal* 50, no. 1 (2007), pp. 226–38.

25. M. Akinola, A. Martin, and K. Phillips, "To Delegate or Not to Delegate: Gender Differences in Affective Associations and Behavioral Responses to Delegation," *Academy of Management Journal* 61 (2018), pp. 1467–91.

26. "How to Delegate More Effectively," *Community Banker*, February 2009, p. 14; B. Nefer, "Don't Be Delegation-Phobic," *Supervision*, December 2008; J. Mahoney, "Delegating Effectively," *Nursing Management* 28, no. 6 (June 1997), p. 62; and J. Lagges, "The Role of Delegation in Improving Productivity," *Personnel Journal*, November 1979, pp. 776–79.

27. G. Matthews, "Run Your Business or Build an Organization?" *Harvard Management Review*, March–April 1984, pp. 34–44.

28. A. Arya, H. Frimor, and B. Mittendorf, "Decentralized Procurement in Light of Strategic Inventories," *Management Science* 61 (2015), pp. 578–85.

29. Company website, www.burgerville.com; and "5 Things We Learned from Burgerville CEO Jeff Harvey," *Portland Business Journal*, April 23, 2015, www.bizjournals.com.

30. A. Basek, "This Pacific Northwest Chain Will Change the Way You Think about Fast Food," *Food & Wine*, December 1, 2017, www.foodandwine.com.

31. R. Forrester, "Empowerment: Rejuvenating a Potent Idea," *Academy of Management Executive* 14, no. 3 (August 2000),

pp. 67–80; and M. L. Perry, C. L. Pearce, and H. P. Sims Jr., "Empowered Selling Teams: How Shared Leadership Can Contribute to Selling Team Outcomes," *Journal of Personal Selling & Sales Management* 19, no. 3 (Summer 1999), pp. 35–51.

32. See company website, www.esdglobal.com.

33. "Raj P. Gupta," Environmental Systems Design company website, www.esdglobal.com, accessed October 6, 2019.

34. E. E. Lawler III, "New Roles for the Staff Function: Strategic Support and Services," in *Organizing for the Future,* J. Galbraith, E. E. Lawler III, and Associates (San Francisco: Jossey-Bass, 1993).

35. D. Ulrich, J. Younger, and W. Brockbank, "The Twenty-First-Century HR Organization," *Human Resource Management* 47, no. 4 (2008), pp. 829–50; and L. Barratt-Pugh and S. Bahn, "HR Strategy during Culture Change: Building Change Agency," *Journal of Management & Organization,* February 10, 2015, pp. 1–14.

36. R. Cross and L. Baird, "Technology Is Not Enough: Improving Performance by Building Organizational Memory," *Sloan Management Review* 41, no. 3 (Spring 2000), pp. 69–78; and R. Duncan, "What Is the Right Organizational Structure?" *Organizational Dynamics* 7 (Winter 1979), pp. 59–80.

37. G. S. Day, "Creating a Market-Driven Organization," *Sloan Management Review* 41, no. 1 (Fall 1999), pp. 11–22.

38. G. Strauss and L. R. Sayles, *Strauss and Sayles's Behavioral Strategies for Managers,* 1980, p. 221. Reprinted by permission of Prentice-Hall, Inc., Englewood Cliffs, New Jersey.

39. Univeler company website, "Our Brands," www.unilever.com/brands/, accessed October 3, 2019; and G. McFarlane, "How Unilever Makes Money (UL)," Investopedia, December 15, 2017, www.investopedia.com.

40. R. Boehm and C. Phipps, "Flatness Forays," *McKinsey Quarterly* 3 (1996), pp. 128–43.

41. B. T. Lamont, V. Sambamurthy, K. M. Ellis, and P. G. Simmonds, "The Influence of Organizational Structure on the Information Received by Corporate Strategists of Multinational Enterprises," *Management International Review* 40, no. 3 (2000), pp. 231–52.

42. V. Afshar, "Salesforce.com Chief Strategy Officer: Companies Must Innovate around the Customer," *Huffington Post,* January 29, 2016, www.huffingtonpost.com.

43. M. Derven, "Managing the Matrix in the New Normal," *T + D* 64, no. 7 (July 2010), pp. 42–29; H. Kolodny, "Managing in a Matrix," *Business Horizons,* March–April 1981, pp. 17–24; J. Battilana and M. Lee, "Advancing Research on Hybrid Organizing: Insights from the Study of Social Enterprises," *Academy of Management Annals* 8 (2014), pp. 397–441; and D. Levinthal and M. Workiewicz, "When Two Bosses Are Better Than One: Nearly Decomposable Systems and Organizational Adaptation," *Organization Science* 29 (2018), pp. 207–24.

44. J. Battilana and M. Lee, "Advancing Research on Hybrid Organizing: Insights from the Study of Social Enterprises," *Academy of Management Annals* 8 (2014), pp. 397–441; D. Levinthal and M. Workiewicz, "When Two Bosses Are Better Than One: Nearly Decomposable Systems and Organizational Adaptation," *Organization Science* 29 (2018), pp. 207–24.

45. M. Derven, "Managing the Matrix in the New Normal," *T + D* 64, no. 7 (July 2010), pp. 42–29; and H. Kolodny, "Managing in a Matrix," *Business Horizons,* March–April 1981, pp. 17–24.

46. D. Cackowski, M. K. Najdawi, and Q. B. Chung, "Object Analysis in Organizational Design: A Solution for Matrix Organizations," *Project Management Journal* 31, no. 3 (September 2000), pp. 44–51; J. Barker, "Conflict Approaches of Effective and Ineffective Project Managers: A Field Study in a Matrix Organization," *Journal of Management Studies* 25, no. 2 (March 1988), pp. 167–78; G. J. Chambers, "The Individual in a Matrix Organization," *Project Management Journal* 20, no. 4 (December 1989), pp. 37–42, 50; and S. Davis and P. Lawrence, "Problems of Matrix Organizations," *Harvard Business Review,* May–June 1978, pp. 131–42.

47. A. Ferner, "Being Local Worldwide: ABB and the Challenge of Global Management Relations," *Industrielles* 55, no. 3 (Summer 2000), pp. 527–29; and C. Bartlett and S. Ghoshal, "Matrix Management: Not a Structure, a Frame of Mind," *Harvard Business Review* 68 (July–August 1990), pp. 138–45.

48. S. Heywood and R. Katz, "Structuring Your Organization to Meet Global Aspirations," McKinsey & Company, 2012, www.mckinsey.com.

49. J. Tata, S. Prasad, and R. Thorn, "The Influence of Organizational Structure on the Effectiveness of TQM Programs," *Journal of Managerial Issues* 11, no. 4 (Winter 1999), pp. 440–53; and S. Davis and P. Lawrence, "Problems of Matrix Organizations," *Harvard Business Review,* May–June 1978, pp. 131–42.

50. R. E. Miles and C. C. Snow, *Fit, Failure, and the Hall of Fame* (New York: Free Press, 1994); and G. Symon, "Information and Communication Technologies and Network Organization: A Critical Analysis," *Journal of Occupational and Organizational Psychology* 73, no. 4 (December 2000), pp. 389–95.

51. See Bombardier's company website, www.bombardier.com, accessed October 6, 2019.

52. "Bombardier," *Forbes,* May 15, 2019, www.forbes.com.

53. R. E. Miles and C. C. Snow, *Fit, Failure, and the Hall of Fame* (New York: Free Press, 1994).

54. J. G. March and H. A. Simon, *Organizations* (New York: Wiley, 1958); and J. D. Thompson, *Organizations in Action* (New York: McGraw-Hill, 1967).

55. P. S. Adler, "Building Better Bureaucracies," *Academy of Management Executive* 13, no. 4 (November 1999), pp. 36–49.

56. J. Hughes, "India Replaces China as World's Biggest Motorcycle-Building Nation," *The Drive,* August 22, 2017, www.thedrive.com; "Production and Sales of China Motorcycle Industry in 2015," *China Motorworld,* February 16, 2016, www.chinamotorworld.com.

57. J. Galbraith, "Organization Design: An Information Processing View," *Interfaces* 4 (Fall 1974), pp. 28–36. See also S. A. Mohrman, "Integrating Roles and Structure in the Lateral Organization," in *Organizing for the Future,* ed. J. Galbraith, E. E. Lawler III, and Associates (San Francisco: Jossey-Bass, 1993); and B. B. Flynn and F. J. Flynn, "Information-Processing Alternatives for Coping with Manufacturing Environment Complexity," *Decision Sciences* 30, no. 4 (Fall 1999), pp. 1021–52.

58. J. Galbraith, "Organization Design: An Information Processing View," *Interfaces* 4 (Fall 1974), pp. 28–36; and S. A. Mohrman, "Integrating Roles and Structure in the Lateral Organization," in *Organizing for the Future,* ed. J. Galbraith, E. E. Lawler III, and Associates (San Francisco: Jossey-Bass, 1993).

59. S. Denning, "How Basecamp Rejects Workaholism and Still Drives Results," *Forbes,* March 17, 2019, www.forbes.com.

60. S. Denning, "How Basecamp Rejects Workaholism and Still Drives Results," *Forbes,* March 17, 2019, www.forbes.com.

61. G. Hamel and C. K. Prahalad, "Competing for the Future," *Harvard Business Review,* July–August 1994, pp. 122–28; and D. J. Teece, "The Foundations of Enterprise Performance: Dynamic and Ordinary Capabilities in an (Economic) Theory of Firms," *Academy of Management Perspectives* 28 (2014), pp. 328–52.

62. G. Hamel and C. K. Prahalad, *Competing for the Future* (Boston: Harvard Business School Press, 1994).

63. D. G. Sirmon, M. A. Hitt, and R. D. Ireland, "Managing Firm Resources in Dynamic Environments to Create Value: Looking Inside the Black Box," *Academy of Management Review* 32, no. 1 (2007), pp. 273–92; D. Larcker and B. Tayan, "How Netflix Redesigned Board Meetings," *Harvard Business Review,* May 8, 2018, www.hbr.org; K. Sterling, "Why Mark Zuckerberg Thinks One-on-One Meetings Are the Best Way to Lead," *Inc.,* September 28, 2017, www.inc.com; and J. Bort, "How Salesforce CEO Mark Benioff Uses Artificial Intelligence to End Internal Politics at Meetings," *Business Insider,* May 18, 2017, www.businessinsider.com.

64. P. Eisenstein, "Hyundai and Uber Team Up to Debut New Flying Taxis at CES," *CNBC,* January 6, 2020, www.cnbc.com.

65. P. Eisenstein, "Hyundai and Uber Team Up to Debut New Flying Taxis at CES," *CNBC,* January 6, 2020, www.cnbc.com.

66. H. Jin and J. Lee, "Uber, Hyundai Motor Team Up to Develop Electric Air Taxi," *CNBC,* January 6, 2020, www.cnbc.com; and A. Goodwin, "Hyundai and Uber Elevate Debut Urban Air Taxi Concept S-A1," CNET, January 6, 2020.

67. G. Slowinski, E. Hummel, A. Gupta, and E. R. Gilmont, "Effective Practices for Sourcing Innovation," *Research-Technology Management,* January–February 2009, pp. 27–34; and S. Albers, F. Wohlgezogen, and E. Zajac, "Strategic Alliance Structures: An Organization Design Perspective," *Journal of Management* 42 (2016), pp. 582–614.

68. P. Senge, *The Fifth Discipline* (New York: Doubleday Currency, 1990); D. A. Garvin, "Building a Learning Organization," *Harvard Business Review,* July–August 1993, pp. 78–91; D. A. Garvin, *Learning in Action: A Guide to Putting the Learning Organization to Work* (Boston: Harvard Business School Press, 2000); and V. J. Marsick and K. E. Watkins, *Facilitating Learning Organizations: Making Learning Count* (Aldershot, Hampshire: Gower, 1999).

69. W. Wilhelm, "What Are Learning Organizations, and What Do They Really Do?" *Chief Learning Officer,* February 22, 2017, www.chieflearningofficer.com.

70. D. A. Garvin, "Building a Learning Organization," *Harvard Business Review,* July–August 1993, pp. 78–91; D. A. Garvin, *Learning in Action: A Guide to Putting the Learning Organization to Work* (Boston: Harvard Business School Press, 2000); V. J. Marsick and K. E. Watkins, *Facilitating Learning Organizations: Making Learning Count* (Aldershot, Hampshire: Gower, 1999); and N. Anand, H. K. Gardner, and T. Morris, "Knowledge-Based Innovation: Emergence and Embedding of New Practice Areas in Management Consulting Firms," *Academy of Management Journal* 50, no. 2 (2007), pp. 406–28.

71. R. J. Vandenberg, H. A. Richardson, and L. J. Eastman, "The Impact of High Involvement Work Process on Organizational Effectiveness: A Second-Order Latent Variable Approach," *Group & Organization Management* 24, no. 3 (September 1999), pp. 300–39; G. M. Spreitzer and A. K. Mishra, "Giving Up Control without Losing Control: Trust and Its Substitutes' Effects on Managers' Involving Employees in Decision Making," *Group & Organization Management* 24, no. 2 (June 1999), pp. 155–87; and S. Albers Mohrman, G. E. Ledford, and E. E. Lawler III, *Strategies for High Performance Organizations–The CEO Report: Employee Involvement, TQM, and Reengineering Programs in Fortune 1000 Corporations* (San Francisco: Jossey-Bass, 1998).

72. S. Dewnarain, H. Ramkissoon, and F. Mavondo, "Social Customer Relationship Management: An Integrated Conceptual Framework," *Journal of Hospitality Marketing and Management* 28 (2019), pp. 172–88.

73. B. Creech, *The Five Pillars of TQM: How to Make Total Quality Management Work for You* (New York: Plume Publishing, 1995); and J. R. Evans and W. M. Lindsay, *Management and Control of Quality* (Cincinnati, OH: South-Western College Publishing, 1998).

74. T. S. Bateman and S. A. Snell, *Management: Leading & Collaborating in the Competitive World,* 9th ed. (New York: McGraw-Hill/Irwin, 2011), p. 558; and D. Brandt, "Lean Six Sigma and the City," *Industrial Engineer* 43, no. 7 (July 2011), pp. 50–52.

75. International Organization for Standardization, "ISO: A Global Network of National Standards Bodies," www.iso.org.

76. See Mead Metals, Inc.'s company website, www.meadmetals.com, accessed October 2, 2019.

77. J. Woodward, *Industrial Organization: Theory and Practice* (London: Oxford University Press, 1965).

78. G. Liu and G. D. Deitz, "Linking Supply Chain Management with Mass Customization Capability," *International Journal of Physical Distribution & Logistics Management* 41, no. 7 (2011), pp. 668–83; J. H. Gilmore and B. J. Pine, eds., *Markets of One: Creating Customer-Unique Value through Mass Customization* (Cambridge, MA: Harvard Business Review Press, 2000); and B. J. Pine, *Mass Customization: The New Frontier in Business Competition* (Cambridge, MA: Harvard Business School Press, 1992).

79. F. Sahin, "Manufacturing Competitiveness: Different Systems to Achieve the Same Results," *Production and Inventory Management Journal* 41, no. 1 (First Quarter 2000), pp. 56–65.

80. S. Wadhwa and K. S. Rao, "Flexibility: An Emerging Meta-Competence for Managing High Technology," *International Journal of Technology Management* 19, no. 7–8 (2000), pp. 820–45.

81. B. A. Peters and L. F. McGinnis, "Strategic Configuration of Flexible Assembly Systems: A Single Period Approximation," *IIE Transaction* 31, no. 4 (April 1999), pp. 379–90; and A. Bozek and M. Wysocki, "Flexible Job Shop with Continuous Material Flow," *International Journal of Production Research* 53 (2015), pp. 1273–90.

82. J. K. Liker and J. M. Morgan, "The Toyota Way in Services: The Case of Lean Product Development," *Academy of Management Perspectives* 20, no. 2 (May 2006), pp. 5–20; "Strategic Reconfiguration: Manufacturing's Key Role in Innovation," *Production and Inventory Management Journal,* Summer–Fall 2001, pp. 9–17; S. R. Morrey, "Learning to Think Lean: A Roadmap and Toolbox for the Lean Journey," *Automotive Manufacturing &*

Production 112, no. 8 (August 2000), p. 147; and F. Sahin, "Manufacturing Competitiveness: Different Systems to Achieve the Same Results," *Production and Inventory Management Journal* 41, no. 1 (First Quarter 2000), pp. 56-65.

83. I. Pozin, "What Happens When Big Companies Make Innovation a Priority," *Inc.,* March 28, 2018, www.inc.com.

84. The Lean Startup company website, "The Lean Startup Case Studies," www.theleanstartup.com, accessed October 2, 2019.

85. F. Sahin, "Manufacturing Competitiveness: Different Systems to Achieve the Same Results," *Production and Inventory Management Journal* 41, no. 1 (First Quarter 2000), pp. 56-65; and G. S. Vasilash, "Flexible Thinking: How Need, Innovation, Teamwork and a Whole Bunch of Machining Centers Have Transformed TRW Tillsonburg into a Model of Lean Manufacturing," *Automotive Manufacturing & Production* 111, no. 10 (October 1999), pp. 64-65.

86. C. H. Chung, "Balancing the Two Dimensions of Time for Time-Based Competition," *Journal of Managerial Issues* 11, no. 3 (Fall 1999), pp. 299-314; and D. R. Towill and P. McCullen, "The Impact of Agile Manufacturing on Supply Chain Dynamics," *International Journal of Logistics Management* 10, no. 1 (1999), pp. 83-96. See also G. Stalk and T. M. Hout, *Competing Against Time: How Time-Based Competition Is Reshaping Global Markets* (New York: Free Press, 1990); and W. Yang and K. Meyer, "Competitive Dynamics in an Emerging Economy: Competitive Pressures, Resources, and the Speed of Action," *Journal of Business Research* 68 (2015), pp. 1176-85.

87. "A Just-In-Time Supply Chain?" UPS Supply Chain Solutions White Paper, 2005, www.ups-scs.com; M. Tucker and D. Davis, "Key Ingredients for Successful Implementation of Just-in-Time: A System for All Business Sizes," *Business Horizons,* May-June 1993, pp. 59-65; and H. L. Richardson, "Tame Supply Chain Bottlenecks," *Transportation & Distribution* 41, no. 3 (March 2000), pp. 23-28.

88. See, for example, "Just-in-Time: Has Its Time Passed?" *Baseline,* September 11, 2006.

89. J. E. Ettlie, "Product Development—Beyond Simultaneous Engineering," *Automotive Manufacturing & Production* 112, no. 7 (July 2000), p. 18; U. Roy, J. M. Usher, and H. R. Parsaei, eds., *Simultaneous Engineering: Methodologies and Applications* (Newark, NJ: Gordon and Breach, 1999); and M. M. Helms and L. P. Ettkin, "Time-Based Competitiveness: A Strategic Perspective," *Competitiveness Review* 10, no. 2 (2000), pp. 1-14.

90. J. Zygmont, "Detroit Faster on Its Feet," *Ward's Auto World,* July 1, 2006.

Managing Human Resources

Learning Objectives

After studying Chapter 8, you should be able to

LO1 Discuss how companies use human resources management to gain competitive advantage.

LO2 Give reasons why companies recruit both internally and externally for new hires.

LO3 Understand various methods for selecting new employees and HR-related laws.

LO4 Evaluate the importance of spending on training and development.

LO5 Explain alternatives for who appraises an employee's performance.

LO6 Describe the fundamental aspects of a reward system.

LO7 Summarize how unions and labor laws influence human resources management.

Joe Scarnici/Stringer/Getty Images

In 1981, Pam Nicholson was a senior in college, and graduation was looming. So when recruiters from Enterprise Rent-A-Car visited campus, she jumped at the chance to interview. For Nicholson, who hoped to manage a business someday, getting an offer to work for Enterprise seemed ideal. She got the job and never looked back.

A little more than three decades later, Nicholson was named president and CEO of Enterprise. She frequently has been listed as one of *Fortune*'s "Most Powerful Women in Business." Today, Enterprise is one of the largest travel companies in the world with an annual revenue of nearly $26 billion.[1]

Industry observers might say that Nicholson's success has something to do with the firm's formula for running a business: Hire ambitious people, provide comprehensive training and mentoring, promote from within, and put customers and employees first. This strategy can be sustained only by effective human resources management.

Nicholson retired at the end of 2019. True to form, in early 2020, Enterprise hired from within when it named Chrissy Taylor its new CEO.[2] Taylor had begun her career at Enterprise 17 years earlier in the firm's Rent-A-Car Management Training Program. Like Pam Nicholson, she too worked her way up through the organization to become its CEO.

Enterprise's approach to business is based on the expectation that success will follow from effective human resources management. **Human resources management (HRM)** focuses on activities that attract, develop, and motivate people—fundamental aspects of work life.

This chapter describes HRM as it relates to strategic management, including its nuts and bolts: staffing, training, performance appraisal, rewards, and labor relations. Throughout the chapter, we also discuss legal issues that affect HRM.

> **LO1** Discuss how companies use human resources management to gain competitive advantage.

1 | STRATEGIC HUMAN RESOURCES MANAGEMENT

HRM plays a vital strategic role as companies attempt to compete through people. The term *human capital* is used today to describe the strategic value of employee knowledge and abilities.[3]

You know that firms can create a competitive advantage when they possess or develop resources that are valuable, rare, inimitable, and organized. The same criteria apply to the strategic impact of human resources:

1. *People create value.* People can add value by helping to reduce costs and provide something unique to customers. Through total quality initiatives and continuous improvement, people at Alcon, Southwest Airlines, Toyota, and other companies strengthen the bottom line.

2. *Talent is rare.* Top companies invest in hiring and training the best and the brightest employees to gain an advantage over competitors.

3. *Well-chosen, motivated people are difficult to imitate.* Competitors struggle to match the unique cultures of Pipedrive, Google, and Airbnb, which get the most from their employees.

4. *People can be organized for success.* Competitive advantage comes when companies combine people's talents rapidly to work collaboratively on new assignments.

These four criteria highlight the importance of people and show the close link between HRM and strategic management.[4] Evidence is mounting that this focus brings positive business results.[5] Data show that effective HRM practices relate to improved net margins, client satisfaction, and lower absenteeism.[6] Because employee skills, knowledge, and abilities are among an organization's most distinctive and renewable resources, strategic management of people is more important than ever.

As contributors to the organization's strategy, HR managers also face greater ethical challenges. Strategic decisions require them to be able to link decisions about staffing, benefits, and other HR matters to the organization's mission and business success. As members of the top management team, HR managers may need to implement drastic downsizing while still retaining top executives through generous salaries or bonuses, or they may hesitate to aggressively investigate and challenge corrupt management practices. In the long run, organizations are best served when HR leaders advocate at least four sets of values: strategic, ethical, legal, and financial.[7]

Rapidly changing business conditions mean exciting HR opportunities as well as tough HR challenges. By leveraging data and analytics (a.k.a. people analytics) to make more informed talent management decisions, companies like Nielsen, Virgin Media, and Clarks can better address future skills shortages.[8] Thus HR professionals are adding a new competency to their skill set. Nearly, two-thirds of CEOs state that HR managers now have more influence in their organizations.[9] Reasons for this growing influence include "increased competition for talent, a shrinking labor pool and a demand for higher salaries."[10] Well-managed firms seize the opportunities and meet the challenges.

Managing human capital to sustain competitive advantage is vital to the HR function. But on a day-to-day basis, HR managers have many other concerns about employees and the entire personnel puzzle: attracting talent; maintaining a well-trained, highly motivated, and loyal workforce; managing diversity; devising effective compensation systems; managing layoffs; and containing health care and pension costs. The best approaches depend on the company's circumstances, such as whether it is growing, declining, or standing still.

1.1 | HR Planning Involves Three Stages

"Get me the right kind and the right number of people at the right time." It sounds simple enough, but meeting an organization's staffing needs requires strategic HR planning—an activity with a strategic purpose derived from the organization's plans.[11] The process occurs in three stages (see Exhibit 8.1):

1. *Planning*—To ensure that the right number and types of people are available, HR managers must know the company's business plans—where it is headed, in what businesses it plans to be, what future growth is expected, and so forth.

2. *Programming*—HR managers implement specific human resources activities, such as recruitment, training, and pay systems.

3. *Evaluating*—HR managers evaluate whether those activities are producing the results needed in pursuing the business plans.

In this chapter, we focus on human resources planning and programming. You will learn more in later chapters about some other factors shown in Exhibit 8.1.

● Aaron Levie, founder and CEO of Box, giving a presentation on his company's file-sharing and content management capabilities. Yoshio Tsunoda/AFLO/Alamy Live News

Demand Forecasts Perhaps the most difficult part of HR planning is conducting *demand* forecasts—that is, determining how many and what types of people are needed. Demand forecasts are derived from organizational plans. To develop the iPhone, Apple had to determine how many engineers and designers it needed to develop and launch such a complex product. Managers also needed to estimate how many iPhones the company would sell. Based on their forecast, they had to determine how many production employees would be required, along with the staff to market the phone, handle publicity for the launch, and answer inquiries about how to use the new product.

Similarly, companies selling an existing product consider current

Exhibit 8.1 HR planning process

Planning	Programming	Evaluating
HR Environmental Scanning • Labor markets • Technology • Legislation • Competition • Economy **HR Planning** • Demand forecast • Internal labor supply • External labor supply • Job analysis	**HR Activities** • Recruitment • Selection • Diversity and inclusion • Training and development • Performance appraisal • Reward systems • Labor relations	**Results** • Productivity • Quality • Innovation • Satisfaction • Turnover • Absenteeism • Health

"Great vision without great people is irrelevant."[12]

—Jim Collins

sales and projected future sales growth as they estimate the plant capacity for future demand, the sales force required, the support staff needed, and so forth. They calculate the number of labor-hours required and then use those estimates to determine the demand for specific types of workers.

Labor Supply Forecasts Managers also must forecast the *supply of labor*—how many and what types of employees are available. In performing a supply analysis, managers estimate the number and quality of current employees and the available external supply of workers. To estimate internal supply, the company typically relies on its experiences with turnover, terminations, retirements, promotions, and transfers.

Externally, organizations look at workforce trends to make projections. In the United States, demographic trends have contributed to a shortage of workers with appropriate skills and education level. Jobs in technical, financial, and health care industries often require much more training and schooling than the traditional labor-intensive jobs that they replaced. Demand for highly qualified employees continues to outpace supply; this is one reason some

jobs are being transferred overseas. A recent survey of IT managers revealed that 82 percent lack employees with adequate cybersecurity skills to protect their organizations from cyberattacks.[13]

Some demographic trends we discussed in Chapter 2 may worsen this situation. Though some Baby Boomers (born 1946–1964) are continuing to work past retirement age, their retirements are removing large numbers of educated and trained employees from the workforce.[14] And in math, science, and engineering graduate schools, fewer than half of the students receiving graduate degrees are American-born. To fill U.S. jobs, companies must hire U.S. citizens or immigrants with permission to work in the United States.

One response to a skills shortage is to automate routine and repetitive tasks.[15] However, technology advances cannot fill the jobs gap in low- and middle-skilled jobs. So, many companies partner with community colleges to provide students with academic and hands-on training. Infosys partnered with a community college in Rhode Island to help students learn new ways to work with new technology, develop marketable skills, and form a professional network.[16]

Sustaining for Tomorrow

Would You Work for a Social Enterprise?

Operating in the space between nonprofit and for-profit organizations, social enterprises generate revenue to achieve social, environmental, or community economic goals. But many social enterprises in the United States are operating at a suboptimal level. Scaling—growing and continuing to perform well—is an important goal for many. A larger organization with more resources and employees generally makes more progress toward fulfilling the enterprise's mission.

Now more than ever, social enterprises are being created and built up on larger scales. Forty-two percent of existing social enterprises appeared in the past 10 years. In fact, the socially conscious tenets of social enterprises are increasingly being adopted by mainstream business. In a recent survey, 65 percent of CEOs listed "inclusive growth" as a top-three strategy concern. In effect, the once rigid divide between nonprofit and for-profit organizations is beginning to soften.

To fuel additional growth, the industry needs more employees who can use commercial strategies to support social initiatives. Younger people expect organizations to be socially responsible, which explains the popularity of companies like Warby Parker and Bombas, which have strong social missions. The next generation coming into the workforce is also choosing to work for socially conscious organizations. A recent poll found that 70 percent of young people are more likely to work for a company with a "strong environmental agenda," and 40 percent would take a pay cut to work in an organization that emphasized sustainability.

Discussion Questions

- Which do you think is more important: for consumers to support socially conscious businesses or for workers to choose socially conscious employers? Explain your reasoning.

- Assume you are the manager of a social enterprise. How would you attract people to work for your organization?

Sources: R. Meyerhoff, "Why Social Entrepreneurs and Big Business Need Each Other More Than Ever," *Forbes*, November 1, 2018, https://www.forbes.com/sites/sap/2018/11/01/why-social-entrepreneurs-and-big-business-need-each-other-more-than-ever/#7bd0367245b4; J. Bersin, "The Rise of the Social Enterprise: A New Paradigm for Business," *Forbes*, April 3, 2018, https://www.forbes.com/sites/joshbersin/2018/04/03/the-rise-of-the-social-enterprise-a-new-paradigm-for-business/#552f68e571f0; R. Abrams, "Don't Hate, Appreciate: Socially Responsible Small Businesses Win Millennials," *USA Today*, March 27, 2019, https://www.usatoday.com/story/money/usaandmain/2019/03/27/socially-responsible-small-businesses-millennials/3271339002/; and A. Peters, "Most Millennials Would Take a Pay Cut to Work at an Environmentally Responsible Company," *Fast Company*, February 14, 2019, https://www.fastcompany.com/90306556/most-millennials-would-take-a-pay-cut-to-work-at-a-sustainable-company.

Companies also increase the labor supply by recruiting workers from other countries. For example, each year the U.S. government awards H-1B (temporary) visas to college-educated people in such high-skilled, high-demand areas as engineering and teaching. Managers at high-tech companies (Microsoft and Alphabet) and consulting firms (Deloitte and EY [formerly Ernst & Young]) rely on H-1B employees to fill key positions.[17]

Earlier forecasts of a diverse workforce have become fact, adding greatly to the pool of available talent. The next chapter is devoted entirely to this topic.

In contrast, earlier forecasts of an increasingly diverse workforce have become fact, adding greatly to the pool of available talent. Minorities, women, immigrants, older and disabled workers, and other groups have made diversity management a vital activity. Because managing the "new workforce" is so essential, the next chapter is devoted entirely to this topic.

Reconciling Supply and Demand Once managers estimate the supply of and demand for various types of employees, they work to reconcile the two. If they need more people than they currently have (a labor deficit), they can hire new employees, promote current employees to new positions, or outsource work to contractors. When organizations have more people than they need (a labor surplus), they can use attrition—the normal turnover of employees—to reduce the surplus if they have planned far enough in advance. The organization also can lay off employees or transfer them to other areas.

When managers need to hire, they can use fair and competitive compensation policies to attract talent. We discuss pay issues later in this chapter.

Job Analysis Issues of supply and demand are considered at an organizational level, but HR planning also focuses on individual jobs. **Job analysis** does two things:[18]

1. A *job description* tells about the job itself—the essential tasks, duties, and responsibilities involved in performing it. The job description for an accounting manager might specify that the position will be responsible for writing monthly, quarterly, and annual financial reports, issuing and paying bills, preparing budgets, ensuring the company's compliance with laws and regulations, working closely with line managers on financial issues, and supervising an accounting department.

job analysis a tool for determining what is done on a given job and what should be done on that job

recruitment the development of a pool of applicants for jobs in an organization

● LinkedIn, the popular online professional networking site, has hundreds of millions of members in more than 100 countries. aradaphotography/Shutterstock

2. A *job specification* describes the knowledge, skills, abilities, and other characteristics (KSAOs) needed to perform the job. For an assistant manager at a retail store like Nike or Patagonia, job requirements might include a degree in management, motivational skills, knowledge of customer service, retail managerial experience, and excellent communication skills.

Job analysis provides the information needed for virtually every human resources activity. It assists with recruiting, training, selection, appraisal, and reward systems. It also may help organizations defend themselves in lawsuits involving employment practices, for example, by specifying clearly what a job requires if someone claims unfair dismissal.[19] Ultimately, job analysis helps increase the value added by employees to the organization because it clarifies what is required to perform well.

LO2 Give reasons why companies recruit both internally and externally for new hires.

2 | STAFFING THE ORGANIZATION

Once HR planning is completed, managers can focus on staffing: recruiting and selecting people, and sometimes providing outplacement services when people are let go.

2.1 | Recruiting Attracts Good Candidates

A 2020 study by The Conference Board found that attracting candidates was a top priority for CEOs and executives.[20] Recruitment activities increase the pool of candidates from

whom to choose. Companies recruit internally (considering current employees for promotions and transfers) and externally. Each approach has advantages and disadvantages.[21]

Internal Recruiting Advantages of internal recruiting are that employers know their employees, and employees know their organization. External candidates who are unfamiliar with the organization may find they don't like working there. For internal candidates, the opportunity to move up can encourage them to remain with the company, work hard, and succeed. Recruiting from outside the company can be demoralizing.

Managers at Minnesota's Mayo Clinic believe in internal promotion. They encourage employees to be lifelong learners who continually build capabilities and engage in new roles and experiences. Turnover at the health care provider is lower than the industry average.[22]

Internal staffing has potential drawbacks, too. If employees lack skills, the limited applicant pool can yield poor or costly promotions. Moreover, an internal recruitment policy can inhibit a company that wants to change the nature or goals of the business by bringing in outside candidates. In changing from a rapidly growing, entrepreneurial organization to a mature business with more stable growth, Dell went outside the organization to hire managers who better fit those needs.

Internal recruiting often uses a *job-posting system* to advertise open positions. Shell Oil and AT&T use job posting. The posted job description includes a list of duties and the minimum skills and experience required and interested employees can express their interest.

External Recruiting External recruiting brings in "new blood" and can inspire innovation. Among the most frequently used sources of outside applicants are Internet job boards, company websites, employee referrals, newspaper advertisements, and college campus recruiting.

Employers prefer referrals by current employees and online job boards.[23] Many encourage employees to refer their friends by offering cash rewards, and most have a formal employee referral program.[24] Word-of-mouth recommendations are the way most job positions get filled. Not only is this method relatively inexpensive, but employees also tend to know who will be a good fit with the company.

Web job boards such as Indeed, Glassdoor, CollegeRecruiter, SimplyHired, and Mashable Jobs have exploded in popularity as a job recruitment tool because they easily reach a large pool of job seekers.

For specialized positions, companies use networking sites such as LinkedIn, Facebook, and Twitter because job boards generate unqualified leads that are overwhelming to process. Many companies accept applications and post job openings at their corporate websites.

Employment agencies are another common recruitment tool, and for important management positions, companies often use specialized executive search firms. Campus recruiting helps companies looking for applicants who have up-to-date training and innovative ideas. However, companies that rely heavily on campus recruiting and employee referrals must take extra care to ensure that these methods do not discriminate by generating pools of applicants who are, say, mostly women or primarily white.[25] Toward its goal of having 50 percent of its workforce female by 2025, Accenture is asking its employees for help. Those who recommend women or underrepresented minorities whom the company then hires receive a referral bonus.[26]

Some organizations go beyond the call of duty to help certain groups of people find gainful employment. Finding jobs for veterans is an important goal; the unemployment rate among veterans since 2001 is higher than that of the general population. To help these veterans, JPMorgan Chase, with the involvement of 11 other companies, committed to hire or help find jobs for 100,000 veterans. Having surpassed that goal, the mission has expanded to over 200 companies that have recruited over 545,000 veterans.

● The United States Chamber of Commerce and the San Francisco Giants baseball team hosted the Hiring Our Heroes job fair.   Justin Sullivan/Getty Images

Known as the "Veteran Jobs Mission," a website (www.veteran-jobsmission.com) helps transitioning military members match their military expertise to job openings. Given the mission's success, the 230 companies now affiliated with the initiative increased their goal to hiring one million veterans.[27]

Did You KNOW

U.S. employees would leave their current organizations for the following reasons (in descending order of importance):[28]

1. Career advancement or promotional opportunities.
2. Pay/benefits.
3. Lack of job fit.
4. Dissatisfaction with management.
5. Flexibility or scheduling.
6. Job security.

©Brand X Pictures/Getty Images

Most companies use some combination of the methods we have been discussing, depending on the job or situation. They might use internal recruiting for existing jobs that need replacements, and external recruiting when the firm is expanding or needs to acquire new skills.

3 | SELECTING THE BEST HIRE

Selection builds on recruiting and is a decision about whom to hire. As important as these decisions are, they sometimes are made carelessly or quickly.

3.1 | Selection Methods

Knowing the selection techniques you will encounter will help you throughout your career.

Applications and Résumés Applications and résumés provide basic information that helps employers make a first cut through candidates. Typically, they include the applicant's name, educational background, citizenship, work experiences, certifications, and the like. Their appearance and accuracy say something about the applicant—spelling mistakes, for example, can disqualify you immediately. Applications and résumés provide useful starting points, but tend not to be useful as the sole basis for final hiring decisions.

Interviews The most popular selection tool is interviewing, and every company does it. Employment interviewers must be careful about what they ask and how they ask it. As we elaborate on later, federal law requires employers to avoid discriminating on criteria such as sex and race; questions that distinguish candidates according to protected categories can be evidence of discrimination.

In an *unstructured* (or nondirective) interview, the interviewer asks different interviewees different questions. The interviewer may also use probes—that is, ask follow-up questions to learn more about the candidate.[29]

In a structured interview, the interviewer conducts the same interview with each applicant. There are two basic types:

1. The *situational interview* focuses on hypothetical situations. Zale Corporation, a major jewelry chain, uses this to select sales clerks. A sample question would be: "A customer comes into the store to pick up a watch he had left for repair. The watch is not back yet from the repair shop, and the customer becomes angry. How would you

selection choosing from among qualified applicants to hire into an organization

structured interview selection technique that involves asking all applicants the same questions and comparing their responses to a standardized set of answers

handle the situation?" Answering "I would refer the customer to my supervisor" might suggest that the applicant felt incapable of handling the situation independently.

2. The *behavioral description interview* explores what candidates have actually done in the past. An interviewer may ask you: "Tell me about a time when you made a mistake at work." Because behavioral questions are based on real events, they often provide useful information about how the candidate will actually perform on the job. Use the acronym STAR to help you remember what employers want to hear from candidates; describe the specific situation, **t**asks, **a**ction, and **r**esults when answering questions.[30] The questions may be scored on a scale of 1 to 5.[31]

Each of these interview techniques offers advantages and disadvantages. Unstructured interviews can help establish rapport and provide a sense of the applicant's personality, but they may not generate enough specific information about the candidate's abilities. Structured interviews tend to be more reliable predictors of job performance because they are based on the job analysis that has been done for the position. They are more likely to be free of bias and stereotypes. And because the same questions are asked of all candidates, structured interviews allow the manager to directly compare candidates' responses.[32]

Reference Checks Résumés, applications, and interviews rely on the applicant's honesty. To make an accurate selection decision, employers have to be able to trust the words of each candidate. Unfortunately some candidates may exaggerate their qualifications or hide criminal backgrounds that could pose a risk. Executives have added false information to their résumés, including a former president and chairman of the U.S. Olympic Committee and former CEOs of Bausch & Lomb, Yahoo!, and RadioShack.[33] Once lost, a reputation is hard to regain.

Because these and more ambiguous ethical gray areas arise, employers supplement candidate-provided information with *reference checks.* Virtually all organizations contact references or former employers and educational institutions to at least confirm dates of employment (or attendance), positions held, and job duties performed. Although checking references makes sense, reference information is difficult to obtain partly due to former managers not wanting to get accused of defamation of character.[34]

Still, talking to an applicant's previous supervisor is a common practice and often does provide useful information, particularly by using specific job-related questions ("Can you give me an example of a project candidate X handled particularly well?").

Background Checks For a higher level of scrutiny, background investigations are standard procedure at many companies. In some states, companies can be held liable for negligent hiring if they fail to do adequate background checks. Types of checks include Social Security verification, past employment and education verification, and a criminal records check. Other checks can pertain to specific jobs, including a motor vehicle record check (for jobs involving driving) and a credit check (for money-handling jobs).

Background checks are also done in a less formal manner. HR managers often check social networking sites to gather additional information about job applicants. Remember this statistic: 84 percent of recruiters and nearly half of hiring managers review job applicants' social media profiles before deciding whether to hire them.[35] CareerBuilder identified the biggest flags on social media that can hurt job candidates' chances of getting hired: posting inappropriate photos, referring to drinking or using drugs, making negative statements about a previous employer or coworker, using poor communication skills, and making discriminatory comments.[36]

Remember too that anything carrying your name online can become information for potential employers, even years down the road. GoodHire specializes in taking background checks to the next level. If you want to do a preemployment self-check, you can ask GoodHire to research and verify your identity, education, and previous work experience. You can also learn about your rights under the Fair Credit Reporting Act and what to do if you want to dispute an error in the background report. The company helps human resource professionals make faster, more informed selection decisions.[37]

Personality Tests Some employers hesitate to use personality tests for employee selection, largely because they are hard to defend in court.[38] But some traits are associated with greater job satisfaction and performance. At some point in your career you will probably complete some personality tests. Paper-and-pencil (or online) inventories measure personality traits such as extraversion and conscientiousness. Typical questions are "Do you like to socialize with people?" and "Do you enjoy working hard?" Some personality tests try to determine working conditions that the candidate prefers, to see if he or she would be motivated and productive in a particular job. For example, if the candidate prefers making decisions on his or her own but the job requires gaining the cooperation of others, another candidate might be a better fit.

Drug Testing Since the passage of the *Drug-Free Workplace Act of 1988,* applicants and employees of federal contractors and Department of Defense contractors

● When based on a job analysis, structured interviews are more reliable predictors of job performance than unstructured interviews.
Chris Ryan/OJO Images/Getty Images

and those under Department of Transportation regulations have been subject to testing for illegal drugs. Well over half of all U.S. companies also conduct preemployment drug tests.

Cognitive Ability Tests Among the oldest employment selection devices are cognitive ability tests. These tests measure intellectual abilities, including verbal comprehension (vocabulary, reading) and numerical aptitude (mathematical calculations). About 20 percent of U.S. companies use cognitive ability tests for selection purposes.[39] Exhibit 8.2 shows some sample test questions.

Performance Tests In a performance test, the test taker performs a sample of the job. Most companies use some type

---

Exhibit 8.2 Sample measures of cognitive ability

Verbal ability
Gratuitous means the same as ____.
  a. dear   c. expensive
  b. paid   d. costless

Reasoning ability
1, 4, 8, 13, 16, 20, 25, ____.
  a. 27   c. 29
  b. 28   d. 30

Quantitative ability
Yesterday, the price of a bike was $90.00. Today, the price was decreased by 15 percent. What is the new price?
  a. $72.50   c. $76.50
  b. $75.00   d. $78.00

Answers: d, b, and c

---

of performance test, especially for administrative assistant and clerical positions. One of the most widely used is the keyboarding test. However, performance tests exist for almost every occupation, including managerial positions.

Assessment centers are the most notable type of managerial performance test.[40] A typical **assessment center** has 10 to 12 candidates participating in various exercises or situations; some involve group interactions, and others are individual. Each exercise taps critical managerial activities, such as leading, decision making, and communicating. Assessors, generally line managers in the company, observe and record information about the candidates' performance.

Integrity Tests To assess job candidates' honesty, employers can administer integrity tests. Polygraphs, or lie detector tests, are banned for most employment purposes.[41] Instead, paper-and-pencil honesty tests attempt to measure people's propensity to be dishonest (or engage in other counterproductive behaviors) at work. The tests include questions such as whether a person has ever thought about stealing and whether he or she believes other people steal. Companies including Payless ShoeSource report that losses due to theft declined when they started using integrity tests, but the tests' accuracy remains debatable.[42]

3.2 | Reliability and Validity Are Essential

Good selection techniques need to be consistent and accurate. Technically, they must be both reliable and valid. The first step is to understand the difference:

1. **Reliability** is the consistency of test scores over time and across alternative measurements. For example, if three different interviewers talked to the same job candidate but drew very different conclusions about the candidate's abilities, the interview's reliability is low.

2. **Validity** goes beyond reliability to assess the test's accuracy.

Criterion-related validity refers to the degree to which a test actually predicts or correlates with job performance. This is assessed by comparing test performance and job performance for a large enough sample of employees to enable a fair conclusion to be reached. For example, if high scores on a cognitive ability test strongly predict good job performance, validity is demonstrated and candidates who score well will be preferred over those who do not. Still, no test by itself perfectly predicts performance, and managers usually consider other criteria before making a final selection.

Content validity concerns the degree to which selection tests accurately measure a representative sample of the knowledge, skills, and abilities required for the job. The best-known example of a content-valid test is a keyboarding test for administrative assistants, because keyboarding is a task a person in that position almost always performs. However, to be completely content-valid, the selection process also should measure other

tasks the assistant would likely perform, such as working with documents and dealing with the public. Content validity is more subjective (less statistical) than evaluations of criterion-related validity, but both are important, particularly when defending employment decisions in court.

3.3 | Sometimes Employees Must Be Let Go

Unfortunately, hiring is not the only type of staffing decision. Labor demand rises and falls, and some employees simply do not perform at the level required. Managers sometimes must make difficult decisions to terminate people.

Layoffs Organizations sometimes downsize—lay off large numbers of managerial and other employees. Dismissing anyone is tough, but laying off a substantial portion of its workforce can rock the company to its foundation.[43] The victims of restructuring face all the difficulties of being fired—loss of self-esteem, the stigma of being out of work, and demoralizing job searches.

Employers can help by offering **outplacement**, helping dismissed people to regain employment elsewhere. Even then, the impact of layoffs extends beyond departing employees and their families. Many who remain experience disenchantment, distrust, and lethargy. The way management deals with dismissals affects the productivity and satisfaction of those who remain. A thoughtful and fair dismissal process eases tensions and helps remaining employees adjust to the new situation.

If laid-off workers receive severance pay and help in finding a new job, remaining workers will be comforted. Companies also should avoid stringing out multiple layoffs that dismiss a few people at a time.

Done appropriately, downsizing can in fact make firms more agile. But even under the best circumstances, downsizing can be traumatic for an organization and its employees. Interestingly, the people who lose their jobs because of downsizing are not the only ones deeply affected. Those who keep their jobs may develop *survivor's syndrome*.[44] They struggle with heavier workloads, wonder who will be next to go, try to figure out how to survive, lose commitment to the company and faith in their bosses, and become narrow-minded, self-absorbed, and risk-averse.

Termination People sometimes "get fired" for poor performance or other reasons. Should an employer have the right to fire a worker? In 1884 a Tennessee court ruled "All may dismiss their employee(s) at will for good cause, for no cause, or even for cause morally wrong." The concept that an employee may be fired for any reason is known as **employment-at-will** or *termination-at-will,* and was upheld in a 1908 Supreme Court ruling.[45] The logic is that if the employee can quit at any time, the employer is free to dismiss at any time.

Courts in most states make exceptions to this doctrine based on public policy—a policy or ruling designed to protect the public from harm. Under the public policy exception, employees cannot be fired for such actions as refusing to break the law, taking time off for jury duty, or "whistleblowing" to report illegal company behavior. So if a worker reports an environmental violation to the regulatory agency and the company fires him or her, the courts may rule that the firing was unfair because the employee acted for the good of the community. Another major exception is union contracts that limit an employer's ability to fire without cause.

Employers can avoid dismissal's legal pitfalls by using progressive and positive disciplinary procedures.[46] Progressive means the manager takes graduated steps in trying to correct unwanted workplace behaviors. For example, an employee who has been absent receives a verbal reprimand for the first offense, and a written reprimand or personal improvement plan (PIP) for the second offense. A PIP documents clearly the performance gaps and the new goals that need to be achieved, plus a timetable.[47] A third offense results in counseling and probation, and a fourth results in a paid-leave day to think about the consequences of future infractions. The employer is signaling that this is the "last straw." Arbitrators are more likely to side with an employer that fires someone when they believe it made sincere efforts to help the person correct his or her behavior.

The **termination interview**, in which the manager discusses a dismissal decision with the employee, is stressful for both parties. The immediate superior should be the one to deliver the bad news to employees. It also is wise to have a third party, such as an HR manager, present for guidance and note-taking. Because a termination upsets people and occasionally leads to a lawsuit, the manager should prepare carefully. Preparation should include learning the facts and reviewing documents to make sure they are consistent with the reason for the termination. Ethics and common sense dictate that the manager should be truthful but respectful, stating the facts and avoiding arguments. Exhibit 8.3 provides some additional practical guidelines for conducting a termination interview.[48]

3.4 | Legal Issues and Equal Employment Opportunity

Many laws govern employment decisions and practices. They will directly affect a good part of your day-to-day work as a manager, as well as the organization's HR function. Managers need to be familiar with Equal Employment Opportunity laws in order to follow (and comply with) best practices and avoid punishments for noncompliance. Over 76,000 charges of illegal discrimination were filed with the U.S. government in 2019, costing employers nearly $347 million in settlements.[49] Uber agreed to pay over $4 million to settle a sexual harassment and retaliation charge, and Dollar General agreed to settle a race discrimination suit for $6 million.[50]

Exhibit 8.4 summarizes many of these major employment laws.

Laws aimed at protecting employees from discrimination include the 1964 *Civil Rights Act,* which prohibits discrimination in employment based on race, sex, color, national origin, and religion. Title VII of the act forbids discrimination in such employment practices as recruitment, hiring, discharge, promotion,

study tip 8

Sleep isn't an option

Do you ever feel like you have too much on your plate? Between school, work, volunteer/community activities, and social/family life, you may not be getting enough sleep. Also hurting your sleep are caffeinated drinks in the late afternoon or evening. What's the bottom line? Getting sufficient sleep on a regular basis can help you study more efficiently and possibly earn higher grades.

Exhibit 8.3	Practical guidelines for conducting a termination interview

Do provide written explanations of severance benefits.

Do provide outplacement services away from company headquarters.

Do be sure the employee hears about the termination from a manager, not a colleague.

Do express appreciation for what the employee has contributed, if appropriate.

Don't leave room for confusion when firing. Tell the individual in the first sentence that he or she is terminated.

Don't allow time for debate during a termination session.

Don't make personal comments when firing someone; keep the conversation professional.

Don't rush a fired employee off site unless security is an issue.

Don't fire people on significant dates, like the 25th anniversary of their employment or the day their mother died.

Exhibit 8.4 — U.S. equal employment laws

Act	Major Provisions	Enforcement and Remedies
Fair Labor Standards Act (1938)	Creates exempt (salaried) and nonexempt (hourly) employee categories, governing overtime and other rules; sets minimum wage, child labor laws.	Enforced by Department of Labor, private action to recover lost wages; civil and criminal penalties also possible.
Equal Pay Act (1963)	Prohibits gender-based pay discrimination between two jobs substantially similar in skill, effort, responsibility, and working conditions.	Fines up to $10,000, imprisonment up to 6 months, or both; enforced by Equal Employment Opportunity Commission (EEOC); private actions for double damages up to 3 years' wages, liquidated damages, reinstatement, or promotion.
Title VII of Civil Rights Act (1964)	Prohibits discrimination based on race, sex, color, religion, or national origin in employment decisions: hiring, pay, working conditions, promotion, discipline, or discharge.	Enforced by EEOC; private actions, back pay, front pay, reinstatement, restoration of seniority and pension benefits, attorneys' fees and costs.
Executive Orders 11246 and 11375 (1965)	Requires equal opportunity clauses in federal contracts; prohibits employment discrimination by federal contractors based on race, color, religion, sex, or national origin.	Established Office of Federal Contract Compliance Programs (OFCCP) to investigate violations; empowered to terminate violator's federal contracts.
Age Discrimination in Employment Act (1967)	Prohibits employment discrimination based on age for persons over 40 years; restricts mandatory retirement.	EEOC enforcement; private actions for reinstatement, back pay, front pay, restoration of seniority and pension benefits; double unpaid wages for willful violations; attorneys' fees and costs.
Vocational Rehabilitation Act (1973)	Requires affirmative action by all federal contractors for persons with disabilities; defines disabilities as physical or mental impairments that substantially limit life activities.	Federal contractors must consider hiring disabled persons capable of performance after reasonable accommodations.
Americans with Disabilities Amendments Act (1990 & 2008)	Extends affirmative action provisions of Vocational Rehabilitation Act to private employers; requires workplace modifications to facilitate disabled employees; prohibits discrimination against disabled.	EEOC enforcement; private actions for Title VII remedies.
Civil Rights Act (1991)	Clarifies Title VII requirements: disparate treatment impact suits, business necessity, job relatedness; shifts burden of proof to employer; permits punitive damages and jury trials.	Punitive damages limited to sliding scale only in intentional discrimination based on sex, religion, and disabilities.
Family and Medical Leave Act (1991)	Requires 12 weeks' unpaid leave for medical or family needs: paternity, maternity, family member illness.	Private actions for lost wages and other expenses, reinstatement.

compensation, and access to training.[51] Title VII also prohibits a specific form of discrimination, *sexual harassment,* which refers to "unwelcome sexual advances, requests for favors, and other verbal or physical conduct of a sexual nature" that impacts an individual's employment, interferes with work performance, or creates a hostile work environment.[52] The *Americans with Disabilities Act* prohibits employment discrimination against people with disabilities. Recovering alcoholics and drug abusers, cancer patients in remission, and AIDS patients are covered by this legislation. The 1991 *Civil Rights Act* strengthened all these protections and permitted punitive damages to be imposed on companies that violate them. The *Age Discrimination in Employment Act* of 1967 and its amendments in 1978 and 1986 prohibit discrimination against people age 40 and over. One reason for this legislation was the practice of dismissing older workers to replace them with younger workers earning lower pay.

One common reason employers are sued for discrimination is adverse impact—when a seemingly neutral employment practice has a disproportionately negative effect on a certain group, such as a group protected by the Civil Rights Act.[53] For example, if equal numbers of qualified men and women apply for jobs but a test results in far fewer women being hired, the test had an adverse impact and it is subject to challenge. An Alaskan mining company paid $690,000 to settle charges that it discriminated against female employees for not providing advancement opportunities for women.[54]

> **adverse impact** when a seemingly neutral employment practice has a disproportionately negative effect on a protected group

Because these issues are so important, many companies have procedures to ensure compliance with labor and equal opportunity laws. For example, they monitor and compare salaries by race, gender, length of service, and other categories to make sure employees across all groups are paid fairly. Written policies can help ensure fair and legal practices in the workplace, although the company may have to demonstrate a record of actually following those procedures. Effective management practices not only motivate employees to do their best work but also help provide legal protection. For example, managers who

training teaching lower-level employees how to perform their current jobs

development teaching managers and professional employees broad skills needed for their current and future jobs

needs assessment an analysis identifying the jobs, people, and departments that need training

orientation training training designed to introduce new employees to the company and familiarize them with policies, procedures, culture, and the like

● Thousands of McDonald's employees across the country staged protests fighting for a $15 minimum wage.
Mike Nelson/Epa/REX/Shutterstock

give their employees regular, specific evaluations can prevent misunderstandings that lead to lawsuits. A written record of those evaluations can demonstrate fair and objective treatment.

Another important law is the *Worker Adjustment and Retraining Notification Act* of 1989, commonly known as the *WARN Act* or *Plant Closing Bill,* requiring covered employers to give affected employees 60 days' written notice of plant closings or mass layoffs.

> **LO4 Evaluate the importance of spending on training and development.**

4 | TRAINING AND DEVELOPMENT

Today's competitive environment requires managers to upgrade the skills and performance of employees—and themselves. Continual improvement makes organization members more useful in their current job and prepares them for new responsibilities. And it helps the entire organization handle new challenges and take advantage of new methods and technologies. As shown in Exhibit 8.5, training and development can address many different topics.[55]

4.1 | Programs Include Four Phases

Training usually refers to teaching lower-level employees how to perform their present jobs, whereas **development** involves teaching managers and professional employees broader skills needed for their present and future jobs.

Phase one usually starts with a **needs assessment**. Managers conduct an analysis to identify the jobs, people, and departments for which training is necessary. Job analysis and performance measurements are useful for this purpose.[56]

Phase two involves designing the programs. Managers use the needs assessment to establish objectives and content. For example, Bank of America creates individualized training and development plans to help its employees meet performance objectives and managers' expectations.[57]

Phase three involves decisions about the delivery methods, such as online, classroom with a trainer, or blended.[58] Other methods include lectures, role-playing, business simulation, behavior modeling (watching videos and imitating what is observed), conferences, and apprenticeships. Bank of America provides its employees with a combination of instructor-led courses, interactive web-based training, and videos.[59]

Another popular method is job rotation, or assigning employees to different jobs in the organization to broaden their experience and improve their skills. Smart managers often request assignment to jobs where they can be challenged and their skills broadened. The methods should be suited to the objectives defined in phase two.

Finally, *phase four* evaluates the program's effectiveness. Measures of effectiveness include employee reactions (surveys), learning (skills tests), improved behavior on the job, and bottom-line results such as sales increases or fewer defects following the training program.

4.2 | Common Objectives and Topics

Companies invest in training and development to enhance individual performance and organizational productivity. Programs to improve an employee's computer, technical, or communication skills are common, and some types have become standard for many organizations. **Orientation training** familiarizes new

Exhibit 8.5	Important training and development topics in 2019
Executive development	
Management/Supervisory training	
Interpersonal skills (e.g., communication, teamwork)	
IT/Systems training (e.g., enterprise software)	
Desktop application training	
Customer service training	
Sales training	
Mandatory or compliance training	

Source: Adapted from "2019 Training Industry Report," *Training,* November–December 2019, www.trainingmag.com.

employees with their work, work units, and the organization in general. Done well, orientation training can increase morale and productivity and can lower employee turnover and the costs of recruiting and training.

Team training teaches employees the skills they need to work collaboratively in teams. After General Mills acquired Pillsbury, it used a team training program called Brand Champions to combine the marketing expertise of the two companies and share their knowledge in functions including sales and research and development. Most of the time, participants engaged in team exercises to analyze brands, target customers, and develop marketing messages.[60]

Diversity training focuses on building awareness of diversity issues and providing skills needed for effective work relationships. Much more on this follows in the next chapter.

As today's decentralized and leaner organizations have put more demands on managers, **management development programs** are common. Such programs often seek to improve managers' *people skills*—their ability to delegate effectively, motivate their subordinates, solve problems, and communicate and inspire others to achieve organization goals. *Coaching*—being developed by an upper manager or a consultant—is usually the most effective and direct management development tool. Managers also participate in training programs that are used for all employees, such as job rotation, or attend seminars and courses designed to help them improve supervisory skills or prepare for future promotion.

> **LO5 Explain alternatives for who appraises an employee's performance.**

5 | PERFORMANCE APPRAISAL

One of the most important responsibilities you will have as a manager is **performance appraisal (PA)**, the assessment of an employee's job performance.[61] Done well, it can help people improve their performance, pay, and chances for promotion; foster communication between managers and employees; and increase the employees' and the organization's effectiveness. Done poorly, it can cause resentment, reduce motivation, diminish performance, and even expose the organization to legal action.

Performance appraisal has two basic, equally important purposes:

1. *Administrative*—PA provides managers with the information they need to make salary, promotion, and dismissal decisions; helps employees understand and accept the basis of those decisions; and provides documentation that can justify those decisions in court.

2. *Developmental*—The information gathered can be used to identify needed training, experiences, or other improvements. Further, the manager's feedback and coaching can help employees improve their performance and prepare them for greater responsibility.

5.1 | What Do You Appraise?

Performance appraisals can assess three basic categories of employee performance: traits, behaviors, and results. *Trait appraisals* involve judgments about employee behavior. The rater indicates the degree to which the employee shows initiative, leadership, and attitudes. Usually these appraisals use a numerical *ratings scale.* For example, if the measured trait is "attitude," the employee might be rated anywhere from 1 (very negative attitude) to 5 (very positive attitude). Trait scales are common because they are simple to use and provide a standard measure for all employees. But they are often not valid as performance measures. Because they tend to be ambiguous as well as highly subjective—does the employee really have a bad attitude, or is he or she just shy?—they often lead to personal bias and may not be suitable for providing useful feedback.

Behavioral appraisals, while still subjective, focus on observable aspects of performance that relate to the job. They use scales describing specific, prescribed behaviors, which can help ensure that all parties understand what the ratings are really measuring. Because they are less ambiguous, they can provide useful feedback. Exhibit 8.6 shows an example of a behaviorally anchored rating scale (BARS) for evaluating quality.

Another common approach is the *critical incident* technique, in which the manager keeps a regular log by recording significant employee behaviors that reflect performance quality ("Eva impressed the client with her effective presentation today"; "Mike was late with his report"). This approach can be subjective and time-consuming, and it may give some employees a sense that everything they do is being recorded. However, it reminds managers what the employee actually did.

Results appraisals tend to be more objective and can focus on productivity data such as sales volume (for a salesperson), units produced (for a line worker), customer complaints resolved (for a customer service employee), or profits (for a manager). One approach, **management by objectives (MBO)**, involves a subordinate and a supervisor agreeing in advance on specific performance goals (objectives). They develop a plan describing the time frame and criteria for determining whether the objectives are reached. The aim is to agree on a set of objectives that are clear, specific, and reachable. An objective of a marketing manager might be "Develop a new social media advertising campaign using influencers on YouTube, Facebook, and Instagram."

team training training that provides employees with the skills and perspectives they need to collaborate with others

diversity training programs that focus on identifying and reducing hidden biases against people with differences and developing the skills needed to manage a diversified workforce

management development programs training for new or experienced managers, often focused on leadership and other "people skills"

performance appraisal (PA) assessment of an employee's job performance

management by objectives (MBO) a process in which objectives set by a subordinate and a supervisor must be reached within a given time period

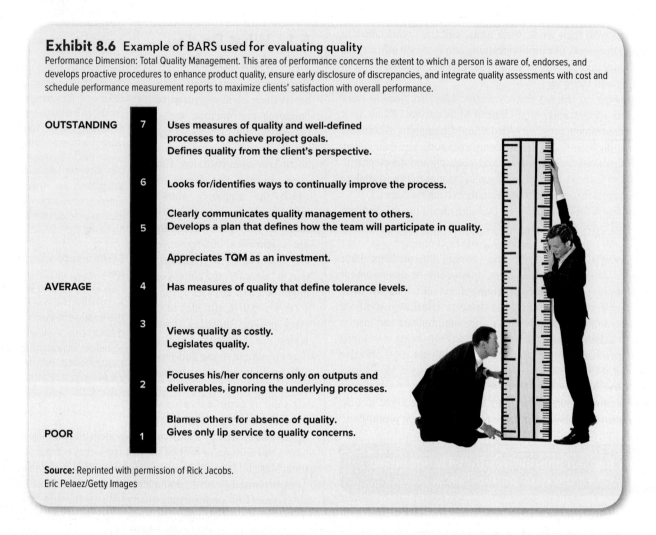

Exhibit 8.6 Example of BARS used for evaluating quality

Performance Dimension: Total Quality Management. This area of performance concerns the extent to which a person is aware of, endorses, and develops proactive procedures to enhance product quality, ensure early disclosure of discrepancies, and integrate quality assessments with cost and schedule performance measurement reports to maximize clients' satisfaction with overall performance.

OUTSTANDING	7	Uses measures of quality and well-defined processes to achieve project goals. Defines quality from the client's perspective.
	6	Looks for/identifies ways to continually improve the process.
	5	Clearly communicates quality management to others. Develops a plan that defines how the team will participate in quality.
		Appreciates TQM as an investment.
AVERAGE	4	Has measures of quality that define tolerance levels.
	3	Views quality as costly. Legislates quality.
	2	Focuses his/her concerns only on outputs and deliverables, ignoring the underlying processes.
POOR	1	Blames others for absence of quality. Gives only lip service to quality concerns.

Source: Reprinted with permission of Rick Jacobs.
Eric Pelaez/Getty Images

MBO has several important advantages. First, it avoids the biases and measurement difficulties of trait and behavioral appraisals. At the end of the review period, the employee either has or has not achieved the specified objective. The employee is judged on actual job performance. Second, because the employee and manager agree on the objective at the outset, the employee is likely to be committed to the goal, and misunderstanding is unlikely. Third, because the employee is directly responsible for achieving the objective, MBO allows empowerment of employees to adapt their behavior so they achieve the desired results.

But the approach has disadvantages as well. Objectives may be unrealistic, frustrating the employee and the manager, or too rigid, leaving the employee without enough flexibility if circumstances change. And, MBO often focuses on short-term achievements at the expense of longer-term goals.

In recent years, companies like Deloitte, The Gap, and Adobe replaced their formal, annual performance appraisals with informal performance check-ins and coaching on a quarterly basis.[62] Crowdsourced feedback can supplement supervisor-provided performance data. Zalando, a European e-retailer, collects real-time feedback about employees' performance in meetings and problem-solving sessions, and on projects. Employees could ask for feedback from supervisors, colleagues, and internal customers.[63]

None of these PA systems is easy to conduct properly, and all have drawbacks. In choosing an appraisal method, certain guidelines help:

- Base performance standards on job analysis.
- Communicate performance standards to employees.
- Evaluate employees on specific performance-related behaviors rather than on a single global or overall measure.
- Document the performance appraisal process carefully.
- If possible, use more than one rater.
- Have a formal appeal process.
- Always take legal considerations into account.[64]

5.2 | Who Should Do the Appraisal?

Just as multiple methods can gather performance appraisal information, several different sources can provide that information:

- *Managers* and *supervisors* are the traditional source because they are often best positioned to know an employee's performance.

> ## "The best minute you spend is the one you invest in people."
> —Ken Blanchard

- *Peers* and *team members* see different dimensions of performance and may be best at identifying interpersonal skills. Some companies use peers and team members to provide input to the performance appraisal.

- *Subordinates* are becoming a more popular source of appraisal information, used by companies such as Xerox and IBM to give managers feedback on how their direct reports view them. Often, this information is given in confidence to the manager and not shared with higher-ups. Even so, this approach can make managers uncomfortable initially. But the feedback is often practical and can help managers improve. Because this process gives employees power over their bosses, it is best used for development purposes only, not for salary or promotion decisions.

- *Internal and external customers* are useful sources of performance appraisal information in companies, such as Ford and Honda, that care about total quality. Restaurants have long used external customers to appraise front-of-the-house employees. Internal customers can mean anyone inside the organization who depends on an employee's work output.

- *Self-appraisals,* in which employees evaluate their own performance, can be highly worthwhile. Although they may be biased upward, the process increases the employee's involvement and is a starting point for setting future goals.

● Performance appraisal feedback is more effective when it's specific and constructive.
Tom Merton/age fotostock

Because each source of information has some limitations, and different people may see different aspects of performance, Westinghouse, Dell, and many other companies use multiple sources for appraisal information. In a **360-degree appraisal**, feedback comes from subordinates, peers, bosses, and often customers—every level involved with the employee. The person being rated can select the appraisers, subject to a manager's approval, with the understanding that the raters' appraisals are confidential. Returned forms don't include appraisers' names, and the results are consolidated for each level.

The 360-degree appraisal delivers a fuller picture of the employee's strengths and weaknesses, and it often captures qualities other appraisal methods miss. For example, an employee may have a difficult relationship with his or her supervisor yet be highly regarded by peers and subordinates. The approach can lead to significant improvement, with people often motivated to improve their ratings. On the downside, people may be unwilling to rate colleagues harshly. Also, the 360-degree appraisal is less useful than more objective criteria, like financial targets. It is usually aimed at employee development, rather than administrative decisions like raises. For those, results appraisals like MBO are more appropriate.[65]

360-degree appraisal process of using multiple sources of appraisal to gain a comprehensive perspective on one's performance

Tips for receiving constructive feedback

Receiving criticism often feels like a negative thing, which makes sense. When we're told we're not our best, it hurts. But getting feedback often helps us improve our skills and our performance. After all, we can't fix what we don't know is broken. Here are a few tips to get you started:

1. Start thinking of criticism as helpful, not hurtful. Defensiveness is a natural response. But we can learn to turn it off—or at least tone it down.

2. Practice active listening. Show the person providing the feedback that you are receptive to their opinion. Try telling them in your own words what you heard them saying.

3. Ask questions. Sometimes you won't understand the feedback you receive. Don't be afraid to ask for specific examples. Ask for ways in which you can work to improve.

4. Reflect on what others share with you. Even if you master the art of receiving feedback, it's still a good idea to set aside time to think about it more deeply. A little time and distance might widen your objectivity lens.

Also, don't forget to thank the person providing the feedback. Being gracious goes a long way in the moment and in the long run.

Sources: S. Heathfield, "How to Receive Feedback with Grace and Dignity," *The Balance*, June 25, 2019, https://www.thebalancecareers.com/receive-feedback-with-grace-and-dignity-1916643; and M. Jenner et al., "How to Master the Art of Receiving Feedback," Hays Recruiting, February 4, 2019, https://social.hays.com/2019/02/04/receiving-feedback-work/.

5.3 | How Do You Give Employees Feedback?

Giving performance feedback can be stressful for managers and subordinates because its multiple purposes often conflict. Providing advice for growth and development requires understanding and support, but the manager must be objective and honest and make tough decisions. Employees want to know how they are doing, but typically they are uncomfortable about getting feedback. Finally, the organization's need to make HR decisions conflicts with the individual employee's need to maintain a positive image.[66] These conflicts often make performance interviews difficult, so managers should conduct them thoughtfully.

Generally, appraisal feedback works best when it is *specific* and *constructive*—related to clear goals or behaviors and clearly intended to help the employee rather than simply criticize. Managers want to not just rate performance but also improve it, and effective appraisals consider both. In addition, the appraisal will be more meaningful and satisfying when the employee can ask questions and respond to the appraisal.

Interviews are most difficult when an employee is performing poorly. When an employee is performing below acceptable standards:

1. Summarize the employee's specific performance. Describe the performance in behavioral or outcome terms, such as sales or absenteeism. Don't say the employee has a poor attitude; rather, explain which employee behaviors indicate a poor attitude.

2. Describe the expectations and standards, and be specific.

3. Determine the causes for the low performance; get the employee's input.

4. Discuss solutions to the problem, and have the employee play a major role in the process.

5. Agree to a solution. As a supervisor, you have input into the solution. Raise issues and questions, but also provide support.

6. Agree to a timetable for improvement.

7. Document the meeting.

Follow-up meetings may be needed.

Performance appraisal is a core component of the much broader, continuous process of performance management (PM). Whereas PA is a discrete (often once-a-year) event, PM (done well) is an ongoing process requiring many activities. Performance management includes a variety of strategically chosen managerial processes,[67] including giving feedback more frequently, leading, motivating, teaming, and communicating (all elaborated in later chapters).

> **LO6** Describe the fundamental aspects of a reward system.

6 | DESIGNING REWARD SYSTEMS

Another crucial set of HRM activities involves reward systems. This section emphasizes monetary rewards such as pay and fringe benefits.

6.1 | Pay Decisions Consider the Company, Position, and Individual

Ideally, reward systems serve the strategic purposes of attracting, motivating, and retaining people. Beyond the body of laws governing compensation, the wage mix is influenced by a variety of factors:[68]

- *Internal factors* include the organization's compensation policy, the worth of each job, each employee's relative worth, and the employer's ability to pay.

- *External factors* include conditions of the labor market, area wage rates, the cost of living, collective bargaining (union negotiations), and legal requirements.

These basic decisions are the core of an effective pay plan:

1. *Pay level*—the choice of whether to be a high-, average-, or low-paying company. Compensation is a major cost for any organization, so low wages can be justified on a short-term financial basis. But being the high-wage employer—the highest-paying in the region—ensures that the company will attract many applicants. Being a wage leader is especially important during times of low unemployment or intense competition.

2. *Pay structure*—the choice of how to price different jobs within the organization. Jobs that are similar in worth are grouped together into job families. A pay grade, with a floor and a ceiling, is established for each job family. Exhibit 8.7 illustrates a hypothetical pay structure.

3. *Individual pay decisions*—different pay rates for jobs of similar worth within the same family. Two criteria determine pay differences within job families. First, some individuals have more seniority than others. Second, some people perform better and therefore deserve higher pay.

Setting low pay rates may become more difficult for employers to sustain in the future, as more employees and job candidates use online resources such as Glassdoor.com, Salary.com, PayScale.com, Indeed.com, and SalaryExpert.com to check whether their pay is above or below the average for similar job titles.[69]

Especially at the individual level, pay decisions are kept confidential. Is that a good thing? Surprisingly, there is little evidence about this practice, even though it affects almost every private-sector employee.[70] Keeping pay decisions secret may help avoid conflicts, protect individuals' privacy, and retain people who are receiving lower-than-average pay. However, secret pay decisions can raise unfounded suspicions about unfairness, and people may be less motivated because they don't see a connection between performance and pay. In an economic sense, labor markets are less efficient when information is unavailable, which can reduce organizations' ability to get the best workers at the optimum pay rates.

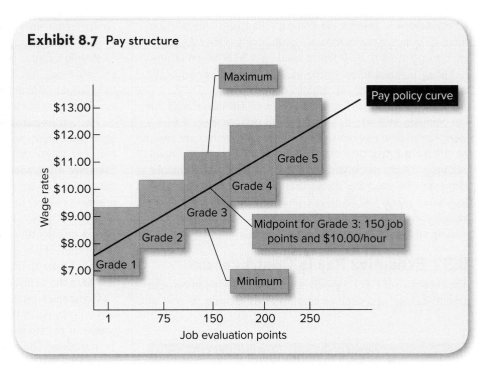

Exhibit 8.7 Pay structure

Given these possible pros and cons of pay secrecy, do you think this practice is wise? Is it ethical? And what about you—do you want to know how much your coworkers earn?

6.2 | Incentive Pay Encourages Employees to Perform

Various incentive systems have been devised to motivate employees to be more productive.[71] The most common are *individual incentive plans,* which compare a worker's performance against an objective standard, with pay determined by the employee's performance. Examples include paying a salesperson extra for exceeding a sales target and awarding managers a bonus when their group meets a target. If effectively designed, individual incentive plans can be highly motivating. For example, Verizon employees can earn compensation above their base salaries if they meet or surpass their individual performance objectives. Depending on how well the company is doing, employee bonuses can be a substantial percentage of base salaries.[72]

Group incentive plans, in which pay is based on group performance, aim to give employees a sense of participation and ownership in the firm's performance. *Gainsharing plans* reward employees for increasing productivity or saving money in areas under their direct control.[73] For example, if the usual waste allowance in a production line has been 5 percent and the company wants production employees to reduce that number, it might offer to split any savings gained with the employees. *Profit-sharing plans* are implemented in the division or organization as a whole, although some incentives may still be tailored to unit performance. The profit-sharing plan is based on a formula for allocating an annual amount to each employee if the company exceeds a specified profit target. Although profit-sharing plans do not reward individual performance, they do give all employees a stake in the company's success and motivate them to improve the company's profitability. Delta Air Lines announced in early 2020 that it would pay $1.6 billion in profit-sharing bonuses to its employees. The record payout is the equivalent of receiving two months of extra pay.[74]

When objective performance measures are unavailable but the company still wants to base pay on performance, it uses a *merit pay system*. Individuals' pay raises and bonuses are based on the merit rating they receive from their boss. Many organizations use merit pay systems to encourage higher performance. However, not everyone agrees that this is the best approach. Individual merit pay plans can undermine teamwork and the achievement of organizational goals; group incentives like gain-sharing and profit sharing avoid these pitfalls.[75]

6.3 | Executive Pay Is Controversial

The sheer size of CEO compensation and the wide gap between executives' pay and average employee pay is wide, as well as

● Workers consider not only salary, but also environment, culture, and benefits in making their employment decisions.
Hello Lovely/Getty Images

controversial. In 2019, CEOs made more than 278 times the average worker's pay.[76]

People differ as to whether or not they approve of such high executive pay, but recent research shows an important bottom line: Bigger differences relate to stronger firm performance in the short term but worse performance in the long run.[77]

The fastest-growing part of executive compensation comes from stock grants and *stock options*. Such options give the holder the right to purchase shares of stock at a specified price. For example, if the company's stock price is $8 a share, the company might award a manager the right to purchase a specific number of shares of company stock at that price. But if the price of the stock rises to, say, $10 a share after a specified holding period—usually three years or more—the manager can exercise the option. He or she can purchase the shares from the company at $8 per share, sell the shares on the stock market at $10, and keep the difference.

Companies issue options to managers to align their interests with those of the company's owners, the shareholders. Of course, if the stock price never rises above $8, the options will be worthless. The assumption is that managers will focus hard on making the company successful, leading to a rise in its stock price. Assuming that the executives continue to own their stock year after year, the amount of their wealth that is tied to the company's performance—and their incentive to work hard for the company—should continually increase.[78]

However, critics say that excessive use of options encourages executives to focus on short-term results to drive up the stock price at the expense of their firm's long-run competitiveness. Plunging stock markets highlight another problem with stock options: Many options become essentially worthless, so they fail to reward employees.[79] In the future, employees may become wary of accepting stock options in lieu of less risky forms of pay.

6.4 | Employees Get Benefits, Too

Benefits make up a far greater percentage of the total payroll than in past decades.[80] The typical employer today pays over 31 percent of payroll costs in benefits.[81] Benefits costs have risen faster than wages and salaries, fueled by the rapidly rising cost of medical care. Accordingly, employers attempt to reduce benefits costs, even as their value to employees is rising. Benefits also receive more attention because of their increased complexity.

Like pay systems, employee benefit plans are subject to regulation. Benefits are divided into those required by law and those optional for an employer. Three basic benefits are required by law:

1. *Workers' compensation* provides financial support to employees suffering a work-related injury or illness.

2. *Social Security,* as established in the Social Security Act of 1935, provides financial support to retirees. In subsequent amendments, the act was expanded to cover employees with disabilities. The funds come from payments made by employers, employees, and self-employed workers.

3. *Unemployment insurance* provides financial support to employees laid off for reasons they cannot control. Companies that terminate fewer employees pay less into the unemployment insurance fund, providing an incentive to minimize terminations.

Many employers also offer benefits that are not required. The most common are pension plans and medical and hospital insurance. However, these programs are changing, partly because in a global economy they put U.S. firms at a competitive disadvantage. For example, U.S. employers spent an average of $15,000 per employee on health benefits in 2018.[83] Overseas firms generally do not bear these costs thanks to government-funded health care, so they can compete more effectively on price. Meanwhile in the United States, health care costs keep rising and companies are asking employees to share more of their cost. A growing share of U.S. companies (more than one-third) offer no medical benefits at all, or they staff more positions with part-time workers and offer coverage only to full-time employees.

At the same time, retirement benefits have moved away from guaranteed (defined benefit) pensions. While a promised monthly pension used to be the norm, only about 4 percent of private company employees have one today (down from 60 percent in the early 1980s).[84] More often, the employee, the employer, or both contribute to an individual retirement account or 401(k) plan, which is invested. Upon retirement, the employee gets the accumulated account balance.

Because of the wide variety of benefit options and the considerable differences in employee preferences and needs, companies often use cafeteria or flexible benefit programs. Employees receive credits, which they "spend" by selecting customized benefit packages, including medical and dental insurance, dependent care, life insurance, and so on.

6.5 | Pay and Benefits Must Meet Legal Requirements

The *Equal Pay Act (EPA)* of 1963 prohibits unequal pay for men and women who perform equal work. Equal work means jobs that require equal skill, effort, and responsibility and are performed under similar working conditions. The law does permit exceptions in which the pay difference is due to a seniority system, merit system, incentive system based on quantity or quality of production, or any factor other than sex, such as market demand.

In contrast to equal-pay-for-equal-work, comparable worth implies that women who perform *different* jobs of *equal* worth

Did You KNOW

While the federal minimum wage remains at $7.25 per hour, 18 states increased their minimum wage rates in 2018. An estimated 4.5 million workers were affected by the pay bump. States that pay $10.00 or more per hour are Alaska, Arizona, California, Colorado, Connecticut, Hawaii, Maine, Maryland, Massachusetts, Minnesota (large employers only), New Jersey, New York, Oregon, Rhode Island, Vermont, and Washington.[82]

cafeteria benefit program an employee benefit program in which employees choose from a menu of options to create benefit packages tailored to their needs

flexible benefit programs benefit programs in which employees are given credits to spend on benefits that fit their unique needs

comparable worth principle of equal pay for different jobs of equal worth

as those performed by men should be paid the same wage.[85] For example, nurses (predominantly female) were paid far less than skilled craftworkers (predominantly male), even though the two jobs were found to be of equal value or worth.[86] Under the Equal Pay Act, this would not constitute pay discrimination because the jobs are so different. But under the comparable worth concept, these findings indicate discrimination because the jobs are of equal worth. To date, no federal law requires comparable worth, and the Supreme Court has made no decisive rulings about it.

However, some states have considered developing comparable worth laws, and others have raised the wages of female-dominated jobs. Over 30 years ago, Minnesota passed a comparable worth law for public-sector employees after finding that women, on average, were paid 25 percent less than men. The gender pay gap has since been reduced to 11 percent.[87] Iowa, Idaho, Montana, Minnesota, New Mexico, Washington, and South Dakota also have comparable worth laws for public-sector employees.[88]

Some laws regulate benefit practices. The *Pregnancy Discrimination Act* of 1978 states that pregnancy is a disability and qualifies a woman to receive the same benefits that she would with any other disability. The *Employee Retirement Income Security Act (ERISA)* of 1974 protects private pension programs from mismanagement. ERISA requires retirement benefits to be paid to those who vest or earn a right to draw benefits, and it ensures retirement benefits for employees whose companies go bankrupt or otherwise cannot meet their pension obligations.

6.6 | Employers Must Protect Health and Safety

The *Occupational Safety and Health Act (OSHA)* of 1970 requires employers to pursue workplace safety by maintaining records of injuries and deaths caused by workplace accidents and submitting to onsite inspections. Large-scale industrial accidents and

Exhibit 8.8

Exhibit 8.8 HR executives cannot neglect safety and health

How many fatal work-related injuries were recorded in 2018?

There were 5,250 work-related fatalities that year, a 2 percent increase over the previous year.

What was the worker fatality rate for all occupations?

The rate was 3.5 per 100,000 full-time employees.

Which occupations experience the most work-related fatalities?

- Drivers/sales workers and truck drivers had 966 fatalities, the highest rate (over 18 percent) of any occupation.

- Logging workers, fishing workers, aircraft pilots and flight engineers, and roofers had more than 10 times the worker fatality rate for all occupations.

- Police and sheriff's patrol officers had over 100 fatalities, a 14 percent increase over 2017.

What are the most common fatal events?

- Transportation incidents are the most frequent type of fatal event, accounting for over 40 percent of work-related deaths.

- Incidents involving contact with objects, like workers caught in running equipment, increased from 695 to 786 from 2017.

- Unintentional overdoses due to nonmedical use of drugs of alcohol while at work increased 12 percent, making it the 6th consecutive annual increase.

Source: "National Census of Fatal Occupational Injuries in 2018," press release, December 17, 2019, Bureau of Labor Statistics, www.bls.gov.

labor relations the system of relations between workers and management

nuclear power plant disasters worldwide have focused attention on the importance of workplace safety. Exhibit 8.8 presents some facts about work-related fatalities in the United States.

One area of particular concern is the safety of young workers, who may lack the confidence to speak up if they see health or safety problems. Many teenage workers are exposed to hazards and use equipment that should be off-limits to teens under federal regulations. The risk of injury is real. Every five minutes a teenager (ages 15–19) is injured at work, and teenagers are almost twice as likely to get injured as employees who are at least 24 years old.[89]

LO7 Summarize how unions and labor laws influence human resources management.

7 | LABOR RELATIONS

Labor relations is the system of relationships and interactions between workers and management. Labor unions recruit members, collect dues, and work to ensure that employees are treated fairly with respect to wages, working conditions, and other issues. When workers organize and negotiate with management, two processes are involved: unionization and collective bargaining. These processes have evolved since the 1930s in the United States to provide important employee rights.[90]

7.1 | What Labor Laws Exist?

Passed in 1935, the *National Labor Relations Act* (also called the *Wagner Act* after its legislative sponsor) ushered in an era of rapid unionization by declaring labor organizations legal, establishing unfair employer labor practices, and creating the National Labor Relations Board (NLRB). Before the act, employers could fire workers who favored unions and use federal troops to put down strikes. Today the NLRB conducts unionization elections, hears complaints of unfair labor practices, and issues injunctions against offending employers. The Wagner Act greatly assisted the growth of unions by enabling workers to use the law and the courts to organize and collectively bargain for better wages, hours, and working conditions. Minimum wages, health benefits, maternity leave, the 40-hour workweek, and other worker protections resulted largely from collective bargaining over many years by unions.

Public policy began on the side of organized labor in 1935, but over the next 25 years, the pendulum swung toward management. The *Labor-Management Relations Act,* or *Taft-Hartley Act* (1947), protected employers' free speech rights, defined unfair labor practices by unions, and permitted workers to decertify (reject) a union as their representative.

The *Labor-Management Reporting and Disclosure Act,* or *Landrum-Griffin Act* (1959), swung the public policy pendulum somewhere between organized labor and management. By declaring a bill of rights for union members, establishing control over union dues increases, and imposing reporting requirements for unions, Landrum-Griffin was designed to curb abuses by union leadership and rid unions of corruption.

● Fast-food workers and activists demonstrate outside the McDonald's corporate campus in Oak Brook, Illinois. They were calling on McDonald's to pay a minimum wage of $15 per hour and offer better working conditions for their employees. Scott Olson/Getty Images

7.2 | How Do Employees Form Unions?

The effort to form a union begins when a union organizer or local union representative describes to workers the benefits they may receive by joining.[91] The union representative distributes authorization cards that permit workers to indicate whether they want an election to certify the union. The National Labor Relations Board will conduct an election if at least 30 percent of the employees sign authorization cards. Management has several choices at this stage: to recognize the union without an election, to consent to an election, or to contest the number of cards signed and resist an election.

If an election is warranted, an NLRB representative conducts one by secret ballot. A simple majority of those voting determines the winner, so apathetic workers who do not vote in effect support the union. If the union wins the election, it is certified as the bargaining unit representative. Management and the union are then legally required to bargain in good faith to obtain a collective bargaining agreement or contract.

Why do workers vote for or against a union? At least four factors play significant roles:[92]

1. *Economic factors,* especially for workers in low-paying jobs—Unions attempt to raise the average wage rate for their members.

2. *Job dissatisfaction*—Poor supervisory practices, favoritism, lack of communication, and perceived unfair or arbitrary discipline and discharge are specific triggers.

3. *Belief that the union has power* to obtain desired benefits.

4. The *image of the union*—Headline stories of union corruption and dishonesty can discourage workers from unionizing.

7.3 | How Is Collective Bargaining Conducted?

In the United States, management and unions engage in a periodic ritual (typically every three years) of negotiating an agreement for wages, benefits, hours, and working conditions. Disputes can arise during this process, and sometimes the workers go on strike to compel agreement on their terms. Such an action, known as an *economic strike,* is permitted by law, but strikes are rare today. Strikers are not paid while they are on strike, and few workers want to undertake this hardship. In addition, managers can legally hire replacement workers during a strike, offsetting some of the strike's effects. Finally, workers are as aware as managers of the tougher competition companies face today; if treated fairly, they will usually share management's interest in coming to an agreement.

After an agreement is signed, the parties may disagree over *interpretation* of the agreement. Usually they settle their disputes through arbitration: the use of a neutral third party, typically jointly selected, to resolve the dispute. The United States uses arbitration while an agreement is in effect to avoid *wildcat strikes* (unplanned work stoppages) in which workers walk off the job in violation of the contract.

Certain clauses are common in a collective bargaining agreement:

- *Security clause*—In a union shop, the contract requires workers to join the union after a set period of time. Right-to-work states, through restrictive laws, do not permit union shops; workers have the right to work without being forced to join a union. The southern United States has many right-to-work states.

- *Wage component*—The contract spells out pay rates, including premium pay for overtime and paid holidays.

- *Individual rights*—These include the use of seniority to determine pay increases, job bidding, and the order of layoffs.

- *Grievance procedure*—This procedure gives workers a voice in what goes on during contract negotiations and administration.[93] In about 50 percent of discharge cases that go to arbitration, the arbitrator either reduces or reverses employer sanctions, reinstating the worker.[94]

Unions have a legal duty of fair representation, which means they must represent all workers in the bargaining unit and ensure that workers' rights are protected.

arbitration the use of a neutral third party to resolve a labor dispute

union shop an organization with a union and a union security clause specifying that workers must join the union after a set period of time

right-to-work legislation that allows employees to work without having to join a union

"Treat your employees exactly as you want them to treat your best customers."

—Stephen R. Covey

7.4 | What Does the Future Hold?

In recent years, union membership has declined to about 10.5 percent overall of the U.S. labor force—down from a peak of over 33 percent at the end of World War II. In the United States in 2017, 34 percent of public-sector employees and 6.5 percent of private-sector employees were union members.[95] The decline may be attributable partly to improved effectiveness of the HR function.

Shrinking union participation is due also to automation eliminating many of the manufacturing jobs that used to be union strongholds. Employees in office jobs are less interested in joining unions and more difficult to organize. Tough global competition has made managers much less willing to give in to union demands, so the benefits of unionization are less clear—particularly to young, skilled workers who no longer expect to stay with one company all their lives.

When companies recognize that success depends on the talents and energies of employees, the interests of unions and managers begin to converge. Rather than one side exploiting the other, unions and managers can find common ground based on developing, valuing, and involving employees. Particularly in knowledge-based companies, the balance of power is shifting toward employees.

Individuals, not companies, own their own human capital. This leaves poorly managed organizations in a particularly vulnerable position. To compete, organizations are searching for ways to obtain, retain, and engage their most valuable resources: people!

Notes

1. Enterprise Holdings website, "Financial Information," https://www.enterpriseholdings.com/en/financial-information.html, accessed March 21, 2020.

2. Enterprise Holdings website. "Chrissy Taylor Named Chief Executive Officer of Enterprise Holdings." December 11, 2019. Retrieved from https://www.enterpriseholdings.com/en/press-archive/2019/12/chrissy-taylor-named-chief-executive-officer-of-enterprise-holdings.html

3. J. Hollenbeck and B. Jamieson, "Human Capital, Social Capital, and Social Network Analysis: Implications for Strategic Human Resource Management," *Academy of Management Perspectives* 29 (2015), pp. 370-85; D. Kryscynski and D. Ulrich, "Making Strategic Human Capital Relevant: A Time-Sensitive Opportunity," *Academy of Management Perspectives* 29 (2015), pp. 357-69; and A. Nyberg and P. Wright, "50 Years of Human Capital Research: Assessing What We Know, Exploring Where We Go," *Academy of Management Perspectives* 29 (2015), pp. 287-95.

4. R. E. Ployhart, "Strategic Organizational Behavior (STROBE): The Missing Voice in the Strategic Human Capital Conversation," *Academy of Management Perspectives* 29 (2015), pp. 342-56; J. Marler, "Strategic Human Resource in Context: A Historical and Global Perspective," *Academy of Management Perspectives* 26 (2017), pp. 6-11; N. Gardner, D. McGranahan, and W. Wolf, "Question for Your HR Chief: Are We Using Our 'People Data' to Create Value?" *McKinsey Quarterly,* March 2011, https://www.mckinseyquarterly.com; D. Ulrich and J. Dulebohn, "Are We There Yet?" What's Next for HR?" *Human Resource Management Review* 25 (2015), pp. 188-204; and C. Ostroff and D. Bowen, "Reflections on the 2014 Decade Award: Is There Strength in the Construct of HR System Strength?" *Academy of Management Review* 41 (2016), pp. 196-214.

5. A. Denisi and C. Smith, "Performance Appraisal, Performance Management, and Firm-Level Performance: A Review, a Proposed Model, and New Directions for Future Research," *Academy of Management Annals* 8 (2014), pp. 127-70; G. Saridakis, Y. Lai, and C. Cooper, "Exploring the Relationship between HRM and Firm Performance: A Meta-analysis of Longitudinal Studies," *Human Resource Management Review* 27 (2017), pp. 87-96; and D. D. Shin and A. Konrad, "Causality between High-Performance Work Systems and Organizational Performance," *Journal of Management* 43 (2017), pp. 973-97.

6. B. Vermeeren, B. Steijn, L. Tummers, M. Lankhaar, R. J. Poerstamper, and S. van Beek, "HRM and Its Effects on Employee, Organizational and Financial Outcomes in Health Care Organizations," *Human Resources for Health,* June 17, 2014, www.ncbi.nlm.nih.gov.

7. P. M. Wright and S. A. Snell, "Partner or Guardian? HR's Challenge in Balancing Value and Values," *Human Resource Management* 44, no. 2 (2005), pp. 177-82.

8. L. Schmidt and D. Green, "This Is Why Data Is Now More Essential Than Ever in HR," *Fast Company,* May 31, 2019, www.fastcompany.com.

9. K. Gurchiek, "HR 'New Frontier' for Data-Driven Business Strategies," Society for Human Resource Management, July 28, 2015, www.shrm.org.

10. K. Gurchiek, "HR 'New Frontier' for Data-Driven Business Strategies," Society for Human Resource Management, July 28, 2015, www.shrm.org.

11. M. Marchington, "Human Resource Management (HRM): Too Busy Looking Up to See Where It Is Going Longer Term?" *Human Resource Management Review* 25 (2015), pp. 176-87; and D. Ulrich and J. Dulebohn, "Are We There Yet? What's Next for HR?" *Human Resource Management Review* 25 (2015), pp. 188-204.

12. J. C. Collins, *Good to Great: Why Some Companies Make the Leap . . . and Others Don't* (New York: HarperBusiness, 2001).

13. K. Sheridan, "Cyber-Security Skills Shortage Leaves Companies Vulnerable," *InformationWeek,* August 1, 2016, www.informationweek.com.

14. The Conference Board, "What Does the Coming Labor Shortage from Retiring Baby Boomers Mean for Your Company?" www.conference-board.org, accessed March 19, 2019; and A. Mathur, "The Baby Boomers Are Doing Just That, Booming," *Forbes,* February 8, 2019, www.forbes.com.

15. R. Dobbs, J. Manyika, and J. Woetzel, "How U.S. Can Fill the Skills Gap," *Fortune,* May 12, 2015, www.fortune.com.

16. J. McDermott, "Infosys Forms Community College Partnership in Rhode Island," *AP News*, February 12, 2019, www.apnews.com.

17. A. Elahi, "What Is an H-1B Visa, and Why Are Tech Companies Worried about Them?" *Chicago Tribune*, February 1, 2017, www.chicagotribune.com.

18. M. T. Brannick, E. L. Levine, and F. P. Morgeson, *Job and Work Analysis: Methods, Research, and Applications for Human Resource Management*, 2nd ed. (Thousand Oaks, CA: Sage, 2007); F. P. Morgeson and M. A. Campion, "Accuracy in Job Analysis: Toward an Inference-Based Model," *Journal of Organizational Behavior* 21, no. 7 (November 2000), pp. 819–27; and J. S. Shippmann, R. A. Ash, L. Carr, and B. Hesketh, "The Practice of Competency Modeling," *Personnel Psychology* 53, no. 3 (Autumn 2000), pp. 703–40.

19. J. S. Schippmann, *Strategic Job Modeling: Working at the Core of Integrated Human Resources* (Mahwah, NJ: Erlbaum, 1999).

20. The Conference Board, "Survey: Business Leaders Start 2020 with Lingering Concerns about Talent Shortages & Recession Risk," press release, January 2, 2020, www.conference-board.org.

21. D. E. Terpstra, "The Search for Effective Methods," *HR Focus*, May 1996, pp. 16–17; H. G. Heneman III and R. A. Berkley, "Applicant Attraction Practices and Outcomes among Small Businesses," *Journal of Small Business Management* 37, no. 1 (January 1999), pp. 53–74; and J. M. Hiltrop, "The Quest for the Best: Human Resource Practices to Attract and Retain Talent," *European Management Journal* 17, no. 4 (August 1999), pp. 422–30.

22. R. Erickson, D. Moulton, and B. Cleary, "Are You Overlooking Your Greatest Source of Talent?" *Deloitte Review*, July 30, 2018, www2.deloitte.com.

23. G. Ruiz, "Print Ads See Resurgence as Hiring Source," *Workforce Management*, March 26, 2007; and G. Ruiz, "Recruiters Cite Referrals as Top Hiring Tool," *Workforce Management*, October 23, 2006.

24. CareerBuilder, "Referral Madness," www.careerbuilder.com.

25. F. Hansen, "Employee Referral Programs, Selective Campus Recruitment Could Touch Off Bias Charges," *Workforce Management*, June 26, 2006.

26. J. Kauflin, "Exclusive: Accenture Commits to Boosting Its Workforce to 50% Women by 2025," *Forbes*, June 14, 2017, www.forbes.com; and E. Peck, "Why Referral Bonuses May Be the Secret to Improving Your Company's Diversity," *Inc.*, February 10, 2016, www.inc.com.

27. Veteran Jobs Mission, "About the Mission," www.veteranjobsmission.com/about-the-mission, accessed October 10, 2019.

28. M. Schwantes, "Why Are Your Employees Quitting? A Study Says It Comes Down to Any of These 6 Reasons," *Inc.*, October 23, 2017, www.inc.com.

29. J. Dana, R. Dawes, and N. Peterson, "Belief in the Unstructured Interview: The Persistence of an Illusion," *Judgment and Decision Making* 8, no. 5 (September 2013), pp. 512–20; M. McDaniel, D. L. Whetzel, F. L. Schmidt, and S. D. Maurer, "The Validity of Employment Interviews: A Comprehensive Review and Meta-Analysis," *Journal of Applied Psychology* 79, no. 4 (August 1994), pp. 599–616; M. A. Campion, J. E. Campion, and P. J. Hudson Jr., "Structured Interviewing: A Note on Incremental Validity and Alternative Question Types," *Journal of Applied Psychology* 79, no. 6 (December 1994), pp. 998–1002; and R. A. Fear, *The Evaluation Interview* (New York: McGraw-Hill, 1984).

30. M. Krumie, "How to Prevent Bad Hires with Behavioral Interviews," ZipRecruiter, www.ziprecruiter.com, accessed March 18, 2020; and "How to Prepare for a Behavioral Interview," Indeed, March 14, 2020, www.indeed.com.

31. "A Guide to Conducting Behavioral Interviews with Early Career Job Candidates," Society for Human Resource Management (2016), www.shrm.org.

32. T. Macan, "The Employment Interview: A Review of Current Studies and Directions for Future Research," *Human Resource Management Review* 19, no. 3 (September 2009), pp. 201–19.

33. H. Restle and J. Smith, "17 Successful Executives Who Have Lied on their Résumés," *Business Insider*, July 15, 2015, www.businessinsider.com; and P. Anand, "5 Big-Shots Who Lied on Their Resumes," *MarketWatch*, September 20, 2014, www.marketwatch.com.

34. S. Lucas, "Your Former Employees Want a Reference. Here Is What Your Attorney Thinks about That," *Inc.*, October 2, 2014, www.inc.com.

35. I. Thottam, "These Social Media Mistakes Can Actually Disqualify You from a Job," Monster, www.monster.com, accessed October 12, 2019.

36. Company website, "According to Annual CareerBuilder Social Media Recruitment Survey," press release, May 14, 2015, www.careerbuilder.com.

37. Company website, "Candidate Help Center," www.goodhire.com.

38. See also M. R. Barrick and M. K. Mount, "The Big Five Personality Dimensions and Job Performance: A Meta-Analysis," *Personnel Psychology* 44 (1991), pp. 1–26; D. P. O'Meara, "Personality Tests Raise Questions of Legality and Effectiveness," *HRMagazine*, January 1994, pp. 97–100; and L. A. McFarland and A. M. Ryan, "Variance in Faking across Noncognitive Measures," *Journal of Applied Psychology* 85, no. 5 (October 2000), pp. 812–21.

39. P. M. Wright, M. K. Kacmar, G. C. McMahan, and K. Deleeuw, "P=f (M X A): Cognitive Ability as a Moderator of the Relationship between Personality and Job Performance," *Journal of Management* 21, no. 6 (1995), pp. 1129–39; P. R. Sackett and D. J. Ostgaard, "Job-Specific Applicant Pools and National Norms for Cognitive Ability Tests: Implications for Range Restriction Corrections in Validation Research," *Journal of Applied Psychology* 79, no. 5 (October 1994), pp. 680–84; F. L. Schmidt and J. E. Hunter, "Tacit Knowledge, Practical Intelligence, General Mental Ability, and Job Knowledge," *Current Directions in Psychological Science* 2, no. 1 (1993), pp. 3–13; M. Roznowski, D. N. Dickter, L. L. Sawin, V. J. Shute, and S. Hong, "The Validity of Measures of Cognitive Processes and Generability for Learning and Performance on Highly Complex Computerized Tutors: Is the G Factor of Intelligence Even More General?" *Journal of Applied Psychology* 85, no. 6 (December 2000), pp. 940–55; and J. M. Cortina, N. B. Goldstein, S. C. Payne, H. K. Davison, and S. W. Gilliland, "The Incremental Validity of Interview Scores over and above Cognitive Ability and Conscientiousness Scores," *Personnel Psychology* 53, no. 2 (Summer 2000), pp. 325–51.

40. F. Lievens and F. Patterson, "The Validity and Incremental Validity of Knowledge Tests, Low-Fidelity Simulations, and High-Fidelity Simulations for Predicting Job Performance in Advanced-Level High-Stakes Selection," *Journal of Applied Psychology* 96, no. 5 (2011), pp. 927–40; W. Arthur Jr., D. J. Woehr, and R. Maldegen, "Convergent and Discriminant Validity of Assessment Center Dimensions: A Conceptual and Empirical Reexamination of the Assessment Center Construct-Related Validity Paradox," *Journal of Management* 26, no. 4 (2000), pp. 813–35; and R. Randall, E. Ferguson, and F. Patterson, "Self-Assessment Accuracy and

Assessment Center Decisions," *Journal of Occupational and Organizational Psychology* 73, no. 4 (December 2000), p. 443.

41. U.S. Department of Labor website, www.dol.gov; A. McFarland and A. M. Ryan, "Variance in Faking across Noncognitive Measures," *Journal of Applied Psychology* 85, no. 5 (October 2000), pp. 812–21; and D. Terpstra, R. Kethley, R. Foley, and W. Limpaphayom, "The Nature of Litigation Surrounding Five Screening Devices," *Public Personnel Management* 29, no. 1 (2000), pp. 43–54.

42. D. S. Ones, C. Viswesvaran, and F. L. Schmidt, "Comprehensive Meta-Analysis of Integrity Test Validities: Findings and Implications for Personnel Selection and Theories of Job Performance," *Journal of Applied Psychology* 78 (August 1993), pp. 679–703.

43. J. A. Oxman, "The Hidden Leverage of Human Capital," *MIT Sloan Management Review* 43, no. 4 (Summer 2002), pp. 78–83; R. L. DeWitt, "The Structural Consequences of Downsizing," *Organization Science* 4, no. 1 (February 1993), pp. 30–40; and P. P. Shah, "Network Destruction: The Structural Implications of Downsizing," *Academy of Management Journal* 43, no. 1 (February 2000), pp. 101–12.

44. "Layoff 'Survivor' Stress: How to Manage the Guilt and the Workload," *HR Focus* 86, no. 8 (August 2009), pp. 4–6; W. F. Cascio, "Strategies for Responsible Restructuring," *Academy of Management Executive* 19, no. 4 (2005), pp. 39–50; W. Cascio, "Downsizing: What Do We Know? What Have We Learned?" *Academy of Management Perspectives* 7, no. 1 (1993), pp. 95–104; and J. Ciancio, "Survivor's Syndrome," *Nursing Management* 31, no. 5 (May 2000), pp. 43–45.

45. See *Adair v. United States,* 2078 U.S. 161 (1908); and D. A. Ballam, "Employment-at-Will: The Impending Death of a Doctrine," *American Business Law Journal* 37, no. 4 (Summer 2000), pp. 653–87.

46. P. Falcone, "Employee Separations: Layoffs vs. Terminations for Cause," *HRMagazine* 45, no. 10 (October 2000), pp. 189–96; and P. Falcone, "A Blueprint for Progressive Discipline and Terminations," *HR Focus* 77, no. 8 (August 2000), pp. 3–5.

47. "How to Establish a Performance Improvement Plan," Society for Human Resource Management, September 16, 2015, www.shrm.org.

48. J. W. Bucking, "Employee Terminations: Ten Must-Do Steps When Letting Someone Go," *Supervision,* May 2008; and M. Price, "Employee Termination Process Is Tough for Those on Both Sides," *Journal Record* (Oklahoma City, OK), October 23, 2008. Bullet points taken from S. Alexander, "Firms Get Plenty of Practice at Layoffs, but They Often Bungle the Firing Process," *The Wall Street Journal,* November 14, 1991, p. 31. Copyright 1991 Dow Jones & Co., Inc. Reproduced with permission of Dow Jones & Co., Inc. via Copyright Clearance Center.

49. U.S. Equal Employment Opportunity Commission, "EEOC Releases Fiscal Year 2018 Enforcement and Litigation Data," April 10, 2019, www.eeoc.gov.

50. See Equal Employment Opportunity Commission website, www.eeoc.gov, accessed March 18, 2020.

51. *Employer EEO Responsibilities* (Washington, DC: Equal Employment Opportunity Commission, U.S. Government Printing Office, 1996); and N. J. Edman and M. D. Levin-Epstein, *Primer of Equal Employment Opportunity,* 6th ed. (Washington, DC: Bureau of National Affairs, 1994).

52. Equal Employment Opportunity Commission website, www.eeoc.gov/facts/fs-sex.html.

53. R. Gatewood and H. Field, *Human Resource Selection,* 3rd ed. (Chicago: Dryden Press, 1994), pp. 36–49; and R. A. Baysinger,

"Disparate Treatment and Disparate Impact Theories of Discrimination: The Continuing Evolution of Title VII of the 1964 Civil Rights Act," in *Readings in Personnel and Human Resource Management,* ed. R. S. Schuler, S. A. Youngblood, and V. L. Huber (St. Paul, MN: West Publishing, 1987).

54. U.S. Equal Employment Opportunity Commission, "Alaska Gold Mine to Pay $690,000 to Settle EEOC Sex Discrimination and Retaliation Lawsuit," June 13, 2019, www.eeoc.gov.

55. "2017 Training Industry Report," *Training,* November–December 2017, www.trainingmag.com.

56. N. Andriotis, "Why You Need to Run a Training Needs Assessment (and How to Do It)," eLearning Industry, April 15, 2019, www.elearningindustry.com.

57. See company website, "Career Mobility–Skill Development," Bank of America, www.bankofamerica.com, accessed March 19, 2020.

58. Organization website, "Training Delivery Guide," Training and Development at MIT, www.web.mit.edu, accessed March 19, 2020.

59. See company website, "Career Mobility–Skill Development," Bank of America, www.bankofamerica.com, accessed March 19, 2020.

60. J. Gordon, "Building Brand Champions: How Training Helps Drive a Core Business Process at General Mills," *Training,* January–February 2007.

61. A. Schleicher et al., "Putting the System into Performance Management Systems: A Review and Agenda for Performance Management Research," *Journal of Management* 44 (2018), pp. 2209–45.

62. L. Bodell, "It's Time to Put Performance Reviews on Notice," *Forbes,* April 27, 2018, www.forbes.com; and A. Smith, "More Employers Ditch Performance Appraisals," Society for Human Resource Management, May 18, 2018, www.shrm.org.

63. "Ahead of the Curve: The Future of Performance Management," *McKinsey Quarterly,* May 2016, www.mckinsey.com.

64. For more information, see K. Wexley and G. Latham, *Increasing Productivity through Performance Appraisal* (Reading, MA: Addison-Wesley, 1994).

65. G. Toegel and J. Conger, "360 Degree Assessment: Time for Reinvention," *Academy of Management Learning and Education* 2, no. 3 (September 2003), p. 297; and L. K. Johnson, "Retooling 360s for Better Performance," *Harvard Business School Working Knowledge,* February 23, 2004, online.

66. M. Edwards and A. J. Ewen, "How to Manage Performance and Pay with 360-Degree Feedback," *Compensation and Benefits Review* 28, no. 3 (May–June 1996), pp. 41–46. See also M. N. Vinson, "The Pros and Cons of 360-Degree Feedback: Making It Work," *Training and Development* 50, no. 4 (April 1996), pp. 11–12; and R. S. Schuler, *Personnel and Human Resource Management* (St. Paul, MN: West Publishing, 1984).

67. R. E. Ployhart, "Strategic Organizational Behavior (STROBE): The Missing Voice in the Strategic Human Capital Conversation," *Academy of Management Perspectives* 29 (2015), pp. 342–56.

68. G. Bohlander, S. Snell, and A. Sherman, *Managing Human Resources,* 12th ed. (Cincinnati, OH: South-Western, 2001).

69. A. Bergen, "7 of the Best Salary Information Websites for Negotiation," Money Under 30, April 19, 2019, www.moneyunder30.com.

70. A. Colella, R. L. Paetzold, A. Zardkoohi, and M. J. Wesson, "Exposing Pay Secrecy," *Academy of Management Review* 32, no. 1 (2007), pp. 55–71.

71. B. Fotsch and J. Case, "How to Build Incentive Plans That Actually Work," *Forbes,* August 24, 2015, www.forbes.com; L. A. Rozycki, "Incentive Plans: A Motivational Tool That Works," *CPA Practice Management Forum* 4, no. 10 (October 2008), pp. 12-16; G. T. Milkovich, J. M. Newman, and B. Gerhart, *Compensation,* 11th ed. (New York: McGraw-Hill/Irwin, 2013); A. Nyberg, J. Pieper, and C. Trevor, "Pay-for-Performance's Effect on Future Employee Performance: Integrating Psychological and Economic Principles toward a Contingency Perspective," *Journal of Management* 42 (2016), pp. 1753-83; S. Gross and J. Backer, "The New Variable Pay Programs: How Some Succeed, Why Some Don't," *Compensation and Benefits Review* 25, no. 1 (January-February 1993), p. 51; B. Gerhart and M. Fang, "Pay for (Individual) Performance Issues, Claims and the Role of Sorting Effects," *Human Resource Management Review* 24 (2014), pp. 41- 52; and L. Bareket-Bojmel, G. Hochman, and D. Ariely, "It's (Not) All about the Jacksons: Testing Different Types of Short-Term Bonuses in the Field," *Journal of Management* 43 (2017), pp. 534-54.

72. U.S. Securities and Exchange Commission, "Administrative Guide of the Verizon Wireless Short-Term Incentive Plan," www.sec.gov.

73. T. Welbourne and L. Gomez-Mejia, "Gainsharing: A Critical Review and a Future Research Agenda," *Journal of Management* 21, no. 3 (1995), pp. 559-609; L. P. Gomez-Mejia, T. M. Welbourne, and R. M. Wiseman, "The Role of Risk Sharing and Risk Taking under Gainsharing," *Academy of Management Review* 25, no. 3 (July 2000), pp. 492-507; D. Collins, *Gainsharing and Power: Lessons from Six Scanlon Plans* (Ithaca, NY: ILR Press, 1998); and P. K. Zingheim and J. R. Schuster, *Pay People Right!* (San Francisco: Jossey-Bass, 2000).

74. J. Sahadi, "Delta Gave Its Employees 2 Months of Extra Pay; Here's Why That's Good Business," *CNN Business,* January 21, 2020, www.cnn.com.

75. F. Hansen, "Merit-Pay Payoff?" *Workforce Management* 87, no. 18 (November 3, 2008), pp. 33-38.

76. L. Mishel and J. Wolfe, "CEO Compensation Has Grown 940% since 1978," Economic Policy Institute, August 14, 2019, www.epi.org.

77. B. Connelly, K. T. Haynes, L. Tihanyi, D. Gamache, and C. Devers, "Minding the Gap: Antecedents and Consequences of Top Management-to-Worker Pay Dispersion," *Journal of Management* 42 (2016), pp. 862-85.

78. M. J. Conyon, "Executive Compensation and Incentives," *Academy of Management Perspectives* 20, no. 1 (February 2006), pp. 25-44.

79. J. D. Glater, "Stock Options Are Adjusted after Many Share Prices Fall," *The New York Times,* March 27, 2009, www.nytimes.com; and D. Nicklaus, "Worthless Options Worry Companies," *St. Louis Post-Dispatch,* April 3, 2009.

80. Bureau of Labor Statistics, "Benefits, Retirement and Savings Make Up Larger Percentage of Government Employee Compensation," December 16, 2015, www.bls.gov; and U.S. Census Bureau, *Statistical Abstract of the United States,* 2007, p. 418.

81. Bureau of Labor Statistics, "Employer Costs for Employee Compensation," September 17, 2019, www.bls.gov.

82. A. Soergel, "24 U.S. States Will See a Minimum Wage Increase in 2020," *U.S. News & World Report,* January 2, 2020, www.usnews.com.

83. S. Miller, "For 2019, Employers Adjust Health Benefits as Costs Near $15,000 per Employee," Society for Human Resource Management, August 13, 2018, www.shrm.org.

84. "Ultimate Guide to Retirement—Just How Common Are Defined Benefit Plans?" *CNN Money,* www.money.cnn.com, accessed March 19, 2020.

85. C. Fay and H. W. Risher, "Contractors, Comparable Worth and the New OFCCP: Deja Vu and More," *Compensation and Benefits Review* 32, no. 5 (September-October 2000), pp. 23-33; and G. Flynn, "Protect Yourself from an Equal-Pay Audit," *Workforce* 78, no. 6 (June 1999), pp. 144-46.

86. S. Snell and G. Bohlander, *Managing Human Resources,* 16th ed. (Chicago: Cengage, 2012).

87. "Pay Equity: The Minnesota Experience," 6th ed., February 2016, Legislative Office on the Economic Status of Women, www.oesw. leg.mn.

88. D. Goldstein, "Minnesota Imposes New Obligations on State Government Contractors," press release, May 19, 2014, Littler Mendelson, P.C., www.littler.com; E. Henry, "Wage-Bias Bill: Study Panel Proposed," *Arizona Business Gazette,* February 28, 2002, pp. 2-4; and S. E. Gardner and C. Daniel, "Implementing Comparable Worth/Pay Equity: Experiences of Cutting-Edge States," *Public Personnel Management* 27, no. 4 (Winter 1998), pp. 475-89.

89. R. Guerin, "Keeping Teens Safe and Healthy at Work: It Takes Teamwork!" NIOSH Science Blog, Centers for Disease Control and Prevention, April 22, 2019, www.blogs.cdc.gov.

90. L. Kahn, *Primer of Labor Relations,* 25th ed. (Washington, DC: Bureau of National Affairs Books, 1994); and A. Sloane and F. Witney, *Labor Relations* (Englewood Cliffs, NJ: Prentice Hall, 1985).

91. S. Premack and J. E. Hunter; "Individual Unionization Decisions," *Psychological Bulletin* 103 (1988), pp. 223-34; L. Troy, *Beyond Unions and Collective Bargaining* (Armonk, NY: M. E. Sharpe, 1999); and J. A. McClendon, "Members and Nonmembers: Determinants of Dues-Paying Membership in a Bargaining Unit," *Relations Industrielles* 55, no. 2 (Spring 2000), pp. 332-47.

92. R. Sinclair and L. Tetrick, "Social Exchange and Union Commitment: A Comparison of Union Instrumentality and Union Support Perceptions," *Journal of Organizational Behavior* 16, no. 6 (November 1995), pp. 669-79. See also S. Premack and J. E. Hunter; "Individual Unionization Decisions," *Psychological Bulletin* 103 (1988), pp. 223-34; and M. Cardador, B. Grant, J. Lamare, and G. Northcraft, "To Be or Not to Be Unionized? A Social Dilemma Perspective on Worker Decisions to Support Union Organizing," *Human Resource Management Review* 27 (2017), pp. 554-68.

93. D. Lewin and R. B. Peterson, *The Modern Grievance Procedure in the United States* (Westport, CT: Quorum Books, 1998).

94. S. Befort and L. Cooper, "Empirical Analysis of How Arbitrators Handle Discharge & Discipline Arbitrations: The Results May Surprise You," ABA Section of Labor and Employment Law, Fifth Annual Labor and Employment Law Conference, Seattle, Washington, November 2, 2011.

95. Bureau of Labor Statistics, "Union Members Summary," January 18, 2019, www.bls.gov.

Design elements: Take Charge of Your Career box photo: ©Tetra Images/ Getty Images; Thumbs Up/Thumbs Down icons: McGraw-Hill Education

Managing Diversity and Inclusion

Learning Objectives

After studying Chapter 9, you should be able to

LO1 Describe how changes in the U.S. workforce make diversity a critical organizational and managerial issue.

LO2 Describe some of the advantages and challenges associated with diversity and inclusion initiatives.

LO3 Define monolithic, pluralistic, and multicultural organizations.

LO4 List steps managers and their organizations can take to cultivate diversity.

LO5 Discuss changes in the global workforce and skills managers need to manage globally.

Geber86/Getty Images

F or all its merits, the technology sector is infamously poor at diversifying its workforce. After years under the microscope, the industry overall isn't making much progress. The major technology companies started publishing diversity reports in 2014. As just one example, Google's female representation that year was 30 percent. In its 2019 report, women still only accounted for 33 percent.[1]

The picture does not look much better for tech start-ups either. Less than half of U.S. tech start-ups have women in leadership positions, and only 30 percent of start-ups have programs to increase the number of women in leadership roles. Not much progress has been made to increase gender parity in the tech industry.[2]

The persistence of this problem is in large part due to a lack of proactive leadership when it comes to diversity and inclusion in tech start-ups. A flexible work environment is a critical factor in job selection for women, yet a third of tech companies have no program for this. Forty percent lack effective recruitment and interview techniques geared toward attracting women. Only a third of tech companies have set diversity as a goal, and less than that have training to address unconscious bias in hiring and promotions.[3]

Creativity and innovation are vital for success and are fostered in an atmosphere that celebrates different perspectives. Few societies have the range of talents available in the United States, with its immigrant tradition and diverse population. And few have as many highly educated women, who now make up 56 percent of U.S. college graduates.[4]

Getting people from different backgrounds to not only work together effectively but to also feel included and empowered is not easy, as is clearly illustrated in the problem confronting the tech industry. For these reasons, managing diversity is one of America's biggest challenges—and opportunities.

The concept of managing diversity and inclusion in organizations has its roots in Equal Employment Opportunity (EEO), meaning "freedom from discrimination on the basis of sex, color, religion, national origin, disability and age."[5] Organizations engage in two types of diversity and inclusion activities: *diversity management,* which is proactive in nature, and *affirmative action* programs, which are more reactive and focus on compliance.

Exhibit 9.1 highlights some differences between these two initiatives. Managing diversity involves basic activities like recruiting, training, promoting, and using to full advantage people with different backgrounds, beliefs, capabilities, and cultures. But it means more than just hiring women and minorities and making sure they are treated equally and encouraged to succeed. It also means understanding and deeply valuing employee differences to

Exhibit 9.1 — Differences between affirmative action and diversity management

Component	Affirmative Action Program (AAP)	Diversity and Inclusion (D&I)
Purpose	Correct historic wrongs and past/current discrimination against minorities, women, and other protected classes.	Value and leverage diversity of all stakeholders—from employees to customers—to achieve competitive advantage.
Origin	Executive Order 11246 and related to Title VII of the Civil Rights Act of 1964.	No precise date; however, data management platforms (DMPs) have become an integral component of most employers' HR strategies.
Approach	Formally written plan to proactively recruit, hire, and promote minorities, women, and other protected classes.	Company-driven plan to foster an inclusive environment in which all stakeholders contribute to organizational objectives.
Required by law?	Yes. Federal, state, and local agencies as well as certain federal contractors and subcontractors are required to have an AAP. It is voluntary for private employers to have one, unless it is court-ordered to correct discriminatory practices.	No. However, the majority of employers have DMPs because they believe that diversity equates to good business. Companies that align the diversity of their employees with that of their customers position themselves for success.
Enforcement	Office of Federal Contract Compliance Programs (OFCCP) in the United States Department of Labor.	An organization's HR department, with input from other internal stakeholders, including diversity councils or advisory groups.
Examples of organizations with program	U.S. Food & Drug Administration, Florida Department of Environmental Protection, Princeton University, Boeing, and the National Association of Basketball Coaches.	Johnson & Johnson, Procter & Gamble, Microsoft, Pepsi, Intel, Kraft Foods, General Electric, Ernst & Young, MasterCard Worldwide, and Kaiser Permanente.

Sources: U.S. Equal Employment Opportunity Commission website, "Diversity and Affirmative Action," www.eeoc.gov; Diversity Inc. Top 50 List, www.diversityinc.com; "Who Supports Affirmative Action?" American Civil Liberties Union, www.aclu.org; "When Would My Company Need to Have an Affirmative Action Program?" Society for Human Resource Management, December 4, 2012, www.shrm.org; "What Is the Difference between EEO, Affirmative Action, and Diversity?" Society for Human Resource Management, September 20, 2012, www.shrm.org; and H. J. Bernardin, *Human Resource Management: An Experiential Approach,* 5th ed. (Boston: McGraw-Hill, 2009), p. 71.

build a more effective and profitable company. Organizations that strive to foster the richness that a diverse workforce brings also work to build bridges between employees to tap their collaborative potential. Such inclusion moves beyond valuing differences to valuing the connections that arise and develop between them.

Related to, but different from, diversity management is **affirmative action**. Many organizations started diversifying their workforce out of concerns for social responsibility and legal necessity. To correct the past exclusion of women and minorities, companies introduced affirmative action—special efforts to recruit and hire qualified members of groups that had been discriminated against.

While many organizations do so voluntarily, contractors and subcontractors with 50 or more employees that receive more than $50,000 in government business are required to develop a written affirmative action program.[6] The intent is not to prefer these group members to the exclusion of others, but to correct for the history of discriminatory practices and exclusion. For example, federal contractor SOS International takes affirmative action in support of its policies to advance diversity and inclusion of minorities, women, veterans, and the disabled. The aerospace and defense firm won the 2019 GovCon award for "Contractor of the Year" in the $300 million and above category.[7]

Yet employment discrimination persists. Despite upward mobility, some groups still lack full participation and opportunity. To move beyond correcting past wrongs and become truly inclusive requires a change in organizational culture—one in which diversity is seen as contributing directly to the attainment of organizational goals.

Viewed in this way, affirmative action and diversity management are complementary, not the same. In contrast to equal employment opportunity (EEO) and affirmative action, managing diversity means moving beyond legislated mandates to embrace a proactive business philosophy that sees differences as positive. In this broader sense, managing diversity involves making changes in organizations' systems, structures, and practices to eliminate barriers that keep people from reaching their full potential. It asks managers to recognize and value the uniqueness of every employee and to see their ideas and perspectives as a source of competitive advantage.

In short, managing diversity goes beyond getting more minorities and women into the organization. It creates an environment in which employees from every background listen to each other and work better together so that the organization

Ariel Skelley/Blend Images

as a whole becomes more effective. This emphasis on coming together to benefit the whole has led many companies to refer to their objective as diversity and inclusion.

This chapter examines the meaning of diversity and inclusion, and the management skills and organizational processes needed to fully leverage the diverse workforce. We identify the changes in society and the workplace that are creating this more diverse U.S. workforce. Next we consider challenges of diversity and ways to address those challenges. Then we explore the practices that support inclusion. Finally, because companies today have a global presence, we end by describing how the global workforce is changing and which skills are needed to manage in environments with economic, cultural, and geographic differences.

> **LO1** Describe how changes in the U.S. workforce make diversity a critical organizational and managerial issue.

1 | DIVERSITY IS DYNAMIC AND EVOLVING

Diversity is not a new challenge for managers. However, U.S. businesses have changed their management approaches.

"Diversity is not about how we differ. Diversity is about embracing one another's uniqueness."

—Ola Joseph

1.1 | Diversity Shaped America's Past

From the late 1800s to the early 1900s, most of the immigrants to the United States came from Italy, Poland, Ireland, and Russia. They were considered outsiders because most did not speak English and had different customs and work styles. They struggled to gain acceptance in the steel, coal, automobile manufacturing, insurance, and finance industries. As late as the 1940s, and sometimes beyond, colleges routinely discriminated against immigrants, Catholics, and Jews, establishing strict quotas that limited their number, if any were admitted at all. Discrimination severely diminished the employment prospects of these groups until the 1960s.

Women's struggle for acceptance in the workplace was in some ways even more difficult. When the Women's Rights Movement launched in Seneca Falls in 1848, most occupations were off-limits to women, and colleges and professional schools were closed to them. In the first part of the 20th century, women began to be accepted into professional schools but were subject to severe quotas. There was also a widespread assumption that certain jobs were done only by men and other jobs only by women.

As recently as the 1970s, classified-ad sections in newspapers listed jobs by sex, with sections headed "Help Wanted–Males" and "Help Wanted–Females." Women who wanted a bank loan needed a male cosigner, and married women could not get credit cards in their own name.[8] This discrimination started to decline when the Civil Rights Act of 1964 and other legislation began to be enforced. Women still are underrepresented at the most senior levels of corporate life, and their average pay rates still lag those of men, but most jobs are now open to women.

The most difficult and wrenching struggle for equality involved America's non-white minorities. Rigid racial segregation of education, employment, and housing persisted for 100 years after the end of the Civil War. After years of courageous protest and struggle, the unanimous *Brown v. Board of Education* Supreme Court decision in 1954 declared segregation unconstitutional, setting the stage for laws we discussed in Chapter 8, including the Civil Rights Act of 1964. Although the struggle for equality is far from complete, many civil rights—equal opportunity, fair treatment in housing, and the illegality of religious, racial, and sex discrimination—received their greatest impetus from the civil rights movement.

The traditional American image of diversity emphasized assimilation. The United States was the "melting pot" of the world, a country where ethnic and racial differences blended into an American purée. But in real life, many ethnic and most racial groups retained their identities but did not express them at work. Deemphasizing their ethnic and cultural distinctions helped employees keep their jobs and get ahead.

1.2 | Diversity Is Becoming Even More Important

In the United States today, nearly half of the workforce consists of women. Some 17 percent of U.S. workers identify as Hispanic or Latino, 13 percent as Black, and 6 percent as Asian.[9] In 2019, nearly 13 million women-owned businesses in the United States employed over 9 million people.[10] Two-thirds

● Freedom marchers in the 1960s were an important part of the American civil rights movement.
National Archives and Records Administration (NWDNS-306-ssM-4A-35-6)

of all global migration is into the United States, making it the top destination for immigrants.[11] U.S. businesses must learn to manage a diverse workforce sooner or better than their competitors do.

Today's immigrants are willing to be part of an integrated team, but they no longer are willing to sacrifice their cultural identities to get ahead. Nor do they have to do so. Many companies know that accommodating employees' differences pays off in business. Customers are becoming increasingly diverse, so a diverse workforce can provide significant competitive advantage.

Diversity means far more than skin color and gender. The term refers to a variety of differences (see Exhibit 9.2), including religious affiliation, age, disability status, military experience, sexual orientation, economic class, educational level, and lifestyle, as well as gender, race, ethnicity, and nationality.

Although within their groups people share many common values, attitudes, and perceptions, great diversity also exists within each category. Every group consists of individuals who are unique in personality, education, and life experiences. There may be more differences among, say, three Asians from Thailand, Hong Kong, and Korea than among a white, an African American, and an Asian all born in Chicago. And people differ greatly in their personal and professional goals and values.

Thus, managing diversity may seem to be inherently contradictory. It means knowing characteristics *common* to a group, while also managing people as *individuals*. Managing diversity means not just tolerating or accommodating all sorts of differences but also supporting, nurturing, and using these differences to the organization's advantage.

Many HR executives say their companies need to or plan to expand their diversity training programs. Although many companies started diversity programs to prevent discrimination, more now see them as a crucial way to expand their customer bases both domestically and worldwide.

Gender Issues

An important development in the U.S. labor market has been the growing number of women working outside the home. Consider:

- Women comprise about 47 percent of the workforce.[12]

- The labor force participation rate of women rose throughout the 1970s through the 1990s and is now holding steady between 58 and 60 percent.[13]

- Almost 60 percent of marriages are dual-earner marriages. In their marriages, women report doing more than men at home, including managing children's schedules and activities.[14]

- Nearly 25 percent of married women in two-income households earn more than their husbands.[15]

Balancing work life and family responsibilities is enormously challenging. Men's roles in our society are changing, but women still carry the bulk of family responsibilities. That puts women at a disadvantage in companies that expect employees, particularly at the managerial level, to put in long hours and sacrifice their personal lives. It also causes companies to lose valuable talent. Some companies therefore offer such benefits as onsite child care, in-home care for elderly family members, flexible work schedules, and technologies that permit more work from home.

The average full-time working woman earns about 81 percent as much as a man in the same job[16] (recall Chapter 8 on equal pay and comparable worth). This pay gap is closing faster for younger women. The female-to-male earnings ratio among 20- to 24-year-olds is 10 percent, while the gap for women 55–64 years of age is twice as high at 22 percent.[17] But the female-to-male earnings gaps for Black women and Latina women are much lower, at 61 percent and 53 percent, respectively.[18]

As women—along with minorities—move up the corporate ladder, they encounter a glass ceiling, a metaphor for an invisible barrier that makes it difficult for women and minorities to move beyond a certain level in the corporate hierarchy.[19] Only 33 women are chief executives of *Fortune* 500 companies—that's just under 7 percent.[20] Still, more women occupy the top spot at a broader range of companies. Some well-known female CEOs include Safra Catz of Oracle, Tricia Griffith of Progressive, and Jill Soltau of JCPenney.[21] Similarly, a handful of minority CEOs are currently leading *Fortune* 500 firms, including Ken Frazier of Merck, Marvin Ellison of Lowe's, Roger Ferguson Jr. of TIAA, Jide Zeitlin of Tapestry, and Lisa Su of Advanced Micro Devices.[22]

Some companies help women break through the glass ceiling. Accenture sponsors monthly networking events for its female employees and offers flexible schedules and part-time arrangements. The following companies are among the 2019 National Association of Female Executives' top companies for executive women:[24]

Allstate	Roche
Edelman	Synchrony
Grant Thornton	PNC Financial
L'Oréal	Verizon
Principal	Whirlpool

> "Leaders can use diversity strategically to create sustainable competitive advantages for their firms."
>
> —Martin N. Davidson, University of Virginia[23]

Exhibit 9.2 Components of workforce diversity

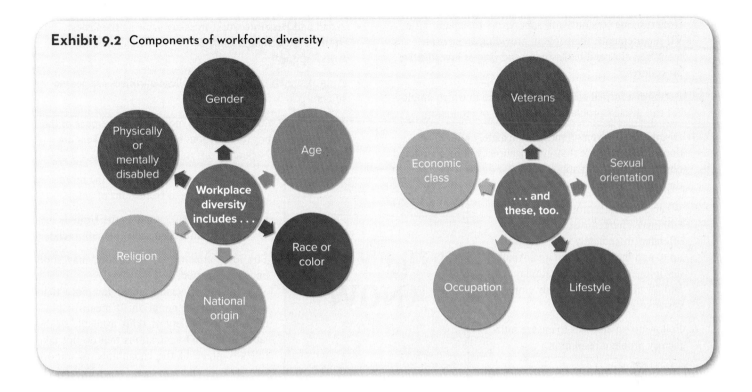

Sexual harassment (introduced in Chapter 8) is unwelcome sexual conduct that is a term or condition of employment. Sexual harassment falls into two categories:

1. *Quid pro quo harassment* occurs when "submission to or rejection of sexual conduct is used as a basis for employment decisions."

2. *Hostile environment* occurs when unwelcome sexual conduct "has the purpose or effect of unreasonably interfering with job performance or creating an intimidating, hostile, or offensive working environment." Behaviors causing hostile work environments include displays of pornography, lewd or suggestive remarks, and demeaning taunts or jokes.

Mark Edward Atkinson/Blend Images

Both categories violate Title VII of the Civil Rights Act of 1964, regardless of the sex of the harasser and the victim (in a recent year, more than 16 percent of complaints filed with the federal government came from males). If an employee files a complaint of sexual harassment with the Equal Employment Opportunity Commission, the commission may investigate and, if it finds support for the complaint, may request mediation, seek a settlement, or file a lawsuit with the potential for stiff fines and negative publicity.

Harassment by hostile work environment is more common than quid pro quo harassment. Managers attempt to maintain proper work environments by ensuring that all employees know what conduct is and is not appropriate and that there are serious consequences for the latter. Even when managers do not themselves harass, if they fail to prevent it or to take appropriate action after receiving legitimate complaints, they and their companies still may be held liable. Managers also need to know that the "hostile work environment" standard applies to same-sex harassment, as well as to non-gender-related cases, such as racial or ethnic slurs.

Managers can help prevent harassment by making sure their organization has an effective and comprehensive harassment policy and by taking these actions (see Exhibit 9.3):[25]

1. Develop a comprehensive organizationwide policy on sexual harassment and present it to all current and new employees. Stress that sexual harassment will not be tolerated under any circumstances.

sexual harassment
conduct of a sexual nature that has negative consequences for employment

2. Hold training sessions with supervisors to explain Title VII requirements, their role in providing an environment free of sexual harassment, and proper investigative procedures.

3. Establish a formal complaint procedure in which employees can discuss problems without fear of retaliation.

4. Discipline a proven offender immediately after allegations. Communicate that investigations will be conducted objectively and with appreciation for the sensitivity of the issue.

5. When an investigation supports employee charges, discipline the offender immediately with penalties up to and including discharge. Apply discipline consistently for similar cases and for managers and hourly employees alike.

6. Follow up on all cases to ensure satisfactory problem resolution.

Gender issues do not apply only to women. The changing status of women has given men a chance to redefine their roles, expectations, and lifestyles. Some men are deciding that there is more to life than corporate success and are scaling back their work commitments to spend time with their families. Worker values are shifting toward personal time, quality of life, self-fulfillment, and family. People today, both men and women, are looking to achieve a balance between career and family.

Minorities and Immigrants Along with gender issues, the importance and scope of diversity are evident in the growth of racial minorities and immigrants in the workforce.[27] Consider:

- Black, Asian, and Hispanic workers occupy more than 35 percent of U.S. jobs.

- Asian and Hispanic workforces are growing the fastest in the United States, followed by the African American workforce.

- Approximately 40 percent of college enrollees are people of color.

- Foreign-born workers make up more than 17 percent of the U.S. civilian labor force. About half of these workers are Hispanic, and 24 percent are Asian.

  - The younger Americans are, the more likely they are to be persons of color.

  - Over 10 million people in the United States identify themselves as multiracial.

The term *minority,* as used now, may soon become outdated.

Managing diversity means far more than eliminating discrimination: It means capitalizing on the variety of skills available in the labor market. Organizations that do not take full advantage of the capabilities of minorities and immigrants are severely limiting their potential talent pool and their ability to understand and capture minority markets. Those markets are growing rapidly, along with their share of purchasing power.

If you sell to businesses, you are likely to deal with minority-owned companies; the number of businesses started by Asian American, African American, and Hispanic entrepreneurs is growing much faster than the overall growth in new companies in the United States. Immigrants founded more than half of the companies that started in California's high-tech Silicon Valley; in a recent year, immigrant-founded engineering and technology companies employed 560,000 employees and earned more than $60 billion in revenue.[28] Exhibit 9.4 lists some well-known immigrant entrepreneurs.

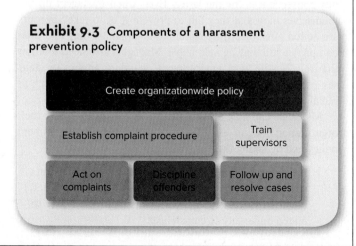

Exhibit 9.3 Components of a harassment prevention policy

Create organizationwide policy

Establish complaint procedure

Train supervisors

Act on complaints

Discipline offenders

Follow up and resolve cases

● Roger Ferguson, president and CEO of TIAA-CREF.
Michael Nagle/Bloomberg/Getty Images

Even so, the evidence shows some troubling disparities. Unemployment rates are higher for Black and Hispanic workers than for whites—twice as high in the case of Black men. Earnings of Black and Hispanic workers consistently trail those of white workers. African Americans and Hispanic Americans are underrepresented in management and professional occupations.[29] This helps perpetuate the problem because aspiring young minorities have fewer role models and mentors.

Discrimination accounts for at least some of these disparities. In one study, fictitious résumés with white-sounding names were nearly twice as likely to get a callback for an interview than the same résumés with African American names. Despite equivalence in credentials, the often unconscious assumptions about different racial groups are difficult to overcome.[30]

But progress is occurring. *Fortune*'s 2019 "50 Best Workplaces for Diversity" list includes Hilton, Five Guys, Farmers Insurance, and Old Navy.[31] Virtually every large organization today has policies and programs for increasing minority representation, including compensation systems that reward managers for increasing the diversity of their operations. PepsiCo, 3M, Yum! Brands, Lowe's, Target, and other companies have corporate diversity officers who help managers attract, retain, and promote minority and women executives. Many organizations, including Merck and Microsoft, support minority internships and MBA studies. The internship programs help students and organizations learn about one another and, ideally, turn into full-time employment opportunities.

People with Mental and Physical Disabilities

The largest unemployed minority population in the United States is people with disabilities. The population with a disability is growing as the average worker gets older and heavier.[32] The Centers for Disease Control and Prevention estimates that over 60 million individuals report some type of disability, with the most common being reduced mobility and impaired cognition.[33] About one in five people with disabilities is employed.[34] On average, employees with disabilities work part-time and make less than their peers without disabilities.[35]

The Americans with Disabilities Act Amendments Act (ADA Amendments Act) defines a disability as a physical or mental impairment that substantially limits one or more major life activities. Examples include those resulting from orthopedic, visual, speech, and hearing impairments; cerebral palsy; epilepsy; multiple sclerosis; HIV infections; cancer; heart disease; diabetes; psychological illness; specific learning disabilities; drug addiction; and alcoholism.[36]

For most businesses, people with disabilities are an unexplored but fruitful labor market. Employers often find that disabled employees are more dependable than other employees, miss fewer days of work, and are less likely to quit. Companies that hire disabled workers receive tax credits and signal to other employees and stakeholders their strong interest in creating an inclusive organizational culture.

Education Levels

When the United States was primarily an industrial economy, many jobs required physical strength, stamina, and skill in a trade. In today's service and technology economy, more positions require college and even graduate or professional degrees, and the share of workers with a bachelor's degree has more than doubled since 1970. People with degrees in science and technology are in especially high demand. Employers often expand their search for scientists and computer professionals overseas, but visa requirements limit that supply.

The share of workers with less than a high school diploma has tumbled from nearly 4 out of 10 in 1970 to below 1 out of 10 today. Among foreign-born workers, about one-fourth have not completed high school.[37]

Age Groups

By 2024, it is estimated that over one-third of workers will be aged 55 or older.[38] As a result, entry-level workers for some positions are in short supply. Today's companies need to compete hard for a shrinking pool of young talent, applicants who know the job market and insist on the working conditions they value and the praise they were raised to expect. Bruce Tulgan, founder of RainmakerThinking, which specializes in researching generational differences, says today's young workers tend to be "high-maintenance" but also "high-performing," having learned to process the flood of information that pours in over the Internet.[39] Many had highly involved parents who filled their lives with "quality" experiences, so employers are designing more stimulating work that includes teamwork, keeping work hours reasonable, giving more positive feedback, and updating recruiting tactics to reach young workers where they are—online.[40]

Exhibit 9.4 Successful immigrant entrepreneurs in the United States

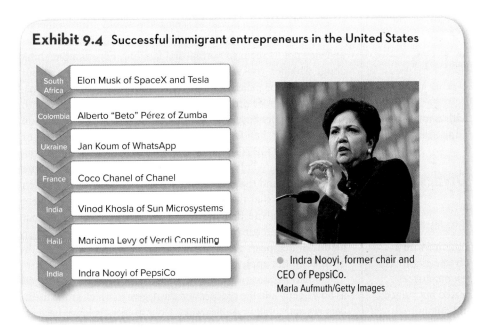

South Africa	Elon Musk of SpaceX and Tesla
Colombia	Alberto "Beto" Pérez of Zumba
Ukraine	Jan Koum of WhatsApp
France	Coco Chanel of Chanel
India	Vinod Khosla of Sun Microsystems
Haiti	Mariama Levy of Verdi Consulting
India	Indra Nooyi of PepsiCo

● Indra Nooyi, former chair and CEO of PepsiCo.
Marla Aufmuth/Getty Images

Most of Rackspace Hosting's 6,000 employees are early-career employees. Its San Antonio headquarters includes a variety of "quirky perqs" to keep its employees happy: a stainless-steel silver two-story slide, a life-sized chessboard, red bouncy balls to use for hallway races, and a video arcade to hold *Mortal Kombat* competitions. This approach is helping Rackspace earn respect and success in the cloud space.[41]

1.3 | The Future Will Be More Diverse Than Ever

During most of its history, the United States experienced a surplus of workers. But that is expected to change. Lower birthrates in the United States and other developed countries are resulting in a smaller labor force. An even more substantial slowdown in labor force growth is projected between now and 2028, as the Baby Boom generation retires.[42]

Industries such as nursing and manufacturing are already facing a tremendous loss of expertise as a result of a rapidly aging workforce. Many other industries ranging from education to nuclear plant maintenance will soon be in a similar situation.[43]

Employers are likely to outsource some work to factories and firms in developing nations where birthrates are high and the labor supply is more plentiful. But they will have to compete for the best candidates from a relatively smaller and more diverse U.S. labor pool. Employers will need to know who these new workers are—and must be prepared to meet their needs.

> **LO2** Describe some of the advantages and challenges associated with diversity and inclusion initiatives.

2 | DIVERSITY AND INCLUSION HAVE ADVANTAGES AND CHALLENGES

As you've learned and will continue to see with management topics, diversity and inclusion create both opportunity and challenge.

2.1 | Potential Advantages of Diversity and Inclusion Initiatives

Managing a diverse workforce well presents many advantages:

- *Attract and retain motivated employees*—Companies with a reputation for providing opportunities for diverse employees have an advantage in the labor market. When employees believe their differences are not merely tolerated but valued, they may become more loyal, productive, and committed.

- *Understand diverse markets*—Just as people may prefer diverse workplaces, they may prefer to do business with such organizations. A diverse workforce provides greater knowledge of diverse markets and can design products and marketing campaigns to meet consumers' needs locally, nationally, and internationally.

- *Leverage creativity and innovation in problem solving*—With a broader base of experience from which to approach problems, diverse teams, when effectively managed, invent more options and create more solutions than homogeneous groups do. They more readily deviate from traditional approaches and practices and are less likely to succumb to "groupthink."[44]

- *Enhance flexibility*—Successfully managing diversity requires a corporate culture that tolerates many different styles and approaches. Less restrictive policies and procedures and less standardized operating methods enable organizations to respond quickly.

- *Performance*—plenty of studies show that diversity can contribute to organizational performance.[45] However, members and managers can deal with it poorly or well, and that can make all the difference.[46] More will be said on this topic in Chapter 12 about teamwork.

2.2 | Challenges Associated with Managing Diversity

Despite equal opportunity laws and the business advantages of diversity and inclusion, thousands of lawsuits are filed over discrimination and unfair treatment.[48] Managers with all the goodwill in the world sometimes find it harder than they expected to get people from different backgrounds to work together for a common goal.[49]

Anyone working in a diverse organization should be aware of and work to overcome common challenges:

Unexamined assumptions—Seeing the world from someone else's perspective can be difficult because our own assumptions and viewpoints seem so normal and familiar. For example, think about whether you would put pictures of loved ones on your work desk. For gender-normative heterosexuals—that is, someone whose gender presentation and sexual attraction align with society's gender-based expectations—the practice is common and accepted; but for lesbian, gay, bisexual, transgender, or questioning (LGBTQ) employees, the decision may cause considerable anxiety.[50] In a résumé study, half of the résumés bore a male name and the other half a female name, and half of each group implied that the applicant was a parent. Employers were less likely to invite the supposed parents for an interview—but only if the name was female.[51] Since the résumés were otherwise identical, it appears that people make assumptions about mothers that do not apply to fathers or to childless women.

Lower cohesiveness—Diversity can decrease *cohesiveness*, defined as how tightly knit the group is and the degree to which group members act and think in similar ways. Cohesiveness is lower because

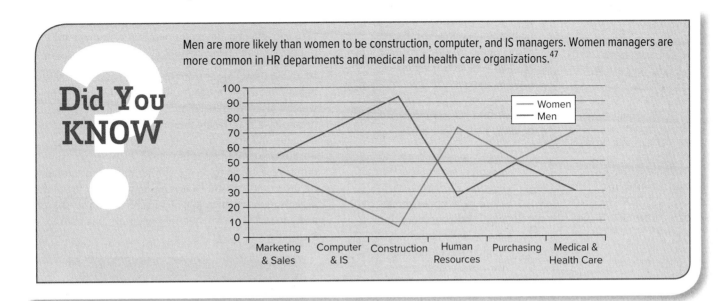
of differences in language, culture, and/or experience. When miscommunication and stress reduce cohesiveness, performance may decline. This may explain the results of a study showing greater turnover among store employees who felt they were greatly outnumbered by coworkers from other racial or ethnic groups.[52]

Communication problems—Perhaps the most common negative effect of diversity, communication problems include misunderstandings, inaccuracies, inefficiencies, and slowness. Speed is lost when not all group members are fluent in the same language or when additional time is required to explain things. Group members may assume they interpret things similarly when they in fact do not, or they may disagree due to different frames of reference.[53] If managers do not actively encourage different viewpoints, some employees may be afraid to speak up, giving the manager a false impression of agreement.

Mistrust and tension—People prefer to associate with others who are like themselves. This normal, understandable tendency can lead to misunderstanding, mistrust, and even fear of those who are different. For example, if women and minority group members are not invited to join white male colleagues for lunch or at business gatherings, they may feel excluded by their colleagues. Similarly, tension can develop between people of different ages—what one generation might see as a tasteless tattoo

may be creative body art for a member of another generation. Such misunderstandings or tensions can cause resentments, making it harder for people to work together productively.[54]

Stereotyping—Group members often stereotype their "different" colleagues rather than accurately perceive and evaluate those persons' contributions, capabilities, aspirations, and motivations.[55] Women may be stereotyped as not dedicated to their careers, older workers as unwilling to learn new skills, minority group members as less educated or capable. Stereotypes may cost the organization dearly by stifling employees' ambition so that they don't fully contribute.

LO3 Define monolithic, pluralistic, and multicultural organizations.

3 | MULTICULTURAL ORGANIZATIONS

To reap the benefits and minimize the costs of a diverse workforce, managers can start by examining their organization's

---

"Among CEOs of *Fortune* 500 companies, 58 percent are six feet or taller. . . . Most of us, in ways we are not entirely aware of, automatically associate leadership with imposing physical stature."

—Malcolm Gladwell

monolithic organization
has a low degree of structural integration—employing few women, minorities, or other groups that differ from the majority—and thus has a homogeneous employee population

pluralistic organization
has a more diverse employee population and works to involve employees from different gender, racial, or cultural backgrounds

multicultural organization values cultural diversity and seeks to utilize and encourage it

prevailing assumptions about people and cultures. Exhibit 9.5 shows some assumptions that are well worth thinking about. Putting assumptions in context, we can classify organizations into several types and describe their implications:

1. A monolithic organization has very little *cultural integration;* its employee population is highly homogeneous. In hiring, an organization might favor alumni of the same college, perhaps targeting members of fraternities and football fans. When a monolithic organization does employ people from groups other than the norm, they primarily hold low-status jobs. Minority group members must adopt the norms of the majority to survive. This fact, coupled with small numbers, keeps conflicts among groups low. Discrimination prevails, informal integration is almost nonexistent, and minority group members do not identify strongly with the company.

2. Pluralistic organizations have a more diverse employee population and take steps to involve people from different backgrounds. These organizations use an affirmative action approach, actively trying to hire and train a diverse workforce and to prevent discrimination against minority group members. They have much more integration than do monolithic organizations, but minority group members still tend to be clustered at certain levels or in particular functions. Because of greater cultural integration, affirmative action programs, and training programs, the pluralistic organization accepts minority group members into informal networks and discriminates much less if at all. Minority members feel greater identification with the organization, but some resentments, coupled with greater numbers of women and minorities, can create conflict.

3. In multicultural organizations, diversity not only exists but is valued. In contrast to the pluralistic organization, which fails to address cultural integration, these organizations fully integrate minority group members both formally and informally. But managers in such organizations do not focus primarily on employees' visible differences, like race or sex. Rather, they value and draw on the *experience* and *knowledge* employees bring to the organization and help it achieve agreed-upon strategies and goals.[56] The multicultural organization is marked

Stephen Lew/CSM/REX/Shutterstock

Exhibit 9.5	Misleading and more accurate assumptions about diversity	
Dimension	**Misleading Assumption**	**More Accurate Assumption**
Homogeneity–heterogeneity	We are a melting pot; we are all the same.	We are more like a stew. Society consists of different groups.
Similarity–difference	"They" are all just like me. There are no real differences.	People exhibit both differences and similarities compared to me.
Parochialism–equifinality	Our way of living and working is the only way.	There are many distinct ways of reaching goals, living, and working.
Ethnocentrism–culture contingency	Our way is the best way; all other approaches are inferior versions of our way.	There are many different and equally good ways to reach goals; the best way depends on the people involved.

Source: Adapted from N. J. Adler, "Diversity Assumptions and Their Implications for Management," *Handbook of Organization,* 1996.

by an absence of prejudice and discrimination and by low levels of intergroup conflict. It *creates* a synergistic environment in which all members contribute to their maximum potential and the advantages of diversity can be fully realized.[57]

4 | ORGANIZATIONS CAN CULTIVATE A DIVERSE WORKFORCE

An organization's plans for becoming multicultural and making the most of its diverse workforce should include these components:

1. Securing top management's leadership and commitment.

2. Assessing the organization's progress toward goals.

3. Attracting employees.

4. Training employees in diversity.

5. Retaining diverse employees.

A major 30-year study of hundreds of companies found the greatest diversity where managers had explicit diversity responsibilities. Moderate change occurred in companies with mentoring and networking programs. Formal diversity training programs had little effect unless the organizations also used the other methods.[58] Thus, cultivating diversity needs to be a well-planned organizationwide effort in which individual managers champion each element, addressing this issue as seriously as they do other challenges.

The National Basketball Association (NBA) has long cultivated diversity at executive levels; in 2019, the league had the highest percentage of minority and female owners in the history of men's sports. In that same year, 33 percent of NBA teams' head coaches were people of color, and the league had four female assistant coaches—the highest number in NBA history.[59]

4.1 | Start by Securing Top Managers' Commitment

Obtaining top management's leadership and commitment is critical for diversity efforts to succeed. Otherwise, the rest of the organization will not take the effort seriously. One way to communicate this commitment—to all employees and to the external environment—is to incorporate attitudes about diversity values into the corporate mission statement and into strategic plans and objectives. Managers' compensation can be linked directly to accomplishing diversity goals. Adequate funding must be allocated to the diversity effort. Top management can set a personal example by participating in diversity programs and making participation mandatory for all managers.

The work of managing diversity cannot be done by top management or diversity directors alone. Many companies rely on minority advisory groups or task forces to monitor organizational policies, practices, and attitudes; assess their impact on diverse groups; and provide feedback and suggestions to top management. At Equitable Life Assurance Society, employee groups meet regularly with the CEO to discuss issues pertaining to women, African Americans, and Hispanics and make recommendations for improvement. At Honeywell, employees with disabilities formed a council to discuss their needs. They proposed and management accepted an accessibility program that went beyond federal regulations for accommodating disabilities.

As you can see, progressive companies are moving from asking managers what they think minority employees need and toward asking the employees themselves what they need.

4.2 | Conduct an Organizational Assessment

Management can periodically assess the organization's workforce, culture, policies, and practices in areas such as recruitment, promotions, benefits, and compensation. They can determine whether they are attracting diverse candidates from the labor pool and whether customer needs are well served by the current workforce. The objective is to identify problem areas

Peace requires everyone to be in the circle—wholeness, inclusion.

—Isabel Allende

chapter 10
Leadership

Learning Objectives

After studying Chapter 10, you should be able to

LO1 Explain how a good vision helps you be a better leader.

LO2 Discuss the similarities and differences between leading and managing.

LO3 Identify sources of power in organizations.

LO4 Know the three traditional approaches to understanding leadership.

LO5 Understand the important contemporary perspectives on leadership.

LO6 Identify types of opportunities to be a leader.

Chris Whitehead/Getty Images

What is leadership? The answer is complex. But to start, a leader influences others to attain goals. The more followers, the greater the influence. And the more successful the attainment of worthy goals, the more evident the leadership. But we must explore further to understand what good leaders really do and to learn what it takes to become an outstanding leader.

The best leaders combine good critical thinking and effective interpersonal processes to formulate and implement strategies that produce strong, long-term results.[1] They may launch enterprises, build organizational cultures, or otherwise change the course of events.[2]

Merck invested tens of millions of dollars in the project. Because the vaccine primarily is used for impoverished people in underdeveloped parts of the world, Merck stands to earn little if any money from it. During an Ebola outbreak in May of 2018, the vaccine proved effective; only 33 people died and the virus vanished almost as quickly as it appeared. The U.S. Food and Drug Administration fully approved the vaccine (now called Ervebo) in December 2019, and it is now the frontline defense against Ebola virus outbreaks.[5]

Showing just how effective Frazier has been as a leader, Merck's board of trustees did away with their long-standing policy that the CEO must step down upon

> "Leadership is about the team—the culture they keep and embrace, it's about empathy for your customers, clients, employees and the communities where you do business, it's about doing the right thing for the right reasons, being confident enough to take risks and responsible enough to think of those who your decisions and risks may affect."
>
> —Kat Cole, COO & President of FOCUS Brands

Such leadership is exemplified by Kenneth Frazier, CEO of Merck, a multinational pharmaceutical company. Frazier took over as CEO in 2011 during a challenging time in Merck's long history. A spate of events caused the company's stock and reputation to slide.[3] Frazier's leadership over the past decade has been a steadying force. Merck's stock and revenue have soared during his tenure, but Frazier views the company's mission as more than catering to shareholders' desire for profits. Says Frazier, "While a fundamental responsibility of business leaders is to create value for shareholders, I think businesses also exist to deliver value to society.... Our salient purpose in the world is to deliver medically important vaccines and medicines that make a huge difference for humanity."[4]

For years, Merck developed a vaccine to fight the spread of Ebola, the lethal, fast-spreading virus that has terrorized people in various parts of Africa for decades.

turning 65.[6] Why? Frazier reached this age. Clearly great leadership is difficult to part with.

What do people want from their leaders? Broadly speaking, they want help in achieving their goals.[7] Besides pay and promotions, these goals include support for personal development; clearing obstacles to high-level performance; and treatment that is respectful, fair, and ethical. Leaders serve people best by helping them develop their own initiative and good judgment, enabling them to grow, and helping them become better contributors.

What do organizations need? Organizations need people at all levels to be leaders. Leaders throughout the organization are needed to do the things that their people want but also to help create and implement strategic direction. Organizations place people in formal leadership roles so that they will achieve the organization's goals.

These two perspectives—what people want and what organizations need—are neatly combined in a set of five key behaviors identified by James Kouzes and Barry Posner, two well-known authors and consultants.[8] The best leaders, say Kouzes and Posner, do five things:

1. *Challenge the process*—They challenge conventional beliefs and practices, and they create change.

2. *Inspire a shared vision*—They appeal to people's values and motivate them to care about an important mission.

3. *Enable others to act*—They give people access to information and give them the power to perform to their full potential.

4. *Model the way*—They don't just tell people what to do; they are living examples of the ideals they believe in.

5. *Encourage the heart*—They show appreciation, provide rewards, and use various approaches to motivate people in positive ways.

You will read about these and other aspects of leadership in this chapter. The topics we discuss not only will help you become a better leader but also will give you benchmarks for assessing the competence and fairness with which your boss manages you.

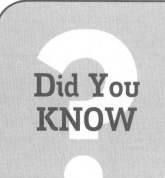

Did You KNOW ?

A Gallup survey reported that only one in four employees strongly agreed that manager feedback helped them improve their job performance. Managers can increase the value of their feedback by providing coaching aimed at improving employees' work.[9]

points are that (1) a vision is necessary for effective leadership; (2) a person or team can develop a vision for any job, work unit, or organization; and (3) many people, including managers who do not develop into effective leaders, fail to develop a clear vision—instead they focus on performing or surviving day by day.

Put another way, leaders must know what they want.[14] And other people must understand what that is. The leader must be able to articulate the vision, clearly and often. Other people throughout the organization should understand the vision and be able to state it clearly themselves. That's a start. But the vision means nothing until the leader and followers take action to turn the vision into reality.[15]

A metaphor reinforces the important concept of vision.[16] Putting a jigsaw puzzle together is much easier if you have the picture on the box cover in front of you. Without the picture, or vision, the lack of direction is likely to result in frustration and failure. That is what communicating a vision is all about: making clear where you are heading.

Not just any vision will do. Visions can be inappropriate, and even fail, for a variety of reasons:[17]

- It may reflect only the leader's personal needs. Such a vision may be unethical or may fail to gain acceptance by the market or by those who must implement it.

- Related to the first reason, a poor vision may ignore stakeholder needs.

> **LO1** Explain how a good vision helps you be a better leader.

1 | VISION

"A vision is not just a picture of what could be; it is an appeal to our better selves, a call to become something more," stated Rosabeth Moss Kanter of the Harvard Business School.[10] Having a vision for the future and communicating that vision to others are known to be essential components of great leadership. "We want to open up space for humanity, and in order to do that, space must be affordable," said Elon Musk, CEO of SpaceX (and Tesla).[11] Sir Richard Branson, CEO of the Virgin Group, envisions that by 2050 the entire world will be powered by renewable energy.[12] Practicing businesspeople are not alone in understanding the importance of vision; academic research shows that communicating a clear vision leads to higher organizational performance.[13]

Visions can be small or large and can exist throughout all organizational levels. The important

● Like with a jigsaw puzzle, a clear picture or vision of what needs to be accomplished provides direction and purpose. Gajus/Shutterstock

Employees outside the Infosys headquarters, in Bangalore, India.
Jagadeesh Nv/EPA/Shutterstock

- Although effective leaders maintain confidence and persevere despite obstacles, the facts may dictate that the vision must change. You will learn more about change and how to manage it later.

Where do visions come from?[18] Leaders should be sensitive to emerging opportunities, develop the right capabilities or worldviews, and not be overly invested in the status quo. You can capitalize on networks of people who have ideas about the future. Some visions are accidental; a company may stumble into an opportunity, and the leader may get credit for foresight. Some leaders and companies launch many new initiatives and, through trial and error, hit occasional home runs. If the company learns from these successes, the "vision" emerges.

tailoring supermarket offerings to neighborhoods.[20] As a result, he is credited by the grocery industry for making supermarkets less cookie-cutter and more interesting places to shop.[21]

2 | LEADING AND MANAGING

Effective managers are not necessarily true leaders. Many administrators, supervisors, and even top executives perform their responsibilities successfully without being great leaders. But these positions afford an opportunity for leadership. The ability to lead effectively sets the excellent managers apart from the rest.

2.1 | Comparing Leaders and Managers

Management must deal with the ongoing, day-to-day complexities of organizations, but true leadership includes effectively orchestrating important change.[22] While managing requires planning and budgeting routines, leading includes setting the direction—creating a vision—for the firm. Management requires structuring the organization, staffing it with capable people, and monitoring results; leadership goes beyond these functions by inspiring people to attain the vision. Great leaders keep people

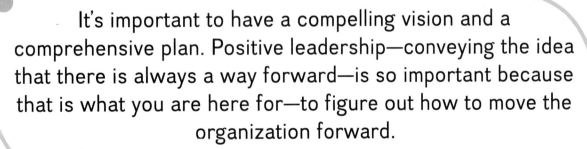

It's important to have a compelling vision and a comprehensive plan. Positive leadership—conveying the idea that there is always a way forward—is so important because that is what you are here for—to figure out how to move the organization forward.

— Alan Mulally

Employees of the Texas-based H-E-B grocery store chain gave their CEO, Charles C. Butt, a 99 percent approval rating on Glassdoor's "Top CEOs in 2019" list.[19] Since taking over the family business in 1971, Butt's vision focused on innovation by offering private-label foods, incorporating technology, and

focused on moving the organization toward its ideal future, motivating them to overcome any obstacles.

It is important to be clear that management and leadership are both vitally important. To highlight the need for more leadership is not to minimize the importance of management

supervisory leadership behavior that provides guidance, support, and corrective feedback for day-to-day activities

strategic leadership behavior that gives purpose and meaning to organizations, envisioning and creating a positive future

power the ability to influence others

or managers. But leadership involves unique processes that are distinguishable from basic management processes.[23] Also, the requirement for different processes does not necessarily call for separate people. The same individual may manage and lead effectively—or may not.

Some people dislike the idea of distinguishing between management and leadership, maintaining that it is artificial or derogatory toward the managers and the management processes that make organizations run. Perhaps a more useful distinction is between supervisory and strategic leadership:[24]

- Supervisory leadership is behavior that provides guidance, support, and corrective feedback for day-to-day activities.

- Strategic leadership gives purpose and meaning to organizations by anticipating and envisioning a viable future for the organization and working with others to initiate changes that create such a future.[25]

2.2 | Good Leaders Need Good Followers

Organizations succeed or fail not only because of how well they are led but also because of how well followers follow. As one leadership scholar puts it, "Executives are given subordinates; they have to earn followers."[26] But it's also true that good followers help produce good leaders.

As a manager, you will be asked to play the roles of both leader and follower. As you lead the people who report to you, you will report to your manager. You will be a member of some teams and committees, and you may head others. While leadership roles are often coveted, followers must perform their responsibilities conscientiously. Good followership is not merely obeying orders, although some bosses may view it that way.[27] The most effective followers can think independently while remaining actively committed to organizational goals.[28] Robert Townsend, who led a legendary turnaround at Avis, says the most important characteristic of a follower may be the willingness to tell the truth.[29]

Effective followers also distinguish themselves by their enthusiasm and commitment to the organization and to a person or purpose—an idea, a product—other than themselves or their own interests. They master skills that are useful to their organizations, and they hold performance standards that are higher than required. Effective followers may not get the glory, but they know their

contributions to the organization are valuable. And as they make those contributions, they study leaders in preparation for their own leadership roles.[30]

3 | POWER AND LEADERSHIP

Central to effective leadership is power—the ability to influence other people. In organizations, this influence often means the ability to get things done or accomplish one's goals despite resistance from others.

One of the earliest and still most useful approaches to understanding power, offered by French and Raven, describes the following potential power sources (also shown in Exhibit 10.1):[31]

1. *Legitimate power*—A leader with legitimate power has the right, or the authority, to tell others what to do; employees are obligated to comply with legitimate orders. For example, when a supervisor tells an employee to design a new social media marketing campaign, the direct report needs to get it done. In contrast, when a staff person (e.g., HR recruiter) lacks the authority to give an order to a line manager (e.g., digital marketing manager), the staff person has no legitimate power over the manager.[32]

2. *Reward power*—The leader who has reward power influences others by controlling valued outcomes; people comply with the leader's wishes in order to receive those rewards. For example, an employee works hard to earn an outstanding performance review, which results in a big pay raise from his boss. In contrast, if company policy dictates that everyone is to receive the same salary increase, a leader's reward power decreases, because she is unable to give higher raises.

3. *Coercive power*—A leader with coercive power has control over punishments; people obey to avoid those punishments. For instance, a manager implements an absenteeism policy that administers disciplinary actions

Exhibit 10.1	Sources of power in organizations

Source of Power	Example of How Source of Power Is Used in Organizations
Legitimate	Your supervisor asks you to work an extra shift and you agree.
Reward	The manager gives you a large bonus for exceptional performance.
Coercive	The accounting director assigns you several unpopular tasks.
Referent	Your boss is a great person, so you're willing to work hard for her.
Expert	The marketing team leader is very experienced, so you listen to him.

Source: Adapted from J. R. P. French and B. Raven, "The Bases of Social Power," in *Studies in Social Power*, ed. D. Cartwright (Ann Arbor, MI: Institute for Social Research, 1959).

to offending employees. A manager has less coercive power if, say, a union contract limits his ability to punish subordinates.

4. *Referent power*—A leader with referent power has personal characteristics that appeal to others; people comply because of admiration, personal liking, a desire for approval, or a desire to be like the leader. For example, young, ambitious managers emulate the work habits and personal style of a successful, charismatic executive. An executive who is incompetent, aggressive, disliked, and commands little respect has little referent power.

5. *Expert power*—A leader who has expert power has useful expertise or knowledge; people comply because they believe in, can learn from, or can otherwise gain from that expertise. For example, a sales manager gives his salespeople some tips on how to close a deal. The salespeople then alter their sales techniques because they respect the manager's expertise. However, this manager may lack expert power in other areas, such as finance, so his salespeople may ignore his advice concerning financial matters.

People who are in a position that gives them the right to tell others what to do, who can reward and punish, who are well liked and admired, and who have expertise on which other people can draw will be powerful members of the organization. All of these sources of power are potentially important. In general, lower-level managers have less legitimate, coercive, and reward power than do middle- and higher-level managers.[34] But although it is easy to assume that the most powerful bosses are those who have high legitimate power and control major

● Elon Musk is accustomed to making history. Since cofounding PayPal, he founded Tesla Motors (the an all-electric auto manufacturer) and Space Exploration Technologies (SpaceX). Next, Musk is developing a "hyperloop" ultra-high-speed train that will move passengers between Los Angeles and San Francisco at a speed of over 700 miles per hour.[33] This image shows the Hyperloop One test run in North Las Vegas, Nevada, in May 2016.
Hyperloop/Cover Images/Newscom

rewards and punishments, it is important not to underestimate the more "personal" sources like expert and referent power.[35]

What does having authority and power over others "do" to people?[36] A fascinating stream of research by Northwestern University's Adam Galinsky and colleagues provides evidence-based answers. Formal power holders tend to pay more attention to the big picture than details, are less likely to take others' perspectives into account, judge other people's ethics more strongly than their own, have more confidence in their own knowledge than in others', are more optimistic than others, are more action-oriented, express themselves more freely, and more often violate social norms while feeling less guilty about doing so.

Tendencies, of course, don't describe every official power holder. It's worth reading the list of attributes again and thinking about them from a personal perspective: Which ones might describe you, and which ones do you want to embrace or avoid?

LO4 Know the three traditional approaches to understanding leadership.

4 | TRADITIONAL APPROACHES TO UNDERSTANDING LEADERSHIP

There are three traditional approaches to studying leadership: the trait approach, the behavioral approach, and the situational approach.

4.1 | Certain Traits May Set Leaders Apart

The trait approach is the oldest leadership perspective; it focuses on individual leaders and tries to determine the personal characteristics (traits) that great leaders share. What set Mahatma Gandhi, Margaret Thatcher, Abraham Lincoln, and Martin Luther King Jr. apart from the crowd? The trait approach assumes the existence of a leadership personality and that leaders are born, not made.

From 1904 to 1948, researchers conducted more than 100 leadership trait studies.[37] At the end of that period, management scholars concluded that no particular set of traits is necessary for a person to become a successful leader. Enthusiasm for the trait approach diminished, but some research on traits continued. By the mid-1970s, a more balanced view emerged: Although no traits *ensure* leadership success, certain characteristics are

● Teenage student leaders in Parkland, Florida, demonstrated a strong sense of purpose, despite having no previous affiliation with any defined political or action group. Rmv/Shutterstock

potentially useful. The current perspective is that some personality characteristics—many of which a person need not be born with but can strive to acquire—do distinguish effective leaders from other people:[38]

1. *Drive.* Drive refers to a set of characteristics that reflect a high level of effort, including high need for achievement, constant striving for improvement, ambition, energy, tenacity (persistence in the face of obstacles), and initiative. In several countries, the achievement needs of top executives were shown to be related to the growth rates of their organizations.[39] But the need to achieve can be a drawback if leaders focus on personal achievement and get so involved with the work that they do not delegate enough work to others.

2. *Leadership motivation.* Great leaders *want* to lead. So it helps to be *extraverted*—extraversion relates to leadership emergence and leadership effectiveness.[40] But introverts have great strengths as well. Try to think in general, flexible terms of what strengths you can capitalize on and what approaches to change.[41] Also important is a high need for power, a preference to be in leadership rather than follower positions.[42] When the power need is exercised in moral and socially constructive ways, leaders inspire more trust, respect, and commitment to their vision. If you consider yourself to be introverted, as so many of us do, you might want to heed the words of Mahatma Gandhi: "In a gentle way, you can shake the world." And listen to author Susan Cain, who writes that introverts are underrated as leaders and are the people who can help us "think deeply, strategize, solve complex problems, and spot canaries in your coal mine."[43]

3. *Integrity.* Integrity is the correspondence between actions and words. Honesty and credibility, in addition to being desirable characteristics in their own right, are especially important for leaders because these traits inspire trust in others.

4. *Self-confidence.* Self-confidence is important because the leadership role is challenging, and setbacks are inevitable. A self-confident leader overcomes obstacles, makes decisions despite uncertainty, and instills confidence in others. Of course, you don't want to overdo this; arrogance and cockiness have triggered more than one leader's downfall.

5. *Knowledge of the business.* Effective leaders have a high level of knowledge about their industries, companies, and technical matters. Leaders must have the intelligence to interpret vast quantities of information. Advanced degrees are useful in a career, but ultimately they are less important than acquired expertise in matters relevant to the organization.[44]

6. *Dark traits.* Recent years have generated a great deal of interest in the dark side of leadership. The "Dark Triad" traits are Machiavellianism (manipulative belief in expediency over principle), narcissism (inflated view of self, self-love, and fantasies of control, admiration, and successes), and psychopathy (the most serious; lack of empathy, lack of remorse, and lack of guilt when harming others). Consider also three less-studied but severely labeled "Nightmare Traits": dishonesty, disagreeableness, and carelessness.[45]

behavioral approach a leadership perspective that attempts to identify what good leaders do—that is, what behaviors they exhibit

task performance behaviors actions taken to ensure that the work group or organization reaches its goals

group maintenance behaviors actions taken to ensure the satisfaction of group members, develop and maintain harmonious work relationships, and preserve the social stability of the group

Leadership styles are often heavily influenced by their cultures. American CEOs are routinely criticized for focusing far more on short-term financial and stock performance than long-term growth. Wall Street rewards CEOs with short-term bounces in stock prices when companies announce major layoffs. But, longer-term consequences of drastic workforce reductions often include lower employee morale, high turnover of valued employees, and reduced organizational performance.

Chinese business leaders exhibit well-known—and useful-to-know—cultural tendencies. *Guanxi* is a Chinese concept loosely defined as friendship with expectations of continuously exchanged favors. Chinese leaders operate from this norm, plus a position of national pride that maintains their country's honor and reputation. Leaders in other countries might do the same, but these mindsets might not be shared to the same degree.

What is the bottom line? Leaders from different cultures might share some attitudes, behaviors, and beliefs, but certain other attitudes and behaviors are shaped by their unique cultures.[47]

Finally, there is one personal skill that may be the most important: the ability to perceive the needs and goals of others and to adjust one's personal leadership approach accordingly.[48] Effective leaders do not rely on one leadership style; rather, they are capable of using different styles as the situation warrants.[49] This quality is the cornerstone of the situational approach to leadership, which we will discuss shortly.

Effective leaders need to exhibit both task performance and group maintenance behaviors. Rawpixel.com/Shutterstock

> "Leadership is not about titles, positions or flowcharts. It is about one life influencing another."
>
> —John C. Maxwell

4.2 | Certain Behaviors May Make Leaders Effective

The behavioral approach to leadership tries to identify what good leaders do. Should leaders focus on getting the job done or on keeping their followers happy? Should they make decisions autocratically or democratically? The behavioral approach downplays personal characteristics in favor of the actual behaviors that leaders exhibit. Studies of leadership behavior have considered the degree to which leaders emphasize task performance versus group maintenance and the extent to which leaders invite employee participation in decision making.

Task Performance and Group Maintenance

Leadership requires getting the job done. Task performance behaviors are the leader's efforts to ensure that the work unit or organization reaches its goals. This dimension is variously referred to as *concern for production, directive leadership, initiating structure,* or *closeness of supervision.* It includes a focus on work speed, quality and accuracy, quantity of output, and following the rules.[50] This type of leader behavior improves leader performance and group and organizational performance.[51]

Leadership is inherently an interpersonal, group activity.[52] In exhibiting group maintenance behaviors, leaders take action to ensure the satisfaction of group members, develop and maintain harmonious work relationships, and preserve the group's social stability. This dimension is sometimes referred to as *concern for people, supportive leadership,* or *consideration.* It includes a focus on people's feelings and comfort, appreciation of them, and stress reduction.[53] This type of leader behavior has a strong positive impact on follower satisfaction and motivation and also on leader effectiveness.[54]

What *specific* behaviors do performance- and maintenance-oriented leadership imply? To help answer this question, assume you have been asked to rate your boss on these two dimensions. If a leadership study were conducted in your organization, you would be asked to fill out a questionnaire in which you answer questions like those listed in Exhibit 10.2.

Leader–member exchange (LMX) theory highlights the importance of leader behaviors not just toward the group as a whole but toward individuals on a personal basis.[55] The focus in the original formulation, which has since been expanded, is primarily on the leader behaviors historically considered group maintenance.[56] According to LMX theory, and as supported by research evidence, maintenance behaviors such as trust, open communication, mutual respect, mutual obligation, and mutual loyalty form the cornerstone of relationships that are satisfying and perhaps more productive.[57]

Remember, though, the potential for cross-cultural differences. Maintenance behaviors are important everywhere, but the specific behaviors can differ from one culture to another. For example, in the United States, maintenance behaviors include dealing with people face-to-face; in Japan, written memos are preferred over giving directions in person, thus avoiding confrontation and permitting face-saving in the event of disagreement.[58]

Participation in Decision Making

How should a leader make decisions? More specifically, to what extent should leaders involve their people in making decisions?[60] As a dimension of leadership behavior, *participation in decision making* can range from autocratic to democratic:

- **Autocratic leadership** makes decisions and then announces them to the group.

- **Democratic leadership** solicits input from others. Democratic leadership seeks information, opinions, and

Exhibit 10.2	Relating to your boss's leadership style

If your boss exhibits task performance leadership behaviors, then . . .

Be detailed and specific when providing verbal updates and written reports about the project.

Follow instructions, and when there is a change to the original plan, clear it with your boss.

Expect your boss to closely monitor your work. Be responsive and don't take it personally.

Be prepared for constructive criticism and encouragement to do the best job possible.

Provide your boss with frequent updates about your progress on the project.

Deliver the finished project on time. Don't miss the deadline or ask for an extension.

If your boss displays group maintenance behaviors, then . . .

Share more freely about personal challenges you are facing at work.

Expect your boss to ask for your opinion about how to solve challenges at work.

Try to be a good team player and seek a consensus with others on key decisions.

Expect your boss to treat you and your coworkers in a fair and consistent manner.

Communicate in an open and transparent manner with others in the work environment.

Give credit to team members for helping with projects and problem solving.

Sources: Adapted from J. Misumi and M. Peterson, "The Performance-Maintenance (PM) Theory of Leadership: Review of a Japanese Research Program," *Administrative Science Quarterly* 30 (June 1985), pp. 199–223; T. Judge, R. Piccolo, and R. Ilies, "The Forgotten Ones? The Validity of Consideration and Initiating Structure in Leadership Research," *Journal of Applied Psychology* 89 (2004), pp. 36–51; and T. Hammer and J. Turk, "Organizational Determinants of Leader Behavior and Authority," *Journal of Applied Psychology* 72 (1987), pp. 674–83.

> "The growth and development of people is the highest calling of leadership."[59]
>
> —Harvey Firestone, founder of Firestone Tire and Rubber Company

preferences, sometimes to the point of meeting with the group, leading discussions, and using consensus or majority vote to make the final choice.

Effects of Leader Behavior

How the leader behaves influences people's attitudes and performance. Studies of these effects focus on autocratic versus democratic decision styles or on performance- versus maintenance-oriented behaviors.

Decision styles. The classic study comparing autocratic and democratic styles found that a democratic approach resulted in the most positive attitudes, but an autocratic approach resulted in somewhat higher performance.[61] A **laissez-faire** style, in which the leader essentially made no decisions, led to more negative attitudes and lower performance. These results seem logical and probably represent the prevalent beliefs among managers about the general effects of these approaches.

Democratic styles, appealing though they may seem, are not always the most appropriate. When speed is of the essence, democratic decision making may be too slow, or people may want decisiveness from the leader.[62] Whether a decision should be made autocratically or democratically depends on the characteristics of the leader, the followers, and the situation.[63] Thus a situational approach to leader decision styles, discussed later in the chapter, is appropriate.

Performance and maintenance behaviors. The performance and maintenance dimensions of leadership are independent of each other. In other words, a leader can behave in ways that emphasize one, both, or neither of these dimensions. Some research indicates that the ideal combination is to engage in both types of leader behaviors.

Pioneering studies at two Big Ten universities in the 1950s laid the foundation for understanding leadership as a process related to both task performance and people. An Ohio State research team investigated the effects of leader behaviors in a truck manufacturing plant of International Harvester.[64] Supervisors scoring high on *maintenance behaviors* (which the researchers termed *consideration*) had fewer grievances and less turnover in their work units than supervisors who were low on this dimension. The opposite held for *task performance behaviors* (called *initiating structure*). Supervisors high on this dimension had more grievances and higher turnover rates.

When maintenance and performance leadership behaviors were considered together, the results were more complex. But one conclusion was clear: When a leader rates high on performance-oriented behaviors, he or she should also be maintenance-oriented. Otherwise, the leader will face high levels of employee turnover and grievances.

Conducted at roughly the same time, a research program at the University of Michigan studied the impact of the same leader behaviors on groups' job performance.[65] Among other things, the researchers concluded that the most effective managers engaged in what they called *task-oriented behavior:* planning, scheduling, coordinating, providing resources, and setting performance goals. Effective managers also exhibited more *relationship-oriented behavior:* demonstrating trust and confidence, being friendly and considerate, showing appreciation, keeping people informed, and so on. As you can see, these dimensions of leader behavior are essentially the task performance and group maintenance dimensions.

After the Ohio State and Michigan findings were published, it became popular to talk about the ideal leader as one who is always both performance- and maintenance-oriented. The best-known leadership training model to follow this style is Blake and Mouton's Leadership Grid®.[66] In grid training, managers are rated on their performance-oriented behavior (called *concern for production*) and maintenance-oriented behavior (*concern for people*). Then their scores are plotted on a two-dimensional grid where concern for production and concern for people are represented by a score from 1 (low) to 9 (high). Managers who score less than a 9,9–for example, those who are high on concern for people but low on concern for production–would then receive training on how to become a 9,9 leader.

For a long time, grid training was warmly received by U.S. business and industry. Later, however, it was criticized for embracing a simplistic, one-best-way style of leadership and ignoring the possibility that 9,9 is not best under all circumstances. For example, even 1,1 leadership can be appropriate if employees know their jobs (so they don't need to receive directions). Also, they may enjoy their jobs and coworkers enough that they do not care whether the boss shows personal concern for them. Still, if the manager is uncertain how to behave, it probably is best to exhibit behaviors that relate to both task performance and group maintenance.[67]

In fact, a wide range of effective leadership styles exists. Organizations that understand the need for diverse leadership styles will have a competitive advantage in the modern business environment over those in which managers believe there is only "one best way."

4.3 | The Best Way to Lead Depends on the Situation

According to proponents of the situational approach to leadership, universally important traits and behaviors don't exist. Rather, effective leader behaviors vary from situation to situation. *The leader should first analyze the situation and then decide what to do.* In other words, look before you lead.

A head nurse in a hospital described her situational approach to leadership this way: "My leadership style is a mix of all styles. In this environment I normally let people participate. But in a code blue situation where a patient is dying I automatically become very autocratic: 'You do this; you do that; you, out of the room; you all better be quiet; you, get Dr. Mansfield.' The staff tell me that's the only time they see me like that. In an emergency like that, you don't have time to vote, talk a lot, or yell at each other. It's time for someone to set up the order."[68]

Sometimes leaders make unpopular decisions to address a particularly challenging situation. Captain Brett E. Crozier, commander of a U.S. aircraft carrier, put the safety of his crew before his naval career.[69] He sent a letter describing his concerns about a coronavirus outbreak on the ship to several people, but he chose not to send it to his immediate superior.[70] After the letter was leaked to the media, acting Navy Secretary Thomas Modly announced the captain was relieved of his command for a "loss of confidence."[71] As Captain Crozier disembarked from the carrier for the final time, he was met by hundreds of sailors clapping and cheering "Captain! Crozier!"[72]

situational approach leadership perspective proposing that universally important traits and behaviors do not exist, and that effective leadership behavior varies from situation to situation

Vroom model a situational model that focuses on the participative dimension of leadership

Fiedler's contingency model of leadership effectiveness a situational approach to leadership postulating that effectiveness depends on the personal style of the leader and the degree to which the situation gives the leader power, control, and influence over the situation

The first situational model of leadership was proposed in 1958 by Tannenbaum and Schmidt. In their classic *Harvard Business Review* article, these authors described how managers should consider three factors before deciding how to lead:[73]

1. *Forces in the manager* include the manager's personal values, inclinations, feelings of security, and confidence in subordinates.

2. *Forces in the subordinate* include his or her knowledge and experience, readiness to assume responsibility for decision making, interest in the task or problem, and understanding and acceptance of the organization's goals.

3. *Forces in the situation* include the type of leadership style the organization values, the degree to which the group works effectively as a unit, the problem itself and the type of information needed to solve it, and the amount of time the leader has to make the decision.

Consider which of these forces makes an autocratic style most appropriate and which dictates a democratic, participative style. By engaging in this exercise, you are constructing a situational theory of leadership.

Although the Tannenbaum and Schmidt article was published a half century ago, most of its arguments remain valid. Since that time, other situational models have emerged. We will focus here on four: the Vroom model for decision making,

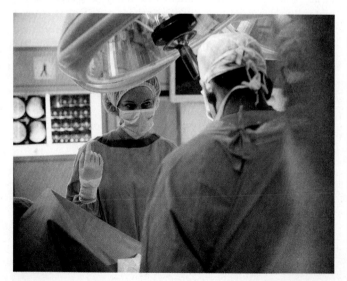

Sam Edwards/Getty Images

Fiedler's contingency model, Hersey and Blanchard's situational theory, and path–goal theory.

The Vroom Model of Leadership In the tradition of Tannenbaum and Schmidt, the Vroom model emphasizes the participative dimension of leadership: how leaders go about making decisions. The model uses the basic situational approach of assessing the situation before determining the best leadership style.[74] The following situational factors are used to analyze problems:[75]

- *Decision significance*—The significance of the decision to the success of the project or organization.

- *Importance of commitment*—The importance of team members' commitment to the decision.

- *Leader's expertise*—Your knowledge or expertise in relation to this problem.

- *Likelihood of commitment*—The likelihood that the team would commit itself to a decision that you might make on your own.

- *Group support for objectives*—The degree to which the team supports the organization's objectives at stake in this problem.

- *Group expertise*—Team members' knowledge or expertise in relation to this problem.

- *Team competence*—The ability of team members to work together in solving problems.

Each of these factors is based on an important attribute of the problem the leader faces and should be assessed as either high or low. The Vroom model operates like a funnel. You answer (and sometimes skip) a series of questions in a decision tree about the problem, until you reach one of 14 possible endpoints. For each endpoint, the model states which of five decision styles—decide, one-on-one consultation, consult the group, facilitate, or delegate—is most appropriate. Several different leader decision styles may work, but the style recommended is the one that takes the least time. The styles indicate that there are several shades of participation, not just autocratic or democratic.[76]

Of course, not every managerial decision warrants this complicated analysis. But the model becomes less complex after you work through it a couple of times. Also, using the model for major decisions ensures that you consider the important situational factors and alerts you to the most appropriate style to use.

Fiedler's Contingency Model According to Fiedler's contingency model of leadership effectiveness, effectiveness depends on two factors: the personal style of the leader and the degree to which the situation gives the leader power, control, and influence over the situation.[77] Exhibit 10.3 illustrates this model. The upper half of the exhibit shows the situational analysis, and the lower half indicates the appropriate style. In the upper portion, three questions are used to analyze the situation:

1. Are leader–member relations good or poor? (To what extent is the leader accepted and supported by group members?)

2. Is the task structured or unstructured? (To what extent do group members know what their goals are and how to accomplish them?)

3. Is the leader's position power strong or weak (high or low)? (To what extent does the leader have the authority to reward and punish?)

These three sequential questions create a decision tree (from top to bottom in the exhibit) in which a situation is classified into one of eight categories. The lower the category number, the more favorable the situation is for the leader; the higher the number, the less favorable the situation. Fiedler originally called this variable "situational favorableness," but now it is known as "situational control." Situation 1 is the best: Relations are good, task structure is high, and power is high. In the least favorable situation (8), the leader has very little situational control, relations are poor, tasks lack structure, and the leader's power is weak.

Different situations dictate different leadership styles. Fiedler measured leadership styles with an instrument assessing the leader's *least preferred coworker* (*LPC*)—that is, the attitude toward the follower the leader liked the least. This was considered an indication more generally of leaders' attitudes toward people. If a leader can single out the person she likes the least, but her attitude is not all that negative, she receives a high score on the LPC scale. Leaders with more negative attitudes toward others would receive low LPC scores. Based on the LPC score, Fiedler considered two leadership styles:

1. **Task-motivated leadership** places primary emphasis on completing the task and is more likely exhibited by leaders with low LPC scores.

2. **Relationship-motivated leadership** emphasizes maintaining good interpersonal relationships and is more likely from high-LPC leaders.

These leadership styles correspond to task performance and group maintenance leader behaviors, respectively.

The lower part of Exhibit 10.3 indicates which style is situationally appropriate. For situations 1, 2, 3, and 8, a task-motivated leadership style is more effective. For situations 4 through 7, relationship-motivated leadership is more appropriate.

Fiedler's theory was not always supported by research. It is better supported if we replace the eight specific levels of situational control with three broad levels: low, medium, and high. The theory was controversial in academic circles, partly because it assumed leaders cannot change their styles but must be assigned to situations that suit their styles. However, the model has withstood the test of time and still receives attention. Most important, it called attention to the significance of finding a fit between the situation and the leader's style.

task-motivated leadership leadership that places primary emphasis on completing a task

relationship-motivated leadership leadership that places primary emphasis on maintaining good interpersonal relationships

Exhibit 10.3 Fiedler's analysis of situations in which the task- or relationship-motivated leader is more effective

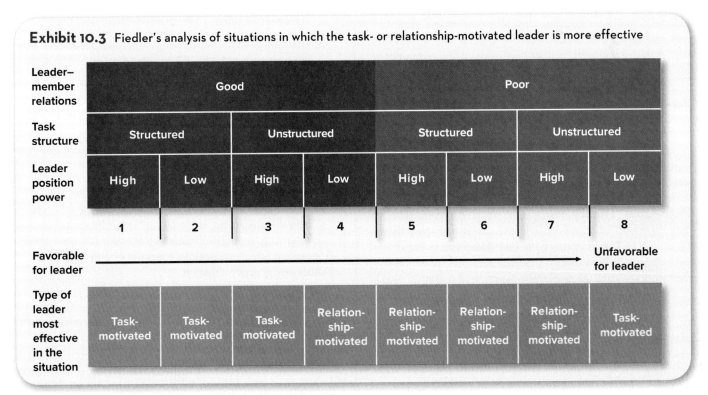

Leader–member relations	Good				Poor			
Task structure	Structured		Unstructured		Structured		Unstructured	
Leader position power	High	Low	High	Low	High	Low	High	Low
	1	2	3	4	5	6	7	8

Favorable for leader →→→ Unfavorable for leader

| Type of leader most effective in the situation | Task-motivated | Task-motivated | Task-motivated | Relationship-motivated | Relationship-motivated | Relationship-motivated | Relationship-motivated | Task-motivated |

Source: D. Organ and T. Bateman, *Organizational Behavior*, 4th ed., McGraw-Hill.

situational theory a life cycle theory of leadership developed by Hersey and Blanchard postulating that a manager should consider an employee's psychological and job maturity before deciding whether task performance or maintenance behaviors are more important

job maturity the level of the employee's skills and technical knowledge relative to the task being performed

psychological maturity an employee's self-confidence and self-respect

path–goal theory a theory that concerns how leaders influence subordinates' perceptions of their work goals and the paths they follow toward attainment of those goals

Hersey and Blanchard's Situational Theory

Hersey and Blanchard developed a situational model that added another factor the leader should take into account before deciding whether task performance or maintenance behaviors are more important. In their situational theory, originally called the *life-cycle theory of leadership,* the key situational factor is the maturity of the followers.[78] Job maturity is the level of the followers' skills and technical knowledge relative to the task being performed; psychological maturity is the followers' self-confidence and self-respect. High-maturity followers have the ability and the confidence to do a good job.

The theory proposes that the more mature the followers, the less the leader needs to engage in task performance behaviors. Maintenance behaviors are not important with followers with low or high maturity but are important for followers of moderate maturity. For low-maturity followers, the emphasis should be on performance-related leadership; for moderate-maturity followers, performance leadership is somewhat less important and maintenance behaviors become more important; and for high-maturity followers, neither dimension of leadership behavior is important.

Little academic research has been done on this situational theory, but the model is popular in management training seminars. Regardless of its scientific validity, Hersey and Blanchard's model provides a reminder that it is important to treat different people differently. Also, it suggests the importance of treating the same individual differently from time to time as he or she changes jobs or acquires more maturity in her or his particular job.[79]

Path–Goal Theory

Perhaps the most comprehensive situational model of leadership effectiveness is path–goal theory. Developed by Robert House, path–goal theory gets its name from its concern with how leaders influence followers' perceptions of their work goals and the paths they follow toward goal attainment.[80]

Path–goal theory has two key situational factors:

1. Personal characteristics of followers.

2. Environmental pressures and demands with which followers must cope to attain their work goals.

These factors determine which leadership behaviors are most appropriate.

The theory identifies four pertinent leadership behaviors:

1. *Directive leadership,* a form of task performance-oriented behavior.

2. *Supportive leadership,* a form of group maintenance-oriented behavior.

3. *Participative leadership,* or decision style.

4. *Achievement-oriented leadership,* or behaviors geared toward motivating people, such as setting challenging goals and rewarding good performance.

These situational factors and leader behaviors are merged in Exhibit 10.4. As you can see, appropriate leader behaviors—as determined by characteristics of followers and the work environment—lead to effective performance.

The theory also specifies *which* follower and environmental characteristics are important. Three key follower characteristics determine the appropriateness of various leadership styles:

1. *Authoritarianism* is the degree to which individuals respect, admire, and defer to authority. Path–goal theory suggests that leaders should use a directive leadership style with subordinates who are highly authoritarian because such people respect decisiveness.

2. *Locus of control* is the extent to which individuals see events as under their control. People with an internal locus of control believe that what happens to them is their own doing; people with an external locus of control believe that it is luck or fate. For subordinates who have an internal locus of control, a participative leadership style is appropriate because these individuals prefer to have more influence over their own work and lives.

3. *Ability* is people's beliefs about their own capabilities to do their assigned jobs. When subordinates' ability is low, a directive style will help them understand what has to be done.

Appropriate leadership style is also determined by three important environmental factors:

- *Tasks*—Directive leadership is inappropriate if tasks already are well structured.

- *Formal authority system*—If the task and the authority or rule system are dissatisfying, directive leadership will create greater dissatisfaction. If the task or authority system is dissatisfying, supportive leadership is especially appropriate because it offers one positive source of gratification in an otherwise negative situation.

- *Primary work group*—If the primary work group provides social support to its members, supportive leadership is less important.

Path–goal theory offers many more propositions. In general, the theory suggests that the functions of the leader are to (1) make the path to work goals easier to travel by providing coaching and direction, (2) reduce frustrating barriers to goal attainment, and (3) increase opportunities for personal satisfaction by increasing payoffs to people for achieving performance goals. The best way to do these things depends on your people and on the work situation. Again, analyze, and then adapt your style accordingly.

Substitutes for Leadership Sometimes leaders don't have to lead, or situations constrain their ability to lead effectively. The situation may be one in which leadership is unnecessary or has little impact. Substitutes for leadership can provide the same influence on people as leaders otherwise would have.

Certain follower, task, and organizational factors are substitutes for task performance and group maintenance leader behaviors.[81] For example, group maintenance behaviors are less important and have less impact if people already have a closely knit group, they have a professional orientation, the job is inherently satisfying, or there is great physical distance between leader and followers. So physicians who are strongly concerned with professional conduct, enjoy their work, and work independently do not need social support from hospital administrators.

Task performance leadership is less important and will have less of a positive effect if people have a lot of experience and ability, feedback is supplied to them directly from the task or by computer, or the rules and procedures are rigid. If these factors are operating, the leader does not have to tell people what to do or how well they are performing.

The concept of substitutes for leadership provides useful and practical prescriptions for how to manage more efficiently.[82] If the manager can develop the work situation where a number of these substitutes for leadership are operating, she can spend less time attempting to influence people and have more time for other important activities.

substitutes for leadership factors in the workplace that can exert the same influence on employees as leaders would provide

Substitutes for leadership may be better predictors of commitment and satisfaction than of performance.[83] These substitutes are helpful, but you can't put substitutes in place and think you have completed your job as leader.

And as a follower, consider this: If you're not getting good leadership, and if these substitutes are not in place, create your own "substitute" for leadership—self-leadership. As but one example, proactive employees can inject ethical behavior into a work environment where the boss is not creating a culture of ethics.[84] Take the initiative to motivate yourself, lead yourself, create positive change, and lead others.

> **LO5 Understand the important contemporary perspectives on leadership.**

5 | CONTEMPORARY PERSPECTIVES ON LEADERSHIP

So far, you have learned the major classic approaches to understanding leadership, all of which remain useful today. Several

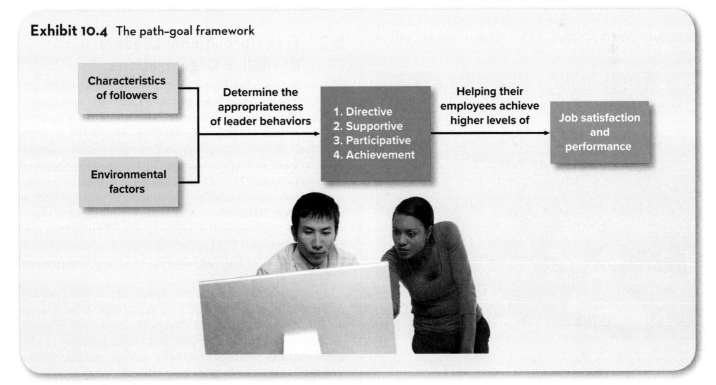

Exhibit 10.4 The path-goal framework

Characteristics of followers / Environmental factors → Determine the appropriateness of leader behaviors → 1. Directive 2. Supportive 3. Participative 4. Achievement → Helping their employees achieve higher levels of → Job satisfaction and performance

Sam Edwards/age fotostock

charismatic leader a person who is dominant, self-confident, convinced of the moral righteousness of his or her beliefs, and able to arouse a sense of excitement and adventure in followers

transformational leaders leaders who motivate people to transcend their personal interests for the good of the group

transactional leaders leaders who manage through transactions, using their legitimate, reward, and coercive powers to give commands and exchange rewards for services rendered

new developments are revolutionizing our understanding of this vital aspect of management.

5.1 | Charismatic Leaders Inspire Their Followers

Like many successful leaders, Nelson Mandela had charisma. So did Winston Churchill. In business, Oprah Winfrey, Howard Schultz, Indra Nooyi, Satya Nadella, and Richard Branson also are charismatic leaders.

Charisma is an elusive concept—easy to spot but hard to define.[85] What *is* charisma, and how does one acquire it? According to one definition, "Charisma packs an emotional wallop for followers above and beyond ordinary esteem, affection, admiration, and trust. . . . The charismatic is an idolized hero, a messiah and a savior."[86] Many people, particularly North Americans, value charisma in their leaders. But some people don't like the term *charisma;* it can be associated with the negative charisma of evil leaders whom people follow blindly.[87] Yet charismatic leaders who display appropriate values and use their charisma for appropriate purposes serve as ethical role models for others.[88]

Charismatic leaders are dominant and exceptionally self-confident, and they have a strong conviction in the moral righteousness of their beliefs.[89] They strive to create an aura of

● Martin Luther King Jr. was a charismatic leader with a compelling vision: a dream for a better world.
National Archives and Records Administration [542068]

competence and success and communicate high expectations for and confidence in followers. Ultimately, charismatic leaders satisfy other people's needs.[90]

The charismatic leader articulates ideological goals and makes sacrifices in pursuit of those goals.[91] Martin Luther King Jr. had a dream for a better world, and John F. Kennedy spoke of landing a human on the moon. Such leaders have a compelling vision and arouse a sense of excitement and adventure. When speaking, charismatic leaders exhibit superior verbal skills, which help communicate the vision and motivate followers. Walt Disney mesmerized people with his storytelling; had enormous creative talent; and instilled in his organization strong values of good taste, risk taking, and innovation.[92]

Leaders who do these things inspire in their followers trust, confidence, acceptance, obedience, emotional involvement, affection, admiration, and higher performance.[93] Charisma not only helps CEOs inspire employees but also may help them influence external stakeholders, including customers and investors.[94] Evidence for the positive effects of charismatic leadership has been found in a wide variety of groups, organizations, and management levels, and in countries including India, Singapore, the Netherlands, China, Nigeria, Japan, and Canada.[95]

Charisma has been shown to improve corporate financial performance, particularly under conditions of uncertainty—that is, in risky circumstances or when environments are changing and people have difficulty understanding what they should do.[96] Uncertainty is stressful, and it makes people more receptive to the ideas and actions of charismatic leaders. By the way, too, as an organization's (or team's) performance improves under a person's leadership, others see that person as increasingly charismatic as a result of the higher performance.[97]

5.2 | Transformational Leaders Revitalize Organizations

Charisma can contribute to transformational leadership. Transformational leaders get people to transcend their personal interests for the sake of the larger community.[98] They generate excitement and revitalize organizations. At age 104, Frances Hesselbein believes leadership must be based on an organization's mission and values. As the CEO of the Girl Scouts of America for nearly 25 years, she earned a reputation for her pioneering work in leadership and social service.[99] For her work at the nonprofit, Hesselbein was awarded the Presidential Medal of Freedom, the highest U.S. civilian honor.[100] Hesselbein now is the president and CEO of her namesake Leadership Forum at the University of Pittsburgh and sits on several nonprofit and private-sector boards.[101]

The transformational process moves beyond the more traditional *transactional* approach to leadership. Transactional leaders view management as a series of transactions in which they use their legitimate, reward, and coercive powers to give commands and exchange rewards for services rendered. Unlike transformational leadership, transactional leadership is dispassionate; it does not excite, transform, empower, or inspire

Sustaining for Tomorrow

The B Team Says "Plan A Is No Longer Acceptable"

The B Team, founded in 2013, describes itself as a group of "global business and civil society leaders working to confront the current crisis of conformity in leadership." This organization of leaders aims to develop a "Plan B," meaning an alternative to business as usual. The problem with the status quo model is that it's driven primarily by profit and is unsustainable. Business as usual has led to a "world of broken trust, rapidly rising temperatures, and increasing inequality."

In contrast, The B Team is attempting to transform leadership so that business becomes a force for social, environmental, and economic good. Members start their own companies and then work together to bring potential solutions to a global scale. They go wherever they can to make a positive difference.

One of the group's major initiatives is to help the world achieve a net-zero greenhouse gas emissions economy by 2050 to avoid the most severe predicted effects of climate change. In support of this effort, The B Team also is trying to establish new norms of climate governance and a "just transition" for workers, so they are guaranteed well-paying jobs during this transformation.

Among The B Team's early leaders are Muhammad Yunus, founder of Grameen Bank and winner of the Nobel Peace Prize for his

The B Team is a not-for-profit initiative comprised of business leaders, including Vice-Chair Sharan Burrow, dedicated to a "better way of doing business for the well-being of people and the planet." Will Bunce/Shutterstock

innovations in microlending; Marc Benioff, CEO of Salesforce.com, a leader in *Fortune*'s list of the world's best places to work; Arianna Huffington, founder of HuffingtonPost.com; and Sir Richard Branson, founder of the Virgin Group. About The B Team, Branson commented: "I believe business must be leading, and not waiting on, the shift toward an inclusive future. I joined The B Team to stand at the forefront of this movement and inspire others to join."

Discussion Questions

- Do you agree with Branson, that business must lead the way on these issues? Why or why not?

- It takes strong leadership to convince stakeholders to engage in green initiatives. Based on your understanding of this chapter, how might B Team members persuade other business leaders to adopt Plan B?

Sources: "Who We Are," The B Team, https://bteam. org/who-we-are/leaders and https://bteam.org/who-we-are/mission, accessed April 10, 2020; and "Our Work," The B Team, https://bteam.org/our-work/causes/climate, accessed April 10, 2020.

people to focus on the interests of the group or organization. Transactional approaches may be more effective for individualists than for collectivists.[102] Also, some managers may use both approaches to leadership, depending on the situation.

Generating Excitement Transformational leaders generate excitement in several ways:[104]

- They are *charismatic,* as described earlier.

> ## "It's kind of fun to do the impossible."[103]
> ### —Walt Disney

- They give their followers *individualized attention.* They delegate challenging work to deserving people, keep lines of communication open, and provide one-on-one mentoring to develop their people. They do not treat everyone alike because not everyone *is* alike.

- They are *intellectually stimulating.* They arouse in their followers an awareness of problems and potential solutions. They articulate the organization's opportunities, threats, strengths, and weaknesses. They stir the imagination and generate insights. As a result, problems are recognized, and high-quality solutions are identified and implemented with the followers' full commitment.

Skills and Strategies At least four skills or strategies contribute to transformational leadership:[105]

1. *Having a vision*—Leaders have a goal, an agenda, or a results orientation that grabs attention.

2. *Communicating their vision*—Through words, manner, or symbolism, leaders relate a compelling image of the ultimate goal.

3. *Building trust*—Being consistent, dependable, and persistent, leaders position themselves clearly by choosing a direction and staying with it, thus projecting integrity.

4. *Having positive self-regard*—Leaders do not feel self-important or complacent, but rather recognize their personal strengths, compensate for their weaknesses, nurture and continually develop their talents, and know how to learn from failure. They strive for success rather than merely trying to avoid failure.

Transformational leadership occurs in industry, the military, politics, and education, in part by engaging multiple stakeholders.[106] Examples of transformational leaders in business include Henry Ford (founder of Ford Motor Company), Herb Kelleher (former CEO of Southwest Airlines), and Anne Mulcahy (in her former role as leader of Xerox).[107] As with studies of charisma, transformational leadership and its positive impact on follower satisfaction and performance have been demonstrated in countries the world over, including India, Egypt, Germany, China, England, and Japan.[108] A study in Korean companies found that transformational leadership predicted employee motivation, which in turn predicted creativity.[109] Under transformational leadership, people view their jobs as more intrinsically motivating (see Chapter 11 for more on this) and are more strongly committed to work goals.[110] And top management teams agree more clearly about important organizational goals, which translates into higher organizational performance.[111]

Transforming Leaders Importantly, transformational leadership is not the exclusive domain of presidents and chief executives. In the military, leaders who received transformational leadership training had a positive impact on followers' personal development. They also were successful as *indirect* leaders: military recruits under the transformational leaders' direct reports were stronger performers.[112] Don't forget, though: The best leaders are those who can display both transformational and transactional behaviors.[113]

Ford Motor Company, in collaboration with the University of Michigan School of Business, put thousands of middle managers through a program designed to stimulate transformational leadership.[114] The training included analysis of the changing business environment, company strategy, and personal reflection and discussion about the need to change. Participants assessed their own leadership styles and developed a specific change initiative to implement after the training—a change that would make a needed and lasting difference for the company.

Over the next six months, the managers implemented change on the job. Almost half of the initiatives resulted in transformational changes in the organization or work unit; the rest of the changes were smaller, more incremental, or more personal. Whether managers made small or transformational changes depended on their attitude going into the training, their level of self-esteem, and the amount of support they received from others on the job. Although some managers did not respond to the training as hoped, almost half embraced the training, adopted a more transformational orientation, and tackled significant transformations for the company.

Level 5 leadership, a term well known among executives, is considered by some to be the ultimate leadership style.

● Henry Ford, founder of Ford Motor Company.
Library of Congress Prints & Photographs Division [LC-USZ62-111360]

Level 5 leadership is a combination of strong professional will (determination) and personal humility that builds enduring greatness.[115] Thus, a Level 5 leader is relentlessly focused on the organization's long-term success while behaving modestly, directing attention toward the organization rather than him- or herself. Examples include Dr. Anthony Fauci, Director of the National Institute of Allergy and Infectious Diseases and leading expert on the coronavirus pandemic; Darwin E. Smith, ex-CEO of Kimberly-Clark; and IBM's former chief executive, Louis Gerstner. Gerstner is widely credited with turning around a stodgy IBM by shifting its focus from computer hardware to business solutions. Following his retirement, Gerstner wrote a memoir that details what happened at the company but says little about himself. Although Level 5 leadership is seen as a way to transform organizations to make them great, it requires first that the leader exhibit a combination of transactional and transformational styles.[116]

Robert Chapman, CEO of Barry-Wehmiller Companies (B-W), had to act decisively when sales at his family's packaging equipment and services firm plunged. He and his management team developed a company vision aimed at balanced and sustainable growth and a commitment to "people-centric leadership." B-W managers must care about their employees, give them authority to make important decisions, and clarify how their contributions enhance the company's vision.

"We measure success by the way we touch the lives of people" captures Chapman's belief that companies can change the world through their impact on individual employees. "The usual corporate-culture buzzwords, like engagement, productivity, and performance, are self-serving to companies," says Bob Chapman. "We want to release human potential." Challenging employees to contribute to the corporate vision gives them a chance to feel that their efforts matter; recognition programs show them that they are appreciated. The result is what Chapman calls an "inspirational environment." With recent sales revenue of $1.7 billion, the company is realizing its potential, too.[117]

5.3 | Authentic Leadership Adds an Ethical Dimension

In general, authentic leadership is rooted in the ancient Greek philosophy "To thine own self be true."[118] In your own leadership, you should strive for authenticity in the form of honesty, genuineness, reliability, integrity, and trustworthiness. Authentic individuals who also are transformational leaders care about public interests (community, organizational, or group), not just their own.[119] They are willing to sacrifice their own interests for others, and they can be trusted. They are ethically mature; people view leaders who exhibit moral reasoning as more transformational than leaders who do not.[120]

Pseudotransformational leaders are the opposite: They talk a good game, but they ignore followers' real needs as their own self-interests (power, prestige, control, wealth, fame) take precedence.[121]

LO6 Identify types of opportunities to be a leader.

6 | YOU CAN LEAD

Every organization has plenty of leadership opportunities available. Employees, team leaders, and higher-level managers alike can work with others within the organization to get things done.

6.1 | Seek Opportunities to Lead

A common view of leaders is that they are superheroes acting alone, swooping in to save the day. But especially in these complex times, leaders cannot and need not act alone.

study tip 10

Lead a study group

Study Tip 7 pointed out the benefits of forming a study group. One way to get more out of this experience is for you to take the lead in forming and managing the group. This should help you (for example) build servant–leadership and group maintenance leadership skills. The first step might be to recruit three or four students from your class to join the group. During the first meeting, ask the attendees in which areas of the course they are struggling and what topics they think the group should spend time discussing. Before ending the meeting, ask members what they want to accomplish in the next session. Then add the date, time, and place to your calendars.

Eric Raptosh Photography/Blend Images LLC

Effective leadership must permeate the organization, not reside in one or two superstars at the top. The leader's job becomes one of spreading leadership abilities throughout the firm.[122] Make people responsible for their own performance. Create an environment in which each person can figure out what needs to be done and then do it well. Point the way and clear the path so that people can succeed. Give them the credit they deserve. Make heroes out of *them*. Thus what is now required of leaders is less the efficient management of resources and more the effective unleashing of people and their intellectual capital.

This perspective uncovers a variety of nontraditional leadership roles that are emerging as vitally important.[123] The term servant–leader was coined by Robert Greenleaf, a retired AT&T executive. The term is paradoxical in the sense that "leader" and

"servant" are usually opposites; the servant–leader's relationship with employees is more like that of serving customers. For the person who wants to both lead and serve others, servant–leadership is a way to serve others' needs and enhance their personal growth while strengthening the organization.[124]

A number of other nontraditional roles provide leadership opportunities. Bridge leaders are those who leave their cultures for a significant period of time.[125] They live, go to school, travel, or work in other cultures. Then they return home, become leaders, and through their expanded repertoire they serve as bridges between conflicting value systems within their own cultures or between their culture and other cultures.

With work often being team based, shared leadership occurs when leadership rotates to the person with the key knowledge, skills, and abilities for the issue facing the team at a particular time.[126] Shared leadership is most important when tasks are interdependent, complex, and require creativity. High-performing teams engaged in such work exhibit more shared leadership than poor-performing teams.[127] In consulting teams, the greater the shared leadership, the higher their clients rated the teams' performance.[128] The hierarchical leader remains important—the

● Alcoa Russia. Daniel Acker/Bloomberg/Getty Images

Take Charge of Your Career

Hone your leadership skills

As with most things, being a good leader takes hard work. Great musicians and athletes don't rely on natural gifts alone. They practice, learn, and hone their skills over a lifetime.

You can take the same approach with your leadership skills. Being an effective leader takes time, but in the meantime, you can develop yourself as a leader in other ways. Here are some tips to developing skills that will serve you well when leading people in both the short and long term:

1. **Build a strong network of successful leaders.** Learn early from those you know as they can help you grow and improve as a leader. Seek leadership mentors and opportunities to lead within any organization you are a part of.

2. **Get involved.** Join business associations. Join one or more charities or other nonprofits that operate in your community. In doing so, you can develop leadership skills in diverse contexts.

3. **Be an active listener.** Take time to actively listen to others who have more leadership experience than you. When you're actively listening, you're more apt to learn.

4. **Consider leading to be not a goal but a journey.** Leadership as a goal has an endpoint. Once you've reached the end, you might become complacent. Leadership as a journey, on the other hand, has no end. You continue to learn and grow as a leader for as long as the process sustains you (and those you lead).

Sources: J. Michael, "Three Challenges Young Leaders Face and How Coaching Can Help," *Forbes*, November 8, 2019, https://www.forbes.com/sites/forbescoachescouncil/2019/11/08/three-challenges-young-leaders-face-and-how-coaching-can-help/#63821e41363b; and D. Patel, "12 Habits of Successful Young Leaders," *Forbes*, September 24, 2017, https://www.forbes.com/sites/deeppatel/2017/09/24/12-habits-of-successful-young-leaders/#497183b04940.

---

formal leader still designs the team, manages its external boundaries, provides task direction, emphasizes the importance of the shared leadership approach, and engages in the transactional and transformational activities described here. But at the same time, the metaphor of geese in V-formation adds strength to the group: The lead goose periodically drops to the back, and another goose moves up and takes its place at the forefront.

Lateral leadership does not involve a hierarchical, superior–subordinate relationship but instead invites colleagues at the same level to solve problems together. You alone can't provide a solution to every problem, but you can create processes through which people work collaboratively. If you can get people working to improve methods collaboratively, you can help create an endless stream of innovations. In other words, it's not about you providing solutions to problems; it's about creating better interpersonal processes for finding solutions.

6.2 | Good Leaders Need Courage

To be a good leader, you need the courage[129]—to create a vision of greatness for your unit; identify and manage allies, adversaries, and fence sitters; and execute your vision, often against opposition.

This does not mean you should commit career suicide by alienating too many powerful people; it does mean taking reasonable risks, with the good of the firm at heart, in order to produce constructive change.

> **lateral leadership** style in which colleagues at the same hierarchical level are invited to collaborate and facilitate joint problem solving

Take Bill O'Rourke, who served as the president of Alcoa Russia from 2005 to 2008. While Russia had a reputation as a difficult place to do business, Alcoa was attracted to the country by its substantial aluminum alloy deposits. O'Rourke was charged with revitalizing the Russian operation to meet Alcoa's world-class standards.

Turning around a multimillion-dollar operation would have been challenging for any leader, but O'Rourke faced additional stressors. After refusing to pay bribes and engage in other types of extortion and corruption, things became more complicated. His life was threatened by a government official who said, "If this was five years ago, I would kill you, and I would get away with it."

The harassment didn't stop there. While transport trucks were delivering a $25 million furnace to the plant in Belaya Kalitva,

---

> ## "When you connect with a purpose greater than yourself, you are fearless; you think big."
>
> —Nancy Barry, pictured nearby, on leaving her executive position at the World Bank to become president of Women's World Banking, which makes microloans to impoverished women around the world[130]

JAVIER LIRA Notimex/Newscom

the local police stopped them outside the city—the trucks were not allowed to move until the company paid $25,000 to a government official. O'Rourke didn't budge and refused to pay a dime. After about three days, the trucks were released to complete their delivery to the plant.

By resisting the culture of corruption, O'Rourke and Alcoa built a profitable, safe, and well-managed operation in Russia. The organization became an employer in which Russian nationals could work their way into leadership positions.

Fulfilling your vision will require some of the following acts of courage:[131]

- Seeing things as they are and facing them head-on, making no excuses and harboring no wishful illusions.

- Saying what needs to be said to those who need to hear it.

- Persisting despite resistance, criticism, abuse, and setbacks.

Courage includes stating the realities, even when they are harsh, and publicly stating what you will do to help and what you want from others. This means laying the cards on the table honestly: Here is what I want from you. . . . What do you want from me?[132]

Notes

1. W. Bennis and B. Nanus, *Leaders* (New York: Harper & Row, 1985), p. 27.

2. W. Bennis and B. Nanus, *Leaders* (New York: Harper & Row, 1985).

3. P. Loftus "Why Merck Is Betting Big on One Cancer Drug," *The Wall Street Journal,* April 15, 2018, https://www.wsj.com/articles/why-merck-is-betting-big-on-one-cancer-drug-1523790000.

4. A. Ignatius, "Businesses Exist to Deliver Value to Society," *Harvard Business Review,* March–April 2018, https://hbr.org/2018/03/businesses-exist-to-deliver-value-to-society.

5. A.Dunn, "FDA Approves Merck's Ebola Vaccine, a Historic First against Deadly Virus," *BioPharma Dive,* December 20, 2019; and C. Leaf, "Deploying the Profit Motive to Beat Ebola," *Fortune,* August 20, 2018, http://fortune.com/2018/08/20/merck-ebola-outbreak-vaccine/.

6. "Merck's Frazier to Remain CEO beyond 2019," Reuters, September 26, 2018, https://www.cnbc.com/2018/09/26/mercks-frazier-to-remain-ceo-beyond-2019.html.

7. E. E. Lawler III, *Treat People Right! How Organizations and Individuals Can Propel Each Other into a Virtual Spiral of Success* (San Francisco: Jossey-Bass, 2003).

8. J. Kouzes and B. Posner, *The Leadership Challenge,* 2nd ed. (San Francisco: Jossey-Bass, 1995).

9. B. Wigert and N. Dvorak, "Feedback Is Not Enough," Gallup, May 16, 2019, www.gallup.com.

10. P. Fitch, "The Value of Vision," *Canadian Journal of Hospital Pharmacy* 70, no. 6 (November–December 2017), pp. 472–73.

11. J. Cheng and R. Harrington, "12 of the Smartest Things Elon Musk Has Said about the Future of Our Planet," *Business Insider,* March 5, 2018, www.businessinsider.com.

12. "Branson Outlines World Powered by Wind, Solar Power," Phys.org, September 25, 2015, www.phys.org.

13. A. M. Carton, C. Murphy, and J. R. Clark, "A (Blurry) Vision of the Future: How Leader Rhetoric about Ultimate Goals Influences Performance," *Academy of Management Journal* 57 (2014), pp. 1544–70; A. Ruvio, Z. Rosenblatt, and R. Hertz-Lazarowitz, Entrepreneurial Leadership Vision in Nonprofit vs. For-Profit Organizations," *Leadership Quarterly* 21 (2010), pp. 144–58; and J. Baum, E. A. Locke, and S. Kirkpatrick, "A Longitudinal Study of the Relation of Vision and Vision Communication to Venture Growth in Entrepreneurial Firms," *Journal of Applied Psychology* 83 (1998), pp. 43–54.

14. W. Bennis and R. Townsend, *Reinventing Leadership* (New York: William Morrow, 1995).

15. W. Bennis and R. Townsend, *Reinventing Leadership* (New York: William Morrow, 1995).

16. J. Kouzes and B. Posner, *The Leadership Challenge,* 2nd ed. (San Francisco: Jossey-Bass, 1995).

17. J. A. Conger, "The Dark Side of Leadership," *Organizational Dynamics* 19 (Autumn 1990), pp. 44–55.

18. J. Conger, "The Vision Thing: Explorations into Visionary Leadership," in *Cutting Edge: Leadership 2000,* eds. B. Kellerman and L. Matusak (College Park, MD: James MacGregor Burns Academy of Leadership, 2000).

19. See company website, "Glassdoor Reveals Employees' Choice Awards for the Top CEOs in 2019," press release, June 18, 2019, www.glassdoor.com.

20. M. Halkias, "Texas' Most Popular CEO Runs a Family Business with an Insanely Loyal Following," *Dallas News,* June 19, 2019, www.dallasnews.com.

21. M. Halkias, "Texas' Most Popular CEO Runs a Family Business with an Insanely Loyal Following," *Dallas News,* June 19, 2019, www.dallasnews.com.

22. D. Ready, "4 Things Successful Change Leaders Do Well," *Harvard Business Review,* January 2016, www.hbr.org; and J. P. Kotter, "What Leaders Really Do," *Harvard Business Review* 68 (May–June 1990) pp. 103–11.

23. G. Yukl, *Leadership in Organizations,* 3rd ed. (Englewood Cliffs, NJ: Prentice Hall, 1994).

24. R. House and R. Aditya, "The Social Scientific Study of Leadership: Quo Vadis?" *Journal of Management* 23 (1997), pp. 409–73.

25. R. D. Ireland and M. A. Hitt, "Achieving and Maintaining Strategic Competitiveness in the 21st Century. The Role of Strategic Leadership," *Academy of Management Executive* (February 1999), pp. 43–57.

26. J. Gardner, "The Heart of the Matter: Leader–Constituent Interaction," in *Leading & Leadership,* ed. T. Fuller (Notre Dame, IN: University of Notre Dame Press, 2000), pp. 239–44, quote on p. 240.

27. M. Uhl-Bien, R. Riggio, K. Lowe, and M. Carsten, "Followership Theory: A Review and Research Agenda," *The Leadership Quarterly* 25 (2014), pp. 83–104.

28. R. E. Kelly, "In Praise of Followers," *Harvard Business Review* 66 (November–December 1988), pp. 142–48.

29. W. Bennis and R. Townsend, *Reinventing Leadership* (New York: William Morrow, 1995).

30. R. E. Kelly, "In Praise of Followers," *Harvard Business Review* 66 (November–December 1988), pp. 142–48.

31. J. R. P. French and B. Raven, "The Bases of Social Power," in *Studies in Social Power,* ed. D. Cartwright (Ann Arbor, MI: Institute for Social Research, 1959).

32. G. Yukl and C. Falbe, "Importance of Different Power Sources in Downward and Lateral Relations," *Journal of Applied Psychology* 76 (1991), pp. 416–23.

33. J. Kasperkevic, "Elon Musk's Hyperloop Could Head to Europe before California," *The Guardian,* March 11, 2016, www.theguardian.com.

34. G. Yukl and C. Falbe, "Importance of Different Power Sources in Downward and Lateral Relations," *Journal of Applied Psychology* 76 (1991), pp. 416–23.

35. G. Yukl and C. Falbe, "Importance of Different Power Sources in Downward and Lateral Relations," *Journal of Applied Psychology* 76 (1991), pp. 416–23.

36. R. E. Sturm and J. Antonakis, "Interpersonal Power: A Review, Critique, and Research Agenda," *Journal of Management* 41 (2015), pp. 136–63.

37. R. M. Stogdill, "Personal Factors Associated with Leadership: A Survey of the Literature," *Journal of Psychology* 25 (1948), pp. 35–71.

38. "How to Become a Better Leader," *MIT Sloan Management Review* 53, no. 3 (Spring 2012), pp. 51–60; and S. Kirkpatrick and E. Locke, "Leadership: Do Traits Matter?" *The Executive* 5 (May 1991), pp. 48–60.

39. G. A. Yukl, *Leadership in Organizations,* 2nd ed. (Englewood Cliffs, NJ: Prentice Hall, 1989).

40. T. Judge, J. Bono, R. Ilies, and M. Gerhardt, "Personality and Leadership: A Qualitative and Quantitative Review," *Journal of Applied Psychology* 87 (2002), pp. 765–80.

41. A. Grant, F. Gino, and D. Hofmann, "The Hidden Advantages of Quiet Bosses," *Harvard Business Review,* December 2010, www.hbr.org; "Analyzing Effective Leaders: Why Extraverts Are Not Always the Most Successful Bosses," Knowledge@Wharton, November 3, 2010, https://knowledge.wharton.upenn.edu/article/analyzing-effective-leaders-why-extraverts-are-not-always-the-most-successful-bosses/.

42. R. Foti and N. M. A. Hauenstein, "Pattern and Variable Approaches in Leadership Emergence and Effectiveness," *Journal of Applied Psychology* 92 (2007), pp. 347–55.

43. S. Cain, *Quiet: The Power of Introverts in a World That Can't Stop Talking* (New York: Broadway Books, 2013); and L. A. Clack, "Book Review: Quiet: The Power of Introverts in a World That Can't Stop Talking," *Frontiers in Psychology* 8 (2017), p. 185.

44. J. P. Kotter, *The General Managers* (New York: Free Press, 1982).

45. R. de Vries, "Three Nightmare Traitsin Leaders," *Frontiers in Psychology,* June 4, 2018, www.frontiersinpsychology.com.

46. J. Kotter, *Leading Change* (Boston: Harvard Business Review Press, 2012).

47. D. De Cremer and T. Tao, "Huawei's Culture Is the Key to Its Success," *Harvard Business Review,* June 11, 2015, www.hbr.org; P. McDonald, "Maoism versus Confucianism: Ideological Influences on Chinese Business Leaders," *Journal of Management Development* 30, no. 7/8 (2011), pp. 632–46; P. Galagan, "The Biggest Losers: The Perils of Extreme Downsizing," *T & D* 64, no. 11 (November 2010), pp. 27–30; G. Hofstede, "Asian Management in the 21st Century," *Asia Pacific Journal of Management* 24 (May 16, 2007), pp. 411–20; and "Are Indian Business Leaders Different?" Knowledge@Wharton, November 1, 2007, https://knowledge.wharton.upenn.edu/article/are-indian-business-leaders-different/.

48. S. Zaccaro, R. Foti, and D. Kenny, "Self-Monitoring and Trait-Based Variance in Leadership: An Investigation of Leader Flexibility across Multiple Group Situations," *Journal of Applied Psychology* 76 (1991), pp. 308–15.

49. M. D. Watkins, "Picking the Right Transition Strategy," *Harvard Business Review* 87, no. 1 (January 2009), pp. 47–53; and D. Goleman, "Leadership That Gets Results," *Harvard Business Review,* March–April 2000, pp. 78–90.

50. J. Misumi and M. Peterson, "The Performance-Maintenance (PM) Theory of Leadership: Review of a Japanese Research Program," *Administrative Science Quarterly* 30 (June 1985), pp. 198–223.

51. T. Judge, R. Piccolo, and R. Ilies, "The Forgotten Ones? The Validity of Consideration and Initiating Structure in Leadership Research," *Journal of Applied Psychology* 89 (2004), pp. 36–51.

52. G. Thomas, R. Martin, and R. Riggio, "Leading Groups: Leadership as a Group Process," *Group Processes & Intergroup Relations* 16 (2013), pp. 3–16.

53. J. Misumi and M. Peterson, "The Performance-Maintenance (PM) Theory of Leadership: Review of a Japanese Research Program," *Administrative Science Quarterly* 30 (June 1985), pp. 198–223.

54. T. Judge, R. Piccolo, and R. Ilies, "The Forgotten Ones? The Validity of Consideration and Initiating Structure in Leadership Research," *Journal of Applied Psychology* 89 (2004), pp. 36–51.

55. G. Graen and M. Uhl-Bien, "Relationship-Based Approach to Leadership: Development of Leader-Member Exchange (LMX) Theory of Leadership over 25 Years: Applying a Multi-Level Multidomain Perspective," *Leadership Quarterly* 6, no. 2 (1995), pp. 219–47.

56. R. House and R. Aditya, "The Social Scientific Study of Leadership: Quo Vadis?" *Journal of Management* 23 (1997), pp. 409–73.

57. G. Han, "Trust and Career Satisfaction: The Role of LMX," *Career Development International* 15, no. 5 (2010), pp. 437–58; and C. R. Gerstner and D. V. Day, "Meta-Analytic Review of Leader-Member Exchange Theory: Correlates and Construct Issues," *Journal of Applied Psychology* 82 (1997), pp. 827–44.

58. R. House and R. Aditya, "The Social Scientific Study of Leadership: Quo Vadis?" *Journal of Management* 23 (1997), pp. 409–73.

59. L. Daskall, "The 100 Best Leadership Quotes of All Time," *Inc.,* April 3, 2015, www.inc.com.

60. T. L. Russ, "Theory X/Y Assumptions as Predictors of Managers' Propensity for Participative Decision Making," *Management Decision* 49, no. 5 (2011), pp. 823–36; and J. Wagner III, "Participation's Effect on Performance and Satisfaction: A Reconsideration of Research," *Academy of Management Review,* April 1994, pp. 312–30.

61. R. White and R. Lippitt, *Autocracy and Democracy: An Experimental Inquiry* (New York: Harper & Brothers, 1960).

62. D. Carey, M. Patsalos, and M. Useem, "Leadership Lessons for Hard Times," *The McKinsey Quarterly* 4 (2009), pp. 52–61; and J. Muczyk and R. Steel, "Leadership Style and the Turnaround Executive," *Business Horizons,* March–April 1999, pp. 39–46.

63. A. Tannenbaum and W. Schmidt, "How to Choose a Leadership Pattern," *Harvard Business Review* 36 (March–April 1958), pp. 95–101.

64. E. Fleishman and E. Harris, "Patterns of Leadership Behavior Related to Employee Grievances and Turnover," *Personnel Psychology* 15 (1962), pp. 43–56.

65. R. Likert, *The Human Organization: Its Management and Value* (New York: McGraw-Hill, 1967).

66. R. Blake and J. Mouton, *The Managerial Grid* (Houston: Gulf, 1964).

67. J. Misumi and M. Peterson, "The Performance-Maintenance (PM) Theory of Leadership: Review of a Japanese Research Program," *Administrative Science Quarterly* 30 (June 1985), pp. 198–223.

68. J. Wall, *Bosses* (Lexington, MA: Lexington Books, 1986), p. 103.

69. H. Cooper, T. Gibbons-Neff, and E. Schmitt, "The Navy Fired the Captain of the Theodore Roosevelt. See How the Crew Responded," *The New York Times,* April 3, 2020, www.nytimes.com.

70. C. Kube and M. Gains, "Navy Relieves Captain Who Raised Alarm about Coronavirus Outbreak on Aircraft Carrier," *NBC News,* April 3, 2020, www.nbcnews.com.

71. D. Welna, "After Outcry over Navy Captain Relieved of Command, Assurances He Won't Be Expelled," NPR, April 3, 2020, www.npr.org.

72. L. Martinez, "Sailors on Aircraft Carrier Give Their Fired Captain a Rousing Sendoff," *ABC News,* April 3, 2020, www.abc-news.com.

73. A. Tannenbaum and W. Schmidt, "How to Choose a Leadership Pattern," *Harvard Business Review* 36 (March–April 1958), pp. 95–101.

74. V. H. Vroom, "Leadership and the Decision-Making Process," *Organizational Dynamics,* Spring 2000, pp. 82–93.

75. V. H. Vroom, "Leadership and the Decision-Making Process," *Organizational Dynamics,* Spring 2000, pp. 82–93. Copyright 2000 with permission from Elsevier Science.

76. For a review of how the model works, see V. H. Vroom, "Leadership and the Decision-Making Process," *Organizational Dynamics,* Spring 2000, pp. 82–93.

77. F. E. Fiedler, *A Theory of Leadership Effectiveness* (New York: McGraw-Hill, 1967).

78. P. Hersey and K. Blanchard, *The Management of Organizational Behavior* (Englewood Cliffs, NJ: Prentice Hall, 1984).

79. G. A. Yukl, *Leadership in Organizations,* 2nd ed. (Englewood Cliffs, NJ: Prentice Hall, 1989).

80. R. J. House, "A Path Goal Theory of Leader Effectiveness," *Administrative Science Quarterly* 16 (1971), pp. 321–39.

81. J. Howell, D. Bowen, P. Dorfman, S. Kerr, and P. Podsakoff, "Substitutes for Leadership: Effective Alternatives to Ineffective Leadership," *Organizational Dynamics* 19 (Summer 1990), pp. 21–38.

82. R. G. Lord and W. Gradwohl Smith, "Leadership and the Changing Nature of Performance," in *The Changing Nature of Performance,* eds. D. R. Ilgen and E. D. Pulakos (San Francisco: Jossey-Bass, 1999).

83. S. Dionne, F. Yammarino, L. Atwater, and L. James, "Neutralizing Substitutes for Leadership Theory: Leadership Effects and Common-Source Bias," *Journal of Applied Psychology* 87 (2002), pp. 454–64.

84. M. Velez and P. Neves, "Shaping Emotional Reactions to Ethical Behaviors: Proactive Personality as a Substitute for Ethical Leadership," *Leadership Quarterly* 29 (2018), pp. 663–73.

85. D. van Knippenberg and S. Sitkin, "A Critical Assessment of Charismatic Transformational Leadership Research: Back to the Drawing Board?" *Academy of Management Annals* 7 (2013), pp. 1–60.

86. B. M. Bass, *Leadership and Performance beyond Expectations* (New York: Free Press, 1985).

87. S. James, "Evil Charisma: Osama Bin Laden, Hitler and Manson Had It," *ABC News,* May 4, 2011, www.abcnews.go.com; Y. A. Nur, "Charisma and Managerial Leadership: The Gift That

Never Was," *Business Horizons,* July–August 1998, pp. 19–26; and R. J. House, "A 1976 Theory of Charismatic Leadership," in *Leadership: The Cutting Edge,* ed. J. G. Hunt and L. L. Larson (Carbondale: Southern Illinois University Press, 1977).

88. R. Nielsen, J. A. Marrone, and H. S. Slay, "A New Look at Humility: Exploring the Humility Concept and Its Role in Socialized Charismatic Leadership," *Journal of Leadership & Organizational Studies* 17, no. 1 (February 2010), pp. 33–43; and M. Brown and L. Trevino, "Socialized Charismatic Leadership, Values Congruence, and Deviance in Work Groups," *Journal of Applied Psychology* 91 (2006), pp. 954–62.

89. M. Potts and P. Behr, *The Leading Edge* (New York: McGraw-Hill, 1987).

90. J. Howell and B. Shamir, "The Role of Followers in the Charismatic Leadership Process: Relationships and Their Consequences," *Academy of Management Review* 30 (2005), pp. 96–112; and M. A. LePine, Y. Zhang, E. R. Crawford, and B. L. Rich, "Turning Their Pain to Gain: Charismatic Leader Influence on Follower Stress Appraisal and Job Performance," *Academy of Management Journal* 59 (2016), pp. 1036–59.

91. S. Yorges, H. Weiss, and O. Strickland, "The Effect of Leader Outcomes on Influence, Attributions, and Perceptions of Charisma," *Journal of Applied Psychology* 84 (1999), pp. 428–36.

92. M. Potts and P. Behr, *The Leading Edge* (New York: McGraw-Hill, 1987).

93. D. A. Waldman and F. J. Yammarino, "CEO Charismatic Leadership: Levels-of-Management and Levels-of-Analysis Effects," *Academy of Management Review* 24 (1999), pp. 266–85.

94. A. Fanelli and V. Misangyi, "Bringing Out Charisma: CEO Charisma and External Stakeholders," *Academy of Management Review* 31 (2006), pp. 1049–61.

95. R. House and R. Aditya, "The Social Scientific Study of Leadership: Quo Vadis?" *Journal of Management* 23 (1997), pp. 409–73; and I. Wanasika, J. P. Howell, R. Littrell, and P. Dorfman, "Managerial Leadership and Culture in Sub-Saharan Africa," *Journal of World Business* 46, no. 2 (April 2011), pp. 234–41.

96. D. A. Waldman, G. G. Ramirez, R. J. House, and P. Puranam, "Does Leadership Matter? CEO Leadership Attributes and Profitability under Conditions of Perceived Environmental Uncertainty," *Academy of Management Journal* 44 (2001), pp. 134–43.

97. N. Paulsen, D. Maldonado, V. J. Callan, and O. Ayoko, "Charismatic Leadership, Change and Innovation in an R & D Organization," *Journal of Organizational Change Management* 22, no. 5 (2009), pp. 511–23; and B. Agle, N. Nagarajan, J. Sonnenfeld, and D. Srinivasan, "Does CEO Charisma Matter? An Empirical Analysis of the Relationships among Organizational Performance, Environmental Uncertainty, and Top Management Team Perceptions of CEO Charisma," *Academy of Management Journal* 49 (2006), pp. 161–74.

98. J. M. Howell and K. E. Hall-Merenda, "The Ties That Bind: The Impact of Leader-Member Exchange, Transformational and Transactional Leadership, and Distance on Predicting Follower Performance," *Journal of Applied Psychology* 84 (1999), pp. 680–94; and B. M. Bass, "Leadership: Good, Better, Best," *Organizational Dynamics,* Winter 1985, pp. 26–40.

99. R. Reiss, "Wisdom from a Dozen Transformative Leaders in 2019," *Forbes,* November 12, 2019, www.forbes.com.

100. "Clinton Honors 15 with Presidential Medals," *CNN,* January 15, 1998, www.cnn.com.

101. "Frances Hesselbein: President and CEO, The Frances Hesselbein Leadership Institute," Graduate School of Education, University of Pennsylvania, gse.upenn.edu, accessed April 9, 2020.

102. D. I. Jung and B. J. Avolio, "Effects of Leadership Style and Followers' Cultural Orientation on Performance in Group and Individual Task Conditions," *Academy of Management Journal* 42 (1999), pp. 208–18.

103. C. Clifford, "Inspirational Quotes from 100 Famous Business Leaders," *Entrepreneur,* May 2, 2016, www.entrepreneur.com.

104. B. M. Bass, *Leadership and Performance beyond Expectations* (New York: Free Press, 1985).

105. W. Bennis and B. Nanus, *Leaders* (New York: Harper & Row, 1985).

106. B. Bass, B. Avolio, and L. Goodheim, "Biography and the Assessment of Transformational Leadership at the World-Class Level," *Journal of Management* 13 (1987), pp. 7–20; and R. Sun and A. Henderson, "Transformational Leadership and Organizational Processes: Influencing Public Performance," *Public Administration Review* (2017), pp. 554–65.

107. D. Bigman, "Jim Collins: On Leadership in America," *Chief Executive,* November 7, 2017, www.chiefexecutive.net.

108. S. Biswas and A. Varma, "Antecedents of Employee Performance: An Empirical Investigation in India," *Employee Relations* 34, no. 2 (2012), pp. 177–92; B. L. Kirkman, G. Chen, J. L. Farh, Z. X. Chen, and K. B. Lowe, "Individual Power Distance Orientation and Follower Reactions to Transformational Leaders: A Cross-Level, Cross-Cultural Examination," *Academy of Management Journal* 52, no. 4 (August 2009), pp. 744–64; T. A. Judge and J. E. Bono, "Five-Factor Model of Personality and Transformational Leadership," *Journal of Applied Psychology* 85 (2000), pp. 751–65; and B. Bass, "Does the Transactional–Transformational Paradigm Transcend Organizational and National Boundaries?" *American Psychologist* 22 (1997), pp. 130–42.

109. S. J. Shin and J. Zhou, "Transformational Leadership, Conservation, and Creativity: Evidence from Korea," *Academy of Management Journal* 46 (2003), pp. 703–14.

110. R. Piccolo and J. Colquitt, "Transformational Leadership and Job Behaviors: The Mediating Role of Core Job Characteristics," *Academy of Management Journal* 49 (2006), pp. 327–40.

111. A. Colbert, A. Kristof-Brown, B. Bradley, and M. Barrick, "CEO Transformational Leadership: The Role of Goal Importance Congruence in Top Management Teams," *Academy of Management Journal* 51 (2008), pp. 81–96.

112. T. Dvir, D. Eden, B. Avolio, and B. Shamir, "Impact of Transformational Leadership on Follower Development and Performance: A Field Experiment," *Academy of Management Journal* 45 (2002), pp. 735–44.

113. B. M. Bass, *Transformational Leadership: Industry, Military, and Educational Impact* (Mahwah, NJ: Erlbaum, 1998).

114. G. Spreitzer and R. Quinn, "Empowering Middle Managers to Be Transformational Leaders," *Journal of Applied Behavioral Science* 32 (1996), pp. 237–61.

115. J. Collins, "Level 5 Leadership: The Triumph of Humility and Fierce Resolve," *Harvard Business Review* 1 (2005), pp. 136–46; J. Collins, "Level 5 Leadership," *Harvard Business Review* 1 (2001), pp. 66–76; J. Kline Harrison and M. William Clough, "Characteristics of 'State of the Art' Leaders: Productive Narcissism versus Emotional Intelligence and Level 5 Capabilities," *Social Science Journal* 43 (2006), pp. 287–92; and A. Ou, D. Waldman, and S. Peterson, "Do Humble CEOs Matter? An Examination of CEO Humility and Firm Outcomes," *Journal of Management* 44 (2018), pp. 1147–73.

116. D. Vera and M. Crossan, "Strategic Leadership and Organizational Learning," *Academy of Management Review* 29 (2004), pp. 222–40.

117. Company website, www.barrywehmiller.com; S. Leibs, "Putting People before the Bottom Line (and Still Making Money)," *Inc.,* May 2014, www.inc.com; and E. Herlzfeld, "Leadership Leads to Growth," *Official Board Markets,* April 11, 2009.

118. F. Luthans, *Organizational Behavior,* 10th ed. (New York: McGraw-Hill/Irwin, 2005).

119. B. M. Bass, "Thoughts and Plans," in *Cutting Edge: Leadership 2000,* eds. B. Kellerman and L. R. Matusak (College Park, MD: James MacGregor Burns Academy of Leadership, 2000), pp. 5–9; and B. Avolio, T. Wernsing, and W. Gardner, "Revisiting the Development and Validation of the Authentic Leadership," *Journal of Management* 44 (2018), pp. 399–411.

120. N. Turner, J. Barling, O. Epitropaki, V. Butcher, and C. Milner, "Transformational Leadership and Moral Reasoning," *Journal of Applied Psychology* 87 (2002), pp. 304–311.

121. B. M. Bass, "Thoughts and Plans," in *Cutting Edge: Leadership 2000,* eds. B. Kellerman and L. R. Matusak (College Park, MD: James MacGregor Burns Academy of Leadership, 2000).

122. W. Bennis, "The End of Leadership: Exemplary Leadership Is Impossible without Full Inclusion, Initiatives, and Cooperation of Followers," *Organizational Dynamics,* Summer 1999, pp. 71–79.

123. L. Spears, "Emerging Characteristics of Servant Leadership," in *Cutting Edge: Leadership 2000,* eds. B. Kellerman and L. Matusak (College Park, MD: James MacGregor Burns Academy of Leadership, 2000); L. Buchanan, "In Praise of Selflessness: Why the Best Leaders Are Servants," *Inc.,* May 2007, pp. 33–35; and J. Hoch, W. Bommer, J. Dulebohn, and D. Wu, "Do Ethical, Authentic, and Servant Leadership Explain Variance above and beyond Transformational Leadership? A Meta-Analysis, "*Journal of Management* 44 (2018), pp. 501–29.

124. D. van Dierendonck, "Servant Leadership: A Review and Synthesis," *Journal of Management* 37, no. 4 (July 2011), pp. 1228–61; M. Chiniara and K. Bentein, "Linking Servant Leadership to Individual Performance: Differentiating the Mediating Role of Autonomy, Competence and Relatedness Need Satisfaction," *Leadership Quarterly* 27 (2016), pp. 124–41; and R. Liden, S. Wayne, C. Liao, and J. Meuser, "Servant Leadership and Serving Culture: Influence on Individual and Unit Performance," *Academy of Management Journal* 57 (2014), pp. 1434–52.

125. J. Ciulla, "Bridge Leaders," in *Cutting Edge: Leadership 2000,* eds. B. Kellerman and L. Matusak (College Park, MD: James MacGregor Burns Academy of Leadership, 2000), pp. 25–28.

126. C. L. Pearce, "The Future of Leadership: Combining Vertical and Shared Leadership to Transform Knowledge Work," *Academy of Management Executive,* February 2004, pp. 47–57; D. Wang, D. Waldman, and Z. Zhang, "A Meta-Analysis of Shared Leadership and Team Effectiveness," *Journal of Applied Psychology* 99 (2014), pp. 181–98.

127. L. D'Innocenzo, J. Mathieu, and M.Kukenberger, "Meta-analysis of Different Forms of Shared Leadership-Team Performance Relations," *Journal of Management* 42 (2016), pp. 1964–91; V. Nicolaides, K. LaPort, T.Chen, A. Tomassetti, E. Weis, S. Zaccaro, and J. Cortina, "The Shared Leadership of Teams: A Meta-analyses of Proximal, Distal, and Moderating Relationships," *Leadership Quarterly* 25 (2014), pp. 923–42.

128. J. Carson, P. Tesluk, and J. Marrone, "Shared Leadership in Teams: An Investigation of Antecedent Conditions and Performance," *Academy of Management Journal* 50 (2007), pp. 1217–34.

129. M. M. Koerner, "Courage as Identity Work: Accounts of Workplace Courage," *Academy of Management Journal* 57 (2014), pp. 63–93.

130. M. Useem, "Thinking Big, Lending Small," *U.S. News and World Report,* October 22, 2006, www.usnews.com. Note: In 2006, Nancy Barry founded and became president of NBA-Enterprise Solutions to Poverty.

131. P. Block, *The Empowered Manager* (San Francisco: Jossey-Bass, 1991).

132. P. Block, *The Empowered Manager* (San Francisco: Jossey-Bass, 1991).

Motivating People

Learning Objectives

After studying Chapter 11, you should be able to

LO1 Understand principles for setting goals that motivate employees.

LO2 Give examples of how to reward good performance effectively.

LO3 Describe the key beliefs that affect people's motivation.

LO4 Explain how people's individual needs affect their behavior.

LO5 Define ways to create jobs that motivate.

LO6 Summarize how people assess and achieve fairness.

LO7 Identify causes and consequences of employee well-being.

JKstock/Shutterstock

motivation forces that energize, direct, and sustain a person's efforts

otivating employees is one of a manager's most important responsibilities, but it's also one of the most complex and complicated. Simply put, different things motivate different people. To be successful, organizations must tailor their policies and programs to best motivate the types of employees they need to attract and retain for the organization's success.

Take Google. The iconic organization thrives on innovation. It wants and needs a workforce that is able and willing to take chances and think outside the box. But to do so, employees need to know that they are supported and that it's okay to fail. That's why Google emphasizes "psychological safety." It fosters a culture built on asking questions, sharing ideas, and taking risks without feeling afraid of criticism or failure.[1] (We discuss this more in the next chapter.) Such a culture keeps its workforce motivated and innovations humming.

Zappos, the online retailer best known for its shoes, motivates its employees in part through a personalized peer-to-peer rewards program. One of its 10 core values is to "build a positive team and family spirit."[2] The peer-to-peer format promotes this value by providing employees the opportunity to share low-cost rewards with each other, ranging from parking spots to cash bonuses.[3]

Apple cofounder Steve Wozniak said of his company, known for its rewarding work environment, "Motivation is worth more than knowledge.... You can teach all the right things and that doesn't matter. If somebody is motivated and wants to do something ... it's emotional. That's the person that is probably going to go and find a way to actually get it done."[4]

> " Start where you are. Use what you have.
> Do what you can.
>
> —Arthur Ashe "

Understanding why people do the things they do on the job is not an easy task for a manager. *Predicting* their response to management's latest productivity program is harder yet. Fortunately, enough is known about motivation to give the thoughtful manager practical, effective techniques for increasing people's effort and performance.

Motivation refers to forces that energize, direct, and sustain a person's efforts. All behavior, except involuntary reflexes like eye blinks (which have little to do with management), is motivated. A highly motivated person will work hard to achieve performance goals. With adequate ability, understanding of the job, and access to the necessary resources, such a person will be highly productive.

Managers must know what behaviors they want to motivate people to exhibit. Although productive people do a seemingly limitless number of things, most of the important activities can be grouped into five general categories:[5]

1. Join the organization.

2. Remain in the organization.

3. Come to work regularly.

4. Perform—that is, work hard to achieve high *output* (productivity) and high *quality.*

5. Exhibit good citizenship by being committed and performing above and beyond the call of duty to help the company.

On the first three points, you should reject the common notion that loyalty is dead and accept the challenge of creating an environment that will attract and energize people so that they commit to the organization.[6] The importance of citizenship behaviors may be less obvious than sheer productive output, but these behaviors help the organization function smoothly. They also make managers' lives easier.

Many ideas have been proposed to help managers motivate people to engage in these constructive behaviors. The most useful of these ideas are described in the following pages. We start with the most fundamental *processes* that influence the motivation of all people. These processes—described by goal-setting, reinforcement, and expectancy theories—suggest actions for managers to take. Then we discuss the *content* of what people want and need from work, how individuals differ from one another, and how understanding people's needs leads to prescriptions for designing motivating jobs and empowering people to perform at the highest possible levels. Finally, we discuss the most important beliefs and perceptions about fairness that people hold toward their work and the implications for motivation.

LO1 Understand principles for setting goals that motivate employees.

1 | SETTING GOALS

Providing work-related goals is an extremely effective way to stimulate motivation. In fact, it is perhaps the most important, valid, and useful approach to motivating performance.

Goal-setting theory states that people have conscious goals that energize them and direct their thoughts and behaviors toward a particular end.[7] Keeping in mind the principle that goals motivate, managers set goals for employees or collaborate with them on goal setting.

The same rules apply to start-up entrepreneurs. Assume you're about to launch a food ordering and delivery app to compete with established brands like Grubhub, DoorDash and Uber Eats. You and your team might set first-year goals like designing a user-friendly app, creating an efficient business model, hiring reliable drivers to deliver the food to customers, and adding enough new repeating customers to hit the breakeven point.

1.1 | Well-Crafted Goals Are Highly Motivating

As illustrated in Exhibit 11.1, motivational goals share four characteristics. The most powerful goals are *meaningful;* purposes that appeal to people's "higher" values add extra motivating power.[9] New Belgium Brewing is dedicated to continuously improving its sustainability initiatives. Honest Tea sells organic and natural beverages but also wants to improve people's health and well-being. Chick-fil-A has religious commitments that appeal to many of its customers and employees. Huntsman Chemical has goals of relieving human suffering—it sponsors cancer research and treatment through its Cancer Institute and hospitals.

Meaningful goals also may be based on data about competitors; exceeding competitors' performance can stoke people's competitive spirit and desire to succeed in the marketplace.[10]

Did You KNOW?

According to a Gallup poll, the top three reasons why employees quit their jobs are lack of career advancement opportunities, low pay/benefits, and poor job fit.[8]

This point is not just about the values companies espouse and the lofty goals they pursue; it's also about leadership at a more personal level. Compared with followers of transactional leaders, followers of transformational leaders (recall Chapter 10) view their work as more important and as highly congruent with their personal goals.[11]

Goals also should be *acceptable* to employees. This means, among other things, that they should not conflict with people's personal values and that people should have reasons to pursue the goals. Allowing people to participate in setting their work goals—as opposed to the boss setting goals for them—tends to generate goals that people accept and pursue willingly.

Acceptable, maximally motivating goals are *challenging but attainable.* They should be high enough to inspire better performance but not so high that people can never reach them. Google uses an Objectives and Key Results (OKR) goal-setting framework that includes defining goals, tracking progress, and evaluating outcomes. When employees reach all of their objectives, managers encourage them to set more ambitious goals.[12]

Ideal goals do not merely exhort employees in general terms to improve performance and start doing their best. Instead goals should be *specific and quantifiable,* like Toyota's goal of making half its global revenue from electric vehicles by 2025.[13] Bringing these principles together, Microsoft and others motivate with goals that are SMART: specific, measurable, achievable, results based, and time-specific.[14]

1.2 | Stretch Goals Help Employees Reach New Heights

Some firms today set **stretch goals**—targets that are exceptionally demanding and novel,

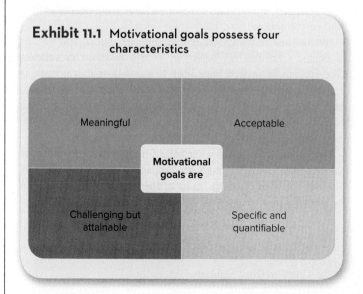

Exhibit 11.1 Motivational goals possess four characteristics

Meaningful

Acceptable

Motivational goals are

Challenging but attainable

Specific and quantifiable

The Photo Works/Alamy Stock Photo

and that some people would never even think of.[15] There are two types of stretch goals:[16]

1. Vertical stretch goals are aligned with current activities, including productivity and financial results.

2. Horizontal stretch goals involve people's professional development, such as attempting and learning new, difficult things.

Impossible though stretch goals may seem to some, they often are, in fact, attainable.

Stretch goals can shift people away from mediocrity and toward major achievement. But if employees try in good faith yet don't meet a stretch goal, don't punish them—remember how difficult these goals are! Base your assessment on how much performance has improved, how the performance compares with that of others, and how much progress has been made.[17]

1.3 | Goal Setting Needs Careful Managing

Goal setting is an extraordinarily powerful management technique. But even specific, challenging, attainable goals work better under some conditions than others. If people lack relevant ability and knowledge, managers might get better results simply by urging them to do their best or setting a goal to learn rather than a goal to achieve a specific performance level.[18] Individual performance goals can be dysfunctional if people work in a group and cooperation among team members is essential to group performance.[19] Individualized goals can create competition and reduce cooperation. If cooperation is important, performance goals should be established *for the team.*

Goals can generate manipulative game playing and unethical behavior.[20] People sometimes find ingenious ways to set easy goals and convince their bosses that they are difficult.[21] Or they may find ways to meet goals simply to receive a reward, without necessarily contributing to the company's success.

Eric Foss, former CEO of Aramark, allegedly decided to cancel bonuses earned by frontline managers in 2018 due to the company missing a profit target set by the board of directors. The managers brought a lawsuit charging that Foss failed to inform them at the start of the fiscal year that the target could impact bonuses. John Zillmer, who replaced Foss as CEO, settled the lawsuit for $21 million.[22]

Another familiar example comes from the pages of financial reports. Some executives have mastered the art of "earnings management"—precisely meeting Wall Street analysts' earnings estimates or beating them by a single penny.[23] The media trumpet, and investors reward, the company that meets or beats the estimates. People sometimes meet this goal by either manipulating the numbers or initiating whispering campaigns to persuade analysts to lower their estimates, making them more attainable. The marketplace wants short-term, quarterly performance, but long-term viability is ultimately more important to a company's success.

It is important *not* to establish a single productivity goal if there are other important dimensions of performance.[24] If the acquisition of knowledge and skills is important, you can also set a specific and challenging learning goal like "identify 10 ways to develop relationships with users of our products." Productivity

study tip 11

Get motivated by setting mini-goals

Try setting mini-goals on a weekly basis to help you stay motivated and get your work done on time. Over the weekend, review the course syllabus and make a to-do list of what needs to get done during the upcoming week. Update your planner with any important due dates. Next, each time you sit down for a study session, take a few goals from your list that you think you can complete, like reading a chapter, completing an online Connect assignment, and so forth. As you complete each task, place a checkmark next to it or cross it off the list. Setting specific, challenging, but attainable study goals (and keeping track of your progress) will help you stay motivated and perform better.

Pixtal/age fotostock

Sustaining for Tomorrow

Stonyfield Organic Motivates Through Its Mission

Samuel and Louise Kaymen founded The Rural Education Center (TREC) in 1979 at Stonyfield Farm in Wilton, New Hampshire. Relying on philanthropy for much of its financial support, the nonprofit center taught rural and homesteading skills to hundreds of students. To earn revenue for the center, the Kaymens expanded the dairy herd to produce and sell more yogurt. Demand for organic yogurt exploded, and what started as a small educational initiative grew into one of the nation's most recognized organic yogurt brands: Stonyfield.

Stonyfield's mission is inspired by its educational farming roots: "healthy food, healthy people, and a healthy planet." Stonyfield's mission motivated the company to establish a "Profits for the Planet" program, which provides funding for four primary categories:

- Promoting family farming.
- Slowing or reversing climate change.
- Engaging in organic agriculture and reducing toxins in the food supply.
- Avoiding adverse health effects of environmental and agricultural practices.

Today, Stonyfield's plant engineers implement ways to get it closer to 100 percent renewable energy use. Recently the company invested $10 million to create an open-source platform to help share ideas among industry and government researchers to develop new sustainable farming practices. The platform is called OpenTEAM, and it's the first open-source platform of its kind.

Britt Lundgren is the Director of Organic and Sustainable Agriculture at Stonyfield Farm. Lundgren believes that farmers are using many good sustainable tools and strategies, but they're not being aggregated to create comprehensive solutions. Lundgren hopes this "smart farming" open platform will jump-start the process.

For nearly 40 years, Stonyfield's founders and employees have been motivated by the company's mission to do well by doing good.

Cofounder and chairman of Stonyfield Organic, Gary Hirshberg (left), believes in socially and environmentally responsible business.
Brian Ach/Chelsea's Table/AP Images

Discussion Questions

- What factors motivated Stonyfield to switch its focus from operating The Rural Education Center to becoming full-time manufacturers of organic yogurt?
- Stonyfield's mission inspires and motivates the company's leaders, employees, and suppliers to behave in ways that support its socially and environmentally friendly business practices. What challenges to maintaining this "green" business strategy might the firm face in coming years?

Sources: Stonyfield website, "Our Story," https://www.stonyfield.com/our-story/history, accessed April 11, 2020; Stonyfield website, "Sponsorship," https://www.stonyfield.com/contact-us/donation-request, accessed April 11, 2020; and "Stonyfield Launches OpenTEAM Platform to Promote Sustainable Farming," Food Tank, September 2019, https://foodtank.com/news/2019/09/stonyfield-launches-openteam-platform-to-promote-sustainable-farming.

goals will likely enhance productivity, but they may also cause employees to neglect other areas, such as learning, tackling new projects, or developing creative solutions to job-related problems. A manager who wants to motivate creativity can establish creativity goals along with productivity goals for individuals or for brainstorming teams.[25]

1.4 | Set Your Own Goals, Too

Goal setting works for yourself as well—it's a powerful tool for self-management. Set goals for yourself; don't just try hard or hope for the best. Create a statement of purpose for yourself comprising an inspiring distant vision, a mid-distant goal along the way, and near-term objectives to start working on immediately.[26] So if you are going into business, you might articulate your goal for the type of businessperson you want to be in five years, the types of jobs that could create the opportunities and teach you what you need to know to become that businessperson, and the specific schoolwork and job search activities that can get you moving in those directions. On the job, apply this chapter's goal-setting advice to yourself.

2 | REINFORCING PERFORMANCE

Goals are universal motivators. So are the processes of reinforcement described in this section. In 1911 psychologist Edward Thorndike formulated the **law of effect**: Behavior that is followed by positive consequences probably will be repeated.[27] This powerful law of behavior laid the foundation for countless investigations into the effects of the positive consequences, called **reinforcers**, that motivate behavior. **Organizational behavior modification** attempts to influence people's behavior and improve performance[28] by systematically managing work conditions and the consequences of people's actions.

2.1 | Behavior Has Consequences

Four key consequences of behavior either encourage or discourage people's behavior (see Exhibit 11.2):

1. **Positive reinforcement**—applying a consequence that increases the likelihood that the person will repeat the behavior that led to it. Examples of positive reinforcers include compliments, favorable performance evaluations, and pay raises. Jim Goodnight, CEO of the $3.3 billion business analytics software company SAS, motivates people to stay with the company by providing a great workplace culture with generous benefits, including a free onsite health care center (with doctors), a free recreation and fitness center, subsidized child care, paid time off for volunteering, and a department dedicated to helping employees maintain work–life balance.[29]

2. **Negative reinforcement**—removing or withholding an undesirable consequence. Teams at Whole Foods vote to decide whether a new hire who has completed a 30- to 90-day probationary period can remain on the team. New hires require a two-thirds positive vote from team members.[30] For those new hires who earn their teammates' approval, the negative reinforcer (probationary status) is removed.

law of effect a law formulated by Edward Thorndike in 1911 stating that behavior that is followed by positive consequences will likely be repeated

reinforcers positive consequences that motivate behavior

organizational behavior modification (OB MOD) the application of reinforcement theory in organizational settings

positive reinforcement applying a consequence that increases the likelihood of a person repeating the behavior that led to it

negative reinforcement removing or withholding an undesirable consequence

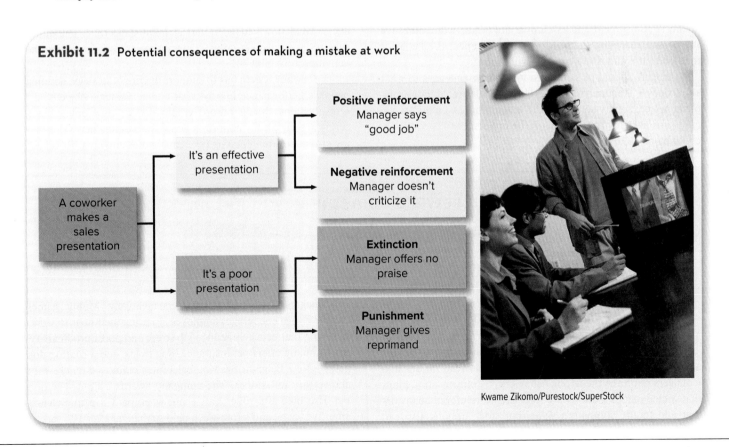

Exhibit 11.2 Potential consequences of making a mistake at work

A coworker makes a sales presentation

→ It's an effective presentation
  → **Positive reinforcement** Manager says "good job"
  → **Negative reinforcement** Manager doesn't criticize it

→ It's a poor presentation
  → **Extinction** Manager offers no praise
  → **Punishment** Manager gives reprimand

Kwame Zikomo/Purestock/SuperStock

punishment administering an aversive consequence

extinction withdrawing or failing to provide a reinforcing consequence

3. **Punishment**—administering an aversive consequence. Examples include criticizing an employee, assigning an unappealing task, reducing work hours, and sending a worker home without pay. Negative reinforcement can involve the *threat* of punishment, with the understanding that satisfactory performance will result in the withholding of punishment. Managers use punishment when they think it is warranted, and they usually concern themselves with following company policy and procedure.[31]

4. **Extinction**—withdrawing or failing to provide a reinforcing consequence. When this occurs, motivation is reduced, and the behavior is *extinguished,* or eliminated. Managers may unintentionally extinguish desired behaviors by not giving a compliment for a job well done, forgetting to say thank you for a favor, setting impossible performance goals so that the person never experiences success, and so on. Extinction can work on undesirable behaviors, too. The manager might ignore long-winded comments during a meeting or fail to respond to unimportant emails in the hope that the lack of feedback will discourage the employee from continuing.

The first two consequences, positive and negative reinforcement, are positive for the person receiving them—the person either gains something or avoids something negative. As a result, the person who experiences them will be motivated to behave in the ways that led to the reinforcement. The last two consequences, punishment and extinction, are negative outcomes for the person receiving them: Motivation to repeat the behavior that led to the undesirable results will drop.

Managers should be careful to match consequences to what employees will actually find desirable or undesirable. For example, a project supervisor upset with an employee who makes too many mistakes might take him off the project. But the employee could be pleased.

Exhibit 11.3	What should (and shouldn't) be rewarded

Solid solutions instead of quick fixes.
Risk taking instead of risk avoiding.
Applied creativity instead of mindless conformity.
Decisive action instead of paralysis by analysis.
Smart work instead of busywork.
Simplification instead of needless complication.
Quietly effective behavior instead of squeaky wheels.
Quality work instead of fast work.
Loyalty instead of turnover.
Working together instead of working against.

reinforce decisions that artificially deliver short-term gains in stock prices, even if they hurt the company in the long run.

Sometimes employees are reinforced with admiration and positive performance evaluations for multitasking—say, typing emails while on the phone or checking text messages during meetings. This behavior may look efficient and send a signal that the employee is busy and valuable, but multitasking slows the brain's efficiency and causes errors.[34] Scans of brain activity show that the brain is not able to concentrate on two tasks at once; it needs time to switch among activities. So managers who praise the hard work of multitaskers may be reinforcing inefficiency and failure to think deeply.

To use reinforcement effectively, managers must identify which kinds of behaviors they reinforce and which they discourage. A well-known adage in management states that "The things that get rewarded get done." One author advises rewarding the activities in Exhibit 11.3.[35]

The reward system has to support the firm's strategy, defining people's performance in ways that pursue strategic objectives.[36] Organizations should reward employees for developing themselves in strategically important ways—for building new skills that are critical to strengthening core capabilities and creating value.

> "Typically, if you reward something, you get more of it. You punish something, you get less of it."
>
> —Daniel H. Pink

2.2 | Be Careful What You Reinforce

You've learned about the positive effects of a transformational leadership style, but giving rewards to high-performing people also is essential.[32] Unfortunately, sometimes organizations and managers reinforce the wrong behaviors.[33] Compensation plans that include stock options are intended to reinforce behaviors that add to the company's value, but stock options also can

Managers should use reinforcers creatively. Mobile games creator Zynga encourages employees to bring their dogs to work. Believing that pets help reduce job stress and boost productivity, the company offers pet insurance, dog treats, and a rooftop dog park.[37] New Belgium Brewing celebrates employee tenure with anniversary milestones. The company awards a limited-edition Fat Tire bike after one year, a one-week paid trip to Belgium after five years, and a four-week paid sabbatical after 10 years.[38]

Innovative managers use nonmonetary rewards, including intellectual challenge, greater responsibility, autonomy, recognition, flexible benefits, and greater influence over decisions. A study found that nearly three-quarters of early-career employees prefer spending money on experiences rather than material goods.[39] The following experiences appealed to younger employees: attending professional conferences, earning an extra vacation day, and going on outings with peers to breweries, sporting events, or adventure parks.[40] These and other rewards for high-performing employees, when creatively devised and applied, can continue to motivate when pay and promotions are scarce.

2.3 | Should You Punish Mistakes?

How a manager reacts to people's mistakes has a big impact on motivation. Punishment is sometimes appropriate, as when people violate the law, ethical standards, important safety rules, or standards of interpersonal treatment, or when they fail to attend or perform like a slacker. But sometimes managers punish people when they shouldn't—when poor performance isn't the person's fault or when managers take out their frustrations on the wrong people.

Managers who overuse punishment or use it inappropriately create a climate of fear in the workplace.[41] Fear causes people to focus on the short term, sometimes creating problems in the longer run. Fear also creates a focus on oneself, rather than on the group and the organization. B. Joseph White, president emeritus of the University of Illinois, recalls consulting for a high-tech entrepreneur who heard a manager present a proposal and responded with brutal criticism: "That's the . . . stupidest idea I ever heard in my life. I'm disappointed in you." According to White, this talented manager was so upset she never again felt fully able to contribute.[42]

To avoid such damage, the key is how to think about and handle mistakes. Recognize that everyone makes mistakes and that mistakes can be dealt with constructively by discussing

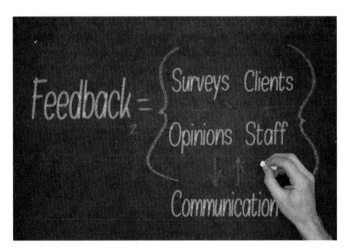

● It is increasingly common for organizations to encourage employees to request feedback about their performance and behavior from fellow employees. Duncan Andison/Shutterstock

and learning from them.[43] Don't punish, but praise people who deliver bad news to their bosses. Treat failure to act when needed as a failure, but don't punish unsuccessful, good-faith efforts. If you're a leader, talk about your mistakes with your people, and show how you learned from them. Give people second chances, and maybe third chances. Encourage people to try new things, and don't punish them if what they try doesn't work out.

2.4 | Feedback Is Essential Reinforcement

Most managers don't provide enough useful feedback, and most people don't receive or ask for feedback enough.[44] As a manager, you should consider all potential causes of poor performance, pay full attention when employees ask for feedback or want to discuss performance issues, and give feedback according to the guidelines you read about in Chapter 8.

Feedback can be offered in many ways.[45] Customers sometimes give feedback directly; you also can request customer feedback and give it to the employee. A manufacturing firm can put the phone number or website of the production team on the product so that customers can contact the team directly. Managers should conduct performance appraisals as discussed in Chapter 8. And bosses should give regular, ongoing feedback—it helps correct problems immediately, provides immediate reinforcement for good work, and prevents surprises when the formal review comes.

For yourself, try not to be afraid of receiving feedback; instead, you should actively seek it. When you get feedback, don't ignore it. Try to avoid negative emotions like anger, hurt, defensiveness, or resignation. Think "It's up to me to get the feedback I need; I need to know these things about my performance and behavior; learning about myself will help me identify needs and create new opportunities; it serves my interest best to know rather than not know; taking initiative on this gives me more power and influence over my career."[46]

LO3 Describe the key beliefs that affect people's motivation.

3 | PERFORMANCE-RELATED BELIEFS

In contrast to reinforcement theory, which describes the processes by which factors in the work environment affect people's behavior, expectancy theory considers some of the cognitive processes that go on in people's heads. According to expectancy theory, the person's work *efforts* lead to some level of

expectancy employees' perception of the likelihood that their efforts will enable them to attain their performance goals

outcome a consequence a person receives for his or her performance

instrumentality the perceived likelihood that performance will be followed by a particular outcome

valence the value an outcome holds for the person contemplating it

performance.[47] Then performance results in one or more *outcomes* for the person. This process is shown in Exhibit 11.4. People develop two important kinds of beliefs linking these three events:

1. *Expectancy,* which links effort to performance.

2. *Instrumentality,* which links performance to outcomes.

3.1 | If You Try Hard, Will You Succeed?

The first belief, **expectancy**, is people's perceived likelihood that their efforts will enable them to attain their performance goals. An expectancy can be high (up to 100 percent), such as when a student is confident that if she studies hard, she can get a good grade on the final exam. An expectancy can also be low (down to a 0 percent likelihood), such as when a suitor is convinced that his dream date will never go out with him.

All else equal, high expectancies create higher motivation than do low expectancies. In the preceding examples, the student is more likely to study hard for the exam than the suitor is to pursue the dream date, even though both want their respective outcomes.

Expectancies can vary among individuals, even in the same situation. For example, a sales manager might initiate a competition in which the top salesperson wins a free trip to the Bahamas. In such cases, the few top people, who have performed well in the past, will be more motivated by the contest than will the historically average and below-average performers. The top people will have higher expectancies—stronger beliefs that their efforts can help them turn in the top performance.

3.2 | If You Succeed, Will You Be Rewarded?

The example about the sales contest illustrates how performance results in some kind of **outcome**, or consequence, for the person. Actually, it often results in several outcomes. For example, turning in the best sales performance could lead to (1) a competitive victory, (2) the free trip to Hawaii, (3) feelings of achievement, (4) recognition from the boss, (5) prestige throughout the company, and (6) resentment from other salespeople.

But how certain is it that performance will result in all of those outcomes? Will winning the contest really generate resentment? Will it really lead to increased status?

These questions address the second key belief described by expectancy theory: instrumentality.[48] **Instrumentality** is the perceived likelihood that performance will be followed by a particular outcome. Like expectancies, instrumentalities can be high (up to 100 percent) or low (approaching 0 percent). For example, you can be fully confident that if you get favorable customer reviews, you'll get a promotion, or you can feel that no matter what your customers say, the promotion will go to someone else.

Each outcome has an associated valence. **Valence** is the value the person places on the outcome. Valences can be positive, as a Hawaiian vacation would be for most people, or negative, as in the case of the other salespeople's resentment.

3.3 | All Three Beliefs Must Be High

For motivation to be high, all three beliefs—expectancy, instrumentalities, and the total valence of all outcomes—must be high. A person will *not* be highly motivated if any of the following conditions exist:

- He believes he can't perform well enough to achieve the positive outcomes that he knows the company provides to good performers (high valence and high instrumentality but low expectancy).

- She knows she can do the job and is fairly certain what the ultimate outcomes will be (say, a promotion and a transfer). However, she doesn't want those outcomes or believes other, negative outcomes outweigh the positive (high expectancy and high instrumentality but low valence).

- He knows he can do the job and wants several important outcomes (a favorable performance review, a raise, and a

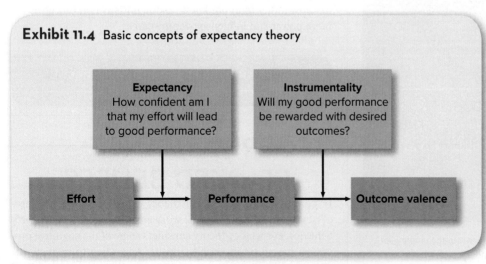

Exhibit 11.4 Basic concepts of expectancy theory

Expectancy
How confident am I that my effort will lead to good performance?

Instrumentality
Will my good performance be rewarded with desired outcomes?

Effort → Performance → Outcome valence

Source: Adapted from D. Organ and T. Bateman, *Organizational Behavior* 4th ed., McGraw-Hill.

promotion). But he believes that no matter how well he performs, the outcomes will not be forthcoming (high expectancy and positive valences but low instrumentality).

3.4 | Expectancy Theory Identifies Leverage Points

Expectancy theory helps the manager zero in on key leverage points for influencing motivation. Three implications are crucial:

1. *Increase expectancies.* Provide a work environment that facilitates good performance, and set realistically attainable performance goals. Provide training, support, required resources, and encouragement so that people are confident they can perform at the expected levels. Recall that charismatic leaders excel at boosting their followers' confidence.

2. *Identify positively valent outcomes.* Understand what people want to get out of work. Think about what their

● Sometimes employees can participate in yoga classes and other wellness activities. To manage rising health care costs, companies sometimes offer financial incentives to employees who pursue healthier lifestyles. Ryan McVay/Getty Images

jobs do and do not (but could) provide them. Consider how people may differ in the valences they assign to outcomes. Know the need theories of motivation, described in the next section, and their implications for identifying important outcomes.

3. *Make performance instrumental toward positive outcomes.* Ensure that good performance is followed by personal recognition and praise, favorable performance reviews, pay increases, and other positive results. The way you emphasize instrumentality may need to be tailored to employees' locus of control. For people who have an external locus of control, tending to attribute results to luck or fate, you may need to reinforce behaviors (more than outcomes) frequently so that they see a connection between what they do and what you reward. It is useful to realize, too, that bosses usually provide (or withhold) rewards, but others do so as well.[49] Peers, direct reports, customers, and others can offer compliments, help, and praise.

Many companies, trying to manage rising health care costs, use monetary incentives to motivate their employees to live healthier lives. At least in the short run, incentives can motivate employees to take their medications; complete health assessments; and participate in weight loss, smoking cessation, or cholesterol reduction programs. One company found that it saved about three dollars for every dollar spent on employee medical and absenteeism costs.[50] Wellness can be a win–win for employees, who become healthier, and their employers, who can use the savings in health-related costs to invest in their businesses.[51]

> **LO4** Explain how people's individual needs affect their behavior.

4 | UNDERSTANDING PEOPLE'S NEEDS

So far, we have described *processes* underlying motivation. The manager who appropriately applies goal-setting, reinforcement, and expectancy theories is creating essential motivating elements in the work environment. But motivation also is affected by characteristics of the person. The second type of motivation theory, *content theory,* identifies the needs that people want to satisfy. People have different needs energizing and motivating them toward different goals and outcomes. The extent to which and the ways in which a person's needs are met or not met at work affect his or her behavior on the job.

The most important theories describing the content of people's needs are Maslow's need hierarchy, Alderfer's ERG theory, and McClelland's needs.

4.1 | Maslow Arranged Needs in a Hierarchy

Abraham Maslow organized five major types of human needs into a hierarchy, as shown in Exhibit 11.5.[52] The **need hierarchy** suggested that when no needs are satisfied—imagine being stranded alone on a deserted island—people will first pursue their lowest-level needs, prioritizing from bottom to top. The needs, in ascending order, are as follows:

1. *Physiological*—food, water, sex, and shelter.

2. *Safety or security*—protection against threat and deprivation.

3. *Social*—friendship, affection, belonging, and love.

4. *Esteem*—independence, achievement, freedom, status, recognition, and self-esteem.

5. *Self-actualization*—realizing one's full potential; becoming everything one is capable of being.

Exhibit 11.5 A hierarchy of human needs

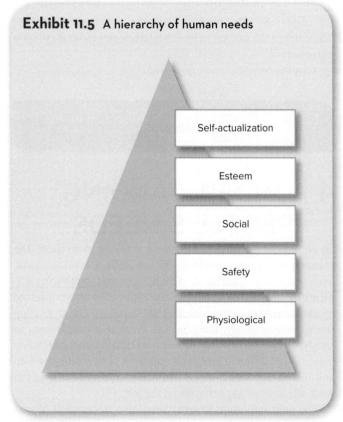

Source: D. Organ and T. Bateman, *Organizational Behavior,* 4th ed. (New York: McGraw-Hill, 1991).

You might recognize this famous pyramid from elsewhere, although Maslow himself did not present his theory in this fashion.[53] Maslow understood that for people not dealing with day-to-day survival, all needs can motivate, sometimes separately and other times simultaneously. In the modern workplace, physiological and safety needs generally are well satisfied, making social, esteem, and self-actualization needs important. But safety issues are still very important in manufacturing, mining, health care, and other work environments.

Maslow's hierarchy is a simplistic and not altogether accurate theory of human motivation.[54] For example, not everyone progresses through the five needs in hierarchical order. But Maslow made three important contributions. First, he identified important need categories, which can help managers create effective positive outcomes. Second, it is helpful to think of two general levels of needs, in which lower-level needs must be satisfied before higher-level needs become important. Third, Maslow alerted managers to the importance of personal growth and self-actualization.

Self-actualization is the best-known concept arising from this theory. According to Maslow, the average person is only 10 percent self-actualized. In other words, most of us are living and working with a large untapped reservoir of potential. The implication is clear: Managers should help create a work environment that provides training, resources, autonomy, responsibilities, and challenging assignments. This type of environment gives people a chance to use their skills and abilities creatively and allows them to achieve more of their full potential.

Thus, managers should treat people not merely as a cost to be controlled but as an asset to be developed.[55] Many companies have programs that offer their people personal and career growth experiences. Enterprise prepares its employees for high-level management positions by assigning them to the company's Management Training Program. Trainees learn customer service, sales, operations, and finance skills while managing Enterprise locations.[56]

4.2 | Alderfer Identified Three Work-Related Needs

A theory of human needs that is more advanced than Maslow's is Alderfer's ERG theory.[57] Maslow's theory has general applicability, but Alderfer aims expressly at understanding people's needs at work. **ERG theory** postulates that three sets of needs can operate simultaneously:

1. *Existence* needs are all material and physiological desires.

2. *Relatedness* needs involve relationships with other people and are satisfied through the process of mutually sharing thoughts and feelings.

3. *Growth* needs motivate people to productively or creatively change themselves or their environment. Satisfaction of the growth needs comes from fully utilizing personal capacities and developing new capacities.

● Starbucks offers U.S. employees who are working at least 20 hours per week development opportunities through its tuition coverage program with Arizona State University. Sorbis/Shutterstock

What similarities do you see between Alderfer's and Maslow's needs? Roughly speaking, existence needs subsume physiological and security needs, relatedness needs are similar to social and esteem needs, and growth needs correspond to self-actualization. ERG theory proposes that several different needs can be operating at once. While Maslow said that self-actualization is important to people only after other sets of needs are satisfied, for Alderfer, people—particularly working people in our postindustrial society—can be motivated to satisfy existence, relatedness, and growth needs at the same time.

Companies can use this knowledge as they design compensation or benefits programs. Kahler Slater, a 135-employee architecture and design firm, faced economic pressures that caused a rollback of employee benefits, including health care coverage. To tailor the cutbacks to its staff, company principals asked employees exactly which benefits meant the most to them. Then the managers came up with a package that worked for all.

One of the most valued benefits was paid time off, and employees gave up less important perks like free pastries in the company office. They also contributed more to their health care coverage. To boost morale and help build camaraderie, the owners reduced their own salaries by 25 percent and began hosting after-work social gatherings. They also offered employees more options for working from home to help them manage their schedules and conflicts. Trusting their employees in this way

helped Kahler Slater earn a spot on Great Place to Work's Best Workplaces lists for several years, including 2019.[58]

Maslow's theory is better known to American managers than Alderfer's, but ERG theory has more research support.[59] Both have practical value in that they remind managers of the types of outcomes that can be used to motivate people. Regardless of whether a manager prefers the Maslow or the Alderfer theory, he or she can motivate people by helping them satisfy their needs, particularly by offering opportunities for self-actualization and growth.

4.3 | McClelland Said Managers Seek Achievement, Affiliation, and Power

David McClelland identified additional basic needs that motivate people. According to McClelland, three needs are most relevant to managers:[61]

1. The need for *achievement*—a strong orientation toward accomplishment and an obsession with success and goal attainment. Most managers and entrepreneurs in the United States have high levels of this need and like to see it in their employees.

2. The need for *affiliation*—a strong desire to be liked by other people. Individuals who have high levels of this need are oriented toward getting along with others and may be less concerned with achieving at high levels.

3. The need for *power*—a desire to influence or control other people. This need can be a negative force (termed *personalized power*) if it is expressed through aggressively manipulating and exploiting others. People high on the personalized-power need want power purely for the pursuit of their own goals. But the need for power also can be a positive motive, called *socialized power,* which is channeled toward people, organizations, and societies.

Different needs predominate for different people. Now that you have read about these needs, think about yourself—which one(s) is most and least important to you?

Low need for affiliation and moderate to high need for power are associated with managerial success for both higher- and lower-level managers.[62] One reason the need for affiliation is not necessary for leadership success is that managers high on this need have difficulty making tough but necessary decisions that will upset some people.

> ## You will either step forward into growth or you will step back into safety.
>
> —Abraham Maslow[60]

extrinsic reward reward given to a person by the boss, the company, or some other person

intrinsic reward reward a worker derives directly from performing the job itself

LO5 Define ways to create jobs that motivate.

4.4 | Do Need Theories Apply Internationally?

How do the need theories apply abroad?[63] Although managers in the United States care most strongly about achievement, esteem, and self-actualization, managers in Greece and Japan are motivated more by security. Social needs are most important in Sweden, Norway, and Denmark. "Doing your own thing"—the phrase from the 1960s that describes an American culture oriented toward self-actualization—is not even translatable into Chinese. Being from a collectivist culture, the Chinese are more likely to value belongingness.[64] "Achievement," too, is difficult to translate into most other languages. Researchers in France, Japan, and Sweden would have been unlikely to even conceive of McClelland's achievement motive because people from those countries are more group-oriented (collectivism) than individually oriented.

Clearly, achievement, growth, and self-actualization are profoundly important in the United States, Canada, and Great Britain. But these needs are not universally important. Every manager must remember that need importance varies from country to country and that people may not be motivated by the same needs. One study found that employees in many countries are highly engaged at companies that have strong leadership, work–life balance, a good reputation, and opportunities for employees to contribute, while another found variations from country to country.[65] Employees in Canada were attracted by competitive pay, work–life balance, and opportunities for advancement; workers in Germany by autonomy; in Japan by high-quality coworkers; in the Netherlands by a collaborative work environment; and in the United States by competitive health benefits. Generally, no single way is best, and managers can customize their approaches by considering how individuals differ.[66]

5 | DESIGNING JOBS THAT MOTIVATE

Here's an example of a company that gave a performance "reward" that didn't motivate. One of Mary Kay Ash's former employers gave her a sales award: a flounder fishing light. Unfortunately, she doesn't fish. Fortunately, she later was able to design her own organization, Mary Kay Cosmetics, around two kinds of motivators that *mattered* to her people.[67]

Work can be rewarding in two vital ways:[68]

1. Extrinsic rewards are given to people by the boss, the company, or some other person. Examples include pay, benefits, business class airline travel, or a large office.

2. An intrinsic reward is one that the person derives directly from performing the job itself. This occurs when you feel a sense of accomplishment after completing a challenging task.

An interesting project, an intriguing subject that is fun to study, a completed sale, and the discovery of the perfect solution to a difficult problem all can give people the feeling that they have done something well. This is the essence of the motivation that comes from intrinsic rewards.

Intrinsic rewards are essential to the motivation underlying creativity.[69] A challenging problem, a chance to create something new, and work that is exciting can provide intrinsic motivation that inspires people to devote their time and energy. So do managers who allow people some freedom to pursue the tasks that interest them most. The opposite situations result in routine, habitual behaviors that interfere with creativity.[70] In one study, researchers found that employees in manufacturing facilities initiated more applications for patents, made more novel and useful suggestions, and were rated by their managers as more creative when their jobs were challenging and their managers did not control their activities closely.[71]

Take Charge of Your Career

Are you motivated to find a job you love?

Organizations invest time and resources into recruiting and retaining a hard-working workforce. But there's only so much organizations can do to motivate their employees. Most job postings tell you what extrinsic rewards you can expect, but no posting can tell you how much you will actually enjoy the work if you are hired.

To find a job you love, you need to discover what truly motivates you. After all, you can be lavished with amazing extrinsic rewards, but it doesn't mean you'll be happy doing the work. To be satisfied in a career, you need to be *intrinsically* motivated as well—and you can shape this. Here are some tips to finding a job you love:

1. Before searching for jobs, examine your internal motivations. Think about what really drives you. People who reflexively say "money" may not be thinking hard enough. Once you figure out what brings you joy and satisfaction and is personally meaningful to you, you can start aligning your self-discoveries to organizations that value what you do (not the other way around). You may want to check out online self-assessments for personal motivation.

2. Make a targeted employer list. Look closely at all aspects of the company, from its customer base to its corporate culture. This research will help you judge whether the employers align with your motivational values.

3. Don't just be an interviewee; be an interviewer. Most job seekers are prepared to answer questions, but many aren't prepared to ask them. Don't be afraid to ask about what's most important to you. The more you know, the better you can assess how well the employer fits your needs.

No matter what job you land, take time figuring out how best to motivate yourself to both learn and perform your best.

Sources: J. Haden, "The Brutal Truth about Finding the Job You Love That Few People Are Willing to Admit," *Inc.*, accessed April 11, 2020; and A. Doyle, "Top 5 Tips for Finding a Job You Will Love," *The Balance*, January 3, 2020, https://www.thebalancecareers.com/top-tips-for-finding-a-job-you-will-love-2060996.

Some jobs and organizations create environments that quash creativity and motivation.[72] The classic example of a demotivating job is the highly specialized assembly-line job; each worker performs one boring operation before passing the work along to the next worker. Such specialization, or the "mechanistic" approach to job design, was the prevailing practice in the United States through most of the 20th century.[73] But jobs that are too simple and routine result in employee dissatisfaction, absenteeism, and turnover.

Especially in industries that depend on highly motivated knowledge workers, keeping talented employees may require letting them design their own jobs so that their work is more interesting than it would be elsewhere.[74] Designing jobs in the following ways can increase intrinsic rewards and make them more motivating.

5.1 | Managers Can Make Work More Interesting

With job rotation, workers who spend all their time in one routine task can instead move from one task to another. Rather than dishing out the pasta in a cafeteria line all day, a person might work the pasta, then the salads, and then the vegetables or desserts. Job rotation is intended to alleviate boredom by giving people different things to do at different times.

As you may guess, job rotation may simply move the person from one boring job to another. But job rotation can benefit everyone when done properly, with people's input and career interests in mind. At Anheuser-Busch, future leaders move to different locations around the United States to learn about the business.[75] Blue Cross and Blue Shield of North Carolina hires college graduates straight out of school to join its Rotational

> **job rotation** changing from one routine task to another to alleviate boredom
>
> **job enlargement** giving people additional tasks at the same time to alleviate boredom
>
> **job enrichment** changing a task to make it inherently more rewarding, motivating, and satisfying

Development Program, a two-year program that develops future leaders.[76]

Job enlargement is similar to job rotation in that people are given different tasks to do. But while job rotation involves doing one task at one time and changing to a different task at a different time, job enlargement assigns the worker multiple tasks at the same time. Thus an assembly worker's job is enlarged if he or she is given two tasks to perform rather than one. At a financial services firm, enlarged jobs led to higher job satisfaction, better error detection by clerks, and improved customer service.[77]

With job enlargement, the person's additional tasks are at the same level of responsibility; enriching jobs creates more profound changes. Job enrichment means that jobs are restructured or redesigned by adding higher levels of responsibility. This practice includes giving people not just more tasks but more important ones, such as by delegating decisions downward and decentralizing authority. Enriching jobs is now common in American industry. The first approach to job enrichment was Herzberg's two-factor theory, followed by the Hackman and Oldham model.

5.2 | Herzberg Proposed Two Important Job-Related Factors

Frederick Herzberg's two-factor theory distinguished between two broad categories of factors that affect people working on their jobs:[78]

1. **Hygiene factors** are *characteristics of the workplace:* company policies, working conditions, pay, coworkers, supervision, and so forth. These factors can make people unhappy if they are poorly managed. If they are well managed, and viewed as positive by employees, the employees will no longer be dissatisfied. However, no matter how good these factors are, they will not make people truly satisfied or motivated to do a good job.

2. **Motivators** describe the *job itself*—that is, what people do at work. Motivators are the nature of the work itself, actual job responsibilities, opportunity for personal growth and recognition, and the feelings of achievement the job provides. According to Herzberg, the key to true job satisfaction and motivation to perform lies in this category of factors. When motivators are present, jobs are presumed to be satisfying and motivating for most people.

Herzberg's theory has been criticized by many scholars, so we will not go into more detail about his original theory. But Herzberg was a pioneer in the area of job design and still is a respected name. In addition, even if the specifics of his theory do not hold up to scientific scrutiny, he made several important contributions. Herzberg's theory highlights the important distinction between extrinsic rewards (from hygiene factors) and intrinsic rewards (from motivators). It also reminds managers not to count solely on extrinsic factors to motivate workers but to focus on intrinsic rewards as well. Finally, it set the stage for later theories, such as the Hackman and Oldham model, that explain more precisely how managers can enrich people's jobs.

5.3 | Hackman and Oldham: Meaning, Responsibility, and Feedback Provide Motivation

Following Herzberg's work, Hackman and Oldham proposed a more complete model of job design.[79] Exhibit 11.6 illustrates their model. As you can see, well-designed jobs lead to high

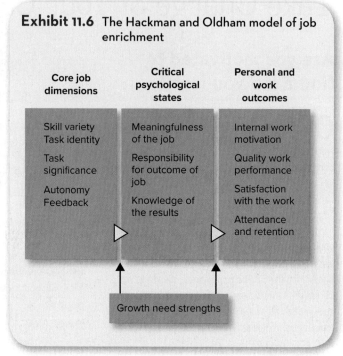

Exhibit 11.6 The Hackman and Oldham model of job enrichment

Source: Adapted from J. Richard Hackman et al., "A New Strategy of Job Enrichment," *California Management Review* 17, no. 4 (1975), pp. 57–71.

motivation, high-quality performance, high satisfaction, and low absenteeism and turnover. These outcomes occur when people experience three critical psychological states (middle column of the figure):

1. They believe they are doing something meaningful because their work is important to other people.

2. They feel personally responsible for how the work turns out.

3. They learn how well they performed their jobs.

These psychological states occur when people are working on enriched jobs—that is, jobs that offer the following five core job dimensions:

1. *Skill variety*—different job activities involving several skills and talents. Management trainees at Kraft Heinz rotate through field sales, manufacturing, and R&D, and do two project rotations before their final placement."[80]

2. *Task identity*—the completion of a whole, identifiable piece of work. At GEICO, agents are independent contractors who sell and provide service for the insurance company's products exclusively. They have built and invested in their own businesses. According to Scott Hordis, a local agent in the Philadelphia area: "There's nothing more rewarding than helping people with their insurance needs."[81]

3. *Task significance*—an important, positive impact on the lives of others. A study of lifeguards found dramatic

improvements in their performance if they were taught about how lifeguards make a difference by preventing deaths. Lifeguards who were told simply that the job can be personally enriching showed no such improvements.[82]

4. *Autonomy*—independence and discretion in making decisions. 3M encourages employees to spend up to 15 percent of their time pursuing exciting, innovative ideas. The company's strategy has resulted in several innovations, including Post-it Notes. Former president and chairman, William McKnight put it succinctly: "Hire good people and leave them alone."[83]

5. *Feedback*—information about job performance. Many companies provide information on productivity, quality, and other performance indicators. Ride-sharing firms like Uber and Lyft encourage customers to submit online reviews of their trip experience—thousands of reviews every day—which is a powerful source of motivation for drivers.

The most effective job enrichment increases all five core dimensions.

A person's growth need strength will help determine just how effective a job enrichment program might be. Growth need strength is the degree to which a person wants personal and psychological development. Job enrichment is more successful for people with high growth need strength. But very few people respond negatively to job enrichment.[84]

5.4 | To Motivate, Empowerment Must Be Done Right

We often hear managers talk about "empowering" their people.[85] Individuals may—or may not—feel empowered, and groups can have a "culture" of empowerment that enhances work unit performance.[86] Empowerment is the process of sharing power with employees, thereby enhancing their confidence in their ability to perform their jobs and their belief that they are influential contributors to the organization.

growth need strength the degree to which individuals want personal and psychological development

empowerment the process of sharing power with employees to enhance their confidence in their ability to perform their jobs and contribute to the organization

employee engagement when employees invest their physical, mental, and emotional energy into performing their jobs, including working hard and producing, taking initiative, and contributing additional citizenship behaviors

Fulton Hotshots Daniel Hammond (left) and Jake Cagle (right), both of Bakersfield, California, set a back burn to help contain a fire in Glacier National Park, Montana. Jennifer DeMonte/Getty Images

Unfortunately, empowerment doesn't always live up to its hype. One problem is that managers undermine it by sending mixed messages like, "Do your own thing—the way we tell you."[87] But empowerment can be profoundly motivating when done properly.[88]

Exhibit 11.7 includes examples of comments from people when they were feeling empowered and disempowered.

Empowerment done well leads to higher levels of employee engagement and overall performance.[89] Engaged employees invest their physical, mental, and emotional energy into

Exhibit 11.7	Reactions to feeling empowered and disempowered

When feeling *empowered*, people may say things like . . .

My supervisor trusts me to purchase office equipment without getting her permission.

After I pitched my new idea to save the company money in cloud storage costs, I was given the green light to move forward with the idea.

After resolving several difficult customer service issues, my boss no longer listens in on my discussions with customers.

The chief financial officer showed me the books.

When feeling *disempowered*, people may make comments like . . .

My manager didn't ask for my opinion during the meeting with my customer.

My subordinates go over my head to my boss because they know I don't have any real power.

No one listens to my ideas around here.

I'm the expert, but I wasn't asked to help train the new employee.

Source: Adapted from J. Kouzes and B. Posner, *The Leadership Challenge,* 2nd ed. (San Francisco: Jossey-Bass, 1995).

equity theory a theory stating that people assess how fairly they have been treated according to two key factors: outcomes and inputs

performing their jobs, including working hard and producing, taking initiative, and contributing additional citizenship behaviors. They persevere in achieving their goals and their leader's vision even in the face of obstacles. Ultimately, managed well, they and their units perform at higher levels.[90]

Genuine empowerment—as opposed to its common use as an empty buzzword—engages employees by changing their beliefs from feeling powerless to believing strongly in their own personal effectiveness.[91] People engage because empowering circumstances allow them to feel self-determined: fulfilling their desires for autonomy, relatedness, and competence.[92] When the job fits their values, empowered employees perceive meaning in their work. And they know they have an impact because they have some influence over important strategic, administrative, or operating decisions or outcomes on the job.

You should not be surprised when empowerment causes some problems, at least in the short term. Empowerment brings responsibility, and employees don't necessarily like the accountability at first.[94] People may make mistakes, especially until they have had adequate training. Because more training is needed, costs are higher. Because people acquire new skills and make greater contributions, they may demand higher wages. But if they are well trained and truly empowered, they will deserve the pay because they contribute more. Both they and the company benefit.

The starting point for understanding how people interpret their contributions and outcomes is equity theory.[96] **Equity theory** proposes that when people assess how fairly they are treated, they consider two key factors:

1. *Outcomes,* as in expectancy theory, refer to the various things the person receives on the job: recognition, pay, benefits, satisfaction, security, job assignments, punishments, and so forth.

2. *Inputs* refer to the contributions the person makes to the organization: effort, time, talent, performance, extra commitment, good citizenship, and so forth.

People generally expect that the outcomes they receive will reflect, or be proportionate to, the inputs they provide—a fair day's pay (and other outcomes) for a fair day's work (broadly defined by how people view all their contributions).

But this comparison of outcomes to inputs is not the whole story. People also pay attention to the outcomes and inputs others receive. At salary review time, for example, most people—from executives on down—try to pick up clues that will tell them who got the biggest raises. As described in the following section, they compare ratios, try to restore equity if necessary, and derive more or less satisfaction based on how fairly they believe they have been treated.

6.1 | People Assess Equity by Making Comparisons

Equity theory describes how people compare the ratio of their own outcomes to inputs against the outcome-to-input

LO6 Summarize how people assess and achieve fairness.

6 | ACHIEVING FAIRNESS

Ultimately, one of the most important issues in motivation surrounds people's view of what they contribute to the organization and what they receive from it in return. Ideally, they will view their relationship with their employer as a well-balanced, mutually beneficial exchange. As people work and realize the outcomes or consequences of their actions, they assess how fairly the organization treats them.[95]

● Employees who lack the power to do their jobs effectively are less likely to feel motivated. JGI/Tom Grill/Getty Images

Exhibit 11.8 Equity theory

Comparing Your Ratio to Other's Ratio		Your Likely Perception	Actions You May Take to Restore Equity
$\dfrac{\text{Your Outcomes}}{\text{Your Inputs}}$ = $\dfrac{\text{Other's Outcomes}}{\text{Other's Inputs}}$		Equitably treated.	No action necessary.
$\dfrac{\text{Your Outcomes}}{\text{Your Inputs}}$ < $\dfrac{\text{Other's Outcomes}}{\text{Other's Inputs}}$		Inequitably treated. Feel underrewarded.	Reduce your inputs (e.g., exert less effort). Try to increase your outcomes (e.g., ask for a raise). Change your perception of inputs or outcomes (e.g., maybe so-and-so really did deserve the bonus).
$\dfrac{\text{Your Outcomes}}{\text{Your Inputs}}$ > $\dfrac{\text{Other's Outcomes}}{\text{Other's Inputs}}$		Inequitably treated. Feel overrewarded.	Increase your inputs by putting in extra effort. Help other person increase her outcomes (e.g., urge her to ask for a larger bonus).

ratio of some comparison person. The comparison person (see Exhibit 11.8) can be a coworker, a boss, or an average industry pay scale.

If the ratios are equivalent, people believe the relationship is equitable, or fair. Equity causes people to be satisfied with their treatment. But the person who believes his or her ratio is lower than another's will feel inequitably treated. Inequity causes dissatisfaction and leads to an attempt to restore balance to the relationship.

Inequity and the negative feelings it creates may appear anywhere. As a student, perhaps you have been in the following situation. You stay up all night and get a C on the exam. Meanwhile, another student studies a couple of hours, goes out for the rest of the evening, gets a good night's sleep, and gets a B. You perceive your inputs (time spent studying) as much greater than the other student's, but your outcomes are lower. You are displeased at the seeming unfairness.

In business, the same thing can happen with pay raises. One manager puts in 60-hour weeks, earned a degree from a prestigious university, and believes she is destined for the top. When her archrival—whom she perceives as less deserving ("she never comes into the office on weekends, and all she does when she is here is butter up the boss")—gets the higher raise or the promotion, she experiences severe inequity.

Many people feel inequity when they learn of the large sums paid to high-profile CEOs. Ironically, one reason for rising CEO pay is an effort to *create* equity. The board of directors compares the CEO's pay with that of chief executives at organizations in a "peer group." Even when a company chooses an appropriate peer group, many boards try to pay their executives in the top one-fourth of the group. The drive to keep everyone's pay above average means the average keeps climbing.[97]

According to the Economic Policy Institute, CEO pay in 1989 was approximately 58 times higher than the average employee's compensation. In 2019, CEOs were making about 278 times more than workers.[98]

Assessments of equity are not made objectively. They are subjective perceptions or beliefs. In the preceding example of the two managers, the one who got the bigger raise probably felt she deserved it. Even if she admits to working fewer hours, she may convince herself she can because she is more efficient. In the example of the students, the one who scored higher may believe the outcome was equitable because (1) she worked harder over the course of the semester, and (2) she's smart (ability and experience, not just time and effort, can be seen as inputs).

6.2 | People Expect and Strive for Equity

People who feel inequitably treated and dissatisfied are motivated to do something to restore equity. They have a number of options that they carry out to change the ratios or to reevaluate the situation and decide it is equitable after all.

The equity equation shown earlier indicates people's options for restoring equity when they feel inequitably treated:

- *Reducing their inputs*—giving less effort, performing at lower levels, or quitting: "Well, if that's the way things work around here, there's no way I'm going to work that hard (or stick around)."

- *Increasing their outcomes:* "My boss is going to hear about this. I deserve more; there must be some way I can get more."

- *Decreasing others' outcomes:* For example, an employee may sabotage work to create problems for his company or boss.[99] People can change their perceptions of an outcome, not just the outcome itself: "That promotion isn't as great a deal as she thinks. The pay is not that much better, and the headaches will be unbelievable."

- *Increasing others' inputs*—Here, too, the change may be in perceptions: "The more I think about it, the more I see he deserved it. He's worked hard all year, he's competent, and it's about time he got a break."

procedural justice using a fair process in decision making and making sure others know that the process was as fair as possible

Thus, a person can restore equity in a number of ways by behaviorally or perceptually changing inputs and outcomes.

People may care about group equity and *may even increase their inputs* to keep a situation equitable for the group. In the first few months of each year, more than 1.3 million accountants face a flood of work related to annual reports and tax preparation.[100] Many work six days a week and several evenings during tax time. Beyond pay and other extrinsic rewards, accountants can draw motivation from seeing their hardworking colleagues working equally long hours.[101]

6.3 | Procedures—Not Just Outcomes—Should Be Fair

Inevitably managers make decisions that have outcomes more favorable for some than for others. Those with favorable outcomes will be pleased; those with worse outcomes, all else equal, will be unhappy. But managers desiring to put salve on the wounds—say, of people they like or respect or want to keep and motivate—can reduce the dissatisfaction. They do this by demonstrating that they provide procedural justice—using a fair process in decision making and helping others know that the process was as fair as possible.[102]

When people perceive procedural fairness, they are more likely to support decisions and decision makers.[103] For example, one year after layoffs, managers' use of procedural justice (in the form of employee participation in decisions) still predicted survivors' organizational commitment, job satisfaction, and trust toward management.[104] Bear in mind, though, that the effects could vary by country and culture.[105]

Thus, even if people believe that their *outcome* was inequitable and unfair, they are more likely to view justice as having been served if the *process* was fair.[106] You can increase people's beliefs that the process was fair by making the process open and visible, stating decision criteria in advance rather than after the fact, making sure that the most appropriate people—those who have valid information and are viewed as trustworthy—make the decisions, giving people a chance to participate in the process, and providing an appeal process that allows people to question decisions safely and receive complete answers.[107]

In contrast, at an elevator plant in the United States, an army of consultants arrived one day, without explanation.[108] The rumor mill kicked in; employees guessed the plant would be shut down or some of them would be laid off. Three months later, management unveiled its new plan, involving a new method of manufacturing based on teams. But management did not adequately answer questions about the purpose of the changes, employees resisted, conflicts arose, and the formerly popular plant manager lost the trust of his people. Costs skyrocketed, and quality plummeted.

LO7 Identify causes and consequences of employee well-being.

7 | EMPLOYEE WELL-BEING

If people feel fairly treated from the outcomes they receive or the processes used, they will be satisfied. A satisfied worker is not necessarily more productive than a dissatisfied one; sometimes people are happy with their jobs because they don't have to work hard! But job dissatisfaction, aggregated across many individuals, creates a workforce that is more likely to exhibit the following characteristics:

- Higher turnover and absenteeism.
- Less good citizenship (going the "extra mile" and helping others at work).[109]
- More grievances and lawsuits.
- Strikes.
- Stealing, sabotage, and vandalism.
- Poorer mental and physical health (which can mean higher job stress, higher insurance costs, and more lawsuits).[110]
- More injuries.[111]
- Poor customer service.[112]
- Lower productivity and profits.[113]

● Mars, Inc. has been named to the 100 Best Companies To Work For list for the past seven years. The list is based on survey responses from employees rating their workplace on more than 50 elements including trust in managers, compensation, fairness, and atmosphere. Roman Samokhin/123RF

All of these consequences of dissatisfaction, either directly or indirectly, are costly. Sadly, most people think about leaving their jobs, and about a third are actively searching. A survey by Mental Health America found that the top contributors to employee dissatisfaction are (1) not being rewarded for strengths and daily contributions, (2) toxic bosses and colleagues, and (3) feeling disengaged from the company's mission.[114]

Job satisfaction is especially important for relationship-oriented service employees such as real estate agents, hair stylists, and stockbrokers. Customers develop (or don't develop) a commitment to a specific service provider. Satisfied service providers are less likely to quit the company and more likely to provide an enjoyable customer experience.[115]

7.1 | Companies Are Improving the Quality of Work Life

Quality of work life (QWL) programs create workplaces that enhance employee well-being and satisfaction.[116] The general goal of QWL programs is to satisfy the full range of employee needs. Promoting QWL is a social and political cause that sprang originally from the establishment of democratic societies and basic human rights.[117]

QWL addresses eight categories:[118]

1. Adequate and fair compensation.

2. A safe and healthy environment.

3. Jobs that develop human capacities.

4. A chance for personal growth and security.

5. A social environment that fosters personal identity, freedom from prejudice, a sense of community, and upward mobility.

6. Constitutionalism—the rights of personal privacy, dissent, and due process.

7. A work role that minimizes infringement on personal leisure and family needs.

8. Socially responsible organizational actions.

Organizations differ drastically in their attention to QWL. Critics claim that QWL programs don't necessarily inspire employees to work harder if the company does not tie rewards directly to individual performance. Advocates of QWL claim that it improves organizational effectiveness and productivity. The term *productivity,* as applied by QWL programs, means much more than each person's quantity of work output.[119] It also includes turnover, absenteeism, accidents, theft, sabotage, creativity, innovation, and especially the quality of work.

All in all, people's satisfaction and well-being have many important consequences, beneficial to both employees and employers.[120] These range from better attitudes and health to work behaviors and performance, and ultimately include firm value[121] and other business outcomes.[122] Win-win solutions are indeed possible in a well-managed workplace.

7.2 | Psychological Contracts Are Understandings of Give-and-Take

The relationship between individuals and employing organizations typically is formalized by a written contract. But in employees' minds there also exists a psychological contract—a set of perceptions of what they owe their employers and what their employers owe them.[123] This contract, whether it is seen as being upheld or violated—and whether the parties trust one another or not—has important implications for employee satisfaction and motivation and the effectiveness of the organization.

Historically, in big companies the employment relationship was stable and predictable. But mergers, layoffs, outsourcing, and other disruptions tore apart the "old deal."[124] In traditionally managed organizations, employees were expected to be loyal, and employers would provide secure employment. Today the implicit contract goes something like this:[125] If people stay, do their own job plus someone else's (who has been downsized), and do additional things like participating in task forces, the company will try to provide a job (if it can), provide gestures that it cares, and keep providing about the same pay (with periodic small increases). The likely result of this not-very-satisfying arrangement: uninspired people in a struggling business.

But a better deal is possible for both employers and employees.[126] Ideally, your employer will provide continuous skill updating and an invigorating work environment in which you can use your skills and will be motivated to stay even though you may have other job options.[127] The employer says, in essence, "If you make us more valuable, we'll make you more valuable," and the employee says, "If you help me grow, I'll help the company grow." The company benefits from your contributions, and you thrive in your work while you also become more marketable if and when you decide to look elsewhere. Employment is an alliance—perhaps temporary, perhaps long term—aimed at helping both employer and employee succeed.[128] The results of such a contract are much more likely to be a mutually beneficial and satisfying relationship and a high-performing, successful organization.

Notes

1. S. Vozza, "This Is How Google Motivates Its Employees." *Fast Company.* September 13, 2018. Accessed from https://www.fast-company.com/90230655/how-google-motivates-its-employees.

2. Zappos website, "What we live by." Accessed from https://www.zappos.com/about/what-we-live-by on April 11, 2020.

3. C. BasuMallick, "4 Companies That Have Nailed Their Employee Recognition Strategy." *HR Technologist.* September 20, 2019. Accessed from https://www.hrtechnologist.com/articles/digital-transformation/employee-recognition-strategy-examples/.

4. C. Clifford, "Apple Co-founder Steve Wozniak: Motivation Is More Important Than Knowledge for Achieving Success," *CNBC,* June 12, 2017, https://www.cnbc.com/2017/06/12/apple-co-founder-wozniak-motivation-is-more-important-than-knowledge.html.

5. D. Katz and R. L. Kahn, *The Social Psychology of Organizations* (New York: Wiley, 1966).

6. C. A. Bartlett and S. Ghoshal, "Building Competitive Advantage through People," *Sloan Management Review,* Winter 2002, pp. 34–41.

7. E. Locke, "Toward a Theory of Task Motivation and Incentives," *Organizational Behavior and Human Performance* 3 (1968), pp. 157–89.

8. M. Schwantes, "Why Your People May Be Quitting," *Inc.,* October 23, 2017, www.inc.com.

9. E. E. Lawler III, *Treat People Right!* (San Francisco: Jossey-Bass, 2003).

10. E. E. Lawler III, *Treat People Right!* (San Francisco: Jossey-Bass, 2003).

11. J. Bono and T. Judge, "Self-Concordance at Work: Toward Understanding the Motivational Effects of Transformational Leaders," *Academy of Management Journal* 46 (2003), pp. 554–71.

12. G. Seif, "Setting and Achieving Your Goals: The Google Way," *Medium,* June 11, 2018, www.medium.com.

13. K. Buckland and N. Tajitsu, "Toyota Speeds Up Electric Vehicle Schedule as Demand Heats Up," Reuters, June 6, 2019, www.reuters.com.

14. K. N. Shaw, "Changing the Goal-Setting Process at Microsoft," *Academy of Management Executive* 4 (November 2004), pp. 139–43.

15. S. B. Sitkin, K. E. See, C. C. Miller, M. W. Lawless, and A. M. Carton, "The Paradox of Stretch Goals: Organizations in Pursuit of the Seemingly Impossible," *Academy of Management Review* 36, no. 3 (2011), pp. 544–66.

16. S. Kerr and S. Landauer, "Using Stretch Goals to Promote Organizational Effectiveness and Personal Growth: General Electric and Goldman Sachs," *Academy of Management Executive* 4 (November 2004), pp. 134–38.

17. S. Kerr and S. Landauer, "Using Stretch Goals to Promote Organizational Effectiveness and Personal Growth: General Electric and Goldman Sachs," *Academy of Management Executive* 4 (November 2004), pp. 134–38.

18. G. P. Latham, "The Motivational Benefits of Goal-Setting," *Academy of Management Executive* 4 (November 2004), pp. 126–29.

19. T. Mitchell and W. Silver, "Individual and Group Goals When Workers Are Interdependent: Effects on Task Strategies and Performance," *Journal of Applied Psychology* 75 (1990), pp. 185–93.

20. M. Schweitzer, L. Ordonez, and B. Douma, "Goal Setting as a Motivator of Unethical Behavior," *Academy of Management Journal* 47 (2004), pp. 422–32.

21. G. P. Latham, "The Motivational Benefits of Goal-Setting," *Academy of Management Executive* 4 (November 2004), pp. 126–29.

22. H. Brubaker, "Under New CEO, Aramark Settles Employee Lawsuits over Canceled Bonuses for $21 Million," *The Philadelphia Inquirer,* November 8, 2019, www.inquirer.com.

23. T. DiChristopher and A. Johnson, "GE's Q1 Industrial Performance 'Impressive': Analyst," *CNBC,* April 17, 2015, www.cnbc.com; M. A. Duran, "Norm-Based Behavior and Corporate Malpractice," *Journal of Economic Issues* 41, no. 1 (March 2007); D. Durfee, "Management or Manipulation?" *CFO,* December 2006; T. Gryta, S. Ng, and T. Francis, "Companies Routinely Steer Analysts to Deliver Earnings Surprises," *The Wall Street Journal,* August 4, 2016, www.wsj.com; and C. Beaudoin, A. Cianci, and G. Tsakumis, "The Impact of CFOs' Incentives and Earnings Management Ethics on Their Financial Reporting Decisions: The Mediating Role of Moral Disengagement," *Journal of Business Ethics* 128 (2015), pp. 505–18.

24. G. Seijts and G. Latham, "Learning versus Performance Goals: When Should Each Be Used?" *Academy of Management Executive* 19 (February 2005), pp. 124–31; P. C. Early, T. Connolly, and G. Ekegren, "Goals, Strategy Development, and Task Performance: Some Limits on the Efficacy of Goal Setting," *Journal of Applied Psychology* 74 (1989), pp. 24–33; and C. E. Shalley, "Effects of Productivity Goals, Creativity Goals, and Personal Discretion on Individual Creativity," *Journal of Applied Psychology* 76 (1991), pp. 179–85.

25. R. C. Litchfield, "Brainstorming Reconsidered: A Goal-Based View," *Academy of Management Review* 33 (2008), pp. 649–68.

26. R. Fisher and A. Sharp, *Getting It Done* (New York: HarperCollins, 1998).

27. E. Thorndike, *Animal Intelligence* (New York: Macmillan, 1911).

28. A. D. Stajkovic and F. Luthans, "Differential Effects of Incentive Motivators on Work Performance," *Academy of Management Journal* 44 (2001), pp. 580–90.

29. "2018-2019 Annual Report," SAS, www.sas.com, accessed April 8, 2020.

30. D. Burkus, "Why Whole Foods Builds Its Entire Business on Teams," *Forbes,* June 8, 2016, www.forbes.com; and J. Mackey and R. Sisodia, "Want to Hire Great People? Hire Consciously," *CNN Money,* January 17, 2013, www.money.cnn.com.

31. K. Butterfield, L. K. Trevino, and G. Ball, "Punishment from the Manager's Perspective: A Grounded Investigation and Inductive Model," *Academy of Management Review* 39 (1996), pp. 1479–512.

32. T. Judge and R. Piccolo, "Transformational and Transactional Leadership: A Meta-Analytic Test of Their Relative Ability," *Journal of Applied Psychology* 89 (2004), pp. 755–68.

33. S. Kerr, "On the Folly of Rewarding A While Hoping for B," *Academy of Management Journal* 18 (1975), pp. 769–83.

34. S. Lohr, "Science Finds Advantage in Focusing, Not Multitasking," *Chicago Tribune,* March 25, 2007, sec. 1, p. 10.

35. M. LeBoeuf, *The Greatest Management Principle in the World* (New York: Berkley Books, 1985).

36. E. E. Lawler III, *Rewarding Excellence* (San Francisco: Jossey-Bass, 2000).

37. S. Caramella, "15 Cool Job Perks That Keep Employees Happy," *Business News Daily,* March 14, 2018, www.businessnewsdaily.com.

38. See New Belgium Brewing's company website, www.newbelgium.com, accessed November 9, 2019.

39. J. Haden, "Rewards That Great Employees Actually Love to Receive," *Inc.,* December 21, 2017, www.inc.com.

40. J. Haden, "Rewards That Great Employees Actually Love to Receive," *Inc.,* December 21, 2017, www.inc.com.

41. J. Pfeffer and R. Sutton, *The Knowing-Doing Gap* (Boston: Harvard Business School Press, 2000).

42. J. S. Lublin, "Recall the Mistakes of Your Past Bosses, so You Can Do Better," *The Wall Street Journal,* January 2, 2007, www.wsj.com.

43. R. Khanna, I. Guler, and A. Nerkar, "Fail Often, Fail Big, and Fail Fast? Learning from Small Failures and R&D Performance in the Pharmaceutical Industry," *Academy of Management Journal* 59 (2016), pp. 436–59.

44. S. Moss and J. Sanchez, "Are Your Employees Avoiding You? Managerial Strategies for Closing the Feedback Gap," *Academy of Management Executive* 18, no. 1 (February 2004), pp. 32–44.

45. E. E. Lawler III, *Treat People Right!* (San Francisco: Jossey-Bass, 2003).

46. S. B. Silverman, C. E. Pogson, and A. B. Cober, "When Employees at Work Don't Get It: A Model for Enhancing Individual Employee Change in Response to Performance Feedback," *Academy of Management Executive* 19, no. 2 (May 2005), pp. 135–47; and J. Jackman and M. Strober, "Fear of Feedback," *Harvard Business Review,* April 2003, pp. 101–07.

47. V. H. Vroom, *Work and Motivation* (New York: Wiley, 1964).

48. R. E. Wood, P. W. B. Atkins, and J. E. H. Bright, "Bonuses, Goals, and Instrumentality Effects," *Journal of Applied Psychology* 84 (1999), pp. 703–20.

49. S. Kerr, "Organizational Rewards: Practical, Cost-Neutral Alternatives That You May Know, but Don't Practice," *Organizational Dynamics* 28, no. 1 (1999), pp. 61–70.

50. S. Oppenheim, "How The Corporate Wellness Market Has Exploded: Meet the Latest Innovators in the Space," *Forbes,* June 11, 2019, www.forbes.com.

51. E. Emerman, "Use of Rewards and Penalties to Drive Employee Health Jumps during 2012," National Business Group on Health, press release, October 25, 2011; and S. J. Wells, "Getting Paid for Staying Well," *HRMagazine* 55, no. 2 (February 2010), pp. 59–63.

52. A. H. Maslow, "A Theory of Human Motivation," *Psychological Review,* July 1943, pp. 370–96.

53. T. Bridgman, S. Cummings, and J. Ballard, "Who Built Maslow's Pyramid? A History of the Creation of Management Studies' Most Famous Symbol and Its Implications for Management Education," *Academy of Management Learning & Education* 18 (2019), https://doi.org/10.5465/amle.2017.0351.

54. M. Wahba and L. Birdwell, "Maslow Reconsidered: A Review of Research on the Need Hierarchy Theory," *Organizational Behavior and Human Performance* 15 (1976), pp. 212–40.

55. M. Marchington, "Human Resource Management (HRM): Too Busy Looking Up to See Where It Is Going Longer Term?" *Human Resource Management Review* 25 (2015), pp. 176–87.

56. E. Moore, "10 Companies That Offer Incredible Professional Development Programs," Glassdoor, May 16, 2019, www.glassdoor.com.

57. C. Alderfer, *Existence, Relatedness, and Growth: Human Needs in Organizational Settings* (Glencoe, IL: Free Press, 1972).

58. Company website, "About Kahler Slater," www.kahler.com; and "Kahler Slater, Inc. Great Place to Work-Certified July 2018-2019," Great Place to Work, www.greatplacetowork.com.

59. C. Pinder, *Work Motivation* (Glenview, IL: Scott, Foresman, 1984).

60. B. Tracy, *How the Best Leaders Lead: Proven Secrets to Getting the Most Out of Yourself and Others* (Nashville, TN: AMACOM, 2010).

61. D. McClelland, *The Achieving Society* (New York: Van Nostrand Reinhold, 1961).

62. D. McClelland and R. Boyatzis, "Leadership Motive Pattern and Long-Term Success in Management," *Journal of Applied Psychology* 67 (1982), pp. 737–43.

63. N. Adler, *International Dimensions of Organizational Behavior,* 2nd ed. (Boston: Kent, 1991); and G. Hofstede, *Cultures and Organizations* (London: McGraw-Hill, 1991).

64. P. A. Gambrel and R. Cianci, "Maslow's Hierarchy of Needs: Does It Apply in a Collectivist Culture?" *Journal of Applied Management and Entrepreneurship* 8, no. 2 (April 2003), pp. 143–62.

65. N. R. Lockwood, "Leveraging Employee Engagement for Competitive Advantage: HR's Strategic Role," *HRMagazine,* March 2007.

66. E. E. Lawler III and D. Finegold, "Individualizing the Organization: Past, Present, and Future," *Organizational Dynamics,* Summer 2000, pp. 1–15.

67. E. E. Lawler III and D. Finegold, "Individualizing the Organization: Past, Present, and Future," *Organizational Dynamics,* Summer 2000, pp. 1–15.

68. E. Gerhart and M. Fang, "Pay, Intrinsic Motivation, Extrinsic Motivation, Performance, and Creativity in the Workplace: Revisiting Long-Held Beliefs," *Annual Review of Organizational Psychology and Organizational Behavior* 2 (2015), pp. 489–521.

69. A. M. Grant and J. W. Berry, "The Necessity of Others Is the Mother of Invention: Intrinsic and Prosocial Motivations, Perspective Taking, and Creativity," *Academy of Management Journal* 54, no. 1 (2011), pp. 73–96; and T. M. Amabile, "A Model of Creativity and Innovation in Organizations," in *Research in Organizational Behavior,* eds. B. M. Staw and L. L. Cummings (Greenwich, CT: JAI Press, 1988), pp. 10, 123–67.

70. C. M. Ford, "A Theory of Individual Creative Action in Multiple Social Domains," *Academy of Management Review* 21 (1996), pp. 1112–42.

71. G. Oldham and A. Cummings, "Employee Creativity: Personal and Contextual Factors at Work," *Academy of Management Journal* 39 (1996), pp. 607–34.

72. T. Amabile, R. Conti, H. Coon, J. Lazenby, and M. Herron, "Assessing the Work Environment for Creativity," *Academy of Management Journal* 39 (1996), pp. 1154–84.

73. M. Campion and G. Sanborn, "Job Design," in *Handbook of Industrial Engineering,* ed. G. Salvendy (New York: Wiley, 1991).

74. E. E. Lawler III and D. Finegold, "Individualizing the Organization: Past, Present, and Future," *Organizational Dynamics,* Summer 2000, pp. 1–15.

75. "Global Management Trainee Program," Anheuser-Busch, www.anheuser-busch.com, accessed November 9, 2019.

76. "Students & Recent Grads," Blue Cross and Blue Shield of North Carolina, www.bluecrossnc.com, accessed April 8, 2020.

77. M. Campion and D. McClelland, "Interdisciplinary Examination of the Costs and Benefits of Enlarged Jobs: A Job Design Quasi-Experiment," *Journal of Applied Psychology* 76 (1991), pp. 186–98.

78. F. Herzberg, *Work and the Nature of Men* (Cleveland: World, 1966).

79. J. R. Hackman, G. Oldham, R. Janson, and K. Purdy, "A New Strategy for Job Enrichment," *California Management Review* 16 (Fall 1975), pp. 57–71.

80. Kraft Heinz company website, www.kraftheinzcompany.com/careers-university-relations.html, accessed November 9, 2019.

81. "Meet Scott Hordis," GEICO, www.geico.com, accessed April 8, 2020.

82. "Motivation in Today's Workplace: The Link to Performance," *HRMagazine,* July 2010, pp. 1–9.

83. "3M Careers," https://www.3m.com/3M/en_US/careers-us/culture/15-percent-culture/, accessed April 1, 2019.

84. M. Campion and G. Sanborn, "Job Design," in *Handbook of Industrial Engineering,* ed. G. Salvendy (New York: Wiley, 1991).

85. Y. Yin, Y. Wang, and Y. Lu, "Why Firms Adopt Empowerment Practices and How Such Practices Affect Firm Performance," *Human Resource Management Review* 29 (2019), pp. 111–24.

86. S. Seibert, S. Silver, and W. A. Randolph, "Taking Empowerment to the Next Level: A Multiple-Level Model of Empowerment, Performance, and Satisfaction," *Academy of Management Journal* 47 (2004), pp. 332–49.

87. C. Argyris, "Empowerment: The Emperor's New Clothes," *Harvard Business Review,* May–June 1998, pp. 98–105.

88. X. Zhang and K. M. Bartol, "Linking Empowering Leadership and Employee Creativity: The Influence of Psychological Empowerment, Intrinsic Motivation, and Creative Process Engagement," *Academy of Management Journal* 53, no. 1 (February 2010), pp. 107–28; and R. Forrester, "Empowerment: Rejuvenating a Potent Idea," *Academy of Management Executive,* August 2000, pp. 67–80.

89. W. Kahn, "Psychological Conditions of Personal Engagement and Disengagement at Work," *Academy of Management Journal* 33 (1990), pp. 692–724; W. Macey and B. Schneider, "The Meaning of Employee Engagement," *Industrial and Organizational Psychology: Perspectiveson Science and Practice* 1 (2008), pp. 3–30; D. Cossin and J. Caballero, "Transformational Leadership Background Literature Review," IMD Global Board Center, June 2013, www.imd.org; and A. Fanelli and V. Misangyi, "Bringing Out Charisma: CEO Charisma and External Stakeholders," *Academy of Management Review* 31 (2006), pp. 1049–61.

90. L. D'Innocenzo, M. Lucian, J. Mathieu, M. Maynard, and G. Chen, "Empowered to Perform: A Multilevel Investigation of the Influence of Empowerment on Performance in Hospital Units," *Academy of Management Journal* 58 (2016), pp. 1290–307.

91. R. C. Liden, S. J. Wayne, and R. T. Sparrowe, "An Examination of the Mediating Role of Psychological Empowerment on the Relations between Job, Interpersonal Relationships, and Work Outcomes," *Journal of Applied Psychology* 85 (2000), pp. 407–16.

92. M. Gagne and E. Deci, "Self-Determination Theory and Work Motivation," *Journal of Organizational Behavior* 26 (2005), pp. 331–62; A. A. Van den Broeck, C. H. Change, and C. Rosen, "A Review of Self-Determination Theory's Basic Psychological Needs at Work," *Journal of Management* 42 (2016), pp. 1195–229.

93. W. B. Wyckoff, "The 25 Best Jobs in 2020," *U.S. News & World Report,* January 7, 2020, https://money.usnews.com/.

94. W. A. Randolph and M. Sashkin, "Can Organizational Empowerment Work in Multinational Settings?" *Academy of Management Executive* 16 (2002), pp. 102–15.

95. J. Colquitt and K. Zipay, "Justice, Fairness, and Employee Reactions," *Annual Review of Organizational Psychology and Organizational Behavior* 2 (2015), pp. 75–99.

96. J. Adams, "Inequality in Social Exchange," in *Advances in Experimental Social Psychology,* ed. L. Berkowitz (New York: Academic Press, 1965).

97. N. Donatiello and B. Tayan, "CEOs and Directors on Pay: 2016 Survey on CEO Compensation," Stanford Business Graduate School and Heidrick & Struggles, www.gsb.stanford.edu; and G. Morgenson, "Peer Pressure: Inflating Executive Pay," *The New York Times,* November 26, 2006, www.nytimes.com.

98. L. Mishel and J. Wolfe, "CEO Compensation Has Grown 940% since 1978," Economic Policy Institute, August 14, 2019, www.epi.org.

99. D. Skarlicki, R. Folger, and P. Tesluk, "Personality as a Moderator in the Relationships between Fairness and Retaliation," *Academy of Management Journal* 42 (1999), pp. 100–8.

100. N. Wells, "Tax Time Is Tough, Especially for an Accountant," *CNBC,* April 18, 2016, www.cnbc.com.

101. A. Blitz, "Teamwork in the Accounting Firm," *Accounting Today,* September 16, 2015, www.accountingtoday.com.

102. J. Brockner, "Making Sense of Procedural Fairness: How High Procedural Fairness Can Reduce or Heighten the Influence of

Outcome Favorability," *Academy of Management Review* 27 (2002), pp. 58–76; and D. DeCremer and D. van Knippenberg, "How Do Leaders Promote Cooperation? The Effects of Charisma and Procedural Fairness," *Journal of Applied Psychology* 87 (2002), pp. 858–66.

103. J. Brockner, "Making Sense of Procedural Fairness: How High Procedural Fairness Can Reduce or Heighten the Influence of Outcome Favorability," *Academy of Management Review* 27 (2002), pp. 58–76; and D. De Cremer and D. van Knippenberg, "How Do Leaders Promote Cooperation? The Effects of Charisma and Procedural Fairness," *Journal of Applied Psychology* 87 (2002), pp. 858–66.

104. M. Kernan and P. Hanges, "Survivor Reactions to Reorganization: Antecedents and Consequences of Procedural, Interpersonal, and Informational Justice," *Journal of Applied Psychology* 87 (2002), pp. 916–28.

105. S. Persson and D. Wasieleski, "The Seasons of Psychological Contract: Overcoming the Silent Transformations of the Employer-Employee Relationship," *Human Resource Management Review* 25 (2015), pp. 368–83; and R. Shao, D. Rupp, D. Skarlicki, and K. Jones, "Employee Justice across Cultures: A Meta-Analytic Review," *Journal of Management* 39 (2013), pp. 263–301.

106. E. Lawler III, *Treat People Right,* (San Francisco, CA: Jossey-Bass, 2003).

107. E. E. Lawler III, *Treat People Right!* (San Francisco: Jossey-Bass, 2003).

108. W. C. Kim and R. Mauborgne, "Fair Process: Managing in the Knowledge Economy," *Harvard Business Review,* July–August 1997, pp. 65–75.

109. T. Bateman and D. Organ, "Job Satisfaction and the Good Sold: The Relationship between Affect and Employee 'Citizenship,'" *Academy of Management Journal,* 1983, pp. 587–95.

110. D. Henne and E. Locke, "Job Dissatisfaction: What Are the Consequences?" *International Journal of Psychology* 20 (1985), pp. 221–40.

111. J. Barling, E. K. Kelloway, and R. Iverson, "High-Quality Work, Job Satisfaction, and Occupational Injuries," *Journal of Applied Psychology* 88 (2003), pp. 276–83.

112. D. Bowen, S. Gilliland, and R. Folger, "HRM and Service Fairness: How Being Fair with Employees Spills Over to Customers," *Organizational Dynamics,* Winter 1999, pp. 7–23.

113. J. Harter, F. Schmidt, and T. Hayes, "Business-Unit-Level Relationship between Employee Satisfaction, Employee Engagement, and Business Outcomes: A Meta-Analysis," *Journal of Applied Psychology* 87 (2002), pp. 268–79.

114. P. Cohan, "3 Reasons Why Your Employees Hate Coming to Work—and What to Do about Them," *Inc.,* September 20, 2018, www.inc.com.

115. T. Bisoux, "Corporate Counterculture," *BizEd,* November–December 2004, pp. 16–20.

116. Matt Straz, "4 Ways to Use Technology in the Workplace to Motivate Employees," *Entrepreneur,* February 23, 2015, https://www.entrepreneur.com/article/242961; and "How Great Leaders Use Technology to Motivate Employees," TechDecisions, June 23, 2016, https://mytechdecisions.com/compliance/how-great-leaders-use-technology-to-motivate-employees/.

117. G. Grote and D. Guest, "The Case for Reinvigorating Quality of Working Life Research," *Human Relations* 70 (2017), pp. 149–67.

118. R. E. Walton, "Improving the Quality of Work Life," *Harvard Business Review,* May–June 1974, pp. 12, 16, 155; and "How Great Leaders Use Technologyto Motivate Employees," TechDecisions, June 23, 2016, https://mytechdecisions.com/compliance/how-great-leaders-use-technology-to-motivate-employees/.

119. E. E. Lawler III, "Strategies for Improving the Quality of Work Life," *American Psychologist* 37 (1982), pp. 486–93; and J. L. Suttle, "Improving Life at Work: Problems and Prospects," in *Improving Life at Work,* eds. J. R. Hackman and J. L. Suttle (Santa Monica, CA: Goodyear, 1977).

120. P. B. Warr, "Well-Being and the Workplace," in *Well-Being: The Foundations of Hedonic Psychology,* eds. D. Kahneman, E. Diener, and N. Schwarz (New York: Russell Sage Foundation, 1999); T. A. Wright and R. Cropanzano, "The Role of Psychological Well-Being in Job Performance: A Fresh Look at an Age-Old Quest," *Organizational Dynamics* 33 (2004), pp. 338–51; and G. Grote and D. Guest, "The Case for Reinvigorating Quality of Working Life Research," *Human Relations* 70 (2017), pp. 149–67.

121. A. Edmans, "The Link between Job Satisfaction and Firm Value, with Implications for Corporate Social Responsibility," *Academy of Management Perspectives* 26 (2012), pp. 1–19.

122. T. Wright and D. Bonett, "Job Satisfaction and Psychological Well-Being as Nonadditive Predictors of Workplace Turnover," *Journal of Management* 33 (2007), pp. 141–60; and J. K. Harter, F. L. Schmidt, and C. L. M. Keyes, "Well-Being in the Workplace and Its Relationship to Business Outcomes: A Review of the Gallup Studies," in *Flourishing: The Positive Person and the Good Life,* eds. C. L. M. Keyes and J. Haidt (Washington DC: American Psychological Association, 2003), pp. 205–24.

123. S. L. Robinson, "Trust and Breach of the Psychological Contract," *Administrative Science Quarterly* 41 (1996), pp. 574–99; J. Robbins, M. Ford, and L. Tetrick, "Perceived Unfairness and Employee Health: A Meta-Analytic Integration," *Journal of Applied Psychology* 97 (2012), pp. 235–72; M. Dahl, "Organizational Change and Employee Stress," *Management Science* 57 (2011), pp. 240–56; and A. M. Ryan and J. Wessel, "Implications of a Changing Workforce and Workplace for Justice Perceptions and Expectations," *Human Resource Management Review* 25 (2015), pp. 162–75.

124. D. Rousseau, "Changing the Deal While Keeping the People," *Academy of Management Executive* 10 (1996), pp. 50–58.

125. E. E. Lawler III, *From the Ground Up* (San Francisco: Jossey-Bass 1996).

126. E. E. Lawler III, *From the Ground Up* (San Francisco: Jossey-Bass 1996).

127. S. Ghoshal, C. Bartlett, and P. Moran, "Value Creation: The New Management Manifesto," *Financial Times Mastering Management Review,* November 1999, pp. 34–37.

128. R. Hoffman, B. Casnocha, and C. Yen, "Tours of Duty: The New Employer-Employee Contract," *Harvard Business Review,* June 2013, pp. 48–58.

Design elements: Take Charge of Your Career box photo: ©Tetra Images/Getty Images; Thumbs Up/Thumbs Down icons: McGraw-Hill Education

Teamwork

Learning Objectives

After studying Chapter 12, you should be able to

LO1 Discuss how teams can contribute to an organization's effectiveness.

LO2 Distinguish the new team environment from that of traditional work teams.

LO3 Summarize how groups become teams.

LO4 Explain why groups sometimes fail.

LO5 Describe how to build an effective team.

LO6 List methods for managing a team's relationships with other teams.

LO7 Give examples of ways to manage conflict.

Organizations are increasingly turning to teams to drive innovation. This is because in today's hypercompetitive, globalized marketplace, innovation is no longer something a business can do on the side; it has become essential for survival.[1] As Deloitte declared in its Human Capital report, "Businesses are reinventing themselves to operate as networks of teams to keep pace with the challenges of a fluid, unpredictable world."[2] Innovation teams generate new ways to stay competitive or, better yet, ahead of the curve.

For example, Stephanie Farsht headed up innovation teams for Target as it came under increasing pressure from online retailers like Amazon. Initially, the idea of a team strictly dedicated to innovation was unheard of within the organization. Overcoming resistance and numerous obstacles, Farsht and her team were able to change the culture. "Our team evolved a tremendous amount over these years and was a critical influencer in how Target operates and thinks about innovation," Farsht says. "But once we made that shift, the company understood that our team's mindset was needed."[3]

Drawing on the team's innovative thinking, Target employed same-day fulfillment options like drive-up, in-store pickup. Such customer-friendly conveniences deserve credit for Target's continued growth and success.[4]

For Target and countless other businesses, teams work.

The goal of this chapter is to help make sure that your management and work teams succeed rather than fail.

Almost all companies use teams to produce goods and services, to manage projects, and to make decisions and run the company.[5] For you, this has two vital implications:

1. You *will* be working in and leading teams.

2. Your *ability* to work in and lead teams is valuable to your employer and important to your career.

Fortunately, coursework focusing on team training can enhance students' teamwork knowledge and skills.[6]

1 | THE CONTRIBUTIONS OF TEAMS

Companies use teams to gain competitive advantage.[7] Used appropriately, teams can be powerfully effective as a *building block for organization structure.* Organizations like L.L. Bean, Lululemon Athletica, Wegmans, and W. L. Gore are structured entirely around teams. 3M's breakthrough products emerge through the use of teams that are small entrepreneurial businesses within the larger corporation.

Teams also can increase *productivity,* improve *quality,* and reduce *costs.* At California's Papa & Barkley, teams increase productivity to manage a 15 percent growth in business every month.[8] Tarang Amin credits teamwork for increasing quality and helping him build successful brands such as Bounty, Pantene, and e.l.f. Cosmetics.[9]

Teams also can enhance speed and be powerful forces for innovation, change, and creativity.[10] Amazon, 3M, Boeing, and many other companies use teams to create new products faster. Cisco relies on teams to keep the firm competitive in the ever-changing field of technology. Nestlé's InGenius program allows employees to collaborate with other employees and external partners to pitch new innovative ideas for business opportunities. It has implemented 48 business ideas in five years.[11]

Teams provide many *benefits for their members.*[12] They are a vital learning vehicle; members learn about the company and themselves, and they acquire new skills and performance strategies. The team can satisfy important personal needs, such as affiliation and esteem. Team members may receive tangible organizational rewards that they could not have achieved working alone.

Team members can give one another feedback; identify opportunities for growth and development; and train, coach, and mentor.[13] A marketing representative can learn about financial modeling from a colleague on a new product development team, and a financial expert can learn about consumer marketing. Experience working together in a team and the development of strong problem-solving capabilities are vital supplements to specific job skills or functional expertise. And, importantly, the skills are transferable to new positions.

> "No one can whistle a symphony. It takes an orchestra to play it."
> —Halford E. Luccock

LO2 Distinguish the new team environment from that of traditional work teams.

2 | THE NEW TEAM ENVIRONMENT

The words *group* and *team* often are used interchangeably.[14] Modern managers sometimes use the word *teams* to the point that it has become cliché; they talk about teams while skeptics perceive no real teamwork. So making a distinction between groups and teams can be useful:

- A **group** is a collection of people who interact to undertake a task but do not necessarily perform as a unit or achieve significant performance improvements.

● At Google, software engineers have freedom and autonomy regarding which projects and teams to join. The firm invests heavily in training its newly hired software engineers, Nooglers, to work productively in teams.
Christiane Oelrich/dpa/Alamy Stock Photo

- A **team** is formed of people (usually a small number) with complementary skills who trust one another and are committed to a common purpose, common performance goals, and a common approach for which they hold themselves mutually accountable.[15]

If you work for Google, chances are good that you will join one or more teams. Its software engineers, the ones who are responsible for developing new products and services like Google Pixel, Google Translate, and Chromecast, typically work in small three- or four-person product development teams. Large teams of 20 or 30 engineers are split into smaller teams that work on specific parts of the overall project, such as designing the Pixelbook Go laptop. The role of leader shifts among members depending on the project's particular requirements. Engineers are free to switch teams without asking management's permission. Google believes that this flexible and hands-off approach to team management spurs innovation and creativity.

Organizations have been using groups for a long time, but today's workplaces are different.[16] Teams are used in many different ways, and to far greater effect, than in the past. Exhibit 12.1 highlights just a few of the differences between the traditional work environment and the way true teams work today. Ideally, people are far more involved, they are better trained, cooperation is higher, and the culture is one of learning as well as producing.

Movement from left to right on the continuum corresponds with more and more worker participation. Toward the right, participation is not trivial and not merely advisory. It has real substance, going beyond suggestions to include action and impact.

2.1 | Organizations Have Different Types of Teams

Your organization may have hundreds of groups and teams, but they can be classified into just a few primary types.[17] **Work teams** make or do things such as manufacture, assemble, sell, or provide service. They typically are well defined, a clear part of the formal organizational structure, and composed of a full-time, stable membership. Work teams are what most people think of when they think of teams in organizations.[18]

Project and development teams work on long-term projects, often over a period of years. They have specific assignments, such as research or new-product development, and members usually must contribute expert knowledge and judgment. These teams work toward a one-time product, disbanding once their work is completed. Then new teams are formed for new projects.

Parallel teams operate separately from the regular work structure of the firm on a temporary basis. Members often come from different units or jobs and are asked to do work that is not normally done by the standard structure. Their charge is to recommend solutions to specific problems. They seldom have authority to act, however. Examples include task forces and quality or safety teams formed to study a particular problem.[19]

management teams teams that coordinate and give direction to the subunits under their jurisdiction and integrate work among subunits

transnational teams work teams composed of multinational members

whose activities span multiple countries

virtual teams teams that are physically dispersed and communicate electronically more than face-to-face

traditional work groups groups that

have no managerial responsibilities

quality circles voluntary groups of people drawn from various production teams who make suggestions about quality

semiautonomous work groups groups

that make decisions about managing and carrying out major production activities but get outside support for quality control and maintenance

autonomous work groups groups that control decisions about

and execution of a complete range of tasks

self-designing teams teams with the responsibilities of autonomous work groups, plus control over hiring, firing, and deciding what tasks members perform

Exhibit 12.1	Comparing traditional and new team work environments	
Activity	**Traditional Work Environment**	**New Team Work Environment**
Work planning	Managers do the planning.	Managers and team members plan together.
Job definition	Narrow set of tasks and duties.	Broad set of skills and knowledge.
Information	Mostly "management property."	Tends to be freely shared at all levels.
Risk taking	Discouraged and punished.	Measured risk taking is encouraged and supported.
Rewards	Based on individual performance.	Based on individual and team performance.
Work process	Managers determine "best methods."	Everyone continuously improves work processes.

Source: Adapted from *Leading Teams* by J. Zenger and Associates.

Management teams coordinate and give direction to the subunits under their jurisdiction and integrate work among subunits.[20] The management team is based on authority stemming from hierarchical rank and is responsible for the overall performance of the business unit. At the top of the organization resides the executive management team that establishes strategic direction and manages the firm's overall performance.

Transnational teams are work teams composed of multinational members whose activities span multiple countries.[21] Such teams differ from other work teams not only by being multicultural but also often by being geographically dispersed, being psychologically distant, and working on highly complex projects having considerable impact on company objectives.

Transnational teams tend to be **virtual teams**, communicating electronically more than face-to-face, although other types of teams may operate virtually as well.[22] A virtual team encounters difficult challenges: building trust, cohesion, and team identity, and overcoming communication barriers and the isolation of virtual team members.[23] Ways that managers can overcome these challenges and improve the effectiveness of virtual teams include ensuring that team members understand how they are supposed to keep in touch, setting aside time at the beginning of virtual meetings to build relationships, ensuring that all participants in meetings and on message boards have a chance to communicate, sharing meeting minutes and progress reports, and recognizing and rewarding team members' contributions.[24]

Ensuring that virtual team members can work together in a seamless manner, companies like Cisco have created powerful collaboration software that integrates voice, video, text, and email for mobile and computer platforms.[25]

2.2 | Self-Managed Teams Empower Employees

Today many different types of work teams exist, with many different labels. The terms can be confusing and sometimes are used interchangeably out of a lack of awareness of actual differences. Generally speaking, some teams are more traditional with little decision-making authority, being under the control of direct supervision. Other teams have more autonomy, decision-making power, and self-direction.[26] Let's define each category:

- **Traditional work groups** have no managerial responsibilities. The first-line manager plans, organizes, staffs, directs, and controls them, and other groups provide support activities, including quality control and maintenance.

- **Quality circles** are voluntary groups of people drawn from various production teams who make suggestions about quality but have no authority to make decisions or execute them.

- **Semiautonomous work groups** make decisions about managing and carrying out major production activities but still get outside support for quality control and maintenance.

- **Autonomous work groups**, or *self-managing teams,* control decisions about and execution of a complete range of tasks—acquiring raw materials and performing operations, quality control, maintenance, and shipping. They are fully responsible for an entire product or an entire part of a production process.

- **Self-designing teams** do all of that and go one step further—they also have control over the design of the team. They decide themselves whom to hire, whom to fire, and what tasks the team will perform.

Sustaining for Tomorrow

Teams Make Social Impact by Design

Cross-functional design teams increasingly work with socially oriented organizations and nongovernmental organizations (NGOs) to help them fulfill their missions. The hope is to use design as a way to solve complex problems in developing countries.

Take team members at IDEO.org, a global design firm. They work together with companies like Hewlett-Packard and Unilever as well as nonprofits like the Rockefeller Foundation and the Lehmann Foundation. For example, the Lehmann Foundation asked IDEO to help reduce functional illiteracy among school-children in Brazil. The IDEO team created a tablet-based digital learning solution loaded with interactive games. The program identifies each student's errors, allowing teachers to diagnose children's difficulties and more effectively help them learn.

The IDEO team is working on another project to help small-scale rural farmers in Myanmar better monitor and cultivate their crops. Partnering with Proximity Designs, a Myanmar-based social enterprise, IDEO created low-cost sensors that "accurately inform

IDEO.org team members, like the one pictured here, use design as a way to bring solutions to basic problems that affect the impoverished in developing countries. Courtesy of IDEO

farmers on irrigation, soil saturation, and what kind of supplies they'll need to maximize their fields."

In these and other ways, teams from design firms like IDEO are using their expertise to create innovations that improve people's lives.

Discussion Questions

- Why do you think organizations like the Lehmann Foundation are launching new products and services designed to have a social or environmental impact? What other goods and services use design this way?

- To better understand problems in developing countries, design teams often spend time getting to know the people, observing their daily behaviors, and interviewing them.

How could these teams use the same research techniques to design new goods and services in more developed economies?

Sources: IDEO website, "A Digital Literacy App for Young Learners," www.ideo.com/case-study/digital-literacy-app-for-young-learners, accessed April 12, 2020; and IDEO website, "Connecting Smallholder Farmers to Low-Cost Sensors," https://www.ideo.org/project/sensor-sensibility, accessed April 12, 2020.

Many companies today use **self-managed teams**, in which workers are trained to do all or most of the jobs in the unit, and they report to higher levels but make decisions previously made by first-line supervisors.[27] Self-managed teams are most often found in manufacturing. People may resist self-managed work teams, in part because they don't want so much responsibility and the change is difficult.[28] In addition, many people don't like to do performance evaluation of teammates or to fire people, and poorly managed conflict may be a particular problem in self-managed teams.[29] But compared with traditionally managed teams, self-managed teams tend to be more productive, have lower costs, provide better customer service, provide higher quality, have better safety records, and be more satisfying for members.[30] In general, autonomous teams are known to improve the organization's overall performance.[31]

self-managed teams autonomous work groups in which workers are trained to do all or most of the jobs in a unit, have no immediate supervisor, and make decisions previously made by first-line supervisors

At Spotify, teams work autonomously to complete long-term projects. Teams decide what projects to develop and how, and who will work on what projects. This team-centric approach has produced innovative services like Rise, which helps launch new artists by integrating them into popular playlists, and Secret Genius, which highlights songwriters through video series and podcasts.[32]

LO3 Summarize how groups become teams.

3 | HOW GROUPS BECOME REAL TEAMS

As a manager, you will want your group to become an effective team. To accomplish this, you need to understand how groups can become true teams and why groups sometimes fail to become teams. Groups become true teams through basic group activities, the passage of time, and team development activities.

Exhibit 12.2 Stages of team development

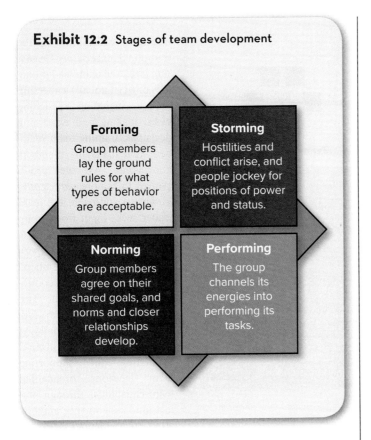

Forming
Group members lay the ground rules for what types of behavior are acceptable.

Storming
Hostilities and conflict arise, and people jockey for positions of power and status.

Norming
Group members agree on their shared goals, and norms and closer relationships develop.

Performing
The group channels its energies into performing its tasks.

3.1 | Group Activities Shift as the Group Matures

Assume you are the leader of a newly formed group—actually a bunch of people. What will you face as you attempt to develop your group into a high-performing team? If groups are to develop successfully, they will typically progress through four broad stages as described in Exhibit 12.2.[33] Groups that deteriorate move to a *declining* stage, and temporary groups add an *adjourning* or terminating stage. Groups terminate when they complete their task or when they disband due to failure or loss of interest, and new groups form as the cycle continues.

Virtual teams also go through these stages of group development.[34] The forming stage is characterized by unbridled optimism: "I believe we have a great team and will work well together. We all understand the importance of the project and intend to take it seriously." Optimism turns into reality shock in the storming stage: "No one has taken a leadership role. We have not made the project the priority that it deserves to be." The norming stage comes at about the halfway point in

the project life cycle, in which people refocus and recommit: "You must make firm commitments to a specific time schedule." The performing stage is the dash to the finish, as teammates show the discipline needed to meet the deadline.

3.2 | Groups Enter Critical Periods

A key aspect of group development is the passage of time. Groups pass through critical periods, or times when they are particularly open to formative experiences.[35] The first critical period is in the forming stage, at the first meeting, when the group establishes rules and roles that set long-lasting precedents. A second critical period is the midway point between the initial meeting and a deadline (e.g., completing a project or making a presentation). At this point, the group has enough experience to understand its work; it comes to realize that time is becoming a scarce resource and the team must "get on with it"; and enough time remains to change its approach if necessary.

In the initial meeting, the group should establish desired norms, roles, and other determinants of effectiveness, which are discussed throughout this chapter. At the second critical period (the midpoint), groups should renew or open lines of communication with outside constituencies. The group can use fresh information from its external environment to revise its approach to performing its task and ensure that it meets customers' and clients' needs. Without these activities, groups may get off on the wrong foot from the beginning, and members may neglect to revise their behavior when they should.[36]

3.3 | Teams Face Challenges

Fast-forming, fast-acting, temporary groups do not have the luxury of time to allow all necessary team processes to develop slowly and naturally. Practices that are particularly helpful in this context[37] include (1) emphasizing the team's purpose, including why it exists, what's at stake, and what its shared values are; (2) building **psychological safety**,[38] making clear that people need to and can freely speak up, be honest, disagree, offer ideas, raise issues, share their knowledge, ask questions, or show fallibility without fear that others will think less of them or criticize them; (3) embracing failure, understanding that mistakes are inevitable, errors should be acknowledged, and learning as we go is a way to create new knowledge while we execute; and (4) putting conflict to work by explaining how we arrive at our views, expressing interest in one another's thinking and analyses, and attempting to fully understand and capitalize on others' diverse perspectives.[39]

Did You KNOW ?

Most early-career employees believe—rightly or wrongly, do you think?—that virtual teams and enhanced communications technology will make face-to-face meetings obsolete in the future.[40] Virtual teamwork skills fall into two broad areas: (1) using online sharing tools like Google Docs, Slack, Yammer, and Dropbox and communication technology like online chat; and (2) human skills such as adapting to different languages and values, overcoming stereotypes, and coordinating across different time zones.[41]

Exhibit 12.3 The path to team leadership

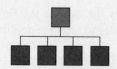 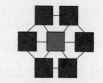

Supervisory leadership	Participative leadership	Team leadership
• Direct people.	• Involve people.	• Build trust and inspire teamwork.
• Explain decisions.	• Get input for decisions.	• Facilitate and support team decisions.
• Train individuals.	• Develop individuals.	• Expand team capabilities.
• Manage one-on-one.	• Coordinate group effort.	• Create a team identity.
• Contain conflict.	• Resolve conflict.	• Leverage team differences.
• React to change.	• Implement change.	• Anticipate and influence change.

Source: Adapted from *Leading Teams* by J. Zenger and Associates.

● Coworkers carry logs in a team-building exercise during a boot camp race.
Barry Diomede/Alamy Stock Photo

3.4 | Some Groups Develop into Teams

As a manager or group member, you should expect the group to engage in all the activities just discussed at various times. But groups are not always successful. They do not always engage in the developmental activities that turn them into effective, high-performing teams.

A useful developmental sequence is depicted in Exhibit 12.3. The figure shows the various activities as the leadership of the group moves from traditional supervision, through a more participative approach, to true team leadership.[42] At the traditional *supervisory leadership* level, the team leader handles most (if not all) leadership duties, including assigning tasks, making and explaining decisions, training team members, and managing members one-on-one. As the group evolves to a more *participative leadership* approach, the team leader seeks input from group members for decisions, provides assignments and experiences to develop members' skills and abilities, and coordinates group effort. At the *team leadership* level, the team leader's job focuses on building trust and inspiring teamwork, facilitating and supporting team decisions, broadening team capabilities through projects and assignments, and creating a team identity.

It is important to understand a couple of points about this model. Groups do not necessarily keep progressing from one "stage" to the next; they may remain permanently in the supervisory level or become more participative but never make it to true team leadership. As a result, progress on these dimensions must be a conscious goal of the leader and the members, and all should strive to meet these goals. Your group can meet these goals—and become a true team—by engaging in the activities in the figure.

4 | WHY DO GROUPS FAIL?

Team building does not necessarily progress smoothly through such a sequence, culminating in a well-oiled team and superb performance.[43] Some groups never do work out. Such groups can be frustrating for managers and members, who may feel that teams are a waste of time and that the difficulties are not worth it.

Several potential barriers can impede team success. Ineffective communication may occur between team members or between the leader and members. Some people overcommunicate, while

> Teamwork is the ability to work together toward a common vision. . . . It is the fuel that allows common people to attain uncommon results.
>
> —Dale Carnegie

others rarely speak up, even when they have something important to contribute. The team leader can help by seeking all members' input. In other cases, the team may lack a charter, vision, or goals. Early in the development process, the team leader and members should define the team's direction and individual roles. When morale and productivity drop, persistence, communication, and forward movement can help them return to higher levels. Or, if team members do not trust each other or their leader, they may spend more time trying to protect their own interests than performing their actual jobs.[44] When trust is present, teams achieve higher performance.[45]

It is not easy to build high-performance teams. *Teams* is often just a word used by management to describe merely putting people into groups. "Teams" sometimes are launched with little or no training or support systems. For example, both managers and group members need new skills to make a group work. These skills include learning the art of diplomacy, tackling "people issues" head-on, and walking the fine line between encouraging autonomy and rewarding team innovations without letting the team get too independent and out of control.[46] Giving up some authority is difficult for managers from traditional systems, but they have to realize they will gain control in the long run by creating stronger, better-performing units.

Teams should be properly empowered,[47] as discussed in the previous chapter. The potential benefits of teams are lost when they are not allowed to make important decisions—in other words, when management doesn't trust them with important responsibilities. If teams must obtain permission for every innovative idea, they will revert to making safe, traditional decisions.[48]

Empowerment enhances team performance even among virtual teams. Empowerment for virtual teams includes thorough training in using the technologies and strong technical support from management. Some virtual teams have periodic face-to-face interactions, which help performance; empowerment is particularly helpful for virtual teams that don't often meet face-to-face.[49]

Failure lies in not knowing and doing what makes teams successful. To be successful, you must apply clear thinking and appropriate practices, as the rest of the chapter describes.[50]

LO5 Describe how to build an effective team.

5 | BUILDING EFFECTIVE TEAMS

All the considerations just described form the building blocks of an effective work team. But what does it really mean for a team to be effective? What, precisely, can a manager do to design a truly effective team? Team effectiveness is defined by three criteria:[51]

1. Team productivity. The output of the team meets or exceeds the standards of quantity and quality expected by the customers, inside and outside the organization, who receive the team's goods or services.

2. Team members realize *satisfaction* of their personal needs.

3. Team members remain *committed* to working together again; that is, the group doesn't burn out and disintegrate after a grueling project. Looking back, the members are glad they were involved. In other words, effective teams remain viable and have good prospects for repeated success in the future.[52]

For help in developing these qualities, teams may use team-building activities or work with an outside coach. Team building usually involves activities focused on relationships among team members. Whether a group discussion or a weekend retreat with physical challenges, the team-building event should fit specific team or company challenges. Participants should consider how they will apply those lessons at work.[53]

Legendary Harvard professor Richard Hackman identified principles of team effectiveness, including this simple rule: Teams need to properly define their membership. However, many don't, perhaps because people hate to exclude someone. When a team problem came to light at a financial services company, the chief executive determined that the chief financial officer was unable to collaborate effectively with others on the executive team. So the CEO asked the financial executive to skip the "boring" team meetings, keeping their communications one-on-one. Without the CFO, the executive team began to function much better.

Another barrier to team effectiveness: People tend to focus too much on harmony, assuming that when team members feel good about their participation, the team is effective. Actually, effectiveness comes first: Team members feel satisfied when their team works effectively. A study of symphony orchestras showed that musicians' job satisfaction came from how they felt *after* a strong performance.

A third mistake is to assume that team members can be together too long, to the point that the team runs out of ideas. But aside from research and development teams, which should periodically add new members, Hackman found that a more frequent problem is the opposite: Team members haven't been together long enough to learn to work well together. Airplane cockpit crews, for example, perform much better when they have flown together previously.[54]

5.1 | Effective Teams Focus on Performance

The key element of effective teamwork is commitment to a common purpose.[55] The best teams are those that have been given an important performance challenge by management and then reached a common understanding and appreciation of their collective purpose. Without such understanding and commitment, a group will be just a bunch of individuals.

The best teams also work hard at developing a common understanding of how they will work together to achieve their purpose.[56] They discuss and agree on such details as how tasks and roles will be allocated and how team members will make decisions. The team should develop norms for examining its performance strategies and be amenable to changing them when appropriate. Teams usually standardize at least some processes, but they should be willing to try creative new ideas if the situation calls for them.[57] With a clear, strong, motivating purpose and effective performance strategies, people pull together into a powerful force that has a chance to achieve extraordinary things. Steve Jobs inspired an Apple team to create the era-defining iPhone in 2007.[58]

The team's general purpose should be translated into specific, measurable performance goals.[59] You already learned about how goals motivate individual performance. Performance can be defined by collective end products, instead of an accumulation of individual products.[60] Team-based performance goals help define and distinguish the team's product, encourage communication within the team, energize and motivate team members, provide feedback on progress, signal team victories (and defeats), and ensure that people focus clearly on team results. Teams with both difficult goals and specific incentives to attain them achieve the highest performance levels.[61]

The best team-based measurement systems inform top management of the team's performance and help the team understand its own processes and gauge its own progress. Ideally, the team plays the lead role in designing its own measurement system. This responsibility is a great indicator of whether the team is truly empowered.[62]

Teams, like individuals, need feedback on their performance. Feedback from customers is especially crucial. Some customers for the team's products are inside the organization. Teams should be responsible for satisfying them and should be given or should seek performance feedback.

Better yet, wherever possible, teams should interact directly with external customers who make the ultimate buying decisions about their goods and services. External customers typically provide the most honest, and most crucial and useful, performance feedback.[63]

5.2 | Managers Can Motivate Effective Teamwork

Sometimes, individuals work less hard and are less productive when they are members of a group. Such social loafing occurs when individuals believe that their contributions are not important, others will do the work for them, their lack of effort will go undetected, or they will be the lone sucker if they work hard but others don't. Perhaps you have seen social loafing in some of your student teams.[64] Conversely, sometimes individuals work harder when they are members of a group than when they are working alone. This social facilitation effect occurs because individuals usually are more motivated in the presence of others, are concerned with what others think of them, and want to maintain a positive self-image.

A social facilitation effect is maintained—and a social loafing effect can be avoided—under the following conditions:[65]

- Group members know each other.

- They can observe and communicate with one another.

- Clear performance goals exist.

- The task is meaningful to the people working on it.

- Group members believe that their efforts matter and that others will not take advantage of them.

- The culture supports teamwork.

Under ideal circumstances, everyone works hard, contributes in concrete ways to the team's work, and is accountable to other team members. Accountability to one another, rather than just to "the boss," is an essential aspect of good teamwork. Accountability inspires mutual commitment and trust.[66] Trust in your teammates—and their trust in you—may be the ultimate key to effectiveness.

Team effort comes also from designing the team's tasks to be motivating. Techniques for creating motivating tasks appear in the guidelines for job enrichment discussed in Chapter 11. Tasks are motivating when they use a variety of member skills and provide high task variety, identity, significance, autonomy, and performance feedback.

Ultimately, teamwork is motivated by tying rewards to team performance.[67] If team performance can be measured validly, team-based rewards can be given accordingly. But it is not easy to move from a system of rewards based on individual performance to one based on team performance and cooperation. It also may not be appropriate unless people are truly interdependent and must collaborate to attain true team goals.[68]

Team-based rewards are often combined with regular salaries and rewards based on individual performance.

If team performance is difficult to measure validly, then desired behaviors, activities, and processes that indicate good teamwork can be rewarded. Individuals within teams can be given differential rewards based on teamwork indicated by active participation, cooperation, leadership, and other contributions to the team.

If team members are to be rewarded differentially, such decisions are better *not* left only to the boss.[69] They should be made by the team itself, through peer ratings or multi-rater evaluation systems. Why? Team members are in a better position to observe, know, and make valid reward allocations. And, the more teams the organization has, and the more a full team orientation exists, the more valid and effective it will be to distribute rewards via gainsharing and other organization-wide incentives.

5.3 | Effective Teams Have Skilled Members

Team members should be selected and trained so that they become effective contributors to the team. Generally, the skills required by teams include technical or functional expertise, problem-solving and decision-making skills, and interpersonal skills. Some managers and teams mistakenly overemphasize some skills, particularly technical or functional ones, and underemphasize the others. In fact, social skills can be critical to team functioning; one worker with a persistently bad attitude—for example, someone who bullies or constantly complains—often sends an entire team into a downward spiral.[70] It is vitally important that all three types of skills be represented, and developed, among team members.

5.4 | Norms Shape Team Behavior

Norms are shared beliefs about how people should think and behave. For example, some people like to keep information and knowledge to

> **norms** shared beliefs about how people should think and behave

Two important sets of roles must be performed:[75]

1. **Task specialist** roles are filled by individuals who have particular job-related skills and abilities. These employees keep the team moving toward accomplishment of the objectives.

2. **Team maintenance specialists** develop and maintain harmony within the team. They boost morale, give support, provide humor, soothe hurt feelings, and generally exhibit a concern for members' well-being.

themselves, but teams should try to establish a norm of knowledge sharing because it can improve team performance.[71]

From the organization's standpoint, norms can be positive or negative. In some teams, everyone works hard; in other groups, employees are opposed to management and do as little work as possible. Some groups develop norms of taking risks, others of being conservative.[72] A norm could dictate that employees speak of the company either favorably or critically. Team members may show concern about poor safety practices, drug and alcohol abuse, and employee theft, or they may not care about these issues (or may even condone such practices). Health consciousness is the norm among executives at some companies, but smoking is a norm at tobacco companies. Some groups have norms of distrust and of being closed toward one another, but as you might guess, norms of trust and open discussion about conflict can improve group performance.[73]

A professor described his consulting experiences at two companies that exhibited different norms in their management teams.[74] At Federal Express Corporation, a young manager interrupted the professor's talk by proclaiming that a recent decision by top management ran counter to the professor's point about corporate planning. He was challenging top management to defend its decision. A hot debate ensued, and after an hour everyone went to lunch without a trace of hard feelings. But at another corporation, the professor opened a meeting by asking a group of top managers to describe the company's culture. There was silence. He asked again. More silence. Then someone passed him an unsigned note that read, "Dummy, can't you see that we can't speak our minds? Ask for the input anonymously, in writing." As you can see, norms are important, and can vary greatly from one group to another.

> **Did You KNOW ?**
>
> Google studied 120 of its high- and low-performing teams over several years and concluded: "To build a successful team, you must find the balance between results and culture." The factors that mattered most to team effectiveness were making members feel psychologically safe, ensuring timely work, setting clear role expectations, and helping members find meaningfulness in their work.[76]

Note the similarity between these roles and the important task performance and group maintenance leadership behaviors you learned about in Chapter 10. Some of these roles will be more important than others at different times and under different circumstances. But these behaviors need not be carried out only by one or two leaders; any member of the team can assume them at any time. Both types of roles can be performed by different people at different times.

What roles should leaders perform? Superior team leaders are better at several things[77] (as illustrated in Exhibit 12.4):

- *Relating*—exhibiting social and political awareness, caring for team members, and building trust.

- *Scouting*—seeking information from managers, peers, and specialists, and investigating problems systematically.

5.5 | Team Members Must Fill Important Roles

Roles are different sets of expectations for how different individuals should behave. Although norms apply generally to all team members, different roles exist for different members within the norm structure.

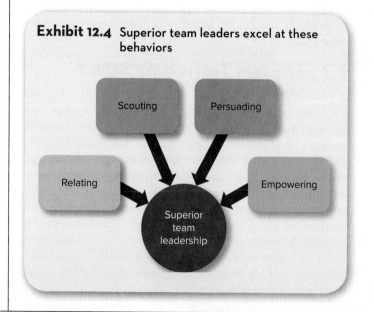

Exhibit 12.4 Superior team leaders excel at these behaviors

- *Persuading*—influencing team members, as well as obtaining external support for teams.

- *Empowering*—delegating authority, being flexible regarding team decisions, and coaching.

Leaders also should roll up their sleeves and do real work to accomplish team goals, not just supervise.[78] Finally, recall from Chapter 10 the importance of shared leadership, in which group members rotate or share leadership roles.[79]

5.6 | Cohesiveness Can Boost Team Performance—Sometimes

One of the most important properties of a team is cohesiveness.[80] **Cohesiveness** refers to how attractive the team is to its members, how motivated members are to remain in the team, and the degree to which team members influence one another. In general, it refers to how tightly knit the team is.

The Blue Angels are a highly cohesive team. Exhibiting a culture of excellence, a select few Navy and Marine Corps officers voluntarily serve with the Navy's premier flight demonstration squadron. Touring around the world, the squadron performs challenging aerial maneuvers that are tightly choreographed and delivered with the utmost precision.[81]

The Importance of Cohesiveness Cohesiveness is important for two primary reasons:

1. It contributes to *member satisfaction*. In a cohesive team, members communicate and get along well with one another. They feel good about being part of the team. Even if their jobs are unfulfilling or the organization is oppressive, people gain some satisfaction from enjoying their coworkers.

● The Blue Angels' demonstration pilots fly the F/A-18 Hornet in shows throughout the United States and abroad. They still use many of the same practices and techniques used in aerial displays from 1946.
U.S. Navy photo by Mass Communication Specialist 1st Class Roger S. Duncan

2. It has a major impact on *performance*.[82] A study of manufacturing teams showed that performance improvements in both quality and productivity occurred in the most cohesive unit, whereas conflict within another team prevented any quality or productivity improvements.[83] Sports fans read about this all the time. When teams are winning, players talk about the team being close, getting along well, and knowing one another's games. In contrast, players attribute losing to infighting and divisiveness.

> **cohesiveness** the degree to which a group is attractive to its members, members are motivated to remain in the group, and members influence one another

Cohesiveness clearly can have positive effects on performance.[84] But exceptions to this intuitive relationship occur. Tightly knit work groups can be disruptive to the organization, such as when they sabotage the assembly line, get their boss fired, or enforce low performance norms.

When does high cohesiveness lead to good performance, and when does it result in poor performance? Ultimately, performance depends on two things:

1. The task.

2. Performance norms.

The Task If the task is to make a decision or solve a problem, cohesiveness can lead to poor performance. Groupthink occurs when a tightly knit group is so cooperative that agreeing with one another's opinions and refraining from criticizing others' ideas become norms. For a cohesive group to make good decisions, it should establish a norm of constructive disagreement. This type of debating is important for groups up to the level of boards of directors.[85] In top management teams, debate improves companies' financial performance.[86]

But the effect of cohesiveness on performance can be positive, particularly if the task is to produce some tangible output. In day-to-day work groups for which decision making is not the primary task, cohesiveness can enhance performance. But that depends on the group's performance norms.[87]

Performance Norms Some groups are better than others at ensuring that their members behave the way the group prefers. Cohesive groups are more effective than noncohesive groups at norm enforcement. But the next question is, Do they have norms of high or low performance?

As Exhibit 12.5 shows, the highest performance occurs when a cohesive team has high-performance norms. But if a highly cohesive group has low-performance norms, that group will have the worst performance. In the group's eyes, it will have succeeded in achieving its goal of poor performance. Noncohesive groups with high-performance norms can be effective from the company's standpoint. However, they won't be as productive as they would be if

Take Charge of Your Career

Build your teamwork skills now

When we think of sports, we think of teams and competition. But when employers want to hire team members, they want to hire people with the willingness and ability to collaborate with others. In fact, teams are a core part of almost any workplace environment. Businesses as wide ranging as Google and Whole Foods rely on teams to drive innovation and success.

But don't wait until later to gain important teamwork skills. You've got plenty of opportunities in school to work on this in-demand skill set.

In business, "teamwork" often serves as an umbrella term that includes many soft skills that employers value. To be a good "team player," you need to be a good communicator, be able to effectively resolve conflict, and be accountable and respectful, to name a few. You can develop these skills in the team projects you do in your courses. Here are a few things to consider:

1. Know that you don't need all the answers; be willing to ask questions and accept help. Not surprisingly, a healthy give-and-take in the spirit of collaboration is key to successful teamwork.

2. Make speaking and listening a two-way street. Everyone has ideas and opinions, but not everyone is able to keep an open mind and consider fairly the ideas and opinions of others.

3. Maintain a positive attitude. Every team faces challenges and conflict. Troubles arise when those challenges and conflict deflate team morale or turn teammates against each other. Teammates who remain positive and constructive through good times and bad have more success.

It's also important to convey teamwork skills on your résumé. How do you do that? Be sure to mention any rewards or recognition you've received for your efforts in a team environment.

List work experience in which teamwork was an integral part of your job. Providing specific examples is key to attracting the attention of recruiters and hiring managers.

Sources: "Developing and Sustaining High-Performance Work Teams," Society for Human Resource Management, https://www.shrm.org/resourcesandtools/tools-and-samples/toolkits/pages/developingandsustaininghigh-performanceworkteams.aspx, accessed April 12, 2020; A. Van Nuys, "New LinkedIn Research: Upskill Your Employees with the Skills Companies Need Most in 2020," December 28, 2019, https://learning.linkedin.com/blog/learning-thought-leadership/most-in-demand-skills-2020; A. Doyle, "Important Teamwork Skills That Employers Value," The Balance, November 24, 2019, https://www.thebalancecareers.com/list-of-teamwork-skills-2063773; "15 Top Tips to Become a Better Team Player at Work," Forbes, December 18, 2018, https://www.forbes.com/sites/forbescoachescouncil/2018/12/18/15-top-tips-to-become-a-better-team-player-at-work/#414668b33f6e; and "Teamwork Skills on Your Resume: List and Examples," Resume Coach, https://www.resumecoach.com/teamwork-skills-on-your-resume-list-and-examples/, accessed April 12, 2020.

Exhibit 12.5 Cohesiveness, performance norms, and group performance

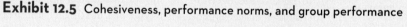
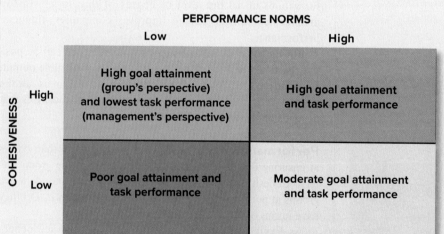

| | PERFORMANCE NORMS | |
	Low	High
COHESIVENESS High	High goal attainment (group's perspective) and lowest task performance (management's perspective)	High goal attainment and task performance
Low	Poor goal attainment and task performance	Moderate goal attainment and task performance

they were more cohesive. Noncohesive groups with low-performance norms perform poorly, but they will not ruin things for management as effectively as cohesive groups with low-performance norms.

5.7 | Managers Can Build Cohesiveness and High-Performance Norms

Managers should build teams that are cohesive and have high-performance norms. The following actions (Exhibit 12.6) can help create such teams:[88]

- *Recruit members with similar attitudes, values, and backgrounds.* Similar individuals are more likely to get along with one another. Don't do this, though, if the team's task requires heterogeneous skills and inputs—a homogeneous committee or board might make poor decisions because it will lack different information and viewpoints and may succumb to groupthink. Educational diversity and national diversity provide more benefits than limitations to groups' information use and application.[89]

Exhibit 12.6 Ways managers can build cohesive teams with high-performance norms

1. Recruit members with similar attitudes, values, and backgrounds.
2. Maintain high entrance and socialization standards.
3. Keep the team as small as possible.
4. Help the team succeed, and publicize its successes.
5. Be a participative leader.
6. Present a challenge from outside the team.
7. Tie rewards to team performance.

- *Maintain high entrance and socialization standards.* Teams and organizations that are difficult to get into have more prestige. Individuals who survive a difficult interview, selection, or training process will be proud of their accomplishment and feel more attached to the team.

- *Keep the team as small as possible* (but large enough to get the job done). The larger the group, the less important members may feel. Small teams make individuals feel like large contributors. Amazon's Jeff Bezos agrees: "If you can't feed a team with two large pizzas, it's too large."[90]

- *Help the team succeed, and publicize its successes.* You can empower teams as well as individuals.[91] Be a path–goal leader who facilitates success; the experience of winning brings teams closer together. Then, if you inform superiors of your team's successes, members will believe they are part of an important, prestigious unit. Teams that get into a good performance track continue to perform well as time goes on, but groups that don't often enter a downward spiral in which problems compound over time.[92]

- *Be a participative leader.* Participation in decisions gets team members more involved with one another and striving toward goal accomplishment. Too much autocratic decision making from above can alienate the group from management.

- *Present a challenge from outside the team.* Competition with other groups makes team members band together to defeat the enemy (witness what happens to school spirit before the big game against an archrival). Some of the greatest teams in business and in science have been completely focused on winning a competition.[93] But don't *you* become the outside threat. If team members dislike you as a boss, they will become more cohesive—but their performance norms will be against you, not with you.

- *Tie rewards to team performance.* To a large degree, teams are motivated just as individuals are: They do the activities that are rewarded. Make sure that high-performing teams get the rewards they deserve and that poorly performing groups get fewer rewards. You read about this earlier. Bear in mind that not just monetary rewards but also recognition for good work are powerful motivators. Recognize and celebrate team accomplishments. The team will become more cohesive and perform better to reap more rewards. Performance goals will be high, the organization will benefit from higher team motivation and productivity, and team members' individual needs will be better satisfied. Ideally, membership on a high-performing team that is recognized as such throughout the organization becomes a badge of honor.[94]

But keep this in mind: Strong cohesiveness encouraging "agreeableness" can be dysfunctional. For problem solving and decision making, the team should establish norms that promote an open, constructive atmosphere, including honest disagreement over issues without personal conflict and animosity.[95]

● Self-managed teams can boost productivity. But people often resist self-managed teams, in part because they don't want so much responsibility and it is difficult to adjust to the change in decision-making process. Yuri Arcurs/E+/Getty Images

LO6 List methods for managing a team's relationships with other teams.

6 | MANAGING LATERAL RELATIONSHIPS

Teams do not function in a vacuum; they are interdependent with other teams. For example, groups of IBM researchers from its 12 labs collaborate to develop practical uses for artificial intelligence, blockchain, and quantum computing.[96]

6.1 | Some Team Members Should Manage Outward

Several vital roles link teams to their external environments—that is, to other individuals and groups inside and outside the organization. One role that spans team boundaries is the **gatekeeper**, a team member who stays abreast of current information in scientific and other fields and tells the group about important developments. Information useful to the group can also include resources, trends, and political support throughout the corporation or the industry.[97]

The balance between an internal and external strategic focus and between internal and external roles depends on how much the team needs information, support, and resources from outside. The team's strategy dictates the team's mix of internally–versus externally–focused roles and the ways the mix changes over time. There are several general team strategies:[98]

- The **informing** strategy entails making decisions with the team and then telling outsiders of the team's intentions.

- **Parading** means that the team's strategy is to simultaneously emphasize internal team building and achieve external visibility.

- **Probing** involves a focus on external relations. This strategy requires team members to interact frequently with outsiders; diagnose the needs of customers, clients, and higher-ups; and experiment with solutions before taking action.

When teams have a high degree of dependence on outsiders, probing is the best strategy. Parading teams perform at an intermediate level, and informing teams are likely to fail. They are too isolated from the outside groups on which they depend.

Informing or parading strategies may be more effective for teams that are less dependent on outside groups—for example, established teams working on routine tasks in stable environments. But for most important work teams—task forces, new-product teams, and strategic decision-making teams tackling unstructured problems in a rapidly changing external environment—effective performance in roles that involve interfacing with the outside is vital.

6.2 | Some Relationships Help Teams Coordinate with Others in the Organization

Managing relationships with other groups and teams means engaging in a dynamic give-and-take that ensures proper coordination throughout the management system. To many managers, this process often seems like a free-for-all. To help understand the process and make it more productive, we can identify and examine the different types of lateral role relationships and take a strategic approach to building constructive relationships.

Different teams, like different individuals, have roles to perform. As teams carry out their roles, several distinct patterns of working relationships develop:[99]

- *Workflow relationships* emerge as materials are passed from one group to another. A group commonly receives work from one unit, processes it, and sends it to the next unit in the process. Your group, then, will come before some groups and after others in the sequence.

- *Service relationships* exist when top management centralizes an activity to which a large number of other units must gain access. Common examples are technology services, research departments and libraries, and administrative staff. Such units must help assist other people accomplish their goals.

- *Advisory relationships* are created when teams with problems call on centralized sources of expert knowledge. For example, staff members in the human resources or legal department advise work teams.

- *Audit relationships* develop when people not directly in the chain of command evaluate the methods and performances of other teams. Financial auditors "check the books," and technical auditors assess the methods and quality of the work.

- *Stabilization relationships* involve auditing before the fact. In other words, teams sometimes must obtain clearance from others—for example, for large purchases—before they act.

- *Liaison relationships* involve intermediaries between teams. Managers often are called on to mediate conflict between two organizational units. Public relations people, sales managers, purchasing agents, and others who work across organizational boundaries serve in liaison roles as they maintain communications between the organization and the outside world.

The fact that teams are interdependent with other teams requires coordination and leadership.[100] For starters, teams should assess each working relationship with another unit by asking basic questions: "From whom do we receive work, and to whom do we send work? What permissions do we control, and to whom must we go for authorizations?" In this way, teams can better understand whom to contact and when, where, why, and how to do so. Coordination throughout the working system improves, problems are avoided or short-circuited before they get too serious, and performance improves.[101]

7 | CONFLICT IS INEVITABLE BUT MANAGEABLE

Conflict is a normal part of life in organizations. Keep in mind, you have many options for managing and resolving it.

7.1 | Conflicts Arise Both Within and Among Teams

The complex maze of interdependencies provides many opportunities for conflict to arise among groups and teams. Conflict is defined as a process in which one party perceives that its interests are being opposed or negatively affected by another party.[102] It can occur between individuals on the same team or among different teams. Many people's view of conflict is that it should be avoided at all costs. However, early management science contributor Mary Parker Follett was the first of many to note its potential advantages.[103] Typically, conflict can foster creativity when it is about ideas rather than personalities. In contrast, at a nonprofit organization, team members were committed to maintaining harmony during meetings, but their unresolved differences spilled over into nasty remarks outside of the office.[104]

Many factors cause great potential for destructive conflict: the sheer number and variety of contacts, ambiguities in jurisdiction and responsibility, differences in goals, intergroup competition for scarce resources, different perspectives held by members of different units, varying time horizons in which some units attend to long-term considerations and others focus on short-term needs, and others. Commonly, subgroups form along conflict fault lines.[105]

Tensions and anxieties are likely to arise in teams that are demographically diverse, include members from different parts of the organization, or are composed of contrasting personalities. Both demographic and cross-functional heterogeneity initially lead to problems such as stress, lower cooperation, and lower cohesiveness.[106]

Over time and with communication, diverse groups actually tend to become more cooperative and perform better than do homogeneous groups. Norms of cooperation can improve performance, as does the fact that cross-functional teams engage in more external communication with more areas of the organization.[107]

7.2 | Conflict Management Techniques

Teams inevitably face conflicts and must decide how to manage them.[108] The aim should be to make the conflict productive—that is, to make those involved believe they have benefited rather than lost from the conflict.[109] People believe they have benefited from a conflict when they see the following outcomes:

conflict a process in which one party perceives that its interests are being opposed or negatively affected by another party

avoidance a reaction to conflict that involves ignoring the problem by doing nothing at all or deemphasizing the disagreement

accommodation a style of dealing with conflict involving cooperation on behalf of the other party but not being assertive about one's own interests

compromise a style of dealing with conflict involving moderate attention to both parties' concerns

competing a style of dealing with conflict involving strong focus on one's own goals and little or no concern for the other person's goals

collaboration a style of dealing with conflict emphasizing both cooperation and assertiveness to maximize both parties' satisfaction

- A new solution is implemented, the problem is solved, and it is unlikely to emerge again.

- Work relationships have been strengthened, and people believe they can work together productively in the future.

People handle conflict in different ways. You have your own style; others' styles may be similar or may differ. Their styles depend in part on their country's cultural norms. For example, the Chinese are more concerned with collective than with individual interests, and they are more likely than managers in the United States to turn to higher authorities to make decisions rather than resolve conflicts themselves.[110]

Culture aside, any team or individual has several options regarding how they deal with conflicts.[111] These personal styles of dealing with conflict, shown in Exhibit 12.7, differ based on how much people strive to satisfy their own concerns (the assertiveness dimension) and how much they focus on satisfying the other party's concerns (the cooperation dimension).

For example, a common reaction to conflict is avoidance. In this situation, people do nothing to satisfy themselves or others. They ignore the problem by doing nothing at all, or address it by merely smoothing over or deemphasizing the disagreement. This, of course, fails to solve the problem or clear the air. When Paul Forti was passed over for a promotion, his new boss was at first too busy to discuss his disappointment and future role in the firm. He avoided conversations, and their working relationship suffered for weeks.[112]

Accommodation means cooperating on behalf of the other party but not being assertive about one's own interests. Compromise involves moderate attention to both parties' concerns, being neither highly cooperative nor highly assertive. This style results in satisficing but not optimizing solutions. Competing is a strong response in which people focus strictly on their own wishes and are unwilling to recognize the other person's concerns. Finally, collaboration emphasizes both cooperation and assertiveness. The goal is to maximize satisfaction for both parties.

Imagine that you and a friend want to go to a movie together, and you have different movies in mind. If he insists that you go to his movie, he is showing the competing style. If you agree, even though you prefer another movie, you are accommodating.

Exhibit 12.7 Conflict management strategies

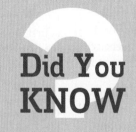

COOPERATION

	Uncooperative		Cooperative
Assertive	Competing		Collaborating
		Compromising	
Unassertive	Avoiding		Accommodating

ASSERTIVENESS

Source: K. Thomas, "Conflict and Conflict Management," in *Handbook of Industrial and Organizational Psychology,* ed. M. D. Dunnette. Copyright © 1976. Reprinted by permission of Kenneth W. Thomas.

Chris Ryan/age fotostock

superordinate goals higher-level goals that take priority over specific individual or group goals

mediator a third party who intervenes to help others manage their conflict

If one of you mentions a third movie that neither of you is excited about but both of you are willing to live with, you are compromising. If you realize you don't know all the options, do some research, and find another movie that you're both enthusiastic about, you are collaborating.

Different approaches are necessary at different times.[114] For example, *competing* can be necessary when cutting costs or dealing with other scarce resources. *Compromise* may be useful when people are under time pressure, when they need to achieve a temporary solution, or when collaboration fails. People should *accommodate* when they learn they are wrong or to minimize loss when they are outmatched. Even *avoiding* may be appropriate if the issue is trivial or resolving the conflict should be someone else's responsibility.

But when the conflict concerns important issues, when both sets of concerns are valid and important, when a creative solution is needed, and when commitment to the solution is vital to implementation, *collaboration* is the ideal approach.[115] Collaboration can be achieved by airing thoughts, addressing all concerns, and avoiding goal displacement by not letting personal attacks interfere with problem

solving. An important technique is to invoke superordinate goals—higher-level organizational goals toward which everyone should be striving and that ultimately need to take precedence over personal or unit preferences.[116] Collaboration offers the best chance of reaching mutually satisfactory solutions based on the ideas and interests of all parties, and of maintaining and strengthening work relationships.

7.3 | Mediating Can Help Resolve a Conflict

Managers spend a lot of time trying to resolve conflict between *other* people. You already may have served as a mediator, a third party who intervenes to help settle a conflict between other people. Third-party intervention, done well, can improve working relationships and help the parties improve their own conflict management, communication, and problem-solving skills.[117]

Some insight comes from a study of human resource (HR) managers and the conflicts with which they deal.[118] HR managers encounter every type of conflict imaginable: interpersonal difficulties from minor irritations to jealousy to fights; operations issues, including union issues, work assignments, overtime, and sick leave; discipline over infractions ranging from drug use and theft to sleeping on the job; sexual harassment and racial bias; pay and promotion issues; and feuds or strategic conflicts among divisions or individuals at the highest organizational levels.

Did You KNOW ?

The U.S. Equal Employment Opportunity Commission's private-sector mediation program resolves thousands of complaints, annually, resulting in well over $100 million in monetary benefits for complainants.[113]

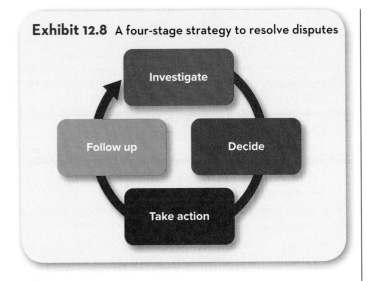

Exhibit 12.8 A four-stage strategy to resolve disputes

- Investigate
- Decide
- Take action
- Follow up

In the study, the HR managers successfully settled most of the disputes. As illustrated in Exhibit 12.8, these managers typically follow a four-stage strategy:

1. They *investigate* by interviewing the disputants and others and gathering more information. While talking with the disputants, they seek both parties' perspectives, remaining as neutral as possible. The discussion should stay issue-oriented, not personal.

2. They *decide* how to resolve the dispute, often in conjunction with the disputants' bosses. In preparing to decide what to do, they should not assign blame prematurely; at this point they should explore solutions.

● Conflicts can arise for any team—the trick is to make them productive.
Phovoir/Shutterstock

3. They *take action* by explaining their decisions and the reasoning, and advise or train the disputants to avoid future incidents.

4. They *follow up* by making sure everyone understands the solution, documenting the conflict and the resolution, and monitoring the results by checking back with the disputants and their bosses.

Throughout, the objectives of HR managers are to be fully informed so that they understand the conflict; to be active and assertive in trying to resolve it; to be as objective, neutral, and impartial as humanly possible; and to be flexible by modifying their approaches according to the situation.

Here are some other recommendations for more effective conflict management.[119] Don't allow dysfunctional conflict to build or hope or assume that it will go away. Address it before it escalates. Try to resolve it, and if the first efforts don't work, try others. Even if disputants are not happy with your decisions, it helps to strive to treat people fairly, make a good-faith effort, and give them a voice in the proceedings. Remember, too, that you may be able to ask HR specialists to help with difficult conflicts.

7.4 | Conflict Isn't Always Face-to-Face

When teams are geographically dispersed, as is often the case for virtual teams, team members tend to experience more conflict and less trust.[120] Conflict management affects the success of virtual teams.[121] In a recent study, avoidance hurt performance. Accommodation—conceding to others just to maintain harmony rather than assertively attempting to negotiate integrative solutions—had no effect on performance. Collaboration had a positive effect on performance. The researchers also uncovered two surprises: Compromise hurt performance, and competition helped performance. Compromises hurt because they often are watered-down, middle-of-the-road, suboptimal solutions. Competitive behavior was useful because the virtual teams were temporary and under time pressure, so having some individuals behave dominantly and impose decisions to achieve efficiency was useful rather than detrimental.

When people have problems in business-to-business e-commerce (e.g., costly delays), they tend to behave competitively and defensively rather than collaboratively.[122] Technical problems and recurring problems test people's patience. The conflict will escalate unless people use more cooperative, collaborative styles. Try to prevent conflicts before they arise; for example, make sure your information system is running smoothly before linking with others. Monitor and reduce or eliminate problems as soon as possible. When problems arise, express your willingness to cooperate, and then *actually be* cooperative. Even technical problems require the social skills of good management.

Notes

1. L. Landry, "How to Build an Effective Innovation Team," Northeastern University Graduate Programs, October 25, 2017, https://www.northeastern.edu/graduate/blog/how-to-build-innovation-team/.

2. T. McDowell, D. Miller, D. Agarwal, T. Okamoto, and T. Page, "Organizational Design: The Rise of Teams," Deloitte Insights, March 1, 2016, https://www2.deloitte.com/us/en/insights/focus/human-capital-trends/2016/organizational-models-network-of-teams.html.

3. D. Walsh, "Three Steps to Help Innovation Teams Succeed at an Established Company," Kellogg School of Management, January 4, 2019, https://insight.kellogg.northwestern.edu/article/three-steps-to-help-innovation-teams-succeed-at-an-established-company.

4. P. Tatevosian, "What's behind the Success of Target's Growth Rejuvenation?" The Motley Fool, December 3, 2019, https://www.fool.com/investing/2019/12/03/whats-behind-the-success-of-targets-growth-rejuven.aspx.

5. "The Power of Many: How Companies Use Teams to Drive Superior Corporate Performance," Ernst & Young, www.ey.com; and K. O'Connor, "9 Ways Great Companies Organize Their Teams for Success," Fast Company, August 21, 2012, www.fastcompany.com.

6. L. Riebe, D. Roepen, B. Santarelli, and G. Marchioro, "Teamwork: Effectively Teaching an Employability Skill," Education and Training 52, no. 6/7 (2010), pp. 528-39; and G. Chen, L. Donahue, and R. Klimoski, "Training Undergraduates to Work in Organizational Teams," Academy of Management Learning and Education 3 (2004), pp. 27-40.

7. T. McDowell, D. Agarwal, D. Miller, T. Okamoto, and T. Page, "Organization Design: The Rise of Teams," Deloitte Insights, March 1, 2016, https://www2.deloitte.com/us/en/insights/focus/human-capital-trends/2016/organizational-models-network-of-teams.html; and T. O'Neill and E. Salas, "Creating High Performance Teamwork in Organizations," Human Resource Management Review 28 (2018), pp. 325-31.

8. J. Weed, "California's Papa & Barkley Cannabis Company Grows with Teamwork," Forbes, June 22, 2018, https://www.forbes.com.

9. S. Siang, "How Mentors, Teamwork and Lessons from Failure Led to Success for CEO of e.l.f. Cosmetics," Forbes, March 11, 2019, https://www.forbes.com.

10. M. Mace, "GoogleLogic: Why Google Does the Things It Does the Way It Does," The Guardian, July 9, 2013, http://www.theguardian.com; and A. Somech and A. Drach-Zahavy, "Translating Team Creativity to Innovation Implementation: The Role of Team Composition and Climate for Innovation," Journal of Management 39 (2013), pp. 684-708.

11. "InGenius: Accelerator Program within Nestlé, Focusing on Employee-Driven Innovation," Nestlé, http://ingeniusaccelerator.nestle.com, accessed March 21, 2019.

12. D. Nadler, J. R. Hackman, and E. E. Lawler III, Managing Organizational Behavior (Boston: Little, Brown, 1979).

13. M. Cianni and D. Wnuck, "Individual Growth and Team Enhancement: Moving toward a New Model of Career Development," Academy of Management Executive 11 (1997), pp. 105-15.

14. S. Cohen and D. Bailey, "What Makes Teams Work: Group Effectiveness Research from the Shop Floor to the Executive Suite," Journal of Management 23, no. 3 (1997), pp. 239-90; and S. Huovinen and M. Pasanen, "Entrepreneurial and Management Teams: What Makes the Difference," Journal of Management and Organization 16, no. 3 (July 2010), pp. 436-54.

15. J. Katzenbach and D. Smith, "The Discipline of Teams," Harvard Business Review, March-April 1993, pp. 111-20.

16. H. Morgan, "5 Workplace Changes Your Boss Is Eyeing for the Future," Money, March 2, 2016, www.money.usnews.com; and J. Lindzon, "6 Ways Work Will Change in 2016," Fast Company, November 2, 2015, www.fastcompany.com.

17. S. Cohen, "New Approaches to Teams and Teamwork," in J. Galbraith, E. E. Lawler III, and Associates, Organizing for the Future (San Francisco: Jossey-Bass, 1993); and J. Hollenbeck, B. Beersma, and M. Schouten, "Beyond Team Types and Taxonomies: A Dimensional Scaling Conceptualization for Team Description," Academy of Management Review 37 (2012), pp. 82-106.

18. S. Cohen and D. Bailey, "What Makes Teams Work: Group Effectiveness Research from the Shop Floor to the Executive Suite," Journal of Management 23 (1997), pp. 239-90.

19. "Developing and Sustaining High-Performance Work Teams," Society for Human Resource Management, July 23, 2015, www.shrm.org.

20. "Developing and Sustaining High-Performance Work Teams," Society for Human Resource Management, July 23, 2015, www.shrm.org.

21. C. Snow, S. Snell, S. Davison, and D. Hambrick, "Use Transnational Teams to Globalize Your Company," Organizational Dynamics, Spring 1996, pp. 50-67.

22. L. Gilson, M. Travis, N. C. J. Young, M. Vartiainen, and M. Hakonen, "Virtual Teams Research: 10 Years, 10 Themes, and 10 Opportunities," Journal of Management 41 (2015), pp. 1313-37; J. Dulebohn and J. Hoch, "Virtual Teams in Organizations," Human Resource Management Review 27 (2017), pp. 569-74; J. Schaubroeck and A. Yu, "When Does Virtuality Help or Hinder Teams? Core Team Characteristics as Contingency Factors," Human Resource Management Review 27 (2017), pp. 635-47; B. Liao, "Leadership in Virtual Teams: A Multilevel Perspective," Human Resource Management Review 27 (2017), pp. 648-59; and N. Hill and K. Bartol, "Empowering Leadership and Effective Collaboration in Geographically Dispersed Teams," Personnel Psychology 69 (2016), pp. 159-98.

23. F. Siebdrat, M. Hoegl, and H. Ernst, "How to Manage Virtual Teams," MIT Sloan Management Review 50, no. 4 (Summer 2009), pp. 63-68; and B. Kirkman, B. Rosen, C. Gibson, P. Tesluk, and S. McPherson, "Five Challenges to Virtual Team Success: Lessons from Sabre, Inc.," Academy of Management Executive 16 (2002), pp. 67-80.

24. A. Malhotra, A. Majchrzak, and B. Rosen, "Leading Virtual Teams," *Academy of Management Perspectives,* February 2007, pp. 60-70, table 1.

25. J. Meggers, "Making Teamwork Simpler," *Cisco Blogs,* May 2015, www.blogs.cisco.com.

26. J. Hess, "Empowering Autonomous Teams," *Ivey Business Journal,* November-December 2013, www.iveybusinessjournal.com; and J. Millikin, P. Hom, and C. Manz, "Self-Management Competencies in Self-Managing Teams: Their Impact on Multi-Team System Productivity," *Leadership Quarterly* 21 (2010), pp. 687-702.

27. C. Blakeman, "Why Self-Managed Teams Are the Future of Business," *Inc.,* November 25, 2014, www.inc.com; D. Yeatts, M. Hipskind, and D. Barnes, "Lessons Learned from Self-Managed Work Teams," *Business Horizons,* July-August 1994, pp. 11-18; and M. Muethel and M. Hoegl, "Shared Leadership Effectiveness in Independent Professional Teams," *European Management Journal* 31 (2013), pp. 423-32.

28. B. Kirkman and D. Shapiro, "The Impact of Cultural Values on Job Satisfaction and Organizational Commitment in Self-Managing Work Teams: The Mediating Role of Employee Resistance," *Academy of Management Journal* 44 (2001), pp. 557-69.

29. B. Kirkman and D. Shapiro, "The Impact of Cultural Values on Job Satisfaction and Organizational Commitment in Self-Managing Work Teams: The Mediating Role of Employee Resistance," *Academy of Management Journal* 44 (2001), pp. 557-69.

30. B. Kirkman and D. Shapiro, "The Impact of Cultural Values on Employee Resistance to Teams: Toward a Model of Globalized Self-Managing Work Team Effectiveness," *Academy of Management Review* 22 (1997), pp. 730-57.

31. M. von Bonsdorff, M. Janhonen, Z. Zhou, and S. Vanhala, "Team Autonomy, Organizational Commitment and Company Performance: A Study in the Retail Trade," *The International Journal of Human Resource Management* 26, no. 8 (2014), pp. 1-12; M. Johnson, J. Hollenbeck, D. DeRue, C. Barnes, and D. Jundt, "Functional versus Dysfunctional Team Change: Problem Diagnosis and Structural Feedback for Self-Managed Teams," *Organizational Behavior and Human Decision Processes* 122 (2013), pp. 1-11; S. Sarker, S. Sarker, S. Kirkeby, and S. Chakraborty, "Path to 'Stardom' in Globally Distributed Hybrid Teams: An Examination of a Knowledge-Centered Perspective Using Social Network Analysis," *Decision Sciences* 42 (2011), 339-70; and B. Macy and H. Isumi, "Organizational Change, Design, and Work Innovation: A Meta-Analysis of 131 North American Field Studies—1961-1991," *Research in Organizational Change and Development* 7 (1993), pp. 235-313.

32. "Most Innovative Companies in 2019: Spotify," *Fast Company,* www.fastcompany.com, accessed April 9, 2020.

33. B. W. Tuckman, "Developmental Sequence in Small Groups," *Psychological Bulletin* 63 (1965), pp. 384-99.

34. S. Furst, M. Reeves, B. Rosen, and R. Blackburn, "Managing the Life Cycle of Virtual Teams," *Academy of Management Executive,* May 2004, pp. 6-20. Quotes in this paragraph are from pp. 11 and 12; D. Mukherjee, S. Lahiri, D. Mukherjee, and T. Billing, "Leading Virtual Teams: How Do Social, Cognitive, and Behavioral Capabilities Matter?" *Management Decision* 50 (2012), pp. 273-90; and S. Humphrey and F. Aime, "Team Microdynamics: Toward an Organizing Approach to Teamwork," *Academy of Management Annals* 8 (2014), pp. 443-503.

35. C. J. G. Gersick, "Time and Transition in Work Teams: Toward a New Model of Group Development," *Academy of Management Journal* 31 (1988), pp. 9-41.

36. J. R. Hackman, *Groups That Work (and Those That Don't)* (San Francisco: Jossey-Bass, 1990).

37. J. R. Hackman, *Groups That Work (and Those That Don't)* (San Francisco: Jossey-Bass, 1990); and A. C. Edmondson, "Teamwork on the Fly," *Harvard Business Review* 90, no. 4 (2012), pp. 72-80.

38. A. Newman, R. Donahue, and N. Eva, "Psychological Safety: A Systematic Review of the Literature," *Human Resource Management Review* 27 (2017), pp. 521-35; M. Frazier, S. Fainshmidt, R. Klinger, A. Pezeshkan, and V. Vracheva, "Psychological Safety: A Meta-Analytic Review and Extension," *Personnel Psychology* 70 (2017), pp. 113-65; and C. Roussin, T. MacLean, and J. Rudolph, "The Safety in Unsafe Teams: A Multilevel Approach to Team Psychological Safety," *Journal of Management* 42 (2016), pp. 1409-33.

39. I. Hoever, D. van Knippenberg, W. van Ginkel, and H. Barkema, "Fostering Team Creativity: Perspective Taking as Key to Unlocking Diversity's Potential," *Journal of Applied Psychology* 97 (2012), pp. 982-96.

40. T. Johns and L. Gratton, "The Third Wave of Virtual Work," *Harvard Business Review,* January 1, 2013, www.hbr.org.

41. "Dell and Intel Future Workforce Study Provides Key Insights into Technology Trends Shaping the Modern Global Workplace," Dell, July 18, 2016, www.dell.com.

42. J. Zenger, E. Musselwhite, K. Hurson, and C. Perrin, *Leading Teams: Mastering the New Role* (Burr Ridge, IL: Irwin Professional Publishing, 1994).

43. R. Cross, "Looking before You Leap: Assessing the Jump to Teams in Knowledge-Based Work," *Business Horizons,* September-October 2000, pp. 29-36.

44. M. E. Palanski, S. S. Kahai, and F. J. Yammarino, "Team Virtues and Performance: An Examination of Transparency, Behavioral Integrity, and Trust," *Journal of Business Ethics* 99, no. 2 (2011), pp. 201-16.

45. M. E. Palanski, S. S. Kahai, and F. J. Yammarino, "Team Virtues and Performance: An Examination of Transparency, Behavioral Integrity, and Trust," *Journal of Business Ethics* 99, no. 2 (2011), pp. 201-16.

46. J. Case, "What the Experts Forgot to Mention," *Inc.,* September 1993, pp. 66-78.

47. N. Lorinkova, M. Pearsall, and H. P. Sims Jr., "Examining the Differential Longitudinal Performance of Directive versus Empowering Leadership in Teams," *Academy of Management Journal* 56 (2013), pp. 573-96; M. T. Maynard, L. Gilson, and J. Mathieu, "Empowerment—Fad or Fab? A Multilevel Review of the Past Two Decades of Research," *Journal of Management* 38 (2012), pp. 1231-81; S. Seibert, G. Wang, and S. Courtright, "Antecedents and Consequences of Psychological and Team Empowerment in Organizations: A Meta-Analytic Review," *Journal of Applied Psychology* 96 (2011), pp. 981-1003; and G. Chen, P. N. Sharma, S. Edinger, D. Shapiro, and J.-L. Farh, "Motivating and Demotivating Forces in Teams: Cross-Level Influences of Empowering Leadership and Relationship Conflict," *Journal of Applied Psychology* 96 (2011), pp. 541-57.

48. J. Middleton, "Leadership Skills for Nurses," *Nursing Times–Leadership Supplement,* August 24, 2011, pp. 1-34; and A. Nahavandi and E. Aranda, "Restructuring Teams for the Reengineered Organization," *Academy of Management Executive,* November 1994, pp. 58-68.

49. B. Kirkman, B. Rosen, P. Tesluk, and C. Gibson, "The Impact of Team Empowerment on Virtual Team Performance: The Moderating Role of Face-to-Face Interaction," *Academy of Management Journal* 47 (2004), pp. 175-92.

50. J. R. Katzenbach and D. K. Smith, *The Wisdom of Teams* (Boston: Harvard Business School Press, 1993).

51. D. Nadler, J. R. Hackman, and E. E. Lawler III, *Managing Organizational Behavior* (Boston: Little, Brown, 1979).

52. D. Nadler, J. R. Hackman, and E. E. Lawler III, *Managing Organizational Behavior* (Boston: Little, Brown, 1979).

53. J. Graves, "The Best Team-Building Exercises," *Money,* September 24, 2014, www.money.usnews.com.

54. D. Coutu, "Why Teams Don't Work," *Harvard Business Review,* May 2009, pp. 99-105 (interview of J. Richard Hackman).

55. J. Katzenbach and D. Smith, "The Discipline of Teams," *Harvard Business Review,* March-April 1993, pp. 111-20.

56. J. Katzenbach and D. Smith, "The Discipline of Teams," *Harvard Business Review,* March-April 1993, pp. 111-20.

57. L. Gibson, J. Mathieu, C. Shalley, and T. Ruddy, "Creativity and Standardization: Complementary or Conflicting Drivers of Team Effectiveness?" *Academy of Management Journal* 48 (2005), pp. 521-31.

58. D. Smith, "'Where Are They Now?' Here's What Happened to Apple's Famous Leadership Team That Launched the First iPhone in 2007," *Business Insider,* July 21, 2019, www.businessinsider.com; and M. Hayes, "Who Invented the iPhone?" *Scientific American,* September 13, 2018, www.blogs.scientificamerican.com.

59. "Developing and Sustaining High-Performance Work Teams," Society for Human Resource Management, July 23, 2015, www.shrm.org.

60. J. R. Katzenbach and J. A. Santamaria, "Firing Up the Front Line," *Harvard Business Review,* May-June 1999, pp. 107-17.

61. A. Kleingeld, H. van Mierlo, and L. Arends, "The Effect of Goal Setting on Group Performance: A Meta-Analysis," *Journal of Applied Psychology* 96, no. 6 (November 2011), pp. 1289-1304; D. Knight, C. Durham, and E. Locke, "The Relationship of Team Goals, Incentives, and Efficacy to Strategic Risk, Tactical Implementation, and Performance," *Academy of Management Journal* 44 (2001), pp. 326-38; D. Blumenthal, Z. Song, A. Jena, and T. Ferris, "Guidance for Structuring Team-Based Incentivesin Health Care," *American Journal of Managed Care* 19 (2013), pp. 64-70; and C. Barnes, J. Hollenbeck, D. Jundt, D. S. DeRue, and S. Harmon, "Mixing Individual Incentives and Group Incentives: Best of Both Worlds or Social Dilemma?" *Journal of Management* 37 (2011), pp. 1611-35.

62. B. L. Kirkman and B. Rosen, "Powering Up Teams," *Organizational Dynamics,* Winter 2000, pp. 48-66.

63. E. E. Lawler III, *From the Ground Up* (San Francisco: Jossey-Bass, 1996).

64. A. Jassawalla, H. Sashittal, and A. Maishe, "Students' Perceptions of Social Loafing: Its Antecedents and Consequences in Undergraduate Business Classroom Teams," *Academy of Management Learning and Education,* 2009, pp. 42-54.

65. M. Erez, "Is Group Productivity Loss the Rule or the Exception? Effects of Culture and Group-Based Motivation," *Academy of Management Journal* 39 (1996), pp. 1513-37; and C. Lam, "The Role of Communication and Cohesion in Reducing Social Loafing in Group Projects," *Business Communication Quarterly* 78, no. 4 (December 2015), pp. 454-75.

66. J. Katzenbach and D. Smith, "The Discipline of Teams," *Harvard Business Review,* March-April 1993, pp. 111-20.

67. C. M. Barnes, J. R. Hellenbeck, D. K. Jundt, D. S. DeRue, and S. J. Harmon, "Mixing Individual Incentives and Group Incentives: Best of Both Worlds or Social Dilemma?" *Journal of Management* 37, no. 6 (November 2011), pp. 1611-35; M. Bolch, "Rewarding the Team," *HRMagazine,* February 2007; P. Pascarelloa, "Compensating Teams," *Across the Board,* February 1997, pp. 16-22; Y. Garbers and U. Konradt, "The Effect of Financial Incentives on Performance: A Quantitative Review of Individual and Team-Based Financial Incentives," *Journal of Occupational and Organizational Psychology* 87 (2014), pp. 102-37; M. Johnson, J. Hollenbeck, S. Humphrey, D. Ilgen, D. Jundt, and C. Meyer, "Cutthroat Cooperation: Asymmetrical Adaptation to Changes in Team Reward Structures," *Academy of Management Journal,* 2006, pp. 103-19; and M. J. Pearsall, M. S. Christian, and A. P. J. Ellis, "Motivating Interdependent Teams: Individual Rewards, Shared Rewards, or Something Between?" *Journal of Applied Psychology* 95 (2010), pp. 183-91.

68. R. Wageman, "Interdependence and Group Effectiveness," *Administrative Science Quarterly* 40 (1995), pp. 145-80.

69. E. E. Lawler III, *From the Ground Up* (San Francisco: Jossey-Bass, 1996).

70. B. Leichtling, "One Bad Apple Spoils the Whole Team," *Charlotte Business Journal,* December 16, 2011, www.bizjournals.com; J. Allen, "One 'Bad Apple' Does Spoil the Whole Office," Reuters, February 12, 2007, www.yahoo.com/news; and J. Wardy, "Don't Let One with Bad Attitude Infect Others," *Daily Record* (Morris County, NJ), April 23, 2007, www.dailyrecord.com.

71. A. Srivastava, K. Bartol, and E. Locke, "Empowering Leadership in Management Teams: Effects on Knowledge Sharing, Efficacy, and Performance," *Academy of Management Journal* (2006), pp. 1239-51.

72. J. M. Levine, E. T. Higgins, and H. Choi, "Development of Strategic Norms in Groups," *Organizational Behavior and Human Decision Processes* 82 (2000), pp. 88-101.

73. K. Jehn and E. Mannix, "The Dynamic Nature of Conflict: A Longitudinal Study of Intragroup Conflict and Group Performance," *Academy of Management Journal* 44 (2001), pp. 238-51; and M. Duffy, K. Scott, J. Shaw, B. Tepper, and K. Aquino, "A Social Context Model of Envy and Social Undermining," *Academy of Management Journal* 55 (2012), pp. 643-66.

74. J. O'Toole, *Vanguard Management: Redesigning the Corporate Future* (New York: Doubleday, 1985).

75. R. F. Bales, *Interaction Process Analysis: A Method for the Study of Small Groups* (Reading, MA: Addison-Wesley, 1950).

76. J. Bariso, "Google Spent Years Studying Great Teams. These 5 Qualities Contributed the Most to Its Success," *Inc.,* September≈10, 2018, www.inc.com.

77. V. U. Druskat and J. Wheeler, "Managing from the Boundary: The Effective Leadership of Self-Managing Work Teams," *Academy of Management Journal* 46 (2003), pp. 435-57.

78. J. R. Katzenbach and D. K. Smith, *The Wisdom of Teams* (Boston: Harvard Business School Press, 1993).

79. J. Carson, P. Tesluk, and J. Marrone, "Shared Leadership in Teams: An Investigation of Antecedent Conditions and Performance," *Academy of Management Journal* (2007), pp. 1217-34; and V. Nicolaides, K. LaPort, T. Chen, A. Tomassetti, E. Weis, S. Zaccaro, and J. Cortina, "The Shared Leadership of Teams: A Meta-Analysis of Proximal, Distal, and Moderating Relationships," *Leadership Quarterly* 25 (2014), pp. 923-42.

80. S. E. Seashore, *Group Cohesiveness in the Industrial Work Group* (Ann Arbor: University of Michigan Press, 1954).

81. See military website, "The Blue Angels Team," www.blueangels.navy.mil, accessed April 11, 2020.

82. A. G. Tekleab, N. R. Quigley, and P. E. Tesluk, "A Longitudinal Study of Team Conflict, Conflict Management, Cohesion, and Team Effectiveness," *Group & Organization Management* 34, no. 2 (April 2009), pp. 170-205; and B. Mullen and C. Cooper, "The Relation between Group Cohesiveness and Performance: An Integration," *Psychological Bulletin* 115 (1994), pp. 210-27.

83. R. Banker, J. Field, R. Schroeder, and K. Sinha, "Impact of Work Teams on Manufacturing Performance: A Longitudinal Field Study," *Academy of Management Journal* 39, no. 4 (1996), pp. 867-90.

84. S. Wise, "Can a Team Have Too Much Cohesion? The Dark Side to Network Density," *European Management Journal* 32 (2014), pp. 703-11; and B. Mullen and C. Cooper, "The Relation between Group Cohesiveness and Performance: An Integration," *Psychological Bulletin* 115 (1994), pp. 210-27.

85. D. P. Forbes and F. J. Milliken, "Cognition and Corporate Governance: Understanding Boards of Directors as Strategic Decision-Making Groups," *Academy of Management Review* 24 (1999), pp. 489-505.

86. T. Simons, L. H. Pelled, and K. A. Smith, "Making Use of Difference: Diversity, Debate, and Decision Comprehensiveness in Top Management Teams," *Academy of Management Journal* 42 (1999), pp. 662-73.

87. S. E. Seashore, *Group Cohesiveness in the Industrial Work Group* (Ann Arbor: University of Michigan Press, 1954).

88. B. Lott and A. Lott, "Group Cohesiveness as Interpersonal Attraction: A Review of Relationships with Antecedent and Consequent Variables," *Psychological Bulletin,* October 1965, pp. 259-309.

89. K. Dahlin, L. Weingart, and P. Hinds, "Team Diversity and Information Use," *Academy of Management Journal* 48 (2005), pp. 1107-23.

90. M. Gupta, "Why 'Two Large Pizza' Team Is the Best Team Ever," *Medium,* January 21, 2018, www.medium.com.

91. B. L. Kirkman and B. Rosen, "Beyond Self-Management: Antecedents and Consequences of Team Empowerment," *Academy of Management Journal* 42 (1999), pp. 58-74.

92. J. R. Hackman, *Groups That Work (and Those That Don't)* (San Francisco: Jossey-Bass, 1990).

93. W. Bennis, *Organizing Genius* (Reading, MA: Addison-Wesley, 1997).

94. M. Cianni and D. Wnuck, "Individual Growth and Team Enhancement: Moving toward a New Model of Career Development," *Academy of Management Executive* 11 (1997), pp. 105-15.

95. K. Jehn, "A Multimethod Examination of the Benefits and Detriments of Intragroup Conflict," *Administrative Science Quarterly* 40 (1995), pp. 245-82; and T. O'Neill and M. McLarnon, "Optimizing Team Conflict Dynamics for High Performance Teamwork," *Human Resources Management Review* 28 (2018), pp. 378-94.

96. Company website, "Transforming Industries and Society," IBM Research, www.research.ibm.com.

97. D. G. Ancona, "Outward Bound: Strategies for Team Survival in an Organization," *Academy of Management Journal* 33 (1990), pp. 334-65.

98. D. G. Ancona, "Outward Bound: Strategies for Team Survival in an Organization," *Academy of Management Journal* 33 (1990), pp. 334-65.

99. L. Sayles, *Leadership: What Effective Managers Really Do, and How They Do It* (New York: McGraw-Hill, 1979).

100. T. A. De Vries, J. R. Hollenbeck, R. B. Davison, F. Walter, and G. S. van der Vegt, "Managing Coordination in Multiteam Systems: Integrating Micro and Macro Perspectives," *Academy of Management Journal* 59 (2016), pp. 1823-44; T. A. De Vries, F. Walter, G. S. van der Vegt, and P. J. M. D. Essens, "Antecedentsof Individuals' Interteam Coordination: Broad Functional Experiences as a Mixed Blessing," *Academy of Management Journal* 57 (2014), pp. 1334-59; H. C. Bruns, "Working Alone Together: Coordination in Collaboration across Domains of Expertise," *Academy of Management Journal* 56 (2013), pp. 62-83; and M. A. Hogg, D. van Knippenberg, and D. E. Rast III, "Intergroup Leadership in Organizations: Leadingacross Group and Organizational Boundaries," *Academy of Management Review* 37 (2012), pp. 232-55.

101. L. Sayles, *Leadership: What Effective Managers Really Do, and How They Do It* (New York: McGraw-Hill, 1979).

102. J. A. Wall Jr. and R. R. Callister, "Conflict and Its Management," *Journal of Management* 21, no. 3 (1995), pp. 515-58.

103. B. R. Fry and T. L. Thomas, "Mary Parker Follett: Assessing the Contribution and Impact of Her Writings," *Journal of Management History* 2, no. 2 (1996), pp. 11-19.

104. P. Lencioni, "How to Foster Good Conflict," *The Wall Street Journal,* November 13, 2008, www.wsj.com; and D. Schachter, "Learn to Embrace Opposition for Improved Decision Making," *Information Outlook,* October 2008.

105. A. Caron and T. Cummings, "A Theory of Subgroups in Work Teams," *Academy of Management Review* 37 (2012), pp. 441-70.

106. J. Chatman and F. Flynn, "The Influence of Demographic Heterogeneity on the Emergence and Consequences of Cooperative Norms in Work Teams," *Academy of Management Journal* 44 (2001), pp. 956-74; and R. T. Keller, "Cross-Functional Project Groups in Research and New Product Development: Diversity, Communications, Job Stress, and Outcomes," *Academy of Management Journal* 44 (2001), pp. 547-55.

107. K. Melymuka, "Managing Multicultural Teams: Winning Strategies from Teams around the World," *Computerworld,* November 20, 2006, www.gale.com.

108. J.-L. Farh, C. Lee, and C. Farh, "Task Conflict and Team Creativity: A Question of How Muchand When," *Journal of Applied Psychology,* 2010, pp. 1173–80; J. Shaw, J. Zhu, M. Duffy, K. Scott, H. A. Shih, and E. Susanto, "A Contingency Model of Conflict and Team Effectiveness," *Journal of Applied Psychology* 96 (2011), pp. 391–400; F. R. C. de Wit, L. Greer, and K. Jehn, "The Paradox of Intergroup Conflict: A Meta-Analysis," *Journal of Applied Psychology* 97 (2012), pp. 360–90; S. Thatcher and P. Patel, "Group Faultlines: A Review, Integration, and Guide for Research," *Journal of Management* 38 (2012), pp. 969–1009; and I. Hoever, D. van Knippenberg, W. van Ginkel, and H. Barkema, "Fostering Team Creativity: Perspective Taking as Key to Unlocking Diversity's Potential," *Journal of Applied Psychology* 97 (2012), pp. 982–96.

109. D. Tjosvold, *Working Together to Get Things Done* (Lexington, MA: Lexington Books, 1986).

110. T. Hout and D. Michael, "A Chinese Approach to Management," *Harvard Business Review,* September 2014, www.hbr.com; and C. Tinsley and J. Brett, "Managing Workplace Conflict in the United States and Hong Kong," *Organizational Behavior and Human Decision Processes* 85 (2001), pp. 360–81.

111. K. W. Thomas, "Conflict and Conflict Management," in *Handbook of Industrial and Organizational Psychology,* ed. M. D. Dunnette (Chicago: Rand McNally, 1976).

112. J. S. Lublin, "How Best to Supervise Internal Runner-Up for the Job You Got," *The Wall Street Journal,* January 30, 2007, www.wsj.com.

113. U.S. Equal Employment Opportunity Commission, www.eeoc.gov.

114. K. W. Thomas, "Toward Multi-Dimensional Values in Teaching: The Example of Conflict Behaviors," *Academy of Management Review* 2, no. 3 (1977), pp. 484–89.

115. D. Tjosvold, A. Wong, and N. Chen, "Constructively Managing Conflicts in Organizations," *Annual Review of Organizational Psychology and Organizational Behavior* 1 (2014), pp. 545–68.

116. C. O. Longenecker and M. Neubert, "Barriers and Gateways to Management Cooperation and Teamwork," *Business Horizons,* September–October 2000, pp. 37–44.

117. P. S. Nugent, "Managing Conflict: Third-Party Interventions for Managers," *Academy of Management Executive* 16 (2002), pp. 139–54.

118. M. Blum and J. A. Wall Jr., "HRM: Managing Conflicts in the Firm," *Business Horizons,* May–June 1997, pp. 84–87.

119. J. A. Wall Jr. and R. R. Callister, "Conflict and Its Management," *Journal of Management* 21, no. 3 (1995), pp. 515–58; and J. Leon-Perez, F. Medina, A. Arenas, and L. Munduate, "The Relationship between Interpersonal Conflict and Workplace Bullying," *Journal of Managerial Psychology* 30 (2015), pp. 250–63.

120. J. Polzer, C. B. Crisp, S. Jarvenpaa, and J. Kim, "Extending the Faultline Model to Geographically Dispersed Teams: How Collocated Subgroups Can Impair Group Functioning," *Academy of Management Journal* 49 (2006), pp. 679–92.

121. M. Montoya-Weiss, A. Massey, and M. Song, "Getting It Together: Temporal Coordination and Conflict Management in Global Virtual Teams," *Academy of Management Journal* 44 (2001), pp. 1251–62.

122. R. Standifer and J. A. Wall Jr., "Managing Conflict in B2B Commerce," *Business Horizons,* March–April 2003, pp. 65–70.

Communicating

Learning Objectives

After studying Chapter 13, you should be able to

LO1 Discuss important advantages of two-way communication.

LO2 Identify communication problems to avoid.

LO3 Describe when and how to use different communication channels.

LO4 Give examples of ways to become a better "sender" and "receiver" of information.

LO5 Explain how to improve downward, upward, and horizontal communication.

LO6 Summarize how to work with the company grapevine.

LO7 Describe the boundaryless organization and its advantages.

Effective communication is an ongoing management responsibility in stable times.[1] It is even more vital in turbulent times, which is what managers in U.S. firms experienced during the coronavirus pandemic of 2020.

As infections rippled through the West Coast and the Northeast, public officials mandated nationwide travel restrictions, shelter-in-place lockdowns, and business closures.[2] Workers across the United States sought reassurance.

Slack's CEO Stewart Butterfield wanted his employees to understand that he empathized with them. He sent an internal memo showing just that: "We got this. Take care of yourselves, take care of your families, be a good partner. It is fine to work irregular or reduced hours. It is fine to take time out when you need it." His prevailing message to his workforce: "I'm with you. Don't stress about work as we cope together through the pandemic."[3]

CEOs showed support for their employees in other ways. Many CEOs announced they were taking pay cuts. Arne Sorenson, CEO of Marriott, relinquished his entire 2020 salary, and executive managers took a 50 percent pay cut.[4] Given Marriott's large size, this forfeiture of compensation will have little effect on its bottom line, but the act conveys empathy to employees—an important message for leaders to communicate.

As Mark Cuban, the billionaire entrepreneur and owner of the NBA's Dallas Mavericks, said, "How companies respond . . . is going to define their brand for decades."[5] That response starts with effective communication from the top.

> **communication** the transmission of information and meaning from one party to another through the use of shared symbols

In this chapter, we present important communication concepts and practical guidelines for improving your own effectiveness. We also discuss communication at the interpersonal and organizational levels.

> **LO1 Discuss important advantages of two-way communication.**

1 | INTERPERSONAL COMMUNICATION

When people in an organization conduct a meeting, share stories in the cafeteria, or deliver presentations, they are making efforts to communicate. To understand why communication efforts sometimes break down and find ways to improve your communication skills, it helps to identify the elements of the communication process. Communication is the transmission of information and meaning from one party to another through the use of shared symbols. Exhibit 13.1 shows a general model of how one person communicates with another.

1.1 | One-Way Communication Is Common

The *sender* initiates the process by conveying information to the *receiver*—the person for whom the message is intended. The sender has a *meaning* she wishes to communicate and *encodes* the meaning into symbols (the words chosen for the message). Then the sender *transmits,* or sends, the message through some *channel,* such as a verbal or written medium.

The receiver *decodes* the message (e.g., reads it) and attempts to *interpret* the sender's meaning. The receiver may provide *feedback* to the sender by encoding a message in response to the sender's message.

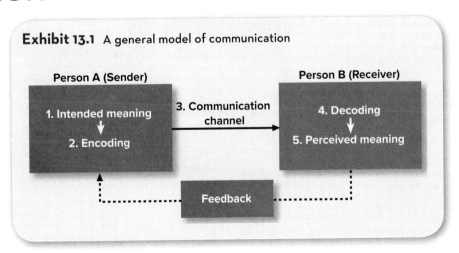

Exhibit 13.1 A general model of communication

Person A (Sender)
1. Intended meaning
2. Encoding

3. Communication channel

Person B (Receiver)
4. Decoding
5. Perceived meaning

Feedback

In **one-way communication**, information flows in only one direction—from the sender to the receiver, with no feedback loop. A manager sends an email to a subordinate without asking for a response. An employee phones the information technology (IT) department and leaves a message requesting repairs for her computer. A supervisor yells at a production worker about defects and then storms away.

The communication process often is hampered by *noise,* or interference in the system, that blocks perfect understanding. Noise could be anything that interferes with accurate communication: phone interruptions, thoughts about other things, or simple fatigue or stress. At times, noise can derail your message. Imagine asking your boss for a raise on the same day that she received a below-average performance review. No matter how effectively you present your case, the likelihood of receiving an affirmative answer is low.

The model in Exhibit 13.1 is more than a theoretical treatment of the communication process: It points out the key ways in which communications can break down. Mistakes can be made at each stage of the model. A manager who is alert to potential problems can perform each step carefully to ensure more effective communication. The general model and two-way communication model exemplified in Exhibit 13.2 help explain the topics discussed next: the differences between one-way and two-way communication, communication pitfalls, misperception, and the various communication channels.

1.2 | Communication Should Flow in More Than One Direction

As shown in Exhibit 13.2, when a receiver (in this case, a student) responds to a sender (here, a professor), **two-way communication** has occurred. One-way communication in situations like those described above can become two-way if the manager's email invites the receiver to reply with any questions, the IT department returns the employee's call and asks for details about the computer problem, and the supervisor calms down and listens to the production worker's explanation of why defects are occurring.

True two-way communication means not only that the receiver provides feedback, but also that the sender is receptive to the feedback. In these constructive exchanges, information is

---

Exhibit 13.2 Zoom is a two-way communication channel

Your professor (*sender*) prepares a lecture (*encodes message*) and delivers it virtually via Zoom (*channel*) to students (*receivers*) who interpret the meaning of the presented material (decoding).

A student (*now the sender*) asks the professor (*now the receiver*) to clarify a concept on one of the slides (*feedback*).

Westend61/Getty Images

Pressmaster/Shutterstock

perception the process of receiving and interpreting information

filtering the process of withholding, ignoring, or distorting information

shared between both parties rather than merely delivered from one person to the other.

Because one-way communication is faster and easier for the sender, it is much more common than it should be. A busy executive finds it easier to dash off an email than to discuss a nagging problem with a subordinate. Also, he doesn't have to deal with questions or face a challenge by someone who disagrees.

Two-way communication is more difficult and time-consuming than one-way communication. However, it is more accurate; fewer mistakes occur, and fewer problems arise later. When receivers have a chance to ask questions, share concerns, and make suggestions or modifications, they understand more precisely what the sender is communicating and what they should do with the information.[6]

As discussed in Chapter 8, performance appraisals typically occur once per year. About one-third of companies—for example, Adobe, Gap, IBM, and OppenheimerFunds—are breaking with tradition by providing employees with "frequent, informal check-ins."[7] These are good examples of two-way communication. Managers provide feedback and constructive suggestions, and employees can ask questions that relate to their current projects, maximizing on-the-job learning.[8]

LO2 Identify communication problems to avoid.

2 | WATCH OUT FOR COMMUNICATION PITFALLS

As we know from personal experience, the sender's intended message does not always get across to the receiver. You are operating under an illusion if you think there is a perfect correlation between what you say and what people hear.[9] Errors can occur in every stage of the process. In the encoding stage, people misuse words, enter decimal points in the wrong places, leave out facts, or use ambiguous phrases. In the transmission stage, a report may get lost on a cluttered desk, the words on the slide may be too small to read from the back of the room, or words may be spoken with ambiguous inflections.

Decoding problems arise when the receiver doesn't listen carefully or reads too quickly and overlooks a key point. And of course receivers can misinterpret a message, as when a reader draws the wrong conclusion from an unclear text message, a listener takes a general statement by the boss too personally, or an extended pause in a conversation is taken the wrong way.

2.1 | Everyone Uses Perceptual and Filtering Processes

More generally, people's perceptual and filtering processes create misinterpretations. **Perception** is the process of receiving and interpreting information. Such processes are not perfectly objective. They are subjective because people's self-interested motives and attitudes toward the sender and the message bias their interpretations. People assume that others share their views and, naturally, care more about their own views than those of others.[10]

But perceptual differences get in the way of consensus. To remedy this, it helps to remember that others' viewpoints are legitimate and to incorporate others' perspectives into your interpretation of issues.[11] Generally, adopting another person's viewpoint is fundamental to working collaboratively. And your ability to take others' perspectives—say, to really understand the viewpoints of customers or suppliers—can strengthen your performance.[12]

Filtering is the process of withholding, ignoring, or distorting information. Senders do this when they tell the boss what they think the boss wants to hear or give unwarranted compliments rather than honest criticism. Receivers also filter information; they may fail to recognize an important message or attend to some aspects of the message but not others. Probably you have heard the saying: "So-and-so hears only what he wants to hear (or sees only what he wants to see)."

Sometimes managers, to avoid demotivating an employee or starting an argument, soften or distort the fact that the employee needs to correct a problem behavior. A manager may sugarcoat the feedback by saying, "That wasn't bad" or "You'll get the hang of it after a while." Honesty, including better ideas or suggestions, works better.[13]

Due to filtering and perceptual differences, you cannot assume the other person means what you think he means or understands the meanings you intend. Managers need to interpret signals and adjust their own communication styles and perceptions to the people with whom they interact.[14]

The human tendencies to filter and perceive subjectively underlie much of the ineffective communication that you will read about in the rest of this chapter—and underscore the need for more effective communication practices.

2.2 | Mistaken Perceptions Cause Misunderstandings

People do not pay attention to everything going on around them. They inadvertently send mixed signals that can undermine the intended messages. Different people attend to different things, and people interpret the same message in different ways. For example, a hiring manager may, at the end of an interview, say, "You seem like a good fit for this position." One interviewee might leave thinking he's getting a job offer, while another might depart feeling less confident because she noticed that the manager avoided eye contact and his voice lacked enthusiasm.

Cross-cultural differences magnify these difficulties.[15] Breakdowns often occur when business transactions take place between people from different countries. McGill University professor Nancy J. Adler, an expert in international management, suggests several tactics for communicating with someone who speaks a different language (see Exhibit 13.3 for some tips).[16]

As the U.S. workforce ages (see Chapter 9), some employers are sending mixed signals regarding how they value older versus

---

Exhibit 13.3 — Overcoming language barriers

Dimensions	Tips for Improving Communication
Verbal communication	• *Clear, slow speech.* Enunciate each word. Do not use colloquial expressions. • *Repetition.* Repeat each important idea using different words to explain the same concept. • *Simple sentences.* Avoid compound, long sentences. • *Active verbs.* Avoid passive verbs.
Nonverbal behavior*	• *Visual restatements.* Use as many visual restatements as possible, such as pictures, graphs, tables, and slides. • *Gestures.* Use more facial and appropriate hand gestures to emphasize the meaning of words. • *Demonstrations.* Act out as many themes as possible. • *Pauses.* Pause more frequently. • *Summaries.* Hand out written summaries of your verbal presentation.
Accurate interpretation	• *Silence.* When there is a silence, wait. Do not jump in to fill the silence. The other person is probably just thinking more slowly in the nonnative language or translating. • *Intelligence.* Do not equate poor grammar and mispronunciation with lack of intelligence; it is usually a sign of nonnative language use. • *Differences.* If unsure, assume difference, not similarity.
Comprehension	• *Understanding.* Do not just assume that they understand; assume that they do not understand. • *Checking comprehension.* Have colleagues repeat their understanding of the material back to you. Do not simply ask if they understand or not. Let them explain to you what they understand.
Design	• *Breaks.* Take more frequent breaks. Second language comprehension is exhausting. • *Small modules.* Divide the material to be presented into smaller modules. • *Longer time frame.* Allocate more time for each module than you usually need for presenting the same material to native speakers of your language.
Motivation	• *Encouragement.* Verbally and nonverbally encourage and reinforce speaking by nonnative language participants. • *Drawing out.* Explicitly draw out marginal and passive participants. • *Reinforcement.* Do not embarrass novice speakers.

* For more information about cross-cultural body language, see www.bodylanguageexpert.co.uk/questionnaire-cross-cultural-body-language.html.

Life_imageS/Shutterstock

younger employees.[17] While companies may deny practicing ageism, their perceptions of older workers tell another story, namely that they resist change, are expensive and hard to train, and lack technology skills.[18]

Perceptions influence behavior. Google agreed to pay $11 million to settle a lawsuit with over 200 older job applicants for "exhibiting preferential hiring toward job candidates under the age of 40."[19] The settlement also required parent company Alphabet to provide age-bias training to employees and managers, and to create a committee on age diversity in recruiting.[20] This contrasts starkly with Google's official policy prohibiting age discrimination.[21]

What signals is Google sending? It values low-cost, younger employees and discriminates against older people. Will people believe the policy, or the actions the lawsuit reveals?

Another way people may undermine an intended message is when they are deceitful in their communication. Ethical communication is accurate, honest, sincere, and not deceptive in any way.[22] In contrast, unethical communicators may exaggerate or manipulate their message, omit negative information, or state opinions as facts to achieve personal gain.[23]

Many problems can be avoided if people take the time to do the following four things:

1. Ensure that the receivers attend to the message being sent.

2. Consider the other party's frame of reference and attempt to convey the message with that viewpoint in mind.

3. Take concrete steps to minimize perceptual errors and improper signals in sending and receiving.

4. Send consistent messages.

You should make an effort to predict people's interpretations of your messages and think in terms of how they could *misinterpret* your messages. It helps to say not only what you mean but also what you *don't* mean. Every time you say, "I am not saying *X,* I am saying *Y,*" you eliminate a possible misinterpretation.[24]

3 | COMMUNICATIONS FLOW THROUGH DIFFERENT CHANNELS

Communication can be sent through a variety of channels (step 3 in Exhibit 13.1), including oral and written. As shown in Exhibit 13.4 the effectiveness of a communication channel depends on the situation.

Oral communication includes face-to-face discussion, telephone conversations, videoconferences, and formal presentations. Advantages are that questions can be asked and answered; feedback is immediate and direct, the receiver(s) can sense the sender's sincerity (or lack of it), and oral communication is more persuasive and sometimes less expensive than written. Yet, oral communication also has disadvantages: It can lead to spontaneous, ill-considered statements (and regret), and there is no permanent record of it (unless an effort is made to record it).

Written communication includes texts, emails, memos, letters, reports, training materials, computer files, and other written documents. Advantages to using written messages are that they can be revised before they are sent, they are permanent records that can be saved, the message stays the same even if relayed through many people, and the receiver has more time to think about the message. Disadvantages are that the sender has no control over where, when, or if the message is read; the sender lacks immediate feedback; the receiver may not understand parts of the message; and the message might not contain all the information others need.[25]

● Face-to-face communication can be more effective than other channels when you want to receive immediate feedback or present your ideas in a persuasive manner. Paul Bradbury/Caiaimage/Getty Images

anonymous contributions, presuming it will add more honesty to internal discussions. Group decision support systems can generate more data sharing and critical argumentation and higher-quality decisions than face-to-face meetings.[36] But anonymity can spur lies, gossip, insults, threats, harassment, and the release of confidential information.[37]

Disadvantages The disadvantages of digital communication include the difficulties involved in solving complex problems that need extended, face-to-face interaction, as well as the inability to pick up subtle, nonverbal, or inflectional clues about what communicators are thinking.

On the other hand, people are more willing to lie online. In online bargaining—even before it begins—negotiators distrust one another more than in face-to-face negotiations. After the negotiation (compared with face-to-face negotiators), people usually are less satisfied with their outcomes, even when the outcomes are economically equivalent.[38]

Although organizations rely heavily on digital communication for group decision making, face-to-face groups generally take less time, make higher-quality decisions, and are more satisfying.[39] Email is most appropriate for routine messages that do not require the exchange of large quantities of complex information. It is less suitable for communicating confidential information, resolving conflicts, or negotiating.[40] Such impersonal forms of communication can hurt feelings, and an upset employee can easily forward messages, which often has a snowball effect that can embarrass everyone involved.

Companies worry about leaks and negative portrayals and may require employees to agree to specific social media guidelines, such as the following:[41]

- Avoid content that could embarrass the company or disclose confidential information.

- Present opinions in a professional manner.

- Clarify whose opinion is being expressed.

Because most digital communications are quick and easy, and at times anonymous, some people hurl insults, vent frustration, snitch on coworkers to the boss, and otherwise breach protocol. Digital channels liberate people to send messages they would not say to a person's face. Without nonverbal cues, "kidding" remarks may be taken seriously, causing resentment and regret. Some people try to clear up confusion with emojis, but those can further muddy the intent.[42]

3.2 | Managing the Digital Load

Experienced managers wonder how they ever worked without digital communication media. But the sheer volume of communication can be overwhelming, especially when it never lets up.[43]

A few rules of thumb can help you manage your digital communications.[44] For information overload, the challenge is to separate the truly important from the routine. Effective managers find time to think about bigger business issues and don't get too bogged down responding to every message that seems urgent but may be trivial. Essential here is to think strategically about your goals, identify the items that are most important, and prioritize your time around those goals. This is easier said than done, of course, but it is essential, and it helps.

More specific suggestions include: Don't hit "reply to all" to an email when you should just hit "reply." Get organized by creating email folders sorted by subject, priority, or sender, and flag messages that require follow-up. It's not a bad idea to have a colleague read nonroutine emails before you send them. And a final email golden rule: Don't hit "send" unless you'd be comfortable having the contents of your email on the front page of a newspaper, being read by your mother or a competitor.

Some companies realize the downsides of digital media overuse. In France, a labor agreement requires employees, once they leave at the end of the workday (and over weekends), to disconnect and not respond to their managers' emails (even on their smartphones).[45] The agreement affects employees from the consulting and technology sectors, including the French groups of PricewaterhouseCoopers, Deloitte, Facebook, and Google.[46]

As overwhelming as digital communications can be, you can take steps to simplify. A global customer account management team established two ground rules:

1. Whenever a member communicated with a customer, the member was to send a briefing to all team members.

2. They designated a primary contact for each customer, with no one else on the team authorized to discuss or decide strategies or policies with the customer.

If contacted by a customer, team members would direct the customer to the appropriate contact person. These steps simplified communication channels and greatly reduced contradictory and confusing messages.[47]

3.3 | The Virtual Office

Based on the philosophy that management's focus should be on what people do, not where they are, the virtual office is a mobile office in which people can work anywhere—their home, car, airport, coffeehouses, customers' offices—as long as they have the tools to communicate with customers and colleagues. Consulting firm Deloitte gives many of its employees the choice to work up to five days a week outside the office. When desired, employees can reserve a workspace at the company for the day, a concept known as "hotdesking."[48]

Many of consulting giant Accenture's employees spend most of their time at clients' workplaces. Under those conditions, cultivating teamwork and connecting with colleagues is difficult. Consultants may have a client on one continent, a supervisor on another, and support staff on a third. To foster communication and collaboration, Accenture created an online social networking platform, Accenture People. The internal platform allows employees to connect, share skills and interests, and collaborate 24/7 from anywhere in the world.[49]

In the short run at least, the benefits of virtual offices appear substantial. Saving money on rent and utilities is an obvious advantage. Hiring and retaining talented people is easier because virtual offices support scheduling flexibility and even may make it possible to keep an employee who wants to relocate—for example, with a spouse taking a new job in another city.

But what will be the longer-term impact on productivity and morale? We may be in danger of losing too many "human moments"—those authentic encounters that happen only when two people are physically together.[50] Some people hate working at home. Some send messages in the middle of the night—and others reply to them. Some work around the clock yet feel they are not doing enough. Long hours of being constantly close to the technical tools of work can cause burnout.

And some companies are learning that direct supervision at the office is necessary to maintain the quality of work, especially when employees are inexperienced and need guidance. The virtual office requires changes in how human beings work and interact, and presents technical challenges. So, although it is much hyped and useful, it will not completely replace real offices and face-to-face work.

3.4 | Use "Richer" Media for Complex or Critical Messages

Some communication channels convey more information than others. The amount of information a medium conveys is called media richness.[51] (See Exhibit 13.6 for a comparison.) The more information or cues a medium sends to the receiver, the "richer" the medium is.[52] The richest media are more personal than technological, provide quick feedback, allow lots of descriptive language, and send different types of cues. Face-to-face communication is the richest medium because it offers a variety of cues in addition to words: tone of voice, facial expression, body language, and other nonverbal signals. It also allows more descriptive language than, say, a memo does. In addition, it affords more opportunity for the receiver to give feedback to and ask questions of the sender, turning one-way into two-way communication.

The phone is less rich than face-to-face communication, electronic mail is less rich yet, and memos are the least rich medium.

Exhibit 13.6 Differences in media richness

↑ **More rich**
Face-to-face coversation, videoconference, and phone call.

↓ **Less rich**
Email, text, blog post, and memo.

In general, you should send difficult and unusual messages through richer media, transmit simple and routine messages through less rich media, and use multiple media for important messages that you want to ensure people attend to and understand.[53] You should also consider factors such as cost, which medium your receiver prefers, and the preferred communication style in your organization.[54]

study tip 13

Visiting your professor

When should you make the time to sit down for a face-to-face chat with your professor? You may want to use this rich communication medium when you have problems or concerns like reviewing the questions you missed on a recent exam, asking advice about how to handle a slacker on your student project team, or requesting a letter of recommendation. You are much more likely to understand better and resolve things faster by talking face-to-face rather than communicating digitally.

● Financial guru Suze Orman is known for her ability to relay financial information in easy-to-understand ways. She uses clear, concise, and direct language. Great business communicators use understandable language to discuss complex issues. Frazer Harrison/Getty Images

4 | IMPROVING COMMUNICATION SKILLS

Employers have long been dismayed by college graduates' poor communication skills. A demonstrated ability to communicate effectively makes you a more attractive job candidate, distinguishing you from others. You can do many things to improve your communication skills, both as a sender and as a receiver.

4.1 | Senders Can Improve Their Communication Skills

To start, be aware that honest, direct, straight talk is important but all too rare. CEOs are often coached on how to slant their messages for different audiences—the investment community, employees, or the board. That's not likely to be straight talk. The focus of the messages can differ, but inconsistencies can cause problems. People should be able to identify your perspective, reasoning, and good intentions.[55] Beyond this basic point, senders can improve their skills in making persuasive presentations, writing, using language, and sending nonverbal messages.

Presentation and Persuasion Skills Throughout your career, you will be called on to state your case on a variety of issues. You will have information and perhaps an opinion or proposal to present to others. Typically, your goal will be to "sell" your idea. In other words, your challenge will be to persuade others to go along with your recommendation. As a leader, you will find that some of your toughest challenges arise when people do not want to do what has to be done. Leaders have to be persuasive to get people on board.[56]

Persuasion is not what many people think: merely selling an idea or convincing others to see things your way. Don't assume that it takes a "my way or the highway" approach, with a one-shot effort to make a hard sell and resisting compromise.[57] Usually, it is more constructive to consider persuasion a process of learning from each other and negotiating a shared solution. Persuasive speakers are seen as authentic, which happens when speakers are open with the audience, make a connection, demonstrate passion, and show they are listening as well as speaking. Practice this kind of authenticity by noticing and adopting the type of body language you use when you're around people you're comfortable with, planning how to engage directly with your listeners, identifying the reasons why you care about your topic, and watching for nonverbal cues as well as fully engaging when you listen to audience comments and questions.[58]

The most powerful and persuasive messages are simple and informative, are told with stories and anecdotes, and convey excitement.[59] People are more likely to remember and buy into your message if you can express it as a story that is simple, unexpected, concrete, credible, and includes emotional content.

Nordstrom motivates employees by passing along stories of times when its people have provided extraordinary service, such as warming up customers' cars while they shopped or ironing a shirt so that a customer could wear it to a meeting.

Writing Skills Effective writing is more than correct spelling, punctuation, and grammar (although these help). Good writing above all requires clear, logical thinking.[60] The act of writing can be a powerful aid to thinking because you have to think about what you really want to say and what the logic is behind your message.[61]

You want people to find your email and reports readable and interesting. Strive for clarity, organization, readability, and brevity.[62] Brevity is much appreciated by readers who are overloaded with documents, including wordy memos. Use a dictionary and a thesaurus, and avoid fancy words.

Your first draft rarely is as good as it could be. If you have time, revise it. Take the reader into consideration. Go through your entire document, and delete all unnecessary words, sentences, and paragraphs. Use specific, concrete words rather than abstract phrases. Instead of saying, "A period of unfavorable weather set in," say, "It rained every day for a week."

Be critical of your own writing. If you want to improve, start by reading *The Elements of Style* by William Strunk and E. B. White and the most recent edition of *The Little, Brown Handbook*.[63]

Language Word choice can enhance or interfere with communication effectiveness. Jargon is a form of shorthand that can make communication more effective when both the sender and the receiver know the buzzwords. But, when people from different functional areas or disciplines communicate with one another, misunderstandings often occur. As in writing, simplicity usually helps.

Whether speaking or writing, you should consider the receiver's background—cultural as well as technical—and adjust your language accordingly. When you are receiving, don't assume that your understanding is the same as the speaker's intentions.

The meaning of word choices also can vary by culture. Japanese people use the simple word *hai* (yes) to convey that they understand what is being said; it does not necessarily mean they agree. Asian businesspeople rarely use the direct "no," using more subtle ways of disagreeing.[64] Global teams fail when members have difficulties communicating because of language, cultural, and geographic barriers. Heterogeneity harms team functioning at first. But when teams develop ways to interact and communicate, they develop a common identity and perform well.[65]

Not just you, but your employer as well, can benefit from knowing other languages.[66] When conducting business overseas, try to learn something about the other country's language and customs. Americans are less likely to do this than are people from some other cultures; few Americans consider a foreign

Take Charge of Your Career

Tips for being an effective public speaker

Companies and recruiters have long complained about college graduates' weak communication skills. Presentations are when stronger skills offer great advantage. Professor Lynn Hamilton of the University of Virginia's McIntire School of Commerce offers 10 tips for making presentations more effective:

1. *Spend adequate time on the **content** of your presentation.* It's easy to get so distracted by PowerPoint slides or concern about delivery skills that the actual content of a presentation is neglected. Know your content inside and out; you'll be able to discuss it conversationally and won't be tempted to memorize. If you believe in what you're saying and own the material, you will convey enthusiasm and will be more relaxed.

2. *Clearly understand the **objective** of your presentation.* Answer this question with one sentence: "What do I want the audience to believe following this presentation?" Writing down your objective will help you focus on your bottom line. Everything else in a presentation—the structure, the words, the visuals—should support your objective.

3. ***Tell** the audience the **purpose** of the presentation.* As the saying goes, "Tell them what you're going to tell them, then tell them, then tell them what you've told them." Use a clear preview statement early on to help the audience know where you're taking them.

4. *Provide **meaning**, not just data.* Today, information is widely available; you won't impress people by overloading them with data. People have limited attention spans and want presenters to help clarify the meaning of data.

5. ***Practice, pr**actice, practice.* Appearing polished and relaxed during a presentation requires rehearsal time. Practice making your points in a variety of ways. Above all, don't memorize a presentation's content.

6. *Remember that a presentation is more like a **conversation** than a speech.* Keep your tone conversational yet professional. Audience members will be much more engaged if they feel you are talking with them rather than at them. Rely on PowerPoint slides or a broad outline to jog your memory.

7. *Remember the incredible power of **eye contact**.* Look at individual people in the audience. Try to have a series of one-on-one conversations with people in the room. This will calm you and help you connect with your audience.

8. ***Allow imperfection.*** If you forget what you were going to say, simply pause, look at your notes, and go on. Don't "break character" and effusively apologize or giggle or look mortified. Remember that an audience doesn't know your material nearly as well as you do and won't notice many mistakes.

9. *Be prepared to **answer tough questions**.* Try to anticipate the toughest questions you might receive. Plan your answers in advance. If you don't have an answer, acknowledge the fact and offer to get the information later.

10. *Provide a **crisp wrap-up** to a question-and-answer session.* Whenever possible, follow the Q&A period with a brief summary statement. Set up the Q&A session by saying, "We'll take questions for 10 minutes and then have a few closing remarks." This prevents your presentation from just winding down to a weak ending. Also, if you receive hostile or hard-to-answer questions, you'll have a chance to have the final word.

Source: Reprinted with permission of Lynn A. Hamilton, University of Virginia.

---

language necessary for doing business abroad, and most U.S. firms do not require expatriates to know the local language.[67] But those who do will have an edge over competitors who do not.[68] Making the effort to learn the local language builds rapport, sets a proper tone for doing business, aids in adjustment to culture shock, and especially can help you "get inside" the other culture.[69] You will learn more about how people think, feel, and behave in their personal and business dealings.

4.2 | Nonverbal Signals Matter, Too

People send and interpret signals other than those that are spoken or written. These nonverbal messages can support or undermine the stated message, and convey information about emotions, power, relationships, and more.[70] Often, nonverbal cues make a greater impact than other signals. In employees' eyes, managers' actions often speak louder than their words.

> "Good communication does not mean that you have to speak in perfectly formed sentences and paragraphs. It isn't about slickness. Simple and clear go a long way."
>
> —John Kotter

In conversation, except when you intend to convey a negative message, you should give nonverbal signals that express warmth, respect, concern, a feeling of equality, and a willingness to listen. Negative nonverbal signals show coolness, disrespect, lack of interest, and a feeling of superiority.[71] The following suggestions can help you send positive nonverbal signals:

- Use *time* appropriately. Don't keep your employees waiting to see you. Devote enough time to your meetings, and communicate frequently, which signals your interest in their concerns.

- Make your *office arrangement* conducive to open communication. A seating arrangement that avoids separating people helps establish a warm, cooperative atmosphere. When you sit behind your desk and your subordinate sits before you, the environment is more intimidating and authoritative.[72]

- Remember your *body language.* Research indicates that facial expression and tone of voice can account for 90 percent of the communication between two people.[73] Several nonverbal body signals convey a positive attitude toward the other person: assuming a position close to the other person; gesturing frequently; maintaining eye contact; smiling; having an open body orientation, such as facing the other person directly; uncrossing the arms; and leaning forward to convey interest.

Silence is an interesting nonverbal situation. The average American is said to spend about twice as many hours per day in conversation as the average Japanese.[74] North Americans tend to talk to fill silences; Japanese allow long silences to develop, believing they can get to know people better. Japanese believe that two people with good rapport will know each other's thoughts. The need to use words implies a lack of understanding.

Nonverbal Signals in Different Countries Here are just a few nonverbal mistakes that Americans might make in other countries.[75] Traditionally, nodding the head up and down in Bulgaria means no. The American thumb-and-first-finger circular A-OK gesture is vulgar in Brazil, Singapore, Russia, and Paraguay. The head is sacred in Buddhist cultures, so you must never touch someone's head. In Muslim cultures, never touch or eat with the left hand, which is thought unclean. Crossing your ankle over your knee is rude in Indonesia, Thailand, and Syria. Don't point your finger toward yourself in Germany or Switzerland—it insults the other person.

You also must correctly interpret the nonverbal signals of others. Chinese might scratch their ears and cheeks to show happiness. Greeks puff air after they receive a compliment. Hondurans touch their fingers below their eyes to show disbelief or caution. Japanese might indicate embarrassment or "no" by sucking in air and hissing through their teeth. Vietnamese look to the ground with their heads down to show respect. Compared with Americans, Russians use fewer facial expressions, and Scandinavians fewer hand gestures, whereas people in Mediterranean and Latin cultures gesture and touch more. Brazilians are more likely than Americans to interrupt, Arabs to speak loudly, and Asians to respect silence.

Use these examples not to stereotype, but to remember that people in other cultures have different styles and to aid in communication accuracy.

4.3 | Receivers Can Improve Their Listening, Reading, and Observational Skills

Once you become effective at sending oral, written, and nonverbal messages, you are halfway toward becoming a complete communicator. However, you must also develop adequate receiving capabilities. Receivers need good listening, reading, and observational skills.

Listening Managers need excellent listening skills. Although people often assume that good listening is easy and natural, in fact it is difficult and far less common than needed. Catherine Coughlin practiced her listening skills as a customer service representative for Union Electric Company during the summers of her college years. Whether someone was calling about an unpaid bill or a power outage, or just looking for an excuse to talk to somebody, Coughlin found that "you've got to respect everyone and their story" and then decide how to respond. Coughlin used that experience to build a successful career with Southwestern Bell Telephone and its successor companies. She was AT&T's

● Learning to observe and interpret accurately people's nonverbal cues will help you communicate more effectively. Dragana Gordic/Shutterstock

executive vice president and global marketing officer until she retired in 2015.[76]

A basic technique called *reflection* helps people listen effectively.[77] Reflection is a process by which a person states what he or she believes the other person is saying. This technique places greater emphasis on listening than on talking. When both parties actively engage in reflection, they get into each other's frame of reference rather than listening and responding from their own. Reflection makes two-way communication more accurate, as will these listening techniques:[78]

1. *Find an area of interest.* Even if you decide the topic is dull, ask yourself, "What is the speaker saying that I can use?"

2. *Judge content, not delivery.* Don't get caught up in the speaker's personality, mannerisms, speaking voice, or clothing. Instead try to learn what the speaker knows.

3. *Hold your fire.* Rather than getting immediately excited by what the speaker seems to be saying, withhold evaluation until you understand the speaker's message.

4. *Listen for ideas.* Don't get bogged down in all the facts and details; focus on central ideas.

5. *Be flexible.* Have several systems for note taking, and use the system best suited to the speaker's style. Don't take too many notes or try to force everything said by a disorganized speaker into a formal outline.

6. *Resist distraction.* Close the door, shut off the radio, move closer to the person talking, or ask him or her to speak louder. Don't look out the window or at papers on your desk.

7. *Exercise your mind.* Some people tune out when the material gets difficult. Develop an appetite for a good mental challenge.

8. *Keep your mind open.* Many people get overly emotional when they hear words referring to their most deeply held convictions—for example, *union, subsidy, import, Republican* or *Democrat,* and *big business.* Try not to let your emotions interfere with comprehension.

9. *Capitalize on thought speed.* Take advantage of the fact that most people talk at a rate of about 125 words per minute, but most of us think at about four times that rate. Use those extra 400 words per minute to think about what the speaker is saying rather than turning your thoughts to something else.

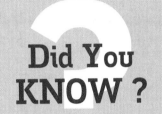

Did You KNOW ?

An employee survey asked: "What is the most critical skill a leader can possess when working with others?" The three most frequent responses were (from most frequent): (1) communication/listening, (2) effective management skills, and (3) emotional intelligence and empathy.[79]

10. *Work at listening.* Spend some energy. Don't just pretend you're paying attention. Show interest. Good listening is hard work, but the benefits outweigh the costs.

For managers, the stakes are high: Failure to listen causes managers to miss good ideas and can even drive employees away. Listening begins with personal contact. Staying in the office, keeping the door closed, and eating lunch at your desk are sometimes necessary to get pressing work done, but that is no way to stay on top of what's going on. Better to walk the halls, initiate conversations, go to lunch even with people outside your area, have coffee in a popular gathering place, and maybe even move your desk onto the factory floor.[80]

When a manager takes time to really listen to and get to know people, they think, "She's showing an interest in me," or "He's letting me know that I matter," or "She values my ideas and contributions." Trust develops. Listening and learning from others are even more important for innovation than for routine work. Successful change and innovation come through lots of human contact.

Reading Illiteracy is a significant problem in the United States; even if it's not a problem where you work, reading mistakes are common and costly. As a receiver, for your own benefit, read important messages as soon as possible, before it's too late to respond. You may skim most of your reading materials, but read important messages slowly and carefully. Note important points for later referral.

And, don't limit your reading to items about your particular job skill or technical expertise; read materials that fall outside your immediate concerns. You never know when a creative and useful idea will be inspired by a novel, a biography, a sports story, or an article about a problem in another business or industry.

Observing Effective communicators are skilled at observing and interpreting. By reading nonverbal cues, a presenter can determine how her talk is going and adjust her approach if necessary. Some companies train their sales force to interpret the nonverbal signals of potential customers. Nonverbal signals can be decoded to determine whether a sender is being truthful or deceitful. In the United States, deceitful communicators tend to maintain less eye contact, make either more or fewer body movements than usual, and smile either too much or too little. Verbally, they may offer fewer specifics than truthful senders.[81]

A vital source of useful observations comes from visiting people, plants, and other locations to get a firsthand view.[82] Many corporate executives rely heavily on reports from the field and don't travel to remote locations to observe what is going on.

downward communication information that flows from higher to lower levels in the organization's hierarchy

coaching dialogue with a goal of helping someone become more effective and achieve his or her full potential on the job

Reports are no substitute for actually seeing things happen in practice. Frequent visits to the field and careful observation can help a manager develop deep understanding of current operations, future prospects, and ideas for how to fully exploit capabilities.[83]

Of course, you must *accurately interpret* what you observe. A Canadian conducting business with a high-ranking official in Kuwait was surprised that the meeting was held in an open office and was interrupted constantly.[84] He interpreted the lack of a big, private office and secretary to mean that the Kuwaiti was of low rank and uninterested in doing business, so he lost interest in the deal. The Canadian observed the facts accurately, but his perceptual biases and limited awareness of cultural differences in norms caused him to misinterpret what he saw.

Japanese are particularly skilled at interpreting nuance of voice and gesture, putting most Westerners at a disadvantage.[85] When one is conducting business in other countries, local guides can be invaluable not only to interpret language but to "decode" behavior at meetings, what subtle hints and nonverbal cues mean, who the key people are, and how the decision-making process operates.

> **LO5** Explain how to improve downward, upward, and horizontal communication.

5 | ORGANIZATIONAL COMMUNICATION

Communicating poorly or well affects individuals, relationships, groups and teams, and entire organizations.[86] Every minute of every day, countless bits of information are transmitted in small interactions and through every corner of every organization. The flow of information affects performance at every level. Communications travel downward, upward, horizontally, and informally.

5.1 | Downward Communication Directs, Motivates, Coaches, and Informs

Downward communication refers to the flow of information from higher to lower levels in the organization's hierarchy. Examples include a manager giving an assignment to an assistant, a supervisor making an announcement to his subordinates, and a company president delivering a talk to her management team. Downward communication that provides relevant information helps employees identify with the company, improve their attitudes, and make decisions consistent with the organization's objectives.[87]

People must receive the information they need to perform their jobs and become—and remain—loyal to the organization. But they often lack adequate information due to:[88]

- *Information overload*—Managers and employees are bombarded with so much information that they can't absorb it all. Much incoming information is not very important, but the volume causes some relevant information to be lost.

- *Lack of openness between managers and employees*—Managers may believe "No news is good news," "I don't have time to keep them informed of everything they want to know," or "It's none of their business, anyway." Some managers withhold information even if sharing it would be useful.

- *Filtering*—As we discussed earlier in the chapter, when messages are passed from one person to another, some information is left out. When a message passes through many people, information can be lost during each transmission. The message also can be distorted as people add words or interpretations. Filtering poses serious problems in organizations when messages are communicated downward through many organizational levels (see Exhibit 13.7).

By the time messages reach their ultimate destination, those receivers may get very little useful information. The fewer authority levels through which communications pass, the less information will be lost or distorted. In flatter organizations, filtering downward is less of a problem.

Coaching Some of the most important downward communications occur when managers give performance feedback to their direct reports. We discussed earlier the importance of giving feedback and positive reinforcement when it is deserved. It is also important to explicitly discuss poor performance and how to improve.

Coaching is dialogue with a goal of helping someone become more effective and achieve his or her full potential on the job.[89]

upward communication
information that flows from
lower to higher levels in the
organization's hierarchy

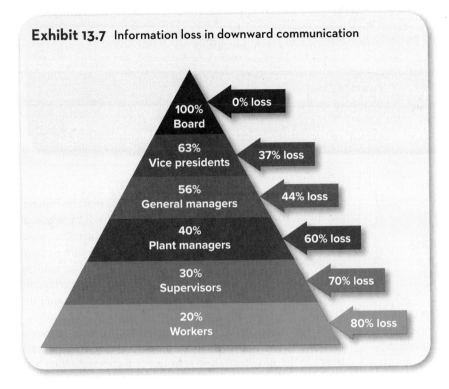

Exhibit 13.7 Information loss in downward communication

100% Board — 0% loss

63% Vice presidents — 37% loss

56% General managers — 44% loss

40% Plant managers — 60% loss

30% Supervisors — 70% loss

20% Workers — 80% loss

Done properly, coaching develops managers and executives, drives engagement, and enhances performance.[90] A survey by the American Management Association found that about half of responding companies used coaching to prepare managers for a promotion or new role.[91]

Companies including Coca-Cola use coaching as an essential part of their executive development process. When done well, coaching is true dialogue between two committed people engaged in joint problem solving. It is far more than an occasion for highlighting poor performance, delivering reprimands, or giving advice. Good coaching requires achieving real understanding of the problem, the person, and the situation; jointly generating ideas for what to do; and encouraging the person to improve. Good coaches ask a lot of questions, listen well, provide input, and encourage others to think for themselves. Effective coaching requires honesty, calmness, and supportiveness, all aided by a sincere desire to help. The ultimate and longest-lasting form of help is enabling people to think through and solve their own problems.

Downward Communication in Difficult Times

Adequate downward communication can be particularly valuable during difficult times.[92] During corporate mergers and acquisitions, employees feel anxious and wonder how the changes will affect them. Ideally (and ethically), top management should communicate with employees about the change as early as possible.

But some argue against that approach, on the grounds that informing employees about the reorganization might cause them to quit too early. Then too, top management often cloisters itself, prompting rumors and anxiety. CEOs and other senior execs are surrounded by lawyers, investment bankers, and so on—people who are paid merely to make the deal happen, not to make it work. Yet with the people who are affected by the deal, you must increase, not decrease, communication.[93]

In a merger of two *Fortune* 500 companies, two plants received very different information.[94] All employees at both plants received the initial letter from the CEO announcing the merger. But after that, one plant was kept in the dark while the other received frequent information about what was happening. Top management told employees about layoffs, transfers, promotions and demotions, and changes in pay, jobs, and benefits.

Which plant do you think fared better as the difficult transitional months unfolded? In both plants, the merger decreased employees' job satisfaction and commitment to the organization and increased their belief that the company was untrustworthy, dishonest, and uncaring. In the plant where employees got little information, these problems persisted for a long time. But in the plant where employees received complete information, the situation stabilized, and attitudes improved toward their normal levels. Full communication helped employees survive an anxious period and also served a symbolic value by signaling management's care and concern. Without such communications, employee reactions to a merger or acquisition may be so negative as to undermine the corporate strategy and future performance.

5.2 | Upward Communication Is Invaluable

Upward communication travels from lower to higher ranks in the hierarchy. Good upward communication is important for several reasons:[95]

- Managers learn what's going on. Management gains a more accurate picture of subordinates' work, accomplishments, problems, plans, attitudes, and ideas.

- Employees gain from the opportunity to communicate upward. People can relieve some of their frustrations, gain a stronger sense of participation in the enterprise, and improve morale.

- Effective upward communication facilitates downward communication as good listening becomes a two-way street.

A manufacturing company relied on upward communication as it prepared to operate shifts around the clock. Managers expected that the change would be difficult for some people, so they created an employee focus group to inform management

Traditional Thinking

Ignore rumors because they are usually baseless; they will go away on their own.

The Best Managers Today

Neutralize potentially destructive rumors by providing factual information.

voice when people speak up with good intentions about work-related issues, rather than remaining silent

horizontal communication information shared among people on the same hierarchical level

about how the new work shifts were affecting workers' families and other commitments, including night school. The change to the new shifts took employees' concerns into account and proceeded smoothly.[96]

The problems common in upward communication resemble those for downward communication. Managers are bombarded with information from different directions and may neglect or miss information from below. In addition, most people are not always open with their bosses; filtering occurs upward as well as downward. People tend to share only good news with their bosses and suppress bad news, for several reasons:

- They want to appear competent.

- They mistrust their boss and so resist sharing confidential information and thoughts.

- They fear the boss will punish the messenger, even if the reported problem is not his or her fault.

- They believe they are helping if they shield their boss from problems.

For these and other reasons, managers may not learn about important problems.[97] As one leadership expert put it, "If the messages from below say you are doing a flawless job, send back for a more candid assessment."[98]

Managing Upward Communication Generating useful information from below requires managers to both *facilitate* and *motivate* upward communication. For example, they can have an open-door policy and encourage people to use it, have lunch or coffee with employees, use surveys, offer incentives for good suggestions, and have town hall meetings. They can ask for employee advice, make informal visits to plants, really think about and respond to employee suggestions, and distribute summaries of new ideas and practices inspired by employee suggestions and actions.[99]

Some executives practice MBWA (management by wandering around). That term, coined decades ago by Ed Carlson of United Airlines, refers simply to getting out of the office, walking around, and talking frequently and informally with employees.[100] Netflix CEO Reed Hastings takes MBWA to another level. He purposely doesn't have an office at headquarters; he connects with people by working at random places around the building.[101]

At an aerospace company with poor management–employee relations, outside consultants assembled a team of employees to study the problem. Their top-priority recommendation was informal walk-arounds in which managers visit employees in their work areas. The team members told management they wanted these visits as a signal that managers cared to get to know them, spend time with them, and listen to them.[102]

Useful upward communication must be reinforced and not punished. Someone who tries to talk to a manager about a problem must not be consistently brushed off. An announced open-door policy must truly be open-door. Ideally, people must trust their bosses and know they will not hold a grudge if they receive negative information. To get honesty, managers should truly listen, not punish the messenger for being honest, and take action on valid concerns and ideas.

What will be your own tendencies regarding what you do and don't convey to your boss? You can exercise voice—speaking up with good intentions about work-related issues, rather than remaining silent—but know that others will perceive your comments as either positive (good ideas and opportunities, usually presented in a positive tone) or negative (problems, sometimes presented in a negative tone and prompting defensiveness).[103] Both types are potentially useful, but bear in mind the importance of presenting them appropriately and offering constructive ideas (not just criticism). Make sure you go through appropriate channels. Some health care professionals who told the public about conditions related to dealing with COVID-19 against the wishes of administrators learned this lesson the hard way.[104]

5.3 | Horizontal Communication Fosters Collaboration

Much information needs to be shared among people on the same hierarchical level. Such horizontal communication can

● Effective managers encourage and facilitate upward and horizontal communication. Jetta Productions/Blend Images, LLC

take place among people in the same work team or in different departments. For example, a purchasing agent discusses a problem with a production engineer, and a task force of department heads meets to discuss a particular concern. Horizontal communication also occurs with people outside the firm, including potential investors.[105]

Horizontal communication serves several important functions:[106]

- It allows units to share information, coordinate work, and solve mutual problems.

- It helps resolve conflicts.

- By allowing interaction among peers, it provides social and emotional support.

All these factors contribute to morale, cohesion, and effectiveness. Google provides space for ongoing horizontal communication in Google Cafés, which are designed to encourage more interaction among employees within and between teams.[107]

Managing Horizontal Communication When decisions in one unit affect another, information must be shared horizontally. Denver Health and Hospital Authority encourages its nurse care teams to use huddles (or quick meetings of key personnel) during each shift change to improve patient safety.[108]

General Electric offers a great team example of how to use horizontal communication as a competitive weapon.[109] GE's businesses could operate independently, but each helps the others. They transfer technical resources, people, information, ideas, and money to one another. GE accomplishes this cooperation through easy access between divisions and the CEO; a culture of openness, honesty, trust, and mutual obligation; and quarterly meetings in which all top executives share information and ideas. Similar activities take place at lower levels as well.

LO6 Summarize how to work with the company grapevine.

6 | INFORMAL COMMUNICATION NEEDS ATTENTION

Communications differ in their formality:

- *Formal communications* are official, management-sanctioned episodes of information transmission. They can move upward, downward, or horizontally and often are prearranged and necessary for performing some task.

- *Informal communication* is more unofficial. People gossip; employees complain about their boss; people talk about their favorite sports teams; work teams tell newcomers how to get by.[110]

The grapevine is the social network of informal communications. Informal networks provide people with information, help them solve problems, and teach them how to do their work. You should develop a good network of people willing and able to help.[111] However, the grapevine can be destructive when irrelevant or erroneous misinformation proliferates and harms operations.[112]

What does this mean for you personally? Don't overdo the gossip, electronic or whispered. Embarrassing messages become public, and lawsuits based on defamation of character and invasion of privacy use email evidence. But don't avoid the grapevine, either.[113] Listen, but evaluate before believing what you hear. Who is the source and how believable? Does the rumor make sense? Is it consistent or inconsistent with other things you know or have heard? Seek more information. Don't stir the pot.

6.1 | Managing Informal Communication

Rumors start over any number of topics, including salaries, job security, costly mistakes, and the identity of people who are leaving or being promoted. Rumors can destroy people's faith and trust in the company—and in each other. But the grapevine cannot be eliminated. So managers need to *work with* the grapevine. You can manage the grapevine in several ways:[114]

- If you hear a story that could get out of hand, you can *talk to the key people* involved to get the facts and their perspectives. Don't allow malicious gossip.

transparency people's beliefs that the information their employer and others send them is of high quality, as defined by accuracy, timeliness, and full disclosure of relevant information

boundaryless organization organization in which there are no barriers to information flow

- To *prevent* rumors from starting, you can explain events that are important but have not been explained, dispel uncertainties by providing facts, and establish open communications and trust over time.[115] These efforts are especially important during times of uncertainty, such as after a merger or layoff or when sales slow down, because rumors increase along with anxiety.

- You should *neutralize* rumors once they have started. Disregard the rumor if it is ridiculous; openly confirm any parts that are true; make public comments (no comment is seen as a confirmation of the rumor); deny the rumor, if the denial is based in truth (don't make false denials); make sure communications about the issue are consistent; select a spokesperson of appropriate rank and knowledge; and hold town meetings if needed.[116]

Some companies use informal rumors to create buzz and excitement in advance of a new product launch. Rumors abounded in 2020 about the second generation of Facebook's popular Oculus Quest virtual reality headset. Questions regarding the Quest 2's release date and cost, plus its processing speed and resolution display flooded the virtual reality gaming space.[117] Fans reacted positively when Facebook announced the Quest 2, at a cost of about $350, would be released for sale to the public on October 13, 2020.[118]

LO7 Describe the boundaryless organization and its advantages.

7 | TRANSPARENT INFORMATION FLOW BUILDS TRUST

Many executives and management scholars today consider open access to information in all directions to be an organizational imperative. You will often hear the relevant term *transparency*: people's beliefs that the information their employer and others send them is of high quality, as defined by *accuracy, timeliness,* and full *disclosure* of relevant information.[119] "Relevant" indicates that not all information—for instance, company secrets or confidential conversations—should be or needs to be shared. Ideally, all relevant stakeholders, internal and external, use those three quality criteria to achieve transparency with one another.

Jack Welch, when he was CEO of General Electric, coined the now-famous word *boundarylessness.* A **boundaryless organization** is one without significant barriers to information flow. Ideas, information, decisions, and actions can move to where they are most needed.[120]

This free flow does not imply a random free-for-all of unlimited communication and information overload. It implies information available *as needed,* moving fast and easily enough that the organization functions far better as a whole than as separate parts.

GE's chief learning officer used the metaphor of the organization as a house having three kinds of boundaries: the floors and ceilings, the walls that separate the rooms, and the outside walls. These barriers correspond to the boundaries between different organizational levels, different units, and the organization and its external stakeholders—for example, suppliers and customers.[121]

GE's famous Workout program is a series of meetings for people across multiple hierarchical levels, characterized by extremely frank, tough discussions that break down even vertical boundaries. From 2007 to 2018, nearly 1.5 million GE people participated in a Workout program.[122] Customers and suppliers participate in Workout programs as well, breaking down external boundaries.

Boundarylessness facilitates dialogue by turning barriers—physical and psychological—into permeable membranes. As the GE people put it, people from different parts of the organization need to learn both "how to talk" and "how to walk."[123] That is, dialogue is essential, but it must be followed by commensurate action.

Consistency between words and action is one type of integrity, which creates trust. Transparency, too, strengthens people's trust in an organization and in one another. Taken together, these are vital contributors to personal, team, and organizational effectiveness.[124]

Notes

1. "Performance Management: Competencies That Support Effective Performance Management," U.S. Office of Personnel Management, www.opm.gov.

2. C. Guse, "New York's Unemployment System Overwhelmed as Coronavirus Shutters Businesses across the State," *MSN,* March 16, 2020, https://www.msn.com/en-us/news/world/new-york-e2-80-99s-unemployment-system-overwhelmed-as-coronavirus-pandemic-shutters-businesses-across-the-state/ar-BB11hc9k.

3. C. Clifford, "CEO of Multibillion-Dollar Company Slack to Employees amid Coronavirus: 'Don't Stress about Work,'" *CNBC,* March 26, 2020, https://www.cnbc.com/2020/03/26/slack-ceo-to-employees-amid-covid-19-dont-stress-about-work.html.

4. C. Duffy, "Why CEOs Are Giving Up Their Salaries during the Coronavirus Crisis," *CNN Business,* March 26, 2020, https://www.cnn.com/2020/03/26/investing/ceo-giving-up-pay-coronavirus/index.html.

5. K. Stankiewicz, "Mark Cuban Says How Companies Treat Workers during Pandemic Could Define Their Brand 'for Decades,'" *CNBC,* March 25, 2020, https://www.cnbc.com/2020/03/25/coronavirus-mark-cuban-warns-against-rushing-employees-back-to-work.html.

6. W. V. Haney, "A Comparative Study of Unilateral and Bilateral Communication," *Academy of Management Journal* 7 (1964), pp. 128–36.

7. P. Capelli and A. Tavis, "The Performance Management Revolution," *Harvard Business Review,* October 2016, www.hbr.org.

8. P. Capelli and A. Tavis, "The Performance Management Revolution," *Harvard Business Review,* October 2016, www.hbr.org.

9. M. McCormack, "The Illusion of Communication," *Financial Times Mastering Management Review,* July 1999, pp. 8–9.

10. R. Cross and S. Brodt, "How Assumptions of Consensus Undermine Decision Making," *Sloan Management Review* 42 (2001), pp. 86–94.

11. S. Mohammed and E. Ringseis, "Cognitive Diversity and Consensus in Group Decision Making: The Role of Inputs, Processes, and Outcomes," *Organizational Behavior and Human Decision Processes* 85 (2001), pp. 310–35.

12. S. Parker and C. Axtell, "Seeing Another Viewpoint: Antecedents and Outcomes of Employee Perspective Taking," *Academy of Management Journal* 44 (2001), pp. 1085–1100.

13. C. Folz, "How to Deliver Bad News," Society for Human Resource Management, August 25, 2016, www.shrm.org.

14. M. Murphy, "My Boss and I Have Different Communication Styles, and It's Destroying Our Relationship," *Forbes,* April 24, 2016, www.forbes.com.

15. L. K. Larkey, "Toward a Theory of Communicative Interactions in Culturally Diverse Workgroups," *Academy of Management Review,* April 1996, pp. 463–91.

16. N. J. Adler, *International Dimensions of Organizational Behavior.* Copyright 1986. Reprinted with permission of South-Western College Publishing, a division of Thomson Learning.

17. P. Milligan, "The Mixed Signals Businesses Send Older Workers," *Forbes,* May 4, 2018, www.forbes.com.

18. S. Sarkis, "Combat Age Discrimination at Work: For Employees and Employers," *Forbes,* September 15, 2019, www.forbes.com.

19. K. Gurchiek, "LA Times to Pay $15.4 Million in Age-Discrimination Case," Society for Human Resource Management, August 22, 2019, www.shrm.org.

20. J. Kelly, "Google Settles Age Discrimination Lawsuit, Highlighting the Proliferation of Ageism in Hiring," *Forbes,* July 23, 2019, www.forbes.com.

21. "Policy on Harassment, Discrimination, Retaliation, Standards of Conduct, and Workplace Concerns (US)," Google, www.services.google.com, accessed April 17, 2020.

22. J. V. Thill and C. L. Bovee, *Business Communication Version 2.0* (Upper Saddle River, NJ: Prentice-Hall, 2005), p. 17.

23. J. V. Thill and C. L. Bovee, *Business Communication Version 2.0* (Upper Saddle River, NJ: Prentice-Hall, 2005), p. 17.

24. C. Deutsch, "The Multimedia Benefits Kit," *The New York Times,* October 14, 1990, sec. 3, p. 25.

25. T. W. Comstock, *Communicating in Business and Industry* (Albany, NY: Delmar, 1985).

26. "Email Statistics Report, 2019–2023," The Radicati Group, February 2019, www.radicati.com.

27. M. Plummer, "How to Spend Way Less Time on Email Every Day," *Harvard Business Review,* January 22, 2019, www.hbr.org.

28. N. Fearn, S. McCaskill, and B. Turner, "Best Online Collaboration Tools of 2020: Software for Shared Work and Communications," *TechRadar,* April 1, 2020, www.techradar.com.

29. See Nike account, Instagram.com, accessed April 17, 2020.

30. C. Conner, "How Top CEOs Leverage Social Media to Build a Following and Brand Loyalty," *Forbes,* March 11, 2018, www.forbes.com.

31. See John Legere's Twitter account, Twitter.com, accessed April 17, 2020.

32. M. Schaefer, "The 10 Best Big Company Blogs in the World," *Business Grow,* January 12, 2015, www.businessesgrow.com.

33. M. Schaefer, "The 10 Best Big Company Blogs in the World," *Business Grow,* January 12, 2015, www.businessesgrow.com.

34. A. LaVito and M. Townsend, "The Hidden Costs of All These Canceled Business Trips," Bloomberg News, March 10, 2020, www.bloomberg.com.

35. S. Patnaik, "Zoom's Daily Active Users Jumped from 10 Million to over 200 Million in 3 Months," Reuters, April 2, 2020, www.reuters.com.

36. S. S. K. Lam and J. Schaubroeck, "Improving Group Decisions by Better Pooling Information: A Comparative Advantage of Group Decision Support Systems," *Journal of Applied Psychology* 85 (2000), pp. 565–73.

37. H. Kelly, "Anonymous Social Apps Provide Forum for Gripes, Gossip," *CNN,* February 28, 2014, www.cnn.com.

38. C. Naquin and G. Paulson, "Online Bargaining and Interpersonal Trust," *Journal of Applied Psychology* 88 (2003), pp. 113–20.

39. B. Baltes, M. Dickson, M. Sherman, C. Bauer, and J. LaGanke, "Computer-Mediated Communication and Group Decision Making: A Meta-Analysis," *Organizational Behavior and Human Decision Processes* 87 (2002), pp. 156–79.

40. R. Rice and D. Case, "Electronic Message Systems in the University: A Description of Use and Utility," *Journal of Communication* 33 (1983), pp. 131–52; and C. Steinfield, "Dimensions of Electronic Mail Use in an Organizational Setting," *Proceedings of the Academy of Management,* San Diego, 1985.

41. "Why Your Business Needs a Social Media Policy and Eight Things It Should Cover," *Forbes,* May 25, 2017, www.forbes.com.

42. H. Brueck, "Nobody Knows What Your Emojis Mean," *Fortune,* April 14, 2016, www.fortune.com.

43. J. Robinson, "Tame the E-mail Beast," *Entrepreneur,* February 12, 2010, www.entrepreneur.com; M. Totty, "Rethinking the Inbox," *The Wall Street Journal,* March 26, 2007, www.wsj.com; Reuters, "BlackBerrys, Laptops Blur Work/Home Balance: Poll," Yahoo! News, April 5, 2007, www.news.yahoo.com; and M. Locher, "BlackBerry Addiction Starts at the Top," *PC World,* March 6, 2007, www.pcworld.com.

44. J. Taylor, W. Wacker, and H. Means, *The 500 Year Delta: What Happens after What Comes Next* (New York: Harper Business, 1997); M. Locher, "BlackBerry Addiction Starts at the Top," *PC World,* March 6, 2007, www.pcworld.com; and G. Hughes, "Quick Guide to IM-ing at Work," Yahoo! Tech, January 24, 2007, tech.yahoo.com.

45. "When the French Clock Off at 6 pm, They Really Mean It," *The Guardian,* April 9, 2014, www.theguardian.com.

46. "When the French Clock Off at 6 pm, They Really Mean It," *The Guardian,* April 9, 2014, www.theguardian.com.

47. V. Govindarajan and A. Gupta, "Building an Effective Global Team," *Organizational Dynamics* 42 (2001), pp. 63–71.

48. "Workplace Flexibility: Take Control of Letting Go," Deloitte, https://www2.deloitte.com/us/en/pages/human-capital/solutions/workplace-flexibility-services.html, accessed April 5, 2019; J. Pochepan, "Here's What Happens When You Take Away Dedicated Desks for Employees," *Inc.,* May 10, 2018, www.inc.com.

49. "Accenture People Enables Collaboration Anytime, Anywhere within Today's Digital Business," Accenture, www.accenture.com, accessed April 17, 2020.

50. E. M. Hallowell, "The Human Moment at Work," *Harvard Business Review,* January–February 1999, pp. 58–66.

51. R. Lengel and R. Daft, "The Selection of Communication Media as an Executive Skill," *Academy of Management Executive* 2 (1988), pp. 225–32.

52. J. R. Carlson and R. W. Zmud, "Channel Expansion Theory and the Experiential Nature of Media Richness Perceptions," *Academy of Management Journal* 42 (1999), pp. 153–70.

53. L. Trevino, R. Daft, and R. Lengel, "Understanding Managers' Media Choices: A Symbolic Interactionist Perspective," in *Organizations and Communication Technology,* ed. J. Fulk and C. Steinfield (London: Sage, 1990).

54. J. Fulk and B. Boyd, "Emerging Theories of Communication in Organizations," *Journal of Management* 17 (1991), pp. 407–46.

55. L. Bossidy and R. Charan, *Confronting Reality: Doing What Matters to Get Things Right* (New York: Crown Business, 2004).

56. J. Guterman, "How to Become a Better Manager by Thinking Like a Designer," *MIT Sloan Management Review* 50, no. 4 (Summer 2009), pp. 39–42; and M. McCall, M. Lombardo, and A. Morrison, *The Lessons of Experience: How Successful Executives Develop on the Job* (Lexington, MA: Lexington, 1988).

57. J. A. Conger, "The Necessary Art of Persuasion," *Harvard Business Review,* May–June 1998, pp. 84–95.

58. N. Morgan, "How to Become an Authentic Speaker," *Harvard Business Review,* November 2008, pp. 115–19.

59. N. Nohria and B. Harrington, *Six Principles of Successful Persuasion* (Boston: Harvard Business School Publishing Division, 1993).

60. N. van Dam and E. van der Helm, "Organizational Cost of Insufficient Sleep," *McKinsey Quarterly,* February 2016, www.mckinsey.com; and E. Markowitz, "Should Your Employees Take Naps?" *Inc.,* August 12, 2011, www.inc.com.

61. C. D. Decker, "Writing to Teach Thinking," *Across the Board,* March 1996, pp. 19–20.

62. M. Forbes, "Exorcising Demons from Important Business Letters," *Marketing Times,* March–April 1981, pp. 36–38.

63. W. Strunk Jr. and E. B. White, *The Elements of Style,* 3rd ed. (New York: Macmillan, 1979); and H. R. Fowler and J. E. Aaron, *The Little, Brown Handbook,* 12th ed. (New York: Longman, 2011).

64. G. Ferraro, "The Need for Linguistic Proficiency in Global Business," *Business Horizons,* May–June 1996, pp. 39–46.

65. P. C. Early and E. Mosakowski, "Creating Hybrid Team Cultures: An Empirical Test of Transnational Team Functioning," *Academy of Management Journal* 43 (2000), pp. 26–49.

66. D. Welch and L. Welch, "Developing Multilingual Capacity: A Challenge for the Multinational Enterprise," *Journal of Management* 44 (2018), pp. 854–59.

67. G. Ferraro, "The Need for Linguistic Proficiency in Global Business," *Business Horizons,* May–June 1996, pp. 39–46.

68. C. Chu, *The Asian Mind Game* (New York: Rawson Associates, 1991).

69. G. Ferraro, "The Need for Linguistic Proficiency in Global Business," *Business Horizons,* May–June 1996, pp. 39–46; and J. F. Puck, M. G. Kittler, and C. Wright, "Does It Really Work? Re-assessing the Impact of Pre-departure Cross-Cultural Training on Expatriate Adjustment," *The International Journal of Human Resource Management* 19, no. 12 (December 2008), pp. 2182–97.

70. S. Bonaccio, J. O'Reilly, S. O'Sullivan, and F. Chiocchio, "Nonverbal Behavior and Communication in the Workplace: A Review and an Agenda for Research," *Journal of Management* 42 (2016), pp. 1044–74.

71. T. W. Comstock, *Communicating in Business and Industry* (Albany, NY: Delmar, 1985).

72. M. Korda, *Power: How to Get It, How to Use It* (New York: Random House, 1975).

73. A. Mehrabian, "Communication without Words," *Psychology Today,* September 1968, p. 52. Cited in M. B. McCaskey, "The Hidden Message Managers Send," *Harvard Business Review,* November-December 1979, pp. 135-48.

74. G. Ferraro, "The Need for Linguistic Proficiency in Global Business," *Business Horizons,* May-June 1996, pp. 39-46.

75. M. Munter, "Cross-Cultural Communication for Managers," *Business Horizons* 36, no. 3 (May-June 1993), pp. 69-78.

76. C. Hall, "Cathy Coughlin, Relentless Crusader of 'It Can Wait' Campaign, Dies at 57," *Dallas News,* April 24, 2015, www.dallas-news.com.

77. A. Athos and J. Gabarro, *Interpersonal Behavior* (Englewood Cliffs, NJ: Prentice-Hall, 1978).

78. R. G. Nichols, "Listening Is a 10-Part Skill," *Nation's Business* 45 (July 1957), pp. 56-60. Cited in *Readings in Interpersonal and Organizational Communication,* ed. R. C. Huseman, C. M. Logue, and D. L. Freshley (Boston: Allyn & Bacon, 1977).

79. "Critical Leadership Skills: Key Traits That Can Make or Break Today's Leaders," Ken Blanchard Companies, www.kenblanchard.com.

80. J. Kouzes and B. Posner, *The Leadership Challenge* (San Francisco: Jossey-Bass, 1995).

81. G. Graham, J. Unruh, and P. Jennings, "The Impact of Nonverbal Communication in Organizations: A Survey of Perceptions," *Journal of Business Communications* 28 (1991), pp. 45-62.

82. G. Graham, J. Unruh, and P. Jennings, "The Impact of Nonverbal Communication in Organizations: A Survey of Perceptions," *Journal of Business Communications* 28 (1991), pp. 45-62.

83. D. Upton and S. Macadam, "Why (and How) to Take a Plant Tour," *Harvard Business Review,* May-June 1997, pp. 97-106.

84. N. Adler, *International Dimensions of Organizational Behavior,* 2nd ed. (Boston: Kent, 1991).

85. C. Chu, *The Asian Mind Game* (New York: Rawson Associates, 1991).

86. J. Keyton, "Communication in Organizations," *Annual Review of Organizational Psychology and Organizational Behavior* 4 (2017), pp. 501-26.

87. A. Smidts, A. T. H. Pruyn, and C. B. M. van Riel, "The Impact of Employee Communication and Perceived External Prestige on Organizational Identification," *Academy of Management Journal* 49 (2001), pp. 1051-62.

88. J. W. Koehler, K. W. E. Anatol, and R. L. Applebaum, *Organizational Communication: Behavioral Perspectives* (Orlando, FL: Holt, Rinehart & Winston, 1981); and X. Qin, R. Ren, Z.Zhang, and R. Johnson, "Fairness Heuristics and Substitutability Effects: Inferring the Fairness of Outcomes, Procedures, and Interpersonal Treatment When Employees Lack Clear Information," *Journal of Applied Psychology* 100 (2015), pp. 749-66.

89. J. Waldroop and T. Butler, "The Executive as Coach," *Harvard Business Review,* November-December 1996, pp. 111-17; and D. O'Neil, M.Hopkins, and D. Bilimoria, "A Framework for Developing Women Leaders: Applications to Executive Coaching," *Journal of Applied Behavioral Science* 51 (2015), pp. 253-76.

90. J. Bersin, "Becoming Irresistible: A New Model for Employee Engagement," Deloitte University Press, January 26, 2015, www.dupress.com; and P. Coate and K. R. Hill, "Why Smart Companies Hire Performance Coaches to Turn Managers into Leaders," *Employment Relations Today* 38, no. 1 (Spring 2011), pp. 35-43.

91. V. Elmer, "Coaching Is Hot. Is It Right for You?" *Fortune,* August 29, 2011, www.fortune.com.

92. R. J. Bies, "The Delivery of Bad News in Organizations: A Framework for Analysis," *Journal of Management* 39 (2013), pp. 136-62.

93. J. Gutknecht and J. B. Keys, "Mergers, Acquisitions, and Takeovers: Maintaining Morale of Survivors and Protecting Employees," *Academy of Management Executive,* August 1993, pp. 26-36.

94. D. Schweiger and A. DeNisi, "Communication with Employees Following a Merger: A Longitudinal Field Experiment," *Academy of Management Journal* 34 (1991), pp. 110-35.

95. W. V. Ruch, *Corporate Communications* (Westport, CT: Quorum, 1984).

96. E. Krell, "The Unintended Word," *HRMagazine,* August 2006.

97. L. Tost, F. Gino, and R. Larrick, "When Power Makes Others Speechless: The Negative Impact of Leader Power on Team Performance," *Academy of Management Journal* 56 (2013), pp. 1465-86.

98. J. Gardner, "The Heart of the Matter: Leader-Constituent Interaction," in *Leading and Leadership,* ed. T. Fuller (Notre Dame, IN: Notre Dame University Press, 2000), pp. 239-44.

99. R. Ashkenas, D. Ulrich, T. Jick, and S. Kerr, *The Boundaryless Organization* (San Francisco: Jossey-Bass, 1995).

100. W. V. Ruch, *Corporate Communications* (Westport, CT: Quorum, 1984).

101. P. Sellers, "How Netflix CEO Hastings Stays Agile," *Fortune,* December 13, 2010, www.fortune.com.

102. L. Dulye, "Get Out of Your Office," *HRMagazine,* July 2006.

103. M. Chamberlin, D. Newton, and J Lepine, "A Meta-Analysis of Voice and Its Promotive and Prohibitive Forms: Identification of Key Associations, Distinctions, and Future Research Directions," *Personnel Psychology* 70 (2017), pp. 11-71.

104. N. Scheiber and B. M. Rosenthal, "Nurses and Doctors Speaking Out on Safety Now Risk Their Job," *The New York Times,* April 9, 2020.

105. A. Hutton, "Four Rules for Taking Your Message to Wall Street," *Harvard Business Review,* May 2001, pp. 125-32.

106. J. W. Koehler, K. W. E. Anatol, and R. L. Applebaum, *Organizational Communication: Behavioral Perspectives* (Orlando, FL: Holt, Rinehart & Winston, 1981); and D. Tjosvold, A. S.H. Wong, and N. Y. F. Chen, "Constructively Managing Conflicts in Organizations," *Annual Review of Organizational Psychology and Organizational Behavior* 1 (2014), pp. 545-68.

107. E. Huynh, "Google's Innovative Workplace," *Medium,* March 6, 2018, www.medium.com.

108. C. Dingley, K. Daugherty, M. Derieg, R. Persing, "Improving Patient Safety through Provider Communication Strategy Enhancements," Agency for Health Care Research and Quality, www.ahrq.gov, accessed April 18, 2020.

109. D. K. Denton, "Open Communication," *Business Horizons,* September–October 1993, pp. 64–69.

110. N. B. Kurland and L. H. Pelled, "Passing the Word: Toward a Model of Gossip and Power in the Workplace," *Academy of Management Review* 25 (2000), pp. 428–38; T. Grosser, V. Lopez-Kidwell, G. Labianca, and L. Ellwardt, "Hearing It through the Grapevine: Positive and Negative Workplace Gossip," *Organizational Dynamics* 41 (2012), 52–61; and L. Abrams, R. Cross, E. Lesser, and D. Levin, "Nurturing Interpersonal Trust in Knowledge-Sharing Networks," *Academy of Management Executive* 17 (November 2003), pp. 64–77.

111. R. Cross, P. Gray, S. Cunningham, M. Showers, and R. Thomas, "The Collaborative Organization: How to Make Employee Networks Really Work," *MIT Sloan Management Review* 52, no. 1 (Fall 2010), pp. 83–90; L. Abrams, R. Cross, E. Lesser, and D. Levin, "Nurturing Interpersonal Trust in Knowledge-Sharing Networks," *Academy of Management Executive* 17 (November 2003), pp. 64–77; and T. Grosser, V. Lopez-Kidwell, G. Labianca, and L. Ellwardt, "Hearing It through the Grapevine: Positive and Negative Workplace Gossip," *Organizational Dynamics* 41 (2012), 52–61.

112. N. Shragai, "How Rumour and Gossip Oil the Wheels of Office Life," *Financial Times,* July 6, 2015, www.ft.com; and R. L. Rosnow, "Rumor as Communication: A Contextual Approach," *Journal of Communication* 38 (1988), pp. 12–28.

113. L. Burke and J. M. Wise, "The Effective Care, Handling, and Pruning of the Office Grapevine," *Business Horizons,* May–June 2003, pp. 71–76.

114. K. Davis, "The Care and Cultivation of the Corporate Grapevine," *Dun's Review,* July 1973, pp. 44–47.

115. N. Difonzo, P. Bordia, and R. Rosnow, "Reining in Rumors," *Organizational Dynamics,* Summer 1994, pp. 47–62.

116. N. Difonzo, P. Bordia, and R. Rosnow, "Reining in Rumors," *Organizational Dynamics,* Summer 1994, pp. 47–62.

117. S. Stein, "Oculus Quest 2: Rumor Roundup and Everything You Need to Know," C | Net, July 30, 2020, www.cnet.com.

118. T. Haselton, "Facebook's Latest Virtual Reality Headset is the Best Yet, but Still Feels Antisocial," CNBC, September 16, 2020, www.cnbc.com.

119. A. Schnackenberg and E. Tomlinson, "Organizational Transparency: A New Perspective on Managing Trust in Organization-Stakeholder Relationships," *Journal of Management* 42 (2016), pp. 1784–1810.

120. R. Ashkenas, D. Ulrich, T. Jick, and S. Kerr, *The Boundaryless Organization: Breaking the Chains of Organizational Structure* (San Francisco: Jossey-Bass, 1995).

121. R. M. Hodgetts, "A Conversation with Steve Kerr," *Organizational Dynamics,* Spring 1996, pp. 68–79.

122. "Number of Employees at General Electric in the U.S. from 2007 to 2018 (in 1, 000s)," Statistica, www.statistica.com, accessed April 5, 2019.

123. R. Ashkenas, D. Ulrich, T. Jick, and S. Kerr, *The Boundaryless Organization: Breaking the Chains of Organizational Structure* (San Francisco: Jossey-Bass, 1995).

124. A. Schnackenberg and E. Tomlinson, "Organizational Transparency: A New Perspective on Managing Trust in Organization-Stakeholder Relationships," *Journal of Management* 42 (2016), pp. 1784–1810.

chapter 14

Managerial Control

Learning Objectives

After studying Chapter 14, you should be able to

LO1 Explain why companies develop control systems.

LO2 Summarize how to design a basic bureaucratic control system.

LO3 Describe the reasons for using budgets as a control device.

LO4 Recognize basic types of financial statements and financial ratios used as controls.

LO5 List procedures for implementing effective control systems.

LO6 Discuss ways in which market and clan control influence performance.

Cindy Ord/Getty Images for Yahoo

Julie Sweet is the CEO of Accenture, one of the top-rated organizations in the world for its diverse and inclusive workplace. How is Accenture accomplishing this? In an interview with *The New York Times*, Sweet shared her strategy: "You first have to decide if diversity is a business priority. If it is, then you need to treat it like a business priority. You set goals, have accountable leaders, you measure progress, and you have an action plan."[1]

Diversity and inclusivity (D&I) initiatives are shifting from a corporate "reporting goal" to a CEO-level business priority. As such, organizations are no longer measuring D&I based only on a demographic profile but are measuring D&I in all facets of operations: recruitment, promotion and pay, investment in training, and promoting diversity worldwide. As firms invest more in proactive D&I

initiatives, they hold managers accountable by comparing their results against other departments and companies.[2]

Accenture set a long-term goal, called "Getting to Equal," to achieve a gender-balanced workforce by 2025. Its board of directors includes individuals from six countries across four continents and is 42 percent female. Accenture has invested nearly a billion dollars in lifelong learning and professional development initiatives and produces publications offering strategies for achieving workplace equality.[3]

Regarding their D&I efforts, Sweet said, "Eventually, leaders will evolve to see profit and culture not as separate endeavors at all, but as tightly interdependent goals, equally crucial to success."[4] She's right, of course, but it will take effective control strategies to get there.

In this chapter, you will learn why control is so essential to good management.

LO1 Explain why companies develop control systems.

1 | SPINNING OUT OF CONTROL?

Control is one of the fundamental forces that keep the organization together and heading in the right direction. Control is any process that directs activities toward the achievement of organizational goals. It is how effective managers make sure things are going as planned.

During challenging economic times when resources are limited and budgets need to be stretched, managerial control becomes crucial for survival. Some managers don't want to admit it, but control problems—the lack of controls or the wrong kinds of controls—often cause irreparable damage. Here are some signs that a company lacks controls:

- *Lax top management*—Senior managers do not emphasize or value the need for controls, or they set a bad example.

- *Absence of policies*—The firm's expectations are not established in writing.

- *Lack of agreed-upon standards*—Organization members are unclear about what needs to be achieved.

- *"Shoot the messenger" management*—Employees feel their careers would be at risk if they reported bad news.

- *Lack of periodic reviews*—Managers do not assess performance on a regular, timely basis.

- *Bad information systems*—Key data are not measured and reported in a timely and easily accessible way.

- *Lack of ethics in the culture*—Organization members have not internalized a commitment to integrity.

control any process that directs the activities of individuals toward the achievement of organizational goals

Employees simply wasting time at work—whether it's using personal email and social media, visiting sports sites, or playing online games—costs U.S. employers billions of dollars in productivity each year![6] Ineffective control systems result in problems ranging from employee theft to lead in the paint of children's toys. Large automakers are not immune. In 2014, Congress questioned Mary Barra, CEO of General Motors, as to why it took GM more than 10 years to recall and fix vehicles with faulty ignition switches. Barra responded that she did not know why the recall took so long and announced an internal investigation. Results showed that faulty switches in some models led to the engine shutting off, causing the loss of power steering, power brakes, and air bags, and resulting in 124 deaths and 275 injuries. GM recalled more than 2.6 million vehicles to replace the ignition switches. Barra said that the 10-year delay was attributable partly to GM's "cost culture" (where reducing costs is the top priority). She added that the auto giant was moving toward a more "customer-focused culture."[7]

Control has been called one of the Siamese twins of management. The other twin is planning. Once managers form plans and strategies, they must ensure that the plans are carried out. Controls help determine whether people are doing what needs

> ## A bad system will beat a good person every time.
> —W. Edwards Deming[5]

bureaucratic control the use of rules, regulations, hierarchy, and authority to guide performance

market control control based on the use of pricing mechanisms and economic information to regulate activities within organizations

clan control control based on the norms, values, shared goals, and trust among group members

standard expected performance for a given goal: a target that establishes a desired performance level, motivates performance, and serves as a benchmark against which actual performance is assessed

to be done and not doing inappropriate things. It provides feedback to managers so they can take steps to correct any problem.

This process is the primary control function of management. To maintain and strengthen quality, speed, and productive output and reduce costs, managers must create and monitor effective controls.

Effective planning aids control, and control aids planning. Planning lays out a framework for the future and provides a blueprint for control. Control systems then regulate resource allocation and use, and facilitate the next planning phases. In today's complex environments, both functions have become harder to implement while becoming more important in every organizational unit. Managers today must control their people, inventories, quality, and costs, to mention just a few.

Managers can apply three general strategies for achieving organizational control:[8]

1. **Bureaucratic control** is the use of rules, standards, regulations, hierarchy, and legitimate authority to guide performance. It includes such items as budgets, statistical reports, and performance appraisals to regulate behavior and results.

2. **Market control** uses prices, competition, and exchange relationships to regulate activities as though they were economic transactions. Business units are profit centers, and they trade resources (services or goods) with one another via such mechanisms. Managers who run these units are responsible for profit and loss.

3. **Clan control** does not assume that the interests of the organization and individuals naturally diverge. Instead it is based on the idea that employees share the values,

expectations, and goals of the organization and act in accordance with them. When members of an organization have common values and goals—and trust one another—formal controls may be less necessary. Clan control is based on interpersonal processes of organizational culture, leadership, and groups and teams.

> **LO2 Summarize how to design a basic bureaucratic control system.**

2 | BUREAUCRATIC CONTROL SYSTEMS

Bureaucratic (or formal) control systems measure progress toward performance goals and apply corrective measures as needed to ensure that performance achieves managers' objectives. Control systems detect and correct significant variations, or discrepancies, in the results of plans and activities.

2.1 | Control Systems Include These Steps

As Exhibit 14.1 shows, a typical control system includes these major steps:

1. Setting performance standards.

2. Measuring performance.

3. Comparing performance against the standards and determining deviations.

4. Taking action to correct problems and reinforce successes.

Step 1: Setting Performance Standards Every organization has goals: profitability, innovation, customer and employee satisfaction, and so on. A standard is the level of expected performance for a given goal. **Standards** are targets that establish desired performance levels, motivate performance, and serve as benchmarks against which to assess actual performance. Standards can be set for any activity—financial activities, operating activities, legal compliance, charitable contributions, and so on.[9]

Exhibit 14.1 The control process

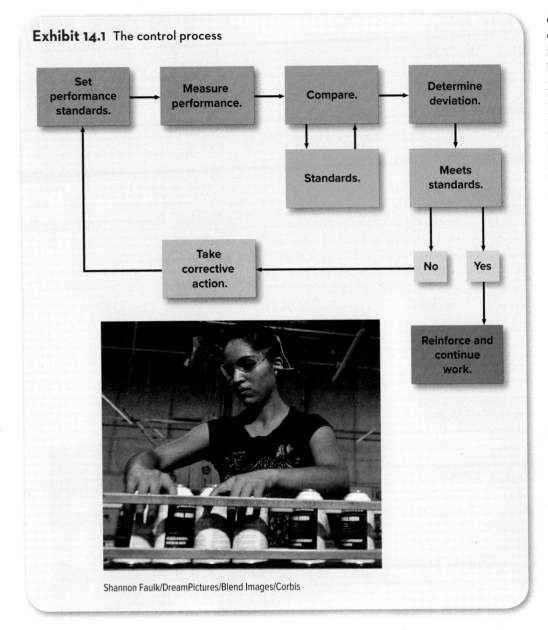

Shannon Faulk/DreamPictures/Blend Images/Corbis

data-gathering and analysis capabilities and the decreasing costs of cloud storage, both large and small companies can gather and retain huge amounts of performance data. One particularly efficient application, the dashboard, helps managers monitor several organizational performance indicators in real time.[10]

1. *Oral reports* allow two-way communication. When a salesperson contacts his or her supervisor each evening to report the day's accomplishments, problems, and customer reactions, the manager can ask questions to gain additional information or clear up any misunderstandings. When necessary, the parties discuss corrective actions.

2. *Personal observation* involves going to the area where activities take place and directly observing work methods, employees' nonverbal signals, and the general operation. Personal observation gives a detailed picture of what is going on, but it does not provide accurate quantitative data; the information is general and subjective. Employees can misunderstand

Performance standards are compared with various production activities (Exhibit 14.2), including volume of output (quantity), defects (quality), on-time availability of finished goods (time used), and dollar expenditures for raw materials and direct labor (cost). Customer service can be measured by the same standards—adequate supply and availability of products, service quality, delivery speed, and so forth.

Step 2: Measuring Performance The second step in the control process is to measure performance. Managers can count units produced, days absent, papers filed, samples distributed, and dollars earned. Performance data commonly are obtained from three sources:

1. *Written reports* are not only developed by people, but are often computer- and AI-generated. Thanks to computers'

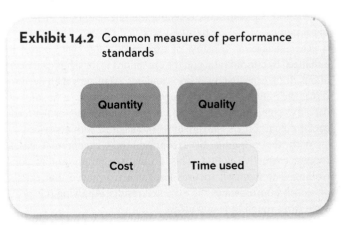

Exhibit 14.2 Common measures of performance standards

Quantity	Quality
Cost	Time used

How to control without being too controlling

Control is one of the most misunderstood areas in management. For many employees, the term conjures up images of a dictatorial boss micromanaging employees. The effects of this version of control on employees are frustration, resentment, and low morale.

This chapter is largely about budgetary, financial, and other numbers-based controls. But a crucial type of control occurs—for better or for worse—interpersonally between "boss" and "subordinate" or direct report. If you supervise others, know that different employees respond to controls in different ways. Some like knowing exactly what needs to be done and appreciate you checking in, while others prefer to be left alone so they can work.

Here are some control tips about interacting personally:

- Develop your technical skills. To provide effective control measures to others, you have to be sure that you know your stuff.

- Develop your communication skills. Control is a two-way street: you have to be able to clearly articulate what you want, but you also need to be receptive to criticisms or concerns. Open lines of communication and active listening skills are key.

- Develop your organizational skills. It is exceedingly difficult to implement effective controls if you can't keep track of them. Many organizations use project management applications such as Asana, Trello, or Basecamp. Make sure you're versed in how best to use these applications.

You don't have to wait until you are a manager to develop control skills. You can work on your self-control. Perhaps begin by implementing organizational strategies to keep you on track with your coursework.

Source: "Management Skills: Definition and Examples," Indeed, November 8, 2018, https://www.indeed.com/career-advice/career-development/management-skills.

---

principle of exception a managerial principle stating that control is enhanced by concentrating on the exceptions to or significant deviations from the expected result or standard

the purpose of personal observation as mistrust ("Why is my boss looking over my shoulder?"). Still, many managers believe in the value of firsthand observation. Personal contact can increase leadership visibility and upward communication. It also can provide valuable information about performance to supplement written and oral reports.

Step 3: Comparing Performance with the Standard

In this process, the manager evaluates the performance. For some activities, small deviations from standard are acceptable, while in others a slight deviation may be serious. In many manufacturing processes, a significant deviation in either direction (e.g., drilling a hole that is too small or too large) is unacceptable. In other cases, a deviation in one direction, such as sales or customer satisfaction below the target level, is a problem, but a deviation in the other—exceeding the sales target or customer expectations—signals better-than-expected results.

The managerial principle of exception states that control is enhanced by concentrating on the exceptions to, or significant deviations from, expected results or standards. Managers then need to direct their attention to the exceptions—for example, a handful of defective components produced on an assembly line, or the feedback from customers who are upset or delighted with a service.

With the principle of exception, only exceptional cases require corrective action. This principle is important in controlling. The manager focuses less on performance that equals or closely approximates the expected results. Applying this principle saves much time and effort.

The accounting and consulting firm of Moody, Famiglietti & Andronico (MFA) uses a control system to ensure exceptional service is tailored to each client's needs and preferences. The Tewksbury, Massachusetts, firm adopted the U.S. Army's

● When Sundar Pichai replaced Larry Page as the CEO of Alphabet in late 2019, he streamlined the company's performance management system known as objectives and key results (OKRs). The move enabled the tech giant's employees to focus their work on one major goal at a time.
Rajat Gupta/EPA/Shutterstock

practice of conducting before-action reviews and after-action reviews to learn from experience and apply those lessons in the future.

When employees are preparing to handle an assignment, they call a short meeting with everyone who has worked with that client during the previous year, plus employees who have handled similar assignments for other clients. During this before-action review, participants trade experiences with and knowledge about the engagement—say, questions that are likely to arise or existing tools for handling common problems. The input helps the team establish goals.

During the assignment, team members meet periodically to assess progress and identify needed adjustments. Soon after project completion, the team reassembles to compare outcomes with goals. Members identify successful actions to recommend in the future, as well as mistakes to avoid next time. Besides noting whether they helped the client meet goals, they also record what they learned about serving the client. Because lessons they learn will come up at future before-action reviews, MFA employees are motivated to fix mistakes and improve methods.[11]

Step 4: Taking Action to Correct Problems and Reinforce Successes

The last step in the control process is to take appropriate action when there are significant deviations. This step ensures that operations are adjusted to achieve the planned results—or to continue exceeding the plan if the manager determines that is possible. If significant variances are discovered, the manager usually takes immediate and vigorous action.

Often, the corrective action can be taken by the operator at the point of the problem. Computer-controlled production technologies use two types of control:

1. *Specialist control*—Operators of computer numerical control (CNC) machines must notify engineering specialists of malfunctions. With this traditional division of labor, the specialist takes corrective action.

2. *Operator control*—Multiskilled operators can rectify their own problems as they occur. This strategy is more efficient because deviations are controlled closer to their source. Operators benefit by having an enriched, satisfying job.

The best corrective action depends on the nature of the problem. The corrective action may involve a shift in marketing strategy (if, say, the problem is lower-than-expected sales), a disciplinary action, a new way to check the accuracy of manufactured parts, or a major modification to a process or system. Sometimes, managers learn they can get better results if they adjust their own practices.

Chipotle is taking food-safety control to the next level. The fast-casual chain recently announced the rollout of Zenput, a mobile food-safety protocol platform used by KFC, Domino's, and others to ensure that all employees at Chipotle's nearly 2,500 stores adhere to food management standards and procedures.

This rollout comes in the wake of another food-safety event at a Powell, Ohio, restaurant where 600 people reported illnesses after eating there.[13] Since the end of 2015, Chipotle has experienced other food-safety events.[14]

study tip 14

Proactively monitor your grades

Most students monitor how their grades are progressing during the semester. However, some don't realize until too late that they're not going to earn their desired grade. You can stay on top of your progress and make adjustments by following the steps in the control process in Exhibit 14.1:

1. Early in the semester, set your performance standard or desired grade.
2. Measure your performance by calculating your grade average after every online assignment, quiz, or exam.
3. Compare your running grade average against your standard.
4. If your grade average is lower than desired, take corrective action like studying more effectively or asking the professor for advice. Alternatively, if your grade average meets your standard, keep doing what you're doing and maybe consider setting a higher standard.

Ryan Smith/Getty Images

feedforward control the control process used before operations begin, including policies, procedures, and rules designed to ensure that planned activities are carried out properly

concurrent control the control process used while plans are being carried out, including directing, monitoring, and fine-tuning activities as they are performed

feedback control control that focuses on the use of information about previous results to correct deviations from the acceptable standard

Did You KNOW ?

A growing number of companies, including Microsoft, IBM, Gap, General Electric, and Accenture, are doing away with annual performance reviews and instead providing employees with more frequent, constructive performance feedback.[12]

Twitter, or social networking sites such as LinkedIn. Human resource policies defining what forms of body art are acceptable to display at work can avoid awkward case-by-case conversations about specific people.[16]

At Donnelly Custom Manufacturing in Alexandria, Minnesota, all 225 employees of this short-run, close-tolerance injection mold manufacturer participated in "error proofing" workshops that taught them to identify and correct errors before they occur. After identifying potential problems, employees develop and then rank-order solutions according to the speed, complexity, and cost of implementing them. They also consider the effectiveness of each alternative solution. Since applying these "error proofing" techniques to several molding jobs with a long-time customer, 75 percent fewer parts were rejected due to human error, and parts-per-million defects dropped by two-thirds.[17]

Some firms, concerned about the pitfalls of workplace romance, have sought a solution in feedforward control. Romantic activities between a supervisor and subordinate create a conflict of interest or lead to sexual harassment. Other employees might infer from lack of action that the company allows a culture of harassment or sanctions personal relationships as a path to advancement. And relationship ups and downs can affect everyone's mood and motivation.

Controls aimed at preventing such problems include training in appropriate behavior (including how to avoid sexual harassment) and even requiring executives and their romantic interests to sign "love contracts" stating that the relationship is voluntary and welcome. The company keeps a copy of the contract in case the relationship dissolves and an unhappy employee blames the company for allowing it in the first place.[18]

2.2 | Bureaucratic Control Occurs Before, During, and After Operations

Bureaucratic control combines three approaches, defined according to their timing:

1. Feedforward control takes place before operations begin and includes policies, procedures, and rules designed to ensure that planned activities will be carried out properly. Examples include inspection of raw materials and proper selection and training of employees.

2. Concurrent control takes place while plans are being carried out. It includes directing, monitoring, and fine-tuning activities as they occur.

3. Feedback control focuses on the use of information about results to correct deviations from the acceptable standard after they arise.

Feedforward Control Feedforward control (sometimes called *preliminary control*) is future-oriented; its aim is to prevent problems before they arise. Instead of waiting for results and comparing them with goals, a manager or employees can exert control by limiting activities in advance. For example, companies have policies defining the scope within which decisions are made. As in Procter & Gamble's Worldwide Business Conduct Manual,[15] a company may dictate that managers must adhere to clear ethical and legal guidelines when making decisions. Formal rules and procedures prescribe people's actions before they occur. Legal experts advise companies to establish policies forbidding disclosure of proprietary information or making clear that employees are not speaking for the company when they post messages on blogs, microblogging sites such as

Concurrent Control Concurrent control, which takes place while plans are carried out, is the heart of any control system. On a manufacturing floor, all efforts are directed toward producing the correct quantity and quality of the right products in the specified amount of time. In an airline terminal, the baggage must get to the right airplanes before flights depart. And in many settings, supervisors watch employees to ensure they work efficiently and avoid mistakes.

Information technology provides powerful concurrent controls, giving managers immediate access to data from the remotest corners of their companies. Managers update budgets instantly from a continuous flow of performance data. In production facilities, monitoring systems that track errors per hour, machine speeds, and other measures let managers correct small production problems before they become disasters. Point-of-sale terminals in store checkout lines send sales data to a retailer's headquarters to show which products are selling in which locations.

"Continuous improvement is better than delayed perfection."

—Mark Twain

Feedback Control Feedback control takes place when performance data have been gathered and analyzed and the results are returned to someone (or something) in the process to make corrections. When supervisors monitor behavior, they are exercising concurrent control. When they point out and correct improper performance, they are using feedback as a means of control.

Timing matters greatly in feedback control. Long time lags often occur between performance and feedback, such as when actual spending is compared with the quarterly budget, instead of weekly or monthly, or when some aspect of performance is compared with the projection made a year earlier. Yet if performance feedback is not timely, managers cannot quickly identify and eliminate the problem and prevent more serious harm.[19]

Some feedback processes are under real-time (concurrent) control, such as a computer-controlled robot on an assembly line. Such units have sensors that continually determine whether they are in the correct position to perform their functions. If they are not, a built-in control device makes immediate corrections.

In other situations, feedback processes take more time. Hertz uses feedback that includes customer ratings of service and car quality. Compliments and complaints help the company reinforce or correct practices at particular facilities. If a customer is upset about something, Hertz wants to know as soon as possible so it can correct the problem.

The Role of Six Sigma In Chapter 7, we introduced six sigma, a particularly robust and powerful application of feedback control. Six sigma is designed to reduce defects in all organizational processes—not just product defects but anything that may result in customer dissatisfaction, such as inadequate service, delayed delivery, and excessively high prices due to high costs or inefficiency. The technique has been widely adopted

and improved upon by companies including Bechtel, Caterpillar, Maersk, Wipro, and Starwood Hotels & Resorts.

Sigma is the Greek letter used in statistics to designate the estimated standard deviation, or variation in a process. It indicates how often defects in a process are likely to occur. The lower the sigma number, the higher the level of variation or defects; the higher the sigma number, the lower the level of variation or defects. For example, as illustrated in Exhibit 14.3, a two-sigma-level process has more than 300,000 defects per million opportunities (DPMO)—not a very well-controlled process. A three-sigma-level process has 66,807 DPMO, which is roughly a 93 percent level of accuracy. Many organizations operate at this level, which on its face does not sound too bad, until we consider its implications—for example, 7 items of airline baggage lost for every 100 processed. The additional costs of such inaccuracy are enormous. As you can see in the exhibit, even at just above a 99 percent defect-free rate, or 6,210 DPMO, the accuracy level is unacceptable.[20]

Exhibit 14.3		Relationship between sigma level and defects per million opportunities
Sigma Level	**DPMO**	**Is Four Sigma Good Enough?**
2	308,537	20,000 lost articles of mail per hour.
3	66,807	Unsafe drinking water 15 minutes per day.
4	**6,210**	5,000 incorrect surgical operations per week.
5	233	200,000 wrong prescriptions each year.
6	3.4	No electricity for 7 hours each month.

Source: Adapted from T. Rancour and M. McCracken, "Applying 6 Sigma Methods for Breakthrough Safety Performance," *Professional Safety* 45, no. 10 (October 2000), pp. 29–32.

At six sigma level, a process is producing fewer than 3.4 defects per million, which means it is operating at a 99.99966 percent level of accuracy. Six sigma companies have close to zero product or service defects, plus lower production costs and cycle times and much higher levels of customer satisfaction. The methodology isn't just for the factory floor, either; accountants use six sigma to improve the quality of their audits investigating risks faced by clients.[21]

The six sigma approach is based on intense statistical analysis of processes that contribute to customer satisfaction.[22]

2.3 | Management Audits Control Multiple Systems

Management audits are a means of evaluating the effectiveness and efficiency of various organizational systems, from social responsibility programs to accounting control. A management audit can be external or internal. Managers conduct external audits of other companies and internal audits of their own companies. Some of the same tools and approaches are used for both types of audits.[23]

External Audits An **external audit** occurs when one organization evaluates another organization. Typically, an external body such as a certified public accountant (CPA) firm conducts financial and accounting audits. But any company can conduct external audits of competitors or other companies for its own strategic decision-making purposes. This type of analysis investigates other organizations for possible merger or acquisition, determines the soundness of a company to be used as a supplier, or discovers the strengths and weaknesses of a competitor to maintain or better exploit a competitive advantage.[24]

External audits provide essential feedback control when they identify legal and ethical lapses that could harm the organization and its reputation. They also are useful for preliminary control because they can prevent problems from occurring. If a company seeking to acquire other businesses gathers adequate, accurate information about possible candidates, it is more likely to acquire the most appropriate companies and avoid unsound acquisitions.

Internal Audits Your organization may assign a group to conduct an **internal audit** to assess what the company has done

for itself and what it has done for its customers or other recipients of its goods or services. The audit can assess a number of factors, including financial stability, production efficiency, sales effectiveness, human resources development, earnings growth, energy use, public relations, civic responsibility, and other effectiveness criteria. The audit reviews the company's past, present, and future, including any risks the organization should be prepared to face.[25]

Management audits uncover common undesirable practices such as unnecessary work, work duplication, poor inventory control, uneconomical use of equipment and machines, procedures that are costlier than necessary, and wasted resources. Strong audit committees do a better job of finding and eliminating undesirable practices.[26] Stock prices of companies with highly rated audit committees tend to rise faster than shares of companies with lower-rated internal auditors.[27]

2.4 | Sustainability Audits and the Triple Bottom Line

Companies that are serious about sustainability conduct audits to evaluate how effectively they are serving all stakeholders and protecting the environment. Sustainability audits typically evaluate performance in terms of a **triple bottom line**—that is, the company's financial performance, environmental impact, and impact on people in the company and the communities where it operates. Adapting a slogan coined by Shell in the 1990s, an easy way to remember the three bottom lines is *profit, planet, and people.*[28]

In practice, reporting a triple bottom line is not standardized and regulated the way financial reporting is. A company might report its profitability in the traditional way, its environmental impact in terms of efficiency of resource use, and its human impact in terms of general policies. Specific practices vary, but performing a sustainability audit can serve as a first step toward measuring and reinforcing sustainable business practices.

LO3 Describe the reasons for using budgets as a control device.

3 | BUDGETARY CONTROLS

Budgetary control is one of the most widely recognized and commonly used methods of managerial control. It ties together feedforward control, concurrent control, and feedback control, depending on the point at which it is applied. *Budgetary control* is the process of finding out what's being done and comparing the results with the corresponding budget data to verify accomplishments or remedy differences. Budgetary control commonly is called **budgeting**.

Exhibit 14.4   A sales-expense budget

	January		February		March	
	Estimate	Actual	Estimate	Actual	Estimate	Actual
Sales	$1,200,000		$1,350,000		$1,400,000	
Expenses						
General overhead	$ 310,000		$ 310,000		$ 310,000	
Selling	242,000		275,000		288,000	
Producing	327,000		430,500		456,800	
Research	118,400		118,400		115,000	
Office	90,000		91,200		91,500	
Advertising	32,500		27,000		25,800	
Estimated gross profit	$ 80,100		$ 97,900		$ 112,900	

3.1 | Fundamental Budgetary Considerations

In business, budgetary control begins with an estimate of sales and expected income. Exhibit 14.4 shows a budget with a forecast of expected sales (the *sales budget*) on the top row, followed by several categories of estimated expenses for the first three months of the year. In the bottom row, the profit estimate is determined by subtracting each month's budgeted expenses from the sales in that month's sales budget. Columns next to each month's budget provide space to enter the actual accomplishments so managers can readily compare expected amounts and actual results.

Although we focus here on the flow of money into and out of the company, budgeting information is not confined to finances. The entire enterprise and any of its units can create budgets for their activities, using units other than dollars, if appropriate. For example, many organizations use production budgets forecasting physical units produced and shipped, and labor can be budgeted in skill levels or hours of work.

All budgets are prepared for a specific time period—often one, three, or six months or one year. The period chosen depends on the primary purpose and the enterprise's complete normal cycle of activity. For example, seasonal variations might affect production and sales. The budget period commonly coincides with other control devices, such as managerial reports, balance sheets, and statements of profit and loss. Selection of the budget period also should consider the extent to which reasonable forecasts can be made.

Exhibit 14.5 shows the stages of the budgetary control process. Although specific practices vary, a member of top management often serves as budget coordinator. Usually the chief financial officer (CFO) has these duties. He or she resolves conflicting interests, recommends adjustments when needed, and gives official sanction to the budgetary procedures and final budget. In a small company, budgeting responsibility generally rests with the owner.

Exhibit 14.5 Three stages of budgetary control

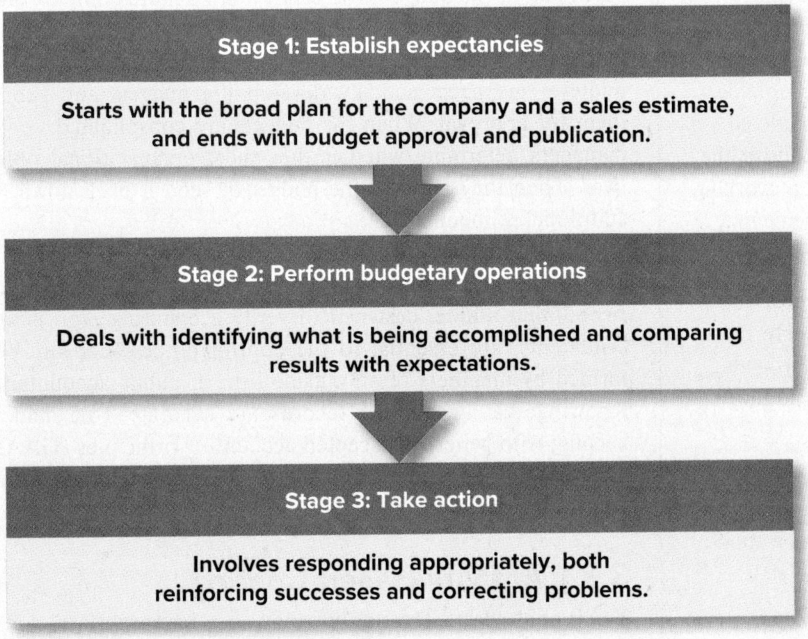

Stage 1: Establish expectancies

Starts with the broad plan for the company and a sales estimate, and ends with budget approval and publication.

Stage 2: Perform budgetary operations

Deals with identifying what is being accomplished and comparing results with expectations.

Stage 3: Take action

Involves responding appropriately, both reinforcing successes and correcting problems.

3.2 | Types of Budgets

Common types of budgets include:

- *Sales budget.* Usually data for the sales budget include forecasts of sales by month, sales area, and product.

- *Production budget.* The production budget commonly is expressed in physical units. Required information for preparing this budget includes types and capacities of machines, quantities to produce, and availability of materials.

- *Cost budget.* The cost budget is used for areas of the organization that incur expenses but no revenue, such as human resources and other support departments. Cost budgets also may be included in the production budget. Costs may be fixed (independent of the immediate level of activity), like rent, or variable (rising or falling with the level of activity), like raw materials.

Sustaining for Tomorrow

The Gates Foundation: Do Even Good Intentions Need to Be Controlled?

As the founder of Microsoft, the world's largest computer software company, Bill Gates is a household name. What might not be as widely known is how impactful he is in terms of philanthropy and social entrepreneurship.

Gates left Microsoft in 2008 to dedicate his attention to the Gates Foundation, a charitable organization he founded with his wife, Melinda. The Gates Foundation isn't a typical social enterprise, a small-scale start-up working on a shoestring budget in a local community. Rather, the Foundation operates in 139 countries and has an endowment of $47 billion, backed in no small part by Bill and Melinda Gates's personal fortune.

Bill and Melinda Gates's vision for the foundation has always been clear: to harness market forces to work for the good of all people, especially those most in need.

Bill Gates refers to this approach as "creative capitalism," whereby "governments, businesses, and nonprofits work together to stretch the reach of market forces so that more people can make a profit, or gain recognition, doing work that eases the world's inequities."

Without doubt, the Gates Foundation has done much good in the world. The Gates's philanthropy has contributed greatly to a wide range of positive social outcomes: from reducing the global child mortality rate, to increasing women's access to contraception in developing countries, to mitigating the effects of diseases such as tuberculosis and malaria (to name just a few).

Yet questions remain about what *precisely* the foundation's impact has been in some areas, whether one private organization should have so much influence over public policy, and how ethically it distributes money, especially to private corporations. The foundation has donated hundreds of millions of dollars to private companies in which it holds stocks, creating potential conflicts of interest. The foundation also has worked to strengthen intellectual property rights, which in turn increase the costs of potentially lifesaving drugs.

Such questions and confusion largely stem from a lack of effective *control*. There is no systematized oversight of the Gates Foundation, nor is there a system of measurable accountability. Due to its vast financial resources and powerful connections, the Gates Foundation seemingly is able to do whatever it wants to do.

Control systems offer transparency, or at least the potential thereof, which could resolve ambiguities relating to the Gates Foundation in observers' minds. This begs the question: Do even good intentions need to be controlled?

Sources: "Foundation Fact Sheet," Gates Foundation, https://www.gatesfoundation.org/who-we-are/general-information/foundation-factsheet, accessed April 23, 2020; M. Levine, "Is the Gates Foundation Out of Control?" *Nonprofit Quarterly,* March 25, 2020, https://nonprofitquarterly.org/is-the-gates-foundation-out-of-control; and S. Boseley, "How Bill and Melinda Gates Helped Save 122m Lives—and What They Want to Solve Next," *The Guardian,* February 14, 2017, https://www.theguardian.com/world/2017/feb/14/bill-gates-philanthropy-warren-buffett-vaccines-infant-mortality.

---

accounting audits procedures used to verify accounting reports and statements

- *Cash budget.* The cash budget is essential to every business. It should be prepared after all other budget estimates are completed. The cash budget shows the anticipated receipts and expenditures, the amount of working capital available, the extent to which outside financing may be required, and the periods and amounts of cash available.

- *Capital budget.* The capital budget is used for the cost of fixed assets like plants and equipment. Such costs are usually treated not as regular expenses but as investments because of their long-term nature and importance to the organization's productivity.

- *Master budget.* The master budget includes all the major activities of the business. It brings together and coordinates all the activities of the other budgets. Think of it as a "budget of budgets."

Traditionally, senior management imposed budgets *top-down,* setting specific targets for the entire organization at the beginning of the budget process. In today's more complex organizations, the process is more likely to be *bottom-up,* with top management setting the general direction while lower-level and midlevel managers actually develop the budgets and submit them for approval. When the budgets are consolidated, senior managers determine whether they meet organizational objectives. Then they approve the budget or send it back down for additional refinement.

Accounting records must be inspected periodically to ensure that they have been properly prepared and are correct. Accounting audits, designed to verify accounting reports and statements, are essential to the control process and are performed by members of an outside firm of public accountants. Knowing that accounting records are accurate, true, and in keeping with generally accepted accounting principles (GAAP) creates confidence that a reliable base exists for sound overall controlling purposes.

3.3 | Activity-Based Costing

Traditional cost accounting may be inappropriate today because it is based on the outdated, rigid hierarchical organization. Instead of assuming that organizations are bureaucratic "machines" with separate component functions, many companies use activity-based costing (ABC) to allocate costs across business processes.[29]

ABC starts with the assumption that organizations are collections of people performing many different but related activities to satisfy customer needs. The ABC system identifies streams of activity and then allocates costs to those business processes. The basic procedure (Exhibit 14.6) works as follows: First, employees are asked to break down what they do each day in order to define their *basic activities.*

Second, managers look at total expenses computed by traditional accounting—fixed costs, supplies, salaries, fringe benefits, and so on—and spread total amounts over the activities according to the amount of time spent on each. As you can see in Exhibit 14.6, both the traditional and ABC systems reach the same bottom line. However, because the ABC method allocates costs across business processes, it provides a more accurate picture of how costs should be charged to goods and services.[30]

This heightened accuracy can give managers a more realistic picture of how the company is actually allocating its resources. It can highlight where wasted activities are occurring or whether activities cost too much relative to the benefits provided. Managers can then act to correct the problem. The most expensive activity is sales order processing, so its managers will try to lower that cost, freeing up resources for other tasks. Thus ABC is a valuable method for streamlining business processes.

activity-based costing (ABC) a method of cost accounting designed to identify streams of activity and then allocate costs across particular business processes according to the time employees devote to particular activities

balance sheet a report that shows the financial picture of a company at a given time and itemizes assets, liabilities, and stockholders' equity

assets the values of the various items the corporation owns

liabilities the amounts a corporation owes to various creditors

stockholders' equity the amount accruing to the corporation's owners

---

LO4 Recognize basic types of financial statements and financial ratios used as controls.

4 | FINANCIAL CONTROLS

In addition to budgets, businesses commonly use other statements for financial control. Two financial statements that help control overall organizational performance are the balance sheet and the profit and loss statement.

4.1 | Balance Sheet

The balance sheet shows the financial picture of a company at a given time. This statement itemizes three elements:

1. Assets are the values of the various items the corporation owns.

2. Liabilities are the amounts the corporation owes to various creditors.

3. Stockholders' equity is the amount accruing to the corporation's owners.

The relationship among these three elements is as follows:

Assets = Liabilities + Stockholders' equity

Exhibit 14.7 shows an example of a balance sheet. During the year, the company grew because it enlarged its building and acquired more machinery and equipment by means of long-term debt in the form of a first mortgage. Additional stock was

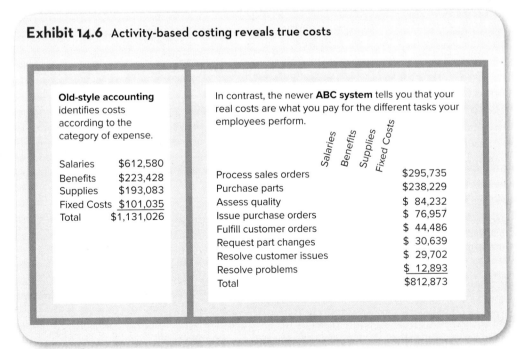

Exhibit 14.6 Activity-based costing reveals true costs

Old-style accounting identifies costs according to the category of expense.

Salaries	$612,580
Benefits	$223,428
Supplies	$193,083
Fixed Costs	$101,035
Total	$1,131,026

In contrast, the newer **ABC system** tells you that your real costs are what you pay for the different tasks your employees perform.

Salaries   Benefits   Supplies   Fixed Costs

Process sales orders	$295,735
Purchase parts	$238,229
Assess quality	$ 84,232
Issue purchase orders	$ 76,957
Fulfill customer orders	$ 44,486
Request part changes	$ 30,639
Resolve customer issues	$ 29,702
Resolve problems	$ 12,893
Total	$812,873

Source: Adapted from Dana Holding Corporation.

Exhibit 14.7   A comparative balance sheet

Comparative Balance Sheet for the Years Ending December 31

	This Year	Last Year
Assets		
Current assets:		
Cash	$ 161,870	$ 119,200
U.S. Treasury bills	250,400	30,760
Accounts receivable	825,595	458,762
Inventories:		
Work in process and finished products	429,250	770,800
Raw materials and supplies	251,340	231,010
Total current assets	1,918,455	1,610,532
Other assets:		
Land	157,570	155,250
Building	740,135	91,784
Machinery and equipment	172,688	63,673
Furniture and fixtures	132,494	57,110
Total other assets before depreciation	1,202,887	367,817
Less: Accumulated depreciation and amortization	67,975	63,786
Total other assets	1,134,912	304,031
Total assets	$3,053,367	$1,914,563
Liabilities and stockholders' equity		
Current liabilities:		
Accounts payable	$ 287,564	$ 441,685
Payrolls and withholdings from employees	44,055	49,580
Commissions and sundry accruals	83,260	41,362
Federal taxes on income	176,340	50,770
Current installment on long-term debt	85,985	38,624
Total current liabilities	667,204	622,021
Long-term liabilities:		
15-year, 9 percent loan, payable in each of the years 2008–2023	210,000	225,000
5 percent first mortgage	408,600	
Registered 9 percent notes payable	——	275,000
Total long-term liabilities	618,600	500,000
Stockholders' equity:		
Common stock: authorized 1,000,000 shares, outstanding last year 492,000 shares, outstanding this year 700,000 shares at $1 par value	700,000	492,000
Capital surplus	981,943	248,836
Earned surplus	75,620	51,706
Total stockholders' equity	1,757,563	792,542
Total liabilities and stockholders' equity	$3,043,367	$1,914,563

sold to help finance the expansion. At the same time, accounts receivable were increased, and work in process was reduced. Observe that Total assets ($3,043,367) = Total liabilities ($677,204 + $618,600) + Stockholders' equity ($700,000 + $981,943 + $75,620).

Summarizing balance sheet items over time uncovers important trends and gives a manager further insight into overall performance and areas in which adjustments are needed. This company might decide that it would be prudent to slow down its expansion plans.

4.2 | Profit and Loss Statement

The profit and loss statement is an itemized financial statement of the income and expenses of a company's operations. Exhibit 14.8 shows a comparative statement of profit and loss for two consecutive years. In this illustration, the company's operating revenue increased. Expenses also went up, but at a lower rate, resulting in a higher net income.

Some managers draw up tentative profit and loss statements and use them as goals. Then they measure performance against these goals or standards. From comparative statements of this type, a manager can identify trouble areas and correct them.

Controlling by profit and loss is most commonly used for the entire enterprise and, in the case of a diversified corporation, its divisions. However, controlling can be by departments, as in a decentralized organization in which department managers have control over both revenue and expense. In that case, each department has its own profit and loss statement. Each

profit and loss statement an itemized financial statement of the income and expenses of a company's operations

current ratio a liquidity ratio that indicates the extent to which short-term assets can decline and still be adequate to pay short-term liabilities

debt–equity ratio a leverage ratio that indicates the company's ability to meet its long-term financial obligations

return on investment (ROI) a ratio of profit to capital used, or a rate of return from capital

department's output is measured, and each is charged a cost including overhead. Expected net income is the standard for measuring departmental performance.

4.3 | Financial Ratios

An effective approach for checking an enterprise's overall performance is to use key financial ratios, which indicate strengths and weaknesses. Key ratios are calculated from selected items on the profit and loss statement and the balance sheet:

1. *Liquidity ratios* indicate a company's ability to pay short-term debts. The most common liquidity ratio is *current assets to current liabilities*, called the current ratio or *net working capital ratio*. This ratio indicates the extent to which current assets can decline and still be adequate to pay current liabilities. Some analysts set a ratio of 2 to 1, or 2.00, as the desirable minimum. Looking at Exhibit 14.7, the liquidity ratio for this company is about 2.3 ($1,918,455/$677,204). The company's current assets are more than capable of supporting its current liabilities.

2. *Leverage ratios* show the funds supplied by creditors and shareholders. An important example is the debt–equity ratio, which indicates the company's ability to meet its long-term financial obligations. If this ratio is less than 1.5, the amount of debt is not considered excessive. In Exhibit 14.7, the debt–equity ratio is only 0.35 ($618,600/$1,757,563). The company has financed its expansion almost entirely by issuing stock rather than by incurring significant long-term debt.

3. *Profitability ratios* indicate management's ability to generate a financial return on sales or investment. For example, return on investment (ROI) is a ratio of profit to capital used, or a rate of return from capital (equity plus long-term debt). This ratio lets managers and shareholders assess how well the firm is doing compared with other investments. In Exhibit 14.7, if the company's net income were $300,000 this year, its return on capital would be 12.6 percent [$300,000/($1,757,563 + $618,600)], normally a reasonable rate of return.

| Exhibit 14.8 | A comparative statement of profit and loss |

Comparative Statement of Profit and Loss for the Years Ending June 30

	This Year	Last Year	Increase or Decrease
Income:			
Net sales	$253,218	$257,636	$4,418*
Dividends from investments	480	430	50
Other	1,741	1,773	32
Total	255,439	259,839	4,400*
Deductions:			
Cost of goods sold	180,481	178,866	1,615
Selling and administrative expenses	39,218	34,019	5,199
Interest expense	2,483	2,604	121*
Other	1,941	1,139	802
Total	224,123	216,628	7,495
Income before taxes	31,316	43,211	11,895*
Provision for taxes	3,300	9,500	6,200*
Net income	$ 28,016	$ 33,711	$5,695*

* Decrease

Using Financial Ratios

Although ratios provide useful performance standards and indicators of what has occurred, relying exclusively on financial ratios can cause problems. Ratios usually are expressed in limited time horizons (monthly, quarterly, or yearly), so they often cause *management myopia*—managers focus on short-term earnings and profits at the expense of their longer-term strategic obligations.[31] To reduce management myopia and focus attention further into the future, control systems can use long-term (say, three- to six-year) targets.

A second negative effect of ratios is that managers relegate other important considerations to secondary positions. Managers focused on ratios may not pay enough attention to research and development, management development, progressive human resource practices, environmental sustainability, and other important considerations. Therefore, other control measures should supplement financial ratios. Organizations can hold managers accountable for market share, number of patents granted, sales of new products, human resource development, energy efficiency, waste reduction, and other performance indicators.

4.4 | People Are Not Machines

While control systems are used to constrain employee behavior and make their future behavior predictable, people are not machines that automatically fall into line as the designers of control systems intend. In fact, control systems can lead to dysfunctional behavior. Managers need to consider how people will react to the control systems they put in place, including potential negative responses such as rigid bureaucratic behavior, tactical behavior, and resistance.[32]

Rigid Bureaucratic Behavior People want to look good on the control system's measures. This focuses people on needed behaviors but can lead to rigid, inflexible behavior

geared toward doing *only* what the system requires. For example, we noted that six sigma emphasizes efficiency over innovation. After 3M began using six sigma extensively, it fell below its goal of having at least one-third of sales come from new products. When George Buckley took the CEO post, he began relying less extensively on efficiency controls because "Invention is by its very nature a disorderly process."[33]

3M now spends big money to create "disruptive platforms" that will lead to new products for multiple markets. 3M developed a new scratch- and stain-resistant surface material for computer touchpads, appliances, and other surfaces.[34] Other new products include Flex & Seal, shipping material that requires no tape or filler,[35] and residential roofing shingles that contain smog-reducing granules to improve air quality.[36] The control challenge, of course, is for 3M to be both efficient and creative.

Rigid bureaucratic behavior occurs when control systems prompt employees to stay out of trouble by sticking strictly to every single and outdated rule. Inflexibility often leads to poor customer service and makes the entire organization slow to act.

We have all been victimized at some time by rigid bureaucratic behavior, and veterans are no exception. Administrators falsified medical records and appointment times at the Phoenix Veterans Administration (VA) Medical Center. They did this to "comply" with a VA policy that veteran patients would see a doctor within 14 days of making an appointment. According to an employee who worked at the medical center, administrators were waiting "6 to 20 weeks" to make appointments. In the wake of these revelations, the VA's bureaucracy and leadership received much of the blame, culminating in the resignation of Eric Shinseki, the secretary of the Department of Veterans Affairs. Blame also was leveled at the underfunded VA budget that contributes to shortages of medical centers and primary care physicians who care for nearly 10 million veterans.[37]

Stories like these give bureaucracy a bad name. Some managers do not even use the term *bureaucratic control* because of its potentially negative connotation. However, the existence of a control system is not the problem. The problems occur when it is no longer viewed as a tool for running the business, but as a collection of rules dictating rigid behavior.

Tactical Behavior People sometimes engage in tactics aimed at "beating the system." The most common tactical behaviors are manipulating information or reporting false performance data. People can produce invalid data about what *has* been done and about what *can* be done.

False reporting about the past is less common because it is easier to identify someone who misreports what happened than someone who incorrectly predicts or estimates what

● A Post-it ad announcing the launch of Super Sticky notes in England.
PA Images/Alamy Stock Photo

might happen. Still, managers sometimes change their accounting systems to "smooth out" the numbers. Also, people may intentionally feed false information into a management information system to cover up errors or poor performance.

An employee at a large financial services firm was told by his new manager that as long as he continued to do a great job, he would have nothing to worry about regarding his job security. Nearly a year passed with minimal contact with the manager, so the employee took this as a good sign. About 10 months after the initial meeting, the manager surprised the employee by giving him a very negative performance review, even though the manager never previously complained about the employee's work. The employee transferred out of the department to work for a different manager. Later, the employee learned that the manager lied about his performance so the position could be given to someone else.[38]

More commonly, people falsify their predictions or requests for the future. When asked to give budgetary estimates, they often ask for larger amounts than they need. On the other hand, people sometimes submit unrealistically *low* estimates when they believe that will help them get a budget or a project approved. Budget-setting sessions can become tugs of war between subordinates trying to get slack in the budget and superiors attempting to minimize slack.

Managers use similar tactics when they negotiate low performance goals for themselves so they will have little trouble meeting them; salespeople when they make low sales forecasts so they will look good by exceeding them; and workers when they slow down the work pace while analysts are setting work pace standards. In these sorts of cases, people care about their own performance numbers more than the overall performance of their departments or companies.

Resistance to Control People often resist control systems, for several reasons:

- Comprehensive control systems increase the accuracy of performance data and make employees more accountable for their actions. Control systems uncover mistakes, can threaten people's job security and status, and decrease people's autonomy.

- Control systems can change expertise and power structures. Management information systems can speed up the costing, purchasing, and production decisions previously made by managers, who may as a result lose decision-making authority, expertise, and power.

- Control systems can change an organization's social structure. They can create competition and disrupt social groups and friendships. People may end up competing against those with whom they formerly had comfortable, cooperative relationships. People's social needs are important, so they will resist control systems that reduce satisfaction of those needs.

- Control systems may be seen as an invasion of privacy, lead to lawsuits, and cause low morale.

LO5 List procedures for implementing effective control systems.

5 | MORE EFFECTIVE CONTROL SYSTEMS

Effective control systems maximize potential benefits and minimize dysfunctional behaviors. To achieve this, management needs to design control systems that meet several criteria:

- The systems are based on valid performance standards.

- They communicate adequate information to employees.

- They are acceptable to employees.

- They use multiple approaches.

- They recognize the relationship between empowerment and control.

5.1 | Establish Valid Performance Standards

The most effective standards are expressed in quantitative terms; they are objective more than subjective. In addition, the measures should be difficult to sabotage or fake. Moreover, the system must incorporate all important aspects of performance. Unmeasured behaviors get neglected. A company that focuses only on sales volume without also looking at profitability might soon go out of business.

Management also must defend against another problem: too many measures that create overcontrol and employee resistance. To make many controls tolerable, managers can emphasize a few key areas while setting "satisfactory" performance standards in others. Or they can set simple priorities, such as directing a purchasing agent to meet targets in a priority order: quality, availability, cost, inventory level. Managers also can set tolerance ranges, as when financial budgets include optimistic, expected, and minimum levels.

Many companies' budgets set cost targets only. This causes managers to control spending but neglect earnings. At Emerson Electric, profit and growth are key measures. If an unanticipated opportunity to increase market share arises, managers can spend what they need to go after it. And during market downturns, the company still expects its managers to find ways to expand profits and drive growth.[39]

This principle applies to nonfinancial aspects of performance as well. At many customer service call centers, control aims to maximize efficiency by focusing on the average time each agent spends handling each phone call. But the business objectives of call centers should also include other measures such as customer satisfaction, first-class resolution, and customer retention.

T-Mobile made a sweeping change in how the company served its customers. Callie Field and her team led the initiative to develop ways to enhance customer experience. They created teams with technology experts and experienced customer service representatives who knew how to solve complex customer problems. After three years, T-Mobile reported a 31 percent decrease in calls escalated to supervisors and a 48 percent reduction in annual turnover of customer representatives.[40]

Summarized in Exhibit 14.9, business consultant Michael Hammer identified seven "deadly sins" of performance measurement to avoid.[41] The following examples suggest how these sins might exhibit themselves in an organization:

1. *Vanity*—A company might measure order fulfillment in terms of whether products are delivered by the latest date promised by the organization rather than by the tougher and more meaningful measure of when the customers request to receive the products.

2. *Provincialism*—If a company's transportation department measures only shipping costs, it won't attend enough to shipping reliability (delivery on a given date).

3. *Narcissism*—A maker of computer systems measured on-time shipping of each component; if 90 percent of the system's components arrived at the customer on time, it was 90 percent on time. But from the customer's point of view, the system wasn't on time at all; the customer needed *all* the components to use the system.

4. *Laziness*—An electric power company assumed customers cared about installation speed, but in fact customers cared most about receiving an accurate installation schedule.

● Many companies administer pre-hire and random drug tests as a way to control illicit drug use among employees. Radius Images/Getty Images

Exhibit 14.9	The seven "deadly sins" of performance measurement
Vanity	Using measures that make managers and the organization look good.
Provincialism	Limiting measures to functional/departmental responsibilities rather than the organization's overall objectives.
Narcissism	Measuring from the employee's, manager's, or company's viewpoint rather than the customer's.
Laziness	Neglecting to expend the effort to identify what is important to measure.
Pettiness	Measuring just one component of what affects business performance.
Inanity	Failing to consider the way standards will affect real-world human behavior and company performance.
Frivolity	Making excuses for poor performance rather than taking performance standards seriously.

Source: Adapted from M. Hammer, "The Seven Deadly Sins of Performance Measurement and How to Avoid Them," *MIT Sloan Management Review* 48, no. 3 (Spring 2007), pp. 19–28.
Photo: John Lund/Drew Kelly/Blend Images LLC

5. *Pettiness*—A clothing manufacturer might assume that it should consider only manufacturing cost rather than all costs of providing stores with exactly the right products when customers demand them.

6. *Inanity*—A fast-food restaurant targeted waste reduction and was surprised when restaurant managers began directing employees to hold off on cooking anything until customers placed orders.

7. *Frivolity*—In some organizations, more effort goes into blaming others than into correcting problems.

The correction to these "sins" is to carefully select standards that look at entire business processes and identify which actions make those processes succeed. Then, accurately measure performance against these standards, making people responsible for their performance and rewarding success. These are the basics of effective control.

5.2 | Provide Adequate Information

Management must communicate to employees the importance and nature of the control system. Then people must receive performance feedback. Feedback motivates people and provides information that enables them to correct their own deviations from performance standards. Allowing people to initiate their own corrective action encourages self-control and reduces the need for outside supervision.

Information should be as accessible as possible, particularly when people must make decisions quickly and frequently. A national food company with its own truck fleet wanted drivers to go through customer sales records every night, insert new prices from headquarters every morning, and still make their rounds—an impossible set of demands. To solve this control problem, the company installed computer terminals in more than 1,000 delivery trucks. Now drivers use their terminals for constant communication with headquarters. Each night drivers send information about the stores, and each morning headquarters sends prices and recommended stock mixes.

Micha Weber/Shutterstock

In general, a manager designing a control system should evaluate the information system by asking the following questions:[42]

- Does it provide people with data relevant to the decisions they need to make?

- Does it provide the right amount of information to decision makers throughout the organization?

- Does it provide enough information to each part of the organization about how other, related parts of the organization are functioning?

5.3 | Ensure Acceptability Plus Empathy

Employees are less likely to behave in counterproductive ways if they find the system acceptable. They are more likely to accept systems that have reasonable, achievable performance standards but are not overly controlling. Ideally, the control system will emphasize positive behavior rather than focus solely on controlling negative behavior.

In more than two decades, Johnson & Johnson's Ethicon San Lorenzo facility has never had to recall a product. The company makes sutures, meshes, and other supplies for surgery—an industry in which quality must be perfect and recalls are all too common. To achieve these outstanding results, the company created the Do It Right Framework, which includes training, employee involvement in process improvements, and open communication about company objectives.[43]

One of the best ways to establish reasonable standards and gain employee acceptance is to develop them together. As you learned in Chapter 5, participation in decision making secures people's understanding and cooperation and results in better decisions. Allowing employees to collaborate in decisions that affect their jobs will help overcome resistance to the system. In addition, employees on the front line are more likely to know which standards are most important and practical, and they can inform their bosses about issues. Moreover, when deviations from standards occur, it's easier to obtain cooperation in problem solving if standards were established collaboratively.

5.4 | Maintain Open Communication

Employees should feel willing and able to report deviations from a standard so the problem can be addressed. If they believe their bosses want to hear only good news, or worse, if they fear reprisal for reporting bad news even if it is not their fault, then controls are much less likely to be effective. Problems may go unreported; solutions later are much more expensive or difficult. But if managers create an environment of openness and honesty and appreciate even negative information shared in timely fashion, employees will help make sure that the control system works well.

5.5 | Use Multiple Approaches

No single control will suffice; multiple controls are needed. Banks need controls on risk so they don't lose a lot of money

balanced scorecard
control system combining four sets of performance measures: financial, customer satisfaction, business processes, and learning and growth

from defaulting borrowers, as well as profit controls including sales budgets that aim for growth in accounts and customers.

As you know, control systems generally include both financial and nonfinancial performance targets and incorporate aspects of preliminary, concurrent, and feedback control. Many companies now combine targets into a **balanced scorecard**, a combination of four sets of performance measures (see Exhibit 14.10): (1) financial, (2) customer satisfaction, (3) business processes, and (4) learning and growth.[44]

The general goal is to broaden management's horizon beyond short-term financial results to strengthen performance for the long-term. For example, JPMorgan Chase uses a

Exhibit 14.10 A strategy map and balanced scorecard for performance improvement at a hospital

Strategy Map

Financial	Steady growth	Return on investor capital	Productivity
Customer Satisfaction	Service leadership	Patient satisfaction	Operational excellence
Business Processes	Improve quality and timeliness of services	Continuously improve staff's skills	Improve patient value
Learning & Growth	Promote culture of quality service	Align employee competencies with strategy	Implement technology to support innovation

Balanced Scorecard

Objectives	Measurement	Target
Grow sales revenue Increase profit	Balance sheet Profit and loss statement	10% annually 5% annually
Increase satisfaction Attract repeat patients	Satisfaction surveys Track in database	90% highly satisfied 80% return rate
Increase expertise of staff Reduce error rates	Completion rate of online training modules Number of incorrect dosages	90% passed with score of 85% or higher 2% or lower
Communicate importance of high quality Develop succession plan	Number of emails and mentions during meetings Percentage completed and times updated	One email and mention per week 90% by year-end and one time per month

Sources: Adapted from R. S. Kaplan and D. P. Norton, "Having Trouble with Your Strategy? Then Map It," *Harvard Business Review*, September–October 2000, pp. 167–72; and R. S. Kaplan and D. P. Norton, *The Balanced Scorecard: Translating Strategy into Action* (Boston: Harvard Business School Press, 1996), p. 76.

balanced scorecard approach that extends beyond earnings to address such questions as (1) Are we recruiting and developing great people? (2) Are we innovating better products? (3) Are we relentlessly improving our core processes? and (4) Are we making good returns on capital?[45]

The balanced scorecard is adaptable to nonprofit settings as well.

transfer price price charged by one unit for a good or service provided to another organizational unit

---

> **LO6 Discuss ways in which market and clan control influence performance.**

6 | THE OTHER CONTROLS: MARKETS AND CLANS

Formal bureaucratic control systems are pervasive (and the most talked about in management textbooks), but they alone don't ensure optimal control. Market controls and clan controls offer more flexible, though no less potent, approaches to regulating and ensuring performance.

6.1 | Market Controls Let Supply and Demand Determine Prices and Profits

Unlike bureaucratic controls, market controls use economic forces—and the pricing mechanisms that accompany them—to regulate performance. The system works like this: When a person, department, or business unit delivers output having value to others, they can negotiate a price for its exchange. As a market for these transactions becomes established, two effects occur:

- Price indicates the value of the good or service.

- Price competition controls productivity and performance.

The basic principles that underlie market controls operate at the levels of the corporation, the business unit (or department), and the individual. Exhibit 14.11 shows a few ways in which market controls operate.

> **Exhibit 14.11** Examples of market control
>
> CEO uses market controls (such as profitability or market share) to evaluate performance of business unit heads.
>
> Managers use transfer pricing to establish values for internal transactions among units.
>
> Market rates determine the base wage/salary for managers and employees.

Market Controls at the Corporate Level Large diversified companies use market controls to regulate independent business units. Large conglomerates act as holding companies, treating business units as profit centers that compete with one another. Top executives may place few bureaucratic controls on business unit managers, but use profit and loss data to evaluate their performance. Decision making and power are decentralized to the business units, and market controls ensure that business unit performance is in line with corporate objectives.

Using market control mechanisms is criticized for not adequately reflecting environmental sustainability or the organization's total value. And employees often suffer as diversified companies are repeatedly bought and sold based on market controls.

Market Controls at the Business Unit Level Market control also is used within business units to regulate exchanges among departments and functions. One way organizations try to apply market forces to internal transactions is through transfer pricing. A transfer price is the internal charge by one organizational unit for a good or service that it supplies to another unit. In automobile manufacturing, transfer prices may be affixed to components and subassemblies before they are shipped to subsequent business units for final assembly. Ideally, the transfer price reflects what the receiving business unit would have to pay for that good or service in the external marketplace.

As organizations can outsource goods and services to external partners, market controls such as transfer prices provide natural incentives to keep costs down and quality up. Managers stay in close touch with prices in the marketplace to make sure their own costs are in line, and they try to improve the service they provide to increase their department's value to the organization. Consider the situation in which human resources activities can be done internally or outsourced to consulting firms. If HR cannot supply services at a reasonable price, for instance in a small company, it may make sense to outsource the service. Or maybe the company doesn't even need an HR department.

Market Controls at the Individual Level Market controls also are used at the individual level. For example, in situations where organizations are hiring, the supply and demand for particular skills influence the wages employees can expect and the rates organizations will pay. Employees or job candidates who have more valuable skills tend to be paid a higher wage. Wages don't always reflect market rates—sometimes they are based (perhaps arbitrarily) on internal resource considerations—but the market rate is often the best indicator of an employee's potential worth to a firm.

Boards of directors use controls to manage CEOs. Although many people think of CEOs as the people controlling everyone else in the company, a CEO is accountable to the board of directors, and the board must ensure that the CEO acts in its interest. Absent board control, CEOs may act in ways that make them

● Are the sometimes incredibly high salaries of today's professional athletes truly indicative of the players' skills and worth?
Rena Schild/Shutterstock

● To enhance their agility, speed, and responsiveness, some companies use clan control based on employee empowerment, trust, and organizational culture. Comstock/Getty Images

look good personally (such as making the company bigger or more diversified) but that do not lead to higher profits. And as recent corporate scandals have shown, without board control, CEOs may artificially inflate the firm's earnings or not fully declare expenses, making the firm look much more successful than it really is.

Board members are supposed to exercise careful control over the company's financial performance, including oversight of the CEO's compensation package. Traditionally, boards try to control CEO performance mainly through incentive pay, including bonuses tied to short-term profit targets. In large U.S. corporations, most CEO compensation is tied to the company's performance. Boards also use long-term incentives linked to the firm's share price, usually through stock options (discussed earlier). And, balanced scorecards can keep CEOs focused on the company's longer-term health.

6.2 | Clan Control Relies on Empowerment and Culture

Control systems based solely on bureaucratic and market mechanisms are not enough for today's workforce, for several reasons:

- *Employees' jobs have changed.* More work is intellectual and therefore invisible compared to producing a tangible product. There is no one best way to perform creative tasks, so programming or standardizing jobs is extremely difficult. Close supervision is unrealistic because it is nearly impossible to supervise activities such as thinking and creative problem solving.

- *Management has changed.* Managers used to know more about work than employees did. Today, many employees know more about their jobs than their bosses do. When real expertise exists at low organization levels, hierarchical control loses power.[46]

- *The employment relationship has changed.* The social contract at work is being renegotiated. Employees once were most concerned about pay and job security. Now more employees want fully engaging work, involvement in decision making, and the opportunity to solve interesting problems and tackle challenging assignments. They want to use their brains.

For these reasons, *empowerment* has become a necessary part of a manager's control repertoire. With no "one best way" to approach a job and no way to scrutinize what employees do all day, managers must learn to trust employees to act in the firm's best interests. This does not mean giving up control; it means creating a strong culture of high standards and integrity so that employees will exercise some control on their own.

Recall our discussion of organizational culture in Chapter 3. A culture that encourages the wrong behaviors will severely hinder an effort to impose effective controls. But if managers create and reinforce a strong culture in which everyone understands management's values and expectations and is motivated to act in accordance with them, then clan control can be highly effective.[47]

Clan control involves creating relationships built on mutual respect and encouraging each individual to take responsibility for his or her actions. Employees work within a guiding framework of values, and they are expected to use good judgment. For example, clan control at Starbucks helps shape and guide employee behavior by emphasizing satisfying customers more than pleasing the managers.[48] Managers tolerate well-intended mistakes, view them as opportunities to learn, and want team members to learn together.

Here are a few practical guidelines for managing in an empowered world:[49]

- *Put control where the operation is.* Hierarchical layers and close supervision are being replaced with self-guided teams.

For centuries even the British Empire—as large as it was—never had more than six levels of management, including the Queen.

- *Use real-time rather than after-the-fact controls.* Issues and problems must be solved at the source by the people doing the actual work. Managers can identify resources to help the team.

- *Rebuild the assumptions underlying management control to build on trust rather than distrust.* Today's "high-flex" organizations are based on empowerment, not just obedience. Information must facilitate decision making, not police it.

- *Move to control based on peer norms.* Clan control is a powerful thing. Some workers in Japan commit suicide rather than disappoint colleagues or lose face. Although this is extreme, it underlines the power of peer influence. Build constructive group norms along with managing by the numbers.

- *Rebuild incentive systems to reinforce responsiveness and teamwork.* The twin goals of adding value to the customer and team performance must become the dominant raison d'être of measurement systems.

Clan control can be a double-edged sword. It takes a long time to develop and even longer to change. This provides stability and direction during periods of upheaval. Yet if managers want to establish a new culture—a new version of clan control—they must help employees unlearn the old values and embrace the new. We will talk more about this transition process in our concluding chapter.

Notes

1. D. Gelles, "Julie Sweet of Accenture Could See Her Future. So She Quit Her Job," *The New York Times,* January 2, 2019, https://www.nytimes.com/2019/01/02/business/julie-sweet-accenture-corner-office.html.

2. J. Bourke, S. Garr, A. van Berkel, and J. Wong, "Diversity and Inclusion: The Reality Gap," *Deloitte Insights,* February 28, 2017, https://www2.deloitte.com/insights/us/en/focus/human-capital-trends/2017/diversity-and-inclusion-at-the-workplace.html.

3. "No. 7 - Accenture," DiveristyInc., www.diversityinc.com, accessed September 21, 2020.

4. M. Ward, "C-Suite Leaders Are Making a Big Assumption about Their Workforce—and It's Bleeding the Economy of $1.05 Trillion," *Business Insider,* March 4, 2020, https://www.businessinsider.com/accenture-report-perception-gap-shows-economic-cost-lack-of-diversity-inclusion.

5. "Deming Quotes," The W. Edwards Deming Institute, quotes.deming.org.

6. C. Morris, "Here's How You're Wasting 8 Hours per Work Week," *Fortune,* July 25, 2017, www.fortune.com; and G. Bresiger, "This Is How Much Time Employees Spend Slacking Off," *New York Post,* July 29, 2017, www.nypost.com.

7. P. Valdes-Dapena and T. Yellin, "GM: Steps to a Recall Nightmare," *CNN Money,* www.money.cnn.com; K. Korosec, "Ten Times More Deaths Linked to Faulty Switch Than GM First Reported," *Fortune,* August 24, 2015, www.fortune.com; J. Muller, "Exclusive: Inside New CEO Mary Barra's Urgent Mission to Fix GM," *Forbes,* May 28, 2014; T. Krisher and M. Gordon, "New CEO Barra Faces Tough Task in Shedding Old GM," *Bloomberg Businessweek,* April 2, 2014, www.businessweek.com; and P. Barrett, "The One Important Thing GM CEO Mary Barra Told Congress," *Bloomberg Businessweek,* April 1, 2014, www.businessweek.com.

8. W. G. Ouchi, "A Conceptual Framework for the Design of Organizational Control Mechanisms," *Management Science* 25 (1979), pp. 833–48; and W. G. Ouchi, "Markets, Bureaucracies, and Clans," *Administrative Science Quarterly* 25 (1980), pp. 129–41.

9. E. D. Pulakos, S. Arad, M. A. Donovan, and K. E. Plamondon, "Adaptability in the Workplace: Development of a Taxonomy of Adaptive Performance," *Journal of Applied Psychology* 85, no. 4 (August 2000), pp. 12–24; J. H. Sheridan, "Lean Sigma Synergy," *Industry Week* 249, no. 17 (October 16, 2000), pp. 81–82; and K. A. Merchant and T. Sandino, "Four Options for Measuring Value Creation: Strategies for Managers to Avoid Potential Flaws in Accounting Measures of Performance," *Journal of Accountancy* 208, no. 2 (2009), pp. 34–38.

10. G. Anadiotis, "Business Analytics: The Essentials of Data-Driven Decision-Making," *ZDNet,* June 11, 2018, www.zdnet.com.

11. "Before and After Reviews of Client Engagements: How One Firm Fine-Tuned the Process," *Inside Public Accounting,* www.cpareport.com; and L. Buchanan, "Leadership: Armed with Data," *Inc.,* March 2009, www.inc.com.

12. C. Woolston, "Why Appraisals Are Pointless for Most People," *BBC,* May 2, 2019, www.bbc.com; A. Elejalde-Ruiz, "Companies Are Scrapping Annual Performance Reviews for Real-Time Feedback," *Chicago Tribune,* April 22, 2016, www.chicagotribune.com.

13. D. Klein, "Chipotle Goes Mobile with New Food-Safety Platform," *QSR,* September 2018, www.qsrmagazine.com.

14. D. Klein, "Chipotle Goes Mobile with New Food-Safety Platform," *QSR,* September 2018, www.qsrmagazine.com.

15. Procter & Gamble's Worldwide Business Conduct Manual, https://us.pg.com/policies-and-practices/worldwide-business-conduct-manual/.

16. J. D. Bible, "Tattoos and Body Piercings: New Terrain for Employers and Courts," *Labor Law Journal* 61, no. 3 (Fall 2010), pp. 109–23; B. Roberts, "Stay Ahead of the Technology Use Curve," *HRMagazine,* October 2008; K. A. Carr, "Broaching Body Art," *Crain's Cleveland Business,* September 29, 2008, www.gale.com; "Dress & Appearance: Tattoos/Piercings: May Employers Have Dress Code Requirements That Prohibit All Visible Tattoos and Piercings?" Society for Human Resource Management, May 25, 2015, www.shrm.org; and B. Miller, K. Nicols, and J. Eure, "Body Art in the Workplace: Piercing the Prejudice?" *Personnel Review* 38, no. 6 (2009), pp. 621–40.

17. Company website, www.donnmfg.com; and "Error Proofing Your Staff," *Quality* 50, no. 3 (March 2011), pp. 54–55.

18. M. Gwin, "Love Contracts: What Restaurant Owners Should Know about Consensual Relationships between Employees," *Modern Restaurant Management,* August 2, 2018, www.modern-restaurantmanagement.com; M. Berman-Gorvine, "Let Love Bloom at Work, but Very Carefully," *Bloomberg BNA,* January 30, 2017, www.bna.com; "Office Romances and 'Love Contract?'" *National Law Review,* February 2, 2016, www.natlawreview.com.

19. "Feedback Is Critical to Improving Performance," U.S. Office of Personnel Management, www.opm.gov; V. U. Druskat, "Effects and Timing of Developmental Peer Appraisals in Self-Managing Work Groups," *Journal of Applied Psychology* 84, no. 1 (February 1999), p. 58; M. Kownatzki, J. Walter, S. Floyd, and C. Lechner, "Corporate Control and the Speed of Strategic Business Unit Decision Making," *Academy of Management Journal* 56 (2013), pp. 1295–1324; and B. Kuvaas, "The Interactive Role of Performance Appraisal Reactions and Regular Feedback," *Journal of Managerial Psychology* 26 no. 2 (2011), pp. 123–37.

20. S. Waddock and N. Smith, "Corporate Responsibility Audits: Doing Well by Doing Good," *MIT Sloan Management Review* 41, no. 2 (Winter 2000), pp. 75–83; L. L. Bergeson, "OSHA Gives Incentives for Voluntary Self-Audits," *Pollution Engineering* 32, no. 10 (October 2000), pp. 33–34; T. Rancour and M. McCracken, "Applying 6 Sigma Methods for Breakthrough Safety Performance," *Professional Safety* 45, no. 10 (October 2000), pp. 29–32; and S. M. Shafer and S. B. Moeller, "The Effects of Six Sigma on Corporate Performance: An Empirical Investigation," *Journal of Operations Management* 30; no. 7–8 (November 1, 2012), pp. 521–32.

21. R. Kepczyk, "How to Implement Lean Six Sigma in an Accounting Practice," *CPA Practice Advisor,* September 12, 2014, www.cpapracticeadvisor.com.

22. A. Dehghann, A. Shahin, and B. Zenouzi, "Service Quality Gaps & Six Sigma," *Journal of Management Research* 4, no. 1 (2012), pp. 11–12; and A. Laureani, J. Antony, and A. Douglas, "Lean Six Sigma in a Call Centre: A Case Study," *International Journal of Productivity and Performance Management* 59, no. 8 (2010), pp. 757–68.

23. RT. Rancour and M. McCracken, "Applying 6 Sigma Methods for Breakthrough Safety Performance," *Professional Safety* 45, no. 10 (October 2000), pp. 29–32; and G. Eckes, "Making Six Sigma Last," *Ivey Business Journal,* January–February 2002, p. 77.

24. J. L. Colbert, "The Impact of the New External Auditing Standards," *Internal Auditor* 5, no. 6 (December 2000), pp. 46–50.

25. S. Aghili, "A Six Sigma Approach to Internal Audits," *Strategic Finance,* February 2009, pp. 38–43, www.sfmagazine.com; Y. Giard and Y. Nadeau, "Improving the Processes," *CA Magazine,* December 2008; G. Cheney, "Connecting the Dots to the Next Crisis," *Financial Executive,* April 2009, pp. 30–33; "Establishment of Internal Audit Function," KPMG, www.kpmg.com, accessed April 6, 2019; and J. Pett and D. Poritz, "A More Effective Approach for Internal Audit," *Journal of Accountancy,* March 1, 2018, www.journalofaccountancy.com.

26. M. Alic and B. Rusjan, "Contribution of the ISO 9001 Internal Audit to Business Performance," *International Journal of Quality and Reliability Management* 27 (2010), pp. 916–37.

27. J. D. Glater, "The Better the Audit Panel, the Higher the Stock Price," *The New York Times,* April 8, 2005, p. C4

28. J. Tullberg, "Triple Bottom Line—a Vaulting Ambition?" *Business Ethics: A European Review* 21, no. 3 (June 2012), pp. 310–24; G. Davis, "The Triple Bottom Line Goal of Sustainable Businesses," *Entrepreneur,* April 24, 2013, www.entrepreneur.com; R. Coons, "Corporate Social Responsibility: Pursuing the Triple Bottom Line," *IHS Chemical Week,* May 27–June 3, 2013, pp. 21–23; and L. A. Henry, T. Buyl, and R. J. G. Jansen, "Leading Corporate Sustainability: The Role of Top Management Team Composition for Triple Bottom Line Performance," *Business Strategy and the Environment* 28 (2019), pp. 173–84.

29. D. C. Nowak and C. Linder, "Do You Know How Much Your Expatriate Costs? An Activity-Based Cost Analysis of Expatriation," *Journal of Global Mobility* 4 (2016), pp. 88–107.

30. "Understanding Activity Based Accounting," *CBS News Money Watch,* July 16, 2007, www.cbsnews.com; *The Executive's Journal* 13, no. 2 (Winter 1997), pp. 6–16; and T. P. Pare, "A New Tool for Managing Costs," *Fortune,* June 14, 1993, pp. 124–29.

31. K. Merchant, *Control in Business Organizations* (Boston: Pitman, 1985); and C. W. Chow, Y. Kato, and K. A. Merchant, "The Use of Organizational Controls and Their Effects on Data Manipulation and Management Myopia," *Accounting, Organizations, and Society* 21, nos. 2/3 (February–April 1996), pp. 175–92.

32. E. E. Lawler III and J. Rhode, *Information and Control in Organizations* (Pacific Palisades, CA: Goodyear, 1976); A. Ferner, "The Underpinnings of 'Bureaucratic' Control Systems: HRM in European Multinationals," *Journal of Management Studies* 37, no. 4 (June 2000), pp. 521–39; and M. S. Fenwick, "Cultural and Bureaucratic Control in MNEs: The Role of Expatriate Performance Management," *Management International Review* 39 (1999), pp. 107–25.

33. B. Hindo, "At 3M, a Struggle between Efficiency and Creativity," *Bloomberg Businessweek,* https://www.bloomberg.com/news/articles/2007-06-10/at-3m-a-struggle-between-efficiency-and-creativity; and J. J. Dahling, S. L. Chau, and A. O'Malley, "Correlatesand Consequences of Feedback Orientation in Organizations," *Journal of Management* 38, no. 2 (2012), pp. 531–46.

34. L. Krauskopf, "3M's New Technology Chief Has a Bigger Budget, Bigger Goal," Reuters, June 1, 2015, www.reuters.com.

35. K. Schwab, "No More Cardboard Boxes? 3M Invents an Ingenious New Way to Ship Products," *Fast Company,* July 29, 2019, www.fastcompany.com.

36. "All New 3M Products to Include Sustainability Value," *Sustainable Brands,* December 5, 2018, www.sustainablebrands.com.

37. J. Craig, "VA Medical Scandal Presents Opportunity to Right a Wrong," *The Pitt News,* June 10, 2014, pittnews.com; and M. Shear and R. Oppel, "V.A. Chief Resigns in Face of Furor on Delayed Care," *The New York Times,* May 31, 2014, www.nytimes.com.

38. L. Ryan, "I Got Ambushed at My Performance Review—and I Just Found Out Why," *Forbes,* May 21, 2018, www.forbes.com.

39. "2020 Emerson Investor Conference," Emerson, www.emerson.com, accessed April 26, 2020.

40. M. Dixon, "Reinventing Customer Service," *Harvard Business Review,* November–December 2018, www.hbr.org.

41. M. Hammer, "The Seven Deadly Sins of Performance Measurement and How to Avoid Them," *MIT Sloan Management Review* 48, no. 3 (Spring 2007), pp. 19–28.

42. E. E. Lawler III and J. Rhode, *Information and Control in Organizations* (Pacific Palisades, CA: Goodyear, 1976); and J. A. Gowan Jr. and R. G. Mathieu, "Critical Factors in Information System Development for a Flexible Manufacturing System," *Computers in Industry* 28, no. 3 (June 1996), pp. 173–83.

43. "Our Promise," Ethicon, www.ethicon.com, accessed April 6, 2019; and A. Selko, "Ethicon: Employee Engagement Results in Zero Product Recalls," *Industry Week,* January 17, 2013, http://www.industryweek.com.

44. R. S. Kaplan and D. P. Norton, *The Balanced Scorecard: Translating Strategy into Action* (Boston: Harvard Business School Press, 1996); A. Gumbus and R. N. Lussier, "Entrepreneurs Use a Balanced Scorecard to Translate Strategy into Performance Measures," *Journal of Small Business Management* 44, no. 3 (July 2006); R. Massingham, P. R. Massingham, and J. Dumay, "Improving Integrated Reporting: A New Learning and Growth Perspective for the Balanced Scorecard," *Journal of Intellectual Capital* 20 (2019), pp. 60–82; and Z. Hoque, "20 Years of Studies on the Balanced Scorecard: Trends, Accomplishments, Gaps and Opportunities for Future Research," *The British Accounting Review,* March 2014, pp. 33–59.

45. Company website, www.jpmorgan.com.

46. F. Edgar, A. Geare, and P. O'Kane, "The Changing Dynamic of Leading Knowledge Workers," *Employee Relations* 37, no. 4 (2015), pp. 487–503; and K. Moores and J. Mula, "The Salience of Market, Bureaucratic, and Clan Controls in the Management of Family Firm Transitions: Some Tentative Australian Evidence," *Family Business Review* 13, no. 2 (June 2000), pp. 91–106.

47. P. H. Fuchs, K. E. Mifflin, D. Miller, and J. O. Whitney, "Strategic Integration: Competing in the Age of Capabilities," *California Management Review* 42, no. 3 (Spring 2000), pp. 118–47; M. A. Lando, "Making Compliance Part of Your Organization's Culture," *Healthcare Executive* 15, no. 5 (September–October 1999), pp. 18–22; and K. A. Frank and K. Fahrbach, "Organization Culture as a Complex System: Balance and Information in Models of Influence and Selection," *Organization Science* 10, no. 3 (May–June 1999), pp. 253–77.

48. "Control," Starbucks, www.starbucks.com, accessed May 2, 2017.

49. G. H. B. Ross, "Revolution in Management Control," *Management Accounting,* November 1990, pp. 23–27. Reprinted with permission.

Design elements: Take Charge of Your Career box photo: © Tetra Images/ Getty Images; Thumbs Up/Thumbs Down icons: McGraw-Hill Education

Innovating and Changing

After studying Chapter 15, you should be able to

LO1 Summarize how technology fuels innovation.

LO2 Identify the criteria on which to base technology decisions.

LO3 Compare key ways of acquiring new technologies.

LO4 Evaluate the elements of an innovative organization.

LO5 Discuss what it takes to be world-class.

LO6 Describe how to lead change effectively.

LO7 Describe strategies for creating a successful future.

As we write this concluding chapter in 2020, the coronavirus has been hitting the world hard. We could report here the numbers of confirmed COVID-19 cases and deaths, plus business shutdowns and job losses. But the published measures are inaccurate, and the true numbers change constantly. Later, when you read this, the totals will be much higher, but otherwise unpredictable.

At a time like this, it might seem like a trivial pursuit to recall the traditional management functions outlined in Chapter 1: planning, organizing, leading, and controlling. But rather than becoming obsolete, these activities are more important than ever. Profound, disruptive changes require the best possible managers, leaders, and collaborators.

Coping with current challenges and creating the best possible futures will require bold and ethical leadership, dynamic strategic planning, new forms of intelligent organization, and sound control systems. These all set the stage for finding ways to change for the better, successfully and continually.

In these efforts, we need to innovate, finding new ways to operate as we try to lean into the futures that we desire. For example, the pandemic exposed systemic flaws in global supply chains, slowing the delivery of medical equipment and exacerbating the crisis. Managers in all organizations will need to leverage new technologies to reimagine how to distribute, coordinate, and track goods and services to increase efficiencies and strengthen the future.[1]

The innovative ideas and actions spawned during the COVID-19 era might change the very nature of business itself. As you've read, some but not all entrepreneurs and corporate leaders question the profit-at-all-costs approach to business, characterized by intense competition. But quickly finding the best vaccine and implementation strategies—effective, safe, and ideally not too costly—might require interorganizational and multinational collaborations, even among rivals.

A common observation as government officials and business owners debate when to "reopen the economy" is that our era will be defined by a monumental inflection point: the period before COVID-19 and whatever "next new normal" will emerge.[2]

To tackle the pandemic and move toward a future new normal, some of the world's largest pharmaceutical companies, including Roche, Eli Lilly, and Johnson & Johnson, agreed to share information and resources.[3] Eli Lilly CEO David Ricks stated, "I have never seen the kind of collaboration across industry partners, biotech, academia that I am seeing now."[4] Such cooperation can bring together the best scientific and management minds and develop innovative products and manufacturing and distribution processes. To make and disperse a successful vaccine to the entire world will require levels of cooperation and coordination never before seen. No single firm—or sector—can do that alone.

The pandemic is not the primary subject matter of this chapter, but it does highlight some key themes, especially the importance of managing change. A change in the external environment, such as the pandemic, necessitates changes in work, not to mention life. Most organizations, like most countries, adapt better than some and worse than others. On a person level, your everdeveloping, long career will be an exercise in dealing with change.

Technological innovations (such as treatments and vaccines for a new virus) help solve problems and capture opportunities. Human decision making and behavior are the keys that aid or hinder progress. This chapter is about innovating—especially making decisions about new technologies, leading productive change, and creating our best possible futures.

Innovation and change can be daunting in their complexity; both organizations and people must manage them well. We begin with technological change.

We defined *technology* in Chapter 7 as the systematic application of scientific knowledge to a new product, process, or service. In this sense, technology is embedded in every product, service, and procedure used or produced.[5]

When technology is used to create a new good or service, or a new way of working, it is a form of innovation. Innovation differs from invention, or turning new ideas into realities, which may or may not add value to an organization. In the management context, *innovation* is any new way of working that creates value.

Innovations can be of these fundamental types:[6]

1. *Product innovation* is a change in the outputs (goods or services) the organization produces. If BP's research into biofuels results in a new kind of fuel to sell, this is an example of product innovation.

2. *Process innovation* is a change in the way outputs (goods or services) are produced. If BP's research into biofuels reveals a more efficient way to produce fuel from sugarcane, it's a process innovation. Other examples of process innovation include the flexible manufacturing processes discussed in Chapter 7, including mass customization, just-in-time, and concurrent engineering.

3. *Business model innovation* is a change in how the organization uses existing technologies and processes to deliver its current products in a more productive and profitable manner. The change may affect any component of a company's business model: its customer value proposition (the basic problem it solves, such as eco-friendly fuel for about the same cost as fossil fuels), its profit formula (the financial road map for its success), and its key resources (people, technology, facilities, brand).

These three categories cover all sorts of creative ideas: new product offerings, the nature of the customer experience provided, process efficiency and effectiveness, and the brand associated with the organization and its products.[7]

Understanding the forces driving technological development can help you anticipate, monitor, and manage technologies effectively. Key driving forces include:

- There must be—potentially at least—a *need,* or *demand,* for the technology. Without this there is no reason for technological innovation to occur.

- Meeting the need must be theoretically possible, and the *knowledge* to do so must exist.

- We must be able to *convert* relevant scientific knowledge into practice in engineering and economic terms.

- Necessary *funding, skilled labor, time, space,* and *other resources* must be available.

- *Entrepreneurial initiative* must identify and pull all the necessary elements together.

This chapter discusses how technology affects competitiveness and how managers identify useful technologies to adopt. Then we describe how companies develop or acquire those technologies, including the decisions that help new technologies succeed.

Of course, technology is not the only way organizations innovate and change. The chapter looks more broadly at innovation, including change efforts aimed at achieving world-class status, the process of leading change, and strategies you can use to actively shape your career.

1 | DECIDING TO ADOPT NEW TECHNOLOGY

Technological innovations typically follow a predictable pattern called the *technology life cycle,* shown in Exhibit 15.1. Early progress can be slow as competitors continually experiment with product design and operational characteristics to meet consumer needs. This stage is where the rate of product innovation tends to be highest.

Eventually the new technology begins to reach the upper limits of both its performance capabilities and the spread of its use. Development slows and becomes costlier, and the market saturates (there are few new customers). The technology might remain in this mature stage for some time—as with autos—or can be replaced quickly by another technology offering superior performance or economic advantage.

Developing technology continually increases the benefits, makes it easier to use, and generates new applications. In the process, the technology spreads to new adopters.

1.1 | Deciding When to Adopt New Technology

Like the technology life cycle, the adoption of new technology over time follows an S-shaped pattern (top line in Exhibit 15.2). The percentage of people using the technology is small in the beginning, but increases

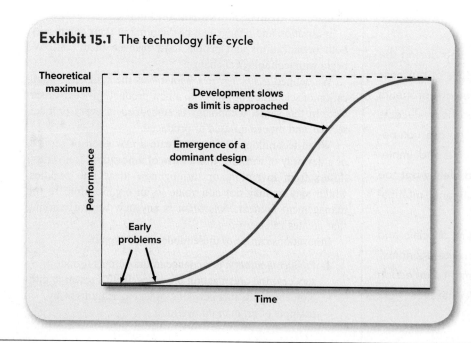

Exhibit 15.1 The technology life cycle

Exhibit 15.2 Technology dissemination pattern and adopter categories

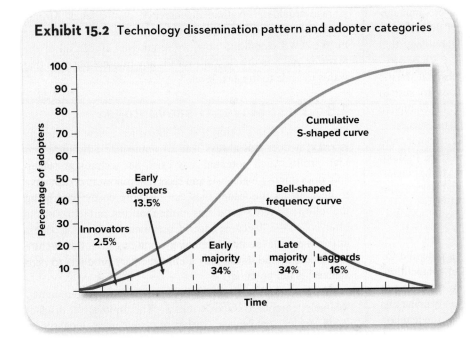

1.2 | Being a Technology Leader

Discussions about technology life cycles and diffusion patterns can imply that technological change occurs naturally or automatically. But just the opposite is true: Change is neither easy nor natural. Innovation decisions are highly strategic, and managers need to approach them systematically and thoughtfully.

In Chapter 5 we discussed two generic strategies a company can use to position itself in the market: low cost and differentiation. With low-cost leadership, the company maintains an advantage because it operates at lower cost than its competitors. With a differentiation strategy, the advantage comes from having a unique good or service for which customers are willing to pay a premium price.[9] Technological innovations can support either of these strategies: gaining cost advantage through pioneering lower-cost product designs and low-cost ways to operate, and differentiating by pioneering unique goods or services that increase buyer value and thus command premium prices.

1.3 | Sometimes Innovative Technology Is Disruptive

As with recorded music, technology can completely change the rules of competition within an industry. Clayton Christensen coined the term **disruptive innovation** to describe situations in which a product, service, or business model takes root in simple applications and takes over the market.[10] Disruptive innovations that transformed entire industries include online learning disrupting traditional classroom education; MP3 file technology and digital music platforms like Apple's iTunes replacing CDs in the music industry; tablets and smartphones replacing desktop and laptop computers; smartphones replacing many stand-alone music devices and cameras; and low-cost airlines like Southwest outperforming many traditional hub-and-spoke carriers.[11]

Many disruptive innovations are taking place as part of the Internet of Things (IoT). Approximately 21 billion e-devices and everyday objects were connected to the Internet in 2020.[12] Examples include wearable items like the Fitbit fitness tracker and Garmin smartwatch, and home devices like Ring video doorbells, Google Home Voice Controller, and Philips Hue personal lighting.[13]

As transformative industry shifts occur, even good managers miss their significance when improving their core businesses incrementally. This tendency, known as the *innovator's dilemma,*

dramatically as the technology succeeds and spreads through the population. Eventually the number of users peaks and levels off when the market saturates. This pattern has been verified with many new technologies and ideas in a wide variety of industries and settings.[8]

The adopters of a new technology fall into five groups (see the bottom line in Exhibit 15.2). Each group presents different challenges and opportunities to managers.

Innovators are the first group to adopt a new technology and typically are adventurous and willing to take risks. They pay a premium for the latest new technology or product and champion it if they like it. The enthusiasm of innovator-adopters is no guarantee of success—for example, the product may still be too expensive for the general market. But a lack of enthusiasm in this group often signals serious problems and a need for further development.

Early adopters are the next group to embrace a new technology. This group is crucial and includes well-respected opinion leaders. Early adopters often are those to whom others look for leadership, up-to-date technological information, and suggestions.

The next group to adopt is the *early majority.* These adopters are more deliberate, taking longer to decide to use something new. Often they are important members of a community or industry, but not the leaders. It may take a while for the technology or new product to spread to this group, but once it does, use will begin to proliferate into the mainstream.

The next group is the *late majority.* The members of this group are more skeptical of technological change and approach innovation with caution, often adopting only because of economic necessity or social pressure. The final group are the *laggards.* Often isolated and conservative in their views, laggards are highly suspicious of innovation and change.

poses the following challenge: "How can executives simultaneously do what is right for the near-term health of their current businesses, plus capitalize on the disruptive technology that could lead to their downfall?"[14]

Most companies face this dilemma. Companies that wrestle with and successfully balance the two objectives—to sustain and grow core businesses plus invest wisely in disruptive innovations—greatly increase their chances of long-run success.[15]

Industry leaders such as 3M, Amazon, Nike, Google, and Merck built and maintain their competitive positions through early development and application of new technologies. However, technology leadership imposes costs and risks, and it is not always the best approach (see Exhibit 15.3).[16]

1.4 | First-Mover Advantages

Technology leadership is attractive thanks to its potential for first-mover advantage, higher prices due to lack of competition, and high profits. Greater profits then can allow lower prices and attract more customers. These early advantages can become sustainable, depending on competitors' ability to copy the technology and the firm's ability to keep improving quickly enough to outpace the competition.

Technology leaders can use patents and other institutional barriers to block competitors. The big players in the pharmaceutical industry invest heavily in research and development; patents give them several years to sell their new drugs without competition before generic versions are permitted.[17] As blockbuster drug patents expire, pharmaceutical companies face a tremendous challenge to develop the next new drugs.

The first mover can preempt competitors by capturing the best market niches. If it can establish high switching costs for repeat customers, these positions become difficult to penetrate. Amazon Web Services (AWS) controls nearly half of the cloud infrastructure market—three times more than its nearest competitor, Microsoft Azure.[18] Customers of AWS like Netflix, LinkedIn, and ESPN rely on the cloud service to store voluminous amounts of data generated from their applications.[19] Switching costs, the fixed costs buyers face when they change suppliers (see Chapter 3), are high for customers as it can be difficult to migrate large amounts of data to a different cloud

| Exhibit 15.3 | Advantages and disadvantages of technology leadership |

Advantages	Disadvantages
First-mover advantage	Greater risk
Little or no competition	Cost of technology development
Greater efficiency	Costs of market development and customer education

If technology leadership increases a firm's efficiency relative to competitors, it achieves a cost advantage. The advantage generates greater profits and can attract more customers through lower prices. And if a company is first to market, it might charge a premium price because it faces no competition. Higher prices and greater profits defray the costs of developing new technologies.

storage provider.[20] Nathan Blecharczyk, cofounder of Airbnb, states: "As our company continued to grow, so did our reliance on the AWS cloud and now, we've adopted almost all of the features. AWS is the easy answer for any Internet business that wants to scale to the next level."[21]

1.5 | First-Mover Disadvantages

On the other hand, being first to introduce a new technology is risky; it does not always lead to immediate advantage and high profits. Such potential may exist, but technology leadership does impose high costs and risks that followers do not have to bear. Being the leader thus can be more costly than being the follower; there's good reason the forefront of technology is often called the "bleeding edge." Costs include educating buyers unfamiliar with the new technology, building an infrastructure to support it, and developing complementary products to help achieve its full potential.

Google launched the world's first consumer head-mounted wearable computer, Google Glass. The innovative product faced major challenges, including "immature technology, privacy rights, Wi-Fi signal health concerns, and too much media hype."[22] Two years later, Google Glass was discontinued. Inspired by Google's bold experiment, several companies launched new brands of smartglasses like North Focals, Vuzix Blade, and Solos.[23]

Being a pioneer carries other risks, as well. If raw materials and equipment are new or have unique specifications, there could be no ready supply at reasonable cost. Or the technology may not be fully developed, having problems that will need to be resolved. Unproven markets offer uncertain demand, and the new technology may have an adverse impact on existing business. It may cannibalize current products or make current investments obsolete.

1.6 | Sometimes Following Is the Best Option

Not all companies are equally prepared to be innovation leaders, nor does leadership benefit each organization equally. In deciding whether to be an innovation leader or follower, managers must consider their company's competitive strategy, the benefits to be gained through the technology, and the characteristics of their organization.[24]

Technology followership shares a feature with technology leadership: It too can be used to support both low-cost and differentiation strategies. If the follower learns from the leader's experience, it can avoid the costs and risks of leadership, thereby establishing a low-cost position. Generic drug makers use this strategy. Followership also can support differentiation. By learning from the leader, followers can adapt the products or delivery systems to fit buyers' needs more closely.

Microsoft built great success on this type of followership. The company launched many products, including music players, video game consoles, spreadsheet and word-processing software, and web browsers, after technology leaders paved

> ## "If the rate of change on the outside exceeds the rate of change on the inside, the end is near."
>
> —Jack Welch, former CEO of General Electric

the way. Likewise, Facebook came to dominate social networking only after Friendster and MySpace burned through money introducing the concept. Newer competitors, such as Instagram, Snapchat, and WhatsApp entered the market hoping to lure away users with better services than Facebook. This follower strategy is more challenging once an industry leader enjoys widespread customer loyalty.

1.7 | Measuring Current Technologies

A **technology audit** helps clarify which technologies the organization most depends upon. One technique sorts technologies into categories (Exhibit 15.4) according to their competitive value:[25]

- *Emerging technologies* are still under development but significantly alter the rules of future competition. Managers should monitor emerging technologies, but they might not want to invest in them until they are developed more fully.

- *Pacing technologies* have yet to prove their full value but have the potential to alter the rules of competition. When first installed, computer-aided manufacturing was a pacing technology. Its potential was not fully understood, but

companies that used it effectively realized major speed and cost advantages.

technology audit process of clarifying the key technologies on which an organization depends

- *Key technologies* have proved effective but provide advantage because not everyone knows or uses them. Eventually alternatives to key technologies emerge, but until then they make it harder for new entrants to pose a threat.

- *Base technologies* are commonplace in the industry; everyone must have them. They provide little competitive advantage, but managers have to invest to ensure their organization's continued competence.

Technologies can evolve rapidly through these categories. Electronic word processing was an emerging technology in the late 1970s. It became a pacing technology by the early 1980s. With continued improvements and more powerful computer chips, it quickly became a key technology. Costs dropped, usage spread, and it enhanced productivity dramatically. By the late 1980s, it was a base technology in most applications, and now it is used widely and routinely.

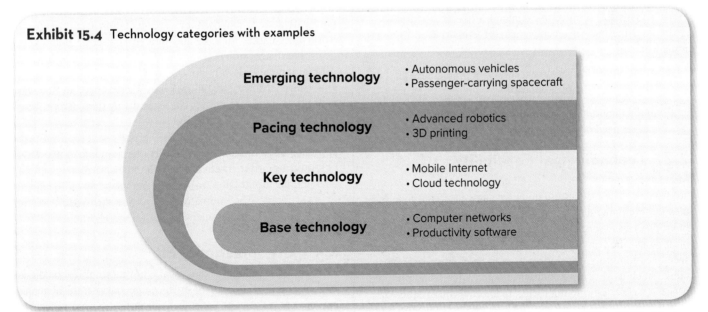

Exhibit 15.4 Technology categories with examples

Emerging technology
- Autonomous vehicles
- Passenger-carrying spacecraft

Pacing technology
- Advanced robotics
- 3D printing

Key technology
- Mobile Internet
- Cloud technology

Base technology
- Computer networks
- Productivity software

Sources: Adapted from R. E. Oligney and M. I. Economides, "Technology as an Asset," *Hart's Petroleum Engineer International* 71, no. 9 (September 1998), p. 27; "The Driverless, Car-Sharing Road Ahead," *The Economist,* January 9, 2016, www.economist.com; C. MacKechnie, "What Are the Types of Business Technology?" *Chron,* http://smallbusiness.chron.com; and J. Manyika, M. Chul, J. Bughin, R. Dobbs, P. Bisson, and A. Marrs, "Disruptive Technologies: Advances That Will Transform Life, Business, and the Global Economy," *McKinsey & Company Report,* May 2013, www.mckinsey.com.

2 | BASE TECHNOLOGY DECISIONS ON RELEVANT CRITERIA

After managers have thoroughly analyzed their company's current technological position, they can plan how to develop or exploit emerging technologies.

system that offers renewable energy whenever and wherever it is needed.[27] Similarly, automakers' efforts to develop electric cars are hindered by the difficulty of designing a battery that can power longer trips.

2.3 | Economic Viability

Apart from whether a firm can "pull off" a technological innovation, executives must consider whether there is a good financial incentive for doing so. The use of hydrogen-powered fuel cell technology for automobiles is almost feasible technically, but its costs are still too high. Even if those costs come down to more acceptable levels, the absence of a supporting infrastructure—such as hydrogen refueling stations—remains a barrier to economic viability.

> "I have not failed. I've just found 10,000 ways that don't work."
>
> —Thomas Edison

2.1 | Anticipated Market Receptiveness

The first consideration in developing a strategy around technological innovation is market potential. Many innovations are stimulated by external demand for new goods and services. For example, the share of Internet users who use a language other than English has been growing rapidly. This trend fueled demand for the ability to search the web in different languages. Companies are creating a variety of innovative apps (e.g., Google Translate) to meet this demand.

In assessing market receptiveness, executives need to determine whether:

1. In the short run, the new technology should have an immediate, valuable application.

2. In the long run, the technology must be able to satisfy a market need or needs.

2.2 | Technological Feasibility

Managers also must consider whether technological innovations are feasible. The makers of computer chips face continual hurdles in developing newer and faster models. But the frontier of microprocessor technology is restricted by the combined forces of physics and economics. To continue boosting processor speed economically, developers have to be creative, using techniques such as shrinking components and embedding multiple processor cores on one microchip to shorten the distance data must travel between processors.[26]

Other industries face similar hurdles. In the sustainable energy industry—such as solar cell and wind turbine production—explosive growth is impossible without an economical storage

Managers must analyze new technologies' costs versus benefits. Major changes require substantial, long-term resource commitments. Uber is investing heavily in driverless car technologies, hoping to make rides more efficient and purchase prices lower for customers.[28] The strategy will replace human drivers with computers; drivers account for 80 percent of total per mile cost.[29] Uber is betting that the benefits of investing will outweigh the (financial) costs.

Economic viability must consider intellectual property theft plus patent and copyright protection. Globalization offers a worldwide market for fake and pirated (low-cost) pharmaceuticals, handbags, athletic shoes, and other products. Millions of people annually illegally download TV shows, movies, music, and games. Music streaming keeps increasing, but the vast majority of songs are not purchased, causing tremendous financial losses for artists and the industry.[30]

Worldwide, lost sales from the theft of intellectual property approach $500 billion a year. Netflix is responding in two ways: (1) lowering prices in countries with extensive piracy, and (2) data mining pirate sites to identify popular shows to add to its own library. The company's innovative goal is to "convert pirates into Netflix customers."[31]

2.4 | Organizational Fit

The decision to adopt technological innovations also should take into account the culture of the organization, the interests of managers, and the expectations of stakeholders. With regard to technology adoption, we can consider three broad types of organizations:

- *Prospector firms*—These proactive innovators, like Samsung and Capital One, have cultures that are outward-looking and

make-or-buy decision
the question of whether an organization should acquire new technology from an outside source or develop it itself

opportunistic. Executives give priority to developing and exploiting technological expertise, and have bold, intuitive visions for the future. Technology champions articulate competitively aggressive, first-mover strategies. Executives tend to be more concerned about the opportunity costs of not taking action than they are about potential failure.

- *Defender firms*—These companies adopt a more cautious posture toward innovation. They tend to operate in stable environments, so they focus on deepening their capabilities through technologies that extend rather than replace their current ones. Strategic decisions are likely to be based on careful analysis and experience in the industry setting.

- *Analyzer firms*—These hybrid organizations need to stay technologically competitive but tend to let others demonstrate solid demand in new arenas before acting. Such companies often adopt an early-follower strategy to grab a dominant position more from their strengths in marketing and manufacturing than from technological innovation.

Companies have different capabilities to deal with new technologies. *Early adopters* tend to be larger, more profitable, and more specialized. They can absorb the risks associated with early adoption while profiting from its advantages. The people involved are highly educated, can deal with abstraction, can cope with uncertainty, and have strong problem-solving skills. Thus, early adopters can better manage the challenges they face.[32]

Managers evaluating technologies also should consider the effects on employees. A new technology brings process changes that directly affects people's work and environment. In response, employees can become anxious and resist the changes. This is often a major factor in determining how difficult and costly the change will be. We discuss how best to manage change later in this chapter.

3 | KNOW WHERE TO GET NEW TECHNOLOGIES

Developing new technology conjures up visions of scientists and product developers working in research and development (R&D) laboratories. In many industries, the primary sources of new technology are the organizations that use it. However, new technologies do come from many sources, including suppliers, manufacturers, users, other industries, universities, the government, and overseas companies.

How to acquire new technology is a **make-or-buy decision**: Should the organization develop the technology itself or acquire it from an outside source? That decision is not simple. As shown in Exhibit 15.5, each of many alternatives has advantages and disadvantages. Here are the most common options:

- *Internal development*—Developing a new technology within the company can keep the technology proprietary—exclusive to the organization. However, internal development usually requires dedicated staff and funding for long periods. Even if the development succeeds, considerable time elapses before practical benefits arrive.

- *Purchase*—Most technologies already in use can be purchased openly. Usually, this is the simplest, easiest, and most cost-effective way to acquire new technology. However, the technology itself will not offer a competitive advantage.

- *Contracted development*—If the technology is not available and a company can't or won't develop it internally, it can contract the development from other companies, independent research laboratories, and university and government institutions.

- *Licensing*—Technologies that are not easily purchased can be licensed for a fee. One such technology for manufacturing and marketing beauty products is Makeup Genius (made by Image Metrics). The free app allows users to do a virtual makeover or try out a new color eyeliner before purchasing the products.

The *Fleabag* after-party, after winning the 2019 Emmy for Outstanding Comedy Series. Todd Williamson/January Images/Shutterstock

Exhibit 15.5	Advantages and disadvantages of make-or-buy technology alternatives	
Alternatives	**Advantage(s)**	**Disadvantage(s)**
Internal development	Technology is proprietary and provides competitive advantage.	Expensive, time-consuming.
Purchase	Simple to implement and cost-effective.	Does not provide competitive advantage.
Contracted development	Allows a firm without internal development capabilities to acquire technology.	Higher monitoring costs and risk that the technology eventually appears in marketplace.
Licensing	Permits firms to access unique technology for a fee; more economical than development.	Firm does not own or control the unique technology; it depends on another firm.
Technology trading	Speeds learning curve and reduces costly trial-and-error approach to using technologies.	Some information is not directly applicable, and not all industries are willing to share information.
Research partnerships and joint ventures	Two or more firms share costs.	Coordination costs can be high and organizational cultures can clash, limiting the outcomes.
Acquisition of a technology owner	Firm gains control and ownership.	Purchase can be expensive.

- *Technology trading*—Some companies are willing to share technology. Google and Tencent share their patents to develop future products. Google has teamed up with China's largest company to expand into the sizeable Chinese market. Tencent hopes to expand its reach beyond China's borders into other markets.[33]

- *Research partnerships and joint ventures*—A research partnership jointly develops a new technology. Typically, each member contributes a unique set of skills or resources, as when an established company contributes money and management know-how, and a start-up contributes technical expertise.

- *Acquisition of a technology owner*—A company lacking and desiring a technology might purchase a company that owns

it. The transaction can be an outright purchase of the company or a minority interest sufficient to gain access to the technology.

Choosing among these make-or-buy options becomes easier by asking these questions:

1. Is it important (and possible) in terms of competitive advantage that the technology remain proprietary?

2. Are the time, skills, and resources for internal development available?

3. Is the technology readily available outside the company?

As Exhibit 15.6 shows, the answers to these questions guide the manager to the most appropriate acquisition approach.

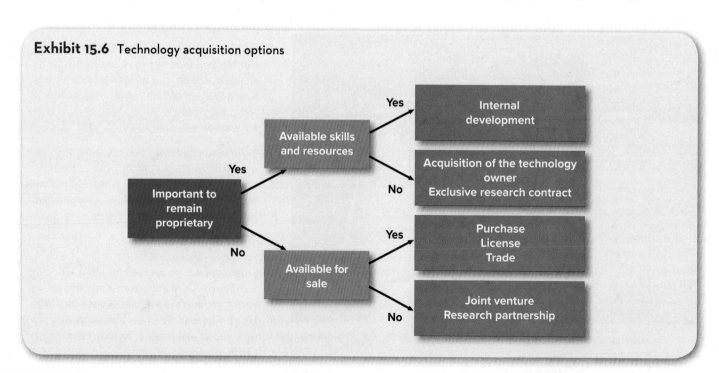

Exhibit 15.6 Technology acquisition options

Managers take additional steps to ensure that the acquisition will make sense for the long term. They try to ensure that key people remain with the firm instead of leaving and taking essential expertise with them. As with any large investment, managers carefully assess whether the financial benefits will justify the price.

LO4 Evaluate the elements of an innovative organization.

4 | ORGANIZING FOR INNOVATION

Successful innovation is a lot more than a great idea. A Boston Consulting Group study showed that a lack of good ideas is hardly ever the obstacle to profitable innovation. More often, ideas fail to generate financial returns because the organization isn't set up to innovate. The culture is risk-averse, projects get bogged down, efforts aren't coordinated, and management can't figure out where to direct financial and other resources.[34]

In Chapter 7 we introduced *learning organizations*— companies that excel at solving problems, seeking and finding new approaches, and sharing new knowledge. Learning organizations are well positioned to innovate.[36]

Some innovations *exploit existing capabilities*—to keep improving production speed or product quality, for example. Other innovations *explore new knowledge,* seeking to develop new products and processes.[37] Companies need to strive for ambidexterity: to both exploit (capitalize on) what they know and explore for new knowledge and ideas.[38] Innovative learning organizations use their strengths to improve their operations and thus their bottom lines, plus they encourage people to explore new possibilities that will ensure long-term success.

4.1 | Who Is Responsible for New Technology Innovations?

Technology was traditionally the responsibility of vice presidents for the research and development function, overseeing corporate and divisional R&D laboratories. But companies today usually have the position of chief information officer (CIO) or chief technology officer (CTO). The CIO is a corporate-level senior executive with broad responsibilities: coordinating the technological efforts of the business units, representing technology in the top management team, identifying ways that technology can support the company's strategy, supervising new technology development, ensuring the security of company data, managing employees' use of personal devices for work, and assessing the technological implications of major strategic initiatives such as acquisitions, new ventures, and strategic alliances. CIOs also lead the information technology (IT) group.[39]

> **ambidexterity** the ability of a company to exploit existing capabilities and explore new knowledge

Without the CIO's integrative role, different departments might adopt different technology tools and standards, leading to much higher equipment and maintenance expense and difficulties in connecting the different units. CEOs supervise the firm's technology experts and help ensure that technology is aligned with strategic goals.

Other people play other critical roles. The *entrepreneur* invents new products or finds new ways to produce old products, opening up new possibilities that can change industries. Within organizations, managers and employees play key roles in acquiring and developing new technologies:[40]

- The *technical innovator* develops or installs and operates the new technology. This person possesses technical skills but perhaps not the managerial skills needed to advance the idea and secure resources for the project.

- The *product champion* promotes the idea throughout the organization, searching for support and acceptance, often at the risk of his or her position and reputation.

- Sponsorship comes from the *executive champion,* who has the status, authority, and financial resources to support the project and protect the product champion.

4.2 | To Innovate, Unleash Creativity

Intuit, 3M, and Google have long histories of producing great new technologies and products. What sets these and other continuous innovators apart is an organizational culture that encourages innovation.[41]

Consider the 3M legend about inventor Francis G. Okie. In the early 1920s, Okie dreamed up the idea of using sandpaper instead of razor blades for shaving. The aim was to reduce the risk of nicks and avoid sharp instruments. The idea failed, but rather than punishing Okie for the failure, 3M encouraged him to champion other ideas, which included 3M's first blockbuster success: waterproof sandpaper. A culture that permits failure fosters the creative thinking and risk taking that innovation requires.

As strange as it may seem, *celebrating* failure can be vital to an innovation culture.[42] Failure (we hope) prompts learning, growing, and succeeding. In innovative companies, many people are trying many new ideas. Even if a majority of the ideas fail, a few big hits can make a company an innovative star. This type of management attitude can foster creative efforts throughout the ranks.

4.3 | Don't Let Bureaucracy Squelch Innovation

Bureaucracy is an enemy of innovation. Its main purpose is maintaining orderliness and efficiency, not pushing the creative envelope. Developing radically new goods and services requires a fluid and flexible (organic) structure that does not restrict thought and action.

However, such a structure can be chaotic and disruptive. Thus, although 3M was long admired for its culture of innovation, it became inefficient, with unpredictable profits and an unimpressive stock price. That has been changing lately as new product launches of medical equipment to protect people against the COVID-19 virus—such as powered air-purifying respirators and personal protection masks—are revitalizing 3M's profits.[43]

To balance innovation with other business goals, companies may create temporary project structures that are isolated from the rest of the organization and allowed to operate under different rules. These units go by many names, including "skunkworks," "greenhouses," and "reserves."

To support its innovation culture, Intuit holds a quarterly event called Innovation Days. Company R&D engineers work in teams for three days to improve the company's products and platform.[44] The events generate hundreds of ideas for new products and enhancing the customer experience.[45] Intuit's commitment to innovation earned it a spot on Fast Company's 2019 Best Workplaces for Innovators list.[46]

4.4 | Development Projects Can Drive Innovation

A development project is a focused organizational effort to create a new product or process via technological advances.[47] Development projects typically feature a special cross-functional team working together on an overall concept or idea. The team interacts with suppliers and customers. Because of their strategic importance, most development teams work under intense time and budget pressures.

One particular type of development process, agile design, guides IT, product, and service development projects in a flexible and interactive manner.[48] Compared to traditional approaches where a company designs and fully develops a new concept internally before rolling it out to customers, the agile design process is more collaborative, faster, and less expensive. It relies on frequent iterations with clients to continually develop, test, and refine new goods or services so the new concept meets customer expectations.[49] The agile design process takes out some risk and improves customer satisfaction.[50]

Thus, development projects create new products and processes. They also provide another vital benefit: They cultivate skills and knowledge useful for future innovative efforts. These new capabilities can be turned into competitive advantage. Thus, *how much the organization learns*—that is, its people – is an important indicator of a project's success.

4.5 | Job Design and Human Resources Make Innovation Possible

Adopting a new technology may require changes in job design. The work people do changes due to the demands of the technology. Ignoring peoples' reactions means full potential won't be reached. People need to adopt new skills and social relationships; otherwise, overall productivity will suffer.

The sociotechnical systems approach to work redesign addresses this problem. Introduced in Chapter 2, this approach redesigns tasks in ways that jointly optimize social and technical

● Project FROG (Flexible Response to Ongoing Growth) wants to revolutionize the construction industry. The San Francisco–based company designs and sells modular components that assemble easily into energy-efficient, green buildings for uses including retail, health care, and classrooms. rarrarorro/Shutterstock

efficiencies. Introduced in studies of new coal-mining technologies in 1949, the sociotechnical systems approach focused on small, self-regulating work groups.[51] Later studies found that such work arrangements operated effectively only in an environment where bureaucracy was limited. Today's trends in bureaucracy bashing, lean and flat organizations, work teams, and workforce empowerment are logical extensions of the sociotechnical philosophy. At the same time, the technologies of the information age—in which people at all organizational levels have access to vast amounts of information—make leaner and less bureaucratic organizations possible.

Technology can limit people's responsibilities and "de-skill" the workforce, turning workers into servants of the technology. Or managers can select and train workers to master the technology, using it to achieve great things and improve work and life. Technology, *managed well,* can empower workers as it strengthens organizations.[52]

Previous reward systems might reinforce old behaviors that will be counterproductive in the new system. Thus, managers need to consider how changing HR practices can help introduce new technologies. For example, advanced manufacturing technology usually requires people with high levels of skill, a commitment to continuous learning, and the ability to work in teams. Adequate training and pay systems that attract and reward people with these skills will help.[53] Reward systems must fit the new technologies, rewarding contributions that make the changes work.

To adapt to a dynamic marketplace, organizations need to reshape themselves. Leading change and organizational learning can drive an organization toward world-class performance.

> **LO5 Discuss what it takes to be world-class.**

5 | BECOMING WORLD-CLASS

Managers want, or perhaps *should* want, their organizations to become *world-class*.[54] It requires applying the best and latest knowledge and ideas, being able to operate at the highest standards of any place anywhere, and being one of the very best at what you do.[55]

To some people, world-class excellence seems a lofty, impossible, unnecessary goal. But it can serve as a worthy stretch goal in a competitive world.

World-class companies create high-value products and earn superior profits over the long run. They demolish the obsolete methods, systems, and cultures of the past that impede progress, and they apply more effective and competitive strategies, structures, processes, and management of human resources. The result is an organization that can compete—and even serve society—on a global basis.[56]

5.1 | Build Companies for Sustainable, Long-Term Greatness

Two Stanford professors, James Collins and Jerry Porras, studied 18 corporations that had achieved and maintained greatness for half a century or more.[57] The companies included Sony, American Express, Motorola, Marriott, Johnson & Johnson, Disney, 3M, Hewlett-Packard, Citicorp, and Walmart. Over the years, these companies have been widely admired as premier institutions in their industries and have made a real impact on the world. Although every company experiences downturns, these companies continue to prevail across the decades. They turn in extraordinary performance over the long run rather than fleeting greatness. This study is reported in the book, *Built to Last.*[58]

The researchers sought to identify the essential characteristics of enduringly great companies. These companies have strong core values they believe in deeply, and they express and live the values consistently. They are driven by goals—not just incremental improvements or business-as-usual goals, but stretch goals (recall Chapter 11). They change continuously, driving for progress via adaptability, experimentation, trial and error, entrepreneurial thinking, and fast action. And they do not focus on beating the competition; they focus primarily on beating themselves. They continually ask, "How can we improve ourselves to do better tomorrow than we did today?"

Underneath the action and the changes, the companies' core values and vision remain steadfast. For example, American Express's core values and mission include facilitating commerce and enabling its customers to do and achieve more in life. Walt Disney's values and mission include fanatical attention to detail, continuous progress through creativity, commitment to preserving Disney's "magic" image, delivery of happiness and "wholesome American values," and a lack of cynicism.

Note that the values are not all the same. In fact, no set of common values consistently predicts success. Instead the critical factor is that the great companies *have* core values, *know* what they are and what they mean, and *live* by them—year after year.

5.2 | Replace the "Tyranny of the *Or*" with the "Genius of the *And*"

Many companies, and individuals, are plagued by what the authors of *Built to Last* call the "tyranny of the *or*"—binary thinking, or the belief that things must be either A or B and cannot be both.[59] However, beliefs that only one goal can be attained often are invalid.

An alternative to the "tyranny of the *or*" is the "genius of the *and*"—the ability to achieve multiple objectives at the same time.[60] This ability—organizational ambidexterity—develops via strategic decisions at the top and the actions of many individuals throughout the organization.

organization development (OD) the systemwide application of behavioral science knowledge to develop, improve, and reinforce the strategies, structures, and processes that lead to organizational effectiveness

Earlier, we discussed the importance of delivering multiple competitive values to customers, performing all four management functions, reconciling hard-nosed business logic with ethics, leading and empowering, and exploiting knowledge while exploring new possibilities. And in this concluding chapter, we opened with a discussion of the COVID-19 pandemic. We cannot let immediate pandemic demands derail needed longer-term efforts to deal with climate change. An ambidextrous, "genius of the *and*" perspective can help find synergistic solutions to mitigating both pandemics and climate change.[61]

Built to Last authors Collins and Porras offered examples of tensions that seem conflicting but can be optimized:[62]

- Purpose beyond profit *and* pragmatic pursuit of profit.

- Relatively fixed core values *and* vigorous change and movement.

- Conservatism with the core values *and* bold business moves.

- Clear vision and direction *and* experimentation.

- Stretch goals *and* incremental progress.

- Control based on values *and* operational freedom.

- Long-term thinking and investment *and* demand for short-term results.

- Visionary, futuristic thinking *and* daily, nuts-and-bolts execution.

Your organization and its managers collectively should not lose sight of any of these tensions, or apparent paradoxes,[63] in your thoughts or actions. To achieve organizational goals, which ebb and flow over time, requires the continuous and effective management of change.

5.3 | Don't Just Change, Develop

How do organizations apply the "genius of the *and*," become more ambidextrous, and move in the other positive directions described throughout this book? Several general approaches can create such positive change through processes of organization development.

Organization development (OD) is a systemwide application of behavioral science knowledge to develop, improve, and reinforce the strategies, structures, and processes that lead to organization effectiveness.[64] Throughout this course, you have acquired knowledge about behavioral science and the strategies, structures, and processes that help organizations become more effective. The "systemwide" component of the definition means OD is not a narrow improvement in technology or operations but a broader approach to changing organizations, units, or people.

The "behavioral science" component means OD is not focused directly on economic, financial, or technical aspects of the organization—although these should benefit through changes in the behavior of the people in the organization. The other key part of the definition—to develop, improve, and reinforce—refers to the actual process of changing for the better and for the long term.

Two features of organization development are essential.[65] First, it aims to increase organizational effectiveness—improving the organization's ability to respond to customers, stockholders, governments, employees, and other stakeholders. This results in better-quality products, higher financial returns, and high quality of work life. Second, OD has an important underlying value orientation: It supports human potential, development, and participation in addition to performance and competitive advantage.

Exhibit 15.7 shows some OD techniques under this philosophical umbrella. You learned about these topics throughout your management course, and you will learn more about creating change in the rest of this concluding chapter.

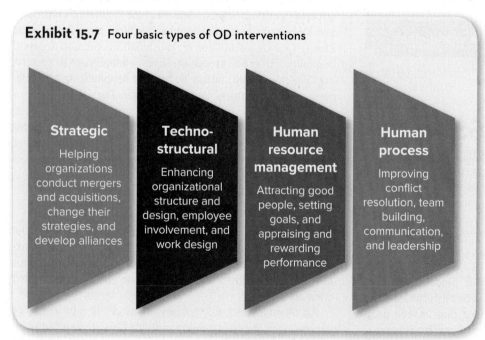

Exhibit 15.7 Four basic types of OD interventions

Strategic
Helping organizations conduct mergers and acquisitions, change their strategies, and develop alliances

Techno-structural
Enhancing organizational structure and design, employee involvement, and work design

Human resource management
Attracting good people, setting goals, and appraising and rewarding performance

Human process
Improving conflict resolution, team building, communication, and leadership

Source: Adapted from T. Cummings and C. Worley, *Organization Development and Change,* 8th ed. (Mason, OH: Thomson/South-Western, 2005).

5.4 | Certain Management Practices Make Organizations Great

A major study of 200 management techniques employed by 160 companies over 10 years identified the specific management practices that lead to sustained, superior performance.[66] The authors boiled their findings down to four key factors:

1. *Strategy* that is focused on customers, continually fine-tuned based on marketplace changes, and clearly communicated to employees.

2. *Execution* by good people, given decision-making authority on the front lines, who are doing quality work and cutting costs.

3. *Culture* that motivates, empowers people to innovate, rewards people appropriately (psychologically as well as economically), entails strong values, challenges people, and provides a satisfying work environment.

4. *Structure* that makes the organization easy to work in and easy to work with, characterized by cooperation and the exchange of information and knowledge throughout the organization.

You have been learning about these concepts throughout this course.

People are the key to successful change.[67] For an organization to be great, people have to care about its fate and know how they can contribute. But typically leadership lies with a few people at the top. Too few take on the burden of change; too few care deeply and make innovative contributions. People throughout the organization need to take a greater interest and a more active role in helping the business as a whole. Ideally they identify with the entire organization, not just with their unit and close colleagues.

Did You KNOW ?

A McKinsey study found that for transformational change efforts to succeed, organizations must involve employees at all levels. The most successful changes had senior leaders communicating compelling change stories plus line managers showing their personal commitment to the initiative.[72]

LO6 Describe how to lead change effectively.

6 | LEADING CHANGE

Change happens, constantly and unpredictably. Any competitive advantage you may have depends on particular circumstances at a particular time, but circumstances change.[68] New competitors appear, new markets emerge, and the economic environment shifts. While economic recessions devastate countless organizations from companies to state governments to nonprofit agencies, they force managers to see innovation as a key to survival. The "business as usual" mindset gives way to a "change to survive" mentality.

The challenge for organizations is not just to produce innovative new products, but to balance a culture that is innovative and builds a sustainable business.[69] For individuals, the ability to cope with change is related to their job performance and the rewards they receive.[70]

The success of most change efforts requires *shared leadership;* people must be not just *supporters* of change but also *implementers.*[71] This shared responsibility for change is not unusual in start-ups and very small organizations, but it often is lost with growth and over time. In large, traditional corporations, it is rare. Organizations must rekindle individual responsibility and creativity. The essential task is to motivate people to keep adapting to new business challenges.

6.1 | Motivate People to Change

People must be *motivated* to change. But often they resist changing. Some people resist change more than others, but managers generally underestimate the amount of resistance they will encounter.[73]

To implement positive change, managers must understand why people often resist change. Some reasons arise regardless of the actual content of the change:[74]

- *Inertia.* The old ways of doing things are comfortable and easy, so people don't want to try something new. For example, it is easier for some managers to provide performance feedback to employees once a year than on a real-time, frequent basis.

- *Timing.* If managers or employees are unusually busy or under stress, or if relations between management and workers are strained, the timing is bad. Where possible, managers should introduce change when people are receptive.

- *Surprise.* If a change is sudden, unexpected, or extreme, resistance may be the initial reaction. The change leaders need to allow time for others to think about the change and prepare for it.

- *Peer pressure.* Work teams often resist changes coming from above. Peer pressure may cause individuals to resist even reasonable changes. Change leaders who invite—and listen to—ideas from team members may find that peer influence becomes a driving force behind the change's success.

● The Zappos corporate office in Las Vegas.
James Leynse/Corbis News/Getty Images

---

unfreezing realizing that current practices are inappropriate and new behavior is necessary

performance gap the difference between actual performance and desired performance

moving instituting the change

force-field analysis an approach to implementing Lewin's unfreezing/moving/refreezing model that involves identifying the forces that prevent people from changing and those that will drive people toward change

---

Other causes of resistance arise from the specific nature of a proposed change:[75]

- *Self-interest.* Most people will resist a change if they think it will cause them to lose something of value. What could people fear to lose? At worst, their jobs, if management is considering closing an operation, merging with another company, or introducing new technology.

- *Misunderstanding.* Even when management proposes a change that will benefit everyone, people may resist because they don't fully understand it. People may not see how the change fits with the firm's strategy, or they simply may not see the change's advantage over current practices.[76]

- *Different assessments.* Employees receive different—and usually less—information than management receives. Such discrepancies cause people to develop different assessments of proposed changes. Some may be aware that the benefits outweigh the costs, while others may see only the costs.

Employees' assessments can be more accurate than management's; employees may know a change won't work even if

management doesn't. In this case, resistance to change benefits the organization. Thus, even though management typically views resistance as an obstacle to overcome, it may actually be an important signal that the proposed change requires further, more open-minded scrutiny.[77]

6.2 | A Three-Stage Model Shows Ways to Manage Resistance

Motivating people to change often requires three basic stages, shown in Exhibit 15.8: unfreezing, moving to institute the change, and refreezing.[78]

Unfreezing During the unfreezing stage, management realizes that its current practices are no longer appropriate and the company must break out of (unfreeze) its present mold by doing things differently. People must come to recognize that some of the past ways of thinking, feeling, and doing things are obsolete.[79] A direct and sometimes effective way to do this is to communicate the negative consequences of the old ways by comparing the organization's performance with that of its competitors. Management can also share with employees data about costs, quality, and profits.[80] Sometimes employees just need to understand the rationale for changing.

An important contributor to unfreezing is to recognize a performance gap: the difference between actual performance and the performance that should or could exist.[81] A gap typically implies poor performance, as when sales, profits, stock price, or other financial indicators are down. This situation attracts management's attention, and management introduces changes to try to correct things.

Another very important form of performance gap occurs when performance is good but someone realizes it could be better. The gap is between what is and what *could be*. This is where entrepreneurs seize opportunities and companies gain a competitive edge. In the realm of change, employees are best motivated by combining the sense of urgency that comes from identifying a problem with the sense of excitement that comes from identifying an opportunity.

Moving The next step, moving to institute the change, begins with establishing a vision of the desired future. You learned about vision in the leadership chapter. The vision can be realized through strategic, structural, cultural, and individual change.

A technique that helps to manage the change process, force-field analysis, involves identifying the specific forces that prevent people from changing and the specific forces that will drive people toward change.[82] In other words, managers investigate the forces acting on people in opposite directions. Then they select forces to add or remove; eliminating the restraining forces helps people unfreeze, and increasing the driving forces motivates them to move forward.

Refreezing may not be the best final step if it creates new behaviors that are as rigid as the old ones. The ideal new culture is one that applies agility and organizational learning to adapt to continuous change. Refreezing is appropriate when it

Exhibit 15.8 Motivating people to change

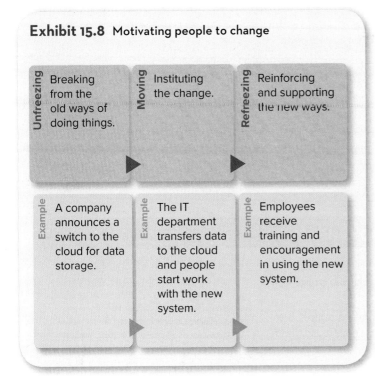

Unfreezing	Moving	Refreezing
Breaking from the old ways of doing things.	Instituting the change.	Reinforcing and supporting the new ways.
Example: A company announces a switch to the cloud for data storage.	Example: The IT department transfers data to the cloud and people start work with the new system.	Example: Employees receive training and encouragement in using the new system.

Exhibit 15.9 How to overcome resistance to change

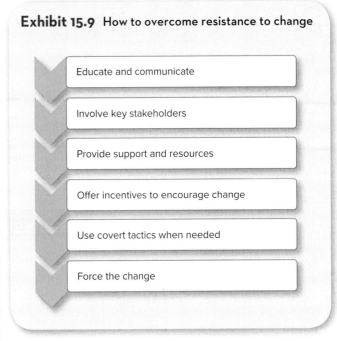

- Educate and communicate
- Involve key stakeholders
- Provide support and resources
- Offer incentives to encourage change
- Use covert tactics when needed
- Force the change

permanently installs behaviors that maintain essential core values, such as a focus on important business results and the values maintained by companies that are "built to last." But refreezing should not create new rigidities that might become dysfunctional as the business environment continues to change.[83] The best "refreezing" also promotes continued adaptability, flexibility, experimentation, assessment of results, and continuous improvement. In other words, lock in key values, capabilities, and strategic mission, but not necessarily specific practices and procedures.

6.3 | Certain Strategies Enlist Cooperation

You can try to command people to change, but the key to long-term success is to use multiple approaches.[84] Developing true support is better than "driving" a program forward.[85]

Most managers underestimate the number of different ways they can influence people to care about a change,[86] as summarized in Exhibit 15.9.

- *Educate and communicate*—Management should educate people about upcoming changes before they occur. It should communicate the *nature* of the change and its *logic.* As COVID-19 spread in early 2020, public officials and workplace managers announced policies to shelter in place and work remotely, and conveyed the reasons for doing so.[87] The logic was obvious to some people and less so to others. Public health and the economy seemed to oppose one another—a false choice if results could be optimally balanced. Decision makers continually reconsidered the costs and benefits of closings and openings as circumstances, risks, and uncertainties kept changing. Leaders sent mixed messages, and their logic was often unclear, with widely varying results.

- *Involve key stakeholders*— For important changes, the people who are affected by a change should participate in its design and implementation. For major, organizationwide change, involvement in the process can extend from top to bottom.[88] People who participate in decisions understand them more fully and are more committed to them.

- *Provide support and resources*—Management should make the change as easy as possible for employees and support their efforts. Facilitation can include providing the training and other resources people need to carry out the change and perform well under the new circumstances. Change is stressful, so managers need to help employees by listening to problems, understanding if performance drops temporarily or the change is not perfected immediately, and showing consideration during a difficult period.[89]

- *Offer incentives to change*—When necessary, management can offer concrete incentives for cooperating with the change. Perhaps job enrichment is acceptable only with a higher wage rate, or a work rule change is resisted until management agrees to a concession on some other rule (say, about taking breaks). Job assignments and reward systems perhaps can be restructured to reinforce the change.[90] Managers can make sure people know their own benefits from the changes.[91]

- *Use covert tactics when needed*—Sometimes, managers use more subtle, covert tactics to implement change. Co-optation involves giving a resisting individual a desirable role in the change process. For example, management

Sustaining for Tomorrow

TerraCycle Is Changing How We Look at Garbage

Many products today are made from various types of waste—old tires, scrap metal, plastic bottles. Companies look for ways to recycle and reuse just about every material imaginable. Tom Szaky's company TerraCycle is addressing that need. Szaky's long-term objective is ambitious: "Our goal is to eliminate the idea of waste by creating collection and solution systems for anything that today must be sent to a landfill."

The company converts traditionally hard-to-recycle waste (including drink pouches, chip bags, toothbrushes, and more) into a variety of consumer products, including flip-flops, backpacks, office supplies, park benches, and playgrounds. TerraCycle's products sell through major retailers such as Target and Home Depot. The company has also launched operations internationally. To date, over 200 million people across 21 countries have helped to collect and recycle waste through TerraCycle, helping to raise $44 million for charities around the world.

TerraCycle expanded its operations in 2019, launching a home recycling delivery service called Loop. Consumers can toss their empty containers into a tote provided by TerraCycle, which then sterilizes the packaging to be used again. Consumers don't even have to clean the containers. The system is still in its infancy, but the goal is to shift the focus from "recycle" to "reuse," which in Szaky's estimation is ultimately cheaper and more efficient.

Discussion Questions

- Do you think Loop has offered enough incentive to change the way people dispose of waste?

- Given how TerraCycle has evolved over the past 10 years, how might it continue to innovate in the future?

Sources: D. Karas, "Tom Szaky Started TerraCycle to Help 'De-junk' the World," *CS Monitor,* February 4, 2016, https://www.csmonitor.com/World/ Making-a-difference/2016/0204/Tom-Szaky-started-TerraCycle-to-help-de-junk-the-world; TerraCycle website, "About TerraCycle," https://www.terracycle.com/en-US/about-terracycle?utm_campaign=admittance&utm_medium=menu&utm_source=www.terracycle.com, accessed April 24, 2020; and S. Min, "The Company Refilling Your Household Goods Is Expanding to More States." *CBS News,* July 10, 2019, https://www.cbsnews.com/news/terracycle-loop-zero-waste-products-procter-gamble-nestle-household-brands-expanding/.

---

might invite a union leader to be a member of an executive committee or ask a key member of an outside organization to join the company's board of directors. As people become involved in the change, they become more familiar with what's happening and often less resistant.

- *Force the change*—Sometimes managers resort to using punishments or threats against those who resist change. A manager might insist that subordinates cooperate with the change and threaten them with job loss, denial of a promotion, or an unattractive work assignment. Sometimes, you just have to lay down the law.

Each approach to overcoming resistance has advantages and drawbacks. Effective change managers are familiar with the various approaches and apply them according to the situation.

> "A small group of thoughtful people could change the world. Indeed, it's the only thing that ever has."
>
> —Margaret Mead

Throughout the process, change leaders need to build in stability. Recall that built-to-last companies have essential and stable core values that people can latch onto in the midst of change, turmoil, and uncertainty.[92] Keeping key managers visible and values and mission constant can serve this stabilizing function. Strategic principles can be additional anchors during change.[93] Thus managers should announce the important things that will *not* change. Such anchors will reduce anxiety and help overcome resistance.

6.4 | Harmonize Multiple Changes

No silver bullet exists to make every change successful. Single shots rarely hit a challenging target. Usually, many issues need simultaneous attention, and any single small change will be absorbed by the prevailing culture and disappear. *Total organizational change* involves introducing and sustaining multiple policies, practices, and procedures across multiple units and levels.[94] Such change affects the thinking and behavior of everyone in the organization, can enhance the organization's culture and success, and can be sustained over time.

Because companies introduce new changes constantly, people complain about their companies' "flavor of the month" approach to change. Employees often see change efforts as just the company's jumping on the latest fad or bandwagon. The more these fads come and go, the more cynical people become, and the harder it is to get them committed to making the change a success.[95]

One solution is to identify which change efforts are really worthwhile. Here are some specific questions to ask before embarking on a change project:[96]

- What is the evidence that the approach really can produce positive results?

- Is the approach relevant to your company's strategies and priorities?

- What are the costs and potential benefits?

- Does it really help people add value through their work?

- Does it help the company focus better on customers and what they value?

- Can you go through the decision-making process described in Chapter 5, understand what you're facing, and feel that you are taking the right approach?

Management also needs to integrate the various efforts into a coherent picture that people can see, understand, and get behind.[97] You do this by understanding each change program and its goals, identifying similarities and differences of the programs, and dropping programs that don't meet priority goals or demonstrate clear results. Most important, you do it by communicating to everyone concerned the common themes of the various programs: their common rationales, objectives, and methods. You

show them how the parts fit the strategic big picture and how the changes will improve things for the company and its people. You must communicate these benefits thoroughly, honestly, and frequently.[98]

6.5 | Managers Must Lead Change Actively

Successful change requires managers to lead it actively. The essential activities of leading change are summarized in Exhibit 15.10.

The managers that lead change most effectively *establish a sense of urgency.*[99] They examine current realities and pressures in the marketplace and the competitive arena, identify crises and opportunities, and are frank and honest about them. In this sense, urgency is a reality-based sense of determination, not just fear-based busyness. The immediacy of the need for change is important partly because so many large companies grow complacent.

To stop complacency and create urgency, a manager can talk candidly about the organization's weaknesses relative to competitors, making a point to back up statements with data. Other tactics include setting stretch goals, putting employees in direct

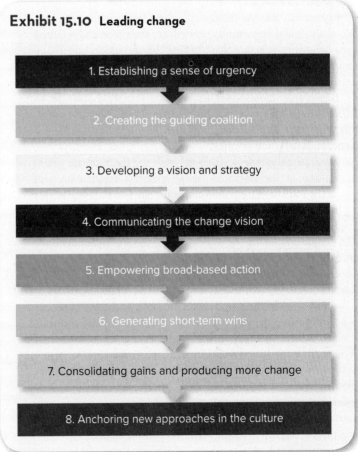

Exhibit 15.10 Leading change

1. Establishing a sense of urgency
2. Creating the guiding coalition
3. Developing a vision and strategy
4. Communicating the change vision
5. Empowering broad-based action
6. Generating short-term wins
7. Consolidating gains and producing more change
8. Anchoring new approaches in the culture

Source: J. P. Kotter, *Leading Change* (Boston: Harvard Business School Publishing, 1996).

contact with unhappy customers and shareholders, and highlighting the future opportunities that the organization so far has failed to pursue.

Ultimately, urgency is driven by compelling business reasons to change. Survival, competition, and winning in the marketplace are compelling; they provide a sense of direction and energy around change. Change becomes a business necessity.[100]

Leading change requires creating a guiding coalition, putting together a group with enough power to make the change happen. Change efforts fail for lack of a powerful coalition.[101] Major organizational change requires leadership from top management, working as a team. But over time, the support must expand outward and downward throughout the organization. Middle managers and supervisors are essential. Groups at all levels can keep change efforts moving forward.[102]

Change leaders develop a vision and strategy to direct the change effort. Because confusion is common during major organizational change, this image of the future state must be as clear as possible and must be communicated to everyone.[103] This image, or vision, can clarify expectations, dispel rumors, and mobilize energies.

Communicating the change vision requires using every possible channel and opportunity to reinforce the vision and required new behaviors. It is said that aspiring change leaders undercommunicate the vision by a factor of 10, 100, or even 1,000, seriously undermining the chances of success.[104]

Empowering broad-based action means removing obstacles to success, including systems and structures that constrain rather than facilitate. Engage people by providing information, knowledge, authority, and rewards.

Generate short-term wins. Don't wait for the ultimate grand realization of the vision. As small victories accumulate, you make the transition from an isolated initiative to an integral part of the business.[105] Plan for and create small victories that show everyone when progress occurs. Visibly recognize and reward the people who made the wins possible; you want people notice and the positive message to reach everyone.

Consolidate gains and produce more change. With the well-earned credibility that successes confer, keep changing things in ways that support the vision. Hire, promote, and develop people who will further the vision. Reinvigorate the company and your change efforts with new projects and change agents. Remain agile while continuously changing and innovating.

Finally, *anchor new approaches in the culture.*[106] Highlight positive results, communicate the connections between the new behaviors and the improved results, and keep developing new change agents and leaders. Continually increase the number of people joining you in taking responsibility for change.[107]

7 | SHAPING THE FUTURE

Most change is reactive. A better way to change is to be proactive. *Reactive change* means responding to pressure after a problem has arisen. It implies being a follower. *Proactive change* means anticipating and preparing for an uncertain future. It implies being a leader and *creating* the future you want.

If you think only about the present or worry about the uncertainties of the future, your future is just a roll of the dice. It is far better to exercise foresight, set an agenda for the future, and pursue it with everything you've got.

Newsweek and others predict dramatic changes in the future: Earth's growing population will severely stress our food and water supplies, and people will live longer and require long-term health treatments. Renewable energy sources will grow, as will the Internet of Things, artificial intelligence, and robotics.[108]

Authors Shoshana Zuboff and Jim Maxim declare that the era of industrial capitalism is over, traditional business enterprises are disappearing, vast new markets exist, new kinds of companies are ready to be created, and the new business model hasn't yet emerged.[109] New business concepts are always interesting to contemplate.

7.1 | Create the Future

As companies prepare to compete in an uncertain future, they can try different strategic postures. **Adapters** take the current industry structure and its future evolution as givens and choose where to compete. Most companies take this posture by conducting standard strategic analysis and choosing how to compete within given environments. In contrast, **shapers** try to change the structure of their industries, creating a future competitive landscape of their own design.[110]

Researchers studying corporate performance over a 10-year period found that 17 companies in the *Fortune* 1000 increased total shareholder return by 35 percent or more per year.[111] How did they achieve such impressive results? They completely reinvented industries. Harley-Davidson turned around by selling not just motorcycles, but nostalgia. Amgen broke the rules of the biotech industry by focusing not on what customers wanted, but on great science. Starbucks took a commodity and began selling it in trendy stores. CarMax and other companies reinvented the auto industry.

You need to create advantages. Rather than maintaining your position in the current competitive arena, the challenge is to create new competitive arenas, transform your industry, and imagine a future that others don't see.[112]

Creating advantage is better than playing catch-up. At best, working to catch up buys time; it cannot get you ahead of the pack or buy world-class excellence.[113] To create new markets or transform industries—these are perhaps the ultimate forms of proactive change.[114]

Exhibit 15.11 shows the vast opportunity to create new markets. Articulated needs are those that customers acknowledge and try to satisfy. Unarticulated needs are those that customers have not yet experienced. Served customers are those to whom your company is now selling, and unserved customers are untapped markets.

While business as usual concentrates on serving only articulated needs, the leaders who re-create the game are constantly trying to create new opportunities to satisfy unarticulated and unserved needs.[115] You can pursue these goals by imagining how you can satisfy a larger proportion of your customers' total needs. Employees at Apple Stores are trained to listen for customers' expressed and unexpressed needs. A customer purchasing a Mac computer or laptop for the first time might be anxious about changing from a PC. Upon sensing this trepidation, Apple employees are quick to recommend free training classes at the Apple Store to help the new Mac owner jump-start the learning process.[116]

All things considered, which should you and your firm do?

- Preserve old advantages or create new advantages?
- Lock in old markets or create new markets?
- Take the path of greatest familiarity or the path of greatest opportunity?
- Be a benchmarker or a pathbreaker?
- Place priority on short-term financial returns or on making a real, long-term impact?
- Do only what seems doable or what is difficult and worthwhile?
- Change what is or create what isn't?
- Look to the past or live for the future?[117]

7.2 | Shape Your Own Future

If your organization operates in traditional ways, consider with your boss what changes to try to make so your company doesn't become a dinosaur of the modern era.[118]

But maybe you are not going to lead a revolution. Maybe you just want a successful career and a good life. You still must deal with an economic environment that is increasingly competitive and fast-moving.[119] To create the future you want for yourself, you have to set high personal standards.

Don't settle for mediocrity; don't assume that "good" is necessarily good enough—for yourself or for your employer. Think about how to exceed, not just meet, expectations; how to break free of apparent constraints that are unimportant, arbitrary, or imagined; and how to seize opportunities instead of letting them pass by.[120]

You can continually add value to your employer—and also to yourself—as you upgrade your skills and ability to contribute. This helps you gain security with your current employer and find alternative employment if necessary. The most successful people take charge of their own development the way an entrepreneur takes charge of a business.[121]

More advice from the leading authors on career management:[122] Consciously and actively manage your own career.

Exhibit 15.11 Unmet needs equal opportunity

OPPORTUNITY
Serve current customers' unarticulated needs

TODAY
Serving current customers' articulated needs

OPPORTUNITY
Serve future customers' unarticulated needs

Source: Adapted from G. Hamel and C. K. Prahalad, *Competing for the Future* (Boston: Harvard Business School Press, 1994).

"You can't go back and change the beginning, but you can start where you are and change the ending."

—C.S. Lewis

Take Charge of Your Career

Is a side hustle in your future?

The gig economy has changed the way we think about work. A contributor to *Forbes* magazine recently wrote, "We have to run our careers differently now. We are all entrepreneurs in the new-millennium workplace, even when we work for other people. . . . Your career is a business! It's your business to run. You are the CEO."

This new way of thinking about your career puts the responsibility squarely on you to develop your skills and promote them. About two-thirds of early-career employees reportedly want to start their own businesses, attracted by the ability to be their own boss and set their own hours and pay rates. So, you may want to give yourself a head start by taking up a side hustle—an additional source of income—that showcases your talents and adds an entry to your résumé.

Common side hustles in recent years included ride-sharing (being a Lyft or Uber driver), offering fitness training or coaching, doing freelance or consulting work, running an e-commerce site, tutoring, teaching, and babysitting. Most of these brought in less than $350 a month, but the payoffs can be much higher. Blogging, vlogging, and podcasting were last on the list and brought in the least money, paying an average of $3 per hour.

Think about what you're good at. Can you play an instrument? Speak a foreign language? Cook? Somewhere there is a market for your talent. It's all up to you.

Sources: L. Ryan, "Job Security Is Disappearing— What Does It Mean for You?" *Forbes,* May 23, 2017, www.forbes.com/sites/lizryan/2017/05/23/job-security-is-disappearing-what-does-it-mean-for-you/#3b3018582173; A. Hess, "These Are the 22 Most Common Side Hustles—Here's How Much They Pay," *CNBC,* March 9, 2018, www.cnbc.com/2018/03/09/these-are-the-22-most-common-side-hustles-heres-how-much-they-pay.html.

Develop marketable skills, and keep developing more. Make career choices based on personal growth, development, and learning opportunities. Look for positions that stretch you and for bosses who develop their protégés. Seek environments that provide training and the opportunity to experiment and innovate. And know yourself—assess your strengths and weaknesses, your true interests, and ethical standards. If you are not already thinking in these terms and taking commensurate action, you can start now.

Additionally, become indispensable to your organization. Be enthusiastic in your job and committed to doing great work, but don't be blindly loyal to one company. Be prepared to leave if necessary. View your job as an opportunity to prove what you can do and increase your skill set, not as a comfortable niche for the long term.[123] Go out on your own if it meets your talents and temperament.

You need to maintain your options. More and more, contemporary careers include leaving a large organization and going entrepreneurial, becoming self-employed in the "postcorporate world."[124] In such a career, independent individuals make their own choices, and must adapt quickly to demands and opportunities. Developing start-up ventures, consulting, accepting temporary employment, doing gigs for one organization and then another, working in professional partnerships, being a constant deal maker—these can be the elements of a successful career. Ideally, this self-employed model balances working with personal life.

This go-it-alone approach can sound ideal, but it also has downsides. Independence can be frightening, the future unpredictable. It can isolate "road warriors" who are always on the go, working from their cars and airports, and can interfere with social and family life.[125] Effective self-management is essential to keep career and family obligations in perspective and under control.

Coping with uncertainty and change is easier if you develop resilience. To become more resilient, practice thinking of the world as complex but full of opportunities; expect change, but view it as interesting and potentially rewarding, even if changing is difficult. Maintain a sense of purpose; set priorities for your time; be flexible; and take an active role in the face of change, rather than waiting for change to happen to you.[126]

7.3 | Learn and Lead the Way

Continuous learning is a vital route to renewable advantage.[127] People in your organization—and you, personally—should constantly explore, discover, and take action, repeating this cycle as you progress in your career:[128]

1. *Explore* your current reality, being as honest and precise as possible about what is happening. Identify your problems and areas of opportunity. Gather data. Check with professors, colleagues, bosses, customers, suppliers, and others. Uncover hidden issues, and look for root causes. Rethink based on what you've learned.

2. *Discover* a deeper understanding of the current reality. The issues and choices should become clearer. Identify possible solutions or ways to take advantage of opportunities. Plan what to do, anticipating problems that may arise.

3. *Act* by testing solutions, implementing your plan, and evaluating the results. Recognize problems; this will prepare you for repeating the cycle. Be sure to enjoy your successes, too.

With this approach, you can learn what is effective and what is not, and then adjust and improve accordingly. Continuous learning helps your company achieve lower costs, higher quality, better service, superior innovation, and greater speed—and helps you develop professionally and personally.

Commit to lifelong learning. Be willing to seek new challenges, and reflect honestly on successes and failures.[129] Lifelong learning requires occasional risk taking. Move outside your comfort zone (sorry for the cliché, but it's true), honestly assess the reasons behind your successes and failures, ask for and listen to other people's information and opinions, and stay open to new ideas.

A leader—and this could include you—should be able to create an environment in which "others are willing to learn and change so their organizations can adapt and innovate [and] inspire diverse others to embark on a collective journey of continual learning and leading."[130] *Learning leaders* exchange knowledge freely; commit to their own continuous learning as well as to others'; examine their own behaviors and personal biases, especially those that may inhibit their learning; devote time to their colleagues, suspending their own opinions while they listen thoughtfully; and develop a broad perspective, recognizing that organizations are an integrated system of human relationships.[131]

"Leaning into the future" is one of our favorite metaphors. It comes from merging the words *leading* and *learning.*[132] These dual activities, which may appear inconsistent, are powerful and synergistic when pursued in complementary ways. A successful future derives from adapting to the world *and* shaping the future, being responsive to others' perspectives *and* being clear about what you want to change, encouraging others to change *while* recognizing what you need to change about yourself, understanding current realities *and* passionately pursuing your vision, learning *and* leading.

Repeating some key concepts and goals: Strive for ambidexterity, for yourself and your organization. And live the genius of the *and.*

7.4 | A Collaborative, Sustainable Future?

As you lead and learn into the future, we urge you to (1) think long term, along with handling the immediate demands you face; and (2) consider collaboration as a key to sustained success.

You've learned about many of today's big challenges, including the pandemic and public health as discussed in the chapter opener. The good news is that new business models and new forms of collaboration are taking root, and others are waiting to be created.[133] Entrepreneurs with societal goals are driving new approaches to commerce. Organizations in every sector—private, public, and nonprofit—are tackling social and environmental issues, enacting market-based approaches to delivering services, and pursuing sustainable business models.

Business and tomorrow's leaders in every sector will help determine the world's future. It would be naïve to think that long-term considerations will guide everyone's behavior more than do the short-term pressures for immediate results. And controversy persists over what the obligations of business really are. But a long-term perspective, balanced with prudent near-term considerations, will sustain your purpose enduringly over time.

Collaboration will not replace competition. Competition has upsides and downsides, and although new competitors continually appear, some former competitors become collaborators when they realize the potential advantages.[134] Certainly at local levels and sometimes at regional and global levels, multisector clusters of businesses, schools, universities, nonprofits, and governments are collaborating in mutually beneficial and effective ways. People are learning how to work more effectively together—not just within but across organizational, industry, geographical, and sector boundaries—to produce new models for action that revitalize commerce and will indeed create the future.[135]

Notes

1. J. Kilpatrick, "COVID-19: Managing Supply Chain Risk and Disruption," Deloitte, https://www2.deloitte.com/global/en/pages/risk/articles/covid-19-managing-supply-chain-risk-and-disruption.html, accessed May 2, 2020.

2. K. Sneader and S. Singhal. "Addressing climate change in a post-pandemic world" April 7, 2020. Accessed from https://www.mckinsey.com/business-functions/sustainability/our-insights/addressing-climate-change-in-a-post-pandemic-world?cid=other-eml-alt-mip-mck&hlkid=c2394c9ba72b4854a5bad0fc5ee-659a5&hctky=9616900&hdpid=ff20671c-232b-4fda-97ad-e4048175cbcf; C. Clifford, "These are the new hot spots of innovation in the time of coronavirus." CNBC. April 15, 2020. Accessed from https://www.cnbc.com/2020/04/15/hot-spots-of-innovation-as-a-result-of-coronavirus-pandemic.html

3. M. Scholz and N. C. Smith, "In the Face of a Pandemic, Can Pharma Shift Gears?" *MIT Sloan Management Review,* April 16, 2020, https://sloanreview.mit.edu/article/in-the-face-of-a-pandemic-can-pharma-shift-gears/.

4. A. Nawrat, "Covid-19 outbreak: pharma's big players discuss pandemic response," *Pharmaceutical Technology,* March 20, 2020. Accessed from https://www.pharmaceutical-technology.com/features/covid-19-pharma-pandemic-response/.

5. R. A. Burgelman, M. A. Maidique, and S. C. Wheelwright, *Strategic Management of Technology and Innovation* (New York: McGraw-Hill, 2000); and P. Ganotakis and J. H. Love, "The Innovation Value Chain in New Technology-Based Firms," *Journal of Product Innovation Management* 29, no. 5 (September 2012), pp. 839–60.

6. K. Girotra and S. Netessine, "Four Paths to Business Model Innovation," *Harvard Business Review,* July–August 2014, www.hbr.org; D. C. L. Prestwood and P. A. Schumann Jr., "Revitalize Your Organization," *Executive Excellence* 15, no. 2 (February 1998), p. 16; C. Y. Baldwin and K. B. Clark, "Managing in an Age of Modularity," *Harvard Business Review* 75, no. 5 (September–October 1997), pp. 84–93; S. Gopalakrishnan, P. Bierly, and E. H. Kessler, "A Reexamination of Product and Process Innovations Using a Knowledge-Based View," *Journal of High Technology Management Research* 10, no. 1 (Spring 1999), pp. 147–66; M. Johnson, C. Christensen, and H. Kagermann, "Reinventing Your Business Model," *Harvard Business Review,* December 2008, pp. 50–59; C. M. Christensen, *The Innovator's Dilemma* (Boston: Harvard Business Publishing, 1997); and C. M. Christensen, S. D. Anthony, and E. A. Roth, *Seeing What's Next* (Boston: Harvard Business Publishing, 2004).

7. M. Sawhney, R. C. Wolcott, and I. Arroniz, "The 12 Different Ways for Companies to Innovate," *MIT Sloan Management Review* 47, no. 3 (Spring 2006), pp. 75–81; and J. Birkinshaw, G. Hamel, and M. J. Mol, "Management Innovation," *Academy of Management Review* 33 (October 2008), pp. 825–45.

8. H. M. O'Neill, R. W. Pounder, and A. K. Buchholtz, "Patterns in the Diffusion of Strategies across Organizations: Insights from the Innovation, Diffusion Literature," *Academy of Management Review* 23, no. 1 (January 1998), pp. 98–114; E. M. Rogers, *Diffusion of Innovations* (New York: Free Press, 1995); and B. Guilhon, ed., *Technology and Markets for Knowledge: Knowledge Creation, Diffusion and Exchange within a Growing Economy,* Economics of Science, Technology and Innovation 22 (Dordrecht, Netherlands: Kluwer Academic Publishing, 2000).

9. M. E. Porter, *Competitive Strategy* (New York: Free Press, 1980).

10. See www.claytonchristensen.com.

11. "The Last Kodak Moment?" *The Economist* 402, no. 8767 (January 14, 2012), p. 63; and M. E. Raynor, "Getting to New and Improved," *The Conference Board Review* 48, no. 4 (Fall 2011), pp. 61–67.

12. "Number of IoT Devices in Use Worldwide from 2009 to 2020," Statista, www.statista.com, www.statista.com, accessed April 27, 2020.

13. "18 Most Popular IoT Devices in 2020," Software Testing Help, April 16, 2020, www.softwaretestinghelp.com; and A. Meola, "A Look at Examples of IoT Devices and Their Business Applications in 2020," *Business Insider,* December 18, 2019, www.businessinsider.com.

14. C. M. Christensen, *The Innovator's Dilemma: The Revolutionary Book That Will Change the Way You Do Business* (New York: Harper Paperbacks, 2003), p. xvi.

15. C. M. Christensen, *The Innovator's Dilemma: The Revolutionary Book That Will Change the Way You Do Business* (New York: Harper Paperbacks, 2003), p. xvi.

16. S. A. Zahra, S. Nash, and D. J. Bickford, "Transforming Technological Pioneering in Competitive Advantage," *Academy of Management Executive* 9, no. 1 (1995), pp. 17–31; and M. Sadowski and A. Roth, "Technology Leadership Can Pay Off," *Research Technology Management* 42, no. 6 (November–December 1999), pp. 32–33.

17. C. Andrew, "Drug Competition, the Patent Game, and Generic Cialis," *Canadian Pharmacy World,* March 6, 2017, www.canadianpharmacyworld.com; and "Can't Buy Love? Sex Drug Prices Put Medicines Out of Reach for Some," *CBS News,* December 5, 2016, www.cbsnews.com.

18. J. Su, " Amazon Owns Nearly Half of the Public-Cloud Infrastructure Market Worth over \$32 Billion," *Forbes,* August 2, 2019, www.forbes.com.

19. B. Kindig, "I Predicted Microsoft Would Win the Pentagon Contract a Year Ago—Here's What Amazon Is Missing," *Forbes,* December 17, 2019, www.forbes.com.

20. J. Alves, "Understanding Amazon's Economic Moats," *Medium,* August 14, 2017, www.medium.com.

21. See company website, "Airbnb Grows with Flexibility and Responsiveness Using AWS," Amazon, www.aws.amazon.com, accessed May 1, 2020.

22. "First-Mover Disadvantage: 9 Reasons Being the First to Market May Harm Your Business," *Medium,* April 13, 2017, www.medium.com.

23. M. Freeman-Mills, "The Best AR Glasses and Smartglasses 2020: Snap, Vuzix, North and More," *Wareable,* October 15, 2020, www.wearable.com.

24. M. Semadeni and B. S. Anderson, "The Follower's Dilemma: Innovation and Imitation in the Professional Services Industry,"

Academy of Management Journal 53 (October 2010), pp. 1175–93; R. E. Oligney and M. I. Economides, "Technology as an Asset," *Hart's Petroleum Engineer International* 71, no. 9 (September 1998), p. 27; C. MacKechnie, "What Are the Types of Business Technology?" *Chron,* http://smallbusiness.chron.com, accessed June 15, 2014; and J. Manyika, M. Chul, J. Bughin, R. Dobbs, P. Bisson, and A. Marrs, "Disruptive Technologies: Advances That Will Transform Life, Business, and the Global Economy," *McKinsey & Company Report,* May 2013, http://www.mckinsey.com.

25. R. E. Oligney and M. I. Economides, "Technology as an Asset," *Hart's Petroleum Engineer International* 71, no. 9 (September 1998), p. 27.

26. See, for example, B. Ames, "IBM Speeds Chips with DRAM Memory," *PC World,* February 12, 2007, www.pcworld.com; S. Ferguson, "Intel Plans Push into Mobility, Emerging Markets," *eWeek,* May 3, 2007, www.eweek.com; and S. Ferguson, "AMD's Next Gen Mobile Chip, Platform to Conserve Power," *eWeek,* May 18, 2007, www.eweek.com.

27. J. Brady, L. Paterson, and L. Sommer, "Solar and Wind Energy May Be Nice, but How Can We Store It?" National Public Radio, April 5, 2016, www.npr.org; and M. Kanellos, "The Most Important Man in Energy Storage? Try Archimedes," *Forbes,* March 26, 2013, www.forbes.com.

28. K. Korosec, "Uber Spent $457 Million on Self-Driving and Flying Car R&D Last Year," *TechCrunch,* April 11, 2019, www.techcrunch.com.

29. S. Shetty, "Uber's Self-Driving Cars Are a Key to Its Path to Profitability," *CNBC,* January 28, 2020, www.cnbc.com.

30. H. McIntyre, "Americans Streamed 164 Billion Songs Last Year, and That Could Help the Music Industry," *Forbes,* January 6, 2016, www.forbes.com.

31. J. Bowman, "How HBO and Netflix, Inc. Are Fighting Back against Piracy," *The Motley Fool,* June 3, 2016, www.fool.com.

32. R. Dewan, B. Jing, and A. Seidmann, "Adoption of Internet-Based Product Customization and Pricing Strategies," *Journal of Management Information Systems* 17, no. 2 (Fall 2000), pp. 9–28; P. A. Geroski, "Models of Technology Diffusion," *Research Policy* 29, no. 4/5 (April 2000), pp. 603–25; E. M. Rogers, *Diffusion of Innovations* (New York: Free Press, 1995); and R. Reinhardt and S. Gurtner, "Differences between Early Adopters of Disruptive and Sustaining Innovations," *Journal of Business Research* 68 (2015), pp. 137–45.

33. L. Chen, "Google, Tencent Agree to Share Patents in Global Tech Alliance," *Bloomberg,* January 18, 2018, www.bloomberg.com.

34. J. Andrew, K. Haanaes, D. Michael, H. Sirkin, and A. Taylor, *Measuring Innovation 2009: The Need for Action,* Boston Consulting Group, April 2009, www.bcg.com.

35. "6 Myths about Innovation That Hold You Back," *Fast Company,* December 15, 2015, www.fastcompany.com.

36. J. G. March, "Exploration and Exploitation in Organizational Learning," *Organization Science* 2, no. 1 (1991), pp. 71–87.

37. T. Burns and G. Stalker, *The Management of Innovation* (London: Tavistock, 1961); and W. Sine, H. Mitsuhashi, and D. Kirsch, "Revisiting Burns and Stalker: Formal Structure and New Venture Performance in Emerging Economic Sectors," *Academy of Management Journal* 49 (2006), pp. 121–32.

38. J. G. March, "Exploration and Exploitation in Organizational Learning," *Organization Science* 2, no. 1 (1991), pp. 71–87; and S. C. Kang and S. A. Snell, "Intellectual Capital Architectures and Ambidextrous Learning: A Framework for Human Resource Management," *Journal of Management Studies* 46, no. 1 (2009), pp. 65–92.

39. J. Miller, "How the CIO Role Is Changing as Business Needs Evolve," *CIO,* October 6, 2014, www.cio.com; T. Hoffman, "Change Agents," *Computer World,* April 23, 2007; Center for CIO Leadership, "Center for CIO Leadership Unveils 2008 Survey Results," news release, November 18, 2008, www.marketwire.com; and Center for CIO Leadership, "CIO Leadership Survey Executive Summary," abstract, 2008, www.cioleadershipcenter.com; "Information Resources: The Evolution of R&D," *Research-Technology Management,* May–June 2011, pp. 65–66; and J. C. Spender and B. Strong, "Who Has Innovative Ideas? Employees," *The Wall Street Journal,* August 23, 2010, http://online.wsj.com.

40. D. L. Day, "Raising Radicals: Different Processes for Championing Innovative Corporate Ventures," *Organization Science* 5, no. 2 (May 1994), pp. 148–72; C. Siporin, "Want Speedy FDA Approval? Hire a 'Product Champion,'" *Medical Marketing & Media,* October 1993, pp. 22–28; C. Siporin, "How You Can Capitalize on Phase 3B," *Medical Marketing & Media,* October 1994, p. 72; and E. H. Kessler, "Tightening the Belt: Methods for Reducing Development Costs Associated with New Product Innovation," *Journal of Engineering and Technology Management* 17, no. 1 (March 2000), pp. 59–92.

41. A. Ritika, "Here's How 5 Companies Create Remarkably Innovative Cultures," *Lean Startup Co.,* May 14, 2015, www.leanstartup.co; L. He, "Google's Secrets of Innovation: Empowering Its Employees," *Forbes,* March 29, 2013, www.forbes.com; and S. Kaplan, "6 Ways to Create a Culture of Innovation," *Fast Company,* December 21, 2013, www.fastcompany.com.

42. J. Gibson, "Celebrating Failure: How to Make a Hit out of Misses," *Entrepreneur,* March 19, 2014, www.entrepreneur.com; and S. Shellenbarger, "Better Ideas through Failure: Companies Reward Employee Mistakes to Spur Innovation, Get Back Their Edge," *The Wall Street Journal,* September 27, 2011, p. D1.

43. Company website, "3M Reports Sales Information for Month of August 2020," Press release, September 15, 2020, https://news.3m.com/English/press-releases/press-releases-details/2020/3M-Reports-Sales-Information-for-Month-of-August-2020/default.aspx.

44. R. Arasu, "Intuit: How Unstructured Collaboration Fuels Innovation and Creativity," LinkedIn, August 17, 2018, www.linkedin.com.

45. R. Arasu, "Intuit: How Unstructured Collaboration Fuels Innovation and Creativity," LinkedIn, August 17, 2018, www.linkedin.com.

46. "The 50 Best Workplaces for Innovators," *Fast Company,* August 5, 2019, www.fastcompany.com.

47. H. K. Bowen, K. B. Clark, C. A. Holloway, and S. C. Wheelwright, "Development Projects: The Engine of Renewal," *Harvard Business Review,* September–October 1994, pp. 110–20; C. Eden, T. Williams, and F. Ackermann, "Dismantling the Learning Curve: The Role of Disruptions on the Planning of Development Projects," *International Journal of Project Management* 16, no. 3 (June 1998), pp. 131–38; and M. V. Tatikonda and S. R. Rosenthal, "Technology Novelty, Project Complexity, and

Product Development Project Execution Success: A Deeper Look at Task Uncertainty in Product Innovation," *IEEE Transactions on Engineering Management* 47, no. 1 (February 2000), pp. 74-87.

48. S. Comella-Dorda, S. Lohiya, and G. Speksnijder, "An Operating Model for Company-wide Agile Development," *McKinsey Digital,* May 3, 2016, www.mckinsey.com; and L. Williams, "Agile Project Management and Its Flavors: Where Does Scrum End and Kanban Begin?" *Stanford University Blog,* July 30, 2014, swsblog.stanford.edu.

49. "Understanding Agile Design and Why It's Important," *Design Shack,* June 19, 2013, www.designshack.net.

50. J. Huhn, "What Is Agile Learning Design?" *Bottom Line Performance,* May 7, 2013, www.bottomlineperformance.com.

51. E. Trist, "The Evolution of Sociotechnical Systems as a Conceptual Framework and as an Action Research Program," in *Perspectives on Organizational Design and Behavior,* ed. A. Van de Ven and W. F. Joyce (New York: Wiley, 1981), pp. 19-75; G. Baxter and I. Sommerville, "Socio-technical Systems: From Design Methods to Systems Engineering," *Interacting with Computers* 23, no. 1 (2011), pp. 4-17; and A. Molina, "Insights into the Nature of Technology Diffusion and Implementation: The Perspective of Sociotechnical Alignment," *Technovation* 17, nos. 11/12 (November/December 1997), pp. 601-26.

52. D. Stone, D. Deadrick, K. Lukaszewski, and R. Johnson, "The Influence of Technology on the Future of Human Resource Management," *Human Resource Management Review* 25 (2015), pp. 216-31; W. F. Cascio and R. Montealegre, "How Technology Is Changing Work and Organizations," *Annual Review of Organizational Psychology and Organizational Behavior* 3 (2016), pp. 349-75; L. Aiman-Smith and S. G. Green, "Implementing New Manufacturing Technology: The Related Effects of Technology Characteristics and User Learning Activities," *Academy of Management Journal* 45 (April 2002), pp. 421-30; and T. L. Griffith, "Technology Features as Triggers for Sensemaking," *Academy of Management Review* 24 (July 1999), pp. 472-88.

53. S. A. Snell and J. W. Dean Jr., "Strategic Compensation for Integrated Manufacturing: The Moderating Effects of Jobs and Organizational Inertia," *Academy of Management Journal* 37 (1994), pp. 1109-40.

54. C. Giffi, A. Roth, and G. Seal, *Competing in World-Class Manufacturing: America's 21st Century Challenge* (Homewood, IL: Business One Irwin, 1990).

55. R. M. Kanter, *World Class: Thriving Locally in the Global Economy* (New York: Touchstone, 1995).

56. C. Giffi, A. Roth, and G. Seal, *Competing in World-Class Manufacturing: America's 21st Century Challenge* (Homewood, IL: Business One Irwin, 1990); and R. M. Kanter, "How Great Companies Think Differently," *Harvard Business Review,* November 2011, pp. 66-78.

57. J. Collins and J. Porras, *Built to Last: Successful Habits of Visionary Companies* (London: Century, 1996).

58. J. Collins and J. Porras, *Built to Last: Successful Habits of Visionary Companies* (London: Century, 1996).

59. J. Collins and J. Porras, *Built to Last: Successful Habits of Visionary Companies* (London: Century, 1996).

60. C. Gibson and J. Birkinshaw, "The Antecedents, Consequences, and Mediating Role of Organizational Ambidexterity," *Academy of Management Journal* 47 (2004), pp. 209-26.

61. https://ssir.org/articles/entry/the_magic_of_multisolving

62. J. Collins and J. Porras, *Built to Last: Successful Habits of Visionary Companies* (London: Century, 1996).

63. D. A. Waldman and D. E. Bowen, "Learning to Be a Paradox-Savvy Leader," *Academy of Management Perspectives* 30 (2016), pp. 316-27; and E. Miron-Spektor, A. Ingram, J. Keller, et al., "Microfoundations of Organizational Paradox: The Problem Is How We Think about the Problem," *Academy of Management Journal* 61 (2018), pp. 26-45.

64. T. Cummings and C. Worley, *Organization Development and Change,* 8th ed. (Mason, OH: Thomson/South-Western, 2005).

65. T. Cummings and C. Worley, *Organization Development and Change,* 8th ed. (Mason, OH: Thomson/South-Western, 2005).

66. N. Nohria, W. Joyce, and B. Roberson, "What Really Works," *Harvard Business Review,* July 2003, pp. 42-52.

67. C. Ayers, M. Graeber, R. Gruman, and B. Sethi, "Successfully Drive Change through the Organization," Price water house-Coopers, www.pwc.com; D. R. Conner, *Managing at the Speed of Change* (New York: Random House, 2006); and R. Teerlink, "Harley's Leadership U-Turn," *Harvard Business Review,* July-August 2000, pp. 43-48.

68. C. M. Christensen, "The Past and Future of Competitive Advantage," *Sloan Management Review,* Winter 2001, pp. 105-9; V. Bruno and H. Shin, "Globalization of Corporate Risk Taking," *Journal of International Business Studies* 45 (2014), pp. 800-820; M. Reeves and M. Deimler, "Adaptability: The New Competitive Advantage," *Harvard Business Review,* July-August 2011, pp. 135-41; and J. Bower, H. Leonard, and L. Paine, "Global Capitalism at Risk: What Are You Doing about It?" *Harvard Business Review,* September 2011, pp. 105-12.

69. M. Schrage, "Getting Beyond the Innovation Fetish," *Fortune,* November 13, 2000, pp. 225-32.

70. T. A. Judge, C. J. Thoresen, V. Pucik, and T. M. Welbourne, "Managerial Coping with Organizational Change: A Dispositional Perspective," *Journal of Applied Psychology* 84 (1999), pp. 107-22; and M. Fugate, A. Kinicki, and G. Prussia, "Employee Coping with Organizational Change: An Examination of Alternative Theoretical Perspectives and Models," *Personnel Psychology* 61 (2008), pp. 1-36.

71. E. E. Lawler III, *Treat People Right!* (San Francisco: Jossey-Bass, 2003).

72. "The People Power of Transformations," McKinsey & Company, February 2017, www.mckinsey.com.

73. D. R. Conner, *Managing at the Speed of Change* (New York: Random House, 2006); E. Lamm and J. R. Gordon, "Empowerment, Predisposition to Resist Change, and Support for Organizational Change," *Journal of Leadership & Organizational Studies* 17, no. 4 (November 2010), pp. 426-37; S. Oreg, "Resistance to Change: Developing an Individual Differences Measure," *Journal of Applied Psychology* (2003), pp. 680-93; and P. Zigarmi and J. Hoekstra, "Leadership Strategies for Making Change Stick," *Perspectives* (Ken Blanchard Companies, 2008), http://www.kenblanchard.com.

74. J. Stanislao and B. C. Stanislao, "Dealing with Resistance to Change," *Business Horizons,* July–August 1983, pp. 74–78; B. Shimoni, "What Is Resistance to Change? A Habitus-Oriented Approach," *Academy of Management Perspectives* 31 (2017), pp. 257–70; J. D. Ford and L. W. Ford, "Decoding Resistance to Change," *Harvard Business Review,* April 2009, pp. 99–103; J. P. Kotter and L. A. Schlesinger, "Choosing Strategies for Change," *Harvard Business Review,* March–April 1979, pp. 106–14; and P. Zigarmi and J. Hoekstra, "Leadership Strategies for Making Change Stick," *Perspectives* (Ken Blanchard Companies, 2008), http://www.kenblanchard.com.

75. J. P. Kotter and L. A. Schlesinger, "Choosing Strategies for Change," *Harvard Business Review,* March–April 1979, pp. 106–14.

76. D. Zell, "Overcoming Barriers to Work Innovations: Lessons Learned at Hewlett-Packard," *Organizational Dynamics,* Summer 2001, pp. 77–85.

77. E. B. Dent and S. Galloway Goldberg, "Challenging Resistance to Change," *Journal of Applied Behavioral Science,* March 1999, pp. 25–41; J. D. Ford and L. W. Ford, "Decoding Resistance to Change," *Harvard Business Review,* April 2009, pp. 99–103; P. Zigarmi and J. Hoekstra, "Leadership Strategies for Making Change Stick," *Perspectives* (Ken Blanchard Companies, 2008), http://www.kenblanchard.com; and J. Ford, L. Ford, and A. D'Amelio, "Resistance to Change: The Rest of the Story," *Academy of Management Review* 33 (2008), pp. 362–77.

78. G. Johnson, *Strategic Change and the Management Process* (New York: Basil Blackwell, 1987); and K. Lewin, "Frontiers in Group Dynamics," *Human Relations* 1 (1947), pp. 5–41.

79. E. H. Schein, "Organizational Culture: What It Is and How to Change It," in *Human Resource Management in International Firms,* ed. P. Evans, Y. Doz, and A. Laurent (New York: St. Martin's Press, 1990).

80. M. Beer, R. Eisenstat, and B. Spector, *The Critical Path to Corporate Renewal* (Cambridge, MA: Harvard Business School Press, 1990).

81. D. Hellriegel and J. W. Slocum Jr., *Management,* 4th ed. (Reading, MA: Addison-Wesley, 1986).

82. K. Lewin, "Frontiers in Group Dynamics," *Human Relations* 1 (1947), pp. 5–41; and S. Cummings, T. Bridgman, and K. Brown, "Unfreezing Change as Three Steps: Rethinking Kurt Lewin's Legacy for Change Management," *Human Relations* 69 (2016), pp. 33–60.

83. E. E. Lawler III, *From the Ground Up* (San Francisco: Jossey-Bass, 1995).

84. Q. Nguyen Huy, "Time, Temporal Capability, and Planned Change," *Academy of Management Review* 26 (2001), pp. 601–23.

85. B. Sugarman, "A Learning-Based Approach to Organizational Change: Some Results and Guidelines," *Organizational Dynamics,* Summer 2001, pp. 62–75; and J. Shin, M. Taylor, and M. Seo, "Resources for Change: The Relationships of Organizational Inducements and Psychological Resilience to Employees' Attitudes and Behaviors toward Organizational Change," *Academy of Management Journal* 55 (2012), pp. 727–48.

86. J. P. Kotter and L. A. Schlesinger, "Choosing Strategies for Change," *Harvard Business Review,* March–April 1979, pp. 106–14.

87. E. Varbeemen and S. B. D'Amico, "Why Remote Working Will Be the New Normal, Even after COVID-19," EY, April 9, 2020, www.ey.com.

88. R. H. Miles, "Beyond the Age of Dilbert: Accelerating Corporate Transformations by Rapidly Engaging All Employees," *Organizational Dynamics,* Spring 2001, pp. 313–21.

89. M. S. Dahl, "Organizational Change and Employee Stress," *Management Science* 57, no. 2 (February 2011), pp. 240–56; J. R. Darling and V. L. Heller, "The Key for Effective Stress Management: Importance of Responsive Leadership," *Organizational Development Journal* 29, no. 1 (Spring 2011), pp. 9–26; and O. Robinson and A. Griffiths, "Coping with the Stress of Transformational Change in a Governmental Department," *Journal of Applied Behavioral Science* 41, no. 2 (June 2005), pp. 204–21.

90. D. A. Nadler, "Managing Organizational Change: An Integrative Approach," *Journal of Applied Behavioral Science* 17 (1981), pp. 191–211.

91. D. Rousseau and S. A. Tijoriwala, "What's a Good Reason to Change? Motivated Reasoning and Social Accounts in Promoting Organizational Change," *Journal of Applied Psychology* 84 (1999), pp. 514–28.

92. C. R. Leana and B. Barry, "Stability and Change as Simultaneous Experiences in Organizational Life," *Academy of Management Review* 25 (2000), pp. 753–59; and B. Sugarman, "A Learning-Based Approach to Organizational Change: Some Results and Guidelines," *Organizational Dynamics,* Summer 2001, pp. 62–75.

93. O. Gadiesh and J. Gilbert, "Transforming Corner-Office Strategy into Frontline Action," *Harvard Business Review,* May 2001, pp. 72–79; and R. Suddaby and W. Foster, "History and Organizational Change," *Journal of Management* 43 (2017), pp. 19–38.

94. B. Schneider, A. Brief, and R. Guzzo, "Creating a Climate and Culture for Sustainable Organizational Change," *Organizational Dynamics,* Spring 1996, pp. 7–19; and J. Bartunek, J. Balogun, and B. Do, "Considering Planned Change Anew: Stretching Large Group Interventions Strategically, Emotionally, and Meaningfully," *Academy of Management Annals* 5 (2011), pp. 1–52.

95. N. Nohria and J. Berkley, "Whatever Happened to the Take-Charge Manager?" *Harvard Business Review,* January–February 1994, pp. 128–37.

96. D. Miller, J. Hartwick, and I. Le Breton-Miller, "How to Detect a Management Fad—and Distinguish It from a Classic," *Business Horizons,* July–August 2004, pp. 7–16.

97. Price Waterhouse Change Integration Team, *Better Change: Best Practices for Transforming Your Organization* (Burr Ridge, IL: Irwin, 1995).

98. Price Waterhouse Change Integration Team, *Better Change: Best Practices for Transforming Your Organization* (Burr Ridge, IL: Irwin, 1995).

99. E. M. Heffes, "You Need Urgency Now!" *Financial Executive,* January–February 2009 (interview with John P. Kotter); J. P. Kotter, "Accelerate!" *Harvard Business Review,* November 2012, pp. 46–58; and Kotter International, "Our Principles: Urgency," http://www.kotterinternational.com.

100. E. E. Lawler III, *From the Ground Up* (San Francisco: Jossey-Bass, 1995).

101. J. P. Kotter, *Leading Change* (Boston: Harvard Business School Publishing, 1996).

102. B. Schneider, A. Brief, and R. Guzzo, "Creating a Climate and Culture for Sustainable Organizational Change," *Organizational Dynamics,* Spring 1996, pp. 7–19.

103. R. Beckhard and R. Harris, *Organizational Transitions* (Reading, MA: Addison-Wesley, 1977).

104. J. P. Kotter, *Leading Change* (Boston: Harvard Business School Publishing, 1996).

105. G. Hamel, "Waking Up IBM," *Harvard Business Review,* July-August 2000, pp. 137–46; and A. Deutschman, *Change or Die: The Three Keys to Change at Work and in Life* (New York: Harper Business, 2007).

106. J. P. Kotter, *Leading Change* (Boston: Harvard Business School Publishing, 1996).

107. D. Smith, *Taking Charge of Change* (Reading, MA: Addison-Wesley, 1996).

108. J. Schlanger, "Forget 2015–2050 Is the Year for Predictions," *Newsweek,* January 4, 2015, www.newsweek.com.

109. S. Zuboff and J. Maxim, *The Support Economy* (New York: Penguin, 2004).

110. H. Courtney, J. Kirkland, and P. Viguerie, "Strategy under Uncertainty," *Harvard Business Review,* November-December 1997, pp. 66–79.

111. J. O'Shea and C. Madigan, *Dangerous Company: The Consulting Powerhouses and the Businesses They Save and Ruin* (New York: Times Books, 1997).

112. W. C. Kim and R. Mauborgne, *Blue Ocean Strategy* (Boston: Harvard Business Review Press, 2015).

113. G. Hamel and C. K. Prahalad, *Competing for the Future* (Boston: Harvard Business School Press, 1994).

114. G. Hamel and C. K. Prahalad, *Competing for the Future* (Boston: Harvard Business School Press, 1994); and W. C. Kim and R. Mauborgne, *Blue Ocean Strategy* (Boston: Harvard Business Review Press, 2015).

115. G. Hamel and C. K. Prahalad, *Competing for the Future* (Boston: Harvard Business School Press, 1994).

116. C. Gallo, "Stop 'Listening' and Start Anticipating Your Customers' Needs," *Forbes,* May 28, 2014, www.forbes.com.

117. G. Hamel and C. K. Prahalad, *Competing for the Future* (Boston: Harvard Business School Press, 1994).

118. J. P. Kotter, *The New Rules: How to Succeed in Today's Post-Corporate World* (New York: Free Press, 1995).

119. J. P. Kotter, *The New Rules: How to Succeed in Today's Post-Corporate World* (New York: Free Press, 1995).

120. T. Bateman and C. Porath, "Transcendent Behavior," in *Positive Organizational Scholarship,* ed. K. Cameron, J. Dutton, and R. Quinn (San Francisco: Berrett-Koehler, 2003).

121. L. A. Hill, "New Manager Development for the 21st Century," *Academy of Management Executive,* August 2004, pp. 121–26;

and D. A. Ready, J. A. Conger, and L. A. Hill, "Are You a High Potential?" *Harvard Business Review* 88 (June 2010), pp. 78–84.

122. E. E. Lawler III, *From the Ground Up* (San Francisco: Jossey-Bass, 1995); and J. P. Kotter, *The New Rules: How to Succeed in Today's Post-Corporate World* (New York: Free Press, 1995).

123. E. E. Lawler III, *Treat People Right!* (San Francisco: Jossey-Bass, 2003).

124. "Life after a Layoff," *Kiplinger's Personal Finance,* February 2012, www.kiplinger.com; and M. Peiperl and Y. Baruck, "Back to Square Zero: The Post-Corporate Career," *Organizational Dynamics,* Spring 1997, pp. 7–22.

125. "Life after a Layoff," *Kiplinger's Personal Finance,* February 2012, www.kiplinger.com; and M. Peiperl and Y. Baruck, "Back to Square Zero: The Post-Corporate Career," *Organizational Dynamics,* Spring 1997, pp. 7–22.

126. D. R. Conner, *Managing at the Speed of Change* (New York: Random House, 2006), pp. 235–45.

127. J. W. Slocum Jr., M. McGill, and D. Lei, "The New Learning Strategy Anytime, Anything, Anywhere," *Organizational Dynamics,* Autumn 1994, pp. 33–37.

128. G. Binney and C. Williams, *Leaning Into the Future: Changing the Way People Change Organizations* (London: Nicholas Brealey, 1997).

129. J. P. Kotter, *The New Rules: How to Succeed in Today's Post-Corporate World* (New York: Free Press, 1995).

130. L. A. Hill, "New Manager Development for the 21st Century," *Academy of Management Executive,* August 2004, p. 125.

131. J. A. Raelin, "Don't Bother Putting Leadership into People," *Academy of Management Executive,* August 2004, pp. 131–35.

132. G. Binney and C. Williams, *Leaning Into the Future: Changing the Way People Change Organizations* (London: Nicholas Brealey, 1997).

133. P. Omidyar, "How Great Companies Think Differently: eBay's Founder on Innovating the Business Model of Social Change," *Harvard Business Review,* September 2011, pp. 41–44; M. Porter and M. Kramer, "Creating Shared Value," *Harvard Business Review,* January-February 2011, pp. 62–77; H. Sabeti, "The For-Benefit Enterprise," *Harvard Business Review,* November 2011, pp. 99–104.

134. P. Adler, "Alternative Economic Futures: A Research Agenda for Progressive Management Scholarship," *Academy of Management Perspectives* 30 (2016), pp. 123–38; and R. Gulati, F. Wohlgezogen, and P. Zhelyazkov "The Two Facets of Collaboration: Cooperation and Coordination in Strategic Alliances," *Academy of Management Annals* 6 (2012), pp. 531–83.

135. P. Adler, "Alternative Economic Futures: A Research Agenda for Progressive Management Scholarship," *Academy of Management Perspectives* 30 (2016), pp. 123–38; and R. Gulati, F. Wohlgezogen, and P. Zhelyazkov "The Two Facets of Collaboration: Cooperation and Coordination in Strategic Alliances," *Academy of Management Annals* 6 (2012), pp. 531–83.

Design elements: Take Charge of Your Career box photo: © Tetra Images/ Getty Images; Thumbs Up/Thumbs Down icons: McGraw-Hill Education

Index

Note: Page numbers followed by n refer to notes; page numbers followed by e refer to exhibits.

Butler, T., 321n
Butt, Charles, 229
Butterfield, K., 273n
Butterfield, Stewart, 301
Buyl, T., 346n
Buzzword, 310
B-W. *See* Barry-Wehmiller Companies (B-W)
BYD, 18
Byrd, M. J., 145n
Byrne, J., 225n
Byron, K., 224n

C

Caballero, J., 274n
Cachila, J., 67n
Cackowski, D., 174n
CAD/CAM. *See* Computer-aided design and computer-aided manufacturing (CAD/CAM)
Caesar, Abraham, 216
Caesar Rivise, 216
Cafeteria benefit program, 197
Cagle, Jake, 267
Cain, S., 247n
Cairncross, F., 23n
Calamities, 129
Callan, V. J., 249n
Callister, R. R., 298n
Cameron, K., 64n, 374n
Cameron, K. S., 68n
Cammisecra, Antonio, 40
Camp, R. C., 173n
Campbell Soup, 83
Campion, M., 274n
Campion, M. A., 201n
Campus recruiting, 179, 183-184
Canada, 240, 264, 314
Canadian Social Insurance number, 77
Canal, E., 147n
Cancer Institute, 254
Candee, D., 89n
Cannon-Bowers, J. A., 120n
Cantalupo, James, 99
Capell, P., 225n
Capella Space, 131
Capelli, P., 319n
Capital budget, 334
Capital One Financial, 7, 354-355
Capital requirements, 52
Cappellen, T., 22n
Caramella, S., 273n
Carbon emissions, 86
Cardador, M., 203n
CareerBuilder, 186
Career development, diversity and, 217
Career tips
  constructive feedback, 194
  control, 328
  entrepreneurship, 129, 368
  ethics, 78
  extrinsic/internal rewards, 265
  history, 35
  internship, 162
  job search management, 111
  leadership skills, 245
  mentor, 218
  organizational culture, 63
  public speaking, 311
  side hustles, 368
  student entrepreneurs, 129, 368
  studying abroad, 15
  teamwork skills, 288
Carell, Steve, 9
Carey, A., 41n
Carey, D., 248n
Carlson, Ed, 316
Carlson, J. R., 320n

CarMax, 366
Carnegie, Dale, 283
Caron, A., 298n
Carpenter, J. W., 118n
Carr, L., 201n
Carroll, A., 83n, 90n
Carson, J., 250n, 297n
Carstedt, G., 91n
Carsten, M., 247n
Carton, A. M., 246n, 272n
Case, D., 320n
Case, J., 41n, 296n
Cash budget, 334
Cash cows, 104e, 105
Casio, W. F., 202n
Casnocha, B., 275n
Catalyst, 63
Caterpillar, 331
Catz, Safra, 208
Caux Principles for Business, 73
Cavat, P., 66n
CB Insights, 137
Centralization, 34e, 57e
Centralized organization, 157-158
CEO. *See* Chief executive officer (CEO)
CEO pay, 76
Certainty, 109
CFO. *See* Chief financial officer (CFO)
Chaco sandals, 52
Chafkin, M., 119n, 147n
Chakraborty, S., 295n
Chamberlain, M., 321n
Chambers, G. J., 174n
Chandler, A. D., 41n
Chanel, 211e
Chanel, Coco, 211e
Change
  harmonizing multiple changes, 365
  leadership, 359-366, 365e
  motivating people to change, 361-362, 363e
  overcoming resistance to change, 361-365, 363e
  reactive/proactive, 366-367
  unfreezing, moving, refreezing, 362-363e
Change, C. H., 274n
Change leader, 365-366
Chapman, Robert, 243
Charan, R., 320n
Charismatic leader, 231, 240-241
Chatman, J., 298n
Chatzky, Jean, 16, 23n
Chau, S. L., 346n
Chen, G., 249n, 274n, 294n, 296n
Chen, L., 67n, 371n
Chen, Leon, 127
Chen, N., 298n
Chen, N. Y. F., 321n
Chen, T., 244, 297n
Chen, X., 225n
Chen, Z. X., 173n, 249n
Chenault, Kenneth, 218
Cheney, G., 346n
Cheng, J., 246n
Chesky, Brian, 65
Chevron, 50, 63-64
Chick-fil-A, 77, 254
Chief ethics officer, 8
Chief executive officer (CEO), 8, 154, 269, 343-344
Chief financial officer (CFO), 333
Chief information officer (CIO), 8, 357
Chief operating officer (COO), 8
Chief technology officer (CTO), 357
Chilcote, A., 173n
Childhood obesity, 50
China

belongingness, 264
  and charismatic leadership, 240, 242
  and competitive advantage, 18
  and conflict, 291
  and COVID-19, 93
  as destination for expatriates, 220
  and globalization, 14
  guanxi, 75, 233
  and innovative advantage, 18
  Internet search engine, 18
  and managerial concepts, 27
  managing globally, 219
  as market for GMC's Cadillac, 56
  market for tech companies, 14
  motorcycle industry, 165
  and nonverbal communications, 312
  tariffs and trade war with United States, 47
  VIPKID, 124
  whistleblowing, 75
  working conditions, 85
Chiniara, M., 250n
Chiocchio, F., 320n
Chipotle, 329
Choi, H., 297n
Chong, C., 119n
Chouinard, Yvon, 137
Chow, C. W., 346n
Christensen, C., 370n
Christensen, C. M., 372n
Christensen, Clayton, 351
Christian, M. S., 297n
Chromecast, 278
Chu, C., 320n-321n
Chugh, D., 88n
Chul, M., 353, 371n
Chung, C. H., 175n
Chung, J. O. Y., 89n
Chung, Q. B., 174n
Churchill, Winston, 240
Cianci, A., 272n
Cianci, R., 273n
Ciancio, J., 202n
Cianni, M., 294n, 297n
Cigna, 101
CIM. *See* Computer integrated manufacturing (CIM)
Cinanci, R., 273n
CIO. *See* Chief information officer (CIO)
Circular economy, 87
Cirque du Soleil, 62
Cisco Systems, 40, 219, 277, 279, 306
Citicorp, 359
Citigroup, 74
Citrix, 306
Ciulla, J., 250n
Civil aspiration, 84
Civil Rights Act (1964), 188-189e, 189, 205e, 207
Civil Rights Act (1991), 189e
Clack, L. A., 247n
Claire, Marie, 144n
Clan control, 326, 343-345
Clan culture, 64, 64e
Clark, J. R., 246n
Clark, K. B., 370n-371n
Clarks, 179
Classical approaches to management
  administrative management, 28, 28e, 33-34
  bureaucracy, 28, 28e, 32-33
  human relations, 28, 28e, 34-36
  scientific management, 28, 28e, 29-32
  systematic management, 28, 28e, 29
Cleary, B., 201n
Clifford, C., 22n, 249n, 272n, 319n, 370n
Clifford, S., 91n
Cline, B. N., 224n
Clinique, 126

Closeness of supervision, 233
Clough, M. William, 250n
Coaching, 191, 314-315
Coalition, 59
Coate, P., 321n
Cober, A. B., 273n
Coca-Cola, 52, 71, 79, 82, 217, 315
Cocheco Company, 29
Cochran, P., 90n
Cochran, P. L., 90n
Coercive power, 230
Cognitive ability test, 186, 186e
Cognizant, 57
Cognizant Technology Solutions, 78
Cohan, P., 274n
Cohen, J., 23n
Cohen, Larry, 109-110, 113
Cohen, S., 294n-295n
Cohen, Stanley, 216
Cohesiveness, 212-213, 287-288, 288e
Colbert, A., 249n
Colbert, J. L., 346n
Colella, A., 202n
Coleman, D., 23n
Colgate-Palmolive, 219
Collaboration
  across organizational boundaries, 14
  boosting performance, 17, 294
  and competition, 369
  conflict managing strategies, 291e
  defined, 291
  horizontal communication to foster, 316-317
Collective bargaining, 195, 198-199
Collectivism, 221
CollegeRecruiter, 183
Colligan, Victoria, 141
Collin, James, 360
Collins, D., 203n
Collins, J., 145n, 250n, 372n
Collins, J. C., 200n
Collins, James, 359-360
Collis, D. J., 67n
Colquitt, J., 249n, 274n
Colt, Sam, 74
Comella-Dorda, S., 372n
Comer, D., 90n
Commercialism, in schools, 76
Commitment and determination, 132
Communication
  blogging, 306, 309e
  boundaryless organization, 318
  channels of, 306-309, 306e
  coaching, 314-315
  and control systems, 341
  coordination and, 166
  cross-cultural differences, 304, 310-312
  defined, 301
  digital media, 306-309
  downward, 314-315, 315e
  e-mail, 308
  ethical versus nonethical, 305
  face-to-face, 305-306, 309
  formal, 317
  general model of, 301e, 302
  grapevine, 317-318
  horizontal, 316-317
  ineffective, and team failure, 283
  informal, 317-318
  information overload, 314, 318
  interpersonal, 301-303
  language, 310-311
  language barriers, 304e
  listening, 312-314
  management by wandering around (MBWA), 316
  media richness, 309